Oracle Real
Application Clusters

Oracle Real Application Clusters

Murali Vallath

ELSEVIER
DIGITAL
PRESS

Amsterdam • Boston • Heidelberg • London • New York • Oxford
Paris • San Diego • San Francisco • Singapore • Sydney • Tokyo

Library of Congress Cataloging-in-Publication Data
A catalog record for this book is available from the Library of Congress.
ISBN 1-55558-288-5

British Library Cataloguing-in-Publication Data
A catalogue record for this book is available from the British Library.

The publisher offers special discounts on bulk orders of this book.
For information, please contact:

Manager of Special Sales
Elsevier
200 Wheeler Road
Burlington, MA 01803
Tel: 781-313-4700
Fax: 781-313-4882

For information on all Digital Press publication available, contact our World Wide Web home page at: http://www.digitalpress.com or http://www.bh.com/digitalpress

Transferred to Digital Printing 2009

To Achan and Amma for bringing me into
existence, for giving their love, guidance, care,
and education.

To my mother in law, who is a symbol of
courage and possibility.

To Jaya, my life partner, who has taken the vow
to stand by my side through the mountains,
valleys, and green pastures of life.

To my children Grishma and Nabhas, who are
the important treasures, without them my life
would have been meaningless.

Contents

Part II: Architecture

Preface

Clustering technology has been around for a long time. It was in the early 1980s that Digital Equipment Corporation (DEC) first introduced the clustered configuration called the *VAXCluster*. Around the same period, I started my computer career working on the PDP-11 systems, also from DEC. PDP-11s were the first platforms that were used by Oracle Corporation to develop the first relational database in 1978, when Oracle released Version 1 of the Relational Database Management System (RDBMS) product. This commercial relational database entered the market nearly 8 years after Dr. E.F. Codd first introduced the relational database model in June 1970 through his white paper entitled, "A Relational Model of Data for Large Shared Data Banks" (published at IBM, San Jose, USA).

After the initial set of VAXClusters entered the market in the early 1980s, DEC introduced a relational database called Rdb.[1] This database used the VAXClusters as their primary platform, thus becoming the first commercial clustered relational database. It was during the late 1980s that I started my career in the relational database world with Rdb on VAXClusters as my first venture into the clustered arena. In 1986, Oracle also introduced the first clustered database solution called Oracle Parallel Server (OPS) with Version 5. In spite of OPS supporting a clustered environment, it did not take advantage of the clustering technology that was available, for example in VAXClusters, namely communicating via the cluster interconnect. This caused a serious performance issue, until Version 9.0 when Oracle, after inheriting some of the clustered database knowledge from Rdb and the technology from Compaq (HP recently acquired Compaq, who had previously acquired DEC), introduced Real Application Clusters (RAC).

All of this experience from VAXClusters to Rdb to OPS to RAC created this motivation to share the knowledge in the form of this book.

---

[1] Oracle Corporation currently owns Rdb. Oracle purchased Rdb from DEC in 1994.

About this book

Compared to its predecessor (OPS), the architecture behind the RAC implementation has changed significantly. The book will discuss in detail subjects that I have never seen discussed elsewhere, for example the internals of RAC operations, cache fusion, fusion recovery, fast reconfiguration of RAC, etc.

Areas such as partitioning, types of indexes, tablespace management, transaction management, backup and recovery principles, and internals of the recovery operation have been covered extensively in this book. What good is a book on RAC that does not provide discussions on tuning? In my view, the coverage of extensive tuning, in over three chapters, starting with tools and utilities such as SQL Trace, STATSPACK, and Oracle Event and Wait interfaces, covering single instance tuning followed by cluster tuning, including tuning the cluster interconnect and cache transfer, makes this book unique.

Throughout the book, examples are provided with file dumps, followed by discussions and analysis of problem solving. The book also provides discussions on migrating to a RAC environment.

Oracle Real Application Clusters provides comprehensive coverage of the features, technology, and principles of Oracle's RAC product, which is part of the Oracle 9*i* release of their RDBMS product. This book is divided into four main parts (Concepts, Architecture, Operations, and Appendices) covering various areas of the application/database design, development, and maintenance life cycles. Starting with the fundamentals, an introduction to the concepts of the various hardware architectures and the clustering technology available, the book discusses the pros and cons, leading into discussion of the RAC technology. After the formal introduction of the concepts of clustering and configurations, the book discusses the various theories of asynchronous (parallel) and synchronous processing and how they could be applied to the database tier of the enterprise architecture.

How to use this book

The chapters are written to follow one another in a logical fashion by introducing topics in the earlier chapters and building on the technology. Thus it is advised that you read the chapters in order. Even if you have worked with clustered databases, you will certainly find a nugget or two that may be new to you. For the experienced reader, the book also highlights wherever applicable the new features introduced in Oracle *9i*, Oracle *9i* Release 2, and Oracle 10*g*. The book's four parts are outlined below.

Part I: Concepts

Information in this part is to get the reader's feet wet. This part contains three chapters.

- *Chapter 1:* Provides an overview of the modern business requirements and the criticality of these requirements in today's Internet-based business.

- *Chapter 2:* Focuses on the hardware concepts, the various types of hardware technologies such as SMP, MPP, NUMA, and the clustered SMP. The chapter also discusses the various components, such as the cluster interconnect technology and the storage systems, including various types of RAID technology.

- *Chapter 3:* Discusses the basic Oracle concepts, starting with what an instance is, then covering the various background and foreground processes, including the various types of files and tablespaces that Oracle supports and uses. Data block dump analysis and data block structure, including transaction layers, are discussed.

Part II: Architecture

Once the reader's feet are wet with regard to the concepts, the second part steps into the clustered database technology starting with the RAC architecture in Chapter 4. This part contains six chapters.

- *Chapter 4:* Takes an in-depth look into the RAC architecture, the various additional background and foreground processes required by RAC, their functions, and how they work together in clustered database architecture. The role of the GCS, GES, and GRD is covered a great detail.

- *Chapter 5:* Discusses the transaction management principles in general, the transaction management in a single instance configuration, and the transaction management in a RAC environment. This chapter discusses, using scenarios, the architecture behind this configuration, how the sharing of data occurs between nodes, and the sharing of data when the cluster has more than two nodes. Through examples, this chapter will explain how cache fusion helps the lock activity between the shared rows, the various lock levels, and how locks are handled, based on requests received from processes on various nodes participating in the cluster. It details the discussions concerning the cache fusion behavior in a transaction; various scenarios of clustered transaction management include the various states of GCS operation such as the PI and XI states of a block.

- *Chapter 6:* Discusses the concepts of parallel processing. The advantages of using parallel processing and the appropriate usage of this feature in today's business computing. Concepts such as working of parallel processing, parallel processing configuration scenarios, problems encountered in using parallel processing, tuning statements for parallel processing, and advantages of using parallel processing are also addressed.

- *Chapter 7:* Discusses the various features of the Oracle product and the technology to be considered in designing databases for the RAC environment. The chapter discusses various types of indexes, data partitioning and materialized views, and the advantages and positive effect of the technology for a RAC environment.

- *Chapter 8:* Covers the various installation and configuration steps required for RAC implementation. The chapter covers both the DBCA utility for database creation and the manual method, including configuration of the GSD, SRVCONFIG, and SRVCTL utilities, and listener configuration.

- *Chapter 9:* Illustrates, lists, and describes the various RAC-related data dictionary views and parameters.

Part III: Operations

After a complete understanding of the architecture, the next step is to understand its operations, taking a step deeper and getting to the bottom of things. This part contains eight chapters.

- *Chapter 10:* Describes the availability and scalability features of RAC, including transparent application failover, Oracle Real Application Cluster Guard, fast reconfiguration, and inclusion and exclusion of instances. It also discusses how to configure TAF using the tnsnames file and by making OCI-based calls directly from a Java application.

- *Chapter 11:* Describes the steps involved during a migration process. Both migrating from a single instance to a clustered database environment and migrating from OPS to RAC are covered.

- *Chapter 12:* Covers the backup features available, including implementation and configuration of RMAN. There are extensive discussions on the various recovery operations, illustrated with trace file analysis, which includes LMON, SMON, and alert log files.

- *Chapter 13:* This is the first of three chapters covering a very important subject, namely performance tuning of a RAC cluster. This chapter discusses the various tools and utilities available such as STATSPACK, SQL_TRACE, Oracle Enterprise Manager (OEM), and methods of analysis by understanding the internals of Oracle, such as using the Oracle Event and Wait interface, are discussed in detail.

- *Chapter 14:* Tuning starts with a single instance; this chapter discusses in detail tuning of a single instance of the database. Starting with a tuning methodology, the chapter approaches tuning from the top down, tuning the application, followed by the instance, and then the database. In this chapter the various wait interface views are drilled down and analyzed to solve specific performance issues. The chapter discusses capturing session level statistics for a thorough analysis of the problem.

- *Chapter 15:* After tuning a single instance of the database, the next step is to tune the cluster. This chapter discusses this key piece to the puzzle. Cluster tuning is tuning of many instances working in a cohesive unit. This means there is sharing of data across middleware. This chapter discusses tuning the cluster interconnect, the shared storage subsystems, and other global cache management areas, including cache transfer and interinstance lock management.

- *Chapter 16:* Discusses the various diagnostic options available for troubleshooting an Oracle database. This includes discussions on common error messages such as ORA-600 and ORA-7445, how to troubleshoot these errors first, and how to gather information to help Oracle support diagnose the problem quickly. This chapter also discusses the Flash Freeze feature, ORADEBUG, and RDA.

- *Chapter 17:* Discusses implementation of RAC on other operating systems, the differences, and additional processes. Primarily, this chapter focuses on Linux and Windows operating systems. It discusses the clustered file system introduced in Oracle *9i* Release 2 for the Windows operating system and the watchdog process for the Linux operating system.

Part IV: Appendices

- Appendix 1: Utilities

- Appendix 2: Scripts

- Appendix 3: References

- Appendix 4: Work Plan

Graphics used

The book uses graphic icons as shown in the following table to quickly locate information or to alert a reader regarding any important information.

Icon	Name	Description
	Note	Notes provide additional information related to the subject area. Important information that the reader should pay attention to is marked with the note icon.
	Caution	Caution indicates that the step should be performed with care.
9i	Oracle 9i New Feature	This feature, command, or parameter was introduced by Oracle in Version 9i Release 1. This indicates that the feature, command, or parameter may not be available in the previous versions of Oracle.
9iR2	Oracle 9iR2 New Feature	This feature, command, or parameter was introduced by Oracle in Version 9i Release 2. This indicates that the feature, command, or parameter may not be available in the previous versions of Oracle.
10g	Oracle 10g New Feature	This feature, command, or parameter is introduced by Oracle in Version 10g Release 1. This indicates that the feature, command, or parameter may not be available in the previous versions of Oracle.

Acknowledgments

First and most importantly, I would like to thank my Achan and Amma who brought me into existence, provided me with education and guided me in the right direction throughout my childhood. No words can illustrate the huge commitments and sacrifices they have taken to educate my sister and me. They may be surprised that I ventured into writing a book—something I myself would have never imagined I would do—but it is their strength and support that has enabled me to do so. It is not only my parents but also my relatives and other close family friends who speak with no hesitation when providing guidance. I would like to thank uncle Eswaran, who suggested that I get into the information technology arena. Thanks also to my sister Ambika, my brother in law Satyan, and my niece Smrithi, who are near and dear to my heart and who I will love forever.

In January of 1990, after about 6 years of working in India in the information technology field, I landed at JFK airport in New York for my first consulting assignment with Digital Equipment Corporation (DEC). I never intended to leave my home country; however, I was promised it would be a small assignment and would be back home before the end of summer. It has been 12 summers and I am still here.

I first met my wife, Jaya, in 1992. When she agreed to become my partner through the journey of life, she never realized how many sacrifices she would have to endure in her married life. Without her, I would not have made it this far. During the past six months, it has been hard on the entire family; writing this book was like a second full-time job. I have to thank my children Grishma and Nabhas, who always said, "Dad, you need to finish the book so that you can spend time with us." Here is a conversation between my son, Nabhas (Nabu), and Jaya in our native language Malayalam, which is spoken in the southern-most state of India, called Kerala. (The state is such a paradise of beauty and freshness that the state's motto is "God's own land.")

Nabhas: Amae, eniku sahayam vanum.

Mother: Monai, achanodu chodiku.

Nabhas: Amae, achanu onum ariella. Achanu, Oracle users group and Oracle Real Application Cluster matharme areullu.

Here is the English version of the conversation.

Nabhas: Mom, I need some help.

Mother: Nabu, ask dad to help you.

Nabhas: Mom, dad only knows about Oracle users group and Oracle Real Application Clusters.

Another important person who has always said "anything is possible if you believe in yourself," is my mother-in-law. She has always encouraged me; in fact, I remember her telling Jaya that she should help me in every possible way. It is remarkable to have a family that is so encouraging.

On my professional front, I would like to thank Joe Deluca, my former manager at DEC. His managerial skills were so individual; the entire atmosphere was one of team spirit through the entire project we worked on, my first experience in corporate America. I have had several managers in my 17-year professional career; Joe is one of three that I loved, and would love to work for again.

I would also like to thank Dave Watts who was my manager while I was on a consulting assignment with Navistar in Springfield, Ohio. Dave was the epitome of commitment and involvement on an assignment. It was a perfect opportunity to learn from his experiences.

As a representative of Navistar, I had the opportunity to attend the Oracle Rdb Advisory council at Oracle's New England development center at New Hampshire, USA. There I met Maxine Campbell, and she suggested I join her DBA team in Charlotte, NC. My sincere thanks go to Maxine, for providing me that opportunity. Followed by a move to Charlotte, I joined the local Oracle users group and was soon elected as the president. It was a remarkable experience to provide service to the Oracle user community, and in the process make tons of friends and learn so much.

I would like to thank all the folks at Oracle Consulting who have shared their RAC knowledge during the various encounters. I also would like to thank folks on the metalink forum and members of the RAC pack team, especially Michael Pettigrew who have directly or indirectly provided valuable information, and the folks at Digex, specifically Tom Jones, for their patience in answering my many questions.

However technically well versed you may be, when you put it in writing, you should ensure that it is correct. This book would be worthless without the technical reviews from the following folks: Fitz Fitzgerald, Bank of America (Fitz is a senior database administrator at Bank of America; in addition to his DBA knowledge, Fitz added great clustering and networking knowledge to the review team); and Sudhir Movva, Elogex Inc. (Sudhir is a software engineer at Elogex who helped me with the Java code examples and with testing the OCI interface to Java using TAF). Other folks at Elogex (in no specific order), Ben Green, Mike Newton, Mike Bassett, Brad Harper, Cameron Herrera, Jo-Anne Saldarini, Terroll Joiner, Damon Green, as well as the folks at DST Interactive, Phil Brehm and Cheryl Rowland, who have contributed bits and pieces to this book project.

For a technical person writing is not an easy task. I would like to thank Amy Rodriguez for helping through the technical edits, and when Amy had to take care of her newborn child, Jaya took on the task of reviewing the remaining chapters.

I would like to thank the managers and leaders at Elogex, Jeff Carter (CTO), Bill Donner (CIO), and Travis Parsons (President), who have always encouraged me and provided support toward writing this book.

It would be the biggest mistake if I did not thank Jennifer Bonk who has been instrumental in helping out with the book abstracts and other related information.

I would have to thank all the folks on the Oracle-L list server where there is a tremendous wealth of knowledge. The list server is a perfect example that Oracle learning never ends. I would like to thank specifically Kirti Deshpande, Jonathan Lewis, Cary Millsap, Steve Adams, Johnson Vardarajan, Tim Gorman, Gaja Krishna Vaidyanatha, and Rachel Carmichael for their in-depth discussions on various technical issues. Reading their discussions and analysis over the years brought about my deep interest in Oracle technology.

The book could not be published without help from the friendly folks at Digital Press. During the proposal phase of this book, I worked with numerous publishing houses. However, none had been as friendly and professional to work with as Theron Shreve and Pam Chester. With such a remarkable team, if I had another opportunity to write a book, I would write again for Digital Press. Thanks are also due to the folks at Keyword;

Jeffrey Boys for the excellent final touches to the technical editing process and Maureen Allen for managing and coordinating the efforts of editing, typesetting, and proof reading, to the final product.

I am proud to have been involved in such an incredible project, and I hope my readers benefit from the efforts of so many to bring this book to life. Enjoy.

Murali Vallath

Part I

Concepts

Requirements Analysis

1.1   Introduction

Computer systems are central to the business strategy of any organization and are perhaps the most visible representation of the organization. This is the case in retail, wholesale, manufacturing, natural resources, financial services, publishing, online services, medical services, law, science, education, government, and military operations. As more advanced technologies become available, the role of the computer becomes more vital as businesses increasingly expect operations to continue 24 hours, 7 days a week throughout the year.

However, as with any equipment or technology, there are limitations on the capabilities of the computer system. The parts, or resources, of the computer (i.e., the Central Processing Unit (CPU), storage disk, disk controller, network card, etc.) are bound to experience failures or have processing power limitations. These resources are capable of handling only a certain workload and this capability is based on the workload that the system has been designed to handle. Increasing the workload of a system beyond this point results in decreased performance of the system.

A computer system comprises resources that are capable of accomplishing tasks. These capabilities and resources may be increased on the computer system in several ways. One of the main resources within a computer system is the CPU, which controls the computer through the interpretation and execution of instructions for the computer and is equal to the amount of computing performed in a unit of time. The addition of extra CPUs increases the capability of the system, which in turn helps to increase the computing power by a percentage of its current capacity.

The amount of data that can be shared between the memory and the storage device depends on the amount of memory and the amount of storage space allocated to the computer system. The availability of more memory means more data can be read from storage devices, assuming the disk subsystem is also capable of handling this increased I/O. This means fewer attempts to get data from disk and this may not provide benefits as required. Increase in performance, along with an increase in resources like CPU, storage, etc., may not provide proportionate benefits or at times may provide negative benefits.

The diminished return with increase in resources could be tied to the theory of economics known as the *Law of Diminishing Returns*. Applying this theory to the current analogy, the law states that *for every additional unit of a resource that is consumed, the benefit that is derived from the additional resource increases at a decreasing rate. In other words, after a certain point with additional resources, no benefit in performance is derived.*

In this chapter the discussions will be focused around the business requirements that drive the information technology in meeting its business goals of the enterprise.

1.2   Modern business requirements

Modern business requirements could be classified by the abilities that the enterprise system should provide, such as availability, reliability, etc., in its day-to-day operations to provide data management to user requests. In this section the various abilities that are expected in today's businesses are discussed along with analysis on how some of these requirements tie into the database tier of the enterprise system.

Modern business requirements are classified by the abilities that a system should provide in its ultimate wisdom of existence. Figure 1.1 is a pictorial representation of the abilities that the modern enterprise system is expected to provide. Overall, these abilities could be assessed as basic requirements in every system. However, with the boom of Internet-based businesses in recent years, abilities such as availability, recoverability, scalability, manageability, and securability (security) have become a necessity. There are those additional elements, not classified under the abilities of a system, that are still vital requirements, such as throughput and response factors of the system. The primary focus of the following discussion will be with respect to the requirements of availability, scalability, manageability, and securability, but will include a brief mention of the other requirements.

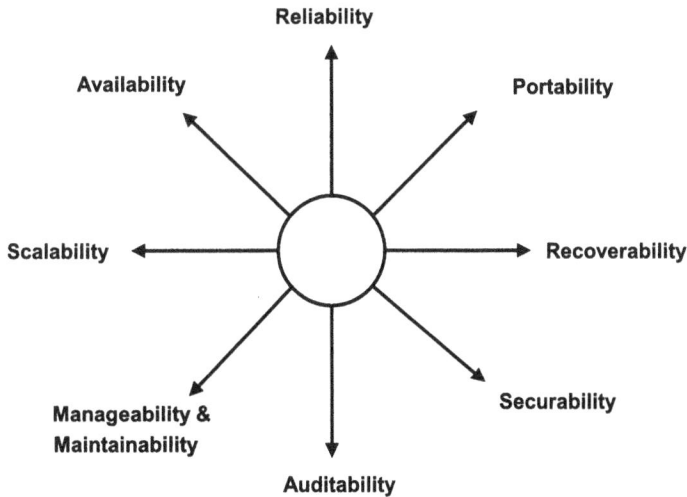

Figure 1.1
*Modern busi-
ness require-
ments (abilities)
of the system.*

1.2.1   Reliability

The reliability requirement says that the system should be reliable, i.e., when a user connects to the system to process a specific request, the system should be guaranteed to provide the expected results or a reasonable response. This requirement applies both to the tools used in the development of the application and to the application logic that is specific to the business. In today's Internet business, if a reliable service cannot be provided, there is the risk of the customer turning to another Internet site for their needs. This obviously would result in lost business.

1.2.2   Portability

Portability is an important requirement that is seldom seriously considered as it relates more to newly established businesses. The requirement of portability ensures that the enterprise systems are portable to various platforms as the business grows and when bigger and more efficient hardware platforms are needed. What this entails is that the development of an application, the supporting tools, the layered products and infrastructure should be organized in such a manner that they could be made available on any hardware platform with minimal or no change. If the requirement of portability is not considered in the early stages of development, the need for it later could potentially require rewrites of the systems, resulting in very expensive development life cycles.

An example under this requirement category would be the selection of the database infrastructure. When businesses start, they normally start small with probably one or two customers, a small server, a database and the application catering to few segments of the total intended market providing the minimal functionality. The reasons for a small start could be many, and definitely, the initial capital investment and the potential business risks. As the business gets established and more customers come aboard, there is the potential concern that the small server that was used to initially start the business may not have the required capacity to handle the additional increased business. At this stage, the enterprise may decide to move to bigger and better platforms. Now the questions normally asked during this process are, will the current application work on this new hardware? Will the infrastructure, including the database on the current hardware, be available on this new hardware? Well, the answer potentially would be maybe, but unless the database platform selected is available on multiple operating systems this may not be possible.

Thus, when selecting important tools and products, it is vital to select those that are supported on most operating systems and hardware platforms. An excellent example in this class would be Oracle RDBMS. Oracle supports almost all operating systems, from Open VMS, to Unix, including Linux and Windows.

1.2.3   Recoverability

Recoverability means that the system should be recoverable from failures with minimal downtime. At a basic level it is the average time required to repair a failed system (for example, an Oracle instance) or the database. Database recoverability directly relates to the quality of the backup strategy in place for the enterprise. A good backup strategy is based on the requirements for recovery time. Ideally, depending on the type of business and its critical nature, the business requirements, or service level agreement (SLA), would state that the system should be up and running quickly after a disaster. The size of a database, the interval at which the backups are being performed and at what level the backups are being taken all affect the recovery time for a database.

Choosing a good backup scheme also depends on the recovery time allowed, or the mean time to recover (MTTR). *MTTR is the desired time required to perform instance or media recovery on the database.* For example, 10 minutes may be set as the goal for media recovery from a disk failure. A variety of factors influence MTTR for media recovery, including the speed of detection, the type of method used to perform media recovery and the size of the database. MTTR of a system should be very low. Under Oracle RDBMS, Recovery Manager (RMAN) provides a good solution toward meeting this business requirement. Features such as block level recovery and backup options such as cumulative, incremental, and full provide a good amount of flexibility to RMAN backup. Using the flashback query option, Oracle provides methods for users to query the database as of a specific time in the past.

System recoverability means that if the system crashes due to reasons such as power surge, power failure, network failure, CPU failure, etc., it should be back up and running in a certain amount of time as defined by the business requirements. In the case of Oracle there is instance recovery, i.e., when a node or instance crashes, recoverability is the mean time required for the instance to perform its recovery operations and be available for users to access. Oracle has made marked progress in this arena of recoverability, with the two-phase recovery process introduced in Oracle *9i*.

1.2.4 Securability

The days when the applications were used in a small finite user community are gone. Under the client server model, the applications were used by a small named set of users and these users were identifiable as they belonged to the same organization.

The Internet-based systems have databases that are accessible from all over the world. Consequently, security of data has become of utmost importance and a high-level requirement. Data is vital to a business and should be protected from hackers. Similarly, the dotcom boom has introduced a new level to sharing applications, through the application service providers (ASP) that allow many organizations and users within these organizations to access data from a common database. Data in this situation should be protected between organizations. That is, data that belongs to one organization should not be visible to others. Oracle has various levels of security available to protect data from outside hackers. Oracle's advanced security option provides encryption of data via the network. Another feature is the private virtual database option, where security could be implemented at the row and column level of tables.

1.2.5 Auditability

Auditability of data refers to the ability to retrieve sufficient information with respect to the creation of data, such as who created the data, why the data was created, who modified the data, when it was modified, etc. This requirement is important and has been in existence since computers were put into use for commercial operations. Organizations are required to maintain their financial related information for many years to meet the legal requirements. Basically, there should be a way to reconstruct a transaction when required. From the database perspective, the system, or tool, should be auditable to track changes that take place against the metadata. Oracle provides various auditing capabilities such as the regular auditing options available to the data block address (DBA) and through some of the new features such as LogMiner and flashback queries. Using the LogMiner feature, the DBA could go back in history (depending on how long the redo logs are retained) to retrieve, track (audit), or roll back changes. In Oracle 9*i*, Oracle has introduced another feature called undo management. Undo management is used in place of rollback segments and will provide abilities to go back in time and examine operations against the database.

1.2.6 Manageability and maintainability

Manageability is a broad area with many aspects. Systems being developed should be easily maintainable and manageable from every tier of the enterprise system. While it may be common to assume that maintainability and manageability is the same thing, the two terms are, in fact, different. Maintainability refers to the everyday continuance or protection of a system, such as the implementation of system and functionality level changes to the system. Manageability refers to the monitoring, tuning, and organization of the system.

Manageability of business requirements entail that the application tier, network tier, database tier, etc., should be easily tunable. From the application tier perspective, there should be considerable options available to manage and monitor the health of the systems. When the business application is developed, the application should provide options to view and tune various thresholds that would help tune application performance. Similarly, development platforms selected should support tools and features that help support these requirements. The tools or methods used should offer visibility into some of the problems and internal operations of the operating system, the layered products, and the infrastructure such as the database, providing a means to understanding the issues and problems and a method for fixing them. For example, Oracle's wait interface (V$SYSTEM_EVENT, V$SESSION_EVENT, V$SESSION_WAIT, and other tools) provides visibility to some of the internals of the Oracle database behavior, providing a better opportunity to approach the issue in a scientific manner.

Every system developed is subject to continuous change throughout its life cycle, from the initial inception or implementation, to upgrades of business functionality, to upgrades of technology, etc. Maintainability of the system is the opportunity to make changes to the system. Thus development servers and database servers selected should allow for configuration changes.

1.2.7 Scalability

Scalability is typically defined in one of two ways, either as the ability to mature the system in accordance with growth in business or as the ability of the application, or enterprise system, to accept additional users in accordance with growth in business without rewriting or redesigning systems. Scalability can be vertical or horizontal (linear). When considering the growth of an enterprise system, linear scalability should be the preferred choice of configuration when compared to vertical scalability. Linear scalability can also provide vertical scalability. While vertical scalability supports more users by increasing the capacity of the existing hardware, linear scalability supports more users by increasing the number of hardware systems (nodes) participating in the configuration. From a systems perspective, a hardware clustering provides this. (*A cluster is a group of independent hardware systems or nodes that are interconnected to provide a single computer source.*) Linear scalability brought about by clustered hardware solutions also provides distribution of user workload among many nodes. Oracle provides a large number of features that support scalability.

Combined with their respective operating systems, hardware clusters provide system level scalability on the database front. Database features, such as Real Application Cluster (RAC), which runs on a clustered operating system, take advantage of clustering. Adding the clustered database configuration to the fusion helps in providing linear scalability at the database tier of the enterprise system.

Under a clustered database configuration such as RAC, as additional users start accessing the system and if there is a resource contention with the existing configuration, additional nodes and additional instances could be added to the system without much difficulty. Oracle Parallel Server (OPS), the predecessor to RAC technology, started with the feature of adding and removing instances as an Oracle solution. By taking advantage of the cluster interconnect technology to transfer and share information, RAC has taken this feature to the next level of scalability.

Another functionality that scalability indirectly provides is throughput for the enterprise system. Scalability helps in higher throughput, especially with linear scalability, when more and more users would connect to the system from more instances providing workload distribution; these instances could all provide the workload that a single instance originally provided, thus providing more data throughput. The system should be able to provide sufficient throughput to meet the demand of users on the system.

1.2.8 Availability

Availability is another important requirement in today's Internet-based business and is often combined with reliability. This combination is due to the fact that, under most circumstances, both reliability and availability are grouped together as one requirement. To illustrate the difference, take the example from the previous section; when a particular item is requested of the system but the user does not get the requested item and instead gets another item, then the system is considered unreliable. However, if the system was not even up to take the request, then the system is said to be not available; consequently, availability becomes the issue. The common ground is in the English terminology; when it is said that if the system is unavailable then it is considered unreliable.

Availability is measured by the system's uptime for a given period of time. Normally, availability is calculated by the number of hours in a year that the system has been up on a continuous basis. The needs of a system could be loosely defined as the crossing point between the system uptime cost and business downtime cost. Uptime increases at a very rapid rate, eventually reaching infinity as it approaches 100% uptime.

An example of this crossover is shown in Figure 1.2. In this example, the best point, according to the given data, would be 99.5% availability, with a lower availability being too costly in terms of business downtime and higher availability in terms of wasted hardware/software resources.

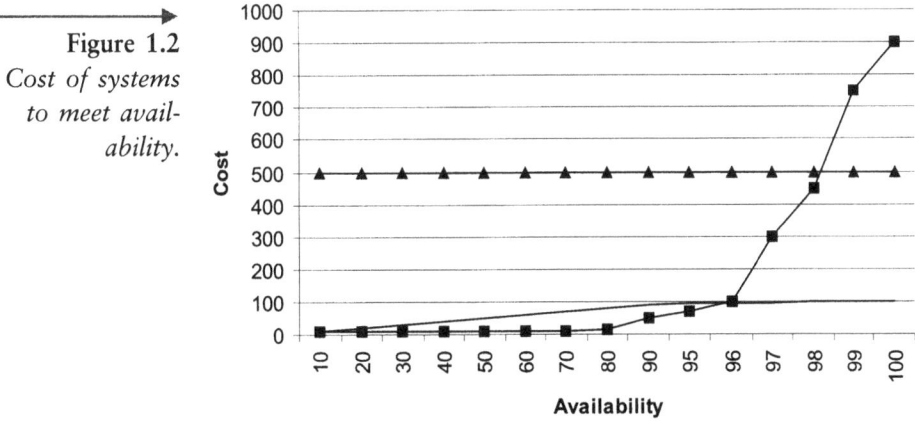

Figure 1.2
Cost of systems to meet availability.

When defining availability requirements, it is important to differentiate between needs at critical times and the needs for other periods. This should be done on separate charts by factoring the cost factor of the operation. Figure 1.2 illustrates this. When the availability requirement is lower, it becomes too costly in business downtime. When higher availability could mean smaller downtime and a smaller loss of business and when downtime is translated into lost revenue, there could be a relationship drawn with wasted hardware/software resources.

Linearly clustered configuration not only provides support for increased workload but also provides distribution of workload amongst many nodes in the cluster. Linear scalability, with appropriate application architecture and products, provides availability of the enterprise systems. If designed and constructed well, the system could provide continuous availability of the application.

Availability is also measured by the amount of time the system has been up and is available for operation. In defining availability of the system, the word "system" does not apply to just the database tier or the application tier, but to the complete enterprise system. This implies that every piece of equipment, including networks, servers, application controllers, disk subsystems, etc., should be considered for availability. Making all tiers of the enterprise system available also means that each tier should provide redundant hardware, helping to provide continuous service when one of the components fails.

Providing this type of availability is based on the actual requirement in place. If the requirement is 99.99% uptime in a 24 hour schedule, 365 days of the year, redundant architecture will become a necessity. However, if some amount of downtime is allowed and does not affect the entire

Table 1.1   *Acceptable Downtime Measurement*

Availability Requirement	Expected Downtime per Year
99.995%	0.5 hours
99.97%	2.5 hours
99.8%	17.5 hours
99.5%	43.2 hours or 1.8 days
99%	88.8 hours or 3.7 days
98%	175.2 hours or 7.3 days
96%	350.4 hours or 14.6 days
6 * 16	All day Sunday and 8 hours/night

business, then all of this redundancy would possibly not be required. Consequently, availability is measured by the amount of downtime that is allowed per year.

Taking a different perspective on the data represented in Figure 1.2, Table 1.1 and Figure 1.3 offer an analysis of the availability and the corresponding hours of downtime allowed. Each percentage value indicates that the system can only be down for a certain number of hours.

Table 1.1 provides the expected downtime per year for the various levels of availability requirements. The table illustrates the fact that the cost of availability rises substantially with each fraction increase in the availability requirement. This table is graphically represented in Figure 1.3,

Figure 1.3
Acceptable downtime measurement.

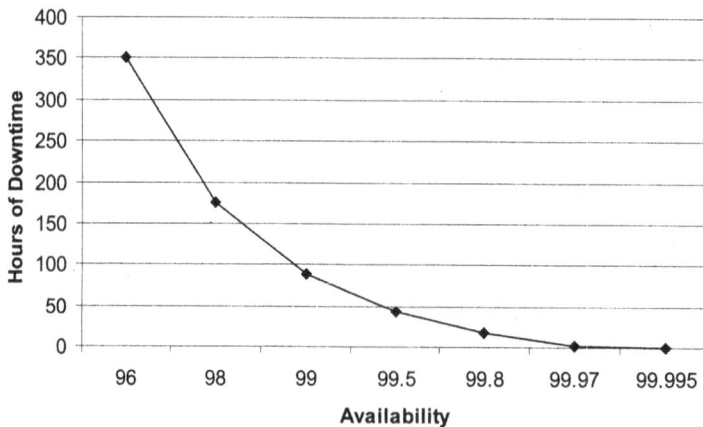

which indicates that a 99.97% availability requirement means that the system could only be down for about 2.5 hours in a year. This means 2.5 hours of downtime for any part of the enterprise system including the database tier. In 2.5 hours on the database tier nothing significant like restores, database recovery, upgrades, etc., is possible, however strong or foolproof the architecture and the supporting infrastructures are. The reality of the situation is that every system is prone to failures, and 2.5 hours per year of downtime is probably not sufficient.

The main factor to consider in determining availability is to keep the mean time between failures (MTBF) high. (*MTBF is the average time (usually expressed in hours) that a component works without failure. It is calculated by dividing the total number of failures into the total number of operating hours observed. The term can also mean the length of time a user can reasonably expect a device or system to work before a failure occurs.*) Keeping the MTBF high to meet this 99.99% availability in a normal configuration (e.g., a single instance Oracle configuration) is difficult in a database tier because every database including Oracle is prone to failure.

Modern business requirements stipulate that systems developed and implemented should be capable of providing continuous availability. Applications developed are prone to failures. The applications cannot provide the requirement of continuous availability unless the underlying infrastructure systems support this requirement. This adds to the requirement that the products, tools, utilities, and the infrastructure selected should also be capable of providing this requirement. The percentage of availability, the right technology, and the actual solution is determined by preparing a cost-benefit analysis.

RAC provides functionality that supports a close to 99.99% availability requirement by providing multiple instances to share a common database. RAC is a two or more node configuration where each instance communicates to a common shared single copy of the physical database. From either node, users could access the database to retrieve information. With some of the database features, such as Transparent Application Failover (TAF),[1] users could be migrated to the available node transparently as if no such failure had happened.

---

1.   TAF is discussed in Chapter 10 (Availability and Scalability).

1.2.9 Response

When compared to the responsiveness of the system, all other business requirements could be deemed less important. Response time from a user's perspective is the time taken for the system to respond to a request. From the system's perspective, response time would be the service time plus the wait time, i.e., the time taken by the system to gather the information requested by the user and the amount of wait time experienced by the system due to other hurdles encountered while gathering the requested information before providing the response to the user. The goal of the application developed should be to meet this important goal of response, because this specific requirement is critical to provide user satisfaction. It is user satisfaction that promotes loyalty of customers to a business and attracts new ones.

The service time depends on the ability of the application to process the information efficiently, which includes the efficiency of the SQL queries (if any) to retrieve data as well as the efficiency of the database tier to respond to these requests.

The wait time is affected by external factors like network latency, disk latency, etc., and is controlled and/or improved by systematically/scientifically approaching the various factors that cause these waits. Oracle has evolved and matured over the years, providing details at the database internals level, and will help to scientifically approach the issues and resolve any waits to improve the response time of the system.

1.3   Conclusion

Business requirements have evolved over the years and have started requiring more tangible factors in enterprise systems. Prior to the Internet boom, this level of requirements was not necessary for the client server application. This is evident through the following:

- Security was considered, but only to the walls of the organization.

- Scalability was considered, but only to the number of users inside the enterprise that would access the system.

- Availability was considered, but only on a smaller scale because downtime only meant affecting and informing the users in the organization.

The Internet has changed every requirement such that each requirement implemented has a matrix and SLA associated with it.

In this chapter we discussed the various modern business requirements, like reliability, availability, scalability, and recoverability, to name a few. The requirements play a very important part in modern businesses where users' dependency on computer systems after the Internet boom has been overwhelming. To keep with this increased demand the main challenge that the various organizations are facing today is to provide for scalability and availability. To meet these basic requirements, all other requirements listed in this chapter play an important part, either directly or indirectly influencing the organization's business direction.

Applications developed to provide the business functions of the organization depend on the underlying layered product technology. It is important that if these underlying layered products do not meet these requirements, this would influence the application and, in turn, the business as a whole.

While analyzing the various requirements we also looked at whether the layered products such as Oracle satisfy these features.

In the next chapter, various hardware architectures, such as SMP, MPP, NUMA, etc., are discussed at length. Also explored is the usage of clustered SMP architecture as a prudent solution for businesses with data processing needs. This architecture allows businesses to provide data storage and retrieval to users and to support increased growth of users through linear scalability. When many systems are joined together to work as a cohesive unit, they support not only the scalability factor but also the availability factor, provided an appropriate clustered operating system is used. When one system or node in the cluster fails, the users have other nodes that could be used to route their request to get to the required information. Consequently, clustering provides linear scalability, which means that more nodes or systems could be added into the mix without much difficulty. More availability is provided due to the fact that when one node in the cluster fails, the failure of one node in the cluster does not down the system, as the other nodes are available to process the required information.

The options and features around other hardware layers such as the storage subsystem, cluster interconnect, and the storage devices will also be discussed in detail.

2

Hardware Concepts

2.1   Introduction

In the previous chapter, we started with a basic introduction to this book and discussed the modern business requirements covering the various abilities that a system should possess, like availability, scalability, manageability, etc. Then we stated that clustered solutions are required to meet most of these requirements. However, to determine if a clustered solution was really the option, we stated that a complete feasibility study followed by a capacity planning is required.

Meeting these requirements ensures that the computer systems that are used today and in the future should be robust enough to handle the dynamic growth of users, both locally within the organization and across the world where users could potentially access any system via the Internet.

This requires that the systems selected to support the various enterprise systems should be able to satisfy the business requirements listed in the previous chapter. While the basic requirements are possible, to maximize the potential to support those requirements depends on the underlying technology that is selected. This stipulates another requirement that, while selecting the technology to run the system, for example, the hardware platform, the hardware technology, storage systems, database systems, etc., considerable care and study should be provided before arriving at a suitable choice.

In this chapter the various hardware architectures such as SMP, MPP, NUMA, etc., will be discussed at length. We will also explore the usage of clustered SMP architecture as a prudent solution for businesses with data processing needs. This architecture allows businesses to provide data storage and retrieval to users and to support increased growth of users through linear scalability. We will discuss areas where many systems are joined together to work as a cohesive unit, how they support not only the scalability factor but also the availability factor. When one system or node in the cluster fails, the users have other nodes that could be used to route their request to get to the required information.

How do these systems meet the scalability requirement? In this chapter we will discuss clustering in relation to the hardware architectures and discuss how clustering will help meet the scalability requirement. Finally, we will also look at the storage subsystems. Selection of the right storage systems helps in meeting the availability requirement. For this, it is important to select the appropriate storage architecture while taking into consideration the performance requirements. The various RAID technologies and the appropriate benefits of using one over the other will be discussed.

2.2   Uniprocessor model

The uniprocessor model has the simplest architecture, including a single processor (that interprets and executes computer instructions) and cache connected to the memory and I/O controllers through a shared bus. Devices on this bus communicate with the CPU and memory bus by a bridge between the two buses. A common example of this type of architecture is the antiquated personal computers (PCs) such as the 486 and 586.

Due to the nature of this architecture, applications, or servers, may not be suitable for this structure. Most application and database engines today have many processes and a single processor environment would be inefficient. This is specifically true in the case of Oracle. Oracle has a multiprocess architecture; its background processes DBWR, LGWR, PMON, SMON, etc., contend for CPU resources, and serious performance concerns arise when they are run in a uniprocessor environment. Consequently, this implies that, at any time, only one person can execute an SQL statement or a PL/SQL package or make an OCI request to the database.

The architecture in Figure 2.1 has only one processing engine in the system. For implementations of Oracle multiprocess architecture, the uniprocessor architecture with just one processor brought about significant restrictions. Uniprocessors are more suited for home computing and simple stand-alone applications that do not require a database environment.

The alternative system to the uniprocessor model is the *multiprocessor* model. As the name indicates, multiprocessor models have two or more CPUs or processors.

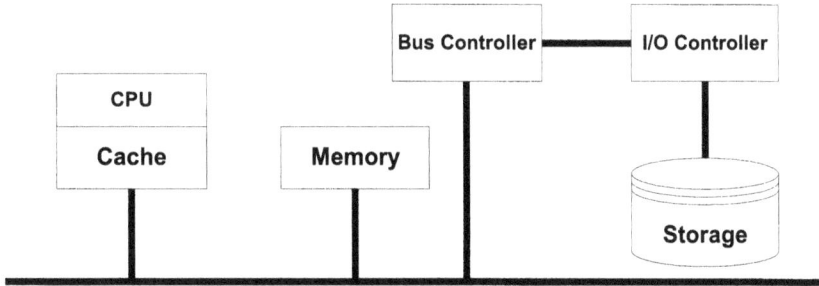

Figure 2.1
*Single processor
(uniprocessor)
architecture.*

2.3   Multiprocessor model

The multiprocessor model is an extension of the uniprocessor model as it has multiple processors and memory subsystems. The most common model under this category is the symmetric multiprocessor (SMP) model. In addition to the SMP model, the multiprocessor model has further extensions such as the massively parallel processing (MPP) model, the non-uniform memory access (NUMA) model, and the clustered SMP model.

In the subsequent sections the following multiprocessor architectures will be briefly discussed:

1.   Symmetric multiprocessor (SMP)

2.   Massively parallel processor (MPP)

3.   Non-uniform memory access (NUMA)

SMP and MPP systems can also be classified under the category of uniform memory access systems.

2.3.1   Symmetric multiprocessor (SMP) architecture

This model is an extension of the uniprocessor model and is the first in the series of multiprocessor models. SMP (symmetric multiprocessing) is the processing of programs by multiple processors that share a common operating system and memory (i.e., all of the memory in the system is directly accessible as local memory by all processors).

In symmetric, or "tightly coupled," multiprocessing, the processors share memory and the I/O bus or data path. A single copy of the operating system is in charge of all the processors. SMP systems are also called "shared everything configuration." The advantages of a shared everything/ tightly coupled system will be discussed in detail later in this chapter.

Figure 2.2
*Symmetric
multiprocessor
(SMP) architec-
ture.*

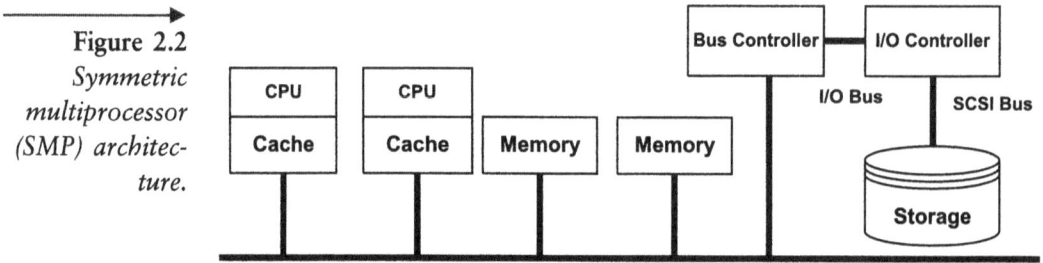

Due to the shared everything architecture, SMP systems are suitable for online transaction processing (OLTP), where many users access the same shared I/O and data paths to the disk systems with a relatively simple set of transactions.

Figure 2.2 illustrates the SMP architecture, where the I/O, memory, bus controllers, and storage systems are shareable. Unlike the uniprocessor machines, these systems can hold multiple CPUs and memory buses, thus providing scalability of the architecture. For this reason they are appropriate for multiprocess systems like Oracle, which has multiple foreground and background processes and is best suited for the SMP architecture.

Another notable advantage of the SMP model is that multiple SMP systems could be clustered together to work as a single unit. The advantages and disadvantages of the clustered SMP model will be discussed in detail later in this chapter following explanation of the MPP and NUMA architectures.

2.3.2 Massively parallel processing (MPP) architecture

A massively parallel processor (MPP) is also known as the "shared nothing configuration." In an MPP configuration, each processor has private, non-shared memory, and possibly its own disk or storage subsystem. MPP architecture allows accessibility from all nodes in the system to local disks. An MPP node has its own operating system, CPUs, disk, and memory. Data is communicated through a message-passing network. MPP systems are considered better than SMP systems for applications that require scaling to a very large database. These include decision support and warehousing applications.

2.3.3 Non-uniform memory access (NUMA)

Non-uniform Memory Access (NUMA) is described as a cross between an SMP and an MPP system. Systems with NUMA architecture have a single operating system and database instance, and provide a single memory address space similar to SMP. CPUs of the local processor node or group are connected to local memory and local disks via a local shared bus and to other processor groups via a high-speed interconnect.

NUMA indicates that it will take longer to access some regions of memory than others. This is due to the fact that some regions of memory are physically on different buses. This may result in poor performance of some programs that are not NUMA-aware. It also introduces the concept of local and remote memory. The memory globally available to the entire cluster is typically the union of all the physical memory banks attached to each physical node (i.e., if node 1 has 2 GB, node 2 has 2 GB, and node 3 has 3 GB, then the collective memory available for the entire cluster is 7 GB of global memory).

With NUMA architecture, the access to a memory location is not uniform in that the memory may be local or remote with respect to the location of which CPU is running the code. The memory is local when the code references physical memory attached to the same node bus where the CPU is attached. The memory is remote when the physical memory referenced is attached to another node.

Shared memory sections map the virtual address spaces of different processes to the same physical address space. In NUMA, the physical address space is spanned among the physical nodes defining the cluster. This allows the shared memory segment to be striped among the available physical nodes.

The NUMA architecture was designed to surpass the scalability limits of the SMP architecture. With SMP, all memory access is posted to the same shared memory bus. This performs well for a relatively small number of CPUs; however, problems arise with the shared bus when there are dozens of CPUs competing for access to the shared memory bus. NUMA alleviates these bottlenecks by limiting the number of CPUs on any one-memory bus, thus connecting the various nodes by means of a high-speed interconnect.

The main benefit of NUMA, as mentioned above, is scalability. It is extremely difficult to scale SMP systems past 8–12 CPUs. Utilizing that many number of CPUs places the single shared memory bus under heavy contention. Using a NUMA-based solution is one way of reducing the number of CPUs competing for access to a shared memory bus. Figure 2.3 represents the NUMA architecture displaying multiple nodes, with each node having its own set of CPUs and other resources, including the storage systems.

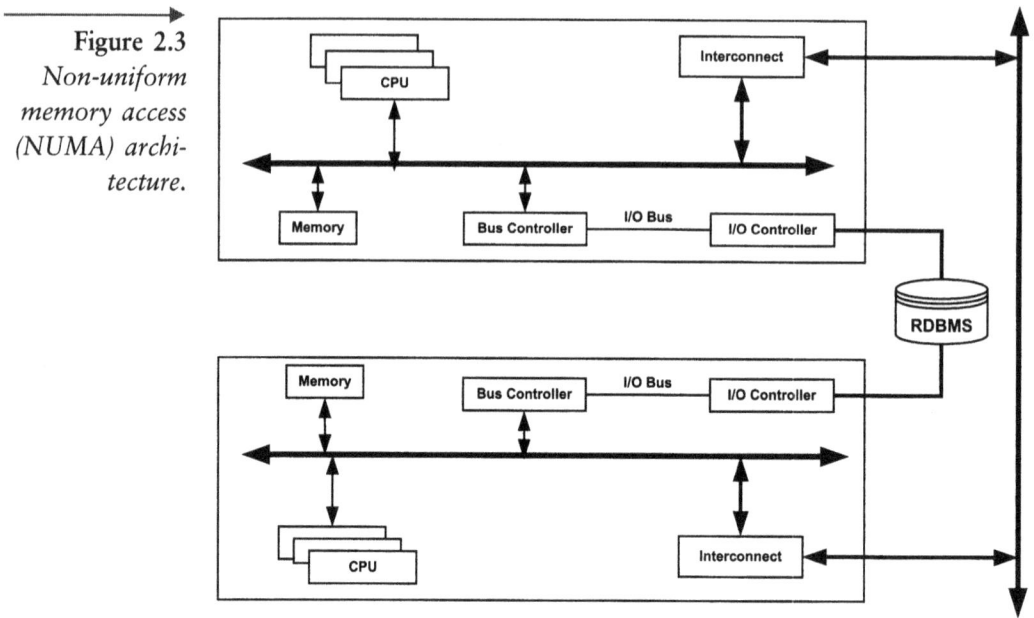

Figure 2.3
*Non-uniform
memory access
(NUMA) archi-
tecture.*

The implementation of Oracle on NUMA architecture may not provide the expected results for many reasons. Firstly, Oracle is a large consumer of shared memory segments. Oracle's architecture comprises multiple background and foreground processors that map to the shared memory segments, or SGA, to access structures like buffer cache, library cache, etc. With the striped concept of memory management in NUMA architecture, the SGA will be striped equally among the physical nodes. This will result in the background and foreground processes running on different CPUs.

Figure 2.4 represents implementation of Oracle on a three-node cluster using the NUMA architecture and illustrates the memory management across multiple nodes. In the figure, Oracle background and foreground processors are running on different CPUs. Also illustrated is the shared memory, which is striped across all the three nodes in the cluster. I/O peripherals such as disks are physically attached to I/O modules accessed by nodes.

While NUMA architecture provides great benefit for processor sharing and efficiency in a clustered configuration, industry maturity on this model is low.

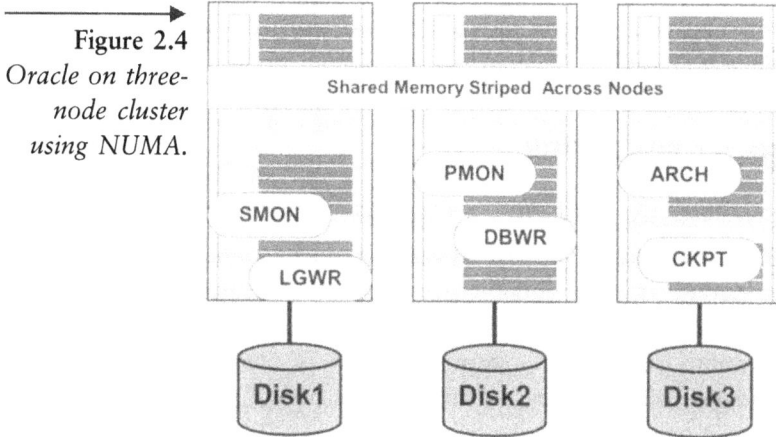

Figure 2.4
Oracle on three-node cluster using NUMA.

2.4   Clustered systems

A clustered system is a number of things of the same sort organized together, or growing together, to form or represent a group of their respective kind. For example, a number of people, flowers, or things grouped together forms a cluster. Similarly, a group of independent hardware systems or nodes that are interconnected to provide a single computer source is referred to as a hardware cluster. Unlike flowers and other objects, if one node in a cluster fails, its workload is automatically distributed among the surviving nodes. This process of automatically distributing the workload to other available nodes reduces downtime of the entire system. Clustering is an architecture that keeps systems running in the event of a single system failure. Clustering provides maximum scalability by grouping separate servers into a single computing facility. Clusters have the potential to provide excellent price/performance advantages over traditional mainframe systems in many areas, such as availability, scalability, manageability, and recoverability. Clustering plays an essential role in various computing paradigms such as Internets, Intranets, and systems that require uninterrupted high-availability solutions.

Digital Equipment Corporation (now acquired by HP) was an early pioneer in clustering. Its primary operating system, VMS, offered built-in clustering support. There are thousands of companies still successfully running Digital VAXClusters. The VMS operating system offered a single system view of the cluster and allowed both the users and the system administrator to use any node indistinguishably from any other. The proprietary nature of VMS (even after Digital pasted the word "open" in front of the operating system name) along with the evolution of super-cheap hardware makes VMS a less demanding product.

2.4.1 Types of clustering

When businesses start small and have low capital budget to invest, it is probable that configurations are minimal, consisting of one or two machines with a storage array to support the database implementation. However, as the business grows, expansion follows and consequently the current configuration (single node, storage system) is not able to handle the increased load due to increased business. It is typical at this point to either upgrade the current hardware by adding more CPUs and other required resources or to add multiple systems to work as a cohesive unit/cluster. However, increasing resources is similar to placing a temporary bandage on the system as it solves the current situation of increased business and demand, but only shifts the issue to be dealt with to a future date as the workload will invariably increase once again. Instead of adding more memory, or CPU, to the existing configuration, which could be referred to as vertical scaling, another system(s) should be added to provide load balancing, workload distribution, and availability. This functionality is achieved by scaling the boxes horizontally, or in a linear fashion, and by configuring these systems to work as a single cohesive unit or a cluster.

Figure 2.5 illustrates the advantages of horizontal scalability over vertical scalability. The growth potential on a vertically scalable system is

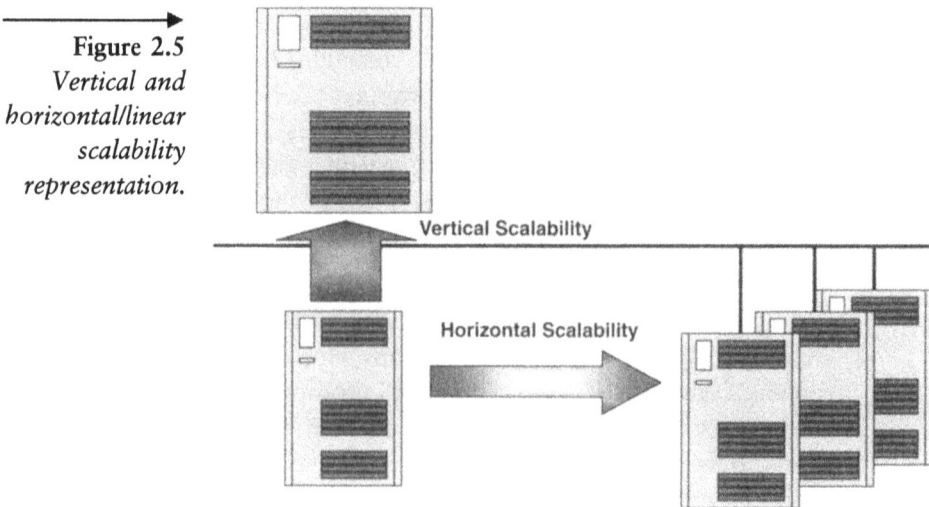

Figure 2.5
Vertical and horizontal/linear scalability representation.

limited and, as explained earlier, reaches a point where the addition of resources does not provide proportionally improved results. Because clusters offer both horizontal (linear) and vertical scalability, the cluster model provides investment protection. Horizontal scalability is the ability to add more nodes to the cluster to provide more functionality. These nodes may be relatively small and/or inexpensive, offering economical upgradeability options that might offer enhancements to a single large system. Vertical scalability is the ability to upgrade individual nodes to higher specifications.

2.4.2 Clustered SMP

A clustered SMP configuration is two SMP systems combined together and managed by one operating system. Working as a cluster provides a single cohesive unit of equipment. Under this configuration, each system has its own processor and memory; however, the storage or disk subsystem is shared between the various systems that participate in the cluster.

Clustering has proven to be a successful architecture of choice for providing high availability and scalability in business-critical computing applications. Clients interact with a cluster as though it were a single entity, or a single high-performance, highly reliable server. If a cluster fails, its workload is automatically distributed among the surviving nodes.

A clustered system is highly integrated by tightly or loosely coupled multiprocessor configurations (or nodes) and storage subsystems communicating with one another for the purpose of sharing data and other resources. In Figure 2.6 it should be noted that each system, or node, has its own CPUs, memory controllers, etc.; however, each shares one common disk system. Such a configuration is best suited for an Oracle Parallel Server (OPS, available with Oracle Versions 7.3 and 8.1) and its successor, Real Application Cluster (RAC, available with Oracle 9*i*).

2.4.3 Tightly vs. loosely coupled

Multiprocessing systems can be either tightly or loosely coupled, depending on how hardware resources are allocated among the processors. Tightly coupled systems share system resources. This makes tightly coupled systems less scalable for applications relying on independent processes and data because of the overhead associated with resource sharing. Tightly coupled clustered configurations do not provide any inherent fault-tolerance. The failure of a single critical component, such as

Figure 2.6
*Clustered SMP
configuration
model.*

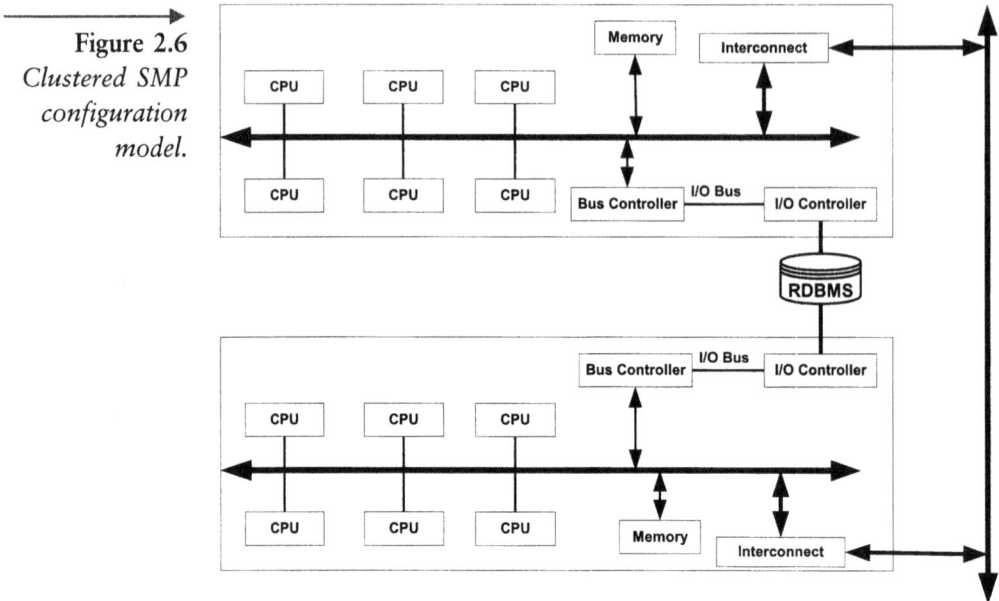

the CPU, could bring the entire system down. Tightly coupled systems are more scalable for applications relying on dependent processes and data because through resource sharing their interprocess communications costs are lower.

The opposite of tightly coupled configurations are the loosely coupled configurations or systems. Loosely coupled clusters eliminate some of the drawbacks of SMP systems, providing improved fault tolerance and easier incremental system growth. These loosely coupled SMP clusters comprise multiple nodes, with each node consisting of a single processing unit (SMP unit) and its own dedicated system memory. The storage systems can be configured as "share nothing" or "shared disk" cluster system with each node having direct access to the disk.

Some of the distinguishing attributes between tightly coupled and loosely coupled multiprocessor configurations are shown in Table 2.1.

Figure 2.7 represents a two-node cluster configuration. In the figure, two nodes participate in the cluster configuration; sharing Disk1 and Disk2 as a single disk configuration on a single bus and communication between the nodes A and B is through a high-speed cluster interconnect.

This enables users to transparently exploit all available resources on a tightly coupled system. For example, in a loosely coupled implementation of a car rental operation (fully deployed using Oracle products), if the

Table 2.1   *Tightly Coupled Vs. Loosely Coupled*

Tightly Coupled	Loosely Coupled
Processors in a tightly coupled system share certain hardware resources in a manner that makes interprocessor timing and synchronization absolutely critical. Thus, the processors that make up the CPU of a tightly coupled system typically conform to the same architecture and execute the same instruction set.	In a loosely coupled configuration, processors can conform to different architectures and therefore can execute different operating systems.
Processors that make up the CPU resource in a tightly coupled configuration typically execute the same operating system. This enforces the same policies for resource allocation, utilization and control.	Loosely coupled configuration processors can conform to different architectures and therefore can execute different operating systems.
Processors in a tightly coupled configuration share hardware resources in a manner that requires all the CPU resources of such a system to be confined to a relatively small area.	In a loosely coupled configuration, the CPU resources are more widely spread apart and lend themselves to a more distributed model.
In a tightly coupled system, resources are generally accessible to all processes in that system. A tightly coupled configuration is usually treated as a single management and security domain.	In the case of a loosely coupled configuration each system has its own security domain, management console and could potentially have a different operating system. This makes it very difficult to manage, support, and operate.

Figure 2.7
*Two-node
cluster
configuration.*

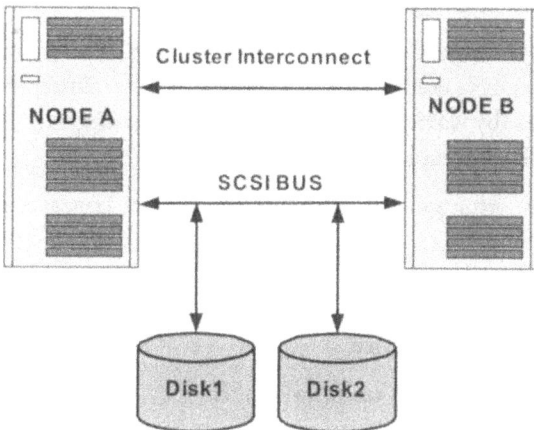

online car availability database system fails, rentals cannot be made, service ultimately suffers, customers are disappointed, and the agency eventually loses business. However, in a tightly clustered configuration, if the system that runs the car availability database system fails, users are transferred to the available node, delivering maximum system availability.

In order to obtain an understanding of "true" clustering, the features in each type of configuration must be understood. To help understand these differences it would be advantageous to compare and contrast the behavior of the following areas under tightly and loosely coupled configurations:

- Resource sharing

- Common system disk

- Cost-effective utilization of resources

- CPU processor composition

- Operating system composition

- File system flexibility

- Flexible user environment

- High availability

- Disaster tolerance

- System management and security

- Failover

- Growth potential and scalability

Resource sharing

In today's high-availability, highly scalable environments, availability of resources is a key concern. Systems in the cluster help in cost-effective measures by saving resources through sharing storage devices, printers, and CPU processors. For example:

- *Disk storage* is used for read/write operation from the nodes participating in the clustered configuration. Nodes that are not configured to write directly to the storage devices can access the storage devices through one of the other nodes that are defined to provide this service.

- *Printers* can be configured such that print jobs can be execute from any of the nodes participating in the clustered configuration.

■   *CPU processors* on one or more systems can synchronize their access to shared resources. For example, three C programs can simultaneously update a file on a shared disk, and a mixture of C, COBOL, and Java programs can update a common shared disk file. Similarly, four CPU processors can concurrently run independent programs that read and update into the same open file.

Common system disk

Every system or computer, clustered or non-clustered, has disks allocated that contain the system files (or the operating system files), which are essential for regular operation of the system. When nodes are coupled together to form a cluster, each node can still have its own system disk, or the operating system disk, or can share a common disk that contains one single copy of the operating system. While there are positives and negatives in either approach, it is ideal to have separate copies of the operating system for each system to provide availability during any disk failure of any one system in the cluster.

We will discuss the storage subsystems in more detail later in this chapter.

Cost-effective utilization of resources

On regular systems, a certain number of disks are assigned or attached to the system. These disks are often backed up and data from them is deleted to create more space for more data. Under circumstances where the data is critical and cannot be deleted, the standard option would be to purchase more storage disks and attach them to the node that requires more space. Similarly, when the system is fully utilized, the options available are to shut down certain processes that are consuming the CPU or to buy more CPUs and plug them into the nodes. Buying such resources is expensive, and the money could be utilized more effectively in other areas.

A loosely coupled clustering configuration provides a solution to this. If the disks are utilized over the limit, and the other disk(s) are idle, then the other disks could be shared amongst the nodes that need more disk storage. *Please note that in today's deployment scenarios, on most systems, the disks are available to all nodes in the cluster. This is also true with the utilization of resources such as the CPU.* If one node of a two-node clustered configuration has its CPUs utilized to the maximum, then certain processors could be transferred to the node that has CPU resources available and executed from there.

CPU processor composition

Timing and synchronization are critical among processors in a single, tightly coupled multiprocessor system. These processors usually conform to the same architecture. Consequently, if a system has two CPUs they should be of the same type and execute the same instruction set, sharing a common in-memory copy of the operating system.

A loosely coupled configuration can incorporate multiple processor types with varying processor types from system to system. In spite of this support being available, this option is seldom practiced, as it is more of a theoretical concept rather than a practical solution. Normally, all nodes in a clustered configuration have the same sets or number of CPUs and are of the same processor types. This helps in load balancing and compatibility in execution of processors when one system fails and users or processes are transferred to the other node in the cluster.

Operating system and file system flexibility

In the case of loosely coupled systems, different operating systems could run on each node in the cluster. These types of configuration add complexity from many aspects. Most operating systems have a different read/write structure and the shared disks cannot share the files across both operating systems. For example, if one node has the Unix operating system and the other has VMS, there could be considerable incompatibility in the file systems for both operating systems. Thus, when a process executing on the VMS system creates a file, it has a specific storage structure based on the internals of the VMS operating system. A process compiled and executing on another operating system, such as Unix, could not normally read this.

However, when both the operating systems are of the same type (for example, Unix is located on both machines), then the file system is compatible. This could create a situation in which the files may be read to or written from either or both nodes 100% of the time.

The same rule holds true in the case of security and protection mechanisms. Varying the operating system could create detrimental situations for system managers and may cause them to deal with multiple security and authentication rules for both operating systems. However, when all nodes participating in the cluster have the same operating system, the difference will not exist and operability is much more simple and convenient.

The cluster file system makes all files visible to and accessible by all cluster members such that all members participating in the clustered configuration hold the same view.

Flexible user environment

Users and resources can easily be distributed to meet the specific needs of the environment, and they can easily be redistributed as those needs change over time.

Certain clustered configurations such as Tru64 Unix clusters[1] allow users to log into a cluster level address called a cluster alias (*a cluster alias is an Internet Protocol (IP) address that makes some or all of the systems in the cluster look like a single system*) and the cluster load balance distributes the user to the appropriate node in the cluster based on availability of resources. The load-balancing feature at the operating system level helps in workload distribution and removes the need for load balancing routers at the hardware level. The load balancing option frees up the clients from having to connect to a specific cluster member for services. In clustered systems that are set up to use cluster aliases, each system in a cluster explicitly joins with the aliases to which it wants to belong. If a member of an alias is unavailable, the cluster stops sending packets to that member and routes packets to active members of that alias.

The cluster alias supports load balancing between the nodes participating in the clustered configuration. The load balancing can be achieved in many different ways; however, the simplest solution is round-robin Domain Name Service (DNS). A round-robin DNS is where a single DNS name is shared among several IP addresses. When a query is made to the DNS server, it reuses the returned IP addresses.

Another major benefit of this configuration is that a client is able to interact with a cluster as though the cluster is a single server, even though many servers may be part of the cluster. The cluster provides a single management entity. As discussed earlier, clustering provides increased availability, greater scalability, and easier management.

High availability

High availability has various meanings in today's computing environment, which differ from person to person. The term "availability," in the context of a computer system, implies that the system is available for use.

---

1.   COMPAQ Tru64 Unix Version 5.1 and above when the clustering version is installed.

Availability of a system is probably the most important property that the computer system should have. If a system is not available to run the workloads it is intended to run and to perform the tasks that are vital to the business, then it does not matter how fast it is or how much memory it has, it basically becomes an expensive pile of useless material.

The term "high availability" means that the system is available most of the time. In today's Internet-based computing environment, this requirement has been defined at 99.999% (or five-nine availability). This means that systems have a continuous uptime including nights and weekends, days, months, and years.

In the fiercely competitive arena of the Internet business, if the web site is not available, or the system is unable to process an order because the backend server is down, it is highly probable that the customer would attempt to access the site a second time, but probably not a third time. This could mean a loss of a potential new customer or damaged relationship with an existing one. All businesses, large and small, need increased availability to stay competitive. Running a business 7 days a week for 24 hours a day has become the standard and a necessity for a company at all levels (small, medium, or large).

High availability is configured in today's systems by providing redundancy at all levels of the system, including connections, network, controllers, nodes, disks, etc. Figure 2.8 represents a two-node total redundancy system with failover options at every level of the equipment. This type of totally redundant configuration supports and provides a higher availability and includes the following functions:

- When a system leaves the cluster, the remaining systems go through a cluster state transition and, during this phase, automatically adjusts the new cluster membership.

- When one path to the storage device fails, the device can be accessed through an alternate path.

- If one communication path fails, systems that are part of the clustered configuration can still exchange information on the remaining communication paths.

- Using volume shadowing and a mirrored disks option provides availability at the disk subsystem/storage level. This means when one disk fails, the information is still available on the other mirrored disk. For example, in a RAID 1 configuration, which is mirror only, a copy of the data is simultaneously saved on disks; that is, the original disk

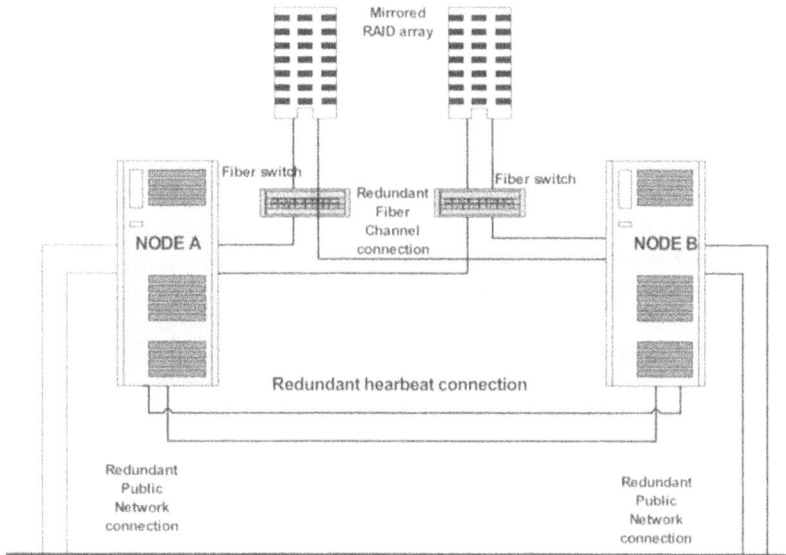

Figure 2.8
Various levels of redundancy for high-availability systems.

and the mirrored disk. When one of the disks is unusable, the system continues operation by accessing the other disk as if no loss was encountered. Because of this, users are not affected.

The high-availability scenario also applies to application systems accessing the clustered configuration. In the event of a server failure (due to hardware, application, or operator fault) another node, configured as the secondary node, automatically assumes the responsibilities of the primary node. At this point, users are switched to that node without operator intervention. This switch minimizes downtime.

A cluster is designed to avoid a single point of failure. Applications are distributed over more than one computer, achieving a degree of parallelism, failure recovery and providing high availability.

In a clustered configuration, applications can be configured or developed to run as:

- Single instance applications

- Multi-instance applications

- Distributed applications

In a single instance application configuration, the application runs on only one node at a time. In case of failure of the original node, the cluster should provide for the starting of the application on the other available node, in order to meet the high-availability specification.

Where multiple instances of an application can run on multiple nodes simultaneously, failure of a single node does not affect the application.

In the case of failure of a single node on a distributed application, the failed node communicates with the cluster interconnect of the failure and coordinates a handshake operation to take care of continuing operations.

Disaster tolerance

An "Act of God" (such as fire, hurricane, tornado, earthquake, flood, or lightning strike) can destroy computer systems, which, in turn, detrimentally affects users, organizations, and customers, leaving them without access to business-critical applications and data.

Systems are disaster tolerant if they can survive the loss of a major computing site due to reasons mentioned above.

Systems may be protected from the "Act of God" scenarios in the clustered configuration when the systems are spread across a large geography.

Using interconnects such as Ethernet and FDDI, systems can be configured such that the computing and storage components are spread over a moderate-sized geography. Using volume shadowing or a RAID 1, data can be duplicated to different sites.

System management and security

Each system maintains its own identity in the cluster configuration. Nodes in the cluster are managed as a single system. Therefore, the systems that participate in the cluster configuration have the same security and system management. Additionally, security policies associated with one system in the cluster are applicable to all other systems participating in the clustered configuration.

For the reasons listed above, it would be ideal to configure all nodes participating in the cluster to have the same operating system. Doing so provides the same security and management structure and supports identical configuration of nodes. This helps the migration of users to the secondary node to be made without much difficulty and to be done in such a way that is transparent to the users.

Failover

On clustered hardware, many nodes access or share the same resources. For example, the database resides on shared disks, visible to two or more nodes. Clustering of nodes helps in node failover. When one node in a cluster fails, the users of the application are transferred to the other machine, or node, allowing the application continuous access (to the database, for example). This failover is done by the operating system and is managed by a cluster manager (CM). The CM provides a service intended primarily to provide failover support for applications such as databases, messaging systems, enterprise resource planning (ERP) applications, and file/print services.

In the event of hardware or software failure occurring in either node, the applications currently running on that node are migrated by the CM to the surviving node and then restarted.

Growth potential and scalability

Computers that perform adequately under current load and business circumstances may not necessarily perform adequately in the future. Any resource in a system is finite. Eventually, it is likely that, as workload increases or as the system is called upon to perform tasks other than those it was originally intended to, resources become constrained and performance is impacted.

As discussed in the early part of this chapter, one possibility in such situations is to increase the resources through options such as the addition of more memory, increasing the number of processors, or increasing further I/O capabilities (i.e., adapters or disks). Adding these additional resources constitutes the vertical scalability of the system and is within the available unit itself.

When considering the scenario where a system is unable to accept any more additional resources, two possible solutions become evident. The first solution, which could be rather costly, is to replace the hardware configurations with a later model that would allow for the expansion of resources. However, this solution could potentially postpone the problem to a later date, as it is probable that the upgraded system would reach maximum capacity too. The second solution would be to add another computer to the system and distribute the work across both machines.

Horizontal scalability provides the ability to add more computers linearly and to distribute work across them. This allows the entire system to scale well beyond the limitations of a single system. The vertical and horizontal/linear scalability of the systems is shown in Figure 2.5. When the computers are vertically scaled, the system configuration increases due to the computer now having additional resources compared to the original configuration. Under the horizontal/linear scalability, the size of the computer remains the same but another computer is added, almost doubling the resources and aiding in distribution of load between both computers. Horizontal scalability also provides higher availability because if one node fails users can be migrated to the other available computer.

2.5   Clustered configuration

From the benefits and functions discussed so far, it should be apparent that clustered configurations provide a great growth or scalability potential compared to traditional systems.

Clustered configurations are ideal for systems that have growth potential; adding nodes to an existing configuration is transparent to the application system or users.[2] It should be noted that when a computer is added within a clustered configuration, the system does not have to be shut down. After addition of a node to the configuration, the computer through its cluster manager immediately makes it cluster aware and is made available for access. The load is distributed from each of the existing nodes to the new node that joined the cluster.

Clustered configurations, apart from direct link address to one or more nodes, provide a single node link address called a cluster alias.[3] A cluster alias is one common address, or identification, given to all the nodes participating in the clustered configuration. It frees clients from having to connect to a specific cluster member for services. Similar to a host, clients can request a variety of services from a cluster alias. The cluster alias acts as a load balancer at the operating system level, monitoring resource availability on the various nodes participating in the clustered configuration and directing new processes to the nodes that have a lower load. These built-in features, available at the clustered configuration level, give applications a great opportunity to perform and scale with minimum effort. This performance and scaling can be done while maintaining high availability of the systems as a whole.

---

2.   COMPAQ Tru64 Unix Version 5.1 and above when the clustering version is installed.
3.   On Open VMS to Alpha-based systems.

While cluster aliases provide the load balancing capability within the nodes participating in the clustered configuration, the communications or requests that one node needs to make to other nodes participating in the cluster happens through another important component called the cluster interconnect.

2.5.1 Cluster interconnects

Nodes in a clustered configuration exchange information with each other by means of physical communication links known as *interconnects*. There are a variety of interconnecting options available with choices depending on the information exchange requirements of the applications running in the environment.

While interconnects provide a great deal of functionality by communicating across nodes in a clustered configuration, the basic strengths of an interconnect should be in the following areas:

- *Throughput:* The throughput of an interconnect is a vital parameter for the performance of the clustered configuration while communicating between the nodes. When considering throughput, the measurement is based on the average and maximum cumulative data transfer rates between nodes during processing of requests across nodes.

- *Availability:* Availability of the application is also a very important requirement for systems that require a clustered configuration. Data transfer between the nodes in the cluster take place via these cluster interconnects; a failure at this level will cause disruption of service between the nodes and will affect the proper functioning of the application. Thus, redundant level interconnects should be provided to ensure continued uptime of the cluster interconnects.

- *Distribution:* A functionality of the interconnect that complements the availability requirement is the support for distributed computing configurations. Because of this, the nodes in the clustered configuration do not have to reside in a small complex of buildings and may be spread throughout or across buildings.

Figure 2.9 represents a cluster interconnect. Nodes in the clustered configuration exchange information with each other by means of physical communication links. The interconnect provides a great deal of functionality by helping communication across nodes in the cluster. There are various kinds of interconnects available and based on the type of hardware systems used, any of the interconnects may be used. In order to

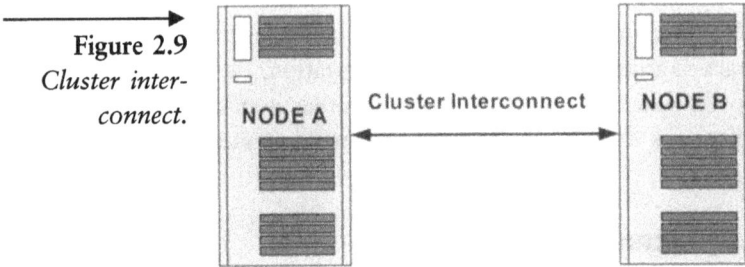

Figure 2.9
*Cluster inter-
connect.*

obtain an appropriate introduction to the various interconnects available, a brief overview for the following interconnects is provided:

- Computer interconnect (CI)

- Local area network interconnects (LAN)

- Gigabit Ethernet interconnects

- InfiniBand

- Virtual interface architecture

- Hyper messaging protocol

Computer interconnect

Computer interconnect (CI) is an early version of the interconnect. VAXClusters used this kind of interconnect with Version 4.0 of VMS. The CI supports the exchange of information at the rate of 70 megabits per second. Data is physically sent to the CI one bit at a time, which makes the CI a serial interconnect. Data is sent as one or more packets with each packet containing at least 7 bytes of information.

The CI provides a dual path access with two distinct signal paths, path A and path B, which are used for communicating among its nodes. These paths are implemented such that none of their components is a potential single point of failure. The CI has high-availability characteristics. Each path in the interconnect has the capacity to transfer data at 70 megabit per second "per path." For example, in a four-node clustered configuration, one node can send data to a second node at 70 megabits per second on path A, while a third node concurrently sends data to a fourth node at 70 megabits per second on path B.

CI is a multidrop interconnect (i.e., each packet transmitted on a CI can be seen by every CI port adapter attached to that CI). Each packet identifies a CI adapter on the node to which the packet is being sent and only the adapter actually accepts the packet from the interconnect.

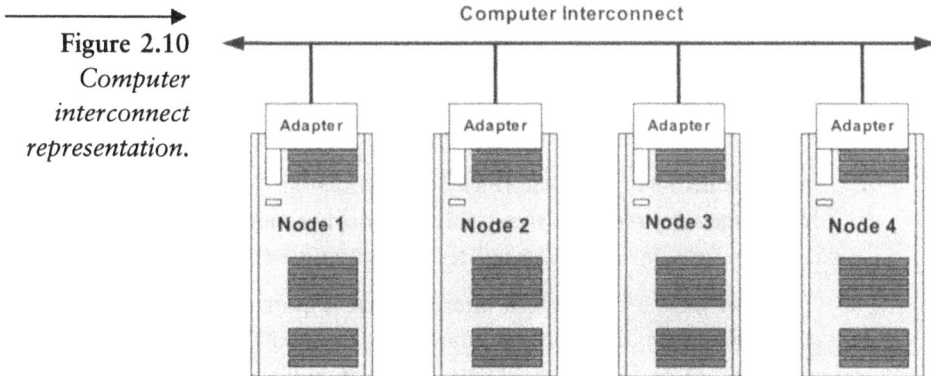

Figure 2.10
*Computer
interconnect
representation.*

When a packet is being transmitted, the configuration module reads data out of the main memory as 32-bit longwords and passes them to the data path (DP) module. The DP module breaks the 32-bit longword down into 8 bit bytes. These bytes are then passed to a packet buffer (PB) module where they are placed in a hardware transmit buffer. Once the entire packet is assembled on the PB module, the data link (LINK) module acquires one path on the CI and then transmits the data in serial format one bit at a time.

Figure 2.10 represents nodes connected together, or communicating with each other, through the CI. The network connections are made directly to the adapters on each cluster member, which in turn is connected to the network line.

When a packet is being received, the LINK module accepts the data in serial format from one path of the CI. The LINK module converts the data into byte format and deposits each byte into the hardware receive buffer on the PB module. Once the entire packet has been received, the data is then fetched as bytes from the hardware receive buffer, moved across the DP module where it is assembled into 32-bit longword and then handed to the configuration module. The configuration module then writes the data into a buffer in the main memory of the node to which the adapter is attached.

Local area network interconnects

The CI discussed above is used to communicate between nodes that reside in a relatively small geographic area. However, nodes that use a traditional network interconnect, such as the Ethernet and the Fiber Distributed Data Interface (FDDI), to communicate with each other can be distributed over a much larger geographical area.

Ethernet has been in existence for almost 25 years now and has progressed along with networking requirements. Invented by Dr. Robert Metcalf and pioneered by Digital and Xerox, Ethernet has become one of the most commonly used LAN technologies worldwide.

As a transport protocol, Ethernet operates at Layers 1 and 2 of the 7-layer Open Source Initiative (OSI) networking model, delivering its data packets to any device connected to the network cable.

Another local area network interface that is quite popular for transfer of packets of information between computers or technical devices is the Fiber Distributed Data Interface (FDDI). FDDI is a fiber optic serial bus that provides for the exchange of information at the rate of 100 megabits per second. FDDI is defined by American National Standard Institute (ANSI) and OSI standards and was originally designed to operate over fiber optic cabling. However, it also includes standard copper media for interconnection. FDDI uses a token ring media access control protocol. A token consists of a special three-octet FDDI frame. A station waits until a token comes by, grabs the token, transmits one or more frames, and releases the token.

Both Ethernet and FDDI are known as local area network (LAN) interconnects. Ethernet is commonly used to support communication among several offices, throughout a building or among several buildings in close proximity to each other. A common application of Ethernet is the networking of computers throughout an automobile assembly plant or a business establishment. FDDI also has a similar use, but it often supports communication over greater distances than Ethernet.

FDDI and Ethernet can coexist on a single network configuration. For example, Ethernet can be used to link together nodes on two sites; FDDI can then be used to link the two sites together into a single network. If computers are distributed across buildings, they could be placed inside an FDDI ring, allowing them to exist as a single configuration. This enables faster data communication between computers in the buildings.

Ethernet is a single-path, multidrop serial bus that supports the exchange of information at the rate of 10 megabits per second or more. A number of different types of wire and fiber optic cable can serve as the physical media within an Ethernet LAN. Specific limitations on cable lengths and distances vary with the media used. While Ethernet has evolved over the years, there are Ethernets that started at 10 megabits per second and have increased to 100 megabits per second. Currently there are Ethernets that support exchange of information at 1000 megabits (1 gigabit) per second.

Gigabit Ethernet interconnects

Gigabit Ethernet has evolved from the original 10 Mbps Ethernet standard, 10 BASE-T and the 100 Mbps Fast Ethernet standards, 100 BASE-TX and 100 BASE-FX. The IEEE and the 10-Gigabit Ethernet Alliance support a 10 Gbps Ethernet standard. Gigabit Ethernet is the latest evolution of networking options providing excellent high-speed communication between devices.

In 1998, IEEE adopted a standard for Gigabit Ethernet over fiber optic cabling and subsequently, in 1999, adopted Gigabit Ethernet over copper as 1000BASE-T. This allowed gigabit speeds to be transmitted over Cat-5 cable. Figure 2.11 represents the two IEEE standards adopted for Gigabit Ethernet over fiber optic cabling and copper.

Benefits of using Gigabit Ethernet over its predecessors, or over fiber optics includes the following:

- Gigabit Ethernet is 100 times faster than regular 10 Mbps Ethernet and 10 times faster than 100 Mbps Fast Ethernet

- Increased bandwidth for higher performance and elimination of bottlenecks

- Full-duplex capacity allowing for the virtual doubling of the effective bandwidth

Figure 2.11
Gigabit Ethernet standards. (Source: Gigabit Alliance).

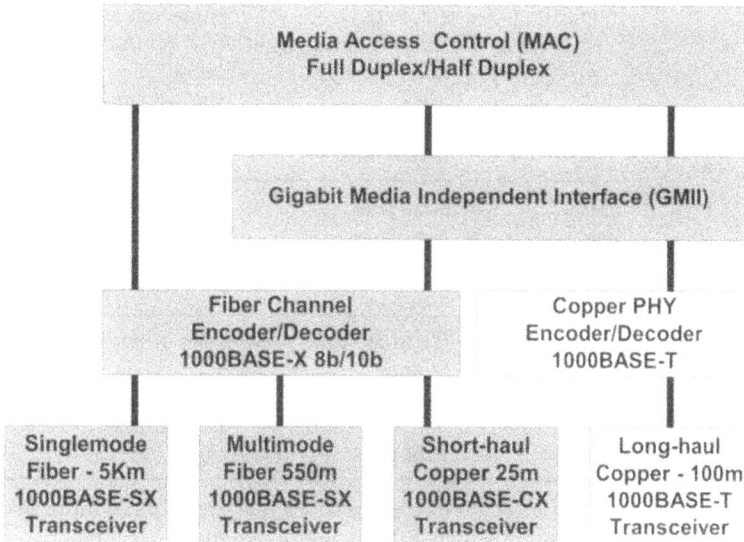

■ Full compatibility with the large installed base of Ethernet and Fast Ethernet nodes

■ Transfer of large amounts of data across network quickly

Ethernet network solutions are used in all major industries where the requirement for high-speed reliable communication is a necessity. Many of these segments continue to use the earlier version of the Ethernet. Due to the high performance benefits with Gigabit Ethernet over the traditional Fast Ethernet, the new Gigabit Ethernet solutions will replace the existing ones in a short to medium time frame.

Table 2.2 illustrates the bandwidth requirements in the various sectors of the information technology arena within the various implementation

Table 2.2 *Summary of Applications Driving Network Growth[a]*

Application	Data Types/Size	Network Traffic Implication	Network Need
Scientific modeling, engineering	• Data files • 100s of megabytes to gigabytes	• Large files increase bandwidth requirement	• Higher bandwidth for desktops and servers
Publications, medical data transfer	• Data files • 100s of megabytes to gigabytes	• Large files increase bandwidth requirement	• Higher bandwidth for desktops and servers
Internet/ Intranet	• Data files now • Audio now • Video is emerging • High transaction rate • Large files, 1 MB to 100 MB	• Large files increase bandwidth required • Low transmission latency • High volume of data streams	• Higher bandwidth for servers and system backbone • Low latency
Data warehousing, network backup	• Data files • Gigabytes to terabytes	• Large files increase bandwidth required • Transmitted during fixed time period	• Higher bandwidth for servers and backbone • Low latency
Desktop video conferencing, interactive whiteboarding	• Constant data stream • 1.5 to 3.5 Mbps at the desktop	• Class of service reservation • High volume of data streams	• Higher bandwidth for servers and backbones • Low latency • Predictable latency

[a]*Source:* "Gigabit Ethernet accelerating the standard for speed," Gigabit Ethernet Alliance, http://www.10gea.org/Tech-whitepapers.htm

Bytes	8	6	6	2	0-1500
	Preamble	Destination Address	Source Address	Length of data field	Protocol header, data and pad

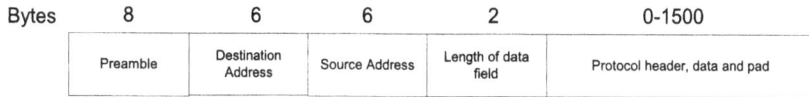

Figure 2.12   *IEEE 802.3 frame specification.*

zones like data warehousing, office automation, online transaction processing systems (OLTP), etc. This details the data transfer sizes and the networking needs to meet these requirements.

Every network connection has two points: an origin and a destination. The origin is the point where the data/message is sent from and the destination is the point to where the data/message is being sent. Data/ messages are transmitted between the two points, and are transferred in packets of information. In an Ethernet connection, the size and packet frame is defined by the IEEE 802.3 specification. (The packet format/frame has not changed between the fast Ethernet and Gigabit Ethernet.)

Figure 2.12 provides a dissection of the Ethernet packet as defined by the IEEE 802.3 specification. This dissection shows the total length of the packet that contains the source, the destination address, and the actual message. While a certain portion of the packet is of a fixed length, the remaining portion that contains the actual message, or data, is of a variable length between 0 and 1500 bytes (i.e., a maximum frame size of 1524 bytes). As indicated above, there has been no change in the frame specification between Fast Ethernet and Gigabit Ethernet; however, the speed of transmitting these packets has increased by a magnitude. This makes it a favorable choice for high-speed data transfer in a data processing environment. It is to be noted that, in most scenarios, there is a tendency for most systems to show a degraded result. In the case of a Gigabit Ethernet connection with an increased load, this was not noticed. A recently performed test by the Gigabit Ethernet Alliance group noted a high linear scalability measurement at various packet sizes. Both the theoretical throughput and actual throughput, in all the various packet sizes, produced the same performance results.

Figure 2.13 represents the Gigabit Ethernet performance at various packet sizes. It should be noted that the performance measurement is linear with increase in packet size.

In a clustered configuration, Gigabit Ethernet plays an important role by providing a higher bandwidth over the traditional Fast Ethernet.

Figure 2.13
*Gigabit
Ethernet perfor-
mance chart.*

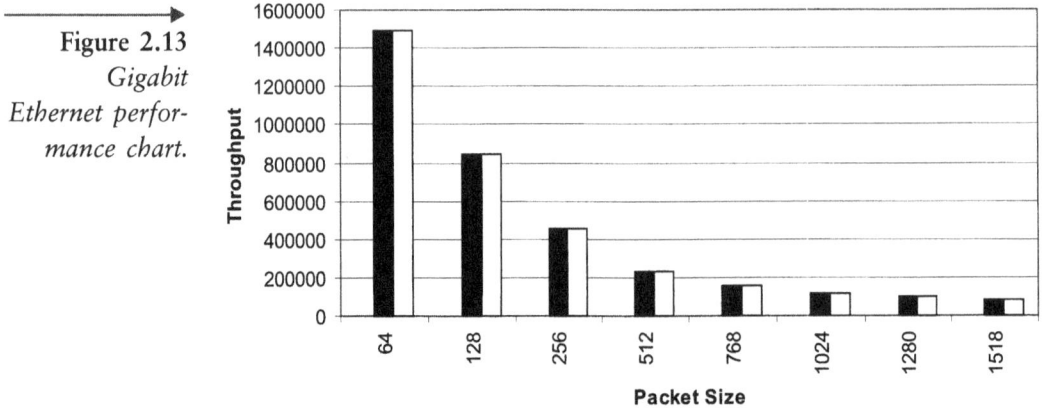

While the Gigabit Ethernet connections are becoming popular, the networking research has not ended. Recently, another technology called InfiniBand[TM] has started to evolve. While Ethernet, fiber channel, and ultra SCSI are the current popular interconnect methods deployed at various locations, InfiniBand technology is becoming popular. InfiniBand technology will be discussed in the following section.

InfiniBand technology

The demands of the Internet and distributed computing are challenging the scalability, reliability, availability, and performance of servers. InfiniBand architecture represents a new approach to I/O technology and is based on the collective research, knowledge, and experience of the industry's leaders and computer vendors. The main developmental goal for this collaborative effort is to establish one standard method of high-speed communication from amongst the many that are currently available.

The evolution of the InfiniBand architecture springs from two competing standards: Next Generation I/O (NGIO) and Future I/O. Through the efforts of key marketing strategies, both standards converged in mid-1999 to form InfiniBand. It is currently represented by Sun Microsystems, Compaq, Intel, Microsoft, IBM, Hewlett-Packard, and Dell, and 140 other organizations have joined as a collective effort.

InfiniBand architecture specifies channels that are created by attaching host channel adapters within a server chassis to host channel adapters in other server chassis. This is done for high-performance interprocess communication (IPC) and to target channel adapters connecting InfiniBand-enabled servers to remote storage and communication networks through InfiniBand switches. InfiniBand links transfer data at 2.5 Gbps,

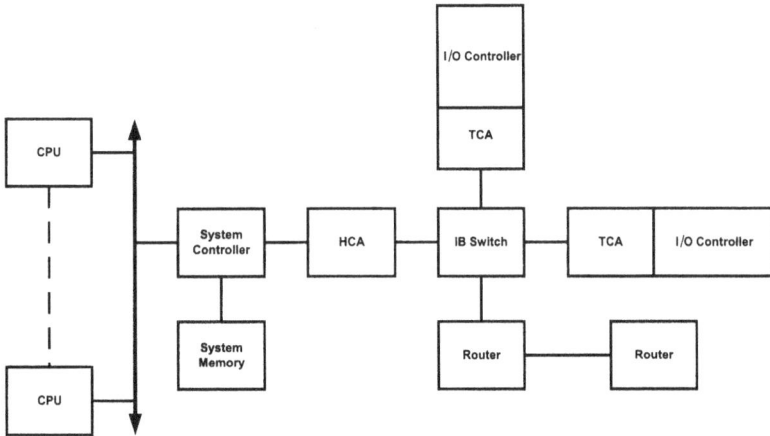

Figure 2.14
InfiniBand architecture.

utilizing both copper wire and fiber optics for transmission. It can carry any combination of I/O, network, and IPC messages.

InfiniBand architecture (Figure 2.14) has the following communication characteristics:

- User level access to message passing

- Remote direct memory access (RDMA) read and write

- Up to a maximum of 2 GB message in a single transfer

The memory protection mechanism defined by the InfiniBand architecture allows an InfiniBand host channel adapter (HCA) to transfer data directly into or out of an application buffer. To protect these buffers from unauthorized access, a process called memory registration is employed. Memory registration allows data transfers to be initiated directly from user mode, eliminating a costly context switch to the kernel. Another benefit of allowing the InfiniBand HCA to transfer data directly into or out of application buffers is that it can remove the need for system buffering. This eliminates the context switch to the kernel, and also eliminates the need to copy data to or from system buffers on a send or receive operation respectively.

InfiniBand architecture also has another unique feature called a memory window. The memory window provides a way for the application to grant remote read and/or write to a specified buffer at a byte-level granularity level to another application. Memory windows are used in conjunction with RDMA read or RDMA write to control remote access to the application buffers. Data can be transferred either by the push or pull method (i.e., either the sending node would send the data over to the requester which is called pushing or the requester could get to the holder and get the data, which is called pulling).

While InfiniBand has just begun, it promises tremendous potential and benefits in a clustered configuration where transfer of data is required to happen via the cluster interconnect.

Virtual interface architecture

The virtual interface (VI) architecture, authored and developed by Compaq (now HP), Intel, and Microsoft, is designed for hardware and software vendors and provides adapters, switches, middleware, and end-user application software that will seamlessly grow as servers or workstations are added and integrated into a clustered system area network (SAN). A SAN relies on high-speed, reliable messaging without the traditional communications protocol overhead as experienced by current LAN or WAN adapters and protocols, such as Ethernet, token ring, fiber channel standard, systems network architecture (SNA), or even asynchronous transfer mode (ATM).

The VI architecture is to be used where server-to-server messages deal with application and data availability, and it allows any server error or failure to cause an immediate transfer of the business critical application to another server for uninterrupted processing. The architecture also allows for parallel application processing and minimizes performance bottlenecks where more traditional communications protocols such as the Remote Procedure Call (RPC), User Datagram Protocol (UDP), and sockets have caused application processing delays due to protocol stack handling and/or network traffic overloads due to collision detection processing. These slowdowns cause application delays or inefficient use of the cluster.

Figure 2.15 illustrates the VI-architecture-based cluster interconnect architecture. That provides high-speed interconnect between Intel-based severs.

VI architecture implementations will consist of three components: SAN media which will be equipped with VI architecture registers and memory, the VI architecture primitive library (VIPL) which will support application use of the architecture, and the VI architecture operating system kernel support services.

Hyper Messaging Protocol (HMP)

Hewlett-Packard (HP), in cooperation with Oracle, has designed a cluster interconnect product specifically tailored to meet the needs of enterprise

Figure 2.15
*Virtual interface
architecture.*

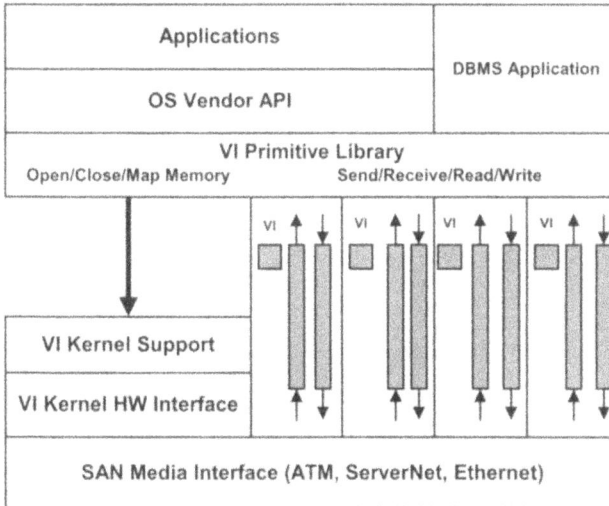

class parallel database applications. HP's Hyper Messaging Protocol (HMP) significantly expands on the feature set provided by TCP/UDP by providing a true reliable datagram model for both RDMA and traditional message semantics. Coupled with operating system bypass capability and the hardware support for protocol offload provided by HyperFabric, HMP provides high bandwidth, low latency and extremely low CPU utilization with an interface and feature set optimized for business critical parallel applications such as Oracle *9i* RAC.

2.6 How clusters work

Clusters work primarily through a mechanism called polling. Polling is an activity similar to pinging, where a message is sent to a target device and the results are examined. If a successful result is received then the polling was successful; otherwise, it is determined to have a problem. All servers participating in the clustered configuration keep polling each other to determine whether each one is working. If something is not right, failover mechanisms leap into action. Polling relies on the cluster interconnect system, the LAN and the device controllers.

Figure 2.16 illustrates a two-node cluster configuration with the cluster interconnect and the SCSI BUS for the LAN. The cluster interconnect is used for polling to determine whether the other node is available while the SCSI BUS is used by the system to determine, based on the initial check

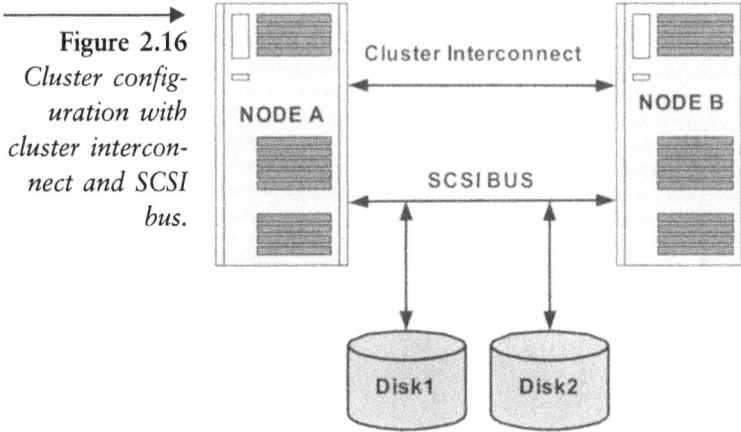

Figure 2.16
Cluster config-
uration with
cluster intercon-
nect and SCSI
bus.

using the cluster interconnect, whether the nodes participating in the cluster are available. Once an initial signal of failure is detected, another validation is performed using the LAN connection before attempting the failover operation.

The interconnect device polls the other node in the cluster to see if the node is available. If the node, or server, does not respond within a time specified internally (time determined by the value of a heartbeat timeout parameter) the polling node tries to find the node through the LAN. *The heartbeat timeout parameter predefines a timeout period after which if there is no response from the target node, it assumes that the node is not available.* Failure or success indicates whether the problem lies with the target node or whether it is with the interconnect device.

If the polling node determines through interconnect and LAN polling mechanism that the other node in the cluster is offline, it will take over the node's disk resources in order to keep them available to the network. When the disabled node goes back online, the substitute relinquishes the appropriated disk resources to their rightful owner as soon as the no-longer "missing" node tries to access them. This is an automatic process and all part of the failover feature of a clustered configuration.

For a failover to occur, the following conditions must be met:

- The interconnect poll must fail.

- The LAN poll must fail.

- The polling node must succeed in taking control of the missing cluster nodes' disk resources.

2.6.1 Cluster failover

The nodes in a clustered configuration communicate via the cluster interconnect, through a heartbeat mechanism. For example, in a two-node clustered configuration using the heartbeat mechanism, node 1 will check the availability of node 2. Similarly, node 2 will check the viability of node 1. The implementations of the various clustered configurations have a different heartbeat value that is used to verify if the other nodes in the cluster are present. For example, Sun and Linux clusters have a default configuration for the heartbeat set at 2 seconds. This means that every 2 seconds the heartbeat mechanism will verify the existence of other nodes in the cluster to ensure that they are up and running.

When one of the nodes does not respond to another member in the cluster after several attempts (based on the heartbeat timeout value, which varies between operating systems), the cluster manager will timeout the heartbeat check against the node that first detected the failure and will declare that the node is not available. The heartbeat timeout value also varies among the various clustered configurations. For example, the heartbeat timeout value on a Sun cluster is 12 seconds, whereas the value on a Linux cluster is 10 seconds. Consequently, if the heartbeat mechanisms do not receive a favorable response within the stipulated period, the node that did not respond is declared as having a failed status.

Once a failure has been ascertained, the next step for the cluster manager is to reconfigure the remaining nodes to form a new configuration. During this process, the remaining nodes drop the failed node from the node/member list and the activities of checking, load balancing, processing, etc., occur among the reconfigured cluster group.

After the reconfiguration process has completed, the cluster manager starts the recovery process. During the recovery process, all user and system activities are brought to a new state that includes information about the failed instance. Also included are removals and/or completion activities that are incomplete by the processes running on the failed node.

At this stage, any database, if present, will start the recovery process. A more detailed look at how the cluster manager and the database (such as Oracle) coordinate this type of activity will be discussed in a later chapter.

2.7   Disk configuration

We looked at the benefits of clustered systems and clustered interconnects in the previous sections. What good are those without the storage systems? Under the hardware configuration, we have seen through evolution of the various technologies like SMP, MPP, etc.; similarly, under the storage tier also we have some details and choices of configurations that should be discussed, like the SAN, NAS, or the traditional direct access architectures. Prior to discussing these configurations, let us look at the basic disk configurations. A disk by itself, like any other equipment, is prone to failures and can have performance issues, especially when many users are accessing one disk. There could be a large amount of I/O contention/ backlogging of user requests, which in turn would create a replicated effect on performance of the system. So the option is to combine multiple disks so that the files could be spread across the disks.

Having multiple disks would not directly solve the issues with I/O contention. It does improve I/O compared to a single disk configuration; however, the contention could still exist and performance issues on the system with a large number of users would remain significantly high.

The next alternative would be to combine these disks and stripe them across all the disks, creating volumes and files that could reside in each volume or stripe. What this means is that multiple users accessing these files could potentially be accessing the files at different locations, thus accessing different disks and reducing performance bottlenecks. In general, striping offers a performance gain by spreading out the I/Os across many channels and devices. This reduces contention and enables throughput beyond the capacity of a single channel or device. The performance gain depends on the database layout, workload, and access patterns. Performance gains should be compared to the costs associated with setting up, managing, and maintaining (extending and reducing) striped volumes.

While striping helps provide distribution of I/O, spreading it across multiple spindles, how about availability? When one disk fails, then data for that stripe probably will not be available. As we discussed in Section 2.4.3 (High Availability), redundancy should be provided at every tier, which includes the storage subsystem. The technology that provides redundancy at the disk level is called *mirroring*, where every time information is recorded onto one disk it is immediately copied over to another disk. Mirroring functionality could be done either via a software process or through hardware configuration.

An ideal solution would be a combination of both, i.e., a disk configuration that has both options of striping and mirroring because proper storage configuration is vital to the performance of the data tier. The industry has various configuration options available today, and each configuration is used for a specific type of implementation. While most of the scenarios work properly, some of them are better for specific implementation categories over the others. Let us look at some details in this area of disk configuration and elaborate on some of the options available in this tier.

2.7.1   RAID

RAID is the technology for expanding the capacity of the I/O system and providing the capability for data redundancy. RAID stands for *redundant array of inexpensive disks*. It is the use of two or more physical disks to create one logical disk, where the physical disks operate in tandem to provide greater size and more bandwidth. RAID provides scalability and high availability in the context of I/O and system performance.

RAID implementations can be made at the hardware level or at the software level. Software-based RAID implementations have considerable overhead and consume resources, including CPU and memory. Hardware RAID implementations are more popular than software RAID implementations because they have less resource overhead.

RAID 0

RAID 0 provides striping, where a single data partition is physically spread across all the disks in the stripe bank, effectively giving that partition the aggregate performance of all the component disks combined. The unit of granularity for spreading the data across the drives is called the stripe size or chunk size. Typical settings for the stripe size are 32 KB, 64 KB, and 128 KB.

The following are benefits that striping provides:

1.   *Load balancing:* In a database environment some files are always busier than other files; therefore, I/O load on the system needs to be balanced. In a non-striped environment this causes a hot spot on the disk and results in poor response times. The exposure to hot spots is

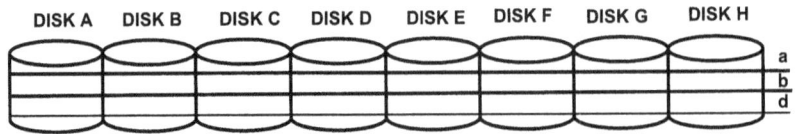

Figure 2.17
RAID 0.

significantly reduced using a striped disk array, because each file is very thinly spread across all the disks in the stripe bank. The result of this spreading of files is random load balancing. This is very effective in a high-volume, high-transactional, very large online transaction processing system (OLTP).

2.   *Concurrency:* In a random access environment the overall concurrency of each file is increased. For example, if a file exists on a single disk, only one read or write can be executed against that file at any one time. The reason for this is physical, because the disk drive has only one set of read/write heads. By striping (RAID 0 configuration), many reads and writes can be active at any one time, up to the number of disks in the stripe set.

The effects of striping in both sequential and random access environments make it very attractive from a performance standpoint. However, the downside of this is that RAID 0 configuration has no built-in redundancy and is highly exposed to failure. If a single disk in a stripe set fails, the whole stripe set is effectively disabled.

In the scenario shown in Figure 2.17 where there are eight disks all striped across in d different stripes or partitions, the MTBF for each disk is now divided by eight, and the amount of data that is not available is eight times that of a single disk.

RAID 1

RAID 1 is known as mirroring and is where all the writes issued to a given disk are duplicated to another disk. This provides for disk availability; if there is a failure of the first disk, the second disk or mirror can take over without any data loss.

The write operation to both disks happens in parallel. When the write is ready to be issued, it is set up and sent to DISK A. Without waiting for that write process to complete (as in a sequential write), the write to DISK B is initiated. However, when the host wants to read from the disk (in a mirrored configuration) it takes advantage of the two disks. Depending on the implementation, the host will elect to round-robin (100% gain in read capacity) all read requests to alternate disks in the mirrored set or to send the request to the drive that has its head closest to the required track.

The biggest advantage in mirrored configuration (RAID 1) is the benefit when one disk or one side of the mirror fails, causing the system to start using exclusively the other side of the mirror for all read/write requests. As a result of this failure the read capability is reduced by 50%. Once replacing or repairing the failed component restores the failed side of the mirror, bringing a disk back online will involve physically copying the surviving mirrored disk onto the replaced peer. This process is called *resilvering*. These mirrored disks can be placed independent of each other or can be placed in a disk array.

In an Oracle environment, RAID 1 is good for both online and archived redo logs. Writing to these files is performed in a sequential fashion. The write head of the disk is located near the last write operation giving performance enhancements. However, more than one RAID 1 volume is required to allow continuous read and write operations to the redo logs and to allow archive logs to read the previous redo logs. This allows for optimal performance, and it is also required to eliminate contention between LGWR and ARCH background processes.

RAID 0 + 1

RAID 0 + 1 (or RAID 01) is a combination of levels 0 and 1. RAID 0 + 1 does exactly what its name implies, that is, stripes and mirrors disks; for example, it stripes first, then mirrors what was just striped. RAID 0 + 1 provides good write and read performance and redundancy without the overhead of parity calculations. Parity is a term for error checking. Parity algorithms contain error correction code (ECC) capabilities, which calculate parity for a given stripe or chunk of data within a RAID volume.

The advantages of both RAID level 0 and RAID level 1 apply in this situation and are illustrated in Figure 2.18, which shows a four-way striped mirrored volume with eight disks (A–H). A given stripe of data (Data 01) in a file is split/striped across disks A–D with the stripe first and then mirrored across disks E–H. The drawback in this RAID configuration/scenario is that when one of the pieces, for example, Data 01 on Disk A, becomes unavailable due to a disk failure on Disk A, the entire mirror member becomes unavailable. The entire mirror member is lost, which reduces the I/O capacity during reads on the volume by 50%.

Figure 2.18
RAID 01.

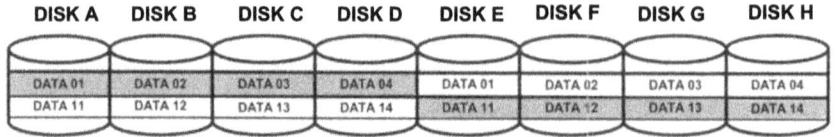

RAID 0 1 figure showing DISK A through DISK H

RAID 1 + 0

RAID 1 + 0 (or RAID 10) is also a combination of the RAID levels 0 and 1 discussed in the previous sections. This combination is also true for RAID 0 + 1. However, in RAID 10 the disks are mirrored and then striped; for example, mirror first, then stripe what was mirrored. All the advantages that apply to the previous RAID configuration apply to this RAID configuration. However, the organization of mirrored sets is different from the previous configuration.

In Figure 2.19, Data 01 is mirrored on the adjoining disks (A and B) and Data 02 is mirrored on the subsequent two disks (C and D), etc. This configuration also contains eight mirrored and striped disks.

The advantage in the RAID 10 configuration over the RAID 01 configuration is, if there is a loss of one disk in a mirrored member, the entire member of the mirrored volume does not become unavailable. This configuration is better suited for high availability. The I/O capacity that results from the failure of a mirror member does not reduce its I/O capacity by 50%. RAID 10 configurations must be the preferred implementation choice for an OLTP implementation.

RAID 5

Under RAID 5, parity calculations provide data redundancy, and the parity is stored with the data. This means that the parity is distributed across the number of drives configured in the volume.

Figure 2.20 illustrates the physical placement of stripes (Data 01 through Data 04) with their corresponding parities distributed across the five disks in the volume. This is a four-way, striped RAID 5 volume where data and parity are distributed.

Figure 2.19
RAID 10.

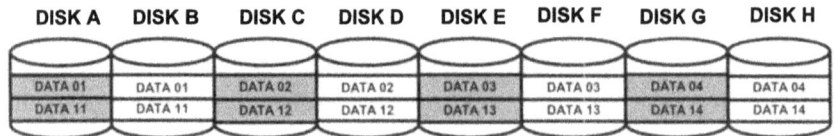

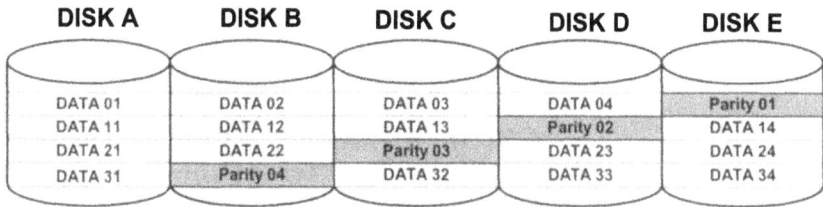

Figure 2.20
RAID 5.

RAID 5 is unsuitable for OLTP because of extremely poor performance of small writes at high concurrency levels. This is because the continuous processes of reading a stripe, calculating the new parity, and writing the stripe back to the disk (with new parity) will make writing significantly slower.

In an Oracle environment, rollback segments and redo logs are accessed sequentially (usually for writes) and are not suitable candidates for being placed on a RAID 5 device. Also, data files belonging to temporary tablespaces are not suitable for placement on a RAID 5 device. Another reason the redo logs should not be placed on RAID 5 devices is related to the type of caching (if any) being done by the RAID system. Given the critical nature of the contents of the redo logs, catastrophic loss of data could ensue if the contents of the cache are not written to the disk, for example, because of a power failure, when Oracle was notified that they had been written. This is particularly true of write-back caching, where the write is assumed to have been written to the disk when it has only been written to the cache. Write-through caching, where the write is assumed to have completed when it has reached the disk, is much safer but still not recommended for redo logs for the reason mentioned earlier.

RAID 5 configurations should be preferred where the read patterns are random and are not very bulky in nature. This is because the spindles in a RAID 5 volume work in an independent fashion. For example, all the disks in a given volume can potentially service multiple I/O requests from different disk locations. RAID 5 should be considered for data warehouse (DW), data mining (DM), and operational data store (ODS) applications where data refreshes occur in the off-hours.

2.7.2   Stripe and mirror everything

The "stripe and mirror everything" concept for disk configuration is more commonly known as SAME. This model is based on two key proposals, (1) stripe all files across all disks using a 1 megabyte stripe width, and (2) mirror data for high availability.

1.   Striping all files across all disks ensures that full bandwidth of all the disks is available for any operation. This equalizes load across disk drives and eliminates hot spots. The recommendation of using a stripe size of 1 megabyte is based on transfer rates and throughputs of modern disks. If the stripe size is very small, more time is spent positioning the disk head on the data, than in the actual transfer of data. Based on internal studies, we have determined that a size of 1 megabyte achieves reasonably good throughput, while anything smaller does not provide adequate throughput.

2.   Mirroring data at the storage subsystem level is the best way to avoid data loss. The only way to lose data in a mirrored environment is to lose multiple disks simultaneously. Given that current disk drives are highly reliable, simultaneous multiple disk failure is a very low probability event.

The primary benefit of the SAME model is that it makes storage configuration very easy and suitable for all workloads. It works equally well for OLTP, data warehouse, and batch workloads. It eliminates I/O hot spots and maximizes bandwidth. Finally, the SAME model is not tied to any storage management solution in the market today and can be implemented with the technology available today.

2.8   Storage system architectures

Storage is a central component and plays a critical role in the overall protection and availability of data. Disks with large capacity (gigabytes) cause performance problems and result in negative performance gains. For good performance the I/O subsystem should be sized for IOPS (I/O operations per second). One of Oracle's suggestions is a size based on, at most, 40 IOPS per drive. Large gigabyte-sized disks do not help in I/O performance. Disks should be purchased by IOPS and not by size. Actually, more disks of smaller capacity would be of significant benefit.

While the disk or storage specifications are important, the architecture used to store and retrieve information from disks (access patterns) is equally if not more important. The following are the three major access patterns standards in the industry today:

1.   Traditional direct attached access model

2.   Storage area network (SAN) access model

3.   Network attached storage (NAS) access model

2.8.1   **Traditional direct attached access model**

This access model involves three basic steps: the client or application server requests data from the database server over the network, the database server does disk I/O, and the result is sent to the user or client over the network (Figure 2.21). Although this has been the most popular model because of its simplicity for a considerably long time, this model has several significant drawbacks. The following drawbacks prevent this model from fitting into the high-availability, high-performance architectural goals:

1.   Physical storage cannot be shared with other systems or applications without being served by the host system to which it is attached.

2.   Storage must be located physically close to the host system because of I/O bus restrictions on distance and performance.

3.   The scalability of number and capacities of devices are limited, depending on the I/O bus and storage technology being used.

4.   Because it depends on a host volume manager, there is no dynamic load balancing, expansion options, or RAID without this.

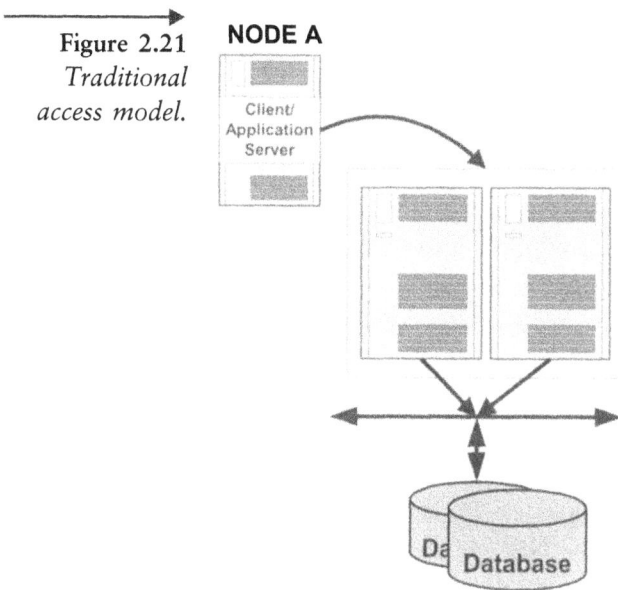

Figure 2.21
Traditional
access model.

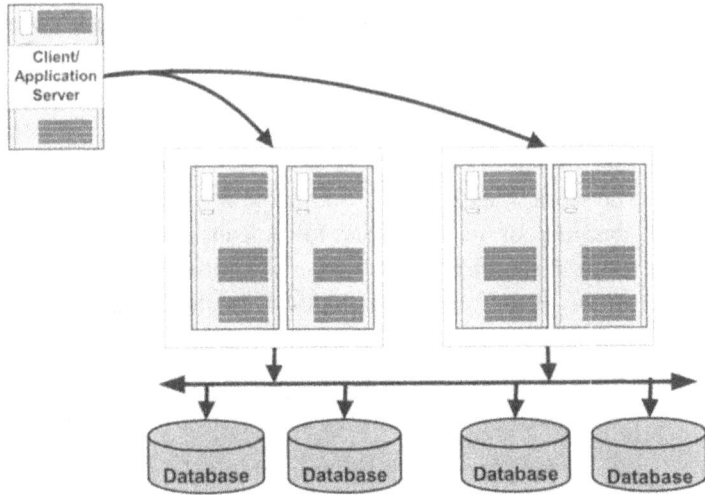

Figure 2.22
SAN access
model.

2.8.2 Storage area network (SAN) access model

Under this access model (Figure 2.22) there are three steps required from the point that a request is made and when it is returned back to the user.

1. The client makes a data request over the network to the database server.

2. The database server performs I/O over a fiber channel I/O bus to a RAID configuration.

3. The database server sends results back to the client over the network.

With the plug-and-play feature of the SAN architecture, more storage systems can be configured and shared from the pool, providing scalability at the storage system level. SAN also supports raw device implementations required for RAC on certain hardware platforms.

2.8.3 Network attached storage (NAS) access model

NAS is a high-performance, platform-independent data storage technology that uses hardware and software that is optimized to perform a specific task, namely file service. NAS devices are part of a growing category of appliance-like servers that are easy to set up and manage. They are particularly well suited to network topologies that have a mixture of clients and servers running different operating systems.

NAS devices are a group of small hard-disk drives that connect to a network, usually by Ethernet. Unlike SAN, NAS devices are not slaves to servers. The NAS model links to a network via an Ethernet card, instead of tying a server directly to a storage device. The NAS device with its processor and operating system acts like a server itself. Using Ethernet, NAS circumvents the need for more expensive fiber channel technology, which serves as the backbone for a SAN.

NAS seeks to eliminate network bottlenecks the same way that SANs do but in an easier and more cost-effective fashion. NAS should cost less than SAN over the long term, because they are cheaper to install and expand than SAN. SAN's relatively high cost is attributable to its use of fiber channel technology.

2.9   Disk allocation

After identifying the best suitable architecture for implementation and selecting the required disk stripe/mirror RAID, the next step would be to determine the implementation of the disk system itself. There are two types of disk allocation: the traditional file system method, or using them directly as raw devices. While the raw device is the basic structure of any disk system, the file system is a software implementation over the raw devices to help create easy manageability and maintenance of the files that are stored on them.

2.9.1   Raw partitions

A raw device partition is a contiguous region of a disk accessed by a Unix character-device interface. This interface provides raw access to the underlying device, arranging for direct I/O between a process and the logical disk. Therefore, the issuance of a write command by a process to the I/O system directly moves the data to the device.

2.9.2   File system

A Unix file system is a hierarchical tree of directories and files implemented on a raw device partition through the file system of the kernel. The file system uses the concept of a buffering cache that optimizes the number of times the operating system must access the disk. The file system releases a process that is executing a write to disk by taking control of the operation, thus freeing the process to continue other functions. The file system then attempts to cache or retain the data to be written until multiple data writes can be done at the same time. This can have the effect of enhancing system performance.

However, system failures before writing the data from the cache can result in the loss of file system integrity. Additionally, the file system adds overhead to any operation that reads or writes data in direct accordance to its physical layout.

Shared file systems allow access from multiple hosts to the same file system data. This reduces the amount of multiple copies of the same data, while distributing the load across those hosts going to the same data.

2.9.3   Tradeoffs

Performance

Bypassing Unix file buffering results in savings on every disk read or write. These savings show up as a throughput improvement only if disk I/O is the system performance bottleneck. Very large database sites with high transaction volumes will certainly have concerns over the performance rates of disk I/O. The conversion to raw device partitions should improve disk I/O performance. These performance gains will be realized to an even greater extent when an online backup is in contention for the physical files that make up the database.

Memory

The memory used by Unix to buffer file I/O can be better used by the RDBMS that does its own I/O and caching. The more memory a machine has, the less effective using raw devices becomes.

Complexity

Using raw device partitions introduces a level of complexity in configuration planning, administration, and movement of databases. Each of these, while important, generally is not a problem because very large database (VLDB) sites tend to have experienced database administrators (DBAs) and this activity of setting up and configuration is more or less a one time activity.

A volume manager (VM) is a software tool that helps a system administrator manage their storage resources. It enables them to group many devices into a single volume group that is then managed as a single entity. This simplifies the management of a large database, and also improves database performance. In many environments, the volume manager is also used to create striped volume sets.

In an Oracle environment, with RAC or an OPS implementation, there is a requirement for a clustered volume manager to set up shared devices. This is required by RAC and OPS to run on clustered and shared devices. By setting these attributes on and off for a single device group, versus many single devices, it enables quick and easier management in a large database configuration.

With OPS the data files must be on raw devices. The archive logs must be on a file system, and the redo logs can reside on either a file system or on a raw partition. Placing the redo logs on a file system requires that the files be cross-mounted using a network file system (NFS). This allows them to be visible from both nodes for recovery. Having the redo logs on a file system simplifies administration but does have an impact on performance. Loss of an NFS mount point due to node failure can cause invisibility of the redo log files. To avoid non-availability of redo log it is recommended that the redo log files be located on raw devices.

With RAC the requirement of raw partitions is removed on most platforms. With the exception of Sun Solaris and HP-UX, for RAC implementation on all other operating systems the requirement to have raw partitions for data files and other optional files is removed. They could be implemented on file systems, like the stand-alone Oracle database.

2.10   Conclusion

Clustering has a history that originates from the VMS days dating back to the early 1980s. In today's Internet-based computing environment, where every second of systems availability is very important for goodwill, reputation, customer retention, and continued business, it is an essential requirement that most application systems are implemented using hardware-clustered configurations. In this chapter, the various advantages that clustered configurations provide to the enterprise were closely considered. The way in which clustering works and how systems interchange information from one node to another was also investigated.

The method of information interchange between systems is very important in order to deduce the availability of the members participating in the clustered configuration.

In an Oracle environment, a clustered configuration perfectly suits the implementation of RAC. RAC is a two or more node configuration running on a clustered operating system connected via a high-speed interprocess communication device (such as a Gigabit Ethernet interface) that shares a common set of storage devices. Each node contains an instance connected to a database that is configured on the shared storage device. Users or applications connect to either of these instances and perform Data Manipulation Language (DML) operations or make queries against the database. These nodes concurrently execute transactions against one shared database, while RAC coordinates the access from each node to the shared device, providing consistency and integrity. Such a configuration offers various benefits that any clustered configuration should provide such as scalability, high availability, transparency, etc.

In the next chapter we will discuss the basic concepts of Oracle. These concepts will help provide an understanding of the current technology and the new enhancements introduced in Oracle 9i. This chapter will help identify the suitable features of Oracle that could be utilized when designing an application system.

3

Oracle Database Concepts

3.1   Introduction

In the previous chapter various hardware architectures, such as SMP, MPP, NUMA, etc., were discussed at length. Also explored was the usage of clustered SMP architecture as a prudent solution for businesses with data processing needs. This architecture allows businesses to provide data storage and retrieval to users and to support increased growth of users through linear scalability. When many systems are joined together to work as a cohesive unit, they support not only the scalability factor but also the availability factor. This is on the assumption that an appropriate clustered operating system is used. When one system or node in the cluster fails, the users have other nodes that could be used to route their request to get to the required information. Consequently, clustering provides linear scalability, which means more nodes or systems could be added into the mix without much difficulty. More availability is provided due to the fact that when one node in the cluster fails, the failure of one node in the cluster does not down the system, as the other nodes are available to process the required information.

These functionalities, or features, provided by the clustered SMP architecture make it a suitable solution for Oracle RAC. In the clustered architecture, the operating system helps provide sharing of resources (e.g., the disk subsystem) between all the participating nodes in the cluster. With RAC, Oracle, which sits on top of the clustered operating system, provides a shared database among two or more Oracle instances, and users access the database via these instances. Such a configuration provides a clustered database solution.

In this chapter, the concepts of a single instance configuration of Oracle, new features in Oracle 9*i* compared against similar features in Oracle 8*i*, and the basic implementation of RAC as an extension to the single, or stand-alone, configuration of Oracle will be discussed. Background processes used in a RAC implementation and their basic functionality along with the changes from the previous versions of RAC will be covered. Additionally, some of the basic extensions in Oracle that would change when implemented with the RAC feature, such as free lists, free list groups, etc., will be highlighted.

The primary focus of this chapter, and future chapters, will be with respect to RAC; however, where it becomes important, the old feature will be discussed from a comparison perspective. The occasional highlights comparing RAC with OPS will provide help to the database administrator migrating from OPS to RAC.

3.2   Oracle components

3.2.1   Instance and database

Every Oracle database is associated with a certain memory area. This area is preallocated from the current systems memory and is used by the database to retain and process user and system requests. Oracle calls this area of memory the system global area (SGA). Once it is established, Oracle also starts various background processes for completing the user requests. The SGA and the corresponding Oracle background process are referred to as the *Oracle instance*.

An Oracle database is composed of various components; their classification is based on the functions that these components perform. These components are broadly classified as the program global area (PGA) and the system global area (SGA).

In Figure 3.1, the various tiers of SGA and PGA are represented. The figure contains the shared pool, database buffer cache, Java pool, large pool, streams pool, and redo log buffer areas that constitute the SGA, and the private SQL area, SQL area, and cursors that constitute the PGA. All of these are areas of memory based on parameter values in a parameter file. When user requests are received, they utilize the memory areas to communicate with the Oracle background processes to accomplish their tasks.

10g   New Feature: Streams Pool is a new memory area introduced in Oracle 10g. This memory area is used for Streams functionality of Oracle.

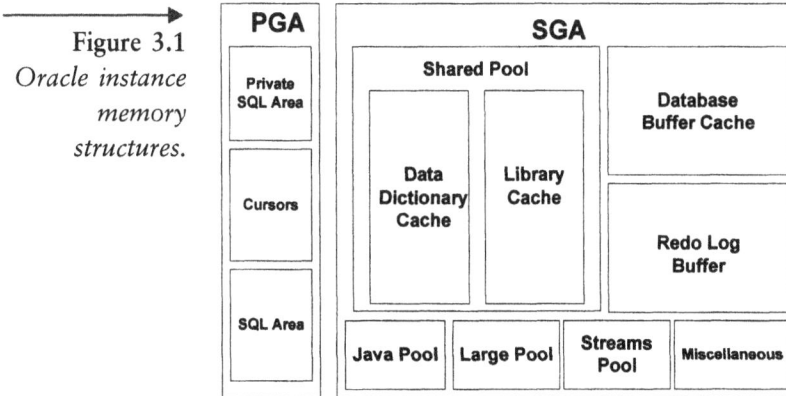

Figure 3.1
Oracle instance memory structures.

PGA

The program (process) global area (PGA) stores session specific information. The PGA is a memory area that contains data and controls information pertaining to a single user process.

To accomplish a task or request against the database, the user has to establish a connection. Oracle provides two methods of operations for this purpose: the shared connection and the dedicated user connection. The shared queue connection feature is implemented using the shared server feature (previously called multithreaded server or MTS). The dedicated connection is established when the dedicated server option is configured, which is the default configuration. When the dedicated connection is used, every user process has a dedicated connection to the server and the PGA contains session-related information that is specific to a user process. Not all data contained in this area is shareable by other processes. As illustrated in Figure 3.1, the PGA in a dedicated connection is outside of the SGA.

In a dedicated configuration, the PGA contains the following:

- Sort area for sorting data before returning it to the user

- Session information, including user privileges pertaining to the session

- Current state of various cursors used by the session

- Area, or stack space, containing variables used in the session

The PGA is created for a single user session when the connection is established to the server and it is deallocated when the session is terminated. This occurs when the user cancels by aborting his or her session or when the session has completed its task through a commit or rollback operation.

9i New Feature: In Oracle 9*i*, in a dedicated server configuration, the size of SQL work areas that are part of the PGA could be automatically and globally managed. This is accomplished by specifying the parameter PGA_AGGREGATE_TARGET. By setting a value to this parameter Oracle will try to ensure that the total amount of PGA memory allocated across all database server processes never exceeds this target.

In earlier versions, the DBAs controlled the maximum size of SQL work area by setting SORT_AREA_SIZE, HASH_AREA_SIZE, BITMAP_AREA_SIZE, and CREATE_BITMAP_AREA_SIZE parameters.

In a shared server setup, user connections are queued to the server and every connection or user process shares one or more connections by a method of queuing to a pool of connections. When a session requires a connection to the database, a connection is allocated from this pool. Since the connections are taken from a pool of pre-established connections, the time and resources required to create these connections are eliminated. The number of connections is based on the configuration parameter, SHARED_SERVER_SESSIONS, defined in the parameter file. In the case of the shared server configuration, the PGA is part of the SGA.

9i New Feature: SHARED_SERVER_SESSIONS replaces the MTS_ SESSIONS parameter that existed in the Oracle 8*i* and before.

The shared server option is useful where a large number of users connect to the database almost simultaneously and/or join and leave the connection quite frequently. To illustrate this let us take a large organization, such as an assembly plant of a truck manufacturer. The manufacturer operates in two shifts. The first shift users start up their computer systems and the second shift users turn them off at the end of their shift. When the first shift users come into work, the first thing the users do is connect to the network to access assembly line information from the database. If the server is configured to use a dedicated connection, these several thousand simultaneous user session requests (depending on the configuration) could potentially cause a traffic jam in the network system. The connections requested by the users will all require memory, time, and resources and could cause network blockage. The blockage would occur when the initial requests are not completed while others are also trying to establish a connection. The end result of this is a huge amount of waits encountered by these users, leading to user session requests ultimately timing out.

In a scenario such as this, where a large number of users are connecting or requesting connection to the system at the same time, the shared server option will help balance the resources. Balance can be achieved because user requests are placed in a queue and a connection is provided from a pool of connections already established. When one user session is making a connection, the request from another user session is waiting in the queue and behind this is another user, and so on. If the system is in the situation of having a large number of users waiting in queues, the shared server option could be configured to have multiple connection pools. This is defined by SHARED_SERVERS parameter in the initialization file.

9i

New Feature: The initi<SID>.ora file used in Oracle 8*i* and previous versions of Oracle has been replaced by Spfile<SID>.ora (server parameter file). The spfile is a binary file and changes to the parameters are done online through an active instance. In Oracle 9*i* most of the parameters used for management of the instance are dynamic and can be changed while the instance is up.

In Oracle 9*i* the multithreaded server (MTS) option has been renamed to SHARED SERVER.

The SHARED_SERVERS parameter replaces the MTS_SERVERS parameter that existed in prior versions of Oracle (Oracle 8*i* and before). This parameter specifies the number of server processes to be created when an instance is started. Another parameter, called SHARED_MAX_SERVERS (called MTS_MAX_SERVERS in prior versions of Oracle), specifies the maximum number of shared server processes allowed to be running simultaneously.

10g

New Feature: With Oracle 10g, Shared Servers do not have to be preconfigured in the parameter file. They can be dynamically configured.

SGA

The system global area (SGA) is the memory structure of an Oracle instance and contains data and control information for the Oracle server. The SGA is a memory area allocated from the virtual memory area of the computer created during database startup through one or more parameters defined in the parameter file. Unlike the PGA (in a dedicated connection), the SGA contains shared information from various processes accessing the Oracle server. As discussed in the previous section, in the case of a shared server configuration, the PGA is part of the SGA and contains shared connections.

The SGA is further divided into the shared pool, Java pool, large pool, the database buffer cache, and the redo log buffer. Each of these components, or areas, within the SGA has their own functional responsibility.

Shared pool

The shared pool consists of the data dictionary cache and the library cache. Its functionality includes keeping the most recently used metadata information in memory for reuse by other users utilizing or executing the same statements.

The transaction life cycle, covered in more detail in Chapter 5 (Transaction Management) later in this book, is an operation comprising multiple phases and covers the entire span of the transaction, from the point that the user makes a request via a query or data manipulation language (DML) statement through the phase that the data is retrieved and returned back to the user. The initial phase of this operation is the parse phase and is the most expensive phase for processing the statement. To help in maintaining lower overheads, the database administrator and the developer have to thoroughly validate and tune the SQL statements. It would also be advisable to encourage reusability of SQL statements. This could be accomplished by developing queries for a specific table generic enough so that it could be shared. Sharing of SQL statements help in lessening utilization of resources.

Oracle computes a hash value for every statement that is parsed by a user and this hash value is stored in the hash bucket when the statement is placed in the library cache. Once the first statement is stored in the library cache, the next time another query is executed, Oracle computes a hash value and then compares it with the one in the bucket. If a match is found, the statement from the library cache is reused and Oracle will not have to reparse the query. (A similar algorithm is also used to find the actual row of data.) However, if a match is not found, Oracle performs the following steps to execute the query:

1.   Parses the statement

2.   Validates authenticity to the tables referenced in the query

3.   Loads metadata information into the dictionary cache

4.   Retrieves the row (if all the validations and authenticity checks were successful)

If any of the validation steps fails, then Oracle cancels the request and returns an error message to the user.

Because of the fact that the hash value is generated based on the contents in the statement, any variation of the statement structure causes a variance in the hash value. A variance in the hash value makes Oracle maintain another copy of the same statement in memory. (It is important to group all SQL queries used inside the application code to maintain a lower variance between the queries.) Another situation in which a variance is created is when a bind variable is used in the WHERE clause of an SQL query statement. Bind variables have values that change based on the application or process, and the memory area allocated for one value may not be sufficient for another statement.

Oracle, by default, assigns a 50-byte memory area for the initial bind value in the bind variable. Suppose the bind value of the initial query is a small string value, for example "SMITH." When another user executes the same query with a longer value greater than 50 bytes, Oracle finds that the existing memory structure cannot hold this new value and allocates another memory structure with this new WHERE clause and bind value. This variation causes SQL query flooding in applications having several queries from various users. Users can see these variations by querying the SQLTEXT column in the V$SQLAREA data dictionary view. Therefore, tuning or validation of SQL statements during the design and development phase of the development cycle can help to achieve a more efficient system.

The variance of SQL queries brings about another complexity. Every query (cursor) is defined in two parts: the cursor header and cursor body. While the cursor head is fixed, the contents do not change and remain in the cache until they are aged out; the cursor body contains the bind variables and execution plan for the statement and can contain multiple versions. There are several reasons for having multiple versions of the cursor body, the primary reason being the high usage of literals instead of bind variables. Another reason is insufficient length being allocated when the bind variables are defined, for example, in PL/SQL definitions.

Java pool

The Java pool is used to configure memory for session-specific Java code and the Java virtual machine (JVM). Depending on whether the dedicated server option or the shared server option is used, the memory allocated via the Java pool is used differently.

Large pool

The database administrator can configure an optional memory area, called the large pool, to provide large memory allocations for:

- Session memory for the shared server option of establishing connections to the database and the Oracle XA interface (used where transactions interact with more than one database)

- I/O server processes

- Oracle backup and restore operations, when RMAN is used

- Parallel execution message buffers, if the initialization parameter PARALLEL_AUTOMATIC_TUNING is set to TRUE (otherwise, these buffers are allocated to the shared pool)

Streams Pool

This pool is new in 10*g* and is used by the Oracle streams component, to store captured events in addition to its use for internal communication during parallel capture and capture. The pool is part of the SGA and is defined using the parameter STREAMS_POOL_SIZE. Like the other pool areas that are part of the SGA, if STREAMS_POOL_SIZE is not defined or is set to a zero value, then up to 10% of memory from the shared pool may be used.

Database buffer cache

The database buffer cache is the portion of the SGA that holds copies of data blocks read from data files. All user processes concurrently connected to the instance share access to the database buffer cache.

As illustrated in Figure 3.2, the buffers in the cache are organized into two areas, the most recently used (MRU) area and the least recently used (LRU) area. In Version 8*i*, Oracle introduced a new concept of managing the data in the buffer cache based on an algorithm called the touch count algorithm (TCA). Over the years Oracle has been improving the buffer management algorithm by constantly providing performance improvements. Unlike the previous versions of the buffer management, under the TCA option, the determination of where the row will reside (MRU or the MRU end of the LRU chain) is based on the number of times the buffer is touched (touch count). Prior to Version 8*i*, the data retrieved was placed on the MRU area of the buffer. Based on the number of times it was used the data was retained at the top of the MRU area. However, if the data

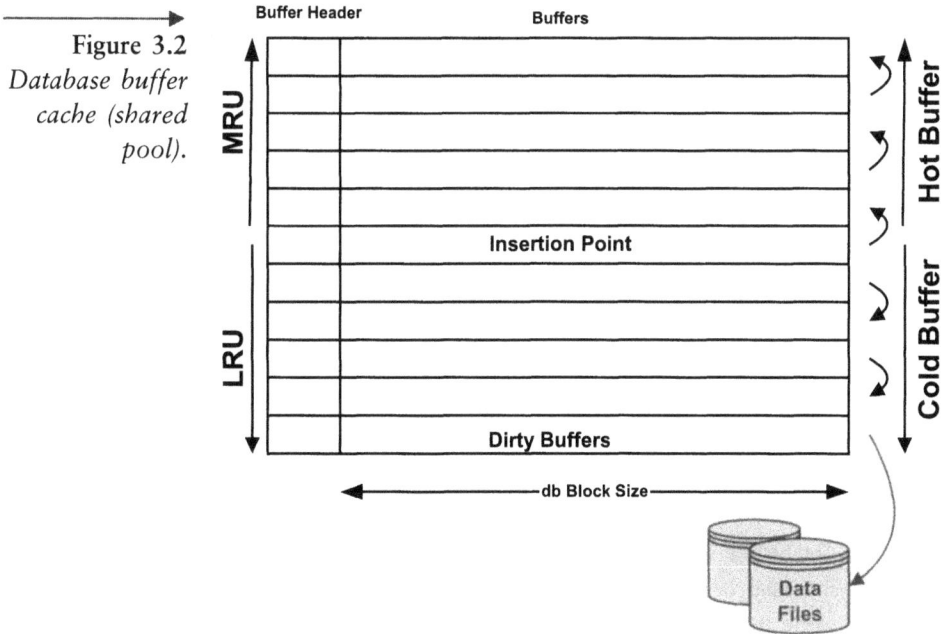

Figure 3.2
Database buffer cache (shared pool).

was not used it was moved to the LRU end of the chain before being marked as dirty and eventually getting flushed out of the cache.

Under the TCA, the buffer cache is equally divided into the two basic areas, the hot buffer area and the cold buffer area. Between the hot buffers and the cold buffers is a midpoint, called the insertion point, or a buffer midpoint. When a block is read from disk and placed into the buffer cache it places the buffer in the middle, that is at the midpoint between the hot and cold buffers with an initial touch count value of one. During this process, Oracle looks for a free buffer to place the block read from disk. If it finds that a block's touch count is greater than two it is moved to the LRU end of the MRU chain. (This value of two is the default value used to determine the initial and future placement of blocks. This is controlled by a hidden parameter.[1]) When a buffer is moved to the MRU end of the LRU chain (i.e., closer to the insertion point), its touch count is usually set to zero. Consequently, if the touch count is not sufficiently incremented quickly enough it could get pushed back to the LRU area of the buffer.

---

1.   Hidden parameters are not visible to the users via the V$PARAMETER view or using the show parameters. The hidden parameters are used by Oracle for controlling certain behavior. Hidden parameters are not guaranteed to be available during a specific future release and hence should be used with caution.

Figure 3.2 represents the database buffer cache and how the data is moved down the buffer space to the LRU end of the buffer. This is based on the data being reused by other processes as well as on the modifications finally written to their respective data files.

How does a buffer move from the MRU end of the LRU chain beyond the midpoint? When a buffer has reached a touch count value to enable movement from a cold buffer region to a hot buffer region, crossing the midpoint, another buffer from the hot region has to provide space for this new hot buffer movement. When this happens, a hot buffer that has, for example, a touch count value of two, when moved over to the cold region, will be reset with a touch count value of one. Now, if the buffer is not frequently touched and the value not incremented, there is a potential that it would be aged out to disk.

As discussed earlier, based on how many times the buffer is touched, the buffer will earn its way to the top of the buffer chain. However, the increase in touch count and movement of buffers do not happen at the same time, rather, they are independent of each other. Additionally, when a touch count is incremented it does not move the buffer up the chain. By default, Oracle only allows a buffer's touch count to be increased once every 3 seconds. Modifying some of the hidden parameters can change this default value of 3 seconds. This process of pushing the rows into the LRU continues until it reaches the edge of the structure and finally gets pushed off. At this point, the data is written to disk. The buffers at the end of the buffer are called dirty buffers.

The database buffer cache contains the data buffers that keep the latest data changes in memory before writing it to disk. As mentioned previously, the changes are kept in memory and pushed down the buffer tree until it reaches the end, when the data is written to disk. This component helps the Oracle engine, or system, to defer the write operation to disk, thus, helping in I/O and diverting the available resources to other parts of the system where it could be used more efficiently.

The data buffers contain data blocks, index blocks, rollback segment blocks, and temporary segment blocks. The database buffer cache contains a buffer for the data and a buffer for the rollback block. The data in the database buffer cache is written to the data files by the database writer process (DBWR).

To gain efficient functioning of the database, the database buffer cache should be rightly sized. The number of buffers in the database buffer cache is defined by the `DB_CACHE_SIZE` parameter defined in the parameter file. The size of each buffer is based on the DB_BLOCK_SIZE parameter, which is also defined in the parameter file. DB_BLOCK_SIZE specifies the size (in bytes) of Oracle database blocks.

9i

New Feature: The DB_CACHE_SIZE parameter replaces the DB_BLOCK_BUFFERS parameter that existed in prior versions of Oracle. This parameter specifies the number of database buffers in the buffer cache.

Oracle *9i* supports multiple block-sized databases; the block size can now be set at the tablespace definition level, thus allowing tablespaces with different block sizes to be created. In addition, up to five non-standard block sizes may be specified. The data block sizes should be a multiple of the operating system's block size, within the maximum limit to avoid unnecessary I/O. Oracle data blocks are the smallest units of storage that Oracle can use or allocate. However, a default DB_BLOCK_SIZE is defined in the parameter file that is used for primary DB_CACHE_SIZE calculation. Additional subcaches could be defined using each of the additional block sizes. This allows for creation of databases supporting multiple purposes, such as an OLTP system and a data warehouse.

When tuning the buffer cache area, while a 95–99% hit ratio is desired, it does not indicate that the database is performing at its peak. This percentage value purely translates to the fact that 95–99% of the time, the system has found a matching buffer hit. It does not indicate that all the buffer requests are met in a sufficiently good time frame. For example, when a user executes a query to retrieve 100,000 rows from a table, depending on the size of the SGA, performing a 2- or 3-table join would show a 95% or higher hit ratio, despite the fact that the response time for the query to return the result set may not be satisfactory. The best method to determine the reasons is to look at Oracle's wait interface by querying the data dictionary view provided by Oracle, such as the V$SESSION_EVENT, V$SESSION_ WAIT, and V$SYSTEM_EVENT.

A more detailed discussion on these views, and other performance related views, are given later in Chapter 13 (Performance Tuning).

Redo log buffers

The redo log buffer keeps all changes, or redo entries, of the data being modified. In the case of system failure and for recovery purposes, this functionality of the component helps in regeneration of changes.

This circular buffer is used to record changes to the database and record if the changes have been committed. The changes made to the database are made by the end user issuing any of the various DML operations (e.g., INSERT, UPDATE, or DELETE). When the Oracle server moves data from the user's memory space, it writes to the redo log buffer. With the after image and before image, the redo log buffer also contains a flag that indicates whether the data has been committed. The log writer (LGWR) writes the data in the redo log buffers to the redo log files. The size of the buffer is specified by the parameter LOG_BUFFER. Though the value in this parameter is used to create the redo log buffer, this allocation of redo log buffer provides a mechanism to create equally sized redo log files. Redo log files are explained later in this section.

The redo entry records the block that has changed, the location of the change, and the new value. The contents of the redo log buffer reflect the state of both the old and the new data. Oracle maintains a flag that indicates whether the data has been committed. Once the user has issued the commit statement, the flag is updated and the data is written to the redo log file on the disk.

It is the generation of redo, and the subsequent writing of that redo to the log file that makes the change real. Once an entry is successfully written in the log file then the change can have been considered to have occurred, regardless of what happens to the database system after this.

The redo log buffer is used sequentially. For example, all changes made to the database are recorded sequentially in the redo log buffer. Hence, the changes made by one transaction may intertwine with changes made by other transactions. Only after the redo record has been built in the redo buffer can the data block buffers be changed.

When the redo log buffer is one-third full, the data from the redo log buffers is flushed into the redo log files.

Other circumstances when the redo buffer information is written to disk include:

- When the user issues a commit statement

- When an LGWR process timeout occurs (which defaults to every 3 seconds)

- Before the DBWR process writes the modified blocks to the data files

9i New Feature: In Oracle *9i*, the SGA can be dynamically managed while the instance is running. The values of the buffer pool, shared pool and large pool could be changed dynamically. However, to protect an uncontrolled change of these areas, Oracle has introduced a new parameter, SGA_MAX_SIZE, that would help define a max value for these parameters.

The size of the SGA is determined by several parameters:

- DB_CACHE_SIZE

- LOG_BUFFER

- SHARED_POOL_SIZE

- LARGE_POOL_SIZE

3.2.2 Files

Figure 3.3 provides an overview of the various types of files that are part of the Oracle architecture. There are other files like the trace files and archive log files that are also part of the architecture.

Control file

The control file contains the information needed to maintain and verify database integrity as well as information related to the database, the

Figure 3.3
Files.

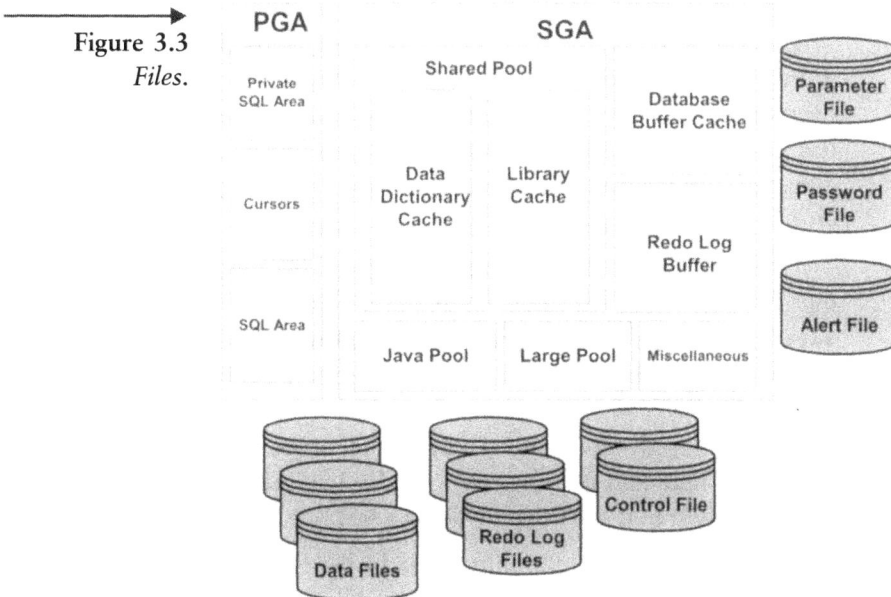

location of data files, tracking of the system change number (SCN), location of archive log information, etc. Since most of the critical information relating to the status of the database is stored in the control file, it is used during the recovery process. The existence of the control file is important for database startup. For this reason, the control file is sometimes considered the backbone of the database. A control file contains information such as:

- Database name
- Timestamp of database creation
- Names and locations of associated data files and online redo log files
- Tablespace information
- Data file offline ranges
- Log history
- Archived log information
- Backup set and backup piece information
- Backup data file and redo log information
- Data file copy information
- Current log sequence number
- Checkpoint information

Every time an instance of an Oracle database is started, the control file identifies the database and redo log files that must be opened for database operation to proceed. If the physical makeup of the database is altered (e.g., if a new data file or redo log file is created), then the control file is automatically modified by Oracle to reflect the change. A control file is also used in database recovery.

Using the human spinal cord as an analogy: the spinal cord is important for a human body because, without the spinal cord, the body would have different forms and may have to move like a caterpillar. Similarly, the control file is important for a system because if a control file is corrupted and no backup is available to re-create the control file, it may cause the database to be in an unrecoverable state. Due to its importance, it is a normal practice to keep a minimum of three control files (and also keep backup copies of control files) in text format by doing a BACKUP TO TRACE.

Table 3.1 illustrates the differences in the control file layout between Oracle 8*i* and 9*i*. The layout has considerably changed, with Oracle storing

Table 3.1   *Control File Layout*

Oracle 8*i*	Oracle 9*i*
Generic file header	Generic file header
Database entry	Database entry
Checkpoint records	Checkpoint progress records
Redo thread records	Extended database entry
Log file records	Redo thread records
Data file records	Log file records
Temp file records	Data file records
Tablespace records	Temp file records
Log file history records	Tablespace records
Offline range records	RMAN configuration records
Archived log records	Log file history records
RMAN information	Offline range records
	Archived log records
	Backup set records
	Backup piece records
	Backup data file records
	Backup log records
	Data file copy records
	Backup data file corruption records
	Data file copy corruption records
	Deletion records
	Proxy copy records
	Incarnation records

more database-related information in the control file. This additional information indicates that the control file would have more activity compared with the previous versions, and its importance also increases because more critical database information is now stored in the control file.

Redo log files

The redo log files contain the record of all transactions made against the database. These records, or logs of transactions, are used by Oracle for recovery in case of a database crash. As redo logs are critical to maintaining data integrity, Oracle writes data to this file on a continuous basis. Based on certain conditions, Oracle writes to the database to make the changes permanent; this write operation is performed in a batch mode and it helps to improve overall performance of the database. To allow for continuous writing to the redo log files and, at the same time, to write the existing data to the database, Oracle's architecture requires a minimum of at least two redo log files. The redo logs are used in a round-robin, or cyclical manner, switching between the files when a file is full. Having just two files for rotation could be dangerous, especially when the redo log files are overwritten. This could mean that if the disk containing one redo log file fails, data in that specific log file is lost. If the data in the database is lost, then data pertaining to the time period when this log file was created is also lost. In other words, there is a single point of failure.

To protect the redo log file from a single point of failure, Oracle recommends the creation of redo log groups. Each group should contain two or more redo log files. In this situation, all files belonging to the group are written to simultaneously.

Figure 3.4 represents a configuration with three redo log groups containing two redo log files each. Data is written simultaneously to both files that belong to a specific group. When the files in Group 1 become full, data is written to files in Group 2, and so on. When data in Group 3 is full, data is written to files in Group 1 and again to files in Group 2, in a cyclical manner between the various groups. When a group is full and data starts getting written to the next group, the existing contents that are contained in the redo log files in the redo log group are overwritten.

Figure 3.4
Redo log groups.

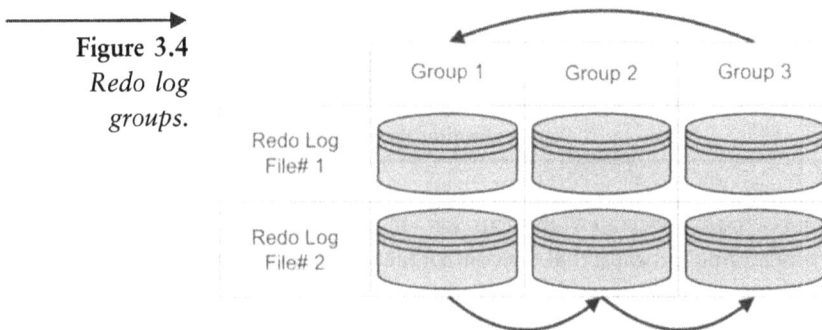

When performing the log switch, the next log to be used must not contain changes required in the event of instance recovery being needed. Oracle ensures that the current thread checkpoint must be beyond that log file, or in other words, the thread checkpoint SCN must be beyond the highest SCN allocated in the log to be switched.

Oracle recommends that the files belonging to each group be placed on different disks. The advantage of this placement is that when one disk containing one of the redo log files fails, Oracle will continue writing to the other redo log file that is part of the same redo log group. This protects the database from a single point of failure from the redo logs and helps to improve performance. If only one file per group was set up, then the database would hang, or crash when a disk containing the redo log file is not available for the write operation. On the other hand, in a group containing two files, when one file is not available, Oracle continues its operation by writing to the other available files in the same group. Before the files in Group 1 are overwritten, the files are copied into an archive media called archive redo logs if archiving is enabled. The message "checkpoint not complete" in the alert log will indicate that LGWR is waiting to switch into an active log file. Under these circumstances increasing the number of log files, the size of the log files or the frequency of checkpointing will help alleviate the issue.

Redo log files are a core component of the Oracle file system; consequently, it is important that considerable effort is given to locate them on high-performance disks for throughput.

While configuring the redo log files it is important that all files in a group, and all groups, are created with the same size. This aids in easy maintenance and consistency in the amount of information stored.

Redo log files are instance-specific because they contain information pertaining to the redo log buffers, which are part of the SGA. Because of this, every instance in a RAC configuration will have its own copy of the redo log files.

Archive redo log files

Archive redo log files, or archive log files, as mentioned above, are offline copies of redo log files that may be necessary to recover the database from media failures. An archive log file is a copy of the redo log files made before being overwritten. For example, when a redo log file becomes full, the redo information starts getting written to the next set of redo log files. (The archive log file is only created if the archive log mode is enabled in the parameter file.) Redo log files help in instance recovery. Archive log files provide for recovery of data not backed up to external media.

For example, when a database needs to be restored to a specific point in time, the following occurs:

1.   The latest backup is restored from the backup media.

2.   All the archive log files from the point that the backup was completed are applied one after the other up to the last archive log file.

In everyday operations, it happens quite often that there is a requirement to restore the database and recover the data lost. To protect the archive log files from any unrecoverable circumstances, it is important to create multiple copies of the archive log files at different locations, to avoid the single point of failure. When one archive log file is corrupt, or is lost due to disk failure, the data from the available archive log file is used for a restore operation. Apart from the situations explained above, archive log files are required for certain backup operations using RMAN; backup and recovery operations using RMAN are explained later in Chapter 12 (Backup and Recovery).

In Figure 3.5, when the redo log files are switched from Group 1 to Group 2, a copy of the redo log files from Group 1 is copied to the archive redo log files. When the files in the next group are filled, the next group (Group 2) is active and the data from Group 2 is written to the archive log directories. Unlike the redo log files, where the files are overwritten in a cyclical manner, the archive redo log files are not. New archive redo log files are created during every redo log switch.

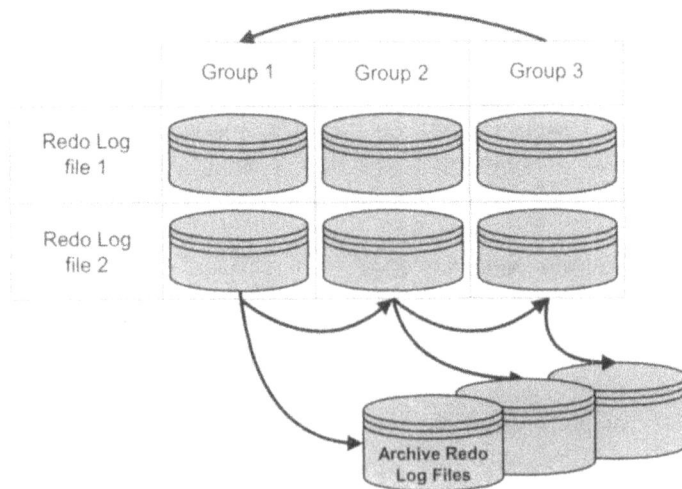

Figure 3.5
Archive redo log groups.

Since the archive logs are copies of the redo log files, they inherit the characteristics (such as the file size) of the redo log files. However, care should be taken in placement of these files. For example, archive log files are critical to the operation of the database and, because of this, they should not be placed on the same disk as the redo log files.

With RAC on systems where the data files must be on a raw partition, the redo logs could be placed on either a file system or on a raw partition, whereas the archive logs must be placed on a file system. Archive redo logs are instance-specific; therefore, every instance will have its own copy of the archive redo log files.

Parameter files

Parameter files are used to define the characteristics of an Oracle instance. With every release, certain parameters become obsolete and new ones are added to improve the efficiency and to introduce new features. The parameter file also contains pointers to important files that Oracle needs to be aware of during startup and shutdown of the database.

When an instance is started, the parameter file is identified. The parameter file contains the location of the control file, and the control file contains the location of all other data files, tablespaces, and system files. The control file also maintains the current state of the database. The parameter file contains details of the destination of the archived log files and certain format parameters for the archive log files. Among other important parameters that are defined in the parameter file is the database name used to identify the database.

Password file

The password file contains relevant information for database authentication. This file is stored in binary format like most other Oracle files. The file is required to be present during the database startup; however, the file can only be updated when the database and instances are up. The password file contains information for remote authentication of users. When a user, through an SQL*Plus client, or one using the Oracle Enterprise Manager[2] (OEM), requires access to the database to perform certain operations, the user is required to have an entry in this file. Privileges such as SYSOPER and SYSDBA require the user name to be present

---

2.   Oracle Enterprise Manager is a database management tool, available from Oracle Corporation. More discussion on usage of this tool is forthcoming in Chapter 13 (Performance Tuning : Tools and Utilities).

in the password file. This file stores the user and the special privileges that he or she has. Like the parameter file discussed above, this file needs to be present for database startup. However, no entries are required when access to the database from a remote location is required. The password file is another file that the control file has no knowledge of but its inclusion in the regular backup strategy of the database is crucial.

Alert files

Alert files (also called alert log files) contain messages generated by the Oracle kernel to inform about any events or changes that happen to the database on a time-to-time basis. Some of the entries found in alert files include:

- Database startup and shutdown information

- Information regarding when the archive processes and the starting and completion of archive operations

- Any errors encountered by the background processes

- Any errors with error number encountered by the Oracle kernel

Unlike the other files mentioned above, this file contains messages to help the database and system administrators monitor and deduce any problems that the database or instance has encountered. Upon observing these errors, the database administrator will take precautionary measures to resolve them. This file is written to on a continuous basis and consequently grows to a considerably large size. However, this file is normally not included in the backup strategy. To avoid having to maintain a large file, it is advisable that this file be copied and deleted periodically and to let the database create a new file.

3.2.3   Background processes

Figure 3.6 displays the various background processes used by Oracle. Each background process has a specific function that it performs. During this process, interaction takes place between the logical storage area of the database and one or more physical storage areas of the database. These background processes interact with the SGA. For example, the DBWR process is used for writing rows of data from the database buffer cache from memory to disk. During this process, the LGWR process writes information from the redo log buffers to disk. Other background processes are the process monitor (PMON), responsible for cleaning up unused

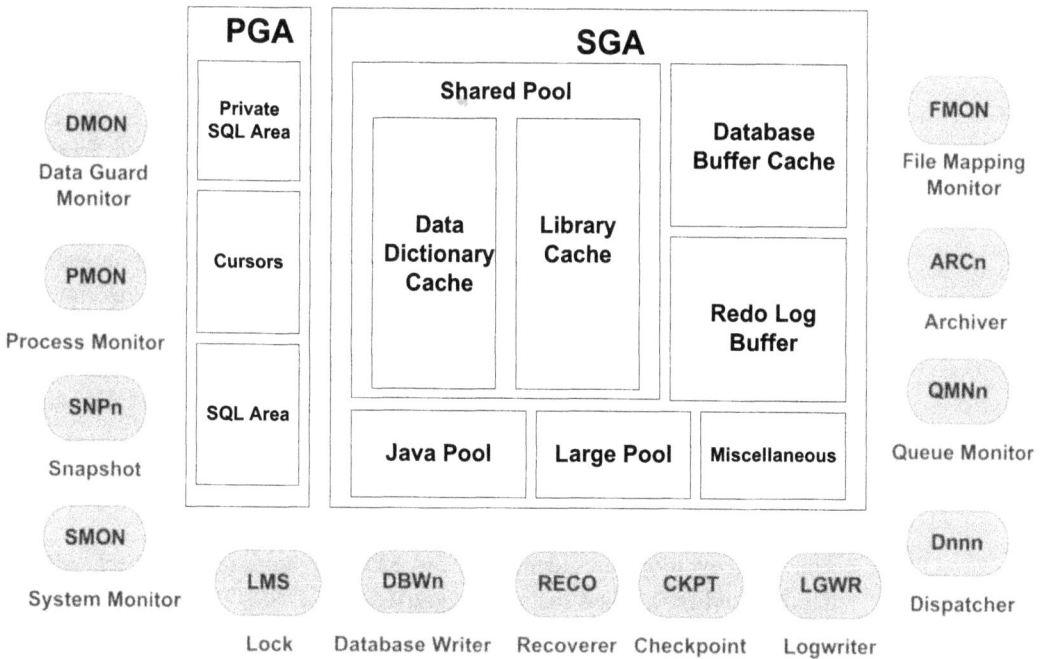

Figure 3.6   *Oracle background processes.*

resources, and system monitor (SMON), responsible for cleaning up unused temporary segments.

An Oracle instance comprises background and foreground processes that are required to service requests from various users. Every instance has several background processes. The background processes essential for the existence of an instance are:

- System monitor (SMON)

- Database writer (DBWn)

- Process monitor (PMON)

- Log writer (LGWR)

- Checkpoint process (CKPT)

These background processes interact as a bridge between the memory (or SGA) of the database and the various permanent storage media (or files). The SGA is an area of memory predefined during database startup to store and share user or process related information.

Process monitor

The process monitor, identified by PMON, is responsible for cleaning up the resources when one of the processes fails. Typically users interrupt their existing process by aborting a session, causing the exit from an SQL*Plus client session without a commit or rollback operation. This occurs when the window is shut down before a query completes. These situations could leave a process on the server machine hanging without a client connection. By performing a rollback of the uncommitted transactions and freeing up resources for other processes to use, PMON takes the responsibility of cleaning up such processes. PMON also releases all locks held by the process and restarts processes that have a failed status during this recovery operation.

System monitor

The system monitor, identified by SMON, initiates recovery of the database when a failed instance is started again. SMON is responsible for cleaning up temporary segments that are no longer required, for coalescing free extents in data files to create larger extents, and recovering terminated transactions skipped during recovery. These transactions are eventually recovered by SMON when the tablespace is brought back online. SMON also coalesces free extents in the dictionary-managed tablespaces to make free space contiguous and easier to allocate. Most of the activities performed by SMON occur during low peak times.

SMON works in a cyclical fashion. For example, SMON does its operation performing multiple passes over the transactions that require a recovery operation. SMON only applies a certain number of undo records per transaction during each pass.

SMON is also responsible for the recovery of transactions that have not been committed when the database is started after a database crash or a shutdown abort operation.

With RAC, the SMON process of one instance can perform instance recovery for failed CPU or instance of other instances that have failed.

Database writer

The database writer, identified by DBWR, is responsible for writing changed data to the database. In the section on the database buffer cache, we discussed the movement of data to the bottom of the LRU stack if the touch count was low when data with a higher touch count required space to move up. The rows at the end of the buffer cache are called dirty buffers. The DBWR writes the dirty buffers to disk. By writing these dirty buffers from the buffer cache to the data files, it ensures sufficient free buffers are available in the database buffer cache. The free buffers allow for new data to be stored in the buffer cache, while removing old data no longer used or required. This writing of dirty buffers from the database buffer cache to disk only happens if space is needed to store new data in the buffer.

This feature of the DBWR to write information from the buffer cache only if needed provides performance benefits. This reduces I/O activity on the database because Oracle does not write the committed rows immediately but instead batches them together.

The actual writing of changed data to disk is done at a later time by the DBWR process. This happens when any of the following events occur:

- *The number of dirty buffers reaches a threshold value:* This value is reached when there is not sufficient room in the database buffer cache for more data. In this situation, Oracle writes the dirty buffers to disk, freeing up space for new data.

- *A process is unable to find free buffers in the database buffer cache while scanning for blocks:* When a process reads data from the disk and does not find any free space in the buffer, this triggers the least recently used data in the buffer cache to be pushed down the stack and finally written to disk.

- *A timeout occurs:* The timeout is configured by setting the required timeout interval (LOG_CHECKPOINT_TIMEOUT) through a parameter defined in the parameter file. On every preset interval, the timeout is triggered to cause the DBWR to write the dirty buffers to disk. This mechanism is used by Oracle for transaction recoverability in case of failure. In an ideal system, where the data is occasionally modified but not written to disk (due to not having sufficient activity that would cause other mechanisms to trigger the write operation), the timeout is helpful.

- *The checkpoint process:* During a predefined interval defined by the LOG_CHECKPOINT_INTERVAL parameter, when the CKPT process is triggered, it causes the DBWR and the LGWR process to write the data from their respective buffer cache to disk.

Configuring multiple database writer processes or using I/O slaves is useful, especially in systems where there is a high transaction rate.

The DBWR process is defined using the DB_WRITER_PROCESSES parameter in the parameter file. Using this parameter, multiple DBWn processes (from DBW0 to DBW9 and from DBWa to DBWj) could be configured. Multiple DBWn processes distribute the work required to identify buffers to be written and also distribute the I/O load over these processes. Selection of the number of DBWn processes required for any system should not be arbitrary, but should be based on analysis of the volume of transactions and the number of buffers required to be scanned before writing to disk. It is also dependent on the number of CPUs that the system currently has; the rule of thumb is to configure one DBWn for every eight CPUs.

Another parameter that supports the DBWn process is the DBWR_IO_SLAVES; configuring this parameter allows I/O load to be distributed over multiple slave processes. I/O slave processes are used when the system has only one CPU available and there is high transactional activity causing slowdown in database writes; under other circumstances, multiple DBWR processes should be preferred over the I/O slaves.

Checkpoint process

The checkpoint process, identified by CKPT, is responsible for updating the database status information whenever changes in the buffer cache are permanently recorded in the database. All of the data, regardless of whether it has been committed or not, is written to the data files. During this event, all the headers of these data files are updated by a checkpoint. The process of writing this checkpoint information into the header ensures that the data files are synchronized. At specific intervals, all modified database buffers in the SGA are written to the data files. This event is called a checkpoint. Though the DBWR processes perform the actual writing of data to the data files, the checkpoint process is responsible for signaling the DBWR processes.

The checkpoint process is activated in the following circumstances:

- *The redo log switch occurs:* The redo log switch occurs under various circumstances described in the LGWR process (below). When a specific redo log file is full, the CKPT processes are activated before the process starts writing to the next available redo log file.

- *The* LOG_CHECKPOINT_INTERVAL *parameter is set:* The LOG_CHECKPOINT_INTERVAL parameter is defined in the parameter file. Giving this parameter an interval value causes the CKPT process to become activated at the specified interval. This value should be set to a high value equal to the size of LGWR processes. Setting this to a small value causes frequent activation of the CKPT process to run and creates a bottleneck for the database operation.

- *The beginning of a tablespace backup:* In the case of a tablespace level backup, when the system is active and in use, the CKPT process is activated at the beginning of a tablespace backup. The tablespace level backup mentioned in this section is also referred to as a hot backup. Hot backups are taken when the system is alive and in use. Due to the state of this process, the data files are active and the CKPT process request ensures that all changes to the file are completed to ensure a cleaner backup copy.

- *The tablespace is taken offline:* When a specific tablespace is taken offline, either manually or through an automated process, the CKPT process is activated to write the current tablespace information to the header of the tablespace and to the control file.

- *The instance is shut down through a normal shutdown process:* When the system is shut down through a normal shutdown process, Oracle RDBMS performs the following:

1.   Activates CKPT processes

2.   Activates the DBWR process in order to update all header files with the latest information

3.   Activates the LGWR processes in order to flush all buffer information to disk

This writing of information to disk ensures synchronization of files and does not cause the recovery process during a database startup operation.

In cases where the database is shut down by an abort or crash operation this information is not written. Therefore, when the database is started again, it goes into a recovery mode.

Log writer

The log writer process, identified by LGWR, is responsible for recording changes registered in the redo log buffer into the redo log files. This is a sequential process and is triggered by the following situations:

- *The redo log buffer is one-third full:* When the redo log buffer is continuously written to and it reaches one-third of its buffer capacity, it triggers the LGWR processes to write the information to disk. This mechanism is to allow for new redo information to be saved in the redo log buffer.

- *A timeout occurs (every 3 seconds):* A default timeout interval is defined at the database level, occurring every 3 seconds. During this timeout, the redo log buffer information is written to disk. If the redo logs are configured as dual files to one group, then both files are written to at the same time. If one of the files is not available due to a bad disk or being taken offline, then the LGWR writes to the available redo log file and continues its operation. However, if none of the redo log files that belongs to the group is available, then the database hangs. This occurs when the redo log file has not been copied when the database is configured in ARCHIVELOG mode.

- *The DBWR process writes the changed blocks from the database buffer cache to the data files:* When the database buffer cache is being flushed to disk it also triggers the LGWR process to write the redo buffer information to the redo log files. The DBWR process writes the dirty buffers to disk when the MRU area is required for new data. During the operation of writing the dirty buffers from the database buffer cache, the LGWR process is triggered.

- *A user or process commits the transaction:* When the user process issues a commit to the transaction, the LGWR writes the redo log buffer to disk. During the commit processes, all redo log buffer information currently in the redo log buffer is flushed to disk. This writing of redo log entries to disk is synchronized for multiple committed transactions, saving I/O and other system resources, after the first transaction's entries are written to the redo log files. When the user commits a transaction, a system change number (or SCN) is assigned to the transaction that is recorded with the transaction's redo entries in the redo log.

Archive process

The archive process, identified by ARCn, is responsible for writing the redo log information to archive log files before allowing for reuse of the redo log files. In the previous section the various types of files used by Oracle and how the archive files are created during redo log file switch activity were discussed. The ARCn background process performs this copy of the redo log to the archive log area.

If the archiving process does not complete before the next redo log file is full, and the switch occurs, the LGWR processes could fail, as the log files are not available for write operation. This could also happen when the log file size is too large, causing the archive to require a significant amount of time to write the information to its destination. Another reason for this delay could be due to slowness of the disk that is used to store the archive log files because of the fact that it is not able to write at the speed at which the data is being read from the file.

The ARCn process is optional and is created when the database is running in ARCHIVELOG mode. The database is set to run under ARCHIVELOG mode by setting the LOG_ARCHIVE_START parameter to TRUE in the parameter file, or by issuing an ALTER command at the database.

An instance can have up to 10 ARCn processes (ARC0 to ARC9). The LGWR process starts a new ARCn process whenever the current number of ARCn processes is insufficient to handle the workload. The starting and stopping of the various archive operations and starting of additional ARCn processes is recorded in the alert file.

Snapshot process

The snapshot process, identified by SNPn, is responsible for refreshing snapshots. The number of SNPn processes is defined by setting the JOB_QUEUE_PROCESSES parameter in the parameter file. The maximum value for this parameter is 36. This means that 36 SNP0...SNPz processes could be started to automatically refresh table snapshots. The process is automatically activated at a predefined interval to refresh any snapshots that are scheduled to be automatically refreshed. With multiple SNPn processes, the workload is shared among these processes.

Lock manager server process

The lock manager server process, identified by LMS, is noticed in a RAC environment and helps the database to communicate with and access shared resources in a database.

Dispatcher process

The dispatcher process, identified by Dnnn, is present in a shared server configuration. There is a dispatcher process for every communication protocol and it is responsible for routing requests from users to available shared server processes and returning results back to the appropriate users.

Recovery process

The recovery process, identified by RECO, is responsible for resolving failures of the database when the database is running in a distributed environment. RECO automatically connects to the other databases involved in an in-doubt distributed transaction and automatically resolves them. During this process it removes from each database pending transaction tables any rows that correspond to the resolved in-doubt transactions.

Queue monitor

The queue monitor process, identified by QMNn, is an optional process that is used with the advanced queuing option. The function of the QMNn process is to monitor the message queues. Approximately 10 QMNn (QMN0 to QMN9) processes could be configured to manage the message queues.

File mapping monitor

The file mapping monitor process, identified by FMON, is a background process started by Oracle when the FILE_MAPPING initialization parameter is set to TRUE. The functionality of this process is to help monitor I/O by mapping files to immediate storage layers and physical devices for I/O monitoring purposes. FMON is responsible for:

1. Building mapping information, which is stored in the SGA. The information is composed of the following structures:

    a. Files

    b. File system extents

    c. Elements

    d. Subelements

2. Refreshing mapping information when a change occurs because of:

    a. Change to size of Oracle data files

    b. Addition or deletion of data files

    c. Changes to the storage configuration

3. Saving mapping information in the data dictionary to maintain a view of the information that is persistent across startup and shutdown operations.

4. Restoring mapping information into the SGA at instance startup. This avoids the need for a potentially expensive complete rebuild of the mapping information on every instance startup.

FMON spawns an external non-Oracle process called FMPUTL. The functionality of this process is to communicate with the vendor-supplied mapping libraries. Based on the availability of the mapping libraries, it obtains information from all levels of the I/O stack.

9iR2

New Feature: The FMON feature is new in Oracle *9i* Release 2. Prior to this version there existed no such process or functionality to provide mapping of external files to Oracle.

Data guard

The data guard process identified by DMON is a background process started by Oracle when the DG_BROKER_START initialization parameter is set to TRUE.

3.3   Oracle data storage

The tablespace is composed of one or more data segments, composed of extents. Each extent comprises one or more Oracle blocks and an Oracle block comprises one or more disk blocks.

3.3.1   Tablespace

Tablespaces are the logical unit of storage in Oracle. A tablespace is used to group related logical structures together. In Oracle, a database is created with a minimum of one tablespace for the system and one or more user-defined tablespaces. Tablespaces help in the distribution of data and in manageability. Within a tablespace a specific number of data block allocations is called an extent.

There are various kinds of tablespace definitions, each having specific features with specific functionality. The different kinds of tablespaces are discussed in the following sections.

Dictionary-managed tablespaces

Before Oracle 8*i,* there were no specific classifications for tablespace management. All tablespaces were managed through the data dictionary. Under this system, Oracle stored all tablespace management information in the data dictionary and thus every change to the tablespace caused a write to the data dictionary. This writing of tablespace management information to the data dictionary causes considerable overhead.

When Oracle requires the allocation of extents to the tablespace (to write data), this operation causes a change in the extent value. This change causes the management of extents and values of current extent and the block address to be managed by writing the information to the data dictionary. When information is written to the data dictionary, it creates rollback entries. The information written to the rollback segments is not for use when the user applies a rollback command, but is for use during the recovery process. When the database is abnormally shut down and the database goes into recovery mode, these rollback entries have to be applied in order to get the database to the current state. Dictionary-managed tablespaces is the default method, meaning no specific syntax is required while defining this type of tablespace.

Locally managed tablespaces

With the release of Oracle 8*i,* the activities of managing extents could be maintained locally within the tablespace. Under this option the tablespace manages its own extents and maintains a bitmap in each data file to keep track of the free or used status of blocks in that data file. In a locally managed tablespace (LMT), each bit in a bitmap corresponds to a block or a group of blocks. Unlike a dictionary-managed tablespace, an update to the dictionary is not made when the allocation of an extent is freed for reuse. However, Oracle server changes the bitmap values to show the new status of the blocks.

Figure 3.7 illustrates the structure of a locally managed tablespace. Apart from the file header information, Oracle also maintains additional information in the form of bitmaps related to the tablespace.

Oracle writes all required information, such as block address, free or used state of blocks, etc., of the tablespace into its header. All information is stored locally in a bitmap format. All required information is stored and managed locally, and since no updates to the dictionary are required, no rollback entries are performed. This only applies to tablespace management and not to the actual data.

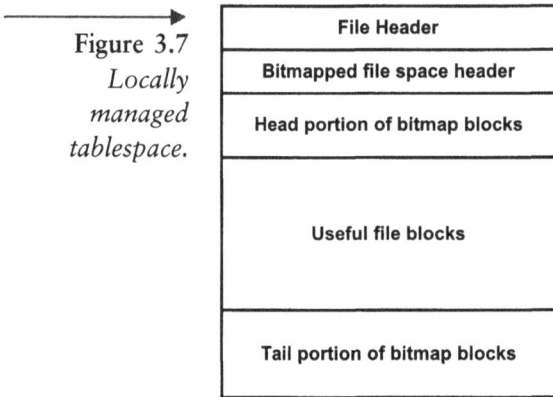

Figure 3.7
Locally managed tablespace.

| File Header |
| Bitmapped file space header |
| Head portion of bitmap blocks |
| Useful file blocks |
| Tail portion of bitmap blocks |

With the reduced update activity to the data dictionary to manage extent activity, locally managed tablespaces have a better performance advantage. Recursive operations are eliminated, because queries against FET$ and UET$ required under dictionary-managed space allocation is not required. While extents are being made, Oracle also checks the adjacent free space and eliminates the need for coalescing of free space.

Locally managed tablespaces are created with a specific LOCAL clause during tablespace creation. Locally managed tablespaces could be converted into dictionary-managed tablespaces, and vice versa.

When adding data files to a locally managed tablespace, additional bytes of space depending on the extent size should be added to the total size of the data file. This additional extent size is used for extent management at the data file level.

When locally managed tablespaces are used, the segment definition parameters such as PCTUSED, FREELIST, and FREELIST GROUPS are ignored. However, parameters such as INITRANS, MAXTRANS, and PCTFREE are valid values.

10g

New Feature: Starting with Oracle 10g, when the MAXTRANS parameter is not required, Oracle assigns the value of 255 by default.

Transportable tablespaces

When data has to be moved from one database to another, the normal methods adopted have been either to export and then import on the target database or to unload and then load. This has been done using tools such as SQL*Loader into the target database or using tools such as Oracle Advanced Replication (OAR).

In Oracle 8*i*, transportable tablespaces were introduced. As the name implies, transportable tablespaces enabled the transport of the tablespace from one database to another. Transportable tablespace helps in movement of data from one database to another very easily as an alternative to copy, export/import or unload/load operations. It is a matter of copying the tablespace to another location, or another machine, and defining the tablespace in the database. Another great usage of the transportable tablespace is for the archive operation. Tablespaces can be archived into media for future restoration if required.

The issues that tablespaces could be copied only between similar operating systems, and that tablespaces could be transported only between Oracle databases, are two limitations that apply to transportable tablespaces.

10g

New Feature: Starting with Oracle 10*g*, tablespaces could be transported between different operating systems. This is achieved by using the RMAN CONVERT command either before the transport or after the transport at the target location.

Temporary tablespaces

Oracle has created the tablespace of type temporary mainly for sort operations. When a sort operation is too large to fit into the local sort area, Oracle uses the temporary tablespace for these operations. Sort operations can occur during various types of SQL query operations, for example when an ORDER BY or GROUP BY operation is involved.

10g

New Feature: Multiple temporary tablespaces could be grouped together and assigned to a user process. This is a new feature in Oracle 10*g*, and alleviates problems caused by one tablespace being inadequate to hold the results of a sort operation. A tablespace group enables parallel execution servers in a single parallel operation to use multiple temporary tablespaces.

Read-only tablespaces

When data in a tablespace is never updated after the initial load, the data in this tablespace is classified as read-only. These tablespaces could be designated as read-only and are protected from any DML operation. These tablespaces do not need backups on a regular basis. The normal method of periodic backup is when the tablespace is made read-only and immediately when the tablespace is made read/write.

A major use of this feature is in a data warehouse, where the specific range set of data is written to this tablespace and no more will be written to the tablespace. These tablespaces could be converted from read-only to read-write or vice versa.

Undo tablespaces

This is a special type of tablespace introduced in Oracle 9*i* to basically store undo information. Undo tablespaces cannot contain other object types like TABLES or INDEXES. When an undo tablespace is implemented, it replaces the rollback segment (RBS) concept used in previous versions of Oracle by providing a read-consistent image of the data to manage undo activity. All characteristics of the RBS options are available under the undo tablespace option also. By allowing Oracle to manage the tablespace, undo tablespaces could be maintained either manually or automatically, like the RBS option. The undo tablespace option is invoked by defining the UNDO_MANAGEMENT parameter in the parameter file to either MANUAL or AUTO. The manual option indicates that the tablespace management will be done manually, and the auto option indicates that Oracle will manage this tablespace automatically without any manual intervention.

The undo tablespace option provides the ability to retain the data in the undo tablespace for a predefined amount of time. This is based on the UNDO_RETENTION parameter defined in the parameter file. Setting this parameter to the right value helps in managing the read-consistent image of data for a specific period of time, thus avoiding the "snapshot too old" error.

Undo tablespaces are created using the locally managed tablespace option.

Bigfile tablespace

Oracle supports the creation of single file tablespaces called BIGFILE tablespaces, which can be up to 8 million terabytes in size. The advantage of using a large tablespace is to reduce the number of tablespaces per database, thus reducing the maintanance on the tablespaces.

The traditional tablespace are now called SMALLFILE tablespace. The specific type of tablespace could be defined:

1.   When the tablespace is created, for example.

```
CREATE BIGFILE TABLESPACE emp_data_p001
  DATAFILE '/u06/ora_data/RAC1/emp_data_001.dbf' SIZE 1T
  EXTENT MANAGEMENT LOCAL
  SEGMENT SPACE MANAGEMENT AUTO;
```

2.   By setting the default tablespace type to either BIGFILE or SMALLFILE when the database is initially created. Once the default tablespace has been defined at the database level, all tablespaces created subsequently are created of this type unless explicitly specified to be of a different type. If no default tablespace type is mentioned the default type is SMALLFILE tablespace.

```
CREATE DATABASE proddb
  SET DEFAULT BIGFILE TABLESPACE
  UNDO TABLESPACE undotbs
  DEFAULT TEMPORARY TABLESPACE temptsl;
```

Due to the large size of these tablespaces, in addition to being able to specify SIZE in kilobytes (K) and megabytes (M) the SIZE can now be specfied in gigabytes (G) or terabytes (T). BIGFILE tablespaces should be created as locally managed with automatic segment space management feature. However, creating BIGFILE temp and undo tablespaces is permitted even though their segments are manually managed.

10g   New Feature: BIGFILE tablespace is a new tablespace type introduced in Oracle 10g to cater to the ultra large databases.

Gigabytes and terabytes size definitions are new in Oracle 10g and have been added to help in defining the ultra large tablespaces.

3.3.2   Data file

A tablespace in an Oracle database consists of one or more physical data files. A data file can be associated with only one tablespace and only one database.

Oracle creates a data file for a tablespace by allocating the specified amount of disk space plus the overhead required for the file header. When a data file is created, the operating system under which Oracle runs is responsible for clearing old information and authorizations from a file before allocating it to Oracle. If the file is large, this process can take a significant amount of time. The first tablespace in any database is always the SYSTEM tablespace, so Oracle automatically allocates the first data files of any database to the SYSTEM tablespace during database creation.

The following is a dump of the data file assigned to tablespace SYSTEM and contains the file header information.

```
DATA FILE #1:
 (name #233) /dev/vx/rdsk/oraracdg/partition1G_3
creation size=0 block size=8192 status=0xe head=233 tail=233 dup=1
tablespace 0, index=1 krfil=1 prev_file=0
unrecoverable scn: 0x0000.00000000 01/01/1988 00:00:00
Checkpoint cnt:139 scn: 0x0000.06ffc050 11/20/2002 20:38:14
Stop scn: 0xffff.ffffffff 11/16/2002 19:01:17
Creation Checkpointed at scn: 0x0000.00000006 08/21/2002 17:04:05
thread:0 rba:(0x0.0.0)
enabled threads: 00000000 00000000 00000000 00000000 00000000 00000000
   00000000 00000000
Offline scn: 0x0000.065acf1d prev_range: 0
Online Checkpointed at scn: 0x0000.065acf1e 10/19/2002 09:43:15
thread:1 rba:(0x1.2.0)
enabled threads: 01000000 00000000 00000000 00000000 00000000 00000000
   00000000 00000000
Hot Backup end marker scn: 0x0000.00000000
aux_file is NOT DEFINED
FILE HEADER:
   Software vsn=153092096=0x9200000, Compatibility
   Vsn=134217728=0x8000000
   Db ID=3598885999=0xd682a46f, Db Name='PRODDB'
   Activation ID=0=0x0
   Control Seq=2182=0x886, File size=115200=0x1c200
   File Number=1, Blksiz=8192, File Type=3 DATA
Tablespace #0 - SYSTEM rel_fn:1
Creation  at  scn: 0x0000.00000006 08/21/2002 17:04:05
Backup taken at scn: 0x0000.00000000 01/01/1988 00:00:00 thread:0
reset logs count:0x1c5a1a33 scn: 0x0000.065acf1e recovered at 11/16/
   2002 19:02:50
status:0x4 root dba:0x004000b3 chkpt cnt: 139 ctl cnt:138
begin-hot-backup file size: 0
Checkpointed at scn: 0x0000.06ffc050 11/20/2002 20:38:14
thread:2 rba:(0x15.31aa6.10)
enabled threads: 01100000 00000000 00000000 00000000 00000000 00000000
   00000000 00000000
Backup Checkpointed at scn: 0x0000.00000000
thread:0 rba:(0x0.0.0)
enabled threads: 00000000 00000000 00000000 00000000 00000000 00000000
   00000000 00000000
External cache id: 0x0 0x0 0x0 0x0
Absolute fuzzy scn: 0x0000.00000000
Recovery fuzzy scn: 0x0000.00000000 01/01/1988 00:00:00
Terminal Recovery Stamp scn: 0x0000.00000000 01/01/1988 00:00:00
```

The header of each data file contains the DB Id field, which is used to verify that this file is associated with the correct database. The file number is the data file number and the file type of value 3 indicates that it is a data file. (Value 6 would indicate a temp file.)

The tablespace number and names indicate that the data file is assigned to tablespace SYSTEM; the rel_fn indicates the relative file number for the data file.

Some of this information can also be obtained by querying the V$DATAFILE_HEADER data dictionary view.

```
SELECT FILE#,STATUS,FORMAT,FUZZY,TABLESPACE_NAME,NAME,
  RFILE# FROM V$DATAFILE_HEADER
/
  FILE# STATUS      FORMAT FUZ TABLESPACE_NAME
----------------------------------------------------------
NAME                                                        RFILE#
----------------------------------------------------------
     1 ONLINE          8 YES SYSTEM
C:\ORACLE\ORADATA\ORA9IDB\SYSTEM01.DBF                           1
     2 ONLINE          8 YES UNDOTBS1
C:\ORACLE\ORADATA\ORA9IDB\UNDOTBS01.DBF                          2
     3 ONLINE          8 YES CWMLITE
C:\ORACLE\ORADATA\ORA9IDB\CWMLITE01.DBF                          3
     4 ONLINE          8 YES DRSYS
C:\ORACLE\ORADATA\ORA9IDB\DRSYS01.DBF                            4
     5 ONLINE          8 YES EXAMPLE
C:\ORACLE\ORADATA\ORA9IDB\EXAMPLE01.DBF                          5
     6 ONLINE          8 YES INDX
C:\ORACLE\ORADATA\ORA9IDB\INDX01.DBF                             6
     7 ONLINE          8 YES ODM
C:\ORACLE\ORADATA\ORA9IDB\ODM01.DBF                              7
     8 ONLINE          8 YES TOOLS
C:\ORACLE\ORADATA\ORA9IDB\TOOLS01.DBF                            8
     9 ONLINE          8 YES USERS
C:\ORACLE\ORADATA\ORA9IDB\USERS01.DBF                            9
    10 ONLINE          8 YES XDB
C:\ORACLE\ORADATA\ORA9IDB\XDB01.DBF                             10

10 rows selected
```

Column FORMAT indicates the compatibility of the data file structure. In this case, although the output is from an Oracle 9i Release 1 database, the FORMAT column continues to show it is in Version 8. In other words the format has not changed between these releases.

Column FUZZY indicates if the file status is in a fuzzy mode or not. This indicates that the file has encountered certain changes since the last checkpoint operation. The fuzzy bit columns in the view and in the data file dump above play an important role during recovery operations.

If the instances were to crash and a copy of the file was saved, the copy would remain in a fuzzy status up to the time of the next crash recovery. A similar marker is also created after crash recovery so that it is possible to know the extent of fuzziness for backups taken after a crash.

The two fuzzy bits used for recovery purposes are:

- *Absolute fuzzy: In* server-managed backups, RMAN in particular calculates the absolute fuzziness of the backup. The absolute fuzzy SCN is the greatest SCN of all the blocks that are changed after the checkpoint. The absolute fuzzy flag is cleared when there is a file checkpoint that advances the SCN beyond the absolute fuzzy SCN.

- *Recovery fuzzy:* This means that the file is in the process of having media recovery applied to it. It is set when media recovery is being applied and is cleared when all the redo logs for that file have been applied.

When a data file is first created, the allocated disk space is formatted but does not contain any user data. However, Oracle reserves the space to hold the data for future segments of the associated tablespace. As the data grows in a tablespace, Oracle uses the free space in the associated data files to allocate extents for the segment.

3.3.3   Segments

A segment is a set of extents allocated for a certain logical database object. All the segments assigned to one object must be in the same tablespace. Extents are allocated to the segments as needed.

There are five types of segments.

Data segment

Every table has a data segment. Data in the tables is stored in the data segment extents. Every table in the database has a data segment in which to store all of its data.

Index segment

Indexes created on the various tables have an index segment that stores data.

Rollback segments

Rollback segments are created for a database for the purpose of temporarily storing undo information. Undo information may be required if the user decides to rollback the transaction and the data has to be restored to the previous state or is required during a recovery operation. Undo information, or the data in these rollback segments, is also required to maintain read consistency.

Information in the rollback segments is stored on a per-transaction basis. Oracle also maintains the order of changes in the rollback segments, which helps Oracle to restore the data to the actual state in case a recovery is required. When a segment is released after use, but is required by another transaction, accessing the rollback data for read consistency could cause an error when the released segment is overwritten with new data. It is advantageous to create many small rollback segments for small transactions and large rollback segments when the transactions or rows retrieved are more in number, for example in a batch processing environment.

Segments comprise one or more extents and an extent comprises one or more data blocks. When a transaction is started, Oracle assigns a rollback segment to the transaction. Other transactions could also use the same rollback segment, and sometimes the same extents. However, only a single transaction could be related to a data block. Oracle uses the extents within a rollback segment in cyclical manner.

Figure 3.8 explains the structure of creation and usage of extents within a rollback segment. A rollback segment has certain initial extents, which are created based on the definition parameters. When a transaction is started, it is assigned to a specific extent within a segment. Many other

Figure 3.8
Structure of creation and usage of extents.

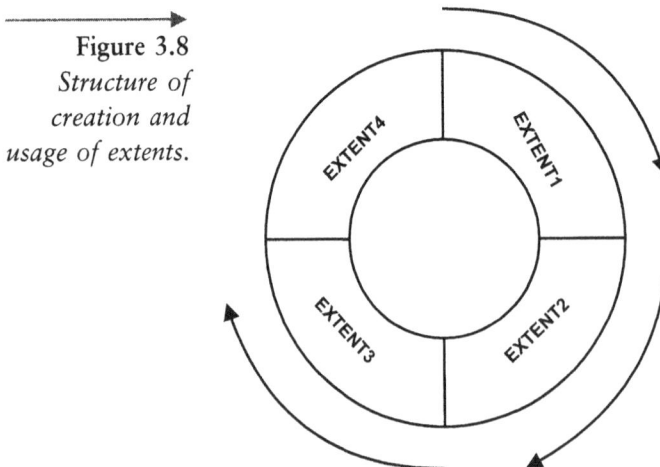

transactions may also be using the same extent. Extents are assigned in a cyclical manner and are deallocated in the reverse order of their creation.

During the process of using the allocated extents, and when Oracle determines the assigned extent was not sufficient, Oracle approaches the next extent for the purpose of writing to it. However, if the specific extent has an active transaction, the next extent is approached. Finally, if all the available extents could not be used, Oracle allocates a new extent. Extents are assigned in a cyclical manner. Similarly, when an extent or segment is not used for a certain amount of time, the extents are deallocated in the reverse order in which they were created, or assigned, to the rollback segment. These deallocated extents are available for future allocation when needed.

Very careful attention should be placed on the creation of rollback segments to ensure that the creation of them is to the right size, which is plentiful enough based on the environment (OLTP, batch, etc.). Not giving proper attention to the size of the rollback segments, based on the data size, could cause a "ORA-22924 snapshot too old" error.

Undo segment

Very much like the traditional rollback segments, in Oracle 9*i* a method of managing undo space has been introduced, called undo segments. With the automatic undo management feature, the undo segment management is also dynamic in nature. Unlike the rollback segments, which are created and managed by the DBAs, the undo segments are created and managed by Oracle. These undo segments house the transactions tables and undo blocks.

More details about the undo management, undo segments, etc., will be covered in Chapter 4 (Real Application Cluster Architecture).

9i   New Feature: In Oracle 9*i*, a new feature is introduced called undo tablespace. With this feature the user has the choice of either using the RBS option or configuring the system to use the undo tablespace. More details on the undo tablespace option can be found in Section 3.3.1.

Temporary segment

A temporary segment is created when a process requires additional temporary space or work area, to complete execution or for large data sorts that cannot be performed in memory. These temporary segment extents are released when the process completes execution. Due to the nature of the segment there is frequent allocation and reallocation of extents based on the need.

3.3.4   Extent management

Dictionary managed

In Oracle, when the initial allocation of blocks has reached its threshold value, Oracle allocates blocks, called extents, to write data. The extent is a specific number of contiguous data blocks during a single allocation.

When a table is created it allocates an initial extent of a specific number of data blocks. This is performed with the intention that, when actual data is written to disk, the table has already allocated and created space to accept the data. When data is written and the initial extent is full, Oracle allocates further extents either equal to the size of the initial extent or greater than the initial extent as specified during table definition. For allocation of extents, Oracle searches the tablespace for a free contiguous set of data blocks equal to or greater than the initial extent. When this is found, it creates the extent.

Oracle finds free space to make an extent based on the following algorithm:

- It finds the first set of contiguous blocks that matches the exact size of the required extent plus one extra block from the free space, or from the space that was released when rows were deleted from the table. If it finds a set of contiguous blocks, it allocates them as extents.

- If it does not find the contiguous block that is the exact size by searching the reusable space, it looks for a set of contiguous blocks greater than the required extent.

- If Oracle is unable to find a contiguous space greater than the required size, it frees up space by coalescing any adjacent free space from the reusable free space.

- If no free space is available for coalescing, then Oracle has no choice but to resize the tablespace by using the autoextension method.

Oracle has to take numerous steps before adding extents to the tablespace. This search for space to create or add an extent is a routine operation when required but adds cost to performance. For this reason, it is very important to size the extents carefully.

Locally managed

Under the locally managed tablespace option, Oracle creates extents based on an internal algorithm. Extents are created using the following method: the first 16 extents are created, in 64 KB size each. Subsequently, when Oracle needs to create additional extents it changes the algorithm and allocates the next 63 extents of 1 MB size each; the next round again there is variation in the number and size of extents, namely 120 extents of 8 MB size each. After this stage extents are created in equal sizes of 64 MB with no variations until the maximum size of the tablespace/file is reached.

3.3.5 Data block

Oracle manages data storage in the data files as units called data blocks. Data blocks are the smallest unit of I/O used by the database. The data block corresponds to a specific number of bytes of physical database space in a data file. The size of a data block is specified at the time of database or tablespace creation. The data block represented by the DB_BLOCK_SIZE defined during database creation is a multiple of the operating system or disk block sizes.

Figure 3.9 is a dissection of an Oracle data block. A data block comprises the block header and the data layer.

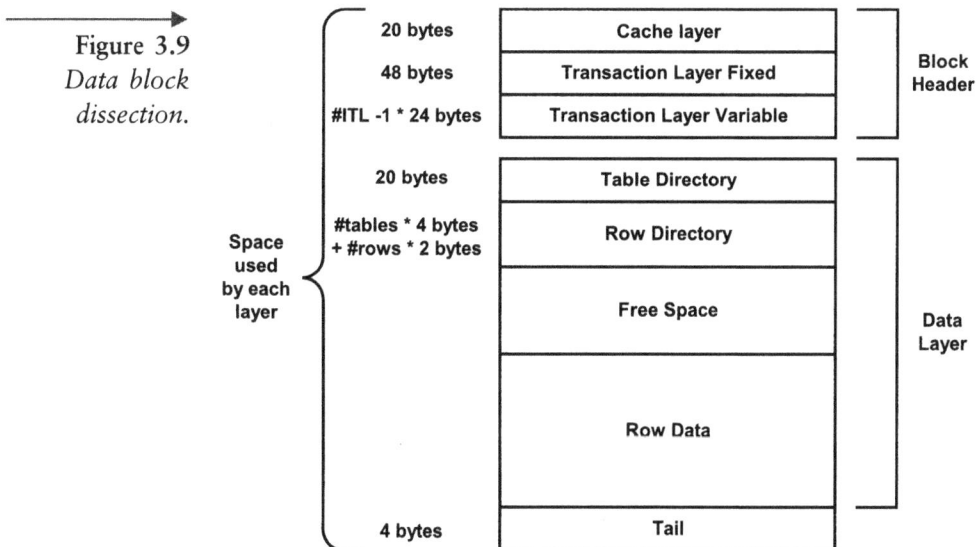

Figure 3.9
Data block dissection.

Block header

The block header comprises the cache layer and the transaction layer.

Cache layer

This is the first layer of the block header and contains structures such as:

- The data block address (DBA)
- The block type
- The block format
- A system change number (SCN)

The cache layer is 20 bytes in size. The block types indicate if the object is a table, index, undo segment, temporary segment, etc. The block format indicates the version format, for example, v8, v9, etc. The SCN number on the cache layer is used for ordering purposes, especially during a recovery operation, to apply records in the order in which they were created.

Transaction layer

This layer has two parts:

- A fixed component contains the transactional block header and one descriptor interested transaction list (ITL). This area contains information about the block/object type, the time of the last block cleanout and the number of ITL entries in the variable portion of the transaction layer, a free list link, and a free space lock.

- The variable portion contains the ITLs necessary for a process to modify rows within the block. By default, Oracle maintains one ITL for a data block containing a table and two ITLs for a data block that contains the index. The default number of ITLs created is influenced by the INITRANS parameter used during table or index creation. The variable portion of the transaction layer will adjust dynamically, expanding as required based on the definitions, provided there is sufficient space available for this purpose. Similarly, the MAXTRANS parameter limits the number of ITLs that can be concurrently allocated and used in the block. If the number of ITLs is not sufficient, then additional entries are allocated dynamically from the free space, provided MAXTRANS is not reached.

Dynamic parameter changes, such as changes to the INITRANS and MAXTRANS values, will not take effect until the next or during subsequent block creations.

Note: Setting the values of INITRANS and MAXTRANS to really high values causes a considerable space allocation in the transaction layer and hence the space in the data layer is reduced. Reduced data area means that more I/O will be required to read the required data set.

When a process wishes to update one or more rows in a data block, it must be allocated an ITL entry. Each row in the data block contains a one-byte field called the lock byte within its row header. This lock byte indicates which ITL entry is or was interested in updating this row. The ITL entry includes a TXID (transaction ID) and an undo block address (UBA) of the last undo record created to update the block for this current transaction.

The UBA consists of a data block address, sequence number/ incarnation number of the undo block, and a record number within the undo block. This is used to directly access the undo records. Other information is also stored in each ITL entry, including transaction status flags, number of rows locked (Lck), and a commit SCN or free space credit (depending on DML type and commit status).

Data layer

The data layer comprises the table directory and row directory, and free space for new data, row data, and a tail.

Table directory

The table directory indicates where the row directory starts. Its usefulness is more obvious in a cluster where more than one table shares the same data blocks. In order to retrieve the rows belonging to one of the tables in the cluster, it is necessary to know exactly where the rows start and finish.

Row directory

Similar in concept to the table directory, the row directory has a similar application. When a data block is accessed using a ROWID, for example, the Oracle server does not need to scan the entire block. Using the slot number contained in the ROWIDs, the Oracle server can read the appropriate offset in the row directory and proceed to read the exact row. Row offsets do not have any specific method of storage; it could be stored anywhere in the data layer. This implies that rows are stored randomly within the data block.

Free space

The free space is used for insertion of new rows into the table. When Oracle is unable to find space from the released blocks it uses space from the free space to insert rows. (The algorithm used by Oracle to obtain this free space is explained in Section 3.3.4.) The free space is based on certain parameter values specified at the table creation time.

Row data

The data area contains the actual rows of data or indexes. Oracle stores data in this area. When the data area is full, Oracle requests space from the free space area. When a user inserts data, through a DML operation either directly or through an application program, the data is inserted into the data blocks via the data files and the tablespace. The data can subsequently be found in the data area. When data is retrieved by a query also, Oracle retrieves the values from this area.

The various areas and sizes allocated for the various layers of the data block could be obtained by querying the V$TYPE_SIZE view:

```
SELECT
     COMPONENT,
     TYPE,
     DESCRIPTION,
     TYPE_SIZE
FROM V$TYPE_SIZE
WHERE COMPONENT LIKE 'K%'
/
```

COMPONENT	TYPE	DESCRIPTION	TYPE_SIZE
K	KDBA	DATABASE BLOCK ADDRESS	4
K	KTNO	TABLE NUMBER IN CLUSTER	1
K	KSCN	SYSTEM COMMIT NUMBER	8
K	KXID	TRANSACTION ID	8
K	KUBA	UNDO ADDRESS	8
KCB	KCBH	BLOCK COMMON HEADER	20
KTB	KTBIT	TRANSACTION VARIABLE HEADER	24
KTB	KTBBH	TRANSACTION FIXED HEADER	48
KDB	KDBH	DATA HEADER	14
KDB	KDBT	TABLE DIRECTORY ENTRY	4
KTE	KTECT	EXTENT CONTROL	44
KTE	KTECH	EXTENT CONTROL	72
KTE	KTETB	EXTENT TABLE	8
KTS	KTSHC	SEGMENT HEADER	8
KTS	KTSFS	SEGMENT FREE SPACE LIST	20
KTU	KTUBH	UNDO HEADER	16
KTU	KTUXE	UNDO TRANSACTION ENTRY	40
KTU	KTUXC	UNDO TRANSACTION CONTROL	104
KDX	KDXCO	INDEX HEADER	16

```
KDX              KDXLE         INDEX LEAF HEADER           32
KDX              KDXBR         INDEX BRANCH HEADER         24
21 rows selected.
```

The above query provides the description of the various layers of the various database components. Of the types listed above, the components of type KCB and KTB are related to the data block.

9i

New Feature: The standard block size is specified by the initialization parameter, DB_BLOCK_SIZE. In addition, up to five non-standard block sizes may be specified. The data block sizes should be a multiple of the operating system's block size, within the maximum limit, to avoid unnecessary I/O. Oracle data blocks are the smallest units of storage that Oracle can use or allocate.

3.4   Optimizer

Oracle optimizer is a critical piece of the architecture and is an important concept that should be understood before going forward. Oracle has two types of optimizer engines, the rule-based optimizer (RBO) and the cost-based optimizer (CBO). From the beginning the RBO has been in use through all versions of Oracle. Under this method Oracle determined the execution path for queries based on a set of predefined rules. That is, if a specific rule was met the execution path was determined based on the set rule.

In Version 7.0, Oracle introduced the CBO. Under this option, the method used to determine the execution path was based on the actual cost of executing the query. To determine the cost, Oracle tried various methods of executing the query on certain statistics that were provided, hence CBO took a mathematical approach to generate the execution plan. Instead of any predefined rules, Oracle uses a certain set of formulas to calculate the cost of an SQL statement. The CBO generates various permutation combinations of execution plans and selects the execution path that has the lowest cost.

Note: Starting with Version 8.0, Oracle has stopped enhancements to the RBO; the RBO remains a feature in the recent versions of Oracle only as a means to encourage users to migrate to the CBO.

Since a mathematical approach is based on data, if sufficient or correct data is not provided, the optimizer does not compute the correct expected result set and hence generates an execution path that is not efficient enough. This happens when no statistics have been gathered or the characteristics of the objects have changed significantly. Statistics are collected using certain built-in packages such as ANALYZE and DBMS_STATS. While ANALYZE was the earlier method to compute statistics, the DBMS_STATS package is a more recent package and provides even better statistics, making the CBO even more efficient.

On large systems, computation of statistics every time with the change in the characteristics of the objects became an expensive process. In order to make this less expensive, in Version 9*i* Oracle introduced the MONITORING option, where statistics were collected in smaller increments and the data was merged to the main collection at user defined intervals.

9i   **New Feature:** In Version 9*i* Oracle has introduced a MONITORING clause for the CREATE OR ALTER TABLE statement that tracks the approximate INSERT, UPDATE or DELETE operations against the table since the last time statistics were gathered.

10g   **Depreciated Feature:** Starting with Oracle 10*g* RBO is deprecated. The only optimizer supported would be the CBO. Along with the deprecation of RBO, the 'RULE' and 'CHOOSE' options used with the OPTIMIZER_MODE parameter has also been deprecated. The only supported options are FIRST_ROWS, FIRST_ROWS_n and ALL_ROWS.

The following is an example to compute statistics using the DBMS_STATS package:

```
DBMS_STATS.GATHER_SCHEMA_STATS(OWNNAME=>MVALLATH,
  granularity=>ALL, cascade=> TRUE);
```

The above package will compute statistics for schema owner MVALLATH with a granularity level of ALL and cascade option to TRUE.

3.5   Dynamic components

It is now possible to dynamically reconfigure the sizes of the shared pool, buffer cache, Java pool, and the large pool. During the dynamic reconfiguration of the size of the SGA, memory is allocated in units called granules. Basically, granules are a unit of allocation used during dynamic reconfiguration of the SGA.

A granule can be 4 MB or 16 MB, depending on the total size of the SGA determined during instance startup. If the size of the SGA is less than 12 MB, the granules are allocated in 4 MB sizes; otherwise they are allocated in 16 MB chunks. The values for the various memory areas are allocated as a multiple of a granule size. If, on instance startup, Oracle determines that the size mentioned is not a multiple of the granule size, Oracle will round the value to the nearest multiple. For example, if the granule size is 16 MB and the DB_CACHE_SIZE allocated is 46 MB, then, Oracle will change the value to 48 MB during instance startup.

Oracle keeps information about the components and their granules in a scoreboard. For each component that owns granules, the scoreboard contains the number of granules allocated to the component, any pending operations against this component, the target size in granules, and the progress made toward the target size. The start time of the operation is also logged. Oracle maintains the initial number of granules and the maximum number of granules for each component.

For operations that modify the number of granules, Oracle logs the operation, the target size, and the start time to the appropriate SGA component in the scoreboard. Oracle updates the progress field until the operation is complete at which time Oracle replaces the current size with the target size and clears the target size field and the progress field. At the end of the operation, a database administrator can see how the number of granules was changed. Oracle updates the initialization parameter values to reflect the updated amount of SGA in use.

Oracle maintains a circular buffer of the last 100 operations made to the scoreboard. Fixed views show the state of the scoreboard and the current contents of the last 100 operations to the scoreboard.

A database administrator grows a component's SGA use with ALTER SYSTEM statements to modify the initialization parameter values. Oracle takes the new size, rounds it up to the nearest multiple of 16 MB and adds or takes away granules to meet the target size. Oracle must have enough free granules to satisfy the request. If the current amount of SGA memory is less than SGA_MAX_SIZE, Oracle can allocate more granules until the SGA size reaches SGA_MAX_SIZE.

3.5.1   **Oracle database configuration**

As discussed above, Oracle RDBMS configuration consists of foreground and background processes that aid in accepting the user process to move

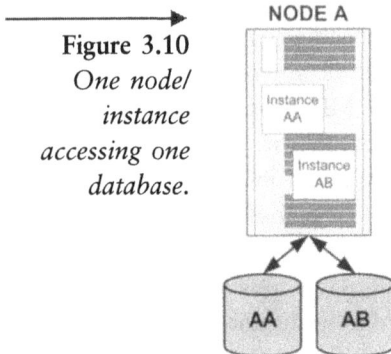

Figure 3.10
*One node/
instance
accessing one
database.*

data from various areas of Oracle's memory into the physical database. A basic configuration of Oracle RDBMS consists of a single instance (also called stand-alone instance) with a single copy of the database. In the sections above we have looked at the various background (Figure 3.6) and foreground processes that constitute the single instance configuration.

In a configuration of this type, where there is only one database and a corresponding instance to support, the instance and the database are identified by the same name. Users accessing the system will make a connection to an instance and, with the help of the background and foreground processes, retrieve and manipulate data in the database.

A single node or system could contain more than one instance; in fact, there are no limits to the number of instances that a single node could hold. It is more of a practical performance limitation to have many instances of Oracle on a single node rather than a physical limitation. Figure 3.10 illustrates how multiple instances can be housed in a single node (node A) and attached to two separate physical databases.

3.5.2   Oracle clustered configuration

Oracle's clustered, or multi-instance, configurations comprise multiple nodes working as a cohesive unit with each node in the cluster consisting of one or more instances talking to a common shared database.

RAC is a configuration where two or more instances are connected to one single shared physical database and users access the database from any of the available instances to retrieve and process data. Unlike the data guard and advanced replication features, the RAC provides availability with data consistency. Because there is no data being transferred between

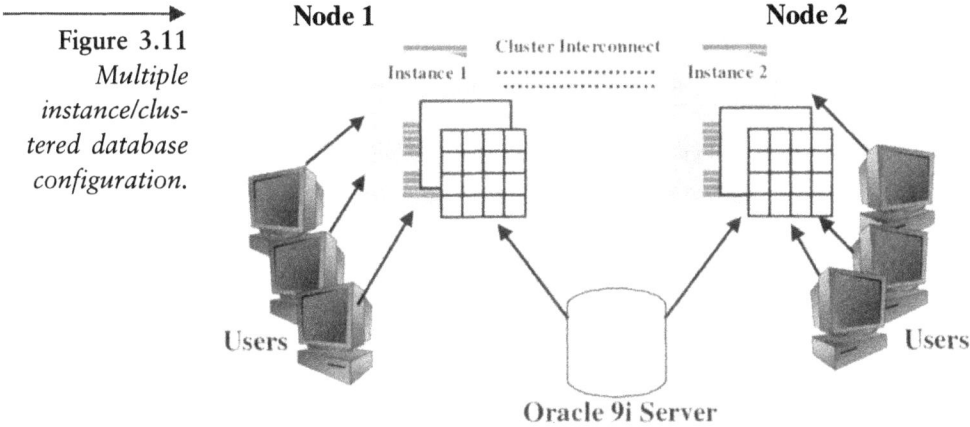

Figure 3.11
*Multiple
instance/clus-
tered database
configuration.*

databases, there is only one physical copy of the database, and only one database is shared by multiple instances.

Oracle's clustered, or multi-instance, configuration is an extension to the single, stand-alone instance configuration. Under this configuration, each instance has its own set of background and foreground processes. These background and foreground processes on each instance talk to one common shared database. Under the multi-instance configuration, the instance and the database do not have the same name or are not identified by the same name. Because there are multiple instances, each instance needs to be uniquely identified. The database that is common has its own identity.

Figure 3.11 illustrates a clustered database configuration, where two nodes, Node 1 and Node 2, containing instance 1 and instance 2 respectively, connect to a common shared Oracle 9*i* database. Users are connected to both instances and can perform database operations.

Having a single, common, shared physical database means that all instances sharing the common database access the same set of data files and control files. This also implies that multiple instances could be requesting the same information.

However, because there are multiple instances accessing the shared database, the instance-specific information, such as the rollback information, redo logs, and archive logs, are maintained uniquely for a specific instance. However, because these files are stored on a shared disk array, they are visible to the other instances. Visibility to these files is critical, especially when a system or instance fails. By having these files on a common shared device, the instance that noticed the failure first would read these files for recovery of failed instance.

9i

New Feature: With the introduction of new data transfer architecture called cache fusion, Oracle has renamed OPS to RAC.

In the next section some of the changes between the two versions of the clustered database will be examined.

Table 3.2 provides the difference between a single instance stand-alone configuration and a clustered database configuration.

Table 3.2   *Single Instance vs. Clustered Configuration*

Single Instance	Real Application Cluster
One instance maps to a single database	Two or more instances share a common physical database
Can run on a single processor hardware configuration or a multi-processor configuration. However, requires only a single node or machine for implementation	Can also run on a single processor hardware configuration or a multi-processor configuration. However, requires hardware clustering and a clustered operating system
Consists of one system global area (SGA) and a set of background and foreground processes	Every instance requires its own SGA (to store instance-specific information), and background and foreground processes. It also consists of additional background processes like LMS and GCS
One copy of the physical database and redo log files	Separate copies of redo logs and archive logs are maintained for every instance
With just one instance attached to one copy of the physical database, no instance level synchronization is required	Multinode synchronization is required. Synchronization between instances is performed using the cache fusion technology via the cluster interconnect
V$ views to monitor and manage instance	V$ views are available and provide visibility to a single instance. For monitoring at the cluster level, Oracle provides GV$ views
Meeting some of the business require-ments (availability, scalability) is limited to a single instance configuration	Modern business requirements of high availability and linear scalability are provided by multiple instances sharing a common physical database

3.6   Changes between OPS and RAC

Administrators who are familiar with OPS technology will know that RAC is the successor to this technology. After the release of OPS with Version 6.2, Oracle evolved this product over the years, and has, during the evolution process, encountered certain performance issues. As with every version of Oracle RDBMS, enhancements to OPS have been under way. With the purchase of Oracle Rdb from Digital Equipment Corporation in 1993, Oracle RDBMS has seen several changes to its core functionality and performance improvements. Most of the enhancements have existed in Oracle Rdb, in some form or another, for quite some time.

Oracle Rdb, primarily functional on Open VMS platforms (pioneers in the clustering technology), has worked in a clustered configuration since its inception into the market. For quite some time Oracle only worked as a single instance configuration. However, with Version 6.2, Oracle has introduced the clustered concept into this product line with OPS.

One of the main performance and scalability concerns in OPS has been around data sharing between multiple instances, as this typically caused pinging activity. *Pinging is forced writing of information in the memory of one instance onto disk, so that this information is available to the other instances requesting access to this information.* An example of pinging is as follows. Instance 1 places a request to read a row from employee table with employee ID = 45987. While reading this row from the disk, Oracle, in its ultimate wisdom to share and expecting the request for the next (thinking ahead), reads the entire block. Reading the entire block also reads in certain additional rows. Depending on the block size and the data being retrieved, typically the previous rows and the subsequent rows are retrieved, for example, rows with employee IDs 45988, 45989, and 45986. Assume another user has connected to another instance, Instance 2, which is part of the clustered configuration, and has requested access to the row for employee ID 45987. While attempting to read the row from disk, Oracle realizes that the row is in a block that has already been acquired by Instance 1. In order to gain access to the row of data, Oracle requests the Instance 1 to write the block back to disk so that Instance 2 can get access to the row in the same block. This writing to disk to allow the Instance 2 to read the row is called *pinging*. This write activity to disk to allow Instance 2 to read the row incurs an I/O operation. This in turn causes performance problems. Pinging activity between instances is a tuning nightmare for database administrators.

While Oracle Rdb also functioned in a clustered configuration and had a similar functionality, it did not cause performance issues during a similar operation. This is because data did not get written to disk in order for the other node to gain access to it but instead was transferred across the cluster interconnect to the other node. In Version 8.1, Oracle had introduced this concept, called *cache fusion*. While cache fusion was only available for read/read operations, with Oracle 9.0 it has been enhanced to provide support for operations of all types (read/read, read/write, and write/write).

The concept of transferring data between cache of one instance to cache of another instance is called *cache fusion*. Cache fusion guarantees cache coherency among multiple cluster nodes without incurring disk I/O costs.

With the new concept of sharing information across the cluster interconnect and other various enhancements to other areas of the system, the product was renamed RAC, potentially to create a new paradigm shift and to remove all the performance concerns surrounding OPS.

Table 3.3 provides a comparison chart between OPS and RAC.

Table 3.3   *OPS vs. RAC*

Oracle Parallel Server	Real Application Clusters
Called Oracle Parallel Server (OPS) in Version 8i and prior versions	Called Real Application Clusters (RAC) in Version 9i
Synchronization of instances only by pinging	Synchronization between instances is using the cache fusion technology via the cluster interconnect
Uses the PCM locking technology	Does not use the PCM locking technology. This has been rewritten in RAC
OPSCTL	SRVCTL
OPS daemon	Global services daemon (GSD)
OPS management	Server management (SRVM)
Parallel cache management	GCS block requests
Lock mastering	Resource mastering
Lock database	Resource database
Block server process (BSPn)	Global cache server process (LMSn)

3.6.1   **Terminology changes**

This section provides a brief introduction to changes in terminology between OPS and RAC. A more detailed discussion about the functionalities will be found in the appropriate sections in the book.

Oracle Parallel Fail Safe (OPFS) is replaced with Oracle Real Application Cluster Guard.

This feature is now integrated with Microsoft's Cluster Server (MSCS) and makes use of Internet protocol (IP) failover and Microsoft's cluster management utilities.

The term distributed lock manager (DLM), is obsolete. The background processes that were formerly aggregated under the DLM in previous cluster software products still exist, but the DLM no longer manages resources under RAC. The two new processes, global cache service (GCS) and global enqueue service (GES), handle the management functions that had been handled by the DLM in OPS.

The OPSCTL utility has been replaced with SRVCTL utility. SRVCTL manages configuration information that is used by several Oracle tools. For example, Oracle Enterprise Manager (OEM) and the Oracle Intelligent Agent use the configuration information that SRVCTL generates to discover and monitor nodes participating in the cluster.

The global service daemon (GSD) has replaced the Oracle Parallel Server communications daemon (OPSD). OPSD under OPS is a process that received requests from the OPSCTL utility to execute administrative job tasks, such as startup and shutdown. Under a RAC the GSD also performs exactly the same function; however, and instead of the OPSCTL utility, it receives requests from the SRVCTL utility. The only difference is that the OPSD service that was not available under Windows for OPS, GSD, is available under windows.

Server Management (SRVM) has replaced Oracle Parallel Server Management (OPSM). OPSM under OPS was used for management of OPS instances, including startup, shutdown, etc. Under RAC, the SRVM process does the same functionality, however, and also provides support to OEM by providing functions such as scheduling jobs, event management, monitoring performance, and the obtaining of statistics of the clustered database. SRVM is part of OEM.

The term parallel cache management (PCM) is obsolete. These operations have been replaced by GCS block requests. PCM locks under

OPS are distributed locks that cover one or more blocks in the buffer cache. With the GCS functionality being introduced the PCM locks are now obsolete with RAC implementation.

The term non-PCM is obsolete. The GES implements the resource management functions.

Lock mastering is obsolete. The equivalent function in RAC is resource mastering.

The lock database under OPS is obsolete. The global resource directory (GRD) handles the equivalent functions in a RAC configuration. Under the OPS implementation, Oracle maintained a lock database to manage cluster-interdependent locks on blocks being accessed by multiple nodes. With the RAC implementation, the lock database concept is obsolete; however, it is replaced with a new functionality called GRD. As in the lock database concept, GRD is maintained on one instance. Each instance portion of the GRD contains the information about the current statuses of all shared resources. Information contained in GRD is used by Oracle during instance failure recovery and during cluster reconfiguration.

3.6.2 Parameter changes

The OPS_INTERCONNECTS parameter is replaced by CLUSTER_INTERCONNECTS.

OPS_INTERCONNECTS, which is an optional undocumented parameter under OPS, provides information about additional cluster interconnects for use in OPS environments. Oracle uses the information from this parameter to distribute traffic among the various interfaces. However, CLUSTER_INTERCONNECTS, another optional, but documented, parameter under RAC, does exactly what OPS_INTERCONNECTS did under OPS.

The PARALLEL_SERVER parameter is replaced by CLUSTER_DATABASE.

PARALLEL_SERVER under OPS, which informs Oracle if the clustered database solution has been enabled, is replaced with the CLUSTER_DATABASE parameter under RAC.

The PARALLEL_SERVER_INSTANCES parameter is replaced by CLUSTER_DATABASE_INSTANCE.

PARALLEL_SERVER_INSTANCES under OPS, which informs Oracle regarding the number of instances that have been enabled, is replaced with CLUSTER_DATABASE_INSTANCE under RAC.

3.6.3 **Data dictionary changes**

In this section only the basic differences between OPS and RAC have been highlighted, a detailed discussion on the various data dictionary views is forthcoming in Chapter 9 (Parameters and Views).

- GV$DLM_MISC is replaced by GV$GES_STATISTICS

- GV$DLM_LATCH is replaced by GV$GES_LATCH

- GV$DLM_CONVERT is replaced by GV$GES_CONVERT_LOCAL

- GV$DLM_CONVERT_REMOTE is replaced by GV$GES_CONVERT_REMOTE

- GV$DML_ALL_LOCKS is replaced by GV$GES_ENQUEUE

- GV$DLM_LOCKS is replaced by GV$GES_BLOCKING_ENQUEUE

- GV$DLM_RESS is replaced by GV$GES_RESOURCE

- GV$DLM_TRAFFIC_CONTROLLER is replaced by GV$GES_TRAFFIC_CONTROLLER

- GV$DLM_LOCK_ELEMENT is replaced by GV$GC_ELEMENT

- GV$BSP is replaced by GV$CR_BLOCK_SERVER

- GV$LOCKS_WITH_COLLISIONS is replaced by GV$GC_ELEMENT_WITH_COLLISIONS

- GV$FILE_PING is replaced by GV$FILE_CACHE_TRANSFER

- GV$TEMP_PING is replaced by GV$TEMP_CACHE_TRANSFER

- GV$CLASS_PING is replaced by GV$CLASS_CACHE_TRANSFER

- GV$PING is replaced by GV$CACHE_TRANSFER

The following new data dictionary views have been added under the RAC implementation:

- V$HVMASTER_INFO: This view describes the current and previous master instances and the number of times remastering of the GES resources has occurred.

- V$GCSHVMASTER_INFO: This view describes the current and previous master instances and the number of times remastering of the GCS resources has occurred, excluding those belonging to files mapped to a particular master.

- V$GCSPFMASTER_INFO: This view describes the current and previous master instances and the number of times remastering of GCS resources that belong to files mapped to instances has occurred.

3.7   Conclusion

In this chapter the basic concepts in Oracle database architecture, the different components, and various types of files and tablespaces used in a single stand-alone configuration of an Oracle database were explored. Because RAC configuration is only an extension to the single stand-alone configuration, many of the features and functions are similar in a RAC configuration. The handling of queries was also briefly discussed during the discussions on database buffer cache. Some new features such as undo tablespace, multiple db block size options, the concept of granules and how they are used in computing the buffer cache requirements were also introduced.

We compared a single instance configuration with a clustered configuration and listed the differences between OPS and RAC.

This concludes the first part of the book. The next part will explore the architecture of RAC. During this process the transaction management, parallel processing concepts, designing databases for RAC, and data dictionary views useful in RAC will be discussed.

Part II

Architecture

Real Application Cluster Architecture

4.1   Introduction

In the previous chapter the basic database concepts of Oracle RDBMS were explored, including areas such as the instance, database, background, and foreground processes for a single instance configuration, as well as the various components of Oracle.

After the initial introduction of a single instance configuration, a RAC configuration was briefly discussed and was compared with some of the changes from its predecessor, OPS.

This chapter covers the architecture of the system, new background processes used by RAC, and new enhancements brought into RAC, such as cache fusion technology for communicating across the interconnect, cache fusion recovery, global services, and clustered database solutions. After discussing information supporting the configuration during its uptime, scenarios covering instance failures will be presented through details of how failover happens, how the resources are handled and how recovery operation is handled in this clustered database environment. For the readers familiar with OPS and/or RAC, this chapter will provide a review of the basic concepts and components surrounding RAC.

4.2   RAC architecture

In Chapter 2 (Hardware Concepts) the clustering options available via the various technologies (SMP, MPP, NUMA, etc.) were discussed extensively. All of these hardware architectures support applications that take advantage of these clustered solutions. One such database application is RAC.

RAC is a clustered database solution that requires a two or more node hardware configuration capable of working together under a clustered operating system. A clustered hardware solution is managed by cluster management software, usually provided by the hardware vendor. The operating system is also responsible for providing access to the shared disk subsystems.

RAC supports all standard Oracle 9i features such as fast commits, group commits and deferred writes. It supports the standard row level locking across instances. Under this new technology, blocks can be shared by multiple transactions, accessing the data from any of the instances participating in the clustered configuration.

Apart from the support for the standard features of a single instance of Oracle, RAC provides additional performance from multiple instances by enabling the following features:

- *Cache fusion:* Cache fusion is a cache coherency mechanism to transfer requests for specific blocks via the cluster interconnect, thus improving performance.

- *Sequence generators:* RAC provides a clustered database solution with the database shared between two or more instances. All objects, including sequence numbers in the shared database, are accessible from one or more instances simultaneously.

- *System change number (SCN):* The system change number generated on one instance is communicated via the cluster interconnect to the other instances providing a single view of the transaction status across all instances. This communication of SCN across the interconnect takes place without any additional overhead, by piggy backing against any message that is passed across the cluster interconnect. An SCN is at least 48 bits long. Thus they can be allocated at a rate of 16,384 SCNs per second for over 534 years without running out of them.

- *Failover:* A clustered configuration consists of two or more nodes participating as a collective configuration. In a clustered database, this type of configuration provides application failover by allowing reconnection to the database using another active instance in case the connection to the original instance is broken.

- *Scalability:* By allowing members in a cluster to leave (in case of node failures, or for maintenance) or join the cluster (in case new nodes are added to the cluster), RAC provides scalability. Scalability helps to add additional configurations based on increased user requirements.

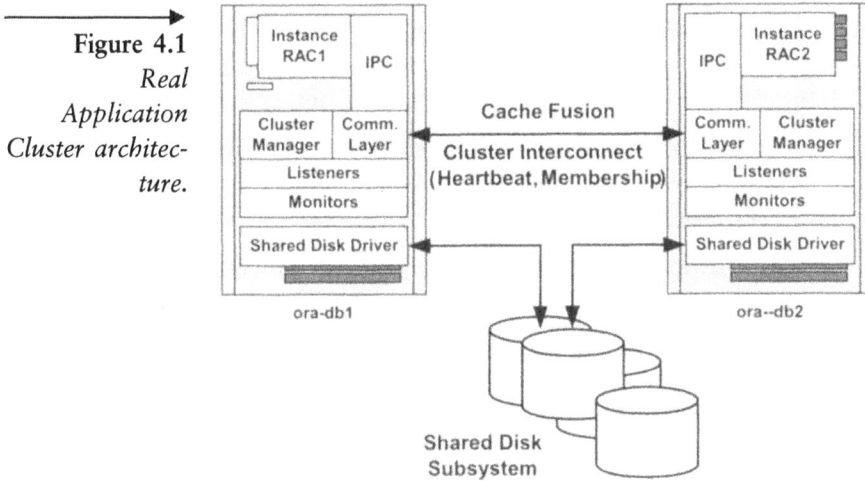

Figure 4.1
Real Application Cluster architecture.

Figure 4.1 illustrates the various components of the clustered hardware configuration. It is composed of:

- Cluster manager (CM)
- Shared disk driver (disk group manager)
- Communication layer
- Interprocess communication protocol (IPC)
- Listeners
- Monitors

Cluster manager (CM) is part of the clustered operating system that is responsible for providing cluster integrity. A high-speed interconnect is used to provide communication between nodes in the cluster. The CM uses the interconnect to process heartbeat messages between nodes. The function of the heartbeat messaging system is to determine which nodes are logical members of the cluster and to update the membership information on the nodes. Basically, the heartbeat messaging system enables the CM to understand how many members are in the cluster at any given point of time.

The communication layer manages the communication between the nodes. Its responsibility is to configure and pass messages across interconnect, to the other nodes in the cluster. While the CM uses the messages returned by the heartbeat mechanism, it is the responsibility of the communication layer to ensure the transmission of the message to the CM.

Interprocess communication protocol (IPC) in a clustered configuration is responsible for packaging the Oracle messages and passing them to and from the communication layer for the interconnect access.

Various monitor processes consistently verify different areas of the system. The heartbeat monitor continually verifies the functioning of the heartbeat mechanism.

The listener monitor verifies the listener process and the instance monitor verifies the functioning of the instance.

The majority of the messages passed via the interconnect are related to GCS which comprises the global enqueues, data blocks, and lock granularity information. GCS uses the cache fusion architecture to communicate between the various caches (cache to cache) of the members in the cluster.

4.3   Clustering Linux systems

Unlike other operating systems, clustering of the Linux systems is done through Oracle Cluster Management Software (OCMS). OCMS consists of two components: the watchdog daemon and the CM.

- The watchdog daemon monitors the CM and passes notifications to the watchdog timer at defined intervals.

- The CM maintains the status of the nodes and the Oracle instances across the cluster. The CM process runs on each node of the RAC. Each node has one CM.

4.4   Background processes in RAC

In the previous chapter, a single instance configuration of Oracle was explored and the various background processes that Oracle utilizes to perform different functions was also discussed. RAC is an extension of a single instance configuration in the sense that a RAC implementation comprises two or more nodes (instances) accessing a common shared database, (i.e., one database is mounted and opened by multiple instances concurrently). In this case, each instance in this configuration will have all the background process used in a stand-alone configuration.

Each instance has its own SGA and several background processes and each instance runs on a separate node having its own CPU and physical memory. Keeping the configurations in all the nodes identical would be beneficial for load balancing when a failover happens and the processes have an identical environment in which to execute.

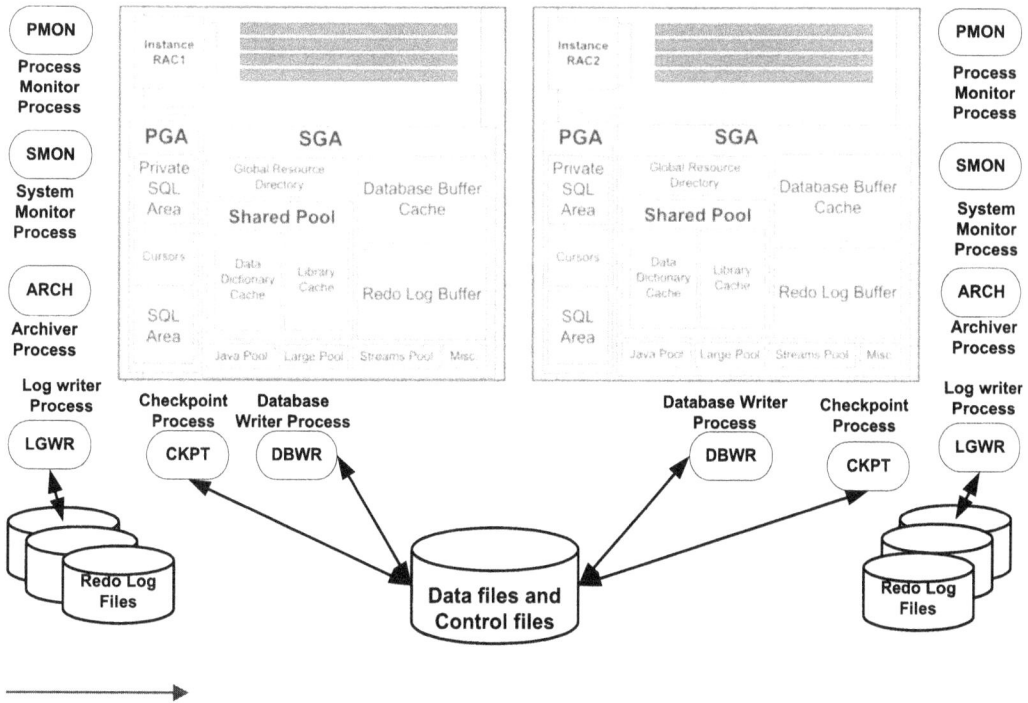

Figure 4.2   *Background processes on multiple instances.*

Figure 4.2 shows multiple instances of Oracle accessing a common shared database. Each instance has its own SGA, PGA, and other background processes. These background processes should be familiar, as, in a RAC configuration, each instance will have a set of these background processes.

The following characteristics are unique to a RAC implementation as opposed to a single instance configuration:

- RAC is a configuration with multiple instances of Oracle running on many nodes.

- Multiple instances of Oracle share a single physical database.

- Multiple instances reside on different nodes and communicate with each other via a cluster interconnect.

- Instances may come and leave the cluster dynamically, provided the number is within the MAX_INSTANCES value defined in the parameter file.

- Instances share a common database that comprises common data files and control files.

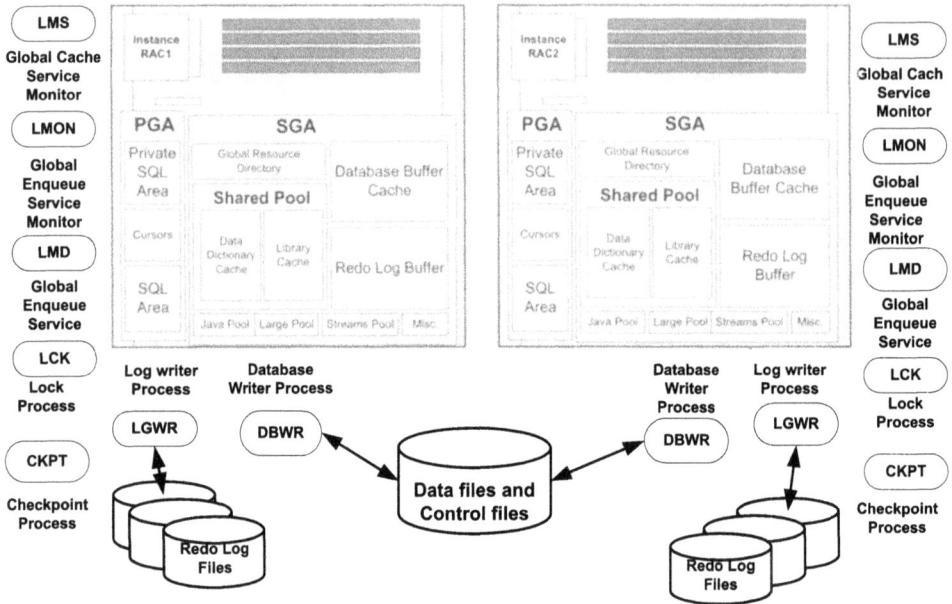

Figure 4.3   *Background processes in RAC.*

- Each instance participating the clustered configuration will have individual log files, rollback segments and undo tablespaces.

- All instances participating the clustered configuration can simultaneously execute transactions against the common shared database.

- Instances participating in the clustered configuration communicate via the cluster interconnect using a new technology called the cache fusion technology.

RAC does have a few unique background processes that do not play any role in a single instance configuration.

Figure 4.3 defines the additional background processes and their role in a RAC implementation. The functionality of these background processes is described below:

LMS   Global cache service processes (LMSn) are processes that, when spawned by Oracle, copy blocks directly from the holding instance's buffer cache and send a read consistent copy of the block to the requesting foreground process on the requesting instance to be placed into the buffer cache. LMS rolls back any uncommitted transactions for any blocks that are being requested for consistent read by the remote instance.

RAC software provides for up to 10 LMS processes (0–9), depending on the amount of messaging traffic. However, there is, by default, one LMS process per pair of CPUs. In general, the number of LMS processes varies depending on the amount of messaging traffic amongst nodes in the cluster.

9i **New Feature:** Global cache services (GCS) were called lock manager services in prior versions of Oracle.

While Oracle has changed the names of several services, the names of these processes have not changed in Oracle *9i*.

LMON The global enqueue service monitor (LMON) is a background process that monitors the entire cluster to manage global resources. By constantly probing the other instances, it checks and manages instance deaths and the associated recovery for GCS. When a node joins or leaves the cluster, it handles reconfiguration of locks and resources. In particular, LMON handles the part of recovery associated with global resources. LMON provided services are also known as cluster group services (CGS).

9i **New Feature:** Global enqueue service monitor was called lock manager monitor in previous versions of Oracle.

LMD The global enqueue service daemon (LMD) is a background agent process that manages requests for resources to control access to blocks and global enqueues. It manages lock manager service requests for GCS resources and sends them to a service queue to be handled by the LMSn process. The LMD process also handles global deadlock detection and remote resource requests (remote resource requests are requests originating from another instance).

GSD The global service daemon (GSD) is a component that receives requests from the SRVCTL control utility to execute administrative job tasks such as startup or shutdown. The command is executed locally on each node and the results are returned to SRVCTL. The GSD is installed on the nodes by default.

9iR2 **New Feature:** In Oracle *9i* Release 2, Oracle has introduced a new utility called GSDCTL to start and stop the GSD process.

Note: Please refer to Appendix 1 for a detailed list of SRVCTL commands.

LCK The lock process (LCK) manages non-cache fusion resource requests such as library and row cache requests and lock requests that are local to the server. LCK process manages instance resource requests and cross-instance call operations for shared resources. It builds a list of invalid lock elements and validates lock elements during recovery. Because the LMS process handles the primary function of lock management, only a single LCK process exists in each instance.

9i **New Feature:** Unlike the prior versions of Oracle, there is only one LCK process per instance in RAC.

DIAG The diagnosability daemon (DIAG) background process monitors the health of the instance and captures diagnostic data about process failures within instances. The operation of this daemon is automated and updates an alert log file to record the activity that it performs.

The following is an extract from the alert log file, showing the various background processes started by Oracle during instance startup.

```
Fri Jul 26 00:51:36 2002
cluster interconnect IPC version:Oracle UDP/IP
IPC Vendor 1 proto 2 Version 1.0
PMON started with pid=2
DIAG started with pid=3
LMON started with pid=4
LMD0 started with pid=5
LMS0 started with pid=6
LMS1 started with pid=7
DBW0 started with pid=8
DBW1 started with pid=9
LGWR started with pid=10
CKPT started with pid=11
SMON started with pid=12
RECO started with pid=13
CJQ0 started with pid=14
Fri Jul 26 00:51:41 2002
```

4.5   Cache fusion

Cache fusion is a new technology that uses a high-speed interprocess communication interconnect to provide cache-to-cache transfer of data blocks between instances in a cluster. This technology for transferring data across nodes through the interconnect became a viable option as the bandwidth for interconnects increased and the transport mechanism improved. Cache fusion architecture is revolutionary in an industry sense because it treats the entire physical distinct RAM for each cluster node logically as one large database SGA, with the interconnect providing the physical transport among them.

Prior to Oracle 9*i* RAC, transferring a data block from one node to another involved writing the block from the database buffer cache of the holding node to the shared disk storage. The requesting node read the data block from disk into its own cache.

Cache fusion, a natural evolution of the OPS architecture, implements cache synchronization using a write-back model. The GCS and GES processes on each node manage the synchronization by using the cluster interconnects for data block movement between nodes. Cache fusion addresses transaction concurrency between instances. This section will provide a brief introduction to the different scenarios of intercluster sharing of blocks and explore how they work.

Note: A more detailed discussion on cache fusion is forthcoming in Chapter 5 (Transaction Management).

- *Concurrent reads on multiple nodes:* This occurs when two or more instances participating in the clustered configuration need to read the same block of information. The block of requested information is shared between the instances via the cluster interconnect. The first instance that reads the block would be the owning block and the subsequent instances that require access to the same block will request for the block via the cluster interconnect.

- *Concurrent reads and writes on different nodes:* This is the common type of concurrency that would be noticed, a mixture of read/write operations against the same block. In this scenario the architecture is similar to that of a single instance except that they happen across the cluster interconnect through a different set of background processes. A block can be read from the current version or from the read-consistent previous version of the block.

- *Concurrent writes on different nodes:* This kind of operation could be classified, or incorporated, into what was just discussed. This is a situation where multiple instances request modification of the same data block frequently. Again, the outcome, or the solution, to complete these requests is via the cluster interconnect.

In all of these transfer of block requests between instances using the interconnect, the GCS process plays a significant role as the master/keeper

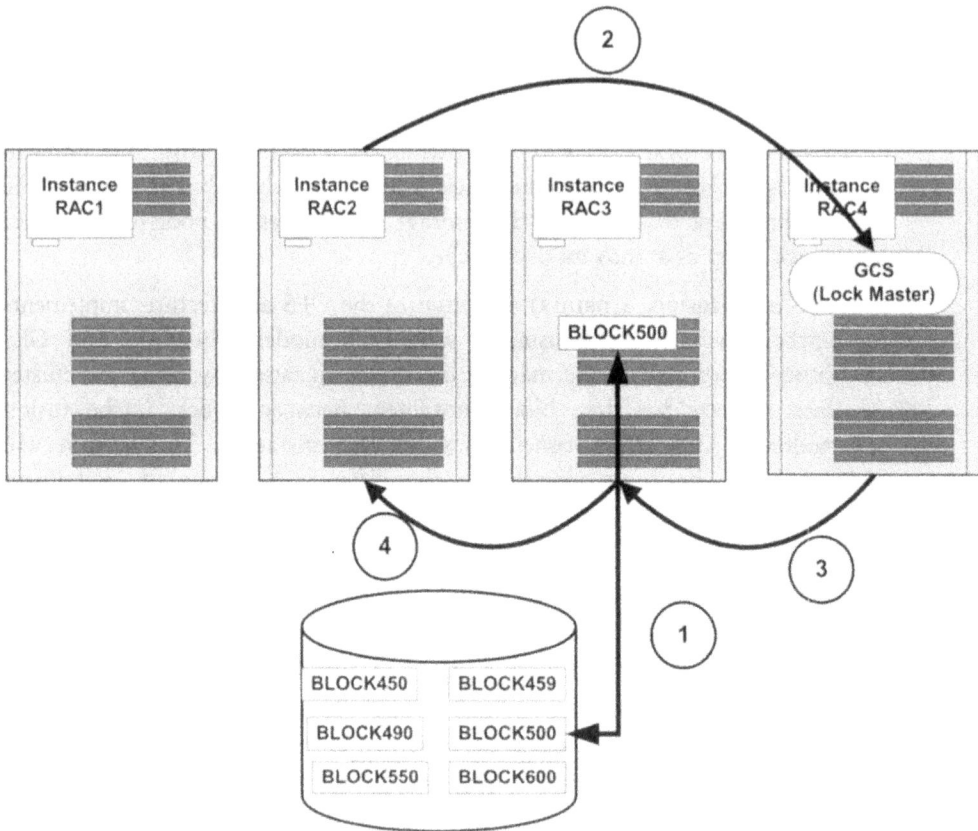

Figure 4.4   *Cache fusion technology.*

of all requests between instances. GCS tracks the location and status of data blocks as well as the access privileges of various instances. Oracle uses the GCS for cache coherency when the current version of a data block is on one instance's buffer cache and another instance requests that block for modification.

Figure 4.4 is a simple illustration of the cache fusion technology. In this example, instance RAC3 has read block 500 from the database and is currently holding the block. Now instance RAC2 requires the same block and makes a request to retrieve it from the database. Instance RAC2 during this process communicates with the GCS process, which could be resident (depending on the resource master) on any of the nodes. For this example, we will place it on instance RAC4. Instance RAC4 understands that instance RAC3 is currently the holder of the block and requests instance RAC3 to transfer the block via the cluster interconnect to instance RAC2.

The resource master for a specific data file is obtained by querying against the GV$GCSHVMASTER_INFO.

```
SQL>SELECT
         INST_ID,
         HV_ID,
         CURRENT_MASTER,
         PREVIOUS_MASTER,
         REMASTER_CNT
FROM GV$GCSHVMASTER_INFO
WHERE REMASTER_CNT > 0;
```

INST_ID	HV_ID	CURRENT_MASTER	PREVIOUS_MASTER	REMASTER_CNT
1	625	0	32767	1
1	626	0	32767	1
1	627	0	32767	1
1	628	0	32767	1
1	629	0	32767	1
1	630	0	32767	1
1	631	0	32767	1
1	632	0	32767	1
1	633	0	32767	1
2	598	0	1	1
2	599	0	1	1

As illustrated above, while most of the sharing of data blocks between instances happens via the cluster interconnect, Oracle continues to maintain cache coherency between instances. Examples are:

- The cache-to-cache data transfer is done through the high-speed IPC interconnect. This virtually eliminates any disk I/O to achieve cache coherency.

- The GCS tracks one or more past images (PI) for a block in addition to the traditional GCS resource roles and modes. (*A past image is the copy of a block retained after the holding instance has shipped the block to the requesting node.*) The amount of work that the GCS is required to perform is proportional to the number of instances participating in the clustered configuration.

When multiple instances require access to a block, and a different node masters the block, it is the GCS resources that track the movement of blocks through the cluster. As a result of block transfers between instances, multiple copies of the same block could be on different nodes. These blocks in different instances have different resource characteristics. These characteristics are identified by the following factors:

1. Resource mode

2. Resource role

Resource mode   Resource mode is determined by various factors, such as who the original holder of the block is, what operation the block was acquired for, what operation the requesting holder intending to perform is, what the outcome of the operation is, etc.

Table 4.1   *Resource Modes*

Resource Mode	Identifier	Description
Null	N	Nodes holding blocks at this level convey no access rights
Shared	S	This level indicates that the block is being held in protected read mode. That is, multiple instances have access to read this block, but cannot modify it
Exclusive	X	A resource held in this mode indicates that it is being held in exclusive mode. While consistent versions of the older blocks are available, other processes or nodes cannot write to the resource

Table 4.1 illustrates the different modes and their descriptions.

Resource role   While the resource modes are being maintained between the instances they could be held by the local instance, where its requirement is of a local nature, or could be utilized by more than one instance, where the requirements would be of a global nature.

Table 4.2   *Resource Roles*

Role	Description
Local	When the block is read for the first time into an instance's cache, and there are no other instances in the cluster that have read the same block or are holding the block, then the block is locally managed
Global	If the block that was originally acquired has been modified by the holding instance and, based on a request from another instance, has transmitted the block over. The block that was originally on one node is now present in multiple nodes and therefore is considered globally managed

Table 4.2 illustrates the different roles and their descriptions.

4.6   **Global resource directory**

The global resource directory (GRD) contains information about the current status of all shared resources. It is maintained by the GCS and GES to record information about resources and enqueues held on these resources. GRD resides in memory and is used by GCS and GES to manage the global resource activity. It is distributed throughout the cluster to all nodes. Each node participates in managing global resources and manages a portion of the GRD.

9i

New Feature: GRD takes the place of the lock database used in OPS. However, unlike the lock database, the information contained in GRD is also used by Oracle for recovery during instance failure and cluster reconfigurations.

When an instance reads data blocks for the very first time, its existence is local, that is, no other instance in the cluster has a copy of the same block. The block in this state is called a current state block (XI). Therefore, the behavior of this block in memory is similar to any single instance configuration, with the exception that GCS keeps track of the block even in a local mode. Multiple transactions within the instance have access to these data blocks. Once another instance has requested for the same block, then the GCS process will update the GRD, taking the state of the data block from a local role to a global role.

Figure 4.5 provides the contents of the GRD. The structure and function of the GRD is similar to a redo log buffer. The redo log buffer contains the current and past images of the rows being modified, while the GRD contains information at a higher level, specifically the current and past image of the blocks being modified by the various instances in the cluster. As illustrated in Figure 4.5, the GRD consists of:

Database block address (DBA)   This is the basic address of the block that is being modified. An example would be block 600. This indicates that block 600 is accessed by a user on its current instance and, based on other values like mode (null, shared, and exclusive) and role (local or global), is determined if the current instance is the original holder or a requester of the block.

Location   This indicates the location of the current version of the data block. (This value is only present if multiple nodes share the block.)

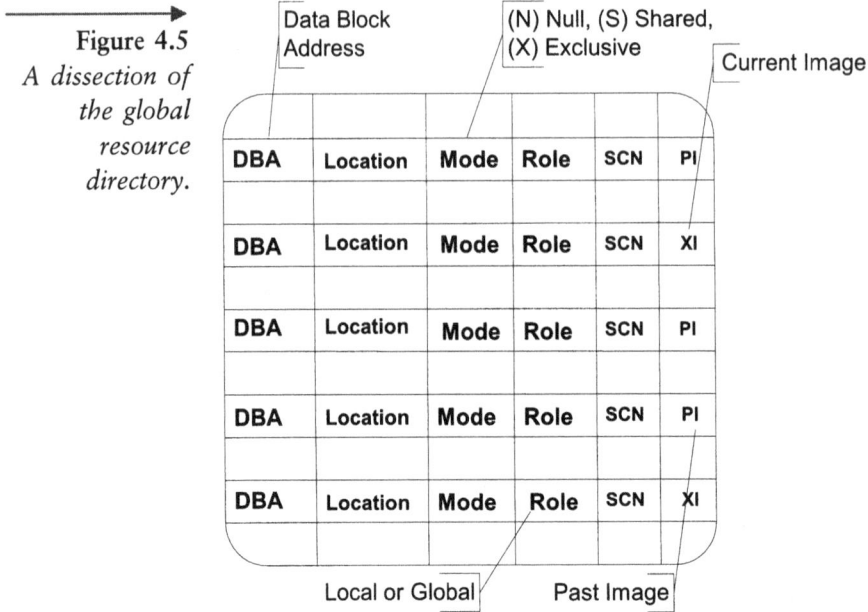

Figure 4.5
A dissection of the global resource directory.

Mode   This indicates the mode in which the data blocks are being held by instances. The various modes are described in Table 4.1.

Role   This indicates the role in which the data block is being held by each instance. The various roles are described in Table 4.2.

System change number (SCN)   The system change number is required in a single instance configuration to serialize activities such as block changes, redo entries, and replay of redo logs during a recovery operation. The SCN has a more robust role in a RAC environment.

In a RAC configuration there are multiple instances with a common shared database. Because more than one instance updates the shared database, data blocks are transferred via the cluster interconnect between the instances. The SCNs play an even more important part, providing synchronization in a RAC environment between various versions of data blocks. To track these successive generations of data blocks across instances, Oracle assigns (uses) a unique logical timestamp or SCN, to each data block that is generated. The SCN is used by Oracle to order the data block change events within each instance and across all instances.

Depending on the type of block request, each instance participating in the transaction maintains a PI of the block being requested. This enables

Oracle to generate redo logs in an orderly manner and to accommodate subsequent recovery processing. Hence, the SCNs generated by all instances have to be synchronized globally.

To make the activity less complex, separate SCNs are generated by each instance. However, with the database being a commonly shared database, and in an effort to keep the transactions in a serial order, these SCNs have to resynchronize their own SCN to the highest SCN known in the cluster.

The method used by Oracle to resynchronize its own SCN to the highest SCN in the cluster is a broadcasting mechanism known as *Lamport generation*. Under this scheme, SCNs are generated in parallel on all instances and Oracle piggybacks an instance's current SCN onto any message being sent via the cluster interconnect to another instance. This allows the SCN to be propagated between instances without incurring any additional message overhead. Once propagated, the GCS process will manage the SCN synchronization process. The default interval is based on the platform-specific message threshold value of 7 seconds.

Note: The Lamport SCN generation scheme is used when the value of MAX_COMMIT_PROPAGATION_DELAY is larger than the platform-specific threshold.

Past image (PI)   The past image is a copy of a globally dirty block image maintained in cache. It is saved when a dirty block is served to another instance after setting the resource role to global. A PI must be maintained by an instance until it, or a later version of the block, is written to disk. The GCS is responsible for informing an instance that its PI is no longer needed, after another instance writes the block. PI can be discarded when an instance writes a current block image to disk. With cache fusion, such writes occur to satisfy checkpoint requests and not to transfer blocks between instances.

Current image (XI)   The current image is a copy of a block held by the last (current) instance in the chain of instances that requested and transferred an image of the block.

The GRD tracks consistent read block images with a local resource in NULL mode. Once tracked, GRD does not have to retain any information about a resource being held in NULL mode by an instance. However, once it has some kind of global allocation, global block resource information is stored in the GRD to manage the history of block transfers even if the resource mode is NULL. With local resources, the GCS discards resource allocation information for instances which downgrade a resource to NULL mode.

4.7   Lock structure

In the above section we stated that when a block held by an instance is requested by another instance, the original holder makes a copy of the block which becomes the past (previous) image of the block. To keep track of these PIs, Oracle uses locking of blocks. Implementing roles and modes enforce these locks. Refer to Tables 4.1 and 4.2 for an explanation of the roles and modes.

When a lock is acquired for the first time by an instance, only that specific instance has a copy of the block. Therefore, the block is acquired with a local role. If the block was acquired from a remote instance, the holding instance will make a copy of the original block before transmitting the block to the requesting instance. This is called the past image. This indicates that there are two possibilities; one where a PI is maintained and the second where a PI is not maintained. These possibilities for the PI are represented by a Boolean value of "yes" or "no." These modes, roles, and instance of the PI all represent the lock structure.

Figure 4.6 represents the three-character lock structure where:

- The first character "M" indicates the mode:

  N for null

  S for shared

  X for exclusive

- The second character "R" indicates the role:

  L for local

  G for global

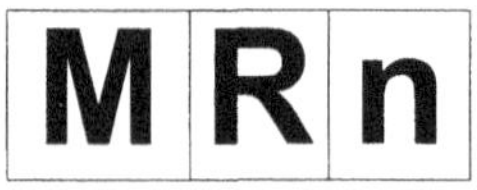

M R n

Figure 4.6   *GCS lock structure.*

■ The third character "n" indicates whether the GRD knows about the PI:

0 for no

1 for yes

Putting these together there are potentially nine types of lock situations.

Table 4.3   *Lock Modes*

Chars	Mode	Description
NL0	Null local 0	Essentially the same as N with no past image
SL0	Shared local 0	Essentially the same as S with no past images
XL0	Exclusive local 0	Essentially the same as X with no past images
NG0	Null global 0	Global N lock and the instance owns a current block image
SG0	Shared global 0	Global S lock with no past images
XG0	Exclusive global 0	Global X lock with ownership to the block
NG1	Null global 1	Global N lock with the instance past image.
SG1	Shared global 1	Global S lock, with instance owning past image
XG1	Exclusive global 1	Global X lock, and instance owns a past image

Table 4.3 lists the various lock modes and their descriptions.

Blocks held by a single instance only have a single copy and each is in control of its modification and writing of the changes to disk. However, when another instance requests for the same block, its status changes from a local to a global state. Only in this situation, where one or more other instances also contains a copy of the current block, does the original instance require to keep the original, or PI, of the block.

4.8   **Global cache management**

Cache fusion brings about interinstance transfer of data blocks between the buffer cache of one instance to the buffer cache of another instance.

It is the GCS that tracks the locations, modes, and roles of data blocks and makes updates to the GRD. By tracking these states, the GCS plays an important role in global cache management, acquiring resources at a cluster-wide level and providing cache coherency when the current version

Figure 4.7
*Global cache
management.*

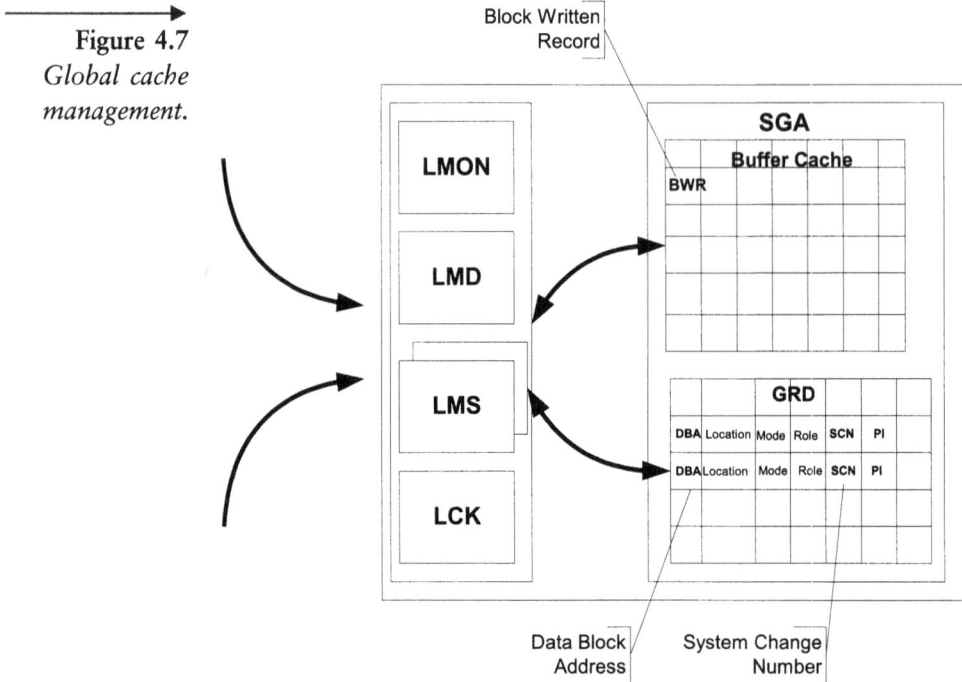

of a data block is in one instance's buffer cache and another instance requests that block for modifications. GCS, in its ultimate wisdom of managing the global cache, also ensures that only one instance could modify a block at a given time.

Figure 4.7 illustrates the global cache management between the various background processes. When a user process from another instances makes a request for a block of data that the current instance is holding, the LMD process builds the initial block and passes it to GRD. If the GRD contains the block information (based on the type of request) it creates a PI, assigns an SCN and passes the block to the LMS process. In turn, the LMS process returns the block to the requesting instance and it finally reaches the user process.

When an instance needs to write a block to disk upon a checkpoint request, the instance checks the role of the resource covering the block. If the role is global, the instance must inform the GCS of the write requirement. The GCS is responsible for finding the most current block image and informing the instance holding the image to perform the block write. The GCS then informs all holders of the global resource that they can release the buffers holding the PI copies of the block, thus allowing the global resources to be released.

As shown in Figure 4.7, a block written record (BWR) is placed in the redo log buffer when an instance writes a block covered by a global resource, or when it is told it can free up a PI buffer. Recovery processes use this record to indicate that redo information for the block is not needed prior to this point.

During interinstance transfer of blocks, there could be a situation when an instance receives a current copy of a block for which it already has a PI copy. If, during the write request operation, an instance receives a current copy of the block for which it already has a PI copy, the instance will keep both the copies of the block. The receiving instance has to serve the block to another instance and the GCS includes an indication of whether a write is in progress that would free the PI.

If a write is not occurring, the instance replaces the old PI with a new PI created from the current image. This creates a single string of redo for the block, terminated by just one BWR when the block is finally written to disk. Under such circumstances the instance creates a new PI from the current image.

When the current image is served, a write-in-progress bit is set in the block if the block is holding an exclusive mode resource. This is required to synchronize block writes when the serving instance holds the original local role resource. The SCN of the PI is used during instance recovery to reconstruct the current and consistent read version of the block.

4.9 Mastering of resources

With the introduction of the cache fusion technology and the use of cluster interconnect to communicate requests between instances, architectural changes that have evolved include resource mastering and remastering features.

Based on the demand for resources on a specific file, the resource is maintained on the node or instances that require its use the most in a multi-instance configuration. For example, suppose that instance RAC1 was reading from data file A1 and data from this file was being processed for an arbitrarily large number of user requests, and another instance, say instance RAC2, also required access to the file A1 for just a few users. Instance RAC1 would have more users accessing this file, making requests and would therefore require this resource the most. Hence, instance RAC1 would be allocated as the resource master for this file and the GRD for this file would be maintained on instance RAC1. Consequently, when instance RAC2 requires information from this file it must coordinate with the GCS and the GRD on instance RAC1 to retrieve/transfer data across the cluster interconnect. This includes all locking and managing of requests.

If users from instance RAC1 have subsequently completed their processing and the number of requests has significantly dropped to a level below what is requested by users on instance RAC2, the GCS and GES processes, in combination, would re-evaluate the situation and transfer the mastering of the resource via the interconnect to instance RAC2. This entire process of remastering of resources is called *resource affinity—the use of dynamic resource remastering to move the location of the resource masters for a database file to the instance where block operations are most frequently occurring.*

Resource affinity optimizes the system in situations where update transactions are being executed on one instance. When activity shifts to another instance the resource affinity will correspondingly move to the new instance. If activity is not localized, the resource ownership is distributed to the instances equitably.

While one instance manages all information regarding a specific resource, information regarding the specific resource is maintained on all nodes that need access to it. Mastering resources on the most required instance enables optimization of resources across the cluster and helps achieve load distribution and quicker startup time. While these are benefits, on a busy system, system performance could be affected if there is a constant change of load on the instances participating the cluster and the resource utilization changes frequently, causing frequent remastering of resources. However, as long as the resource is highly utilized on one single instance with minimal remastering, performance is optimized.

Remastering also happens when instances join and leave the clustered configuration. However, instead of remastering all locks/resources across all nodes, Oracle uses an algorithm called "lazy remastering." Basically, this approach takes a lazy route to do a minimal amount of remastering when an instance departs from the cluster due to failures, when an instance is taken off the cluster, or when an instance joins the cluster.

Figure 4.8 is a two-node cluster with resources mastered on all of them for their respective resources. That is, instance RAC1, instance RAC2, instance RAC3, and instance RAC4 are mastering resources R1, R2, R3, R4, R5, R6, R7, and R8 respectively.

If instance RAC3 crashes, instance RAC1 and instance RAC2 will continue to master their resources, namely R1, R2, R3, and R4. The

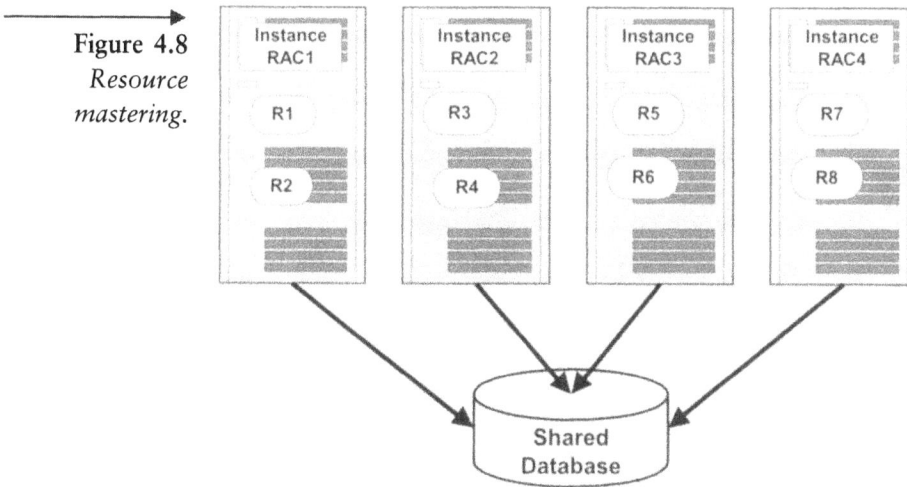

Figure 4.8
*Resource
mastering.*

resources of the crashed instance need to be remastered among the available instances and Oracle uses the lazy mastering concept to remaster only the resources mastered from the failed instance. Consequently, R5 is inherited by instance RAC1, and R6 is inherited by instance RAC2; instance RAC4 is not affected.

Figure 4.9 illustrates the remastering of resources from instance RAC3 to instances RAC1 and RAC2 respectively. It should be noted that Oracle, instead of load balancing the resources by removing all resources and remastering them evenly across instances, only remasters the resources owned by the instance that crashed (in this case).

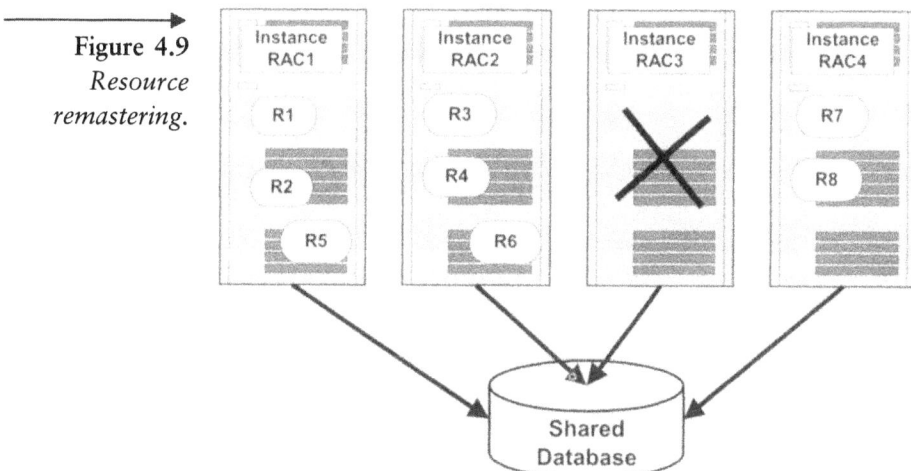

Figure 4.9
*Resource
remastering.*

A similar type of operation happens when an instance joins the cluster. Basically, a resource is removed from each of the available instances and moved to the instance that joined the cluster.

9i **New Feature:** Under the previous versions of Oracle (early OPS), when an instance leaves the cluster, lock remastering occurred by deleting all open global locks/resources on all instances across the cluster and redistributing these locks/resources (including the resources of the failed instance) evenly across surviving instances. During this period all instances went through a freeze period and caused performance concerns. This delay does not exist with dynamic fast remastering of resources under Oracle *9i*.

4.10   Failover

In the earlier chapters it was established that one of the greatest advantages of a clustered configuration is availability and the possibility of users to continue using the system when one node in the cluster fails. In a database-clustered configuration, access to the database is also available through the other nodes when one node in the system fails. Implementation of failover in a RAC implementation can be of two types: server-side failover and host-based failover. On most platforms, server-side failover is different from host-based failover.

Host-based failover   The host-based failover option is normally implemented on a two-node clustered configuration. In situations where the monitoring of services is done on a given cluster node acting as the primary node, and there is failure in the primary system, the services failover to a secondary node. This is implemented by having a node to act as an active node and another to act as the passive node. The monitoring of services from the passive node to the active node initiates failover when the primary node service is unavailable. This feature is supported under RAC with the implementation of the Real Application Cluster Guard feature.

9i **New Feature:** The Real Application Cluster Guard feature replaces the Oracle Fail Safe feature that was available in the prior versions of Oracle.

Server-side failover   The server-side failover option has quite an opposite architecture compared to the host-based failover option. Server-side failover is accomplished by a concurrent active–active node configuration.

A concurrent active–active node configuration is when all instances have applications running on them and have monitoring services, and where one node monitors the services on the other node in a circular fashion. All nodes have access to all disks, as they are shared. When a failure happens there is no ownership to be transferred.

RAC relies on the CM of the operating system for failure detection because the CM maintains the heartbeat functions. Using the heartbeat mechanism, the CM allows the nodes to communicate with the other nodes that are available on a continuous basis at preset intervals, e.g., 2 seconds on Sun and Linux clusters. When a node, or the communication to a node, fails, the heartbeat from the node does not get through. After a timeout period (configurable on most operating systems), remaining nodes detect the failure and attempt to reform the cluster. (*The heartbeat timeout parameter, like the heartbeat interval, varies from operating system to operating system, while the default heartbeat timeout parameter on Sun clusters is 12 seconds and the default on Linux clusters is 10 seconds.*) If the remaining nodes form a quorum, the other nodes reorganize the cluster membership. The reorganization process regroups the nodes that are accessible and removes the nodes that have failed. For example, in a four-node cluster, if one node fails, the CM will regroup among the remaining three nodes. The CM performs this step when a node is added to a cluster or a node is removed from a cluster. This information is exposed to the respective Oracle instances by the LMON process running on each cluster node.

Note: On busy systems, there is a potential that the response required by the heartbeat mechanism may not be received in the required timeframe defined by the timeout parameter. Under such circumstances the CM may signal a false failure of a node. In systems where this could potentially occur, it is advisable to tune the timeout parameter to ensure this does not happen. It is advisable to use a private interconnect isolated from the regular interconnect used for data transfers.

The next step in the failover process is the database recovery operation. During the database recovery process, remastering of GCS from the failed instance, cache recovery (rolling forward all transactions) from the redo logs of the failed instances, and transactions recovery (rolling back all uncommitted transactions) are performed by the remaining nodes. With the redo logs located on a shared disk system (in RAC implementations), the recovery process is even smoother. The instance that first deducted the failure reads from the redo logs and applies them to the database.

4.11   Recovery

Oracle performs recovery operations through a two-phased approach. Under this method of recovery Oracle passes through the required file twice to complete the recovery operation. This feature speeds up the recovery process while making the system available to the users more quickly.

After detection, and during the remastering of GCS of the failed instance and cache recovery, most work in the surviving instance is paused and, while transaction recovery takes place, work occurs at a slower pace. This point is considered full database availability, as now all data is accessible, including that which resided on the failed instance. The application is now responsible for reconnecting the users and repeating any uncommitted work they have done.

As part of the failover process when an instance crashes and the processes fails over to the other surviving nodes, the GCS resources that were previously mastered at the failed instance are redistributed across the surviving instances through the process of resource remastering. Once this is completed, the resources are reconstructed at their new master instances. While resources from the failed instance are distributed among the surviving nodes, all other resources previously mastered at surviving instances are not affected.

For any lock request, there is a $1/n$ chance that the request will be satisfied locally and an $(n-1)/n$ chance that the lock request involves a remote operation. In the case of one surviving instance, all lock operations are satisfied locally.[1]

On completion of the remastering of resources from the failed instance to the surviving instances, Oracle performs a clean-up operation to remove in-progress transactions of the failed instance. This is called instance recovery (IR).

The active instance that first identifies a member in the cluster that is not responding and deduces its failure is responsible for the recovery operation. The active instance that deduced the failure through its LMON process controls the recovery operation by taking over the redo logs files (in a shared disk subsystem the redo logs are visible by all instances participating in the cluster) of the failed instance.

---

1.   Oracle 9*i* Real Application Cluster Concepts Documentation.

Based on the new method of recovery in two passes, the recovery operation is divided into cache recovery and transaction recovery. Apart from these two modes of recovery there is another method that is unique to a RAC implementation called online block recovery.

4.11.1 Cache recovery

Cache recovery is the first pass of reading through the redo logs by SMON on the active instance. The redo logs files are read and applied to the active instance performing the recovery operation through a parallel execution.

During this process, SMON will merge the redo thread ordered by the SCN to ensure that changes are applied in an orderly manner. It will also find the BWR in the redo stream and remove entries that are no longer needed for recovery because they were PIs of blocks already written to disk. SMON recovers blocks found during this first pass and acquires the required locks needed for this operation. The final product of the first pass log read is a recovery set that only contains blocks modified by the failed instance, with no subsequent BWR to indicate that the blocks were later written. The recovering SMON process will then inform each lock element's master node for each block in the recovery list that it will be taking ownership of the block and lock for recovery. Other instances will not be able to acquire these locks until the recovery operation is completed.

This two-phased approach to recovery provides full database access once Oracle has completed replaying of redo log files. After the completion of the first phase of the recovery operation, cache recovery, the second phase, transaction recovery, begins.

4.11.2 Transaction recovery

Compared to the cache recovery scenario where the recovery is of a forward nature, i.e., rolling forward of the transactions from the redo logs, the transaction recovery scenario handles uncommitted transactions, hence rolling them back. Also during this pass, the redo threads for the failed instances are merged by SCN and the redo is applied to the data files.

During this process of rolling back uncommitted transactions, Oracle uses a technology called *fast-start recovery* where it performs the transaction recovery as a deferred process, as a background activity. Under this feature Oracle uses a multiversion and consistency method to provide on-demand rollback of only those rows blocked by expired transactions. This feature helps new transactions by not requiring them to wait for the rollback activity to complete. Fast-start recovery can be of two kinds, fast-start on demand and fast-start parallel rollback.

Fast-start on demand

Under this option, users are allowed to perform regular business not being interfered with by the uncommitted or expired transactions from the other instance.

Fast-start parallel rollback

Fast-start parallel rollback is performed by SMON, which acts as a coordinator and rolls back transactions using parallel processing across multiple server processes. The parallel execution option is useful where transactions run for a longer duration before committing. Under these circumstances the SMON process automatically decides to perform a parallel rollback operation. When using this feature each node spawns a recovery coordinator and recovery process to assist with parallel rollback operations.

Fast-start parallel rollback features is enabled by setting the parameter FAST_START_PARALLEL_ROLLBACK to either low or high. This setting indicates the number of processes to be involved for performing parallel rollback. It should be either twice or four times the CPU_COUNT parameter, for the low and high values, respectively.

Examining some of the data dictionary views could help in the monitoring of the fast-start rollback feature:

- V$FAST_START_SERVERS

- V$FAST_START_TRANSACTIONS

Note: More details about the parallel recovery process will be covered in Chapter 6 (Parallel Processing) and more details regarding these and other data dictionary views will be covered in Chapter 9 (Parameters and Views).

4.11.3 Online block recovery

Online block recovery is another kind of recovery that is unique to the RAC implementation. Online block recovery occurs when a data buffer becomes corrupt in an instance's cache. Block recovery will occur if either a foreground process dies while applying changes or if an error is generated during redo application. If the block recovery is to be performed as a result of the foreground process dying, then PMON initiates online block recovery. However, if this is not the case, then the foreground process attempts to make an online recovery of the block.

Under normal circumstances this involves finding the block's predecessor and applying redo records to this predecessor from the online logs of the local instance. However, under the cache fusion architecture, copies of blocks are available in the cache of other instances and, therefore, the predecessor is the most recent PI for that buffer that exists in the cache of another instance. If, under certain circumstances, there is no PI for the corrupted buffer, the block image from the disk data is used as the predecessor image before changes from the online redo logs are used.

4.12   Database files in RAC

In a RAC environment, most of the database-related files are shared between the various instances. However, there are certain files, such as the redo log files, parameter files, archive log files, etc., that are not shared. In the sections below, the various files and their behaviors in a RAC implementation are explored.

4.12.1   Parameter file

The parameter file contains parameter definitions required for the functioning of an instance. While these parameters are instance-specific, certain parameter values have identical values in all the instances participating in the clustered configuration. It is a common practice to keep the parameters that have identical values separate from the parameters that have values specific to an instance. The main purpose of this isolation is for easy maintenance, allowing only a single point for modification of parameter values across instances. It would also be beneficial under RAC to maintain a single copy of the parameter file that is shareable by both instances. Under Oracle 9*i* this has been made possible.

Parameter files have a new definition syntax that allows storing of all parameters that are unique and common to both instances in one file. This file can then be stored in the shared disk subsystem with soft links, allowing visibility to a single file from both instances.

Examples of parameter values shared across instances would be:

- CONTROL_FILE

- CLUSTER_DATABASE

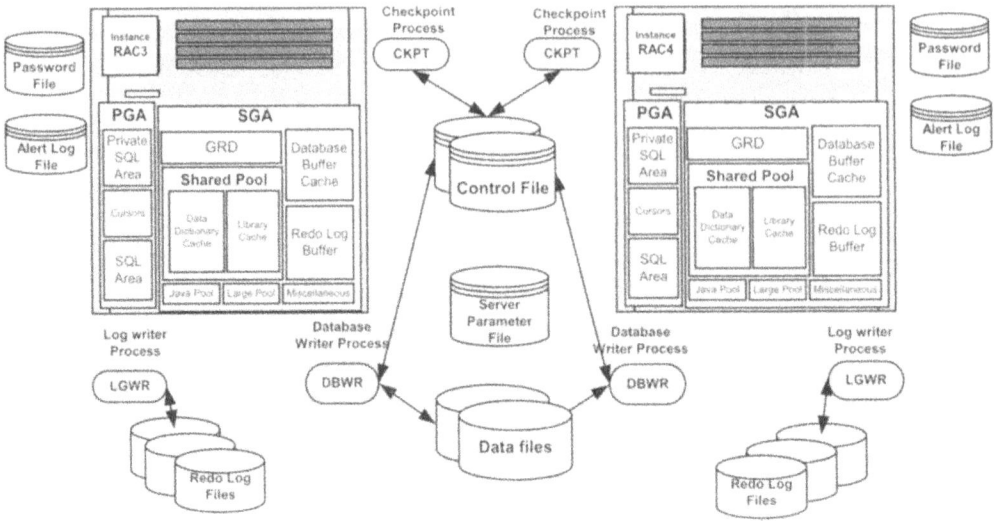

Figure 4.10   *Database files in a RAC configuration.*

By qualifying the parameter with a "*," or the name of the instance, the parameter could be made applicable to either both instances or to a specific instance:

```
*.CONTROL_FILE =
RAC1.UNDO_TABLESPACE = UNDO_TBS1
RAC2.UNDO_TABLESPACE = UNDO_TBS2
*.DB_BLOCK_SIZE = 16K
```

9i **New Feature:** The requirement to maintain separate parameter files in the previous versions of Oracle is removed with the new qualification option available in Oracle 9*i*.

The parameter file that used to be in ASCII text format is replaced with a binary file that could be made shareable. All modifications to this file are through an active instance.

Figure 4.10 illustrates the Oracle instances in a RAC configuration and the files that are common and those that are required for every instance. For example, the control files are common, whereas the alert log files, redo log file, etc., are required for every instance.

4.12.2   Data files

Data files are files that contain data shared by all instances participating in the cluster; those that reside on a shared disk subsystem. In order for an instance to function, all data files should be created as shareable. These files are verified during instance startup and when new data files are added to the database.

4.12.3 Control files

All instances share the control files and should have access to the control files during startup, to keep track of regular activities of the database. In an environment where file systems are not supported, such as Sun clusters, control files should reside on a raw partition.

Since the control file is shared across all instances participating in the cluster, it contains instance-specific information pertaining to redo log files. For example, the redo log thread details, log file history information, archived log records information, etc. All of this information could be viewed by querying the data dictionary views.

4.12.4 Online redo log files

The redo logs contain information relating to an instance and reside in the shared database. This helps in recovery operations during an instance failure. The other instances have access to the file and could use it for recovery purposes.

Users on an instance make changes to the data and these values are stored in a rollback segment or in an undo tablespace. When the LGWR writes the information to disk it updates the log files.

As in a single instance configuration of Oracle, each instance contains at least two groups of the redo log files. To identify a set of redo logs created by an instance from that of another, the redo log files are organized into threads. While group numbers are unique to a database, assignment of threads is arbitrary.

Like in the case of a single instance configuration, there are no restrictions to the number of members in a group; however, it is advisable to create groups that contain the same number of members. Conversely, in a RAC implementation, each instance must have at least two groups of redo log files. When one group fills up, a log switch happens and the instances start writing to the next group. At each log switch Oracle writes information to the control files.

Each log is identified by its thread number, sequence number (within thread), and the range of SCNs spanned by its redo records.

This information is stored in the thread number, sequence number, low SCN, and next SCN fields of the log file header.

The redo records in a log are ordered by SCN, and redo records containing change vectors for a given block occur in increasing SCN order across threads. Only some records have SCNs in their header; however, every record is applied after the allocation of the SCN appearing with or before it in the log. The header of the log contains the low SCN and the next SCN. The low SCN is the SCN associated with the first redo record. The next SCN is the low SCN of the log with the next higher sequence number for the same thread. The current log of an enabled thread has an infinite next SCN, since there is no log with a higher sequence number.

For each log file, there is a control file record that describes it. The index of a log's control file record is referred to its log number. These log numbers are equivalent to log group numbers and are globally unique across all threads.

4.12.5 Archived redo log files

As redo log files store information pertaining to a specific instance, archive files, which are copies of redo log files, also contain information pertaining to that specific instance. As in the case of redo log files, write activities to the archived redo log happen from only one instance. However, for easy recovery, these files should be visible from all instances.

> **Note:** On hardware platforms that require usage of raw partitions for implementation of RAC, it is required that the archived redo log files are stored on file systems. This is due to the fact that archived logs are written to a specific destination. On a raw partition, writing multiple files to the same destination overwrites the existing files, thus losing them.

4.12.6 Other files

Files that contain instance-specific information, such as the alert logs or the trace file generated for the various background and foreground processes, are maintained for every instance.

4.13   Maintaining read consistency in RAC

In order to provide users with a consistent image of the rows while other users are modifying the rows and have not completed their operation, read consistent images of data records are required. A consistent image of the row provides users with access to the previous image before users have made an update or delete operation, but have not yet completed the operation by performing a commit or rollback. Read consistent images of rows can be provided in two different ways:

1.   Rollback segments (traditional)

2.   Undo management (new)

    a.   Rollback segment method

    b.   Undo tablespace method

9i

New Feature: Oracle 9*i* has introduced undo management, which replaces the functionality provided by the traditional method of rollback segments. While either of these options could be implemented at a time, rollback segments is a deprecated feature and is provided for backward compatibility only. Oracle has been encouraging the usage of undo tablespace.

4.13.1   Traditional rollback segments

Rollback segments contain information for maintenance of read consistent images of data in an instance. When a user process modifies a record in the database, the rollback segment maintains the record's past image and current image. The past image is maintained to provide a consistent view of data to user processes that are accessing the row from the database. It is also maintained so that when the user decides that he or she does not require to make this change it could replace the current image with the original record by allowing an undo or rollback operation.

Rollback segments under a RAC configuration are a little different compared to a single instance implementation, as a RAC configuration allows two different types of rollback segment implementation, private and public. Because the rollback segments contain information pertaining to data modified by users connected to that specific instance, the reasons for such an instance-specific relationship are quite understandable.

As the name suggests, private rollback segments are specific to an instance which they were assigned to during creation and instance startup. Private rollback segments are created using the keyword `PRIVATE` clause with the `CREATE ROLLBACK SEGMENT` command. Private rollback segments are private to an instance and are not shareable in the sense that, without DBA intervention, other instances cannot gain access to these segments under any circumstances.

On the other hand, public rollback segments are created in a generic nature and are shareable across instances. Public rollback segments are created using the keyword PUBLIC clause with the CREATE ROLLBACK SEGMENT command. These segments are generic in nature and could be utilized by any instance, provided they are allocated to that instance during startup or allocated to it through the intervention of a DBA.

While implementing the rollback segment feature in a RAC implementation, it is advisable to create a larger number of private rollback segments and a smaller number of public rollback segments. This will guarantee a balanced number of rollback segments to all the instances. If sufficient private rollback segments are not present and there is a crash of all the members of the cluster, when the instances start up under recovery mode and find a number of public rollback segments, Oracle would automatically assign all rollback segments to this instance to complete the recovery operations more quickly. Consequently, when other instances start up, there would be no rollback segments left for use during startup and this could cause the instance to crash.

If, instead, there were a large number of private rollback segments, every instance would be guaranteed to get hold of those rollback segments.

An availability of private and public rollback segments would provide the best of both worlds. During instance startup, every instance is guaranteed the minimum of rollback segments allocated to it. If additional rollback segments are required (like in the case of a recovery operation) the instance will attempt to acquire the required number of rollback segments from the pool of available public rollback segments for the recovery operation. This allocation of public rollback segments is based on a first come, first served basis. Once allocated, it remains attached to that instance for the life of the instance or until intervention of a DBA.

Rollback segments are assigned using the parameter ROLLBACK_ SEGMENTS. The number of rollback segments required by each instance is based on a formula and depends on the load of transactions on the system as defined by the two parameters TRANSACTIONS and TRANSACTION_PER_ROLLBACK_SEGMENT. Using the values in these parameters, Oracle arrives at the number of rollback segments using the formula below:

TRANSACTIONS/TRANSACTIONS_PER_ROLLBACK_SEGMENT

Figure 4.11
Rollback
segment extent
management.

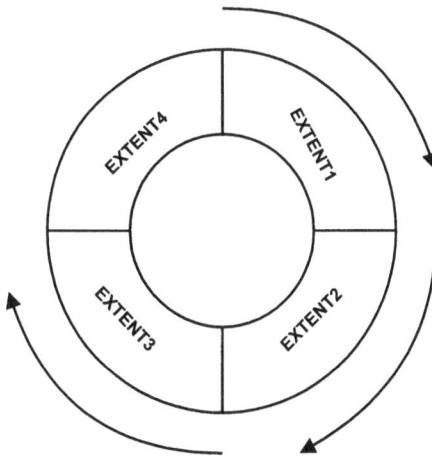

As an example, if the number of TRANSACTIONS defined in the parameter file is of the value 187 and the TRANSACTIONS_PER_ROLLBACK_SEGEMENT is defined as 5, then the number of rollback segments would be 187/5, which equals 37. So, if during instance startup, Oracle finds that the parameter ROLLBACK_SEGMENTS has not been set, it would use the above formula to allocate that many rollback segments from the pool of public rollback segments.

Note: If the TRANSACTIONS parameter is not defined in the parameter file it is dynamically generated using the formula: 1.1 times the number of sessions. This should be the preferred approach of defining the number of transactions and would provide a balanced approach to the rollback segment requirements.

The other parameter that affects the rollback segments is the MAX_ROLLBACK_SEGMENTS. This parameter defines the maximum number of rollback segments that could be allocated to an instance. This is also a user definable parameter. However, if no value is specified, the value equals the number of rollback segments defined under the ROLLBACK_SEGMENTS parameter or equals the value arrived at based on the formula defined earlier.

Figure 4.11 represents the rollback segment extent allocation. Rollback segment extents are used in a circular fashion with transactions moving from one extent to the next after the current extent is filled. To manage transactions, a "head and tail" mechanism is employed such that the head is the pointer location of the current uncommitted transaction record and the tail is the pointer location to the oldest uncommitted transaction record. The RBS mechanism will always try to reuse the next extent in the ring unless there is an active transaction. If an active transaction is found, a new extent is allocated and brought into the ring. Only after a rollback or commit operation will the transaction space be available for other transactions.

Note: The feature of rollback segments is a deprecated feature starting with Oracle 9*i* and is provided for backward compatibility; it is advisable, based on Oracle recommendations, to use the undo tablespace option instead.

4.13.2   Undo management

This is a new feature introduced in Oracle 9*i* that replaces the existing rollback segment feature. Oracle has provided two methods of undo management: the rollback segment, or the manual undo management method, and the undo tablespace, or the automatic undo management method.

Rollback segment method

This method is an extension of the traditional rollback segment approach available in previous versions of Oracle. Under this method, all the normal requirements of the traditional rollback segment approach discussed in the previous section apply. While the entire set of rollback segment related parameters could be used, an additional parameter called UNDO_ MANAGEMENT is set to a value of MANUAL.

10g

New Feature: The rollback segment method is absolute with Oracle version 10*g*. The only undo management method available is the undo tablespace method.

Undo tablespace method

This method is also referred to as the automatic undo management (AUM) approach. By internalizing the interface of these segments, this simplifies the process of managing undo segments (undo segments replace the rollback segments in prior versions). This also reduces the number of parameters traditionally required for the rollback segment management. Advantages of the AUM feature are:

- Eliminates DBA interface traditionally present with rollback segment implementations

- Considerably lowers the number of parameters required to manage undo segments, thus making it easier for the DBA

- Better manages the undo segments, reducing the occurrence of various ORA-15xx errors that generally appear with rollback segments (e.g., ORA-1555 and ORA-1561)

The undo tablespace method brings about changes to the architecture in which undo is being handled both physically and structurally. The undo segments are more transaction aware in that an undo segment of appropriate size is allocated based on the type and length of the transaction; the introduction of the concept of dynamic undo segments makes this possible. To the extent that they also contain transaction tables and undo blocks, dynamic undo segments are very much like rollback segments. However, the manner in which undo segments are managed is quite different from the previous versions.

The AUM feature is enabled by setting the following parameters:

```
*.UNDO_MANAGEMENT = AUTO
RAC1.UNDO_TABLESPACE = (undo tablespace name)
```

The undo tablespace is created with the undo tablespace clause. This clause creates the tablespace as a locally managed tablespace and its space-extent is managed via bitmaps that reside in the file header. The advantage of locally managed tablespaces is that space transaction and management is performed using bitmaps versus performing expensive recursive calls to maintain these values in the data dictionary. This is supportive of information in previous chapters.

Under this method of undo management, the traditional rollback segment methods, or parameters, do not apply. However, under this method, the parameter UNDO_MANAGEMENT is set to a value of AUTO. When set to this value, all undo management activity is automatically performed by Oracle. With this method, Oracle will provide all the functionality provided by the traditional and rollback segment method, such as providing the opportunities for the user to perform rollback operations, and providing a read consistent image of the data, and data for recovery operations.

The management of undo segments is very similar to the rollback segment approach; when the instance starts it will bind an undo tablespace of its own. Therefore, as in the case of rollback segments (private and public), it is required that each instance maps to its own undo tablespace.

At instance startup each undo tablespace will contain 10 undo segments. The number of additional segments brought online during instance startup is based on the SESSIONS parameter. Oracle allocates approximately one undo segment for every five sessions. These are sized according to the auto-allocate algorithm for locally managed tablespaces. The basic algorithm is that the first 16 extents are 64 KB in size. During subsequent allocation the next 63 extents are 1 MB, the next 120 extents are 8 MB and all additional extents are 64 MB.

Under this approach the DBAs will notice entries in the alert log files during allocation and deallocation of undo segments:

```
Fri Jul 26 00:52:01 2002
Undo Segment 1 Onlined
Undo Segment 2 Onlined
Undo Segment 3 Onlined
Undo Segment 4 Onlined
Undo Segment 5 Onlined
Undo Segment 6 Onlined
Undo Segment 7 Onlined
Undo Segment 8 Onlined
Undo Segment 9 Onlined
Undo Segment 10 Onlined
Successfully onlined Undo Tablespace 1.
Fri Jul 26 00:52:01 2002
```

The above output is from the alert log file recorded on instance startup. This output indicates that for every undo tablespace at least 10 segments are allocated at instance startup.

This method of undo management provides quite a few new features or options. One such feature is to go back into history to reconstruct a transaction, and this is enabled by the parameter UNDO_RETENTION. Setting this parameter allows the DBAs to go back into history to retrieve any specific data as it appeared at that point in time. The parameter is set in seconds. Depending on how far back visibility of data is required, this parameter is set that many seconds backwards. For example, if a 24-hour visibility of the past information is required, the parameter is set to a value of 86,400.

The following query queries the undo statistics related information from the data dictionary view:

```
SQL> SELECT
            INST_ID,
            BEGIN_TIME,
            END_TIME,
            UNDOTSN,
            UNDOBLKS,
            MAXQUERYLEN
FROM GV$UNDOSTAT
WHERE MAXQUERYLEN >0;
```

INST_ID	BEGIN_TIME	END_TIME	UNDOTSN	UNDOBLKS	MAXQUERYLEN
2	26-JUL-2002 17:13:54	26-JUL-2002 17:23:54	5	0	3
2	26-JUL-2002 03:13:54	26-JUL-2002 03:23:54	5	0	2
2	26-JUL-2002 01:03:54	26-JUL-2002 01:13:54	5	3	2
2	26-JUL-2002 00:43:54	26-JUL-2002 00:53:54	5	5	13
1	28-JUL-2002 16:11:36	28-JUL-2002 16:21:36	1	0	3
1	28-JUL-2002 10:51:36	28-JUL-2002 11:01:36	1	2	2
1	26-JUL-2002 22:21:36	26-JUL-2002 22:31:36	1	0	3
1	26-JUL-2002 14:41:36	26-JUL-2002 14:51:36	1	0	2
1	26-JUL-2002 00:51:36	26-JUL-2002 01:01:36	1	1	10

While under the traditional and rollback segment method Oracle managed rollback segments using the parameters, TRANSACTIONS and TRANSACTION_PER_ROLLBACK_SEGMENT, when using automatic undo management (AUM), Oracle ignores settings for the TRANSACTIONS parameter. This is due to the fact that Oracle dynamically allocates transaction objects from the SGA for AUM. Also, when using the AUM, Oracle uses the SYSTEM rollback segment. There is only one SYSTEM rollback segment for each database and it resides in the SYSTEM tablespace. Oracle automatically creates it during database creation when the CREATE DATABASE statement is issued.

In RAC environments also, all instances use the same SYSTEM rollback segment and are used for performing system transactions such as creation of transaction tables. There is no maintenance required on this rollback segment.

The output below is a dump of the undo header block. As with any block header, this block header also contains the generic fields such as the Db ID and the database name that helps identify the database. The next few columns indicate the file characteristics such as the block size and the file type.

The next section is the extent control header and contains the extent header information. The undo segment header carries around the high water mark information, which helps efficient management when a user performs a rollback operation. Oracle will ensure that the high water mark is not exceeded.

```
FILE HEADER:
  Software vsn=153092096=0x9200000,Compatibility
    Vsn=134217728=0x8000000
  Db ID=3598885999=0xd682a46f, Db Name='PRODDB'
  Activation ID=0=0x0
  Control Seq=2536=0x9e8, File size=358400=0x57800
  File Number=2, Blksiz=8192, File Type=3 DATA
```

```
Dump all the blocks in range:
buffer rdba: 0x00800099 (2/153)
scn: 0x0000.0898b2d4 seq: 0x01 flg: 0x04 tail: 0xb2d42601
frmt: 0x02 chkval: 0x3639 type: 0x26=KTU SMU HEADER BLOCK
Extent Control Header
---------------------------------------------------------
Extent Header:: spare1: 0 spare2: 0 #extents: 6 #blocks: 527 last map
   0x00000000 #maps: 0 offset: 4080
Highwater:: 0x00800e7b ext#: 5 blk#: 114 ext size: 128
#blocks in seg. hdr's freelists: 0
#blocks below: 0
mapblk 0x00000000 offset: 5
      Unlocked
Map Header:: next 0x00000000 #extents: 6 obj#: 0 flag: 0x40000000
Extent Map
---------------------------------------------------------
0x0080009a length: 7
0x00800071 length: 8
0x00800189 length: 128
0x00800589 length: 128
0x00800309 length: 128
0x00800e09 length: 128

Retention Table
---------------------------------------------------------
Extent Number:0 Commit Time: 1040025723
Extent Number:1 Commit Time: 1040025723
Extent Number:2 Commit Time: 1040025723
Extent Number:3 Commit Time: 1040031124
Extent Number:4 Commit Time: 1040046425
Extent Number:5 Commit Time: 1040046425

TRN CTL::seq:0x08fb chd:0x0026 ctl:0x000d inc:0x00000000
   nfb:0x0002
  mgc:0x8201 xts:0x0068 flg:0x0001 opt:2147483646
   (0x7ffffffe)
  uba:0x00800e7a.08fb.27 scn:0x0000.08987c03
Version: 0x01
FREE BLOCK POOL::
  uba: 0x00800e7a.08fb.27 ext: 0x5 spc: 0xddc
  uba: 0x00800e7b.08fb.01 ext: 0x5 spc: 0x1a3c
  uba: 0x00000000.08e5.22 ext: 0x4 spc: 0x10f2
  uba: 0x00000000.063c.01 ext: 0x2 spc: 0x1fa0
  uba: 0x00000000.063c.01 ext: 0x2 spc: 0x1fa0
TRN TBL::
```

index	state	cflags	wrap#	uel	scn	dba
0x00	9	0x00	0x33df	0x0001	0x0000.08987c3c	0x00800e6d
0x01	9	0x00	0x33d6	0x0013	0x0000.08987c3f	0x00800e70
0x02	9	0x00	0x33e5	0x0005	0x0000.0898920f	0x00800e7a

parent-xid	nub	stmt_num
0x0000.000.00000000	0x00000003	0x00000000
0x0000.000.00000000	0x00000003	0x00000000
0x0000.000.00000000	0x00000001	0x00000000

The undo segment header also contains the transaction table. Oracle ensures that before creation of an undo record, the transaction is created in the transaction table. The transaction table contains slots (or rows), which keeps track of all active transactions within that rollback segment. The rollback segment header is similar in structure to a normal segment header (table, index, or cluster segments). Additional structures in the undo segment header include the free blocks pool, the transaction table, and new in 9*i* is the retention table.

The transaction table holds a pointer to the head and tail of the committed transaction table slots. Each inactive entry in the transaction table points to the next committed (inactive) slot. They are ordered by commit SCN, starting at the oldest transaction to have committed. If the committed list is empty after several attempts at traversing it, the transaction table remains full and an error is reported. This indicates that there are not enough undo segments for the amount of concurrent transactions in the database. However, since AUM tries to allocate each concurrent transaction to their own undo segment, this should be extremely rare to see. If this error does occur, the solution is to increase the size of the undo tablespace to allow more undo segments to be created. Each time the transaction table slot is reused, the slot wrap number is incremented. When the slot has been reused 4,294,967,295 (0xffffffff) times[2] an ORA-1558[3] is reported when trying to increase the wrap number one more time. This should also be extremely rare due to the AUM algorithm of undo segment allocation.

Figure 4.12 illustrates the process followed during allocation of slots in the transaction table.

The transaction table also contains a data block address of the last undo block that was used. Within the header of each undo block is a record index, similar to the way that a data block has a row index. The record index stores the byte offsets for each undo record stored in the block. There is also a structure that indicates the last record number in the block that was created for an active transaction. It is used in a multitude of ways:

- Deferred block cleanout (also known as delayed logging block cleanout) occurs because on issuing a commit, the data blocks are not fully updated to show that the commit has occurred. The next process that accesses the block for consistent read (CR) or updates carries out

---

2.   4,294,967,295 is the maximum value defined internally by Oracle.

3.   ORA-1558: "Out of transaction Ids in rollback segment %s."

Figure 4.12
*Transaction
table slot
allocation.*

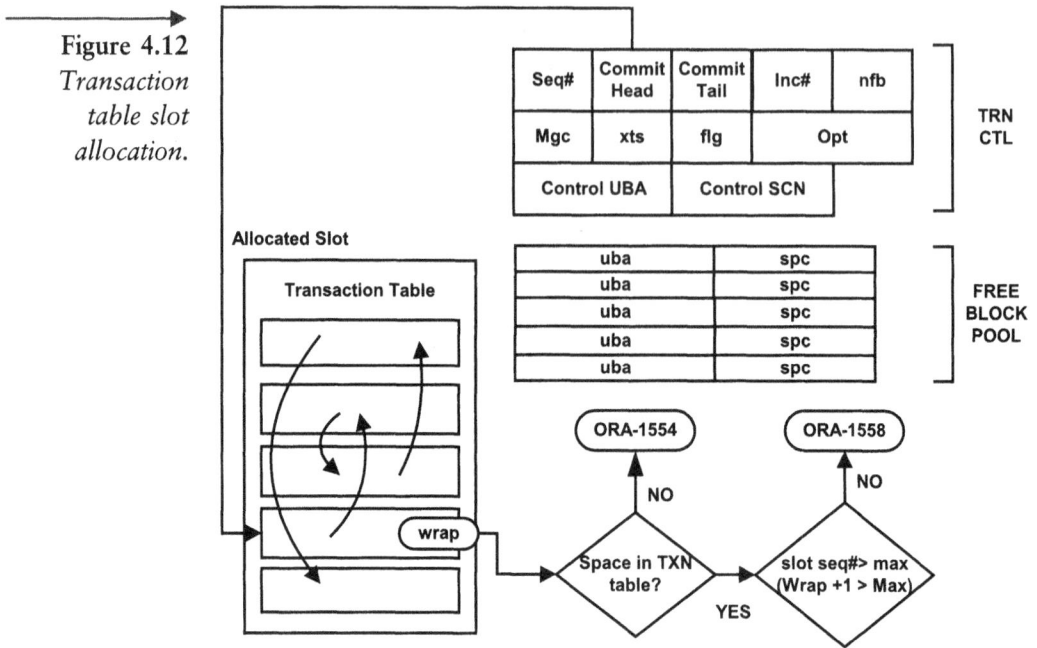

the block updates for this. The transaction table is used during this
process to determine when the commit originally occurred.

- The transaction table is needed to determine if a current transaction
  that is locking a row has committed or is still active. If the transaction
  is committed, a block cleanout is carried out. Otherwise there is a wait
  for the active transaction to complete (commit or rollback).

- During rollback the undo chain is traversed in reverse order to which
  it was created so that the original changes made to the data blocks can
  be undone. The last (most recent) undo block added to the undo chain
  is named in the transaction table entry, along with the number of undo
  blocks used.

- During recovery the transaction tables from each rollback segment are
  read. The slots that contain active transactions are then used to undo
  the transaction. The transaction undo mechanism is the same as
  described in the previous option. Rollback of all transactions is not
  done at startup. The blocks needed for successful startup will be rolled
  back, and the rest will be left for SMON or for any process that
  accesses a block that needs to be rolled back. The processes will roll
  back the whole transaction and not just the data block.

Free block pool table

Within each undo segment header there is free block pool table. Blocks are stored in this pool for reuse (once the last transaction has committed) and to avoid wasted space in the undo segment. When a transaction commits, the last block that was used, if its free space is greater than or equal to 400 bytes, is placed in the pool. If all five slots are filled, current entries can be replaced if it has less free space or is from a non-current extent. When an undo segment fails during an extension, the last block of the last used extent will also be put into the free block pool, assuming it has enough free space.

Retention table

Undo retention allows for better control on the length of time undo information remains in the undo segments. This should help in reducing ORA-1555s. By setting the init<SID>.ora parameter UNDO_RETENTION to a number of seconds, Oracle attempts to not reuse each extent until that number of seconds has passed since the last transaction using each extent has committed. This is controlled by a new structure in the undo segment header and extent map blocks called the retention table. Each time a transaction commits, the retention table is updated with a time value (hundredths of seconds from a known starting point) for all extents that transaction used. During undo segment shrinkage or extent stealing, the retention times are compared with the current time (plus the UNDO_RETENTION time) to decide if the extents have expired.

When allocating an undo block, Oracle tries to use space available in the transaction's undo segment, and when it determines that no space is available, it searches for expired space. If no expired space is available, extents that have not yet expired will be reused. Under this situation the user could potentially encounter an ORA-1555 error.

4.14 Conclusion

In this chapter the architecture of RAC was explored by detailing the various features of the cache fusion technology, how cache fusion operates, how blocks are shared across the instances, and how they are managed in such a way that only one instance makes changes to the block at any moment. Also discussed was the provision to cache memory between the various instances by GCS, how resources are mastered on an instance with a new concept of a resource directory, and how the GCS and GES communicate with the GRD. The additional background and foreground processes available only in a RAC implementation were also investigated.

One of the greatest advantages of a clustered database solution is continual provision of availability of data to the users. It was discussed in brief how failover operation works in a RAC environment and how recovery operation happens during an instance failure. Although Oracle has been configured to recover from failures very quickly, failures can severely disrupt users by dropping connections to the database. Work in progress at the time of the failure is most likely lost. If the user queried, for example 1000 rows from the database, and a failure on the node occurred while the user was scrolling through these rows on his/her browser, the failure would cause the user to re-execute the query and browse through these rows again. This disruption could be eliminated for most situations by masking the failure with the transparent application failover (TAF) option. Features such as TAF and a more detailed discussion about availability and scalability features of RAC are forthcoming in Chapter 10.

How the various files used in a RAC implementation are managed as part of the architecture was also discussed. Certain files such as the data files and control files are shared and others, such as the redo log files and the archived log files, are required to be maintained specifically for an instance. How the parameter file that was previously maintained, specific to an instance, could be configured as shared by using the appropriate qualification (e.g., RAC3.UNDO_TABLESPACE) was explored.

Finally, comparing the traditional method of the rollback segment approach versus the new undo management approach completed architectural discussions about the new features of undo management.

More discussions around the undo management are also forthcoming in a subsequent chapter when the availability and recovery operation in a RAC implementation is discussed.

In the next chapter, the transaction management life cycle in a RAC implementation will be explored along with the use of various test scenarios, beginning with the time a user places a request for information to the point that the data/information is returned back to the user. Transaction management, with respect to queries and DML operations, will also be covered.

5

Transaction Management

5.1   Introduction

In the previous chapter we discussed the architecture of RAC, introducing the various components that distinguish the RAC architecture from a regular single instance Oracle configuration. While RAC acts as an extension to the regular single instance configuration, there are quite a few differences in the management of the components, the additional background process required, the additional files, and the sharing of resources between instances. It is in the RAC configuration that the real difference between a database and an instance is noticed as they are uniquely identified. While this difference does exist in a regular single instance configuration, this is seldom noticed because they are not distinguished from each other like in a RAC configuration. During the process of discussing the various architectural components pertaining to the RAC implementation, we also looked into some common new features like the AUM, GCS, GRD, etc.

Among the many great advantages of using a RAC configuration is availability. In a clustered configuration continuous availability is obtained by load balancing users across multiple instances. When one instance fails, the user process is transferred to one of the other available instances in the cluster. We also discussed the failover and recovery processes. The previous chapter formed an introduction to the architectural features of RAC; we will revisit these features in their respective chapters.

In this chapter we will discuss one such area, namely transaction management, describing how data is shared between instances, and how user requests are processed when they are requested simultaneously from multiple instances. How does the clustered database solution support concurrent transaction management? When users access the same information from multiple instances how is the data shared, how is data integrity maintained, and how is data coherency maintained across these instances and across these requests?

5.2   ACID property of transactional requirements

All the transactional systems are required to possess ACID properties (atomicity, consistency, isolation, and durability).

Atomicity describes the property that all operations taking place under a transaction form a single, indivisible unit of work. The transaction either succeeds as a single unit or fails as a single unit. *Consistency* is the characteristic that all data operations within the same transaction either commit together or they are aborted. Aborted data operations cause modified data to be restored to its original state. The *isolation* property states that the data operations associated with separate transactions do not interfere with one another. Data modifications made by one transaction that have not yet been committed are not visible to other transactions. Data updates are therefore not visible to other transactions until the data modification has been guaranteed to be permanent. This guarantee that committed data is permanently stored is the property of *durability*. Durability means that even if there is a system failure at an inappropriate time (i.e., before the committed data is actually written to disk), it is required that either all the data is saved or all the data is rolled back.

Every transactional system is required to adhere to these basic rules of transaction management. In any business processing transactional information (e.g., enterprise resource planning, supply chain management, transportation logistics, customer care and billing, or defense systems), it is required to follow these basic ACID properties or else data can not be guaranteed to be useful in any form.

One of the prominent rules that would be clear to every transactional management architect, database administrator, or application developer, should be that either the entire transaction completes successfully or none is allowed to succeed. This is required to ensure that all parts of the data are saved to disk. For example, in an inventory system, when a part is issued to the customer, the customer's account should be updated with the item and the item master should be reduced by the item that was removed and sold to the customer. In a situation where the update to the customer's account has completed successfully, but the system failed while making updates to the item master, the entry in the customer's account should not be saved but rather undone. This means that the entire transaction succeeds successfully or no part is allowed to succeed, otherwise in our example above the accounting books would be out of sync. There would be items showing as sold, while the actual quantity of items in stock remained unchanged.

Another example would be a banking operation. A transfer of funds between two accounts (the transaction or logical unit of work) should include the debit to one account (performed by one SQL statement) and the credit to another account (performed by another SQL statement). Both actions should either fail or succeed together as a unit of work; the credit should not be committed without the debit. Other unrelated actions, such as a new deposit to the same account, should not be included in the transfer of funds transaction.

Oracle RDMS is not any different; actually this is one of the databases that strictly follows the implementation of these properties of transactional management. That is probably why most enterprise systems today use Oracle as their primary system of recording transactional data.

In a single instance/stand-alone configuration of Oracle, ACID properties provide read consistency such that users can only view committed data, and there is no visibility of in-flight transactions, i.e., transactions that are in progress are only visible to the process that owns the transaction. These are some of the simple basic rules of transactional integrity that Oracle's architecture ensures in a single or stand-alone configuration.

If Oracle follows this transactional behavior in a single stand-alone configuration of the database, it is guaranteed that these rules are also followed in a given instance on a clustered configuration. However, in a clustered database configuration the transactional behavior does not end with a single instance but with many instances communicating and sharing information through the cluster interconnect. So basically Oracle needs to ensure the transactional behavior at the clustered level plus at the single stand-alone instance level.

In Oracle 9*i*, Oracle has implemented the cache fusion architecture that follows sharing of transactional data across the cluster interconnect making it possible to transfer information much quicker compared to the prior versions such as OPS. (Under this architecture, transaction management has shifted from within a single instance to multiple instances across the network.)

Under OPS, as users familiar with the system would recall, when a block owned by one instance was required by another instance based on a user access, the requesting instance will request the owning instance to write the information back to disk for the requesting instance to read the information back form disk. This writing allowed recovery of the transaction in the case of failure (maintaining transactional integrity). On the other hand, this architecture created performance issues.

Under the new architecture, while the block is not forced to disk, copies of these blocks are retained in memory of the owning instance before a copy is sent across the cluster interconnect to the requesting instance. Retaining a copy or PI helps in the recovery operation when the requesting instance (holding the latest copy of the change) fails.

How does one ensure all this integrity of transactional behavior? How does Oracle ensure that:

- Only completed transactions are visible by multiple users concurrently accessing data from multiple instances?

- Only committed transactions are made visible to users?

- All changes complete successfully or none complete?

We will discuss various scenarios to analyze these transactional behaviors of Oracle under a clustered environment using RAC through the rest of this chapter. First let us start our discussion by examining the transactional behavior in a single instance non-clustered database environment.

5.3   Single instance transaction behavior

In Oracle, a transaction begins when the first executable SQL statement is encountered. This happens when the statement makes a call to the instance and includes any data manipulation language (DML) or data definition language (DDL) operation, or after the SET TRANSACTION command is explicitly issued. However, a transaction ID (TXID) is not allocated until an undo segment and transaction table slot are allocated, which occurs during the first DML statement. SET TRANSACTION only allocates a transaction state object, which is not populated with data until the first DML statement is issued, and a TXID is provided.

When a transaction begins, Oracle assigns the transaction to an undo segment or rollback segment to record the rollback entries for the new transaction and a transaction ends when any of the following occurs:

- A commit or rollback statement is issued without any SAVEPOINT clause.

- A DDL statement such as CREATE, DROP, ALTER, etc., is run.

- The user session with the current transaction is disconnected from Oracle.

- The user session is abnormally terminated, in which case the transaction is automatically rolled back by Oracle.

When a transaction is committed, the following occurs:

- The internal transaction table for the associated rollback segment records that the transaction has committed, and the corresponding unique SCN of the transaction is assigned and recorded in the table.

- The LGWR process writes redo log entries in the SGA's redo log buffers and the transaction's SCN to the online redo log file. The atomic event constitutes the commit of the transaction.

- Oracle releases all the locks held on rows and tables.

- Oracle finally marks the transaction as complete.

When a transaction is rolled back either through a regular rollback operation or when a user session is abnormally terminated, the following occurs:

- Oracle will undo all changes made by all the SQL statements in the transaction by using the corresponding undo or rollback segment.

- Oracle releases all the transaction's locks held on rows and tables.

- Oracle ends the transaction by marking it complete/cancelled.

We have looked at the various background processes and the database files that are used by Oracle in Chapter 3 (Oracle database Concepts). When a user process makes a request to the database to perform an operation, almost all the background, foreground, and database files are involved in some form, either directly or indirectly, to complete the operation and to ensure that the operation has completed in a manner to ensure that its atomicity is maintained.

To analyze the transactional behavior of a user request, let us take an example where a user is attempting to modify existing data in the database. This example will help provide a basic overview of a transaction flow.

Figure 5.1 illustrates the process flow of the example being considered to illustrate the transactional behavior in a single instance system.

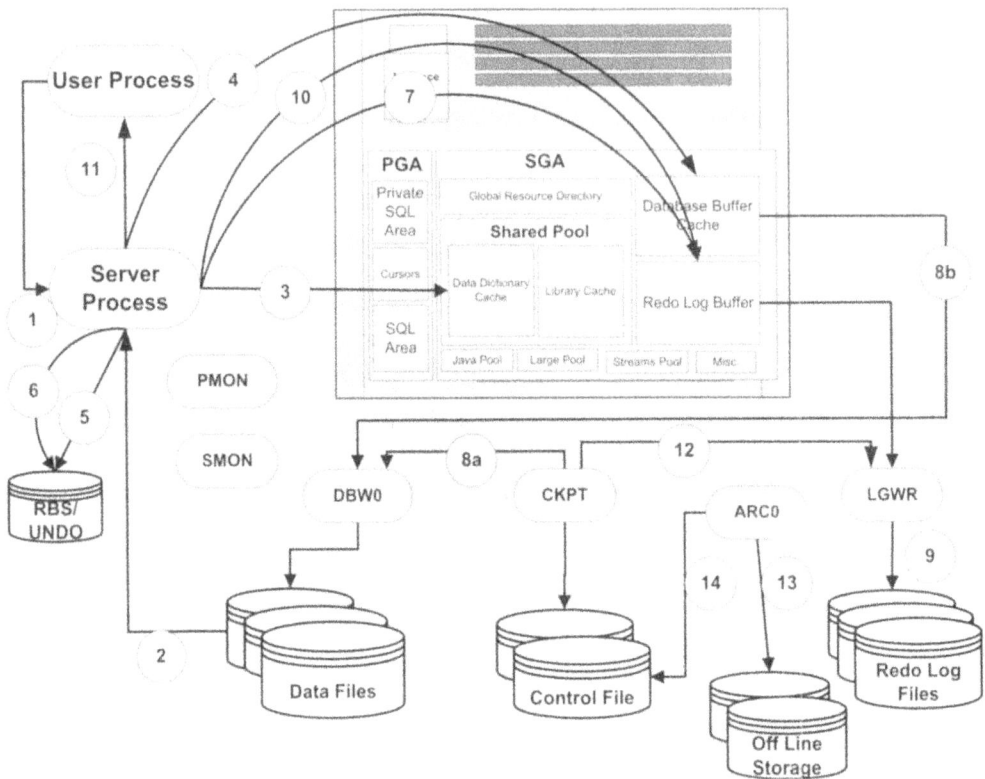

Figure 5.1   *Transactional behavior.*

It illustrates the involvement of the various background, foreground, and database files in completing a user request:

1.   A client workstation or machine running an application in a user process establishes a connection to the server using an Oracle Net service driver. The user process sends the UPDATE statement to the server process with a request to parse or compile the query.

2.   During this step of the operation, Oracle has to perform several internal steps with respect to the transaction.

   a.   A DML operation requires allocation of an undo segment. With an initial rule of thumb to allocate one transaction per undo segment, Oracle performs this operation on a random basis (random number has an upper limit defined by the undo segment number (USN) that has been brought online during instance startup[1]) to even out the distribution. If no suitable undo segment is found, a new number is generated; this process is repeated three times, after which Oracle tries to online an offline undo segment. It then starts its process of looking for undo segments. If this step also fails, that is, there are no more undo segments offline, Oracle tries to create a new segment. This is made online and the search continues. This loop is repeated several times until a point is reached where it is decided (when the undo tablespace is full) that undo segments will have to be shared. At this point Oracle steps down to use the Version 8 algorithm, where the undo segment with the smallest number of active transactions is chosen. Now if this also fails, a round-robin algorithm is used amongst the available undo segments.

b.   Once the segment is obtained, Oracle has to create the transaction table. (An output of the segment header dump illustrating the transaction table was discussed in Chapter 4.)

c.   Once the undo segment has been obtained and the transaction table has been allocated, Oracle allocates a TXID (transaction ID) for the current transaction.

3.   After obtaining the TXID, the server process checks the shared pool for any shared SQL area that contains a similar SQL statement. If an SQL statement is found, then the server process checks the user's access privileges for the requested data and the previously existing shared SQL area is used to process the statement for the required data.

4.   The blocks read are then placed in the buffer cache and the process places a lock on the data to prevent other users from accessing the same row.

Note: More detailed explanation of how Oracle finds an SQL statement in the buffer cache is forthcoming toward the end of this chapter.

The changes are made to the undo segment or redo log buffers with the old value (before image) and the new value (after image), by the server process.

---

1.   Oracle by default brings online 10 undo segments per instance during instance startup.

5.   The before-image is recorded in the rollback block and updates are made to the data layer of the data block. The rollback block and data block are in the database buffer cache. Since the data in the data block and rollback block are not the same as that found on disk, they are marked as dirty buffers.

> **Note:** In the case of an INSERT operation, there is no before-image for the data being inserted. The server process only requires the row location information to be stored in the rollback.

6.   Before making the changes, the server process saves the old value into a rollback or undo segment. This is done by the processes to enable an undo operation when the transaction is rolled back, to maintain read consistency, and for database recovery in the case of failure.

7.   The changes are recorded in the redo log buffers by the server process. The redo log buffer stores redo records, which record changes in the blocks, the location of the change, and the value being changed.

8.   The DBWn process writes the dirty buffers from the database buffer cache to the data files. This writing to the data files is a deferred process and happens when the number of dirty buffers reaches a threshold value, when (a) timeout occurs, or (b) when the server process cannot find enough free blocks.

9.   The LGWR writes entries from the redo log buffer into the redo log files. This writing to the redo log files happens when the redo log buffer is one-third full, when a timeout occurs, or when the transaction commits.

10.   When the user issues a COMMIT statement, the server process assigns an SCN to the transaction; this is used to synchronize data. The commit record along with the SCN is placed in the redo log buffer.

      a. Before allocation of an SCN to the committed record, Oracle verifies if the new value is inferior to a theoretical maximum value based on the hypothesis that there cannot be more than 16,384 commits per second.

      b. The transaction table is updated with the current SCN number.

      c. The last undo block is placed in the free block pool for reuse by other transactions.

       d. The commit times are propagated to the retention tables (to support the undo retention feature introduced in Oracle 9*i*).

Note: SCNs are used for concurrency control, redo log records ordering, and recovery. The SCN base is incremented monotonically for each SCN allocation; however, there may be a jump in the SCN sequence in a distributed or RAC environment.

11. The server process records information that the transaction is complete, the resources are released, and the server process sends a message across the network to the application. If it was not successful for some reason, then an error message is transmitted.

12. When any of the requirements of the LGWR are satisfied, the CKPT process requests the LGWR process to make the redo log file switch.

13. If the database is running in ARCHIVE LOG mode, the redo log switch triggers the ARCO process to make a copy of the redo log file to an offline storage destination. Normally this location is identified by the LOG_ARCHIVE_DEST parameter defined in the parameter file.

14. On successful completion of making a copy of the redo log file to the offline storage, the ARCO process updates the control file of the specific archive log sequence number.

Throughout the entire procedure, the other background processes run, watching for conditions that require intervention. In addition, the database server manages other user transactions and prevents contention between transactions that request the same data.

If the user had executed a ROLLBACK statement instead of a COMMIT statement:

1. The transaction table is visited and the correct slot is read, using the TXID.

2. The data block address is read from the transaction table, and the last undo block is read (maybe from disk).

3. The beginning undo record for rollback is determined, and the offset is read from the record index.

4. The undo record is read, creating the redo vector to change the data block.

5. The redo record is applied, and the next undo record is found. If there are no more undo records, because a SAVEPOINT has been

reached, or the last undo record has been applied, the transaction is considered fully rolled back.

The behavior of a transaction in a single instance configuration is not simple. There are quite a few steps to complete during the entire life cycle. However, all these steps have to be completed precisely and quickly enough to ensure user satisfaction, which includes transactional integrity.

5.3.1 Two-phase commit operation

We looked at handling transactions against a single database, from a single instance. In today's businesses in many cases there exist multiple databases distributed locally or geographically across various parts of the country. *A distributed transaction is a transaction that includes one or more statements that update data on two or more distinct nodes of a distributed database.* Users are required to perform operations or query data that span multiple databases. These operations could be either DML statements or queries. In the case of DML statements that span multiple databases, it is required to follow the ACID properties. The most prominent among these properties is that either the entire transaction against both the databases is successful when a COMMIT statement is issued or the entire operation fails and it is rolled back. This is called a two-phase commit mechanism.

A two-phase commit mechanism guarantees that all database servers participating in a distributed transaction will either all commit or roll back the transaction. Like any DML operation, the two-phase commit mechanism also protects operations performed by integrity constraints, and remote procedure calls and triggers.

In applications that are written using transaction processing monitors (TPM) or application servers such as Oracle 9*i*AS, Web logic, Jboss or Tuxedo, Oracle's answer to a two-phase commit mechanism is the XA compliance.[2] It follows the same two-phase protocol consisting of a prepare phase and a commit phase.

In phase one, the prepare phase, the TPM asks each resource manager (RM) to guarantee the ability to commit any part of the transaction. If this is possible, then the RM records its prepared statement and replies affirmatively to the TPM. If it is not possible, then the RM may roll back

---

2. XA is the standard architecture established for distributed transaction processing by the X/Open transaction processing work group in 1991.

any work and reply negatively to the TPM, and forget any knowledge about the transaction. This protocol allows the application, or any RM, to roll back the transaction unilaterally until the prepare phase is complete.

In phase two, which is the commit phase, the TPM records the commit decision. Then the TPM issues a commit or rollback to all RMs that are participating in the transaction.

XA

XA is an industry standard interface between a TPM and an RM. An RM is an agent that controls a shared, recoverable resource; such a resource can be returned to a consistent state after a failure. For example, Oracle Server is an RM and uses its redo log and undo segments to be able to do this.

A TPM manages a transaction including the commit protocol and, when necessary, the recovery after a failure. Normally, Oracle Server acts as its own TPM and manages its own commitment and recovery. However, using a standards-based TPM allows Oracle to cooperate with other heterogeneous RMs in a single transaction.

Figure 5.2 is a simplified version to illustrate the XA interface component that acts as a bridge between the transaction manager and the resource managers of the application program.

The XA interface is an interface between two system components, not an application program interface. The application program does not write

Figure 5.2
XA interface
components.

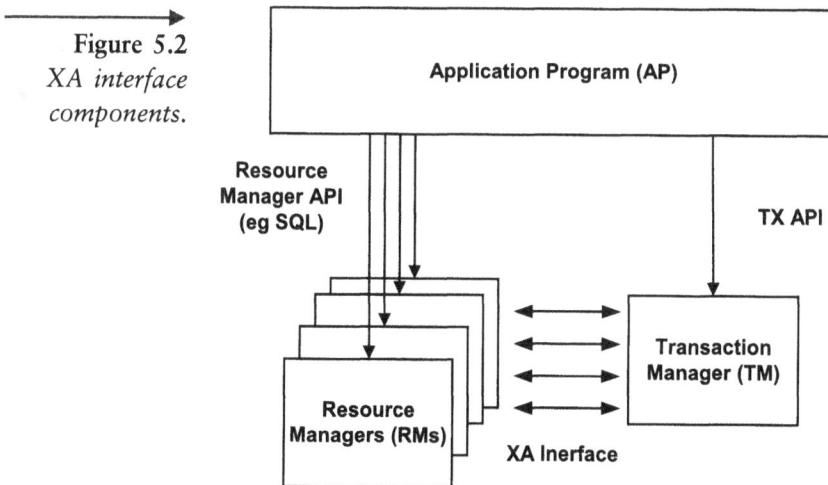

XA calls, nor does it need to know the details of this interface. The TM cannot do transaction coordination without the assistance of the RM; the XA interface is used to get that assistance.

5.3.2 Transaction naming

Transactions inside Oracle are identified by the session and the serial number of the process making the request. With data available in the V$SESSION and the V$TRANSACTION data dictionary views, details of a transaction could be obtained.

9i

New Feature: In Oracle *9i*, a new feature is introduced by which a transaction could be directly identified by a name that is provided to it when the transaction is started. This feature replaces the "commit comment" feature available in the prior versions of Oracle.

To assign a name to a transaction, the session should first execute the following statement before the beginning of the transaction:

```
SET TRANSACTION NAME <name of transaction>
E.g., SET TRANSACTION NAME 'SummerSky';
```

By naming the transaction, the transaction name gets associated with the transaction ID. These names do not have to be unique. Different transactions can have the same transaction name.

This new feature provides considerable benefits:

- It provides easy visibility of long-running transactions and helps resolve in-doubt distributed transactions.

- These names are written to the transaction auditing redo record.

- When using Log Miner to retrieve transactions in the redo logs, these names provide benefits by providing a mechanism for easy search.

- Transactions could be identified by name in the V$TRANSACTION data dictionary views.

- If different names are used, it provides the opportunity to distinguish different transactions by the same owner.

5.3.3 Discrete transaction management

This feature of transaction management allows changes made to any data to be deferred until the transaction commits. Using this feature does not generate rollback segment activity like other regular transactions do; however, rollback segments generated are stored in the PGA. These segments are written to the regular rollback segment space only at commit time.

Using the `BEGIN_DISCRETE_TRANSACTION` procedure enables the discrete transaction feature. This procedure streamlines transaction processing so that short transactions can execute more rapidly.

```
DBMS_TRANSACTION.BEGIN_DISCRETE_TRANSACTION;
```

5.3.4   Autonomous transactions

A regular transaction is an activity invoked by a user to perform a certain database operation. This transaction is complete when a commit or rollback statement is issued from within its context. If from within this transaction, i.e., between the time that a statement is processed and before a commit or rollback operation is made, if another transaction is started as a subtransaction independent of the primary transaction it is called an *autonomous transaction.*

Figure 5.3 illustrates an example of an autonomous transaction. `LOG_PROC` is another procedure that is called from procedure `GET_PRODUCT`. `GET_PRODUCT` contains a transaction that selects rows from the product table, and from this procedure `LOG_PROC` is called at the beginning and end to insert a row into another table. `LOG_PROC` handles

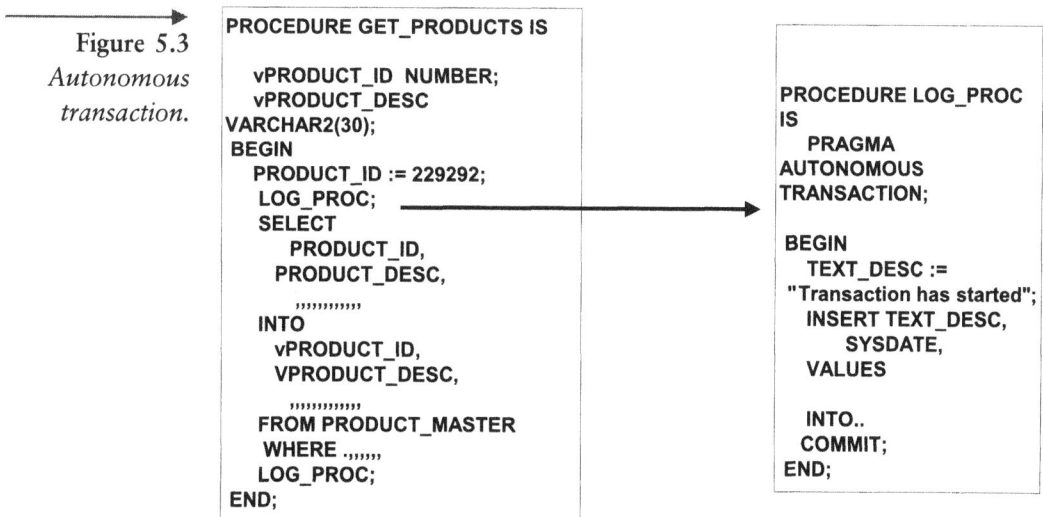

Figure 5.3
Autonomous transaction.

```
PROCEDURE GET_PRODUCTS IS

  vPRODUCT_ID  NUMBER;
  vPRODUCT_DESC
VARCHAR2(30);
 BEGIN
   PRODUCT_ID := 229292;
   LOG_PROC;
   SELECT
     PRODUCT_ID,
     PRODUCT_DESC,
     ,,,,,,,,,,,
   INTO
     vPRODUCT_ID,
     VPRODUCT_DESC,

     ,,,,,,,,,,,,
   FROM PRODUCT_MASTER
   WHERE .,,,,,,
   LOG_PROC;
 END;
```

```
PROCEDURE LOG_PROC
IS
   PRAGMA
AUTONOMOUS
TRANSACTION;

BEGIN
   TEXT_DESC :=
"Transaction has started";
   INSERT TEXT_DESC,
       SYSDATE,
   VALUES

   INTO..
   COMMIT;
END;
```

another transaction that is independent of the transaction handled by GET_PRODUCT, and GET_PRODUCT will wait for LOG_PROC to complete its activities before continuing.

An autonomous transaction starts a new process or transaction that has a different context from the calling transaction, performs some SQL operations, commits or rolls back the operation and then returns to the calling transaction context and continues with that transaction. Such a transaction is totally independent of the main transaction; however, it follows all transactional integrity rules bound by the original transaction. For example, data modified or inserted by the autonomous transaction is not visible to the calling or other transactions unless the data is committed or rolled back. At this point all other transactions could view these changes, while the original or calling transaction has no visibility of this transaction until it commits its current transaction and or starts another.

An autonomous transaction can call another autonomous transaction, causing a nesting of transactions. There is no limit on the number of nested autonomous transactions that could be created. However, care should be provided when using autonomous transactions, as they could cause deadlock errors.

For example, a good usage of an autonomous transactions is when the calling transaction encounters errors, and they need to be written to a table or file while not tying the transactional properties to the main calling transaction.

5.3.5   Transaction isolation levels

A transaction isolation level is the degree to which the intermediate state of the data being modified by a session is visible to other concurrent transactions and the data being modified by other transactions is visible to it. Oracle provides the following isolation levels:

- *Read committed:* This is Oracle's default isolation level. Under this level, queries executed by a transaction will only see data that was committed prior to the start of the current transaction. However, since Oracle does not prevent other transactions from modifying the data read by a query, the data retrieved by a transaction could be modified by another transaction.

- *Serializable:* This type of isolation level provides visibility of only those changes that were committed at the time that the current transaction began, which includes changes made by the transaction itself through an `INSERT`, `UPDATE`, or `DELETE` operation.

Isolation levels are enabled at the beginning as the first step in a session before the execution of any SQL statement. For example:

`SET TRANSACTION ISOLATION LEVEL READ COMMITTED;`

The above statement will start a transaction that only permits read operations against the tables. Isolation levels could be modified or changed midstream by issuing an `ALTER` statement, for example:

`ALTER SESSION SET ISOLATION_LEVEL_READ COMMITTED;`

So far we have looked at the various transaction methods, types and behavioral patterns in a single instance configuration of Oracle. While all of these behaviors apply to a multi-instance or a RAC configuration, RAC has certain additional behavioral patterns; this is because more than one instance could potentially participate in a given transaction.

Before we go into the behaviors that are specific to a RAC implementation through various examples, let us look at the lock management and locking architecture followed in a single instance and analyze this further with respect to a RAC configuration.

5.3.6   Lock management

Oracle uses enqueues as a locking mechanism for managing access to shared resources. In the case of an Oracle implementation, be it a single stand-alone configuration or a multi-instance configuration, there is a considerable amount of sharing of resources between sessions. These resources could be a table definition, a transaction, or any type of structure that is shareable between sessions. To ensure that the right sessions get access to these resources based on their needs to utilize these resources and the type of activity being performed, they would require some type of lock or lock mode to be placed on these resources.

For example, a session trying to perform an SQL query like `SELECT * FROM PRODUCT` will require a shared lock on the `PRODUCT` table. When a number of sessions try to access the same resource, Oracle will serialize the processing by placing a number of these sessions in a wait mode until the work of the blocking sessions has completed.

Then every session requiring access to these resources has to acquire a lock, and when it has completed the function or operation it has to release the lock. This goes on through every session and every resource on the system. Releasing of locks is performed by the sessions when they issue a commit or through a DDL statement or by the SMON process if the session was killed.

Throughout its operation, Oracle automatically acquires different types of locks at different levels of restrictiveness depending on the resource being locked and the operation being performed.

Oracle locks fall into one of the following general categories.

DML locks

These locks protect data. Transactional level row locks are an example of this type of lock. Oracle uses these locks for object level locking during SELECT and DML operations. For example, if a SELECT query has a join between two tables and is using an indexed column in the WHERE clause, then the statement would require a minimum of four locks. If the table were partitioned across three partitions, then the query would require 10 object locks $(4 + 3 + 3)$.

Table 5.1 lists the various lock types and their subtypes with their respective abbreviations. These locks are used during normal DML operations when users issue INSERT, UPDATE, and DELETE statements.

DDL locks

DDL locks protect the definition of a schema object while the object is acted upon or referred to by an ongoing DDL operation. For example, if a

Table 5.1   *DML Lock Abbreviations*

Lock Type	Subtype	Abbreviation
Row Locks		TX
Table Locks		TM
	Row Share Table Locks	RS
	Row Exclusive Table Locks	RX
	Share Table Lock	S
	Share Row Exclusive Table Locks	SRX
	Exclusive Table Locks	X

user is executing a procedure, Oracle will automatically acquire DDL locks on all schema objects referenced in the procedure definition.

Latches and internal locks

Latches are low-level serialization mechanisms to protect shared data structures in the SGA. For example, latches protect the list of users currently accessing the database and protect the data structures.

Internal locks are higher-level more complex mechanisms and serve a variety of purposes. Types of internal locks include:

- Dictionary cache locks
- File and log management locks
- Tablespace and rollback segment locks

Depending on the type of lock requirement, some sessions undergo lock conversion. Lock conversion is allowed if the lock mode required is a subset of the lock mode currently held or is compatible with the lock modes held by other sessions.

Unlike many other databases, Oracle maintains locks at a row level, based on TX enqueues; this is known as transactional locking. When two or more sessions make changes to one row in a table, the first session will place a transaction reference in the block containing the row header. Other sessions will query the lock information and wait on the transaction of the first instance to complete before proceeding. Now when the first session performs a COMMIT operation, the TX resource lock is released and the waiting sessions will start placing a lock on the row.

Table 5.2 describes what lock modes on DML enqueues are actually obtained for which table operations in a standard Oracle installation. It lists the lock modes for each type of DML or DDL operation. How do these DML/DDL operations and the lock modes relate or function in relation to each other? Table 5.3 illustrates the lock mode compatibility matrix. It illustrates how each type of lock is compatible with the other modes.

A RAC implementation is a composition of two or more instances that communicate with a common shared database. Hence all transactional behaviors that apply to a single instance configuration will apply to a RAC implementation.

Apart from the lock management of DML, DDL, latches, and internal locks that apply to a single instance configuration, the lock management in a

Table 5.2   *Lock Modes on DML Enqueues[a]*

Operation	Lock Mode	LMODE	Description
SELECT	NULL	1	NULL
SELECT FOR UPDATE	SS	2	Subshare
INSERT	SX	3	Subexclusive
UPDATE	SX	3	Subexclusive
DELETE	SX	3	Subexclusive
LOCK FOR UPDATE	SS	2	Subshare
LOCK SHARE	S	4	Share
LOCK EXCLUSIVE	X	6	Exclusive
LOCK ROW SHARE	SS	2	Subshare
LOCK ROW EXCLUSIVE	SX	3	Subexclusive
LOCK SHARE ROW EXCLUSIVE	SSX	5	Share/subExclusive
ALTER TABLE	X	6	Exclusive
DROP TABLE	X	6	Exclusive
CREATE INDEX	S	4	Share
DROP INDEX	X	6	Exclusive
TRUNCATE TABLE	X	6	Exclusive

[a]*Source:* http://metalink.oracle.com

multi-instance configuration involves management of locks across instances and across the cluster interconnects. Sharing of resources does not happen within a single instance; however, it happens across multiple instances. Another major difference between single instance configuration and a multi-instance configuration is that while row level locks are still maintained and managed at the instance level, when it comes to interinstance locking, the object level is at a much higher level and the locks are held at the block level. A block contains multiple rows or records of data.

Figure 5.4 represents the lock structure and it illustrates the mode, role, and past image indicator. This figure should be familiar from the previous chapter where we discussed these properties of the lock structure.

Table 5.3 *Lock Mode Compatibility Matrix[a]*

	NULL	SS	SX	S	SSX	X
NULL	YES	YES	YES	YES	YES	YES
SS	YES	YES	YES	YES	YES	NO
SX	YES	YES	YES	NO	NO	NO
S	YES	YES	NO	YES	NO	NO
SSX	YES	YES	NO	NO	NO	NO
X	YES	NO	NO	NO	NO	NO

[a]*Source:* http://metalink.oracle.com

It represents the three-character lock structure in a RAC implementation where:

- The first character indicates the mode:

    N for null

    S for shared

    X for exclusive

- The second character indicates the role:

    L for local

    G for global

- The third character indicates whether the GRD knows about the PI:

    0 for no

    1 for yes

Putting these together there are potentially nine types of lock situations.

Table 5.4 lists the various combinations under which the locks could be held in a RAC implementation. Blocks held by a single instance only have a single copy. This holding instance controls its modification and writes

Figure 5.4 *RAC lock structure.*

Table 5.4 *Lock Modes in a RAC Implementation*

Chars	Mode	Description
NL0	Null Local 0	Essentially the same as N with no past image
SL0	Shared Local 0	Essentially the same as S with no past images
XL0	Exclusive Local 0	Essentially the same as X with no past images
NG0	Null Global 0	Global N lock and the instance owns a current block image
SG0	Shared Global 0	Global S lock with no past images
XG0	Exclusive Global 0	Global X lock with ownership to the block
NG1	Null Global 1	Global N lock with the instance past image
SG1	Shared Global 1	Global S lock, with instance owning past image
XG1	Exclusive Global 1	Global X lock, and instance owns a past image

the changes to disk. When another instance requests for the same block, its status changes from a local to a global state before the block is transferred to the requesting node. Where one or more other instances contain a copy of the current block, the original instance will keep a PI of the block.

5.4 Multi-instance transaction behavior

An instance reads a block from disk when either a user session or a process from another instance based on a similar user request places a request on it. While every single instance could access the block directly from disk (as in the previous version of Oracle), such an access directly from disk could be expensive, especially when another instance is already holding a copy of the block in its buffer and the instance that requires it could get a copy of the block via the cluster interconnect. This operation is as simple as transferring the block via the cluster interconnect to the requesting instance. However, there are other factors involved during this process, for example the block held by the original holder may have been modified and the copy may not have been placed on disk. It could very well be that the instance is holding only a copy of the block, while the original holder is another instance, which means the block has already undergone considerable changes. One of the instances requesting the block could be intending to delete all the rows from the block, while yet another instance is intending to make updates to the block.

How are these changes by multiple instances coordinated? How does Oracle ensure that these blocks are modified and kept track of?

Most of these scenarios are similar to that experienced in a single instance configuration, where Oracle is required to provide read consistency, ensuring that multiple sessions do not see the in-flight transactions or rows that are being modified and have not been saved, etc. However, as discussed earlier, the data movement across the cluster interconnect that we have discussed is at a block level, while the transactions and modifications at the instance level are on a row-by-row basis.

The interesting thing in this situation is that while block level data is held at the instance in a RAC configuration, only a single row from the block behaves like in a regular single instance configuration.

Before we dive into these interesting discussions, let us once again discuss some basic concepts that are part of communication and messaging mechanisms used in a RAC environment.

5.4.1   Cache fusion

Cache fusion is the new term provided to the new architecture adopted by Oracle for movement or sharing of blocks between instances across the cluster interconnect. To perform a similar activity under OPS, Oracle had to write the block to disk and the requesting instance would read it off the disk. This writing and reading from disk was a performance bottleneck, which has been removed under this release through cache fusion technology.

Under the cache fusion architecture, since all of the data transfers happen via the cluster interconnect, it should be based on fast interconnect technologies with a low latency. For example, high-speed Ethernet, GigaNet, etc., are examples of high-speed cluster interconnect. Based on the amount of transactional activity, if a high-speed interconnect is not supported by the hardware, the expected performance benefits from a RAC implementation will not be obtained.

Cache fusion is handled globally by GCS. It is GCS that controls the sharing of blocks between instances and ensures that the proper previous image of the block is maintained. GCS and GES together maintain the GRD to store information pertaining to the current status of all shared resources. The GRD is used by GCS and GES to manage the global resource activity; it resides in memory and is distributed throughout the cluster to all nodes. Each node participates in managing global resources and manages a portion of the GRD.

GRD takes the place of the lock database used in OPS. However, unlike the lock database, the information contained in the GRD is also used by Oracle, during recovery from an instance failure and cluster reconfigurations.

To cover all possible scenarios of cache fusion and sharing of blocks amongst the instances, the following areas of discussion should provide a complete understanding of this new technology:

- Read/read behavior
- Read/write behavior
- Write/write behavior

While these are just the high-level behaviors, there are quite a few possibilities under each of the above high-level behaviors that will be discussed.

Read/read behavior

Under this behavior there are basically two possibilities:

1.   The instance that first requested the block is the only instance holding the block for read purposes.

2.   The first instance is holding the block for read purposes; however, other instances also require access to the same block for read-only purposes.

In the first situation there is absolutely no sharing of resources or block information because everything is owned and operated by one instance.

Read/read behavior with no transfer

Figure 5.5 illustrates the steps involved when an instance acquires the block from disk and no other instance currently holds a copy of the same block. In the first situation, instance PRD3 requests for a shared resource on the block for read-only purposes.

For the purpose of this discussion let us assume that this is the first instance that requested and acquired this block from disk and this block is not currently present in the shared areas of any other instances

GRD - R4

DBA	PRD1	S	L	3908	0	
DBA		Mode	Role	SCN	PI	
DBA		Mode	Role	SCN	Pi	

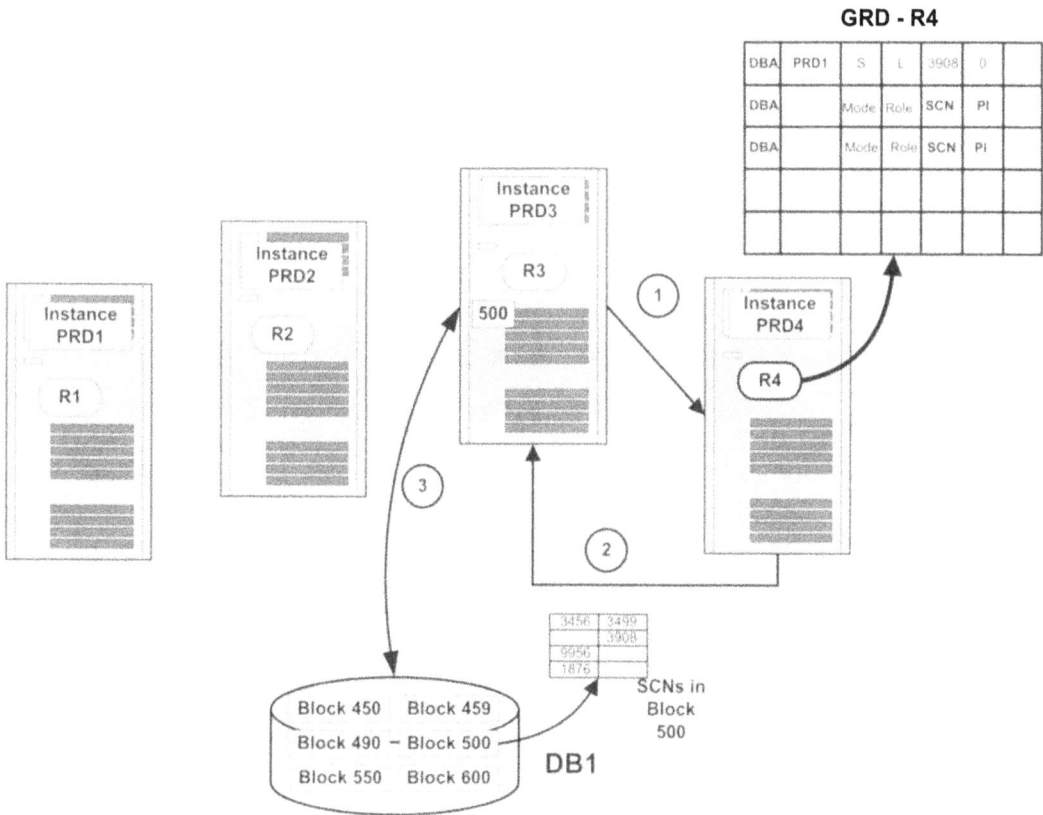

Figure 5.5 *Read/read behavior with no transfer.*

(PRD1, PRD2, PRD4). The following steps are undertaken by PRD3 to acquire the block from disk:

1. A user session or process makes a request for a specific row of data to GCS. The request is directed to instance PRD4 where the GRD for the data file is maintained. Assuming PRD4 is the resource master for the data file being processed. Oracle allocates a node to be the resource master based on the number of sessions accessing this file on that node. If the file access increases on another node, that node becomes the resource master. The designated master keeps shifting around depending on the node where it is required the most.

2. GCS grants the resource in shared mode with a local role. It makes an entry in the GRD on instance PRD4 and informs PRD3 of the grant. PRD3 converts the NULL status on the resource to shared mode with a local role.

3.   Instance PRD3 initiates the I/O request to read the row from disk.
      Let us assume that this row is contained in block 500. The row that
      is requested is contained in block 500, which has an SCN 9956.
      Since Oracle reads a block of data at a time, other rows with
      different SCNs are also retrieved as part of this read operation. On
      completion of the I/O operation the block is read into the buffer of
      instance PRD3. Instance PRD3 now holds the block with SCN 9956
      using a shared local with no PI resource status.

Read/read behavior with transfer

Let us continue with the previous example/illustration. The user queried
the disk to retrieve a row contained in block 500 via instance PRD3. The
block is held in local shared mode, i.e., no other instance has a copy of the
block, hence its role is local. Now let us take this illustration further;
another user requires access to another row that is part of the same data
block 500. This request is made by a user connected to instance PRD2.

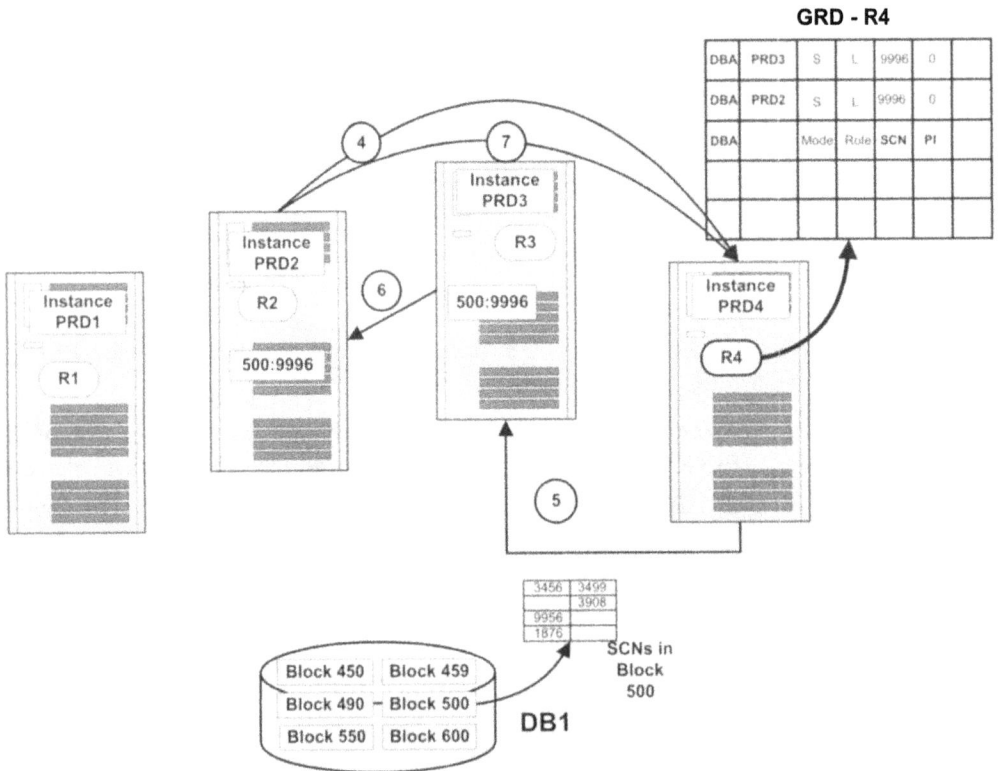

Figure 5.6   *Read/read behavior with transfer.*

Instance PRD2 requests a resource on the block in order to complete the user's query request. In the previous example the block was retrieved by instance PRD3 and is the current holder of the block.

Figure 5.6 illustrates the steps involved when an instance PRD2 requires a block that is currently held by instance PRD3. (*To maintain clarity of the figure, steps 1–3 are not repeated. Readers are advised to see Figure 5.5 in conjunction with Figure 5.6.*)

4.   Instance PRD2 sends a request for a read resource to the GCS. As discussed in steps 1 and 2 earlier, since we are communicating with the same data file, the GRD for this resource is maintained on instance PRD4. So as expected, PRD2 makes a request to PRD4 where the resource is mastered.

5.   Instance PRD4 checks against its GRD regarding the whereabouts of this block and determines that the block is currently held with instance PRD3. GCS in its ultimate wisdom as the global cache manager sends a request to instance PRD3 requesting it to transfer the block for shared access to instance PRD2.

6.   Instance PRD3 ships a copy of the block to the requesting instance PRD2. During this copy operation, PRD3 indicates in the header of the message that is sent over the interconnect that instance PRD3 is only sharing the block (which means it is going to retain a copy of the block). It also informs PRD2 that it is supposed to maintain the block at the same resource level.

9i

New Feature: Under OPS, instance PRD2 would have sent a request for the shared block to the DLM. The DLM would then issue a shared lock for the block and instance PRD2 would then read the block from disk. This entire expensive disk-reading activity is removed with the cache fusion operation.

7.   Instance PRD2 receives the block along with the shared resource level transferred via the message header from instance PRD3. To complete the communication cycle, instance PRD2 sends a message to the GCS that it has received a copy of the block. The GCS now updates the GRD that is maintained on instance PRD4 that instance PRD2 is also another holder of the block.

The above discussion is making an optimistic assumption, namely that everything is available as expected, and all instances have what they are expected to have. Now what if this is not the case and instance PRD3 did not have the block? In such a situation, instance PRD3 would continue with the instruction received from the GCS. However, in this copy process, instance PRD3 would send the message that it no longer has a copy of the block and instance PRD2 is free to get the block from disk. On receipt of this message, instance PRD2 will, after confirming/informing the GCS, retrieve the information directly from disk.

What happens if there is a third node or for that matter a fourth, fifth, or sixth node that is requesting access to this read block? In all these situations the behavior and order of operation is exactly the same. In Figure 5.6, instance PRD3 will copy the block to the respective requesting instances and Oracle controls these copies by maintaining the information in the GRD, in this case on instance PRD4.

Read/write behavior

Let us continue with our previous scenario; a block that was read by instance PRD3 and now copied to instance PRD2 is being requested by instance PRD1 for a write operation. A write operation on a block would require that the instance PRD1 have an exclusive lock on this block to perform this operation. However, since there are other instances currently holding a copy of this block, instance PRD1 could only obtain an exclusive global level lock and not a local lock. Let us go through the steps involved in this process before instance PRD1 gets hold of the block:

8. Instance PRD1 sends a request for an exclusive resource on the block to the GCS on the mastering instance PRD4.

9. GCS after referring to the GRD on instance PRD4 ascertains that the block is being held by two instances, PRD3 and PRD2. GCS sends a message to all (instance PRD2 in our example) but one instance (PRD3) requesting transfer of the block to a NULL location. Transferring the block to a NULL location or status changes the resource from shared mode to local mode. This effectively tells the instances to release the buffers holding the block. Once this is done, the only remaining instance holding the block in a shared mode would be instance PRD3.

10. GCS requests instance PRD3 to transfer the block for exclusive access to instance PRD1.

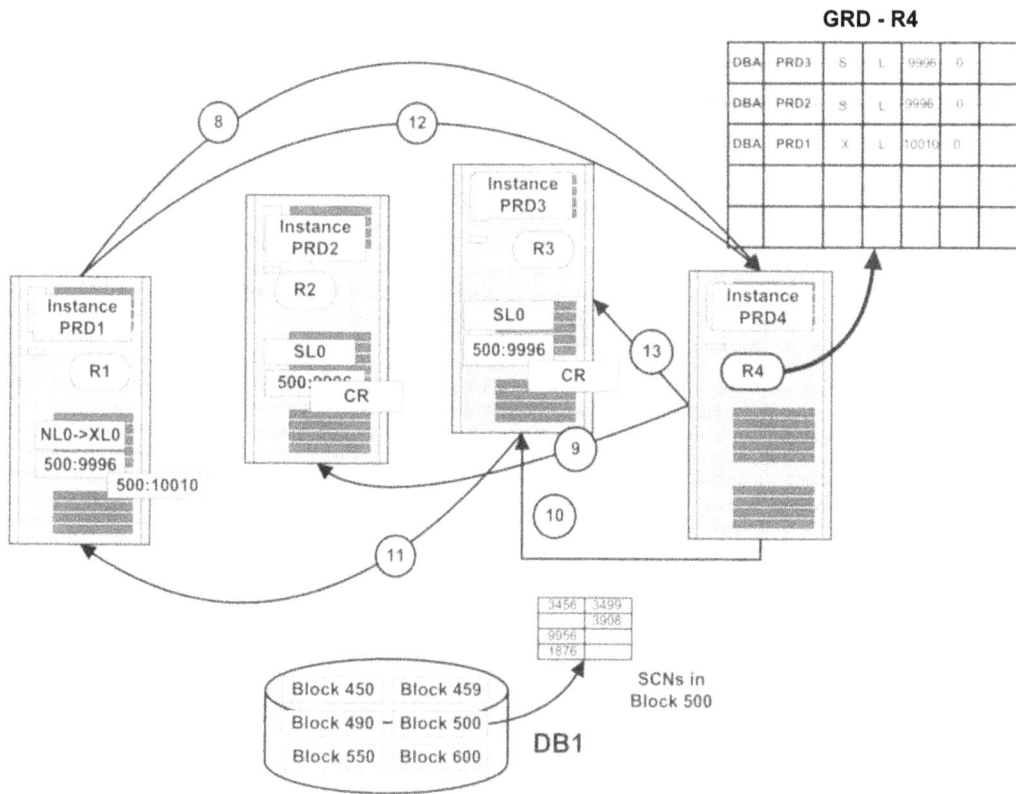

Figure 5.7   *Read/write behavior.*

Figure 5.7 illustrates the steps involved when instance PRD1 requires a copy of the block that is currently held by instance PRD2 and instance PRD3 for a write operation.

11. Instance PRD3, based on the request received from the GCS, will:

   a. Send the block to instance PRD1 along with an indicator that it is closing its own resource and giving an exclusive resource for use by instance PRD1.

   b. After the message has been sent to instance PRD1, it closes its own resource, marking the buffer holding the block image as copy for consistent read (CR) identifying itself that the buffer area is available for reuse.

12. Instance PRD1 converts its resource and sends a message to the GCS indicating/confirming the assumption that it has an exclusive

resource on the block. Along with its regular message it also transfers the message received from instance PRD3 indicating that it has closed its own resource on this block. GCS now updates the GRD regarding the status of the block and instance PRD1 can now modify the block. Please note that at this point, the copies of blocks on other instances would also be removed from the GRD.

As indicated in Figure 5.7, instance PRD1 has now modified the block, and the SCN after this change becomes 10010.

13.   The GCS confirms with instance PRD3 that it has received notification regarding status of the block in its buffer.

9i

New Feature: Under OPS, the read request for instance PRD1 would have been granted by the DLM issuing the exclusive PCM lock to instance PRD1 after forcing instance PRD3 to release the shared lock. However, since the only method to transfer the block to instance PRD1 is to have instance PRD1 read the block from disk, the copy in instance PRD3 would not be used by instance PRD1.

Write/write behavior

We have looked at read/read and read/write behaviors. These behaviors of cache fusion were introduced in Oracle 8*i*. Now in Oracle 9*i* the write/write operation is added.

Previous discussions centered around shareable scenarios like multiple instances having read copies of the same block. Now let us look at how cache fusion operates when multiple instances require write access to the same block. Please note from our previous scenario in Figure 5.7 that the block has been modified by instance PRD1 (new SCN value is 10010); the SCN for the block on disk remains the same at 9996.

In a continuous operation, where there are multiple requests made between instances for different blocks, the GCS is busy with the specific resource documenting all the block activities amongst the various instances. The GCS activity is sequential in the sense that unless it has recorded the information pertaining to previous requests, it does not accept or work on another request. If such a situation occurs, the new request is queued and has to wait for its turn.

GCS activity could be monitored by querying the data dictionary view V$SYSSTAT. For example,

```
SELECT NAME,
 VALUE
FROM V$SYSSTAT
WHERE NAME LIKE '%global cache%'
```

will give a list of tasks that GCS is currently performing.

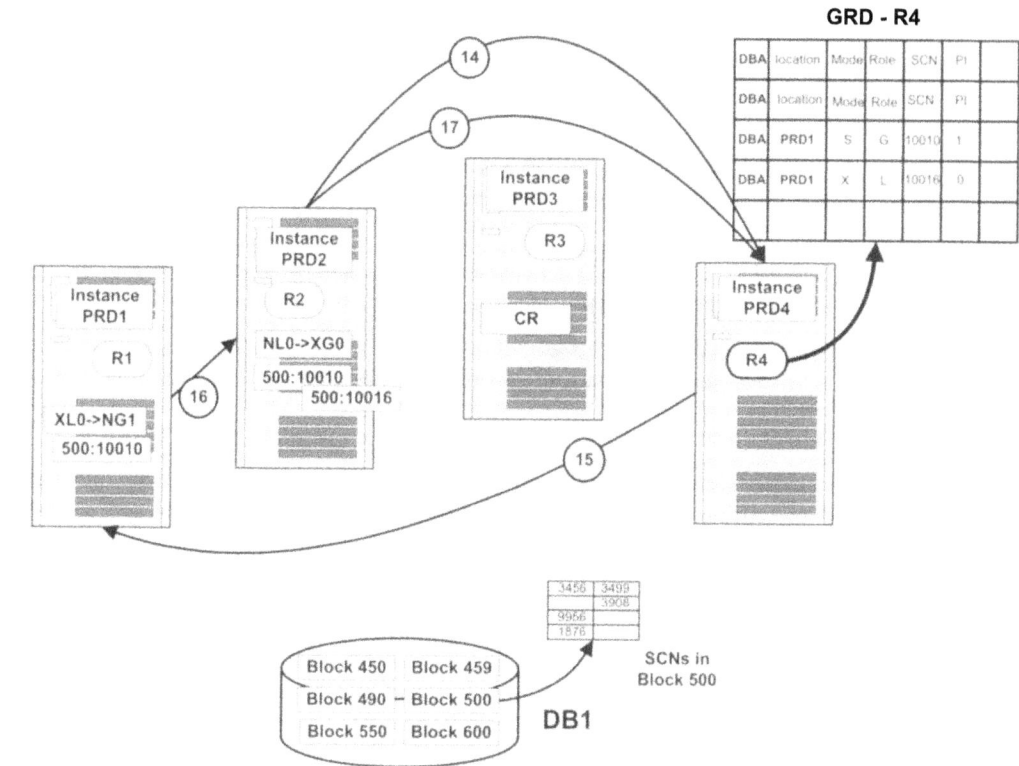

Figure 5.8   *Write/write behavior.*

Figure 5.8 illustrates the steps involved when an instance has acquired a block for write activity and another instance also requires access to the same block for a similar write operation.

14. Instance PRD2, which originally had a read copy of the block, and based on the write request from instance PRD1, received instructions from the GCS to clear the block buffer (marked as CR). Instance PRD2 makes a request to the GCS for an exclusive resource on the block.

15. Assuming that the GCS has completed all previous activities pertaining to other requests, the GCS makes a request to instance PRD1 (the current holder of the block) to give exclusive resource on the block and to transfer the current image of the block to instance PRD2.

16. Instance PRD1 transfers the block over to the requesting instance (PRD2) after ensuring that all activities against this block have been completed. This involves:

     a. Logging any changes to the block and forcing a log flush if this has not already occurred.

     b. Converting its resource to NULL with PI status of 1, indicating that the buffer now contains a PI copy of the block.

     c. Sending an exclusive-keep copy of the block buffer to instance PRD2. This indicates the block image is at SCN 10010, information that the instance PRD1 is holding a PI of the block, and notification that the exclusive resource is available in global mode.

Note: If instance PRD1 had made no changes to the block's content when the message was received, it would send the block image to instance PRD2 and release its resources.

GCS resource conversions and cache fusion block transfers occur completely outside transaction boundaries. That is, an instance does not have to wait for a pending transaction to be completed before releasing an exclusive block resource.

17. After receipt of the message from instance PRD1, instance PRD2 will send a resource assumption message to the GCS. This message informs the GCS that instance PRD2 now has the resource with an exclusive global status and that the previous holder instance PRD1 now holds a PI version of the block SCN 10010. The GCS will update the GRD with the latest status of the block.

Once the GCS has been informed of the status, instance PRD2 can modify the block. The new SCN for the block is 10016.

Instance PRD1 no longer has an exclusive resource on this block and hence cannot make any modifications to the block.

Note: Despite multiple changes to the block made by the various instances, it should be noted that the block's SCN on disk still remains at 9996.

Write/read behavior

We have looked at read/write behavior before; what would be the difference in the opposite situation? That is, when a block is held by an instance after modification and another instance requires the latest copy of the block for a read operation. Unlike the previous read/write scenario, the block has undergone considerable modification and the SCN held by the current holder of the block is different from what is on disk. In a single stand-alone configuration, a query looks for a read consistent image of the row, and clustered configuration is no different; Oracle has to provide a consistent read version of the block. In this example the latest copy of the block is held by instance PRD2 (based on our previous scenario as illustrated in Figure 5.8).

Figure 5.9 illustrates the steps involved when instance PRD3 requires a block for read purposes. From our previous scenario, it is understood that the latest version of the block is currently held by instance PRD2 in exclusive mode.

18. Instance PRD3 once had a read copy of the block; however, based on a request from the GCS it had converted it into a NULL resource. Based on a new query request from a user, it now once again requires a read access to the block. To satisfy this request, instance PRD3 makes a request to GCS for the necessary shared resource.

19. Instance PRD2 is the current holder of the latest copy of the block. To satisfy the request from instance PRD3, the GCS requests instance PRD2 to transfer a shared resource. As discussed before, if there are no resource transactions in progress, this request is immediately processed, or else it is placed in queue and has to wait for its turn.

20. Instance PRD2, on receipt of the message request, completes all required work on the block and sends a copy of the block image to instance PRD3. The block is to be transferred in a shared status with no exclusive rights, hence instance PRD2 has to downgrade its resources to shared mode before transferring the block across to instance PRD3. While the transfer happens, instance PRD2 retains the block's PI.

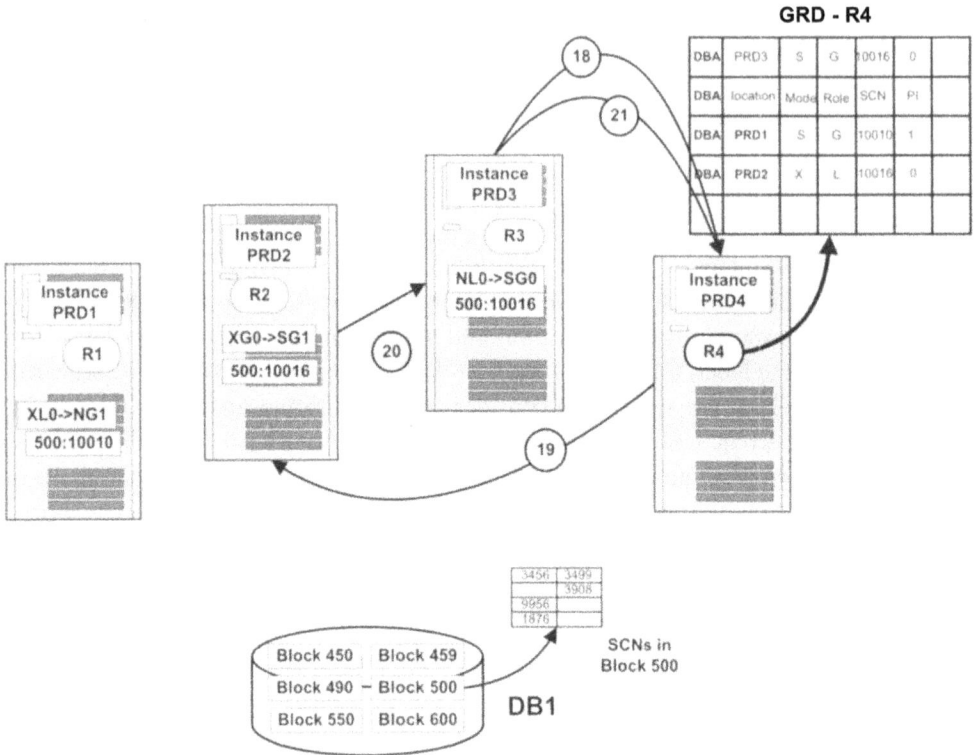

GRD - R4

DBA	PRD3	S	G	10016	0	
DBA	location	Mode	Role	SCN	PI	
DBA	PRD1	S	G	10010	1	
DBA	PRD2	X	L	10016	0	

Figure 5.9   *Write/read behavior.*

Instance PRD1 and instance PRD2 have a PI of their respective blocks with different SCNs.

21.   Instance PRD3 now acknowledges receipt of the requested block, informs the GCS the current status of the block. This includes the SCN of the PI currently retained by instance PRD2. The GCS makes the required updates to the GRD.

Instance PRD3 now has the most recent copy of the block and is now in a global mode.

Write to disk behavior

It is time to discuss what happens when a block needs to be written to disk. Before we step into the mechanics of this, let us recap the current state of the environment:

■   Instance PRD4 continues to be the master of the resource and holds the GRD for the block.

- Instance PRD1 had once modified the block and currently holds block SCN 10010, with a global null resource and a PI of the block.

- Instance PRD2 also contains a modified copy of the block with a block SCN 10016. The current status of the block held by instance PRD2 is in exclusive resource mode. This instance also holds a PI copy of the block.

- Instance PRD3 holds the latest consistent read image version of the block (in shared global mode) received from instance PRD2, which means it is a copy of a block held by instance PRD2.

- The disk, as we have discussed many times, contains the original block SCN 9996.

What could force or stimulate the write activity in a RAC environment? Transactional behavior in a RAC environment is no different when compared to a single instance configuration. All normal rules of single instance, "flushing dirty blocks to disk" apply in this situation also. For example, as discussed in Chapter 3 (Oracle Database Concepts), writing to disk could happen under the following circumstances:

- *The number of dirty buffers reaches a threshold value*: This value is reached when there is not sufficient room in the database buffer cache for more data. In this situation, Oracle writes the dirty buffers to disk, freeing up space for new data.

- *A process is unable to find free buffers in the database buffer cache while scanning for blocks*: When a process reads data from the disk and does not find any free space in the buffer, this triggers the least recently used data in the buffer cache to be pushed down the stack and finally written to disk.

- *A timeout occurs*: The timeout is configured by setting the required timeout interval (LOG_CHECKPOINT_TIMEOUT) through a parameter defined in the parameter file. On every preset interval, the timeout is triggered to cause the DBWR to write the dirty buffers to disk. This mechanism is used by Oracle for transaction recoverability in case of failure. In an ideal system, where the data is occasionally modified but not written to disk (due to not having sufficient activity that would cause other mechanisms to trigger the write operation), the timeout is helpful.

- *The checkpoint process*: During a predefined interval defined by LOG_CHECKPOINT_INTERVAL parameter, when the CKPT process is triggered, it causes the DBWR and LGWR processes to write the data from their respective buffer cache to disk.

However, in a RAC environment, any of the participating instances could trigger this write activity.

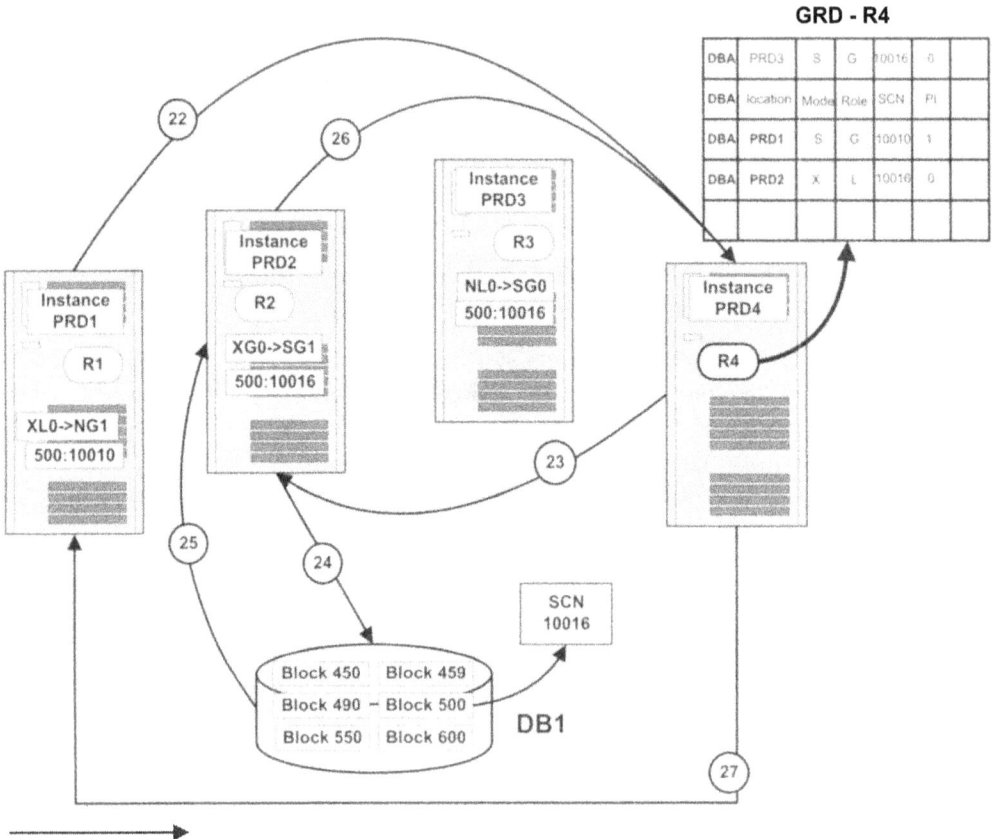

GRD - R4

DBA	PRD3	S	G	10016	0
DBA	location	Mode	Role	SCN	PI
DBA	PRD1	S	G	10010	1
DBA	PRD2	X	L	10016	0

Figure 5.10   *Write to disk behavior.*

Figure 5.10 illustrates the various steps involved during a write to disk activity. In the current scenario instances PRD1 and PRD2 both have a modified version of the blocks.

Let us make the assumption in our scenario that instance PRD1, due to a checkpoint activity during a redo log switch, determines that it needs to write the block information to disk. The following are the steps taken to accomplish this activity:

22. Instance PRD1 sends a write request to the GCS with the necessary SCN. The GCS, after determining from the GRD the list of instances that currently contains PI copies, marks them as requiring modification.

23. The GCS initiates the write operation by requesting instance PRD2, which holds the latest modified block SCN, to perform this operation. During this process, while a write operation is outstanding, the GCS will not allow another write to be initiated until the current operation is completed.

> **Note:** The GCS in its ultimate wisdom as the controller of resources determines which instance will actually perform the write operation. In our scenario, in spite of the fact that instance PRD1 made the request, PRD2 is holding the latest block SCN. The GCS could pick either of the instances to perform the write operation.

24. Instance PRD2 initiates the I/O with a write to disk.

25. Once the I/O operation is complete, a notification message is sent back to instance PRD2. On completion of the write operation, instance PRD2 logs the fact that such an operation has completed and the version is written with a BWR. This activity advances the checkpoint, which in turn forces a log write.

26. Instance PRD2 informs the GCS of the successful completion of the write operation. This notification also informs the GCS of the current resource status of the block, that the resource is going to a local role because the DBWR has written the current image to disk.

27. On receipt of the write notification, the GCS sends to each instance holding a PI an instruction to flush the PI. After completion of this process or if no PI remains, the instance holding the current exclusive resource is told to switch to the local role. In the scenarios discussed above, PRD1 and PRD2 are the two instances holding a PI. When instance PRD2 receives a flush request from the GCS, it logs a BWR that the block has been written, without flushing the log buffer. Once this completes, instance PRD2 will hold the block with an exclusive local resource with no PIs and all other PIs to this block held across various instances are purged.

After the dirty block has been written to disk, any subsequent operation will follow similar steps to complete any requests from users. For example, if an instance requires read access to a block after the block has been written to disk, the instance would check with the GCS and, based on the instruction received from the GCS, would either retrieve the block SCN from disk or retrieve it from another instance that currently has a copy of the block.

The write/write behavior and write to disk behavior are possible behaviors during a DML operation. Similarly, the behavior of the RAC resources will be identical whether it is a single, double or a four-instance configuration.

In all the scenarios it should be noted that, unless absolutely necessary, no write activity to the disk happens. Every activity or state of the block is maintained as a resource in the instance where it was utilized last and reused umpteen number of times from this location.

Now the obvious question that should come to mind is, what happens to all these blocks in memory when a system crashes or a node failure happens? This is a fair question. While we have discussed, in brief, cache fusion recovery, we will discuss this recovery part of the cache fusion technology in more detail in Chapter 12 (Backup and Recovery) later in this book.

9i

New Feature: One new feature introduced in Oracle *9i* is the ability to resume a transaction or a database operation in case of a failure. The feature is called resumable space allocation. This functionality allows the database administrators to make the necessary adjustment or correction to the problem and continue the operation from the point where it failed.

Oracle can manage the transactions across instances efficiently only if the statements contained or participating in the transactions are written efficiently. Efficiency of a statement depends on various factors, like efficient SQL statements, tuned SQL statements, structured formats, etc.

Why are these important? As part of getting an understanding of transaction management, it would be beneficial to understand what happens inside an instance once a user executes a statement. This insight will provide a need to write efficient SQL, providing performance benefits and effective transaction management by Oracle. The most important part of any transaction is the parsing of the statement within Oracle.

5.4.2   Oracle's parse operation

The best approach to understanding the parse operation is to understand its internal operation. Figure 5.11 explains the internals of the parse operation, illustrating the various stages or steps taken, beginning with the time that the cursor is opened by the processes. A similar parse operation

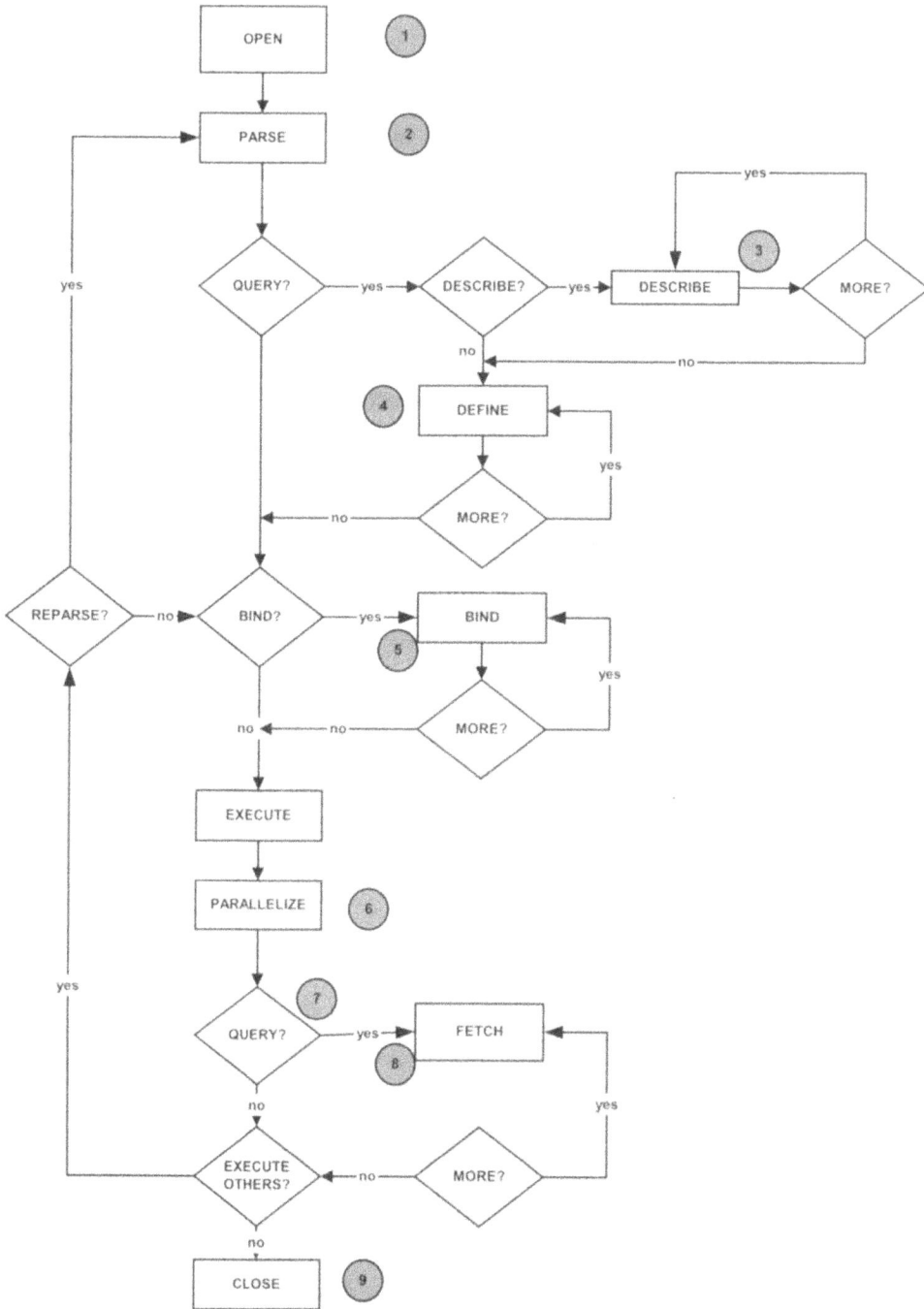

Figure 5.11   *Parse operation flow diagram.*

(not illustrated) is followed, when a PL/SQL procedure and the SQL statements are embedded inside the PL/SQL code. The steps taken by a DML statement, beginning with the point that a query is executed and opened, to the point that it is completed and the results returned, could be broadly grouped into the following nine steps. It should be noted that only the DML statements are required to perform all these steps. DDL statements like create, alter, and drop operations are performed in two steps, namely create and parse.

Step 1: Create a cursor

A cursor can be considered as an association between the data area in a client program and the Oracle server's data structures. When a program is required to process an SQL statement, it is required to open a cursor. The cursor contains a pointer to the current row, and, as the rows get fetched, the pointer moves to the next row until all the rows specified by the condition in the statement have been processed. While the cursor contains the statement, it operates independently of the statement. The cursor is created by a program interface call (OCI) in expectation of an SQL statement. SQL statement processing in general is complex in nature. It has to iterate through various areas of the memory and disk before the results are collected and returned to the user. The various physical components that the SQL statement has to iterate through are:

- Client-side runtime memory
- Server-side runtime memory
- Server-side private SQL area
- Server-side shared SQL area, or the library cache

Step 2: Parse the statement

This is the most complicated and expensive phase of the operation. During this phase the statement is passed from the user's process to Oracle and is loaded into the shared SQL area. Before loading into this area, the following steps have to be completed: the SQL statement is translated and verified, the table and columns checks are performed, and Oracle places a parse lock to prevent definitions from changing. While verifying the definitions, Oracle also checks the user privileges against the referenced objects. Oracle generates the query plan to determine the optimal execution path, followed by loading of the statement into the shared SQL area.

During this phase of operation, Oracle has to determine if the statement being executed is not identical to a previously executed statement. Based on the findings, Oracle will determine whether to use the previous parse information from a previous execution or if the statement has to be parsed before being executed. This is the advantage of the library cache feature. The library cache feature was introduced in Version 7.0 of Oracle, which brought about the concept of sharing SQL statements.

There are two types of parses, soft parse and hard parse. Based on the repeated usage of the statement and Oracle finding the parse information in the library cache, it determines if this is a hard parse or a soft parse.

Hard parse   When a statement is executed for the first time and Oracle is not able to find any information pertaining to this statement in the library cache, Oracle has to do a complete parse operation, which is also referred to as the hard parse. During this initial operation Oracle has to perform these several steps:

■ Syntax checks on the statement

■ Semantic checks on the statement

■ Data dictionary validation for the objects and columns

■ Name translation of the objects (with reference to synonyms)

■ User privileges for the objects referenced in the SQL statement

■ Generation of an execution plan, with the help of the optimizer

■ Loading of the statement into the library cache

Even after all of these steps have been completed and the statement has been loaded into the library cache/shareable area, it actually may not be in a shareable state. This is because Oracle has to place a lock on the cursor/ statement header (cursors created by Oracle have two parts; the cursor header and the cursor body). The lock is placed on the header when the cursor is initially opened, and released when the cursor is closed. Once the cursor is closed, the cursor obtains the shareable state (i.e., other sessions could see this statement in the library cache).

Before storing the statement in the library cache, Oracle computes a hash value and stores it on the hash table. This hash value is compared against a similar query from another user. It should be noted that Oracle, as a first attempt to process an SQL statement, generates a hash value and compares that with the ones in the library cache to determine if any matches exist before the parse operation.

While normally there is only one copy of the header that could be found in the library cache, there could be many copies of the cursor body existing in the library cache. The reason for duplicate cursors, or many cursor bodies for the same cursor header, is due to variations on the SQL statements. Variations in spacing, formatting, non-consistent usage of case, etc., could cause variations, because from Oracle's perspective when it performs a comparison it is going to compare character for character.

After the initial header and body creation, subsequent bodies are created for the same header under the following conditions:

- The threshold of the bind variables changes because the string length of the contents of the bind variable has changed.

- For example, if the books table is initially checked with "Oracle," and the next query checked the books table with "Oracle 9*i* Real Application Clusters New features and Administration," Oracle notices that the length of the bind value has changed and cannot reuse the existing cursor body, therefore it creates another one. The initial space allocation for a bind value is 50 bytes; anything over that requires a new body.

- SQL statements using literals instead of bind variables.

To overcome the difficulties faced by most applications that use literals, Oracle has introduced a new parameter called CURSOR_SHARING = FORCE. This parameter creates bind variables for all literals, thus forcing cursor sharing.

Soft parse   Before parsing the SQL statement, Oracle ensures generation of a hash value and compares the hash value with the statements already in the library cache. To ensure that nothing has changed between the previous execution and now, when the match is found, Oracle may have to do a simpler parse, depending on certain conditions. This parse is a soft parse and could be one of these kinds:

1.   If the user is accessing the SQL statement for the first time and finds it in memory, Oracle has to ensure that the statement is exactly the same as the one that the user has requested and to ensure that the user has authentication to use the objects referenced in the SQL statement.

2.   If the user is accessing the SQL statement for the second time and finds it in the library cache, Oracle still has to validate to ensure that the grants for the objects referenced in the SQL statement have not changed.

The parse operation consumes memory and CPU cycles to complete the query, but reduces the response time considerably.

Step 3: Describe the results

In this step of the process, DESCRIBE provides information about the select list items. This step is more relevant when using dynamic queries using an OCI application.

Step 4: Define query output

While the statement is executed and data is retrieved, appropriate memory variables are required to hold the output information. This step takes care of defining this memory area for the variables.

Step 5: Bind variables

If bind variables are used, Oracle is required to bind them. This gives the Oracle server the address where bind values will be stored in memory. Usage of bind variables is another important factor for efficient usage of memory and the overall performance of the system. Bind variables help in repeated execution of the same statement. Usage of literals (alternative to bind variables) causes statements to be unique and does not allow sharing of SQL statements. The non-shared statements consume memory and cause excessive parse operation.

Step 6: Parallelize the statement

This step is performed only when parallelism is required and configured. When parallelism is chosen, the work of a query is divided among a number of slave processors. If this is required for parsing or if the query is eligible for parallel execution, it is determined during the parse step and the appropriate execution plan has to be defined. The plan is executed during this step of the process.

Step 7: Execute the statement

This step executes the SQL statement and retrieves rows from disk or memory and places the values into the bind variables. This ensures the completion of the statement to produce the desired results.

Step 8: Fetch rows for a query

From the bind variables defined in step 5, the values that are obtained as a result of the statement execution and the placement of values in the bind variables are moved into the output variables of the process. These results are returned in a table format to the calling interface.

Step 9: Close the cursor

Once the data is returned to the calling interface, the cursor is closed.

5.5   Conclusion

In this chapter we looked extensively at the transaction management principles of cache fusion. We looked at the various scenarios or behavioral patterns that are encountered in a normal day-to-day operation in an enterprise in a clustered database configuration. With extensive details including process flows, a step-by-step description of each behavior was given.

In a RAC configuration, as we have discussed, most of the activity is done within the SGA or across the cluster interconnect and a copy maintained within an instance. If one instance required a block that is currently held by another instance, we also looked at how the holding instance would transfer the block to the requesting instance, after making updates to the required GRD on the resource master node.

Under OPS, this was one of the biggest performance nightmares. The transfer of blocks was performed by writing an image or version of the block to disk to allow the requesting instance to read this off the disk. Transferring blocks of information across the interconnect is not cheap, either; when multiple instances are required to transfer large volumes of data, high latency issues could be encountered. This requires the database administrator to tune not only the database servers but also the network cluster interconnect to ensure lower latencies.

We also discussed the internals of transaction management and the steps that take place once a user executes a statement and the results are sent back. These operations are performed via the parse phase of a transaction's life cycle.

In the next chapter we will look at parallel operations, and parallel operations in a clustered database environment. How can database operations be executed in parallel across multiple instances and how does Oracle manage these parallel operations? We will also look into how Oracle decides if the operation should be executed on one node or on multiple nodes.

6

Parallel Processing

6.1   Introduction

In the previous chapter transaction management principles of a single stand alone Oracle configuration were examined. Subsequently, additional steps of a transaction in an RAC environment were also discussed. During these discussions, we examined the normal day-to-day operations, such as when users query the database and when users perform a DML operation.

Almost everyone will have experienced a major traffic jam while driving in one of the major cities on a superhighway. What if these superhighways only had one lane (other lanes are closed due to construction) with every commuter lined up behind another? Clearing traffic jams could potentially take hours. Consequently, superhighways consist of several lanes so that traffic can be distributed over them all. Creating more and more lanes provides for more opportunity for simultaneous or parallel movement of vehicles, thus resulting in a quicker commute time.

The same theory could be applied to the information technology arena. If there were a large number of users making requests to the database simultaneously (or one user making a large request to retrieve a complex set of data) and there was only one CPU to process the request(s), the user(s) would have to wait several hours, or possibly days, for the results. (The length of the wait would be based on the complexity of the query, underlying database design, processing power of the computer, the volume of data being retrieved, etc.). If there were an opportunity for the user(s) to make distributed calls (multiple processors) to the database, the request would complete much more quickly and efficiently. Multiple CPUs on the computer system allow for distribution of requests among the available processors.

The six lanes of traffic movement and processing of data across multiple processors are possible because of the division of work amongst the available resources. This division of work into multiple, or asynchronous processing of a request is called a parallel activity or parallel processing.

In this chapter the concept of parallel processing will be discussed. The advantages and disadvantages of parallel processing, the architecture, implementation and functionality of parallel processing using various options of Oracle will be covered.

Information regarding the basic rules of implementing a parallel processing environment under RAC, how it is configured, what the performance benefits are, and tuning issues around it will also be included.

6.2   What is parallel processing?

Parallel processing is the use of multiple processors to execute different parts of the same program simultaneously.

The main goal of parallel processing is to reduce wall-clock time. Both scenarios discussed in the previous section are examples of parallel processing and both illustrate the goal of distributed processing: the reduction of wait time to solution achievement.

Within the example of the superhighway above, the power and weakness of the parallel approach become visible by taking it to the extreme. In other words, as the number of lanes on the highway is increased, there will be a characteristic *speedup* curve, demonstrating how, up to a certain number of lanes, it is beneficial. However, anything over a certain point probably will give a reduced or negative benefit.

Figure 6.1 represents the increase in the number of lanes to the movement of traffic on a highway. It becomes evident that after a point of six lanes and a speed limit of 70 mph, the curve starts going down, showing a decrease in speed. This is another example of the law of diminishing returns that was discussed earlier in Chapter 1. Too much of something may bring back a lesser satisfaction or benefit. In this case, with the increase in lanes, after a certain point the speed of traffic movement reduces. This is because more vehicles end up crossing lanes, which causes a disruption of fast-moving traffic, either in exiting from the highway or in joining the highway. This back and forth movement of vehicles to cross lanes results in reduced traffic speed. A similar behavior will also be

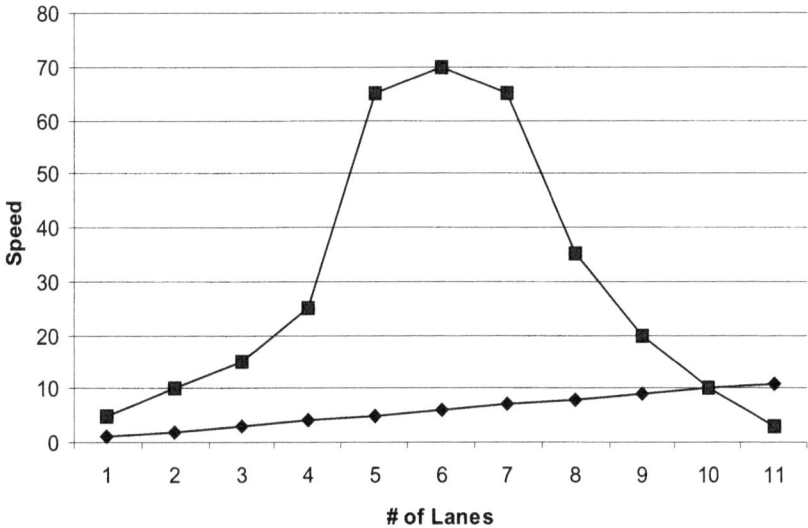

Figure 6.1
Parallel processing example.

noticed in the example related to information technology. Parallel processing is the:

- Division of work into smaller tasks

- Assignment of many smaller tasks into multiple threads to execute simultaneously

- Reduction of wall-clock time for execution of computer programs

6.3   Why parallel processing?

In Chapter 2, the possible degradation of system performance due to an increase in user access was discussed. When this occurs, one solution explored was to increase the processing power of the computer by providing it with additional resources and memory, i.e., vertically scaling the hardware. While this is not ideal in most situations, it does potentially help provide a temporary solution toward supporting the increased number of users.

Another solution was to add additional hardware and scale the number of users in a linear fashion. This would allow for distribution of users across multiple machines, thus providing linear scalability and availability. In this solution, availability would be present because other machines would be available to provide continuous access in the case of failure of one machine.

If we had one large complex process and a computer with a single processor, this would take time to complete depending on many other factors. In this situation, one option is to increase the speed of the existing processor (like increasing the resources on the current hardware) to accept more workload. A given processor is made to specifications, it is made to perform at a certain speed; the same processor could not be increased in speed. However, the processor could be swapped with a higher-speed processor, provided that the hardware that uses it will support this new architecture. This scenario is another flavor of vertical scalability. Instead of replacing the processor with another processor that is of a higher speed, an additional processor is added, providing twice the processing power and aiding in the distribution of work amongst the two processors.

This could be taken even further if you consider three or four processors or multiple computers or nodes each with multiple processors. All these processors and computers or nodes could be put to use simultaneously to perform functions in parallel.

Advantages of moving toward a parallel processing concept include:

- The price of a single CPU grows linearly with speed; however, with parallel processing this linear increase in price cannot be noticed.

- Message-passing parallel computers can be built using off-the-shelf components and processors, thus reducing development time.

- Adding one big processor to do an entire job would be more expensive compared to adding many smaller processors, which provides distribution of workload.

- Running a program in parallel on multiple processors is faster than running the same program on a single processor.

- A system can be scaled or built up gradually. If, over time, a parallel system becomes too small for the tasks needed, additional processors can be added to meet the new requirements.

In Chapter 2, various hardware opportunities that are available to support the parallel concepts, such as clustered SMP, MPP, and clustered NUMA, were examined. These clustered solutions provide linear scalability, help in distribution of workload, and provide availability. Due to the scalability factors built into these hardware architectures, they are all potential platforms for parallel processing.

6.4   **Oracle and parallel processing**

Oracle also supports parallel processing. Oracle's basic architecture (the background and foreground processes) demonstrates a parallel processing architecture if implemented on a hardware that supports multiple processors. While Oracle supports most of the operating systems on most hardware platforms, its architecture may not scale on the smaller platforms that have only one processor but may cause high wait times because one processor has to be shared by the many background and foreground processes.

With platforms that support multiple processors, user requests could be implemented to take advantage of the multiple processors by executing user requests in parallel and returning the results much more quickly. Parallel processing is implemented on either a single stand-alone database configuration or on multi-instance database configurations, such as RAC.

When Oracle executes SQL statements in parallel, multiple processes work together simultaneously to execute a single SQL statement. By dividing the work necessary to execute a statement among multiple processes, Oracle can execute the statement more quickly than if a single process executed it.

Parallel execution dramatically reduces response time for data-intensive operations on large databases such as those typically associated with decision support systems (DSS), data warehouses, certain types of online transaction processing (OLTP), and hybrid systems. Systems that have multiple processors can provide the greatest performance benefits to parallel execution because statement processing can be split up among many CPUs on a single Oracle system.

Parallel execution is useful for many types of operations that access significant amounts of data. Parallel execution improves performance for:

- Queries that are doing a full table scan

- Fast full index scans

- The creation of large indexes

- DML operations doing bulk inserts, updates, and deletes

- Aggregations and copying

- Partitioned index scans

- Database recovery

Parallel execution benefits systems that have the following characteristics:

■ Sufficient I/O bandwidth

■ Underutilization (in the sense that the CPUs are mostly idle)

■ Sufficient memory to handle multiple requests including sorting, hashing, and additional I/O buffers

Basically, parallel processing requires additional resources to accommodate the additional processing requests. Lack of these additional resources to accommodate these requests could potentially cause a negative effect on the system.

There are certain areas of the application where parallel execution will not be beneficial, for example:

■ Applications that have small singleton transactions with a short duration, normally retrieving data from one table.

■ Systems that have fewer resources available to take on this additional load of parallel operation. Basically, systems that are already heavy on CPU usage or are I/O bound are not suitable for parallel executions.

6.5   Parallel query architecture

When a query is executed in parallel, the process that executed the parallel query is called the query coordinator (QC). The QC is a server shadow process of the session running the parallel query. The main function of the QC is to parse the query and partition the work between the slaves. During the parse operation both serial and parallel plans are prepared based on the degree of parallelism defined. The QC then attempts to obtain the number of parallel slaves it wants to run the query. During these attempts, if it is unable to find sufficient slaves, the QC decides to run the query serially. It is the function of the optimizer to use the parallel option only if there are sufficient resources available.

If sufficient resources are available, and the QC is able to get the required number of slaves, the QC sends instructions to the parallel query slaves (PQS). The coordination between the QC and PQS is done by a mechanism of process queues. Process queues are also used for communication between two or more PQS processes and this is handled using queue references.

Queue references are a representation of a link between two process queues. They are always organized in pairs, one for the process at each end of the link. Each queue reference has three message buffers, which are used to communicate between the processes. Every parallel operation is given a unique serial number. All the processes involved as a sanity check on incoming messages use this serial number, as all messages carry this number.

PQS, which is a background process, does most of the work for a parallel query. PQS are allocated in slave sets, which act as either producers or consumers. Determination of number of slave sets to be used is based on the complex nature of the query. For a simple query such as SELECT * FROM PRODUCT, only one slave set may be used, just to scan the table. This set of slaves acts as producers. However, if the query has a more complex nature, such as a multitable join or has a sort or group by operation, then probably more than one slave set would be used, and, in this scenario the slaves act in both the producer and consumer roles. When acting as producers, slaves are making data available to the next step (using the table queues). When acting as consumers, slaves are taking data from a previous table queue and performing operations on it.

Only when there is a need for multiple slave sets (e.g., where statements have ORDER BY or GROUP BY conditions, or statements that have multitable joins) does the consumer come into operation.

This parallelization process is dependent on the current data conditions such as volume, distribution, indexes, etc. Consequently, when data changes, if a more optimal execution plan or parallelization plan becomes available, Oracle will automatically adapt to the new situation.

Passing of data back and forth between the various processes is done using table queues (TQ). TQ is an abstract communication mechanism, which allows child data flow operations to send rows to its parents. Once the QC receives the results back it passes them over to the user that made the original request.

Figure 6.2 represents basic parallel query architecture. The slave set processes (P0 and P1) read data from disk, and, using the queue references and process queues, pass it to the P3 and P2 for sort and merge operation (if the query has GROUP BY or ORDER BY clause). Then it again passes through the queue reference layer to the TQ before returning data back to the QC process. The QC then presents the results back to the client program.

Figure 6.2
*Parallel
processing
architecture.*

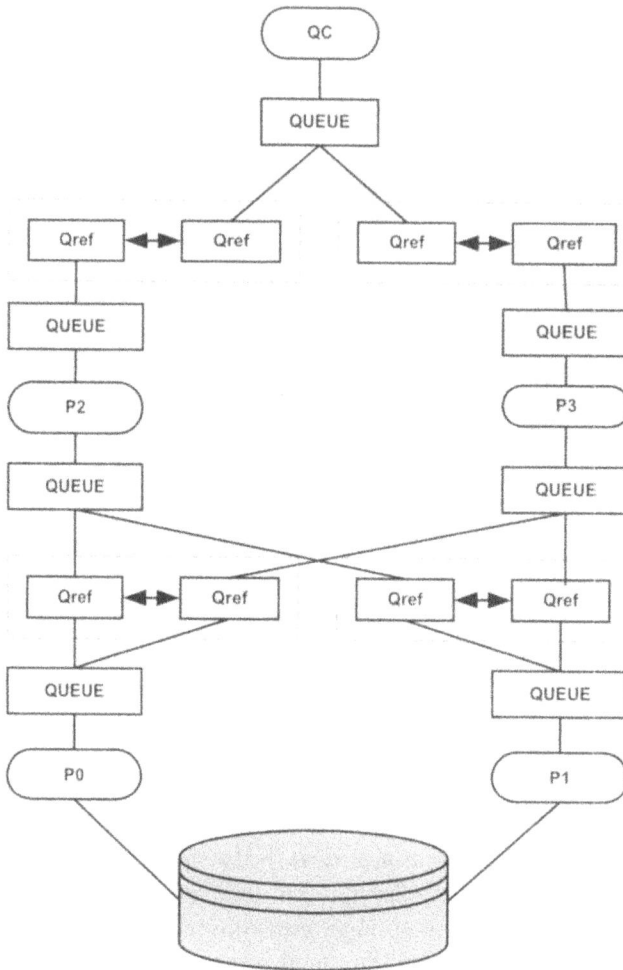

Parallel query slaves bypass the buffer cache and perform a direct I/O to read data from disk. This makes the parallel query operation much faster and also avoids flooding the buffer cache. The data is retrieved directly into the PGA by the PQS process.

Beyond the parallel execution of the statement, in-between processes (e.g., sorting, ordering, joining, etc.) could also be executed in parallel. This kind of operation is called intra-operation parallelism and inter-operation parallelism.

- *Intra-operation parallelism* is the parallelization of an individual operation, where the same operation is performed on smaller sets of rows by parallel execution servers.

- *Inter-operation parallelism* happens when two operations run concurrently on different sets of parallel execution servers with data flowing from one operation into the other.

Let us expand the previous query (SELECT * FROM PRODUCT) with an additional clause of ORDER BY operation.

SELECT * FROM PRODUCT ORDER BY PRODUCT_NAME;

If this query were executed in a regular non-parallel mode, it would perform a full table scan against the PRODUCT table, followed by a sorting of the retrieved rows by PRODUCT_NAME. On the other hand, if the column PRODUCT_NAME does not have an index associated with it and if the degree of parallelism is set to four, i.e., to execute this query in four parallel operations, then each of the two operations (scan and sort) is performed concurrently using its set of parallel execution servers.

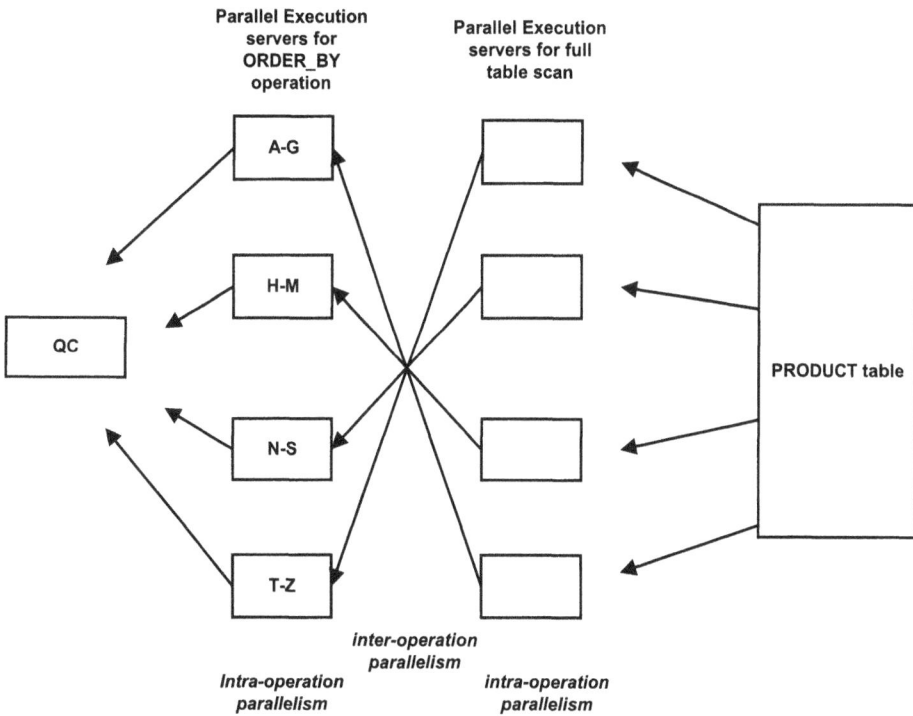

Figure 6.3   *Intra- and inter-operation parallel processing.*

Figure 6.3 represents a pictorial view of the earlier query executed in parallel. The query is parallelized at two stages, the scan phase and the sort phase of the operation, with degree of parallelism of four. However, if you look at the combined execution, it is divided into eight parallel execution servers. This is because it is an inter-operation parallelism where a parent and child operator can be performed at the same time.

It should be noted from Figure 6.3 that the two parallel execution tiers are related to each other in the sense that all the parallel execution servers involved in the scan operation send rows to the appropriate parallel execution server performing the sort operation. For example, if a row scanned by a parallel execution server contains a value of the PRODUCT_NAME column between A and G, that row gets sent to the first ORDER BY parallel execution server. When the scan operation is complete, the sorting processes can return the sorted results to QC, which then returns the complete query results to the user.

6.5.1   Parallel query initialization parameters

PARALLEL_MIN_SERVERS

This parameter specifies the minimum number of parallel execution processes for the instance. The value of 0 indicates that parallel execuion processes will not be created. If a value greater than 0 is defined, then Oracle creates the parallel execution processes at instance startup.

PARALLEL_MAX_SERVERS

This parameter specifies the maximum number of parallel execution processes and parallel recovery processes for an instance. By defining a max value, Oracle will not start too many execution processes. Processes are only added on an as-needed basis.

Careful attention should be given to setting this value. If the value is set too high, this could cause degraded performance, especially when sufficient resources are not available to support this behavior.

However, if this parameter is set to a big number, for example 255, Oracle will limit the effective (real) maximum number of processes, taking into account the number of processors on the machine and the number of threads per processor.

For every process, one chunk of PGA memory is allocated. If a process is loaded in memory during instance startup because the PARALLEL_ MIN_SERVERS initialization parameter was set to a value > zero, the chunk remains allocated until instance shutdown. This chunk of memory allocation is given the attribute of "permanent." Conversely, there are "temporary" processes and "temporary" chunks. For example, if the original values for PARALLEL_MIN_SERVERS and PARALLEL_MAX_SERVERS were set to 10 and 40 respectively, then these values defined in the initialization parameter file would cause the creation of 10 permanent processes and permanent chunks. Now, if the user process requested query parallelism by issuing a command to ALTER this minimum value to 20, this will cause Oracle to dynamically start additional processes to satisfy the user request for parallel execution, namely 10 temporary processes and 10 temporary chunks based on the user request. However, if the user subsequently makes another request to alter the parameter to a value that is greater than the initial definition of PARALLEL_MAX_SERVERS, the command will return an error.

Conversely, if the user sets PARALLEL_MIN_SERVERS to zero (i.e., below the level defined in the parameter file), this change will make all processes and chunks (that are of permanent status) temporary.

PARALLEL_MIN_PERCENT

This parameter is specified in relation to the PARALLEL_MIN_SERVERS and PARALLEL_MAX_SERVERS parameters defined above. This helps specify the minimum percentage of parallel execution processes required for parallel execution. This parameter determines whether the SQL will be executed if all the slaves requested are available.

PARALLEL_ADAPTIVE_MULTI_USER

This parameter enables the adaptive algorithm and, helps improve performance in environments that use parallel executions. The algorithm automatically reduces the requested degree of parallelism based on the system load at query startup time. The effective degree of parallelism is based on the default degree of parallelism, or the degree from the table or hints, divided by a reduction factor.

Having PARALLEL_ADAPTIVE_MULTI_USER set to TRUE causes the degree of parallelism to be calculated as

PARALLEL_THREADS_PER_CPU * CPU_COUNT * (a reduction factor)

The purpose of this parameter is to allow as many users as possible to concurrently run queries in parallel, taking into account the number of CPUs on the machine. As more parallel queries are issued, the number of slaves allocated to each will be reduced, thus preventing parallel queries from being forced to run serially or failing with the error:

`ORA-12827 insufficient parallel query slaves available.`

PARALLEL_AUTOMATIC_TUNING

This parameter determines the default values for the parameters that control parallel execution. When this parameter has been defined, it is required that the table definitions carry the clause `PARALLEL`. This helps Oracle to tune the parallel operations automatically.

When `PARALLEL_AUTOMATIC_TUNING = TRUE`, Oracle attempts to compute a reasonable default for processes which takes into account the additional resources required for parallel execution of SQL statements. The number of parallel processes will be set to the larger of:

1.   What is set in the parameter file (init<SID>.ora), or

2.   The larger of:

`PARALLEL_MAX_SERVERS * 1.2`

or

`PARALLEL_MAX_SERVERS + number of background processes + (CPU_COUNT * 4)`

Under most situations the value from the second formula under option 2 is almost always higher compared to the first formula. The background processes include the number of background processes such as PMON/SMON/LGWR, etc., active in an Oracle instance. The value of this normally would be 11 for a single instance configuration and 15 for a RAC configuration. The additional background processes in a RAC environment are LMS, LMON, LMD, and DIAG. `CPU_COUNT` defaults the actual number of CPUs on the system. When `PARALLEL_ AUTOMATIC_TUNING` is `TRUE`, the `PARALLEL_MAX_SERVERS` is also influenced by the setting of the `PARALLEL_ADAPTIVE_MUTLI_ USER` parameter.

`PARALLEL_MAX_SERVERS = CPU_COUNT*2*5`

`PARALLEL_ADAPTIVE_MULTI_USER` defaults to `TRUE` when `PARALEL_AUTOMATIC_TUNING` is set to `TRUE`.

> **Note:** When setting the `PARALLEL_AUTOMATIC_TUNING` to `TRUE`, caution should be taken in sizing the `LARGE_POOL_SIZE` parameter. If the `LARGE_POOL_SIZE` parameter value is set low, the "`ORA-04031: unable to allocate %s bytes of shared memory`" error.

10g

New Feature: This parameter is deprecated in Oracle Version 10g. Oracle now provides the required defaults for the parallel execution initialization parameters, which are adequate and tuned for most situations.

PARALLEL_THREADS_PER_CPU

This parameter specifies the default degree of parallelism for the instance and determines the parallel adaptive and load-balancing algorithm. It describes the number of parallel execution threads that a CPU can handle during parallel execution.

By setting this value, the parallel execution option is not enabled. This parameter just indicates that such an option is possible. Parallel execution can be enabled by defining the PARALLEL clause at the table level or by adding a PARALLEL hint to the SQL statement.

This parameter is operating-system dependent and the default value of two is adequate in most cases. On systems that are I/O bound, increasing this value could help improve performance.

PARALLEL_EXECUTION_MESSAGE_SIZE

The default value for this parameter is 2148 bytes when PARALLEL_ AUTOMATIC_TUNING is set to FALSE. While the default value of 2148 bytes is sufficient for most applications, increasing this value to 4096 bytes helps in increased performance.

6.5.2 Parallel query using hints

So far we have looked at parallelism in a natural way, not truly natural in the sense of being automatic, but by defining parameters for the entire instance (globally) across all SQL statements. Under this option and based on the statistics collected, the optimizer will determine whether parallel execution would be beneficial.

There is yet another method of using hints to inform the optimizer to behave in a certain way. For example, in the query below, a hint is used requesting a parallel execution:

```
SELECT /*+PARALLEL (PRODUCT 4) ORDERED*/
*
FROM PRODUCT
WHERE PRODUCT_ID =: PRODUCT_ID
GROUP BY PRODUCT
```

The hint /*+PARALLEL (PRODUCT 4) ORDERED*/ tells the optimizer to scan the PRODUCT table using four execution servers and to use a similar parallel approach to ORDER the result set.

There are various kinds of hints that could help the parallel execution behavior such as:

- PARALLEL

- NOPARALLEL

- PQ_DISTRIBUTE

- PARALLEL_INDEX

- NOPARALLEL_INDEX

PARALLEL

The PARALLEL hint specifies the desired number of concurrent servers that can be used for parallel operation. The hint applies to the SELECT, INSERT, UPDATE, and DELETE portions of a statement, as well as to the table scan portion. When using this hint, the number of servers that can be used is twice the value in the PARALLEL hint clause, if sorting or grouping operations also take place.

In queries that join multiple tables and when aliases are used, the hint should use the table alias. The hint can take two values, separated by commas after the table name. The first value specifies the degree of parallelism for the given table and the second value specifies how the table is to be split among the RAC instances. If no value is specified, the default value is used, which is the value specified in the initialization parameter for the degree of parallelism (DOP). It would be beneficial to give an example of a query like this:

```
SELECT /*+PARALLEL (EM 4) ORDERED*/
EMP_ID,
EMP_NAME,
DEPT_NAME
FROM EMPLOYEE_MASTER EM, DEPARTMENT_MASTER DM
WHERE EM.EMP_DEPT_ID = DM.DEPT_ID;
```

NOPARALLEL

The NOPARALLEL hint overrides a PARALLEL specification in the table clause. For example:

```
SELECT /*+ NOPARALLEL PRODUCT */
* FROM PRODUCT
```

PQ_DISTRIBUTE

The PQ_DISTRIBUTE hint improves the performance of parallel join operations. The improvement in performance comes from specifying how rows of joined tables should be distributed among producer and consumer query servers. Using this hint overrides decisions the optimizer would normally make.

6.6   Parallel processing in RAC

With respect to parallel execution, all the features and functions described in the sections above also apply to RAC. Parallel execution in a RAC environment behaves exactly the same way as a parallel execution process on a single instance, with one difference. This difference, which is advantageous to parallel execution, is that portions of the statement can be executed on multiple nodes that are participating as a member in the cluster. The server subdivides the statement into smaller operations that run against a common database residing on a shared disk.

Several CPUs on multiple nodes can each scan part of the table in parallel and aggregate the results. With the cache-fusion-based architecture in RAC, Oracle uses a function shipping strategy to perform work on remote nodes. Oracle's parallel architecture uses function shipping when the target data is located on the remote node. This function shipping technology eliminates unneeded internode data transfers across the cluster interconnect. Participation of multiple nodes in the parallel execution task depends on the volume of work being handled by each of the servers. If the load on the system is minimal, the work will be spread across as many servers as required by the query definition. If the system is fully loaded, then a few local servers will be used to minimize any additional overhead required to coordinate local processes and to avoid any interinstance overhead.

Figure 6.4 illustrates the parallel execution process on a RAC environment. The QC process is on Node 1 because Node 1 is the query initiator. Notice that there are several PQS processes on both Node 1 and Node 2, however there is none on Node 3. There could be several reasons for this behavior. Either Node 3 could be busy and low on resources or the parallel option has not been enabled on the node. However, Node 2 is only partially busy and hence some of the PQS processes are on Node 2.

The number of nodes that can participate in the parallel execution depends on the degree of parallelism (DOP) assigned to each table or index.

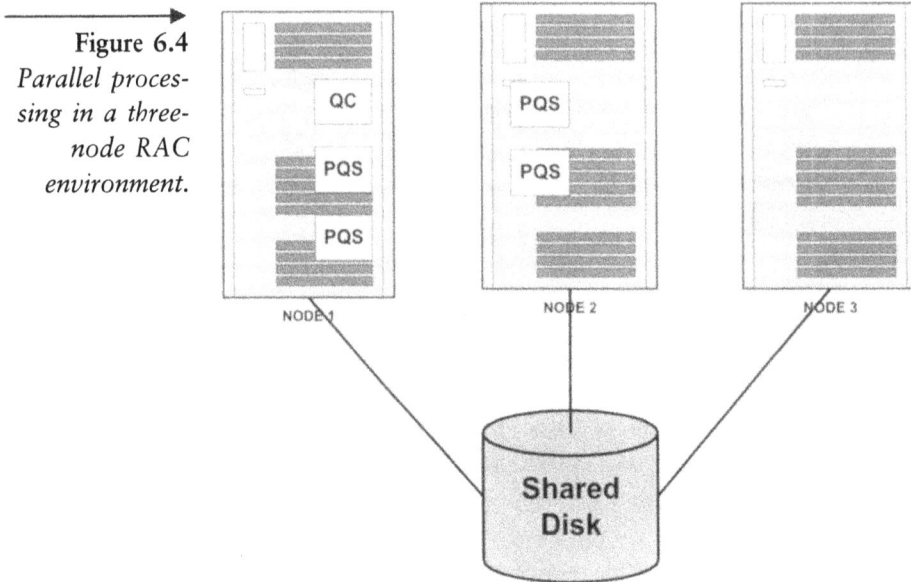

Figure 6.4
*Parallel proces-
sing in a three-
node RAC
environment.*

6.6.1   Degree of parallelism

The parallel execution coordinator may enlist two or more of the instance's parallel execution servers to process an SQL statement. The number of parallel execution servers associated with a single operation is known as the degree of parallelism (DOP).

DOP applies directly to intra-operation parallelism. The total number of parallel execution servers for the statement can be twice the specified DOP. No more than two sets of parallel execution servers can execute simultaneously. Each set of parallel execution servers may process multiple operations. Only two sets of parallel execution servers need to be active to guarantee optimal inter-operation parallelism.

DOP can be applied to the query in several different ways:

- As an attribute of a table or index

- As a hint in a query

- As a default value

- By specifying the DEGREE and INSTANCES parameters

The DOP is calculated as

```
DEGREE * INSTANCES
```

This means that a query on an object with DEGREE set to 1 and INSTANCES set to 5 will run in parallel with five slaves per set. Pre-8*i*, the query would run serially.

Parallel operations could also be performed by grouping or pooling instances together to form a parallel operation cluster. For example if a 12-node cluster is utilized for batch and OLTP processing, certain nodes could be isolated for OLTP purposes and others could be isolated for batch-type operations.

In this case a certain number of instances could be grouped together to form an instance group using the parameter INSTANCE_GROUP. In the example above, if instances RAC6, RAC7, RAC8 are used for batch operations they could be grouped together using the parameter, such as:

- RAC6.INSTANCE_GROUPS = batch
- RAC7.INSTANCE_GROUPS = batch
- RAC8.INSTANCE_GROUPS = batch

During execution, the group name is assigned to the process using the parameter PARALLEL_INSTANCE_GROUP = batch. When the batch process is executed from the instance(s) in which this parameter is defined, it uses the group of instances to execute the operation in parallel.

6.6.2 Parallel DDL

All DDL operations, with the exception of tables with object or LOB columns (datatypes), can use the parallel execution process. Examples of DDL statements are:

- CREATE TABLE AS SELECT
- CREATE INDEX
- ALTER INDEX REBUILD (can be parallelized)
- ALTER TABLE MOVE (or SPLIT in the case of partitioned tables)

The PARALLEL option can be set at table or index level by using the CREATE or ALTER operation as shown below:

```
CREATE TABLE PRODUCT PARALLEL (degree x instances y)
```

where x is the number of slaves to use per instance per slave set and y is the number of instances to be used to parallelize across. Each slave set gets instance x slaves per instance. If the internode parallel query (IPQ) is in use, there will be xy slaves per slave set. If the query being run is complex enough to require producer and consumer slave sets, the actual requirements are $2x$, or, in the IPQ case $2xy$.

The attributes can be checked by querying the data dictionary tables `DBA_TABLES` and `DBA_INDEXES`:

```
COL DEGREE FORMAT A10
COL INSTANCES FORMAT A10
SELECT
     TABLE_NAME,
     DEGREE,
     INSTANCES
FROM DBA_TABLES
WHERE TRIM(DEGREE) != '1';

TABLE_NAME                              DEGREE      INSTANCES
----------------------------            -------     ---------
PRODUCT                                    2            1


SELECT INDEX_NAME,
 DEGREE,
 INSTANCES
FROM DBA_TABLES
WHERE TRIM(DEGREE) != '1';
```

> **Note:** Setting the degree of parallelism for a table or index will force the use of cost-based optimizer (CBO) even in the complete absence of statistics.

6.6.3   Parallel DML

Parallel DML is most often used to speed up DML operations against large objects (e.g., overnight batch updates). The extra statement required to enable PDML is documented (in Oracle documentation) as being too much of an overhead for OLTP transactions. This feature was not intended to be used for small transactions, as the costs involved in calculating how data is to be partitioned amongst parallel execution slaves could actually decrease performance.

All DML (`INSERT`, `UPDATE`, and `DELETE`) operations could use the parallel execution process. Parallel DML uses parallel execution mechanisms to speed up or scale up large DML operations against large database tables and indexes. `INSERT INTO...SELECT FROM` statements that operate against multiple tables as part of single DML operation can also use parallel operations.

Behavior of locks placed on the tables during DML operations is different between serial and parallel DML operations; therefore, it is required that parallel DML be explicitly enabled by issuing the following statement:

```
ALTER SESSION ENABLE PARALLEL DML;
```

Once this statement has been issued, any DML activity against a table with the parallel attribute will occur in parallel if no parallel DML (PDML) restrictions are violated.

This statement must be the first statement of a transaction. If any transaction has not been rolled back or committed before enabling PDML, the following error will be raised:

```
ORA-12841: Cannot alter the session parallel DML state within a trans-
  action
```

Once a PDML statement has been executed, a rollback or commit must be issued before the table can be modified again or queried within the same session. If the transaction is not committed or rolled back, subsequent DML or queries against the table will report:

```
ORA-12838: cannot read/modify an object after modifying it in parallel
```

Each slave process is considered a separate transaction. Therefore, they cannot see any uncommitted data from other transactions, including the other slave processes currently working on the same parent transaction. This is the reason that enabling PDML must be the first statement in a transaction. The coordinator processes (created when connecting to the database) will also create a separate transaction. These processes will not be able to see the data changed by the slave processes until it is committed, hence the ORA-12838 error is raised when trying to view or modify the table.

6.7   Parallel load operations

SQL*Loader is a utility provided by Oracle that helps read data from a flat file and load data based on certain criteria specified in a control file. Oracle provides two methods to load data using SQL*Loader:

- Conventional path method (default)
- Direct path (supports parallel load option)

6.7.1   Conventional path

Conventional path load uses the INSERT statement and a bind array buffer to load data into database tables. All Oracle tools and applications use this method.

When SQL*Loader performs a conventional path load, it competes equally with all other processes for buffer resources. This can slow the load significantly. Extra overhead is added as SQL commands are generated, passed to Oracle, and executed. Oracle looks for partially filled blocks and attempts to fill them on each insert.

6.7.2 Direct path

A direct path load eliminates much of the Oracle database overhead by formatting Oracle data blocks and writing the data blocks directly to the database files. However, while providing us with the benefit of loading data directly and avoiding overhead, this method has a disadvantage in constraint validation. A direct path method disables all database triggers and referential integrity constraints during the load and they must be manually enabled after loads have been completed. Indexes are retained.

Instead of filling a bind array buffer and passing it to Oracle with an SQL INSERT command, a direct path load parses the input data according to the description given in a control file, converts the data for each input field to its corresponding Oracle column data type, and builds a column array structure (an array of <length, data> pairs).

Figure 6.5 illustrates the SQL*Loader architecture, showing the various files that are involved when SQL*Loader loads data into the database. SQL*Loader then uses the column array structure to format Oracle data blocks and to build index keys. The newly formatted database blocks are then written directly to the database (multiple blocks per I/O request using asynchronous writes if the host platform supports asynchronous I/O), bypassing most RDBMS processing. Internally, multiple buffers are used for the formatted blocks. While one buffer is being filled, one or more buffers are being written (if asynchronous I/O is available on the host platform).

The direct path option of SQL*Loader supports loading of data in parallel streams that is based on the definitions in the control file. Data can be loaded into a table, or multiple tables, by reading one or more data files simultaneously in multiple streams. Parallel loads take advantage of the high-speed load option by dramatically reducing the elapsed time needed to perform the load operation. Apart from bypassing all the validation layers of Oracle, direct path loads insert the rows above the high water mark (HWM) of the data file.

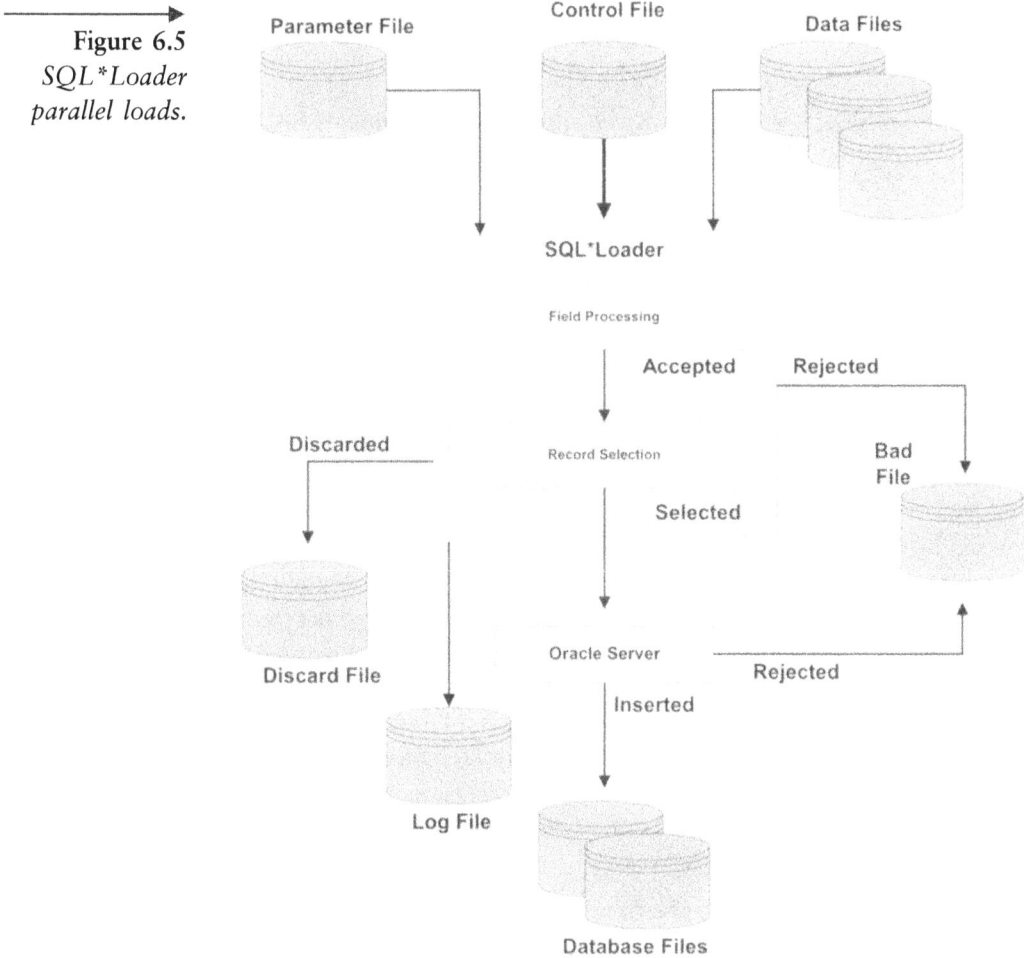

Figure 6.5
*SQL*Loader*
parallel loads.

For example, to load three files simultaneously into the database the DIRECT=TRUE and PARALLEL=TRUE options are enabled:

```
SQLLOAD USERID=MVALLATH/MJGN CONTROL=LOAD1.CTL DIRECT=TRUE
   PARALLEL=TRUE
SQLLOAD USERID=MVALLATH/MJGN CONTROL=LOAD2.CTL DIRECT=TRUE
   PARALLEL=TRUE
SQLLOAD USERID=MVALLATH/MJGN CONTROL=LOAD3.CTL DIRECT=TRUE
   PARALLEL=TRUE
```

Restrictions on parallel direct path loads

The following restrictions are enforced on parallel direct path loads:

- When loading data into a partitioned table, the load can maintain neither local nor global indexes.

- Referential integrity and check constraints must be disabled.

- Triggers must be disabled.

- Rows can only be appended to the already loaded table. When loading data into the same table using the parallel load option, APPEND is the only mode of data loading allowed. REPLACE, TRUNCATE, and INSERT cannot be used (this is because the individual loads are not coordinated). If a table must truncate before a parallel load, it must be done manually.

6.8   Parallel recovery

In the case of a database crash, instance failure, media failure, etc., Oracle performs a recovery operation against the respective files and areas of Oracle. If these files were located on different disks, then using the parallel recovery option would improve performance of these recovery operations. Parallel recovery divides the recovery operation by allocating different processes to different data blocks during the cache recovery phase of recovery. One example of where this could be used is when applying redo information from the redo logs. During recovery, the redo log is read and blocks that require application of redo log information are parsed out. These blocks are subsequently distributed evenly to all recovery processes to be read into the buffer cache. Similarly, crash, instance, and media recovery of data files on different disk drives are good candidates for parallel recovery.

Based on the type of recovery, there are two methods by which parallel recovery is enabled:

3. Setting the RECOVERY_PARALLELISM parameter to the number of concurrent recovery processes for instance or crash recovery could enable parallel recovery. The value of this parameter should be greater than one and should not exceed the value of the PARALLEL_MAX_SERVERS initialization parameter. This parameter only supports recovery of instance or crash recovery.

4. Setting the PARALLEL clause in the RECOVER DATABASE statement. This clause supports media recovery. Parallel media recovery is controlled by the RECOVER_PARALLEL command that selects a degree of parallelism equal to the number of CPUs available on all participating instances times the value of the PARALLEL_ THREADS_PER_CPU initialization parameter. For example, if parallel recovery is performed with PARALLEL 4 and only one

data file needs recovery, then four spawned processes read blocks from the data file and apply records.

Media recovery can also be done against the following:

- Database

- Tablespace

- Data file

For example:

```
RECOVER DATABASE PARALLEL (DEGREE 4 INSTANCES DEFAULT);

RECOVER TABLESPACE <tablespace_name> PARALLEL (DEGREE 4 INSTANCES
   DEFAULT);
```

More details on database recovery will be covered later in Chapter 12 (Backup and Recovery).

6.9   Troubleshooting parallel processing

Some of the basic troubleshooting of the parallel query is explained below.

1. One of the first steps to determine if parallel query is doing any kind of parallel operation is to check the output of an explain plan. If there are no details of parallelism, then parallel query may not be used. The output from the explain plan would indicate if the optimizer has decided on a parallel plan. The PLAN_TABLE in the schema where the explain plan was performed contains a column called OTHER. Checking to determine whether this column contains the SQL generated for use by the slave processes indicates if the parallel query is executing as expected. For example, if this SQL contains hints such as /*+ROWID (PRODUCT)*/, and these hints are clearly not in the original code, then it is likely that PQO is being used. The ROWID hint is one of the internal methodologies used to process PQO queries.

Note: The ROWID hint has a special meaning as it bypasses the buffer cache. In fact, it causes the buffers to be flushed to disk so that direct path I/O can be performed on the base data files.

Oracle provides two scripts to format the query on the PLAN_TABLE, utlxpls.sql and utlxplp.sql. One formats the output for a serial plan and the other can be used to format a parallel plan. Both of these scripts can be found in $ORACLE_HOME/ rdbms/admin directory.

2.   From the session that the query was executed, executing the following statement will, based on the statistics collected, provide an indication of whether or not the parallel query was executed.

```
SELECT * FROM V$PQ_SESSTAT;
```

The output of this query will indicate if the last query that ran under this session was parallelized.

```
STATISTIC                        LAST_QUERY  SESSION_TOTAL
-------------------------------- ----------- -------------
Queries Parallelized                  0            3
DML Parallelized                      0            0
DFO Trees                             0            3
Server Threads                        0            0
Allocation Height                     0            0
Allocation Width                      0            0
Local Msgs Sent                       0          50578
Distr Msgs Sent                       0            0
Local Msgs Recv'd                     0          50570
Distr Msgs Recv'd                     0            0
```

From the above output, the LAST_QUERY column indicates the last query execution statistics and the SESSION_TOTAL column indicates the values that all queries executed in the current session.

The relevant statistics from the above query are:

a.   "Queries Parallelized" indicates the number of SELECT statements that were executed in parallel. In the above scenario a total of three queries were executed in the current session.

b.   "DML Parallelized" indicates the number of DML statements that were executed in parallel. In the current session there were no DML statements executed.

c.   "DFO Trees" indicates the number of times a serial execution plan was converted to a parallel plan. In the above scenario a total of three queries were converted from a serial plan to a parallel plan.

d.   "Server Threads" indicates the number of parallel query slaves used.

e.   "Allocation Height" indicates the degree of parallelism for the instance.

f.   "Allocation Width" indicates the number of instances involved in this operation.

3.   Yet another troubleshooting opportunity is to check the V$ views for slave activity. Executing the following statement several times will indicate if slaves are running:

```
SELECT
    SLAVE_NAME,
    STATUS,
    CPU_SECS_TOTAL
FROM V$PQ_SLAVE;
```

If the query returns no rows, this would indicate that there are no slaves running. If there were no difference in CPU usage between the two runs, this would indicate that there has been no CPU activity for the sampling period.

6.10   Tuning the parallel query

Running queries in parallel, as opposed to running them serially, can have benefits on performance. However when defining parallel queries, the following should be taken into consideration:

- Parallel query has a significant startup cost.

- Multiple slave processes consume more CPU than single processes.

- Each slave process must have its own address space (memory allocation).

Parallel query was designed to reduce execution time for queries that had no option but to read large quantities of data. It maximizes the data throughput by spreading the read workload across multiple processes or slaves. Sort operations are also managed using the slaves' (TQ) structures. This has the effect of increasing the CPU load on the system as a whole. If the system is running at maximum CPU utilization, parallel query will not get any more out of the query. If no more CPU is available, optimizer will, based on the resources available, make the decision to serialize the parallel operations.

The additional I/O requirements of the slave processes reading the data can also stress a heavily loaded I/O subsystem. Distributing data across multiple disk spindles may help alleviate situations where disk I/O may become a bottleneck. Additionally, queries may just run quicker serially. Typically queries that use index lookups are not suited for PQO.

- *Nested loops vs. hash/sort merge joins:* Typically parallel query tries to use full table scan (FTS) to access data, while lookups are divided between slaves on a `ROWID` range basis. Characteristically, nested loop joins are not really efficient with FTS. Hash joins and sort merge options are usually much more efficient at processing large amounts of data. However, there is a downside as hash join and sort merge join do not allow row elimination based on data from a driving row source. This elimination can drastically reduce the data sets involved and can mean that a serial access path using index lookups is quicker than a parallel operation simply due to the volume of data eliminated.

- *Data splitting:* Dividing the data up, passing it through multiple processes and collating the results may make the cost of slave generation greater than retrieving the data serially.

- *Data skew:* Parallel queries divide data between reader slaves on a `ROWID` range basis. Although the same number of blocks is given to each slave it does not mean that these blocks contain identical numbers of rows. In fact, some of the blocks could be completely empty. This can be especially problematic where large quantities of data are archived and deleted as this results in many empty, or sparsely filled, blocks. The effect of this non-uniform data distribution is to cause queries to run slower than they might otherwise. This is because one slave does all the work. Under such situations the only option that is available is to reorganize the data.

6.11   Conclusion

In this chapter the details of parallel processing and the various options and features of parallel execution available under Oracle RDBMS were explored. We demonstrated that parallel processing, with respect to RAC, is not much different from the traditional stand-alone implementation; it is just an extension to the functionality on a single stand-alone instance. The major difference, or advantage, in a RAC environment is that the parallel operation not only can be accomplished on the single instance but also can be processed on the other nodes that participated in the cluster configuration.

Parallel processing in RAC is done not by using the cluster interconnect to transfer information back and forth but rather by using the technology of transferring functional packets across the nodes participating in a cluster.

In the next chapter we will discuss some of the criteria to be considered while designing databases for a RAC implementation. As part of these discussions we will also cover the various features of Oracle that should be considered during the design process to take advantage of the availability and scalability features of RAC.

7

Designing Databases for RAC

7.1   Introduction

In the previous chapter we looked into the concepts of parallel processing, what its benefits are, how this is implemented, and how it is tuned. Parallel processing is not a feature of RAC but a feature that is also available in a single stand-alone configuration of Oracle. However, when used in a RAC environment an additional level of parallelism is obtained when multiple instances are used to process the requests. This helps in the utilization of unused resources because RAC only does parallel processing on single or multiple instances based on the available idle resources.

In Chapter 1 we discussed some of the modern business requirements. Business requirements like availability and scalability are some of the main features that are most often provided by the database vendor through some of their database products. For example, RAC is a feature that is available from Oracle Corporation that provides scalability. With RAC, multiple instances could access a common shared database and as the user base increases additional instances could be added. Similarly, the requirement to provide availability could be implemented using OAR, Oracle Data Guard (ODG), or RAC. Certain business requirements could be implemented directly using certain features of the database technology. Other requirements such as throughput, recoverability, maintainability, manageability, securability, and internationalization also come from a good database design. Database design using a set of features will help obtain these requirements.

Designing a good system is essential, regardless of the software chosen for the layered products including data and application management.

Like in the foundations of a building, if they are not laid out carefully, then there is a potential that the entire building could have a very short life, with potential risk of the building to collapse. So it is of utmost importance that the software foundations follow a good software architecture that is easy to maintain, perform, and scale, and meets the business requirements of the enterprise for the short-term and long-term strategies.

A major step in the software development life cycle is to analyze the requirements, the various functions of the system, and also the system in its entirety. Both the database and application designers approach their common goal from different perspectives. A good analogy is to imagine the application system as a house. The database design is the architectural plan that describes the house; it describes where different rooms are and how many doors or windows each room has. The application design, on the other hand, describes how the house will be used.

From the above analogy of building a house, the database designer must know what rooms the occupants will need and the application designer must make sure that the occupants can get from one room to the next in the manner that they expect.

So careful consideration should be given in designing the house to making it very efficient and this is possible by analyzing all the requirements carefully. Before laying the foundations and designing the house, it is important to start with a clear analysis of the requirements to build a house that is useful and long lasting.

The requirements captured during the analysis phase have to be stored in some form for future use. In earlier days this was done using plane flowcharts and even on paper. Today there are many varieties of tools available to help expedite this in a more concise and precise manner. A few examples are Oracle Designer, ERwin and Systems Architect. Of the modeling tools available, Oracle Designer is a very advanced and robust product. Like most of the Oracle development tools available today, Designer has been kept up-to-date with the enhancements in the Oracle RDBMS arena. All features added to Oracle have found a place in subsequent releases of Oracle Designer.

Figure 7.1 is an introductory screen of Oracle Designer. This snapshot shows all the features available in this product. Entity Relationship Diagrammer, Database Design Transformer, Repository Reports, etc., provide a complete set of features covering the entire design life cycle.

This chapter will focus on designing databases for a RAC environment and as part of these discussions we will look into some of the key features of Oracle RDBMS and their effect in a RAC environment. This includes discussions on partitioning (e.g., application and database partitioning)

Figure 7.1
Oracle Designer Version 6i.

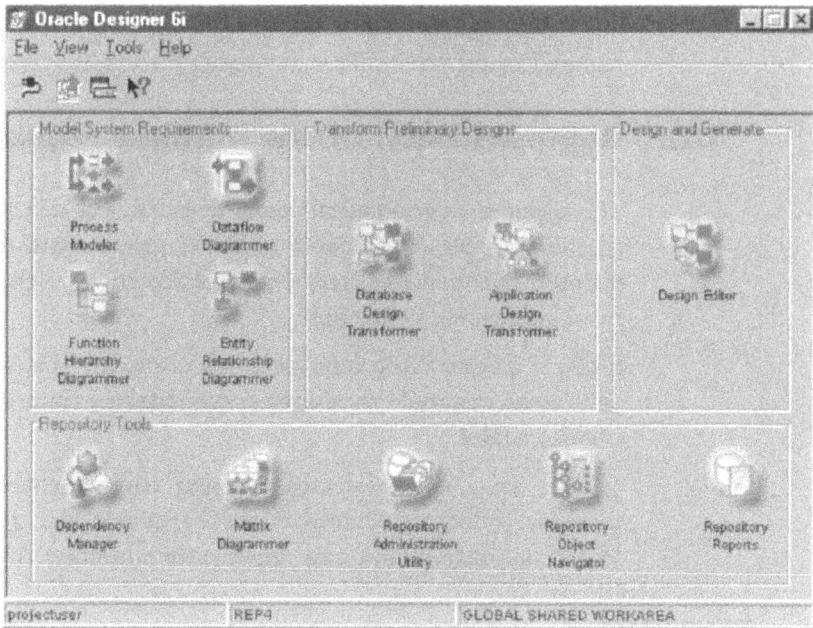

and its benefits and drawbacks, looking at the various data partitioning options available, types of indexes, and the pros and cons of using one type over the other in a RAC environment. These discussions will focus on how designing databases using some of these features will help get a better solution.

7.2   Database design practices

What is a good database design? Some of us may state that if the database follows all the four rules of normalization it is a good design. Others may state that if the database meets the business requirements to store and retrieve data it is a good design. Yet others could also state that the database should be easy to understand, should meet the business rules of the enterprise, and should store and retrieve data efficiently, providing good performance. Meeting the business rules includes scalability and performance.

In fact, all the above capabilities of a database would be desirable and should be the goal of any database design. Yet they are seldom all achieved. Normally, this is due to the fact that most businesses start small and the databases that they designed in the earlier stages do not fit the business model of the enterprise at a later date when the business grows. The database is not able to accommodate the increased growth in users, or the new business rules and new functionality that the application is required to provide while maintaining the current functionality.

7.2.1   Representation of the business requirements

This includes a good logical model that describes the enterprise business in its entirety, providing opportunities for growth with the addition of new features and functions and the implementation of the business rules via relationships and constraints.

Figure 7.2 is an illustration of a logical model. This schema will be used while analyzing and discussing various database features through examples in this chapter.

This stage of the database design covers defining the problem or objective, gathering detailed business requirements, creating a functional, logical or entity model, and implementing business rules and constraints.

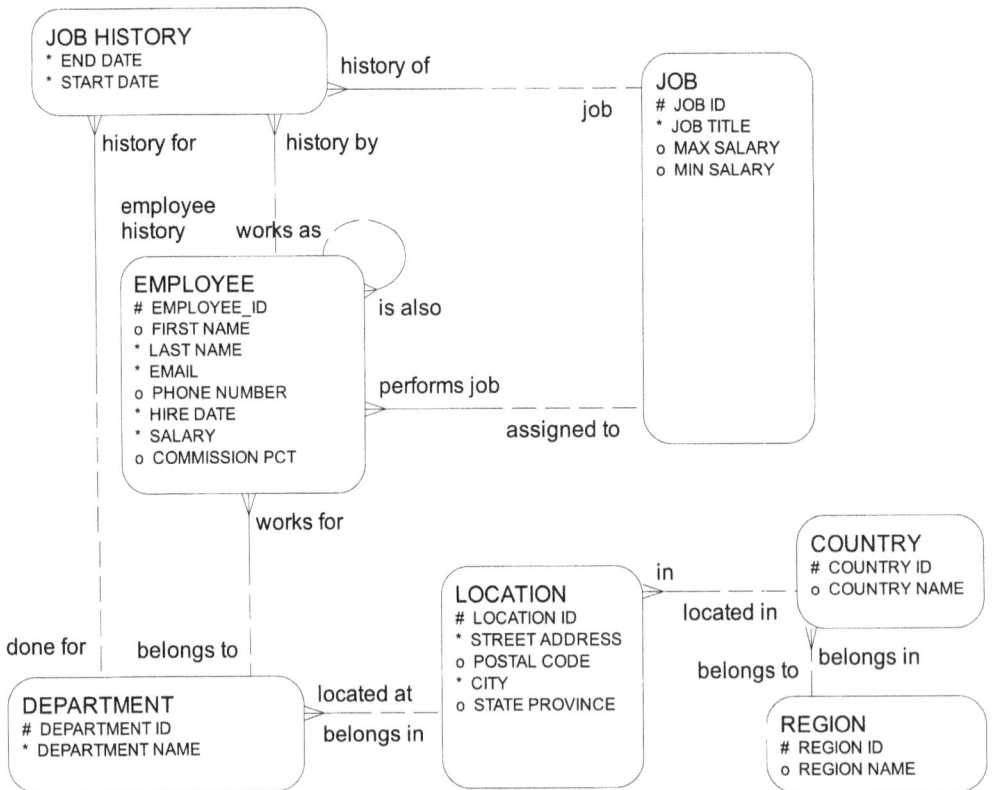

Figure 7.2   *Logical model.*

7.2.2   Representation for the future growth of business

This is the implementation phase of the previous step. That is, once the entity model and the business rules and constraints have been defined, the entity model has to be implemented into a physical form that is usable and which provides throughput, recoverability, securability, maintainability, and manageability of the database system. During this transformation process some design changes to the database model may be implemented to bring efficiency, and may also involve some denormalization. Another method to meet these requirements would be to use some key features of the database product. For example, Oracle provides features such as data partitioning that help maintainability and manageability. Selecting a suitable indexing strategy based on the business model in the previous step would help easy retrieval of data.

Once all the right features of the database have been selected to implement the physical database, another important phase of this step remains, which is the actual implementation itself. During this phase it is important to consider if the database needs to be distributed, if the database needs to be copied over to a different location to meet availability, what level of availability is required, if it is immediate or just to support disaster, and how it will meet scalability. Then there are more details such as the required features of the database (e.g., LMT or dictionary managed), and the various indexing and partitioning strategies that should be considered during the design phase.

7.3   Tablespace management

In Chapter 3 (Oracle Database Concepts) we have discussed the different types of tablespace management, it would be ideal to mention that LMT has considerable performance benefits over the traditional dictionary-managed tablespace (DMT) option. A locally managed tablespace tracks all extent information in the tablespace itself, using bitmaps in each of the data files. This results in increased performance because space allocations and deallocations modify local resources (bitmaps in the header) as opposed to requiring enqueues when the dictionary is updated with this information. Performance is also increased because recursive operations that are sometimes needed during dictionary-managed space allocation are no longer required. Tablespace storage can also be simplified by using an AUTOALLOCATE clause during tablespace creation that causes Oracle to automatically select and manage the extent sizes used in the tablespace with a minimum extent size of 64 KB. As the number of extents increases, the size of subsequent extents will also increase in multiples of 64 KB.

In a RAC implementation the traditional approach (DMT) provides even greater overhead because multiple instances would be inserting data into the same tablespace. If one or more instances encounter a need to add or modify an extent, then it causes considerable contention because the information needs to be written to the data dictionary. On the other hand, LMT maintains a local copy of the information in the data file header and would not require any interinstance updates to the data dictionary.

In versions of the database prior to Oracle 9i, Oracle used data structures called FREELISTS to keep track of blocks within an object, which have enough free space to allow insertion of a new row. The numbers of FREELISTS and FREELIST GROUPS are defined when creating an object. The value of the parameter PCTUSED is used to place a block in and out of the FREELIST.

The new mechanism makes the space management within an object completely transparent by using bitmaps to track the space utilization of each data block allocated to the object. The state of the bitmap indicates how much free space exists in a given data block (i.e., > 75%, between 50 and 75%, between 25 and 50% or <25%) as well as whether it is formatted or not.

LMT eliminates the necessity to tune space-management-related controls (such as FREELISTS, FREELIST GROUPS and PCTUSED) thereby freeing database administrators from manually managing the space within a database object. At the same time, it improves the space utilization, since the database now has a more accurate knowledge of how free a data block is. This enables better reuse of the available free space, especially for objects with rows of highly varying size.

The improvements in performance and management by the automatic segment space management feature are particularly noticeable in a RAC environment. It removes the need to alter the number of FREELISTS and FREELIST GROUPS when new instances are brought online and thereby saves the downtime associated with such table reorganizations.

Using the clause EXTENT MANAGEMENT LOCAL with the tablespace create statement would create an LMT. Oracle also supports creation of uniform extents, meaning that each extent be of the same size.

For example, to create a tablespace for table JOB_HISTORY, the following command will create a locally managed tablespace of size

900 MB with a 2 MB uniform size and with the automatic segment management option:

```
CREATE TABLESPACE JOBHIST_DATA_P001 DATA FILE
  '/dev/vx/oraracdb/partition3G_44' size 2867264K
  EXTENT MANGEMENT LOCAL UNIFORM SIZE 2M
  SEGMENT SPACE MANAGEMENT AUTO;
```

> **Note:** This creates a data file of size 2800 MB plus 64 KB, allowing for the additional size needed to contain the extent management.

When creating tablespaces with a uniform extent size, it is important to understand that Oracle tries to reserve at least 64 KB per data file for the metadata blocks, which includes both file space header as well as bitmap header.

So for a 8 KB block size, there are one space header block and seven bitmap blocks under normal circumstances. Oracle always tries to make sure that there is at least one unit/extent of free space for user data.

In a 100 KB data file, when a tablespace with 50 KB extent size is created, Oracle must leave seven blocks (50 KB rounded to nearest multiple of block size) for the user data. This leaves six blocks for metadata, of which one is used for file header and five for bitmap headers.

In a 100 KB data file, when a tablespace with 10 KB extent size is created, there is enough space to allocate 64 KB for metadata. However, this leaves five unused blocks.

However, since extent sizes are internally rounded up to the nearest multiple of block size, the actual block size is 16 KB, since we need two blocks for each extent. This means that 40 KB of available free space can only accommodate two extents (i.e., four blocks) and only one block is wasted. When creating large database files, add an additional 64 KB to the size of your data file.

Consider the following (bad) example to illustrate the matter:

```
CREATE TABLESPACE USRPRL_DATA_P001 DATA FILE
  '/dev/vx/oraracdb/partition10M_4' size 10M
  EXTENT MANGEMENT LOCAL UNIFORM SIZE 5M;
Statement processed.
```

On executing the following query to determine the amount of free space that is available after the tablespace creation:

```
SELECT BYTES
FROM DBA_FREE_SPACE
```

```
WHERE TABLESPACE_NAME ='USRPRL_DATA_P001'

BYTES

----------

5242880
COL NAME FORMAT A45
SELECT
   DFS.TABLESPACE_NAME,
   DFS.BYTES,
   DFS.BLOCKS,
   DF.NAME
FROM DBA_FREE_SPACE DFS,
   V$DATA FILE DF
WHERE DFS.RELATIVE_FNO = DF.FILE#
```

From the output above, please note that the tablespace USRPL_DATA_P001 was created with 5 MB extents in a 10 MB file. After 64 KB are allocated for the metadata, it is left with one 5 MB extent and one less than 5 MB extent. Because the extents are created of uniform size and the 5 MB that should be remaining are actually less than 5 MB (5 MB–64 KB), it does not get displayed and is wasted.

As noted above, with larger uniform extents when the remainder of space in the data file is just 64 KB short of being able to accommodate an additional uniform extent size the remainder of the space remains unused.

If the same tablespace were created with the following script to allow for the extra 64 KB, there would be a better utilization of the space.

```
CREATE TABLESPACE USRPRL_DATA_P001 DATA FILE
   '/dev/vx/oraracdb/partition10M_4' size 10304K
   EXTENT MANGEMENT LOCAL UNIFORM SIZE 5M;
Statement processed.
```

Note: This creates a data file of size 10,304 KB (10 MB plus 64 KB = 10,304 KB), allowing for the additional size needed to contain the extent management.

On executing the earlier query to determine the space utilization below:

```
SELECT BYTES
FROM DBA_FREE_SPACE
WHERE TABLESPACE_NAME ='USRPRL_DATA_P001'

COL NAME FORMAT A45
SELECT
   DFS.TABLESPACE_NAME,
   DFS.BYTES,
   DFS.BLOCKS,
```

```
   DF.NAME
FROM DBA_FREE_SPACE DFS,
   V$DATA FILE DF
WHERE DFS.RELATIVE_FNO = DF.FILE#
```

When 64 KB were added to the data file size, the full two extents were available (5 MB and 5 MB). LMT should have data files that are 64 KB larger than a multiple of their extent size when using uniform sizing and when the data file size is (Extent Size + 64 KB) or greater.

There is a similar requirement when an additional data file needs to be added to a LMT.

```
ALTER TABLESPACE USPRL_DATA_P001 ADD DATA FILE
   '/dev/vx/rdsk/oraracdg/vertpartition3G_14' size 2867264k
```

7.3.1 Migrating from dictionary managed

Oracle provides the PL/SQL package DBMS_SPACE_ADMIN for additional management of locally managed tablespaces. Almost all of the procedures in the package are used to modify or verify the tablespace bitmaps, in some cases to aid in the recovery process. The DBMS_SPACE_ADMIN package also contains a procedure to migrate a dictionary-managed tablespace to a locally managed tablespace (TABLESPACE_MIGRATE_TO_LOCAL), and a procedure that will migrate a locally managed tablespace to a dictionary-managed tablespace (TABLESPACE_MIGRATE_FROM_LOCAL).

7.4 Selecting the right indexing method

Oracle provides various indexing methods that could be utilized based on the data or column being indexed and the access patterns on the columns. Selecting the right indexing strategy also depends on various factors, type of data being stored, uniqueness of data, cardinality of data, etc.

We have in the previous section looked into indexing options used in a partitioned table, namely local indexes and global indexes. While these are just types of indexes, they could be implemented using various indexing methods, for example, bitmap indexes and B-tree indexes. So the challenge is not in the selection of the type of index, which is easier because it goes one-on-one with the type of implementation (e.g., partitioned indexes) but in the selection of the method used in indexing the tables. The various indexing methods are:

- B-Tree indexes
- Reverse key indexes

- Compressed indexes
- Bitmap indexes
- Bitmap join indexes
- Index organized tables
- Function-based indexes

7.4.1   B-tree indexes

This is the default type of index, i.e., if an index type is not mentioned during the creation of an index, this is the type of index that is created. A B-tree index is a binary tree structure that has branches and leaf nodes. When data is to be retrieved, Oracle will, starting at the root block, step through the branches and leaf blocks to arrive at the correct row that contains the matching data.

A structure of a B-tree index is illustrated in Figure 7.3. From the figure it should be noted that Oracle does not create many tiers of branches and leaf blocks. Initially each index tree has one level. If the data in the table is very small, there may be only one index block. In that case, the leaf block is the same as the branch block. As the data grows, the level increases and then there is a branch block and a leaf block with a parent–child relationship. The maximum number of levels that the B-tree index can grow to is 24 (i.e., 0 to 23), which means that with two rows per index block it can hold approximately 18 billion leaf blocks.

The root block contains data that points to the branch block, which in turn points to the lower level leaf block. The lowest level contains the indexed data values and corresponding ROWIDs required for locating the row.

Figure 7.3
B-tree index.

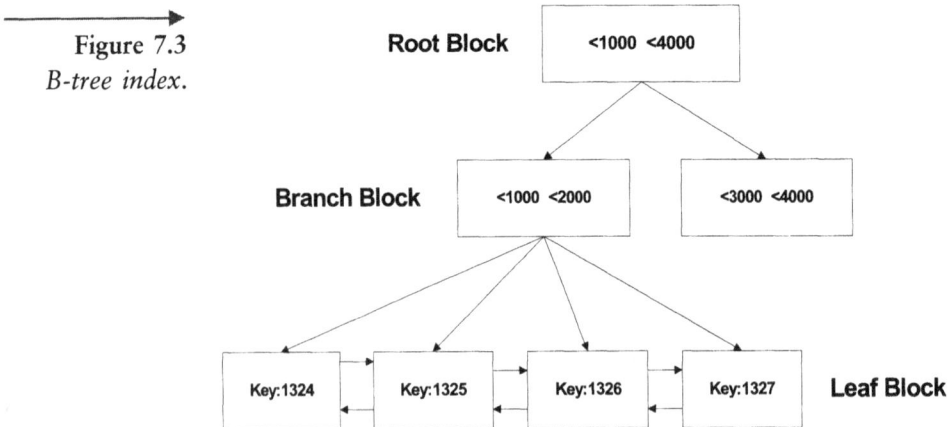

Figure 7.4
*B-tree index leaf
block structure.*

Block Common Header	20 Bytes
Transaction Header	72 Bytes
Index Header	16 Bytes
Index Leaf Header	16 Bytes
Block Size	2 Bytes
Slot Array	2 Bytes
Free Space	
Index Leaf Blocks	
Tail	4 Bytes

Figure 7.4 illustrates the B-tree index leaf block structure. Various index types carry different structures. The B-tree structure has the following advantages:

- All leaf blocks of the tree are at the same depth, so retrieval of any record from anywhere in the index takes approximately the same amount of time. It is important that the index tree does not get very shallow, and hence a tree structure that is more than four levels deep would be inefficient.

- B-tree indexes automatically stay balanced.

- All blocks of the B-tree are three-quarters full on the average.

- B-trees provide excellent retrieval performance for a wide range of queries, including exact match and range searches.

Figure 7.5 illustrates a dissection of the index block. This level of detail is obtained by taking a dump of the index header.

The number of blocks that Oracle has to read before it reaches the actual leaf block is normally low, and depends on the Oracle default block size defined during the database creation.

Note: In the case where a multiblock database is created using Oracle 9*i*, unless specified at the tablespace level, the default block size applies to the number of blocks read by Oracle.

The leaf blocks are created based on the permutation of values that are present during the initial creation of index and subsequent inserts. When

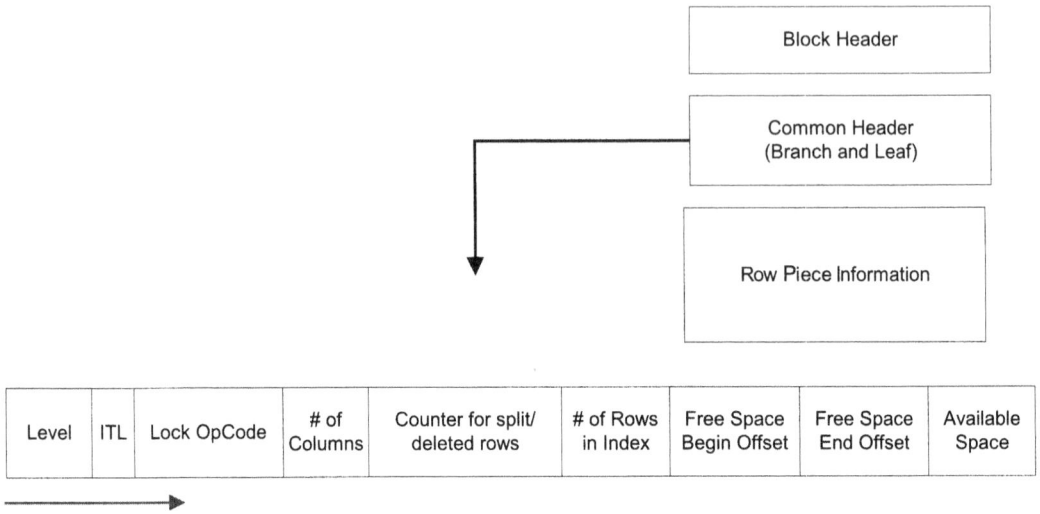

Block Header
Common Header (Branch and Leaf)
Row Piece Information

Level	ITL	Lock OpCode	# of Columns	Counter for split/ deleted rows	# of Rows in Index	Free Space Begin Offset	Free Space End Offset	Available Space

Figure 7.5 *B-tree index block layout.*

a specific index leaf block is filled, another block is allocated by Oracle from the FREELIST (not applicable in the case of locally managed tablespaces). If the index key value falls between the existing keys, Oracle performs an index leaf block split, which means that the upper half of the keys is transferred to the new block while the lower half remains in the old or existing block.

B-tree indexes provide considerable performance benefits where the index key value is unique across the database. Performance degradation of the B-tree index can be noticed when the index key value is non-unique and the number of rows per value gets higher.

B-tree indexes are useful in a RAC environment provided there is no collision of index key values and the inserts into the leaf blocks are not adjacent to each other. If the values being inserted are sequential in nature, which means they are most likely to be inserted into the same leaf block, performance degradation occurs due to frequent index leaf block splits. Under such situations it would be advisable to use the reverse key index option.

7.4.2 Reverse key indexes

A reverse key index reverses the bytes of each column value indexed while keeping the column order. By reversing the keys of the index, the insertions become distributed across all leaf keys in the index. A reverse key index can be used in situations in which the user inserts ascending values and deletes lower values from the table, such as when using sequence-generated (surrogate keys) primary keys.

When using a surrogate key, especially in an insert-intensive application, the lowest level index leaf block will encounter extensive contention. In Figure 7.3 above, the key values 1324, 1325, 1326, etc., are sequentially written in ascending order. This would require a change to the leaf block, and when rows are inserted concurrently it causes block splits to happen more frequently. The end result is a potential performance bottleneck. This overhead is even more significant in the OPS/RAC environment where multiple users insert data from different Oracle instances.

As the word REVERSE implies, the actual key value is reversed before being inserted into the index. For example, if the value of 4567 was reversed its new value would be 7654. We will now see how this works.

When numbers are sequentially generated in ascending order, this has a significant effect in the distribution and scalability for an insert-intensive application. With the reverse option specified with the index creation statement, the potential issues described in Figure 7.3 could be avoided. REVERSE key indexes are created using the following command:

```
CREATE INDEX PK_JBHIST ON JOB_HISTORY (JOBHIST_ID) REVERSE;
```

Figure 7.6
Reverse key index leaf block structure.

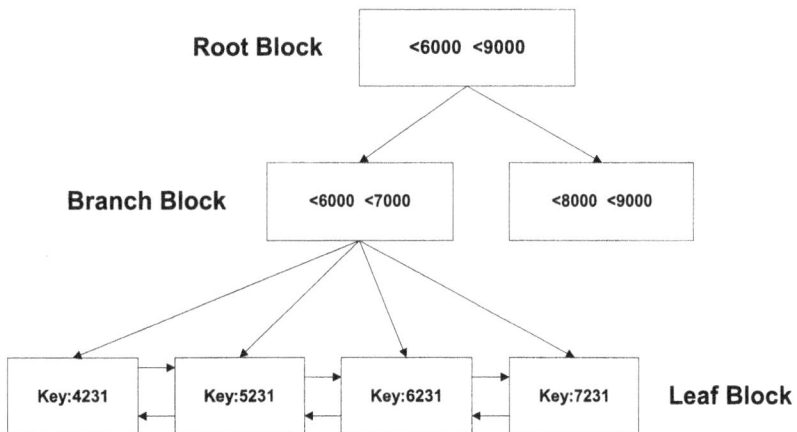

Table 7.1   *Natural and Reverse Key Values*

Natural Key	Reverse Key
1234	4321
1235	5321
1236	6321
1237	7321

Table 7.1 illustrates the corresponding reverse key values to the natural key/surrogate key shown in Figure 7.3.

The following questions become inevitable:

1.   What does this do to accessibility?

2.   Do we have to change code to reflect the reverse structure?

The answer is that there are absolutely *no* effects on accessibility and there is no need to change the code. This is due to the fact that the reverse structure is maintained at the index segment level and is not visible to the application or user.

This is true even when the partitioned options of the database are used, the same rule applies; the index segment is reversed individually rather than the index being reversed and then partitioned. The ROWID is not changed and neither is the column order.

When the REVERSE option is used during index creation, the B-tree index structure at the leaf block level is illustrated in Figure 7.6. (For easy comparison, the example from Figure 7.3 has been used.) Figure 7.6 represents the reverse key structure (the natural key values in this example should be the reverse of what is shown in the leaf blocks.) It is noticeable that the keys are distributed and will help the indexes to scale.

In an OPS/RAC configuration, when an index is based on a column that uses a surrogate key, and two or more instances are inserting data, there is a strong likelihood that both instances will be contending for the same index block. This is because sequential index entries are likely to be in the same block. Reverse key indexes reverse the bytes in each index entry, causing sequential entries to be dispersed and distributed across the index leaf block. This causes reduced contention at the index block. When it comes to performance of insert-intensive applications, the transactions per second (TPS) increase when the reverse option is used on a surrogate key using B-tree indexes, which in turn improves the performance.

In the case of concatenated indexes, the reverse keys feature will also provide similar benefits. This is because the reverse operation is performed individually on each column before they are concatenated. For example, if the model in Figure 7.1 above is implemented and if there exists a concatenated index in the JOB_HISTORY table between the JOBHIST_ID and EMP_ID, the concatenated index when the REVERSE option is implemented would be REVERSE (JOBHIST_ID) | REVERSE (EMP_ID) instead of REVERSE (JOBHIST_ID | EMP_ID).

> **Note:** While this is an excellent choice for OLTP applications where the queries are mostly singleton select and the insert operations are intensive, it is bad for DSS, reporting, and data warehouse applications.

In a DSS or a data warehouse application, queries are not singleton selects but rather retrieval of large numbers of rows requiring a range of data. In Figure 7.6 above, the surrogate keys that have the original values of 1324, 1325, 1325, etc., are in multiple leaf blocks rather than together. When queries make range retrieval, they would have to scan multiple dispersed blocks rather than adjacent blocks. This causes significant performance problems in a DSS or data warehouse application.

When using a reverse key clause, an index block typically references more rows than that contained in each data block for the corresponding table. One major factor for this is the density of the leaf blocks. Unlike a normal B-tree index leaf block, these blocks do not reach 100% density due to the distributed structure.

7.4.3 Compressed indexes

Compressed indexes compress portions of the primary key column values in an index or index-organized table, which reduces the storage overhead of repeated values. Keys in an index comprise two pieces, the grouping piece and a unique piece. If the key is not defined to have a unique piece, Oracle provides one in the form of a row appended to the grouping piece; these pieces are called prefix and suffix, respectively. Oracle provides compression by sharing the prefix among the suffix entries in an index block, while compressing only the leaf level blocks of the B-tree index. In the branch blocks the key suffix can be truncated; however, the key is not compressed.

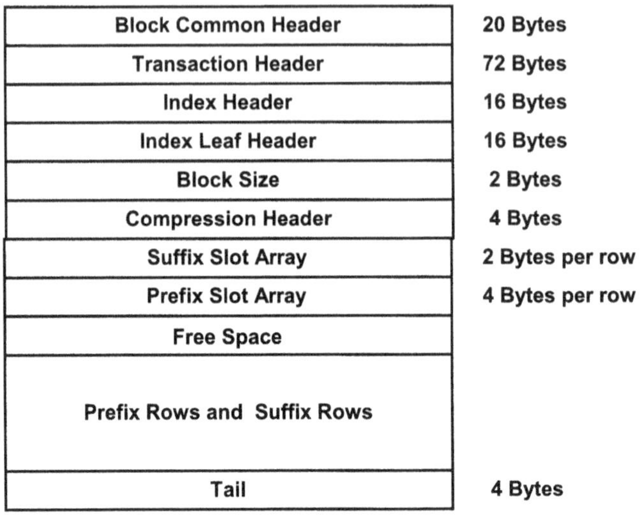

Block Common Header	20 Bytes
Transaction Header	72 Bytes
Index Header	16 Bytes
Index Leaf Header	16 Bytes
Block Size	2 Bytes
Compression Header	4 Bytes
Suffix Slot Array	2 Bytes per row
Prefix Slot Array	4 Bytes per row
Free Space	
Prefix Rows and Suffix Rows	
Tail	4 Bytes

Figure 7.7
B-tree index compressed leaf block structure.

Compressed indexes provide both storage and performance advantages. Compression of the leaf blocks provides a huge saving in space, which allows more keys in each index block, which can lead to less I/O and better performance. However, because the key columns are reconstructed every time during an index scan, there could potentially be additional CPU consumption.

Figure 7.7 represents the index leaf block structure for a compressed B-tree index. Please note that compared to the regular B-tree index, the compressed B-tree index block has more parts and takes more space for the block level information. The structure has additional block level information such as the compression header, and suffix and prefix slots, which are not found in the regular B-tree index.

7.4.4 Bitmap indexes

Bitmap indexes were first introduced in Oracle Version 7.3 and were probably the first type of index outside the traditional B-tree index.

The B-tree indexes are commonly used in an OLTP application where the uniqueness of the key value can be maintained to a great extent. When the uniqueness of the key value changes, or where a value in a column is repeated hundreds or thousands of times, performance of the query to retrieve rows using a B-tree index would be significantly poor. A bitmap index would be ideal in such situations. A bitmap index is typically less than 25% of the size of a regular B-tree index and can be scanned very quickly.

Due to the support for columns with large numbers of duplicate values, a bitmap index is suited for a data warehousing application and is not appropriate for an OLTP application.

The bitmap is compressed before it is stored in the index. If a value in the bitmap changes, then the compressed bitmap must first be uncompressed. After the bits are changed in the bitmap, the bitmap is again compressed for storage in the index. This is another reason why bitmap indexes are suitable in a data warehouse application, because here the data values are seldom modified, and hence such an application does not have this additional overhead.

It should be noted that updates to a table covered by a bitmap index are deferred until the entire DML operation is complete. This means that irrespective of the number of rows being modified, the bitmap will not be updated until the end of the entire operation.

Bitmap indexes are a perfect choice for a data warehouse application implemented on a stand-alone configuration or a RAC implementation.

7.4.5   Bitmap join indexes

A "join index" is an index structure that spans multiple tables and improves the performance of joins of those tables. Bitmap join indexes provide improved performance benefits for a specific class of join queries, namely star queries used in data warehouse schemas.

In the previous section we stated that in a regular bitmap index, each distinct value for the specified column is associated with a bitmap where each bit represents a row in the table. Bitmap join indexes extend this concept such that the index contains the data to support the join query, allowing the query to retrieve the data from the index rather than referencing the join tables.

A bitmap join index uses a compressed storage mechanism to store the join index values, and hence requires less storage space.

Suppose that a data warehouse contains a star schema with a fact table named SALES and a dimension table named PRODUCT, which holds each product brand. A bitmap join index can be created which indexes sales by product brands. Here is the SQL for the index:

```
CREATE BITMAP INDEX PROD_SALES_BJI
ON SALES (PRODUCT.BRAND)
FROM SALES, PRODUCT
WHERE SALES.PRODUCT_ID = PRODUCT.PRODUCT_ID
```

The bitmap join index above could be used to evaluate the following query. In this query, the PRODUCT table will not even be accessed; the query is executed using only the bitmap join index and the sales table.

```
SELECT SUM (SALES.AMOUNT)
FROM SALES, PRODUCT
WHERE SALES.PRODUCT_ID = PRODUCT.PRODUCT_ID
AND PRODUCT.BRAND = 'KELLOGS'
```

If the PRODUCT table is large (and product-based dimension tables can reach tens of millions of records), then the bitmap join index can vastly improve performance by not requiring any access to the PRODUCT table. In addition, bitmap join indexes can eliminate some of the key iteration and bitmap merge work, which is often present in star queries with bitmap indexes on the fact table.

9i New Feature: The bitmap join index is a new type of index introduced in Oracle 9*i*. This feature is specifically useful for data warehouse operations involving star queries.

7.4.6 Index-organized tables

Index-organized tables (IOT) store data in B-tree structures similar to the indexes on a regular table. However, these tables minimize overall storage requirement, because the index and the data are stored together and do not require additional storage for the index structures.

Another major difference between a regular B-tree index and an IOT is that in a regular B-tree, Oracle maps the index to the corresponding row through a ROWID value. IOTs do not have a ROWID.

In an IOT, the B-tree entries at the leaf block level are very large because they consist of both the key and non-key column values. If the index entry gets very large, then the leaf node may end up storing more finite row information, thereby destroying the dense property of the B-tree index.

Figure 7.8 illustrates the leaf block structure of an index-organized table. Please note that while the root and branch blocks are similar to a regular B-tree index, the leaf blocks are different

Applications that could potential benefit from using an IOT are:

- Information retrieval applications

Figure 7.8
IOT leaf block structure.

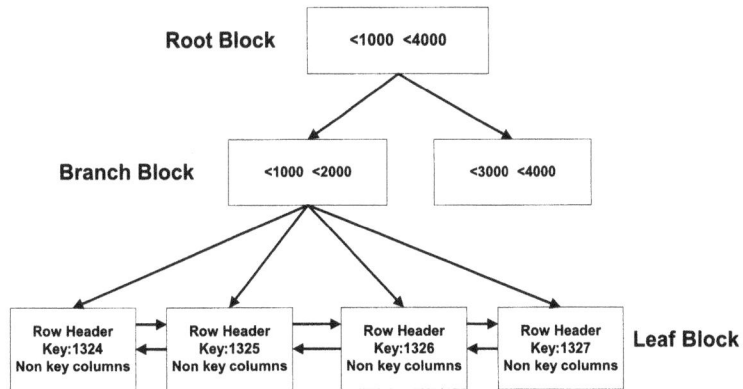

- Spatial applications

- OLAP applications

IOT supports secondary indexes on columns that are neither the primary key nor a prefix of the primary key. These secondary indexes are created using logical row identifiers. Each logical row used in a secondary index is based on the table's primary key and can also include a physical guess, which identifies the block location of the row in the IOT at the time when the secondary index was created or rebuilt.

Logical ROWIDs give the fastest possible access to rows in IOTs by using two methods:

- The physical guess whose access time is equal to that of physical ROWIDs

- Access without the guess (incorrect guess), which performs like a primary key access of the IOT

The guess is based on knowledge of the file and block that a row resides in. If the guess is wrong and the row no longer resides in the specified block, then the remaining portion of the ROWID, the primary key, is used to get the row. Thus if the guess is right, only one block read is required, making performance comparable to that of physical ROWIDs.

7.4.7   Function-based indexes

Most of the time in a query operation, a function or two is used to qualify criteria to retrieve the row. These operations cause full table scans on tables referenced in the query. On large tables such operations cause performance bottlenecks. A function-based index computes the value of the function or expression and stores it in the index. So when a query that contains the function is executed, it directly takes benefit of the stored functional values and makes a quick data retrieval.

Function-based indexes can be created to materialize computational intensive expression in the index, so that the server would not need to compute the value of the expression when processing SELECT and DML statements. For example:

```
CREATE INDEX SALES_MARGIN_INDX
ON SALES (REVENUE-COST);
```

7.5   Hash Clusters

We can create a cluster of instances, which is primarily what RAC is all about. Similarly we can also cluster together data contained in multiple tables using a common field. For example, in a direct-to-home broadcasting industry that uses smartcards as their primary method to determine any transaction. The data in various tables could be clustered together using for example, the smartcard ID column in the various tables. Unlike a regular indexed table, where to retrieve data from these clustered tables requires multiple I/O operations, one to read the clustered index (to determine the key value) and subsequently to read the row from the primary table. If the cluster is a hash cluster, the I/O operations are considerable reduced, because lookup is not based on index values (as in regular indexed or clustered index retrieval) but using hash values. Hash values are generated using hash functions that generate distributed numeric values. Under this option, to find or store a row, Oracle applies the hash function to the row's cluster key value. The resulting hash value corresponds to a data block in the cluster, which is then read or written to on behalf of the issued statement. Unlike the traditional clustered index, Oracle uses the hash function to locate the row in a hash cluster, thus eliminating the extra I/O operation.

A hash cluster is created, by specifying the HASHKEYS clause in the CREATE CLUSTER statement, for example;

```
CREATE CLUSTER smartcard_cluster (smartcard_id NUMBER(18,0))
      PCTUSED 80
      PCTFREE 5
      TABLESPACE smartcard_data_p001
        STORAGE
            (INITIAL 250K
             NEXT 50K
             MINEXTENTS 1
             MAXEXTENTS 3
```

```
           PCTINCREASE 0)
    HASH IS smartcard_id HASKEYS 150;
```

7.5.1   Sorted hash cluster

A sorted hash cluster is where the rows corresponding to each value of the hash function are sorted on a specified set of columns in ascending order. This additional operation could improve performance or response time where repeated operations are required against the clustered data.

Taking the earlier example of the direct-to-home broadcasting industry where viewers can select events on demand using their remote control, in which case a smartcard could have an unlimited number of on demand user selections which are stored as transactions in the database. These events are stored as they happen and are required to be processed in a first-in, first-out order when bills are generated for each customer.

In this situation, using a sorted hash cluster on the timestamp that the event was viewed, a single query on the clustered key would return all rows/event transactions for the customer who owns the smartcard. For example, with the cluster created using

```
CREATE CLUSTER smartcard_cluster (smartcard_id NUMBER(18,0),
                              event_date NUMBER SORT)
      PCTUSED 80
      PCTFREE   5
      TABLESPACE smartcard_data_p001
       STORAGE
           (INITIAL 250K
            NEXT 50K
            MINEXTENTS 1
            MAXEXTENTS 3
            PCTINCREASE 0)
      HASH IS smartcard_id HASKEYS 150;
```

The corresponding clustered table created using

```
CREATE TABLE EVENT_DETAIL
                (smartcard_id    NUMBER(18,0)
                 event_date      NUMBER SORT
                 event_id        NUMBER(18,0))
      CLUSTER smartcard_cluster
            (smartcard_id
             event_date);
```

Given the sorted order of the data, a query on the cluster key would return the event records for the specified hash key (smartcard_id) by the oldest record first.

Since hash keys are created for a given column, they are useful for OLTP applications that use key based retrieval (single-tone selects)

compared to using range scans. This also makes it important that considerable attention should be given during the design phase in selecting the appropriate cluster key.

HASH IS parameter in the CREATE CLUSTER statement should only be used if the cluster key is a single column of datatype NUMBER and contains uniformly distributed integers. If this condition does not apply the HASH IS clause should be omitted.

SIZE parameter is specified to set the average amount of space required to hold all rows for any given hash key. Hence it is important to determine the proper SIZE value based on the characteristics, such as number of rows, length of rows etc. of the data.

10g

New Feature: Sorted hash cluster is a new feature introduced in Oracle version 10g to allow faster retrieval of data for applications where data is consumed in the order in which it was inserted.

7.6   Partitioning

Partitioning helps to divide an object or item into smaller chunks for easy managability and in the case of application or data it helps in easy execution or data retrieval. It works on the principle of "divide and concur." Partitioning could be either an application partitioning or database partitioning. Within the database partitioning, the data could be further partitioned using some built-in features of Oracle.

7.6.1   Application partitioning

Application partitioning is defined as breaking an application into components to improve performance and effectiveness. Application partitioning could be referred to, to compose the various tiers of the enterprise system, but not including the database tier. Thus the application could be partitioned into components such as the business rules tier, web tier, persistence tier, and legacy application tier. Each partition works independently, but requires the existence of the others for their respective tasks. For example, the persistence tier is required to interface with the database when any data needs to be written to or selected from the database. The respective tiers will interface with this persistence tier and the persistence tier will communicate all requests to the database. The

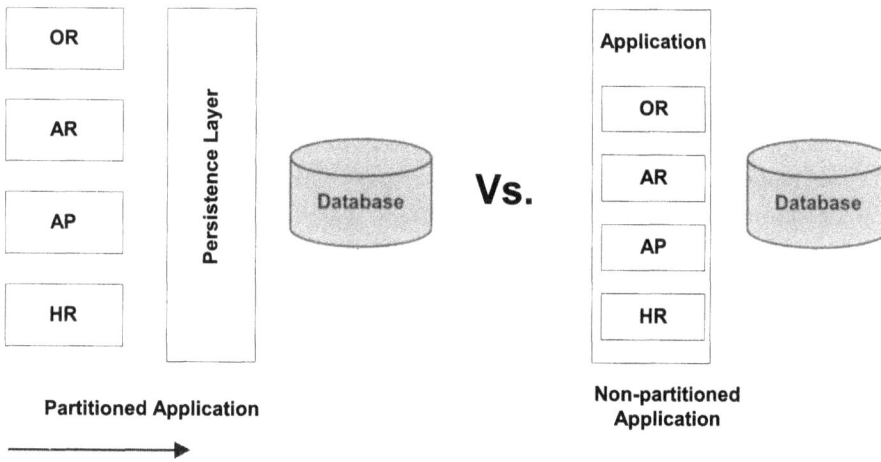

Figure 7.9 *Application partitioning.*

independent behavior of the respective tier allows for easy maintainability because each component could be upgraded or replaced independently.

Figure 7.9 illustrates a comparison using a block diagram of a partitioned and non-partitioned application. Please note that in the partitioned application the persistence layer acts as a common layer to the database. This provides a good amount of isolation of the application from the business logic, and if the database technology needs to be changed, only the persistence layer needs to be modified.

Partitioning helps in distribution of workload amongst various components and provides availability and manageability. Because each component of the application works independently, the resources utilized by each component would be what it actually needs. An example of an application that is partitioned would be an ERP system that could comprise accounts receivable, accounts payable, and payroll components. Each component works independently and communicates when it actually needs to go through some common middle layer.

7.6.2 Database partitioning

Database partitioning could be of the following:

■ Physical partitioning of the database into multiple databases

■ Physical distribution of data within a database into multiple partitions

Physical partitioning of the database into multiple databases takes the same principle as the application partitioning option. For example, there is

a separate database for accounts payable, accounts receivable, payroll, etc.
Each database acts independently. The advantage of this option is that all
transactions are streamlined to a specific database based on need and
usage. When this happens, other databases are idle. This helps distribution
of workload amongst various databases. Another advantage of this
partitioning approach is that databases that are more frequently used
could be provided with additional resources.

The disadvantage of the partitioned database approach is that multiple
databases have to be maintained and supported. Another disadvantage is
that there cannot always be a clean boundary for accessibility between
databases. Sometimes there is common data required by an application that
resides in one or more databases and this adds another level of complexity
because such data have to be stored in a common shareable database.

Figure 7.10 illustrates the database-partitioning scenario. Under this
model each application system could be running one or more functional
areas of the enterprise system. These systems are connected to one of the
instances that operates against a few sets of tables which may be in separate

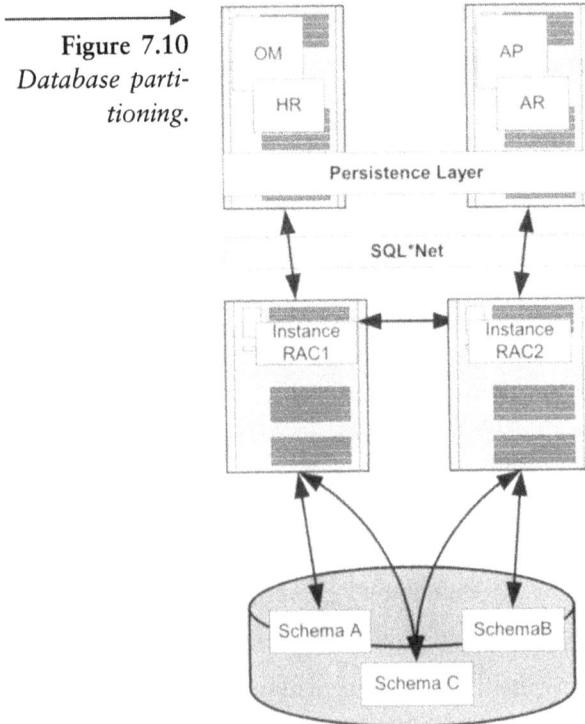

Figure 7.10
*Database parti-
tioning.*

schemas. Also note that access to certain tables by more than one component may be required, and this has to be isolated into a separate schema.

Due to the great amount of pinging activity when data is accessed from multiple instances in an OPS environment, database partitioning provides advantages over common shared single databases. This approach helps reduce pinging because all access to a specific database or schema is done through only one node.

Under the RAC option this feature becomes redundant, because under this new architecture all transfer of data happens via the cluster interconnect and hence there is no pinging activity.

Data partitioning

Physical distribution of data within a database into multiple partitions helps the spreading of data for a table. This addresses a solution to the key problem of supporting very large tables and indexes by allowing users to decompose them into smaller and more manageable pieces called partitions, hence reducing the maintenance windows, workload distribution, recovery times, and impact of failures.

Workload or I/O distribution improves query performance by accessing a subset of partitions, rather than the entire table. Instead of all users' requests being funneled into one file containing all the data, they are now distributed amongst the various data files that contain this data.

Maintainability is achieved because each individual partition can exist independently, which means that if a specific partition needs to be shut down for maintenance or to perform a data restoration from backup, this would be possible. Partitioning also helps concurrent maintenance operations on different partitions on the same table or index.

Manageability is achieved because each partition of a partitioned table or index operates independently, therefore operations on one partition are not affected by the availability of other partitions. If one partition becomes unavailable because of a disk crash or administrative operation, both query and DML operations on data against other partitions are not restricted.

All operations that can be performed on regular tables can also be performed on individual partitions of a partitioned table. For example, administrative activities such as rebuilding of index partitions, and backup and recovery of data partitions, could be done without affecting other partitions.

Note: When using database partitioning the applications have to make specific connections to the respective databases, making these partitions visible to the applications. On the other hand, data partitioning of objects within a database is a physical attribute of a database and such partitioning is transparent to the application.

Partitioning of data could be done in one of several ways. Oracle provides various methods to partition data based on the business requirements, transactions, and actual physical data that are stored.

Partitioning is specified when creating the table by picking a column or set of columns to act as a partitioning key, and this key will determine which data is placed into each partition. Oracle then automatically directs DML operations to the appropriate partition based on the value of the partition key. A partition key:

- Can consist of an ordered list of 1 to 16 columns

- Can contain columns that are `NULLABLE`.

- Cannot contain a `LEVEL`, `ROWID` or a column of type `ROWID`

Note: Partitioning is not part of the default installation; it is an add-on feature that comes bundled with the Enterprise edition of the Oracle database product.

Partitioning is useful for many different types of applications, particularly applications that manage large volumes of data. OLTP systems often benefit from improvements in manageability and availability, while data warehousing systems benefit from performance and manageability.

Oracle provides several partitioning methods:

1.   Range partitioning

2.   Hash partitioning

3.   List partitioning

4.   Composite partitioning

Range partitioning

Data is partitioned based on a range of column values. Each partition is defined by a value list for the partitioning keys, also referred to as the partition bound. A value list defines an open upper bound for the partition, i.e., all rows in that partition have partitioning keys that compare less than the partition bound for that partition. The partition bound for the *n*th partition must compare less than the partition bound for the (*n* + 1)th partition.

The first partition in a range partition is the partition with the lowest bound, and the last partition is the partition with the highest bound. For example, in the script below, the employee table has been partitioned by range on the employee EMPLOYEE_IDs column:

```
CREATE TABLE EMPLOYEE
  (EMPLOYEE_ID     NUMBER(6) NOT NULL
  ,FIRST_NAME      VARCHAR2(20)
  ,LAST_NAME       VARCHAR2(25) NOT NULL
  ,EMAIL           VARCHAR2(25) NOT NULL
  ,PHONE_NUMBER    VARCHAR2(20)
  ,HIRE_DATE       DATE NOT NULL
  ,SALARY          NUMBER(8,2) NOT NULL
  ,COMMISSION_PCT  NUMBER(2,2)
  ,DEPARTMENT_ID   NUMBER(4) NOT NULL
  ,MANAGER_ID      NUMBER(6) NOT NULL
  ,JOB_ID          VARCHAR2(10) NOT NULL
  )
  PARTITION BY RANGE (EMPLOYEE_ID)
  (PARTITION EMP_DATA_P001
   VALUES LESS THAN (300000)
     TABLESPACE EMP_DATA_P001
  , PARTITION EMP_DATA_P002
   VALUES LESS THAN (600000)
     TABLESPACE EMP_DATA_P002
  ,PARTITION EMP_DATA_P003
   VALUES LESS THAN (MAXVALUE)
     TABLESPACE EMP_DATA_P003
)
```

In the illustration above, there are three partitions; all EMPLOYEE_IDs less than 300,000 will go into the first partition and values less than 600,000 will go into the second partition. Since that is all the anticipated immediate requirement, when the enterprise grows beyond this level any values greater than 600,000 will go to the MAXVALUE partition.

Range partitioning can also be done on two or more columns. For example, if the primary key is composed of column *x* and *y*, the range partitioning can be done on *x*, *y*. For example (EMPLOYEE_IDs, DEPARTMENT_ID):

```
CREATE TABLE EMPLOYEE
(EMPLOYEE_ID    NUMBER(6) NOT NULL
,FIRST_NAME     VARCHAR2(20)
,LAST_NAME      VARCHAR2(25) NOT NULL
,EMAIL          VARCHAR2(25) NOT NULL
```

```
,PHONE_NUMBER  VARCHAR2(20)
,HIRE_DATE     DATE NOT NULL
,SALARY        NUMBER(8,2) NOT NULL
,COMMISSION_PCT   NUMBER(2,2)
,DEPARTMENT_ID    NUMBER(4) NOT NULL
,MANAGER_ID       NUMBER(6) NOT NULL
,JOB_ID   VARCHAR2(10) NOT NULL
)
PARTITION BY RANGE (EMPLOYEE_ID, DEPARTMENT_ID)
(PARTITION EMP_DATA_P001
 VALUES LESS THAN (300000,30)
   TABLESPACE EMP_DATA_P001
,PARTITION EMP_DATA_P002
 VALUES LESS THAN (600000,60)
   TABLESPACE EMP_DATA_P002
,PARTITION EMP_DATA_P003
 VALUES LESS THAN (MAXVALUE,MAXVALUE)
   TABLESPACE EMP_DATA_P003
)
```

The above script illustrates the implementation of a range partition when two or more columns are involved in determining the partitioning criteria.

Hash partitioning

Under hash partitioning, records are assigned to partitions using a hash function on values found in columns designated as the partitioning key. The main difference between the range method and hash method is that partitions of tables partitioned using the hash method have no logical meaning to the user. As a consequence, tables partitioned by hash do not support historical data, but will share all the other characteristics of range partitioning. Hash partitioning reduces administrative complexity by providing many of the manageability benefits of partitioning, with minimal configuration effort. The algorithm for mapping rows to tables partitioned by the hash method will aim to provide a reasonably even distribution of rows among partitions and minimize the amount of data movement.

Hash partitioning may be a better choice than range partitioning in certain situations; for example, if it is unknown how much data will map to a given range, or if the size of range partitions may differ substantially.

Due to the way that the partition mapping is implemented, it is recommended to set the number of partitions in the table to a power of 2 (2, 4, 8, 16, and so on) to avoid uneven data distribution.

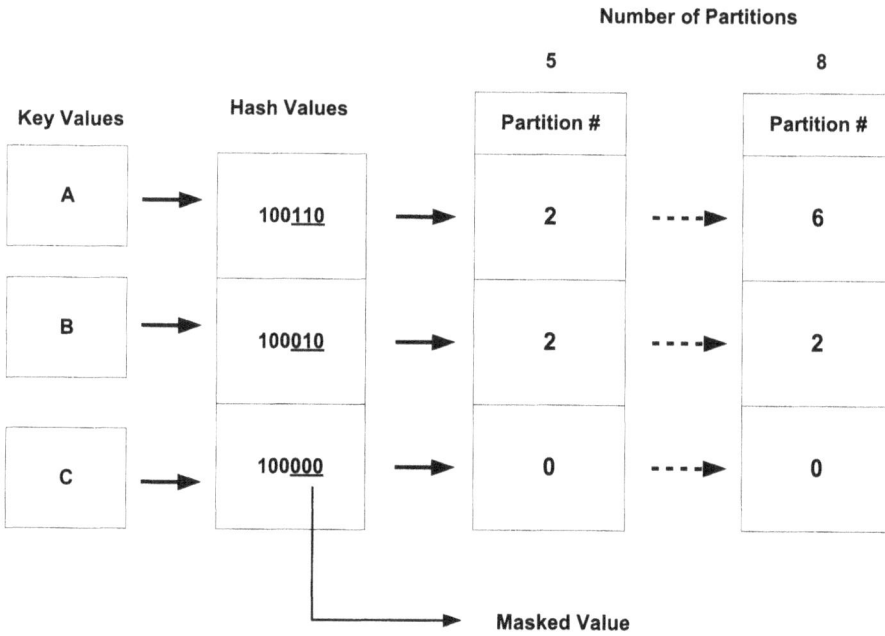

Figure 7.11 *Hash partitioning mapping hash values to partitions.*

Figure 7.11 illustrates how a hash partition value is distributed based on the number of partitions defined. In the figure, if the number of partitions is 5, the values are skewed; however, if the values are to the power of 2, then there is a more even distribution of values amongst the partitions.

The value returned by the hash routine is masked according to the number of partitions in the table. The mask takes the low-order bits necessary to satisfy the number of partitions defined. For example, two partitions will require one bit, four partitions require two, eight partitions require three, and so on. However, as shown in Figure 7.11, if the number of partitions is not a power of 2, data skewing will result because there will be some hash values that do not map to a partition. That is, five partitions will require three bits, but the values 6, 7, and 8 would not correspond to a valid partition number.

Whenever the masked value (110, 010, or 000 in Figure 7.11) is larger than the number of partitions, the low-order bits are used to determine the partition number.

When hash partitions are used, the rows are distributed among partitions in a random fashion. Adjacent rows in a given partition may have no relationship to one another. The only relationship is that their partition key hashes to the same value.

Tables partitioned using the hash method should be used:

- Where partitioning is viewed primarily as a mechanism to improve availability and manageability of large tables

- To avoid data skew between partitions

- To minimize management burden of partitioning

- Where partition pruning and partition-wise joins on a partitioning key is considered important for the database design to provide performance benefits

Partition pruning is limited to equality and in-list predicates under this method.

```
CREATE TABLE DEPARTMENT
  (DEPARTMENT_ID NUMBER(4) NOT NULL
  ,DEPARTMENT_NAME VARCHAR2(30) NOT NULL
  ,LOCATION_ID NUMBER(4) NOT NULL
  )
  PARTITION BY HASH (DEPARTMENT_ID)
  (PARTITION DEPT_DATA_P001 TABLESPACE DEPT_DATA_P001
  ,PARTITION DEPT_DATA_P002 TABLESPACE DEPT_DATA_P002
  ,PARTITION DEPT_DATA_P003 TABLESPACE DEPT_DATA_P003
  ,PARTITION DEPT_DATA_P004 TABLESPACE DEPT_DATA_P004
  )
/
```

The above script illustrates the hash partition. The department table is partitioned on DEPARTMENT_ID and is distributed into four equal partitions. Each partition will map to their respective tablespaces.

If distribution of data into various tablespaces is not a requirement and they could reside in the same tablespace, the following script should also work:

```
CREATE TABLE DEPARTMENT
  (DEPARTMENT_ID NUMBER(4) NOT NULL
  ,DEPARTMENT_NAME VARCHAR2(30) NOT NULL
  ,LOCATION_ID NUMBER(4) NOT NULL
  )
  PARTITION BY HASH (DEPARTMENT_ID) PARTITIONS 16
/
```

The above script will hash partition the department table into 16 different partitions. However, system-generated partition names are assigned to these 16 partitions and the data is stored in the default tablespace of the table.

List partitioning

List partitioning is designed to allow precise control over which data belongs in each partition. For each partition, one can specify a list of possible values for the partitioning key in that partition. In a sense, one can think of this as a user-defined hash-partitioning or range-partitioning scheme.

List partitioning complements the functionality of range partitioning. Range partitioning is useful for segmenting a table along a continuous domain (most often, tables are range partitioned by "time," so that each range partition contains the data for a given range of time values). In contrast, list partitioning is useful for segmenting a table along a discrete domain. Each partition in a list-partitioning scheme corresponds to a list of discrete values. An advantage of list partitioning is that unordered and unrelated sets of data can be grouped and organized in a natural way.

Tables partitioned using list method should be used if:

- The partitioning key consists of discrete data

- The user wants to group together data values that might otherwise be unrelated.

- Partition pruning and partition-wise joins on a partitioning key is considered important for the database design to provide performance benefits

```
CREATE TABLE LOCATION
 (LOCATION_ID     NUMBER(4) NOT NULL
 ,STREET_ADDRESS VARCHAR2(40) NOT NULL
 ,POSTAL_CODE    VARCHAR2(12)
 ,CITY           VARCHAR2(30) NOT NULL
 ,STATE_CODE     VARCHAR2(25)
 ,COUNTRY_ID     VARCHAR2(2) NOT NULL
 )
PARTITION BY LIST (STATE_CODE)
(PARTITION LOC_DATA_P001
 VALUES ('MA','NY','CT','NH','ME','MD','VA','PA','NJ')
 TABLESPACE LOC_DATA_P001
,PARTITION LOC_DATA_P002
 VALUES ('CA,'AZ','NM','OR','WA','UT','NV','CO')
 TABLESPACE LOC_DATA_P002
,PARTITION LOC_DATA_P003
 VALUES ('TX','KY','TN','LA','MS','AR','AL','GA')
 TABLESPACE LOC_DATA_P003
,PARTITION LOC_DATA_P004
 VALUES ('OH','ND','SD','MO','IL','MI','IA')
 TABLESPACE LOC_DATA_P004
,PARTITION LOC_DATA_P005
 VALUES (NULL)
```

```
TABLESPACE LOC_DATA_P005
,PARTITION LOC_DATA_P006
VALUES (DEFAULT)
TABLESPACE LOC_DATA_P006
)
/
```

The above script illustrates the list-partitioning feature. The location table has been list partitioned on the STATE_CODE. Note that there are six partitions in all, with each partition having a list of predefined State codes. Since the State code is not mandatory and could have a null value, a separate partition has been allocated to hold all such rows. Also the last partition, which has been defined as DEFAULT, would contain any State code that has not been listed in partitions 1–4.

Composite partitioning

Composite partitioning is the result of "composing" range and hash or list partitioning. Under composite partitioning, a table is first partitioned using range, called the primary partition, and then each range partition is subpartitioned using the hash or list value. A subpartition of a partition has independent physical entities, which may reside in different tablespaces. Unlike range, list, and hash partitioning, with composite partitioning, subpartitions, rather than partitions, are units of backup, recovery, PDML, space management, etc. This means that a DBA could perform maintenance activities at the subpartition level.

One way of looking at a composite partition would be as a two-dimensional spreadsheet where you can have rows and columns and each row could contain the range values and the columns could contain the hash or list values.

Figure 7.12 illustrates a typical spreadsheet (two-dimensional) view of a composite partitioned table. There is a total of eight range partitions

Figure 7.12
Composite
partition.

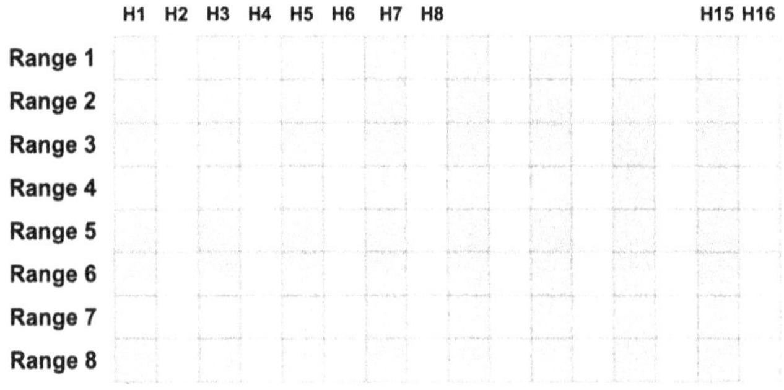

(range 1 through range 8) and each partition is subpartitioned 16 (H1 through H16) ways. Hash partitions should be divisible by 2, hence there are 16 subpartitions.

Hash partitions are implicit in a composite partitioned table. Oracle does not record them in the data dictionary and hence cannot be manipulated using DDL commands. It should be noted that DDL manipulation is permitted on a range partition.

```
CREATE TABLE EMPLOYEE
  (EMPLOYEE_ID      NUMBER(6) NOT NULL
  ,FIRST_NAME       VARCHAR2(20)
  ,LAST_NAME        VARCHAR2(25) NOT NULL
  ,EMAIL            VARCHAR2(25) NOT NULL
  ,PHONE_NUMBER     VARCHAR2(20)
  ,HIRE_DATE        DATE NOT NULL
  ,SALARY           NUMBER(8,2) NOT NULL
  ,COMMISSION_PCT   NUMBER(2,2)
  ,DEPARTMENT_ID    NUMBER(4) NOT NULL
  ,MANAGER_ID       NUMBER(6) NOT NULL
  ,JOB_ID           VARCHAR2(10) NOT NULL
)
PARTITION BY RANGE (DEPARTMENT_ID)
  SUBPARTITION BY HASH (LAST_NAME)
  SUBPARTITION 8 STORE IN
      (EMP_DATA_HSH_P001,
      EMP_DATA_HSH_P002,
      EMP_DATA_HSH_P003,
      EMP_DATA_HSH_P004)
(PARTITION EMP_DATA_RNG_P001
   VALUES LESS THAN (30) TABLESPACE EMP_DATA_RNG_P001
,PARTITION EMP_DATA_RNG_P002
   VALUES LESS THAN (60) TABLESPACE EMP_DATA_RNG_P002
,PARTITION EMP_DATA_RNG_P003
   VALUES LESS THAN (90) TABLESPACE EMP_DATA_RNG_P003
,PARTITION EMP_DATA_RNG_P004
   VALUES LESS THAN (MAXVALUE) TABLESPACE EMP_DATA_RNG_P004
)
/
```

The above script illustrates the composite partitioning feature. In this script the employee table is first range partitioned on the DEPARTMENT_ID column and then hash partitioned on the LAST_NAME column. This produces a 4 by 8 matrix in place of the 8 by 16 matrix illustrated in Figure 7.12.

The records of a composite-partitioned object are assigned to partitions using a range of values found in columns designated as the partitioning key. Rows mapped to a given partition are then assigned to subpartitions of that partition using a subpartitioning method defined for the table.

9i   **New Feature:** A subpartition of the list type is a new feature in Oracle *9i*. Previously in a composite partitioning option, the primary partition used to be range and the subpartition could only be hash partition.

The algorithm used to distribute rows among subpartitions of a partition, subpartitioned by hash or list, is identical to that used to distribute rows between partitions of an object partitioned by the regular hash or list partitions.

```
PROMPT Creating Table 'JOB_HISTORY'
CREATE TABLE JOB_HISTORY
  (JH_ID NUMBER(10,0) NOT NULL
  ,END_DATE DATE NOT NULL
  ,START_DATE DATE NOT NULL
  ,EMPLOYEE_ID NUMBER(6) NOT NULL
  ,JOB_ID VARCHAR2(10) NOT NULL
  ,DEPARTMENT_ID NUMBER(4) NOT NULL
  ,STATE_CODE VARCHAR2(2)
)
PARTITION BY RANGE (START_DATE)
  SUBPARTITION BY LIST (STATE_CODE)
(PARTITION JH_DATA_RNG_P001
  VALUES LESS THAN (TO_DATE('1-APR-2002','DD-MON-YYYY'))
    TABLESPACE JH_DATA_RNG_P001
  (SUBPARTITION JH_DATA_LIST_P001
VALUES ('MA','NY','CT','NH','ME','MD','VA','PA', 'NJ')
    TABLESPACE JH_DATA_LIST_P001
  ,SUBPARTITION JH_DATA_LIST_P002
    VALUES ('CA,'AZ','NM','OR','WA','UT','NV','CO')
    TABLESPACE JH_DATA_LIST_P002
  ,SUBPARTITION JH_DATA_LIST_P003
    VALUES ('TX','KY','TN','LA','MS','AR','AL','GA')
    TABLESPACE JH_DATA_LIST_P003
  ,SUBPARTITION JH_DATA_LIST_P004
    VALUES('OH','ND','SD','MO','IL','MI','IA')
    TABLESPACE JH_DATA_LIST_P004
  ,SUBPARTITION JH_DATA_LIST_P005
    VALUES(NULL)
    TABLESPACE JH_DATA_LIST_P005
  ,SUBPARTITION JH_DATA_LIST_P006
    VALUES(DEFAULT)
    TABLESPACE JH_DATA_LIST_P006)
,PARTITION JH_DATA_RNG_P002
VALUES LESS THAN (TO_DATE('1-JUL-2002','DD-MON-YYYY'))
    TABLESPACE JH_DATA_RNG_P002
  (SUBPARTITION JH_DATA_LIST_P007
VALUES ('MA','NY','CT','NH','ME','MD','VA','PA', 'NJ')
    TABLESPACE JH_DATA_LIST_P006
  ,SUBPARTITION JH_DATA_LIST_P007
    VALUES ('CA,'AZ','NM','OR','WA','UT','NV','CO')
```

```
     TABLESPACE JH_DATA_LIST_P007
 ,SUBPARTITION JH_DATA_LIST_P008
   VALUES ('TX','KY','TN','LA','MS','AR','AL','GA')
     TABLESPACE JH_DATA_LIST_P008
 ,SUBPARTITION JH_DATA_LIST_P009
   VALUES('OH','ND','SD','MO','IL','MI','IA')
     TABLESPACE JH_DATA_LIST_P009
 ,SUBPARTITION JH_DATA_LIST_P010
   VALUES(NULL)
     TABLESPACE JH_DATA_LIST_P010
 ,SUBPARTITION JH_DATA_LIST_P011
   VALUES(DEFAULT)
     TABLESPACE JH_DATA_LIST_P011)
 ,PARTITION JH_DATA_RNG_P003
VALUES LESS THAN (TO_DATE('1-JAN-2003','DD-MON-YYYY'))
     TABLESPACE JH_DATA_RNG_P003
 (SUBPARTITION JH_DATA_LIST_P012
   VALUES ('MA','NY','CT','NH','ME','MD','VA','PA','NJ')
     TABLESPACE JH_DATA_LIST_P012
 ,SUBPARTITION JH_DATA_LIST_P013
   VALUES ('CA,'AZ','NM','OR','WA','UT','NV','CO')
     TABLESPACE JH_DATA_LIST_P013
 ,SUBPARTITION JH_DATA_LIST_P014
   VALUES ('TX','KY','TN','LA','MS','AR','AL','GA')
     TABLESPACE JH_DATA_LIST_P014
 ,SUBPARTITION JH_DATA_LIST_P015
   VALUES ('OH','ND','SD','MO','IL','MI','IA')
     TABLESPACE JH_DATA_LIST_P015
 ,SUBPARTITION JH_DATA_LIST_P016
   VALUES (NULL)
     TABLESPACE JH_DATA_LIST_P016
 ,SUBPARTITION JH_DATA_LIST_P017
   VALUES (DEFAULT)
     TABLESPACE JH_DATA_LIST_P017)
 )
/
```

The above script illustrates a composite partitioning features. In this script the JOB_HISTORY table is first range partitioned on date and then subpartitioned using the list partitioning feature on STATE_CODE.

Objects partitioned using the composite method have logical meaning (defined by their partition bounds) but have no physical presence (since all data mapped into a partition resides in segments of subpartitions associated with it). Subpartitions have no logical meaning beyond the partition to which they belong. As a consequence, objects partitioned using the composite method:

- Support historical data (at partition level)

- Support use of subpartitions as units of parallelism (for PDML), space management, backup, and recovery

- Are subject to partition pruning and partition-wise join on the range, list and hash dimensions
- Support parallel index access

> **Note:** The number of hash partitions or composite partitions, subpartitioned by hash values should be a power of 2 (2, 4, 8, 16, ...).

Partitioned indexes

Data contained in tables can be partitioned, but what about the corresponding indexes? Yes, the index can also be partitioned. Similar to a data partition, index partitioning will help improve manageability, availability, performance, and scalability. Partitioning of indexes can be done in one of two ways, either independent of the data partition, where the index is of a global nature (global indexes) or dependent on the data partition by directly linking to the partitioning method of tables where the indexing is of a local nature (local indexes).

Local indexes

Each partition in a local index is associated exactly with one partition of the table. This enables Oracle to automatically keep the index partitions in sync with the table partitions. Any actions performed by the DBA on one partition, like rebuilding of a partition, reorganization of a partition, etc., only affect that single partition.

Global indexes

Global indexes are opposite to the locally partitioned indexes, in that a global index is associated with more than one partition of the table. The global index by itself could be either partitioned or non-partitioned. In an OLTP environment where a table has multiple indexes to help in query performance, these indexes are normally created as a non-partitioned global index. Under these circumstances, a local index may not provide benefits that a global non-partitioned index would provide, because of the manner in which the rows are distributed.

Global indexes are normally created on columns with duplicate values and these values could be present in any of the underlying data partitions. In these situations a local index would not be feasible because there is no one-to-one mapping between the data partition and the index. When a query needs to determine a row in a global index, it will help identify the row and the corresponding table partition that it belongs in.

7.6.3 Benefits of partitioning

Partitioning provides great benefits to performance in either a single instance environment or a RAC environment. However, compared to a non-partitioned implementation, a partitioned implementation is definitely a better option in a RAC environment. When multiple users access the data from multiple instances, there is no guarantee that users will be accessing data that reside in different partitions; also there is no guarantee that users will be accessing data from the same partitions. However, under situations where users do not access the same data, Oracle will have less lock information to be shared across the cluster interconnect. This is because when users access different partitions, the lock that is placed at the partition is unique to the instance from which the user has accessed the row, hence there is less sharing of lock information across the cluster interconnect.

Apart from the interinstance locking benefits available to a RAC implementation, partitioning provides the following general performance benefits that are common to both a single instance configuration and a parallel instance configuration:

- Partition independence

- Partition pruning

- Partition-wise joins

- Parallel DML

Partition independence

This partitioning feature provides a great amount of flexibility for the DBA. Often, there are maintenance activities like tablespace reorganization, rebuilding of indexes, recovery of data pertaining to a table, etc., that require that the entire database be shut down so that these tasks can be completed. This affects the businesses directly due to interrupted services, and if there is an SLA, this adds to the problem.

With partitioning, only certain partitions need to be shut down for maintenance. This means that only users accessing data from a specific partition will be affected. For example, in an organization that supports many companies (very common in today's Internet-based business), if the data is partitioned based on company, then if a partition is not available only certain companies that belong to that partition are affected. This also allows for scheduled maintenance. The DBA group could inform the appropriate companies of scheduled outages or, if the database only supported one organization and the data was partitioned by region (eastern, western, etc.), outages may be scheduled based on regional activity. This is common in banking applications, where for certain periods of time during the day, customers belonging to a specific region are not allowed access to the data when maintenance is being performed.

Partition pruning

This is one of the most effective and intuitive ways in which partitioning improves performance. Based on the queries optimization plan, it can eliminate one or more unnecessary partitions or subpartitions from the queries execution plan, focusing directly on the partition or subpartition where the data resides.

For example, if the optimizer determines that the selection criteria used for pruning are satisfied by all the rows in the accessed partition or subpartition, it removes those criteria from the predicate list (WHERE clause) during evaluation in order to improve performance. However, there are certain limitations on using certain features; the optimizer cannot prune partitions if the SQL statement applies a function to the partitioning column. Similarly, the optimizer cannot use an index if the SQL statement applies a function to the indexed column, unless it is a function-based index.

Partition pruning occurs when there is an appropriate predicate on the partitioning key of a partitioned table. For range and list partitioning, partition pruning occurs for both equality and inequality predicates. In hash partitioning, partition pruning will occur only for equality predicates.

Note: Partitioning works best with the cost-based optimizer and when the statistics have been collected. This helps Oracle identify and create the best execution plan to get to the right partition that contains the rows.

Partition-wise joins

Another performance benefit of partitioning is partition-wise joins. The performance enhancement is effective for joining tables that are partitioned identically on the join keys (equipartitioned). By recognizing that two tables are equipartitioned, Oracle optimizer will consider new join methods that leverage these partitioning characteristics.

A partition-wise join is a join optimization that you can use when joining two tables that are both partitioned along the join column(s). Partition-wise joins occur when two or more tables and/or indexes are equipartitioned and joined using the partition columns. That is, if the tables and/or indexes have the same partition columns, same number of partitions, and the same range values for range partitions, then the optimizer is able to perform joins partition by partition. By working with smaller sets, the number of rows that need to be joined is smaller, resulting in faster processing.

With partition-wise joins, the join operation is broken into smaller joins that are performed sequentially or in parallel. Another way of looking at partition-wise joins is that they minimize the amount of data exchanged among parallel slaves during the execution of parallel joins by taking into account data distribution.

Figure 7.13 illustrates a comparison with the traditional partition join operation where all the tables of the entire database are joined to complete the operation. However, with the partition-wise join, many smaller partition join operations are performed.

A partition-wise join divides a large join into smaller joins between a pair of partitions from the two joined tables. To use this feature, you must equipartition both tables on their join keys. For example, consider a large

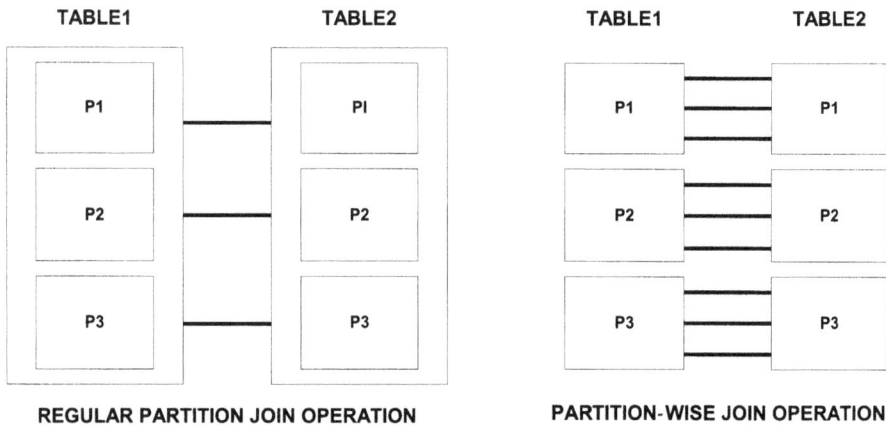

Figure 7.13   *Regular full partition join vs. partition-wise join operation.*

join between a `SALES` table and a `PRODUCT` table on the column `PRODUCT_ID`. The following is an example of this:

```
SELECT
       PRODUCT_NAME,
       COUNT(*)
FROM SALES,
  PRODUCT
WHERE PRODUCT.PRODUCT_ID = SALES.PRODUCT_ID
  AND SALES.SALES_DATE BETWEEN TO_DATE(01-JUN-2002, DD-MON-YYYY) AND
  TO_DATE(01-DEC-2002, DD-MON-YYYY)
GROUP BY PRODUCT.PRODUCT_NAME HAVING COUNT(*) > 1000;
```

This is a very large join typical in data warehousing environments. The entire `PRODUCT` table is joined with one-quarter of the `SALES` data. In large data warehouse applications, it might mean joining millions of rows. The join method to use in that case is obviously a hash join. But you can reduce the processing time for these hash joins even more if both tables are equipartitioned on the `PRODUCT_ID` column. This enables a full partition-wise join.

Partition-wise joins are specifically useful in a RAC environment because they reduce join-processing time and significantly reduce the volume of interconnect traffic amongst the participating instances. Another major benefit in using this feature is that it requires less memory compared to the traditional join operation, where the complete data set of the tables is joined.

Partition-wise joins could be full joins or partial joins. The advantages of partition-wise joins are more visible when used against the composite partitions.

Parallel DML

Parallel execution dramatically reduces response time for data-intensive operations on large databases typically associated with decision support systems (DSS) and data warehouses. In addition to conventional tables, parallel query and PDML can be used with range and hash-partitioned tables. This enhances scalability and performance for batch operations.

7.6.4 Partition maintenance

Like any other DDL operations that are available for maintaining the metadata, partitioning is just another feature and has a similar set of DDL operations that a DBA could apply for regular maintenance on the various partitioning methods.

While we can create a partition, we can also drop, modify, exchange, add, move, and split partitions.

> **Note:** Unless otherwise mentioned, the options below are available for all the partitioning methods.

Split partition

As the name suggests, the SPLIT PARTITION command will split an existing partition into two or more partitions. The current set of data is moved from the existing partition into the new partition based on the partitioning values or ranges. A list or range partition could be split into two or more values:

```
ALTER TABLE <> SPLIT PARTITION <>
  VALUES ( )
INTO (PARTITION <>, PARTITION <>);
```

The EMPLOYEE table used in the previous discussion on range partitions consisted of three partitions:

```
PARTITION BY RANGE (EMPLOYEE_ID)
  (PARTITION EMP_DATA_P001
   VALUES LESS THAN (300000)
     TABLESPACE EMP_DATA_P001
  , PARTITION EMP_DATA_P002
   VALUES LESS THAN (600000)
     TABLESPACE EMP_DATA_P002
  , PARTITION EMP_DATA_P003
   VALUES LESS THAN (MAXVALUE)
     TABLESPACE EMP_DATA_P003
)
```

As the use grows, new employees are added and the MAXVALUE partition becomes so dense that it needs to be repartitioned. Using Oracle's split partitioning feature the MAXVALUE partition could be split into one range partition of 900000 and another continuing to be the new MAXVALUE partition.

```
ALTER TABLE EMPLOYEE SPLIT PARTITION
   PK_EMPLOYEE AT (900000) INTO
( PARTITION EMP_DATE_P003
   VALUES LESS THAN (900000)
     TABLESPACE EMP_DATA_P003
  , PARTITION EMP_DATA_P004
   VALUES LESS THAN (MAXVALUE)
     TABLESPACE EMP_DATA_P004
)
```

Note: After a SPLIT PARTITION has been performed, the underlying
indexes have to be rebuilt to reflect this new partitioning structure.

Merge partition

Again, as the name suggests, the MERGE PARTITION command combines
two or more existing partitions into one. However, only two adjacent
partitions can be combined:

```
ALTER TABLE <> MERGE PARTITION <>.<>,
INTO PARTITION <>;
```

The EMPLOYEE table used in the previous discussion under SPLIT
PARTITION consisted of four partitions (after the split):

```
PARTITION BY RANGE (EMPLOYEE_ID)
  (PARTITION EMP_DATA_P001
   VALUES LESS THAN (300000)
     TABLESPACE EMP_DATA_P001
 , PARTITION EMP_DATA_P002
   VALUES LESS THAN (600000)
     TABLESPACE EMP_DATA_P002
 , PARTITION EMP_DATA_P003
   VALUES LESS THAN (900000)
     TABLESPACE EMP_DATA_P003
 , PARTITION EMP_DATA_P004
   VALUES LESS THAN (MAXVALUE)
     TABLESPACE EMP_DATE_P004
)
```

After a few years when many employees leave and new employees join
the partition, EMP_DATA_P002 may have so few employees that a
separate partition may not required to be maintained. In such
circumstances the EMP_DATA_P002 and EMP_DATA_P003 could be
merged to form one partition.

```
ALTER TABLE EMPLOYEE
MERGE PARTITION EMP_DATA_P002, EMP_DATA_P003
INTO PARTITION EMP_DATA_P003
```

Note: After a MERGE PARTITION has been performed, the underlying
indexes have to be rebuilt to reflect this new partitioning structure.

Drop, truncate, or exchange partition

The DROP PARTITION, TRUNCATE PARTITION, or EXCHANGE
PARTITION command removes an existing partition. When a partition

that is in the middle is dropped, any future data that belongs to the dropped partition will be inserted into the next available partition. When a partition is dropped, the data is also dropped. This operation works exactly the same in all the partitioning methods.

TRUNCATE PARTITION is similar to DROP PARTITION. However, with TRUNCATE PARTITION, all rows are removed from the table partition. If the partition being truncated has a LOCAL index, truncating the table partition will also truncate the corresponding local index partition.

Table definitions could be changed from a non-partitioned to a partitioned structure or from a partitioned to a non-partitioned structure by exchanging their data segments. This feature is useful when migrating from a non-partitioned table structure to a partitioned table structure.

Move partition

The MOVE PARTITION command moves the data from the current partition to another partition. If data in an existing partition is being dropped or truncated, and the data is required, the data could be combined into another partition either using the MERGE PARTITION option or MOVE PARTITION option.

One of the key features of Oracle that would help in meeting the requirements of high volume, high availability, and highly scalable systems is the partitioning option. As discussed, this feature provides a wealth of benefits in performance and distribution of data in a RAC implementation. It would be in the best interest of the enterprise to implement the database with a data-partitioning feature, especially for tables that have a large number of rows.

While data could be distributed into partitions, it must be stored permanently on disk using a storage mechanism. In Chapter 2 (Hardware Concepts) we discussed some of the benefits of the various storage subsystems. There is a layer above the physical storage subsystem and the partition, the tablespace. The tablespace that contains the partition could be managed either using the data dictionary, which is the default, or could be maintained using a bitmap structure at the header using LMT.

7.7   Sequence number

Sequences (numbers) are used in many areas every day; from construction projects, to kitchen projects, to our high-tech computer applications. The construction worker has to follow a sequence when he constructs a house or a building. Similarly, when following a recipe to cook a food item we are required to follow a specific sequence to ensure the food is made the correct way.

In our high-tech computer applications, sequence numbers are used to keep the transactional sequence. They are used in multirow displays for the user interface to show data in a specific order. Additionally they are used for tracking the sequence of events in the case of a billing system or for tracking the sequence of events to be aired by a broadcasting center.

Developers create sequences within their application code to display information on the screen. They are stored as columns in tables or files to keep track of the next value or stored in memory as global variables. Applications that store the values in tables cause significant performance issues in a highly insert-intensive application. This is due to the fact that each time a new number is required the table has to be queried, the number changed and the new value updated. Applications that store these values in global memory variables could lose the values if the system crashed and applications have to determine the next value before starting again. One of the traditional methods of doing this is to scan all the tables to find the maximum values for the key.

Oracle uses sequence numbers inside its architecture in a number of areas; the system change number (SCN) being a prime example. DBAs should recognize the addition of the %S to the archive file names to create log sequence number.

A sequence is a sequential number generator that exists in a database. Some database vendors refer to a sequence as a serial, identity, or auto increment. The Oracle sequence generator reduces serialization where the statements of two transactions must generate sequential numbers at the same time. By avoiding the serialization that results when multiple users wait for each other to generate and use a sequence number, the sequence generator improves transaction throughput and, consequently, a user's wait will be considerably shorter. A sequence is useful for generating transaction-safe numbers for database transactions. The developer/user will have to query the appropriate sequence from the table DUAL. He/she does not have to worry about the additional logic for storing and retrieving of sequence numbers. The command could be simple, as:

```
SELECT JOB_HISTORY_SEQ.NEXTVAL FROM DUAL.
```

In today's database design and development, we can take advantage of this feature by using it as surrogate keys in place of primary keys.

Consider the example in Figure 7.2, the JOB HISTORY entity, which is based on a relationship between the JOB, EMPLOYEE and DEPARTMENT. Creating and maintaining the primary key (for uniqueness) due to the relationship is complicated and consumes a large resource. This complication could be even more significant in the case of a very large table with millions of rows. Most of the time all the columns that are part of the primary key are not used for query lookups.

7.8   Features for data warehouse design

When discussing data warehouse design, immediately the words "star or snowflake schema" should pop up in our minds. That is correct; data warehouses are popular because of this star/snowflake type of schema. The start schema provides a great mechanism to abstract data, based on business functions. While most of the databases today are moving towards a hybrid type of solution, there are others that continue to differentiate between pure OLTP and data warehouse type solutions.

We have discussed some of the database features suitable for an OLTP database or a hybrid database (OLTP or DSS). We also mentioned certain features that would be ideal if implemented in a data warehouse environment; for example, the bitmap index or a bitmap join index.

Another excellent feature added by Oracle in Version 8*i* that benefits a data warehouse implementation is the materialized view option.

7.8.1   Materialized view

Materialized views are different from standard views. A standard view is a database implementation of a query stored permanently as a database object. At runtime, when data is selected from this view, the query is executed and data is returned to the process that executed the query. Data returned by these views is volatile in nature, because once the required row is queried the data in the view is lost and another process that requires the same set of data will requery the view and the data; the underlying query is executed and data is returned again.

In Oracle 8*i*, a feature was introduced where the data in the view, once queried, could be saved on disk like any other database table. Subsequently, when data changes in the underlying tables, the query is refreshed, which automatically refreshes the data. This is called a *materialized view.* From a storage perspective the materialized view behaves exactly like a table. However, data is not directly inserted into it; data is collected and stored from other tables. Oracle treats the materialized view just as it would an Oracle snapshot. The periodic updates to this snapshot are made based on a predefined schedule. Updates are accomplished by way of a refresh interval, which can range from instantaneous rebuilding of the materialized view to a hot refresh that occurs at a predefined interval.

The major advantage of this feature is that all the data is not queried every single time the view is invoked, like in the case of a standard view. In a materialized view the data that is queried during the materialized view creation is saved to disk in a permanent form and any changes to the data set is done through a refresh process, where only the changes are made and no rebuild or requery of the entire collection is required. Like most features, materialized views are not without any restrictions. The major restriction that currently affects many database designers building complex views is the restriction on the usage of subqueries.

However, to overcome this limitation, the workaround would be to use the multitier materialized view option. Under this feature a materialized view is based on other materialized views for their content. That is, a single materialized view will provide the contents of a subquery operation and many such materialized views will be consolidated into one big master materialized view.

Like any other database object, DDL operations are permitted against a materialized view. That is, a materialized view can be created, dropped, altered, etc.

For example, the following statement creates and populates a materialized view MY_SALES_MV. The materialized view will be populated with data as soon as the statement executes successfully and subsequent refreshes will be accomplished by executing the materialized view's query again.

```
CREATE MATERALIZED VIEW my_sales_mv
  TABLESPACE sales_mv_data_p001
    PARALLEL (10)
      ENABLE QUERY REWRITE
        BUILD IMMEDIATE
    REFRESH COMPLETE AS
    SELECT
        TIM.MONTH,
        GEO.STATE,
        SUM(SALES) AS SUM_SALES
```

```
FROM FACT FCT,
    TIME TIM,
    GEOG GEO
WHERE FCT.CUR_DATE=TIM.CUR_DATE
AND FCT.CITY_ID=GEO.CITY_ID
GROUP BY MONTH,
    STATE
```

Cost-based optimizer can use materialized views to improve performance by automatically recognizing when a materialized view can and should be used to satisfy a request. The optimizer transparently rewrites the original query at runtime, to use the materialized view.

Refresh process

A materialized view is a transactionally consistent reflection of its master, as the data exist at a specific point in time. To keep materialized views' data relatively current with the data of its master, the materialized view must be refreshed periodically. They can be refreshed automatically whenever the data is changed in the underlying tables. The refresh method can be incremental (fast refresh) or complete. If data does not change very frequently or if the updates to the underlying tables happen in a controlled environment, the refresh operation could be done manually.

There are many types of refresh options, including:

- *Complete refresh:* Under this option, the materialized view definitions query is executed, which essentially recreates the materialized view. To refresh the materialized view, the result set of the query replaces the existing materialized view data. A complete refresh can take substantially longer to perform than a fast refresh. Once a complete refresh of a materialized view is performed, then the subsequent refresh should also be a complete refresh; if another type of refresh option is used, then the following error message is reported:

```
ORA-12034 mview log is younger than last refresh.
```

- *Fast refresh:* Under this refresh option, the changes that occurred in the master since the most recent refresh of the materialized view are identified and then changes are applied to the materialized view.

- *Force refresh:* To perform a force refresh of a materialized view, the server that manages the materialized view attempts to perform a fast refresh. If a fast refresh is not possible, then Oracle performs a complete refresh.

The refresh options can be invoked either by scheduling a process to happen periodically or can be on-demand where a manual intervention will cause refresh of materialized view groups to immediately propagate the new rows of the master table to associated materialized views.

The on-demand refresh can be done using the following command:

```
EXECUTE DBMS_REFRESH.REFRESH('mview name');
```

Query rewrite

Oracle optimizer automatically recognizes when an existing materialized view can be used to satisfy a request. Once determined, the optimizer transparently rewrites the request to use the materialized view. Queries are then directed to the materialized view and not to the underlying detail tables, resulting in a significant performance gain.

To enable query rewrite the following should be set in the init.ora file or spfile:

```
QUERY_REWRITE_ENABLE=TRUE
```

Since most of the refresh activity in a materialized view happens transparently to the DBA or the users, it uses the job queues to accomplish its activity. Hence it is required to ensure that sufficient job queues are available. Job queues are defined by setting the following parameter in the init.ora or the spfile:

```
JOB_QUEUE_PROCESSES=3
```

Materialized views in RAC environment

Materialized views provide a good amount of benefit in a RAC implementation. When multiple instances have to perform complex queries against multiple tables to retrieve data, there is considerable GCS resource movement between instances. This activity is considerably reduced when materialized views are used in a RAC implementation because only a single object that has preselected rows is queried instead of joining quite a few underlying tables at runtime.

7.9   Conclusion

In this chapter, we looked into the various features available in Oracle RDBMS that should be taken advantage of when designing database systems. We also analyzed the behavior of these features with respect to a RAC implementation.

The chapter started with the introduction of a methodology that should be followed for application development, including logical and physical modeling. Then we looked at some of the best deployment or configuration options that should be considered, like application partitioning and database partitioning, and then at data partitioning. Under data partitioning we looked at the various partitioning options that Oracle provides, like range, hash, composite, and list.

Data is inserted into the database to be retrieved, analyzed, and processed into reports, which are then viewed by users. To retrieve rows efficiently the data needs to be indexed so that retrieval is quick. Various index options were analyzed and their pros and cons compared, and we also discussed the best places where the various types of indexes could be most favorably used.

Then we looked at the feature that would help in making data warehouse applications more efficient, materialized views. A materialized view is a summary table that contains data from a set of underlying tables, which would normally have been retrieved by writing queries against these tables and through complex join operations. The materialized views will store data in a form that would be helpful for easy retrieval.

In the next chapter, let us install Oracle, with the RAC and partitioning options. We will also look at the configuration of a clustered database and some important administrative functions.

8

Installation and Configuration

8.1   Introduction

In the previous chapter we looked at some of the key features that should be considered while designing databases for Oracle, and specifically about designing databases for a clustered solution using RAC. We looked at the various key features that are available within Oracle. These key features help the enterprise in meeting the various business requirements like availability, scalability, and manageability. For example, features such as partitioning provide spreading out of the data instead of concentrating the entire data for a given table into one data file. Partitioning helps in spreading I/O among the various data files which otherwise would have caused users to queue one behind the other to get access to the single data file. These queues cause waits on the disk while retrieving data and thus cause performance bottlenecks. Spreading data across many spindles would noticeably reduce these performance bottlenecks.

We also looked at the various indexing features that Oracle provides. Selecting the right indexing strategy is important to achieve the ideal performance while retrieving data from the database. However, selection of this strategy depends on various factors, such as, is the data retrieved using finite criteria like in an OLTP system or is it retrieved based on a set of range values like in a DSS system?

Finally, we also looked into a key new feature introduced in Oracle 8*i* that helps in the overall performance and scalability of a data warehouse application. The materialized views are a boon in disguise that helps develop complex join operations into more meaningful denormalized structures for easy data retrieval. Updates to the materialized views happen in smaller chunks as data is loaded into the base tables and when the view is refreshed. At runtime it is only this view that the user will have to access to retrieve the data.

What good is a design that is not implemented on a well-configured platform even though it is done with utmost care and has selected the correct features? The underlying database platform should be installed, configured, and managed well to help harvest the potential of a good database design.

Careful planning of the installation, configuration, and administration of the underlying database helps to achieve the overall goal of the business application, basically efficient use and performance. It does not matter how well the system has been laid out, structured, designed, and developed; if the system is not installed, configured, and managed efficiently, achieving the desired result could be far from reality.

In this chapter we will look into the steps taken for installing, configuring, and managing the RAC environment. The first step to the installation process is to follow a standard that will provide a consistent way to define disks and directory structures. One such standard developed and recommended by Oracle is the Optimal Flexible Architecture (OFA). This architecture or standard is widely followed among most customers using the Oracle RDBMS product.

8.2   Optimal Flexible Architecture (OFA)

OFA is a standard configuration recommended by Oracle Corporation for its customers to promote a standard disk configuration or directory structure, for a consistent way of managing disks and directories. Almost any relevant books, including documentation available from Oracle Corporation, will have topics of discussion on the OFA standards. While many companies have not used OFA to configure their directory structure, it is a good practice to follow some form of standard for consistency among the various installations within the organization. This helps in the transfer of knowledge when new associates are hired, and helps in operating under some standard principles.

Implementing the OFA standard is not a requirement for installing and configuring Oracle but rather a general guideline or standard for efficient configuration.

While OFA was originally written and recommended by Oracle for the Unix platforms, many companies have applied and written similar standards for the Windows platform.

Figure 8.1 explains the basic high-level hierarchical view of the directory structures and layouts as defined under the OFA standards.

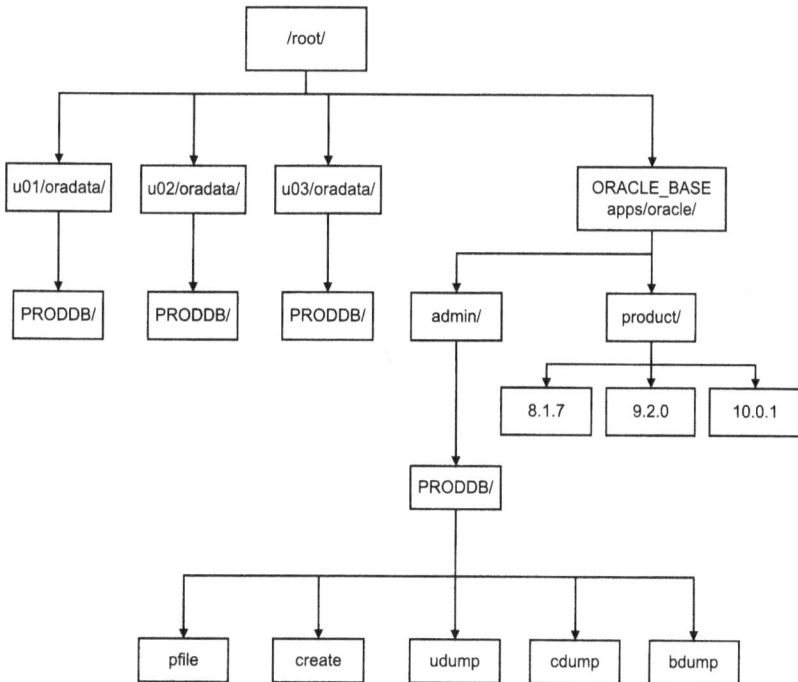

Figure 8.1
Optimal Flexible Architecture (OFA).

This is exactly what the OFA standard is all about, basically a directory structure to keep the files across all installations of Oracle in an enterprise in a consistent manner. From the root level there are *n* levels, based on the disk configuration. OFA recommends 9-, 12-, 18-, or 24-partition disk configuration.

To help explain the structure easily, only four levels have been shown in the diagram, ORACLE_BASE/app/admin and the U01 through U04../oradata structures.

The ORACLE_BASE directory structure and its subdirectories are the main product and database configuration directories. Under the app directory are product and admin directories. The product and admin directories are further split into more subdirectories. Under the product directory is a specific version-related file and under the admin directory is the SID (in the figure it is represented by PRODDB) specific administration file. The parameter file is located under the pfile directory, the alert log file under the bdump directory, and background process files are located under the udump directory.

The above descriptions are all centered on a single instance, single database configuration. In the case of a RAC implementation, this is definitely not the case; we have two or more instances talking to a common shared database. As we have discussed earlier, it is only in a clustered database environment like OPS or RAC that the true definition of an instance and database is laid out.

Now how do we differentiate between these instance-specific information and structure? This discussion covers various areas of a RAC implementation and also depends on what kind of operating system RAC is being installed. For example, if the installation is on a Sun cluster[1] or an HP-UX cluster, Oracle requires that the data files are stored on raw device partitions. However, if RAC is being installed on an HP Tru64 (previously called COMPAQ Tru64) platform, or on either the Linux or Windows operating system (with Oracle Release 9.2.0.1 or higher) the data files could be stored on file systems.

Note: We will look at raw partitions in more detail later in this chapter.

The parameter file used in a RAC configuration is also different compared to a single instance configuration because, in this case, multiple instances would require their own parameter file and certain parameters have the same values, while the others have different values. In Oracle 9*i*, all the parameters that are specific to an instance and that have values common across instances, can be stored on one file; they can also be located on a common disk for providing visibility to all instances participating in the clustered configuration.

Thus the original OFA specification has been slightly modified to accommodate the commonness of the clustered database while also providing an opportunity to identify specific files such as the udump, bdump, archives, etc., located for each instance. So where a configuration that requires Oracle and an O/S for each instance is located on its own disks that are not shared across the cluster, Figure 8.2 shows a way to organize the files using a modified version of the OFA standard. While for the most part, the same standard of hierarchical definition is maintained, in certain areas like the admin layer a slight modification has been made to more specifically identify the Oracle-generated instance specific files. The product and admin directories are further split into more subdirectories.

I   The var VERITAS file system is also available for Sun platforms, in which case raw devices are not required.

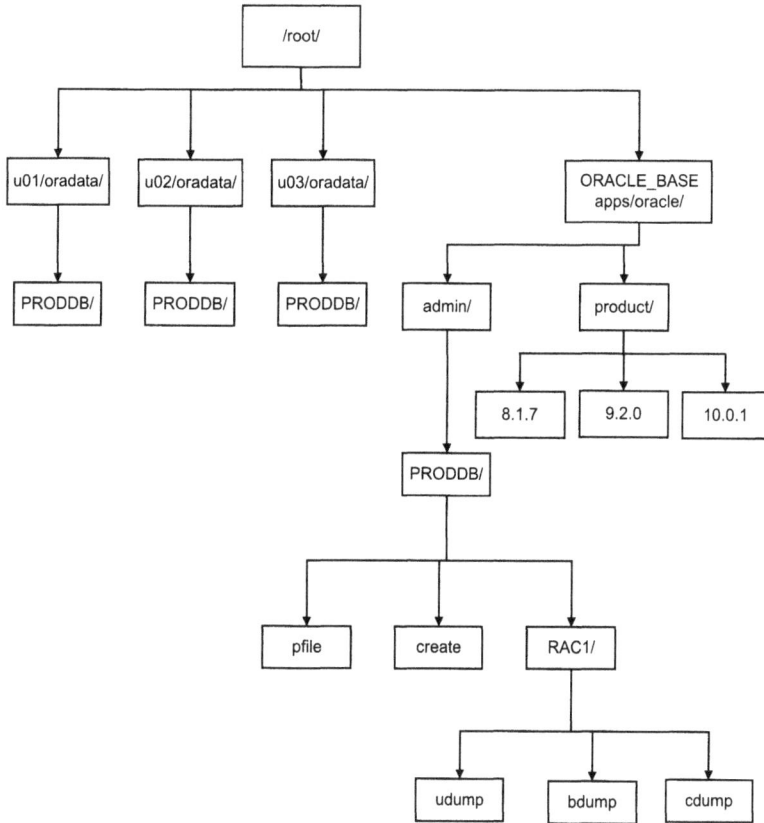

Under the `admin` directory is the database name (in the figure it is represented by `PRODDB`) specific administration file. Under this is the `pfile` and directories that contain files common across instances, or files that are common and also contain prequalified parameter definitions. The instance-specific files like the trace and alert log files are located a level deeper.

As we step through the various phases of installation and configuration of the database a more detailed explanation of the contents of each of these directories will be given.

8.3   Installation

Based on the hardware concepts and technologies discussed in Chapter 2 (Hardware Concepts) an appropriate selection of hardware platform should have been made before proceeding to installation and configuration phase of the product.

As a preinstallation process the following should be completed before installation and configuration of the product. Consideration should be given to a wide variety of details before installing and configuring the database. Such questions could include:

- What should be the physical configuration of the machine?

- What layered products will it have, taking into consideration the basic system requirements of scalability and high availability?

Once this selection has been made, then the next step to the installation process would be to read through the installation guide to determine if any specific needs are to be completed with respect to the O/S of choice. Prior to installation of the product, it is always good to review the release notes and the installation guidelines that are provided. All steps required for the installation should be added to a formal work plan created and reviewed for errors and omissions. Following a work plan of this nature would help to keep track of the work accomplished. It also helps to take follow-up action on any tasks not completed.

Let us review some of the preinstallation steps that should be considered before installing any Oracle-based configuration.

8.3.1 Preinstallation steps

You will need to ensure that:

1. The clustered configuration has been set up, and that you have the correct versions of the clustered operating system and the cluster interconnect configuration.

2. The Oracle version has been certified for the version of the operating system.

3. A work plan to install the product has been completed. (A sample work plan is included in Appendix 4 of this book.)

4. Based on the architecture of the database, all tools and utilities that will be installed from the CD have been preselected.

5. All the latest installation documents have been downloaded and verified for installation procedure and requirements.

6. All required patches for the installation, operating system, and Oracle have been downloaded and verified.

7.   A backup is taken of the entire system. This is a precautionary measure just in case there are any installation issues; the backup can be restored before the system is returned to a prior state.

8.   There is enough disk space and memory as mentioned in the system requirement section of the installation guide.

9.   Disks with sufficient space have been identified for the Oracle product directory including the required swap space. Oracle requires a swap space of about four times the install space during the installation process. This space released after the installation, however, is essential to complete the installation. While allocating space, consideration should be given to future releases of Oracle, as they become available and require installation and/or upgrade. Avoid NFS mounting of disks. Availability and reliability of disks are at risk on NFS-mounted devices.

10. A Unix systems administrator has created all Oracle procedures including Oracle administration user ID, and required directories under the DBA group at the operating system level. As required by Oracle, a user, named Oracle, with an exclusive password, should be created for use in maintaining and administering the database. The Unix systems administrator at the operating system level creates this account. It is required that the product be installed as user Oracle.

11. The required installation directory as required has been defined per OFA specification. Depending on the hardware platform and in the case of a RAC implementation, there is another task, namely configuration of raw devices on certain hardware platforms. Since these partitions are fixed-size partitions, they require a considerable amount of planning and organization.

12. Archive log files should be on file systems. If raw devices are being used, ensure that sufficient disk space on file systems is available for archive log files. If the file systems are NFS mounted (NFS-mounted devices have performance limitations and should be avoided if possible), do not NFS mount archive destinations on all nodes from a single source.

After the selection of the hardware and operating system, and once the preinstallation steps have been verified, the next step to the process would be to configure the hardware itself. A first step to this process would be configuration of a common shared disk subsystem.

Once the storage media has been selected, the next step is the selection of the appropriate RAID technology. The commonly used RAID levels have been discussed in detail in Chapter 2 (Hardware Concepts). Depending on the usage (data warehouse, OLTP, etc.) the appropriate RAID level should be selected.

Once the RAID level has been determined, the next step is to configure the devices.

Device configuration

RAC requires that all instances be able to access either a shared disk subsystem such as a raw device or an Oracle-certified clustered file system. In this section, we will look at both these methods of device configuration.

> Note: While most of the details pertaining to any specific platform have been avoided, certain inclusions and examples are unavoidable.

Raw devices

A raw device partition is a contiguous region of a disk accessed by a Unix character-device interface. This interface provides raw access to the underlying device, arranging for direct I/O between a process and the logical disk. Therefore, the issuance of a write command by a process to the I/O system directly moves the data to the device. Raw devices are precreated using O/S-specific commands before the database can be created. In this section we will look at how to set up and define raw devices.

Setting up the raw devices
The first step in this process of setting up raw devices is the configuration of the shared disk subsystems. To accomplish this step we have to define the raw devices.

Defining raw devices
Each disk attached to the cluster is referred to as a physical volume. These physical volumes, when in use, belong to a volume group, and are divided into physical partitions. Within each volume group, one or more logical volumes are defined. Each logical volume represents a set of information located on the physical volume. The information found on the logical volume appears contiguous to the user, but can be discontiguous at the physical volume layer.

By providing the definition of logical volumes to manage disk space, the volume manager can provide greater availability, performance, and flexibility than a single physical disk. Among other benefits, a volume can be extended across multiple disks to increase capacity, striped across disks to improve performance, and mirrored on another disk to provide data redundancy.

Creation of raw devices
Raw devices need to be defined for the control file, parameter file, data file, and the online redo log files. Apart from these traditional files, another device is also required to store server manager configuration information. These files are of a specific size, because raw devices are prepartitioned to a specific size; it is important to analyze and define a chart containing the various sizes that would be required for the database definitions.

For example, the system tablespace in Oracle 9*i* requires about 500 MB of tablespace. Take into consideration the functionalities such as replication or advanced queuing that could subsequently be added. Providing for this growth, the optimal size of the system tablespace could be somewhere around 800 MB. How many other data files would require a similar size? Such are the questions that need to be asked and answered based on the current database structure.

Consider a system that requires the following partition sizes for the various system files (system, temp, tools, control files, etc.). Based on the example above, the following are the various numbers and sizes of partitions:

1.   100 partitions of 100 MB each

2.   100 partitions of 200 MB each

3.   100 partitions of 500 MB each

4.   50 partitions of 800 MB each

5.   50 partitions of 1000 MB each

Note: On operating systems such as Linux there is a limitation of 128 SCSI disks that could be connected to a machine and this limits the number of partitions per disk to 15, of which only 14 are useable.
The number of raw devices that could be recognized by the Linux kernel is limited to 255.

Configuring raw devices into volume groups and logical volumes

1.   Create all necessary volume groups (VG) and logical volumes on the first node.

2.   Deactivate all the VGs and export the structure of all the VGs to map files by issuing the following command. Remember only one map file per VG is created.

```
vgexport -v -s -p -m /tmp/vg_system.map /dev/vg/system
```

3.   Copy all map files to the remote node, using the `rcp` command.

4.   Log into the other node.

5.   Create all VG directories and group files corresponding to the first node by issuing the following commands; the numbers selected should match the values defined on the first node.

```
mkdir /dev/vg_raw_system
mknod /dev/vg_raw_system/group c 64 0x010000
```

6.   Import the structure of all the VGs by issuing the following command:

```
vgimport -v -s -m /tmp/vg_raw_system.map
  /dev/vg_raw_ssystem /dev/dsk/c2t52d0s2
```

7.   Change the permissions on all the VGs to 777, and change the permissions on all raw LVs to 660, with `oracle:dba` being the owner and group on both nodes. This is accomplished using the following commands:

```
chmod 777 /dev/vg_raw_system
chmod 660 /dev/vg_*/r*
chown oracle:dba /dev/vg_*/r*
```

Once the devices have been configured and made shareable from all nodes participating in the clustered configuration, to complete the installation process another prerequest has to be completed, which is creating a user named `oracle`.

Creation of user

1.   Connect to the node as user root.

2.   Create the groups corresponding to the OSOPER roles in the `/etc/group` file on all nodes of the cluster. The default name for this group is DBA. It is recommended that another group, `oinstall`,

also be created. This group is responsible for installing the Oracle software. The `/etc/group` file has the following format:

```
groupname:password:gid:user-list
```

For example a typical entry should look like this:

```
dba::8500:oracle, mvallath
oinstall::42425:root,oracle
```

3.   Next create an Oracle user account that is a member of the dba group, with the following:

```
$useradd -c ''oracle software owner'' -G dba, oinstall -u 222 -s /bin/ksh
   oracle
```

4.   Create a mount point directory on each node to serve as the top-level directory for Oracle software. The name of the mount point should be identical to that on the initial node. The `oracle` account should have read, write, and execute privileges on this directory.

5.   Depending on from which node the Oracle installation will be performed using the Oracle universal installer, a user equivalence is to be established by adding an entry for all nodes in the cluster. This includes the local node to the `rhosts` file of the Oracle account, or to the `/etc/host` equivalence file.

Before moving to the next step, it is required that all the work performed this far has been verified for accuracy. For example, it is required that the attributes of the Oracle user are the same on all nodes. This could be verified by using the `rlogin` command. If the password is requested, then user equivalence is not set, in which case the remote copy command `rcp` could be used to evaluate user equivalence.

Clustered file system (CFS)

A Unix file system is a hierarchical tree of directories and files implemented on a raw device partition through the file system subsystem of the kernel. Traditional file systems use the concept of a buffering cache that optimizes the number of times the operating system must access the disk. The file system releases a process that executes a write to disk by taking control of the operation, thus freeing the process to continue other functions. The file system then attempts to cache or retain the data to be written until multiple data writes can be done at the same time. This can have the effect of enhancing system performance.

However, system failures before writing the data from the cache can result in the loss of file system integrity. Additionally, the file system adds overhead to any operation that reads or writes data in direct accordance with its physical layout.

Shared file systems allow access from multiple hosts to the same file system data. This reduces the amount of multiple copies of the same data, while distributing the load across those hosts going to the same data.

Oracle supports CFS on certain hardware platforms, such as HP OpenVMS, and HP Tru64. Oracle uses the Direct I/O feature available in CFS. Direct I/O enables Oracle to bypass the buffer cache. Oracle manages the concurrent access to the file itself; this is similar to what it does with the raw devices. On CFS without Direct I/O enabled on files, file access goes through a CFS server. A CFS server runs on a cluster member and serves a file domain. A file domain can be relocated from one cluster member to another cluster member online. A file domain may also contain one or more file systems.

VERITAS file system configuration

VERITAS Database Edition^{TM} Advanced Cluster for Oracle 9*i* RAC enables Oracle to use the CFS. The VERITAS CFS is an extension of the VERITAS File System (VxFS). VERITAS CFS allows the same file system to be simultaneously mounted on multiple nodes. Any node can initiate an operation to create, delete, or resize data; the actual operation is carried out by the master node.

Oracle clustered file system

CFS is a shared file system designed specifically for RAC. CFS eliminates the requirement for Oracle database files to be linked to logical drives and enables all nodes to share a single Oracle home instead of requiring each node to have its own local copy. CFS volumes can span one shared disk or multiple shared disks for redundancy and performance enhancements.

Oracle currently provides CFS for platforms that use Linux and Windows operating systems. These operating systems are in their infancy and do not contain any robust mechanisms for managing clusters to the extent useful for Oracle. Hence, clustered file systems for these operating system platforms have been developed and implemented by Oracle.

Configuring the kernel

Kernel configuration of the operating systems such as Unix and Linux involves sizing the semaphores and the shared memory (Table 8.1). The shared memory feature of the operating system is required by Oracle.

Table 8.1 *Kernel Parameters*

Kernel Parameter	Purpose
SHMMAX	Maximum allowable size of a single shared memory segment. Normally this parameter is set to half the size of the physical memory
SHMMIN	Minimum allowable size of a single shared memory segment
SEMMNI	The number of semaphore set identifiers in the system. It determines the number of semaphores sets that can be created at any one time
SEMMSL	The maximum number of semaphores that can be in one semaphore set. Should be set to the sum of the PROCESSES parameter for each Oracle instance. While setting this value add the largest one twice, and add an additional 10 for each additional instance

The SGA resides in shared memory; therefore shared memory must be available for each Oracle process to address the entire SGA.

Table 8.2 shows the recommended semaphore and shared memory settings for the various O/S. The values for these shared memory and semaphore parameters are set in the kernel configuration file of the operating system. On most systems this file is /etc/systems.

Table 8.2 *Semaphore and shared memory settings*

Operating System	Shared Memory Parameters	Semaphore
Solaris	SHMMAX = 8,388,608 SHMSEG = 20 SHMMNI = 100	SEMMNS = 200 SEMMSL = 50 SEMMNI = 70
HP-UX	SHMMAX = 0x4000000 SHMESG = 12	SEMMNS = 128 SEMMNI = 10
HP Tru64	SHMMAX = 419304 SHMESG = 32	SEMMNS = 200 SEMMNI = 50
Linux ⟋	SHMMAX = Physical memory /2 SHMMIN = 1	SEMMNI = 1024 SEMMSL = 100 SEMOPM = 100 SEMVMX = 32,767

The values of the system-level kernel parameters can be checked (on most systems) using the sysdef command.

Open file descriptors limit

Operating systems maintain two parameters that define the maximum and minimum open file descriptor limits on Unix and Linux platforms. While the maximum value is set to 4096, the minimum value is calculated based on the following formula:

```
db_files * 2 ( twice for equal number of temp files to be opened) + 2 *
  maximum_no_of_log_files_simultaneously_opened +
  maximum_number_of_controlfiles +
  safety_margin_for_misc_files (like trace, alert logs, etc.
  minimum 32 )
```

Hangcheck-timer

The oracm for Linux now includes the use of a Linux kernel module called hangcheck-timer. This module monitors the Linux kernel for long operating system hangs that could affect the reliability of a RAC node and cause a corruption of a RAC database. When such a hang occurs, this module reboots the node. This approach offers the following advantages over the approach used by its predecessor watchdogd:

- Node resets are triggered from within the Linux kernel making them much less affected by system load.

- Oracm on a RAC node can easily be stopped and reconfigured because its operation is completely independent of the kernel module.

9iR2 New Feature: The watchdog daemon process that existed in Oracle Release 9.1 impacted system availability as it initiated system reboots under heavy workloads. This module has now been removed from Oracle. In place of the watchdog daemon (watchdogd), Version 9.2.0.3 of the oracm for Linux now includes the use of a Linux kernel module called hangcheck-timer. The hangcheck-timer module monitors the Linux kernel for long operating system hangs, and reboots the node if this occurs, thereby preventing potential corruption of the database. This is the new I/O fencing mechanism for RAC on Linux.

Configuration parameters

The removal of the watchdogd and the introduction of the hangcheck-timer module require several parameter changes in the CM configuration file, $ORACLE_HOME/Oracm/admin/cmcfg.ora.

1.   The following watchdogd related parameters are no longer valid and should be removed from all nodes in the cluster.

```
WatchdogTimerMargin
WatchdogSafetyMargin
```

2.   A new parameter that identifies the hangcheck module to the oracm is required to be added to the cmcfg.ora file.

```
kernelModuleNam=hangcheck-timer
```

> **Note:** If the module in `KernelModuleName` is either not loaded but correctly specified or incorrectly specified, the `oracm` will produce a series of error messages in the `syslog` system log(`/var/log/messages`). However, it will not prevent the `oracm` process from running. The module must be loaded prior to `oracm` startup.

3.   The following parameter is now a required parameter. This informs the oracm to use the quorum partition.

```
CMDiskFile=<quorum disk directory path>
```

4.   The following new parameters have been introduced; these parameters are used when the hangcheck-timer module is loaded and indicates how long a RAC node must hang before the hangcheck-timer will reset the system.

   - hangcheck_tick – the hangcheck_tick is an interval indicating how often the hangcheck-timer checks on the health of the system.

   - hangcheck_margin – certain kernel activities may randomly introduce delays in the operation of the hangcheck-timer. hangcheck_margin provides a margin of error to prevent unnecessary system resets due to these delays.

   - The node reset occurs when the system hang time > (hangcheck_tick+ hangcheck_margin)

   - For example the addition of the following lines to the `rc.local` script would demonstrate the loading of the hangcheck-timer.

```
#load hangcheck-timer module for ORACM 9.2.0.3
/sbin/insmod/lib/modules/2.4.19-
```

```
4GB/kernel/drivers/char/hangcheck-timer.o hangcheck_tick=30
hangcheck_margin=180
```

The following is the contents of the cmcfg.ora file

```
HeartBeat=15000
ClusterName=Oracle/Cluster Manager, version 9i
KernelModuleName=hangcheck-timer
PollInterval=1000
MissCount=250
PrivateNodenames=mars-int venus-int
PublicNodeNames=mars venus
ServicePort=9998
CmDiskFile=/dev/quorum
HostName=venus-int
```

9iR2   **New Feature:** In place of the watchdog daemon (watchdogd), Version
9.2.0.2 of the oracm for Linux now includes the use of a Linux kernel
module called hangcheck-timer. The hangcheck-timer module monitors the
Linux kernel for long operating system hangs, and reboots the node if this
occurs, thereby preventing potential corruption of the database. This is the
new I/O fencing mechanism for RAC on Linux.

8.3.2   Installing Oracle

As the functionality of the product has increased over the years, the
amount of space required for the installation has increased considerably.
Similarly, the media containing the software also has increased. Oracle is
supplied on multiple CD-ROM disks (Oracle 9i Enterprise Edition is
shipped on 3 CD-ROMs). This means that in order to complete the
installation of the software, it is required to switch the CD-ROMs.
Of course the Oracle Universal Installer (OUI) manages the switching
between CDs. However, if the working directory is set to the CD
device, OUI cannot unmount it. To avoid this problem, ensure that the
directory to the CD-ROM device is not changed before starting the OUI
process.

An alternative method to avoid switching of CD-ROMs is to copy the
contents on to the disk before installation.

Once all the preinstallation steps including the creation of all required
directories required for the product have been completed, the next step is
to install the product. To accomplish this the database administrator
connects to the system as user oracle:

1.   Log in as the oracle user.

2. From the ORACLE_HOME directory, the following command is issued at the command line:

```
oracle$ ./<cdrom_mount_point>/runinstaller
```

The command above invokes the OUI screen. If the installation is on a Windows platform, then the OUI is self-started on insertion of the CD.

> ⚠️ **Caution:** A word of caution is in line at this stage. The OUI software is written using Java, and requires considerable memory to load. The database administrator should ensure that sufficient memory is available when using this tool.

Figure 8.3 shows the first introduction screen of the OUI. This screen provides three options: install/deinstall products, explore CD, and browse documentation. Select the first option to install the Oracle database product.

Figure 8.3
*Oracle
Universal
Installer.*

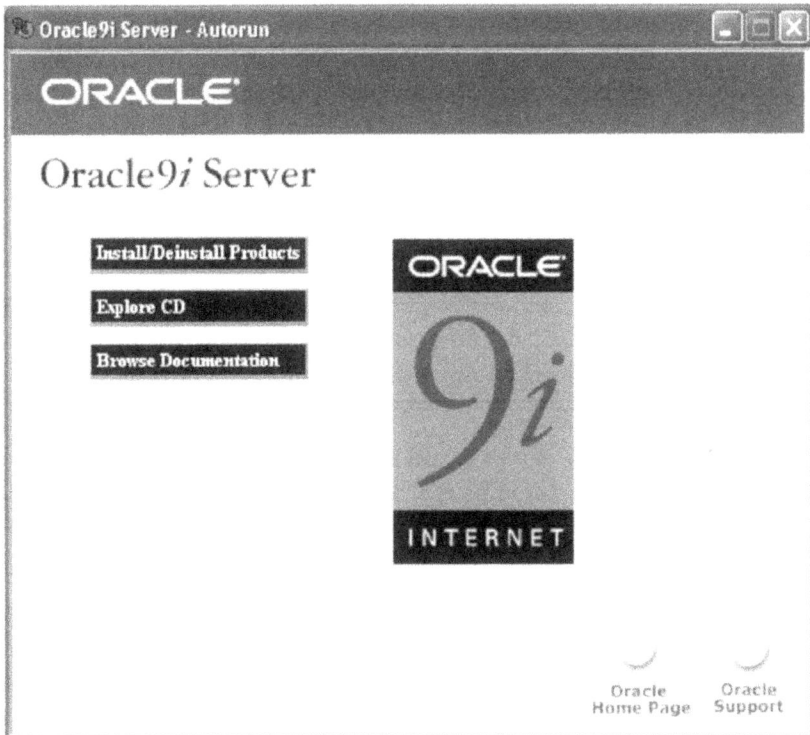

Figure 8.4
Welcome screen.

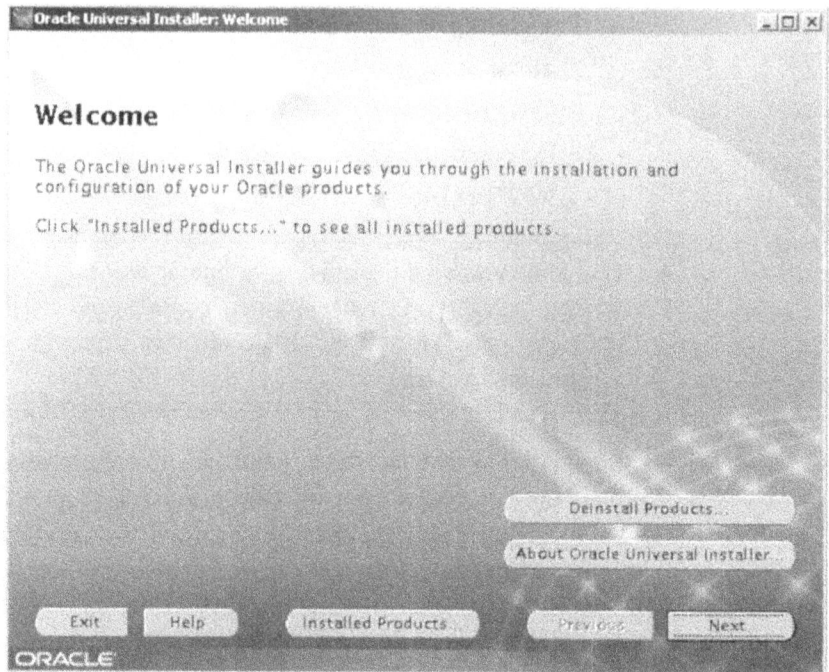

3. The next screen is the welcome screen (Figure 8.4), which gives the user or database administrator the choice to either install the product or to deinstall products already installed during an earlier process. From this screen, select "next" if the intention is to install new software. Prior to Oracle 8*i*, Oracle did not have an OUI product to install the software.

Note: The OUI will deinstall only tools or products that have been installed by the same version of the installer.

4. If this is the first time that the OUI has been run on this system, a prompt appears for the inventory location. This is the base directory into which OUI installs the files. Enter the directory path for the Oracle install directory in the text field and click "OK."

5. The next screen is to select the Unix group name; enter dba as the group name and click "next" to continue. If a window pops up providing instructions to run /orainstRoot.sh, at this point the Unix administrator with the root privileges is required to run the orainstRoot.sh file and click "OK."

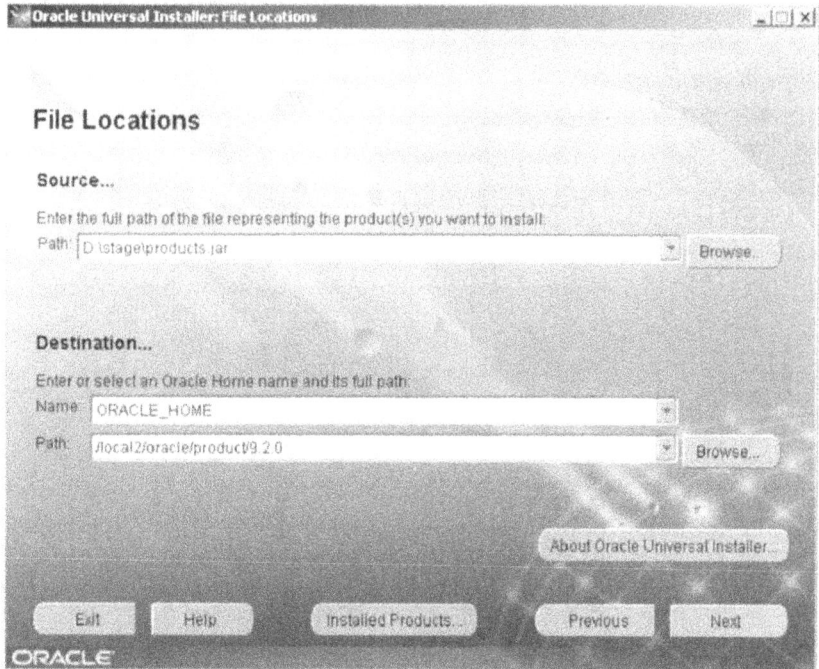

Figure 8.5
*File location
and* ORACLE_
HOME *identifica-
tion screens.*

6.   The next screen (Figure 8.5) identifies the file locations for the media containing the Oracle database product and the destination where the product will be installed. In this screen the default ORACLE_HOME is defined. In a Unix environment this directory is precreated for easy installation. On Windows, if this directory is not already created it will be created by the OUI. The destination paths will vary between operating systems. However, it is a good practice to follow a structure similar to the OFA even in environments such as Windows. For example, the install directory for a Unix operating system install would be /app/oracle/ product/9.2.0/ and following a similar directory path on a Windows platform, the directory structure could be E:\usr\app\ oracle\product \9.2.0.

7.   The OUI loads all high-level product information that the CD contains. Since we are planning on installing the Oracle database product, the next screen should take us to this selection. Figure 8.6 shows the various installation types: Oracle Enterprise Edition (OEE), the standard edition, personal edition, or custom install. Once the type is selected, and based on whether the CD is for the standard edition or OEE, the appropriate options available in the CD are

Figure 8.6
*Selecting the
appropriate
installation type.*

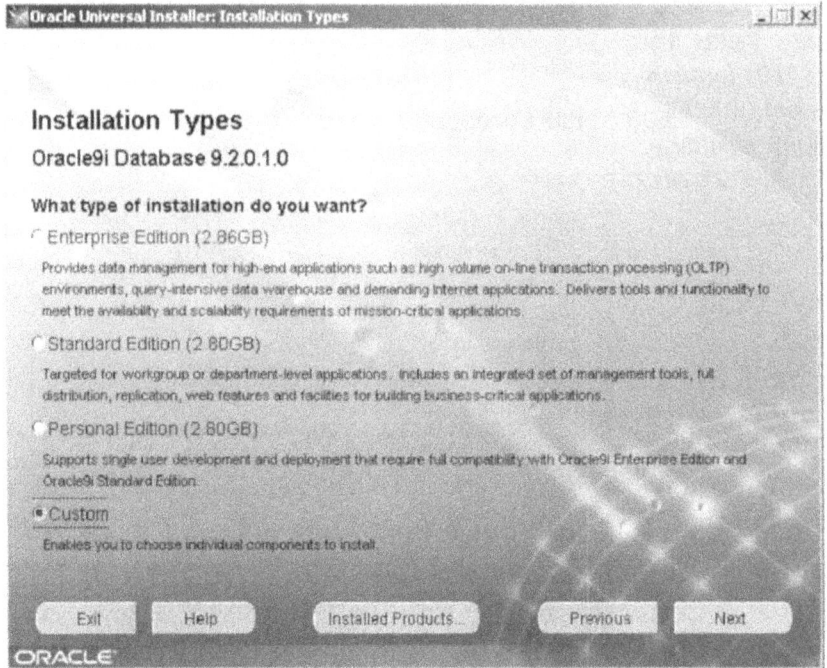

loaded. It should be noted that a similar install and load process is available when installing all products of Oracle. Oracle has standardized the installation of all its products using the OUI interface.

Our main plan is to install the RAC feature with other features identified in Chapter 7 (Database Design). Since the RAC and partitioning features are bundled with OEE, it should be ensured that the correct set of CD-ROMs is available. However, in order to ensure that only the required database components are installed, it would be safer to select the custom option from this screen. Select this option and click "next."

Note: OEE has all tools and utilities that Oracle provides, for example, advanced replication, advanced queuing, database partitioning, Oracle Enterprise Manager, etc. Unless all these features or tools of the database will be used, it is not advisable to install them. Furthermore, every additional option has a price attached to it. Unless the options available under OEE are absolutely necessary (such as RAC), it is not worth purchasing this edition of the product.

8. The next screen is the database configuration screen. In this screen, it is selected whether the database configuration assistant is to be used to install the RAC database.

9. The next screen is the cluster node selection screen, which basically helps to identify the other nodes in the cluster onto which the Oracle RDBMS software is to be installed. After making the selection click "next."

10. Once the cluster nodes have been identified, the next screen is the raw device identification screen to hold the configuration file. This device should be on a common shared device visible to all instances in the cluster. After entering the device name, click "next."

Note: The raw partition or device selected for the configuration file should be at least 100 MB in size.

11. The next screen is the custom selection screen.

Note: The custom software selection screen appears only if the custom option was selected in Figure 8.6. If OEE was selected, then a summary screen is displayed instead of the custom software selection screen.

Figure 8.7 gives a list of components provided by the OUI. The database administrator will select the components that he or she would like to install and deselect those that are not required. While installing the software it is a good practice to install a copy of the OUI with the components, which will help in easy install and deinstall of products, if required at a later date. Confirm that the Oracle 9*i* RAC database software will be installed and click "next."

Note: The RAC option will show on the list of products to be installed, provided the clustered file system or raw device has been configured correctly as per specifications/recommendations for the appropriate hardware platform.

The next few steps required for the installer process are self-explanatory in the sense that they have sufficient information for easy navigation.

Figure 8.7
*Custom soft-
ware selection
screen.*

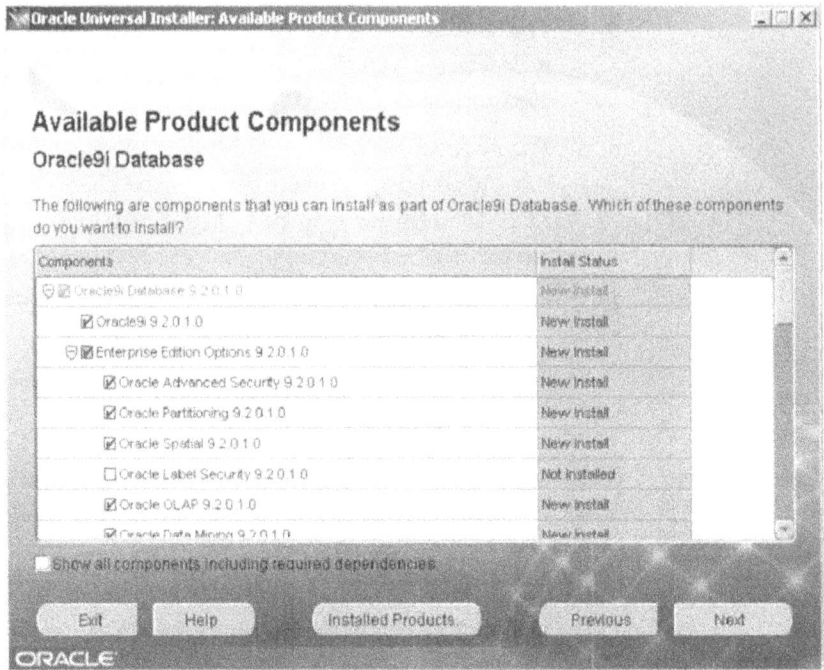

Another important precaution that needs to be observed concerns the amount of memory. With every release of Oracle some additional memory could be required and it is always a good practice to monitor the progress of the installation.

12. The next screen is invoked automatically and provides information about the configuration tools that will be installed. Figure 8.8 displays the various configuration tools that need to be set up. For example, if required, the database administrator could use the Oracle Net Configuration Assistant to install the required Oracle Net files like the listener and the tnsnames.ora files. These files are required to get the Oracle Net component functioning. If the database administrator chooses to configure these components manually, he or she could select "next" and proceed to the next part of the installation.

13. For first-time database administrators installing and configuring the database files, it is advised to use the configuration assistants, which guides the user through the required installation. Figure 8.9 gives the various options available for the Oracle Net Configuration Assistant. Using this tool, the Oracle Net, which includes the tnsnames and listener, can be installed and configured.

Figure 8.8
*Configuration
tools selection.*

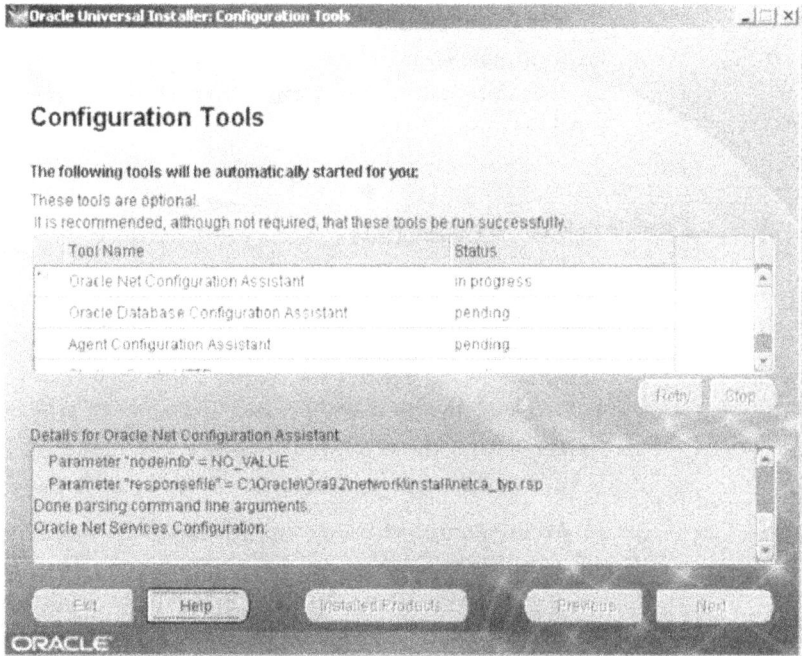

Figure 8.9
*Oracle Net
Configuration
Assistant.*

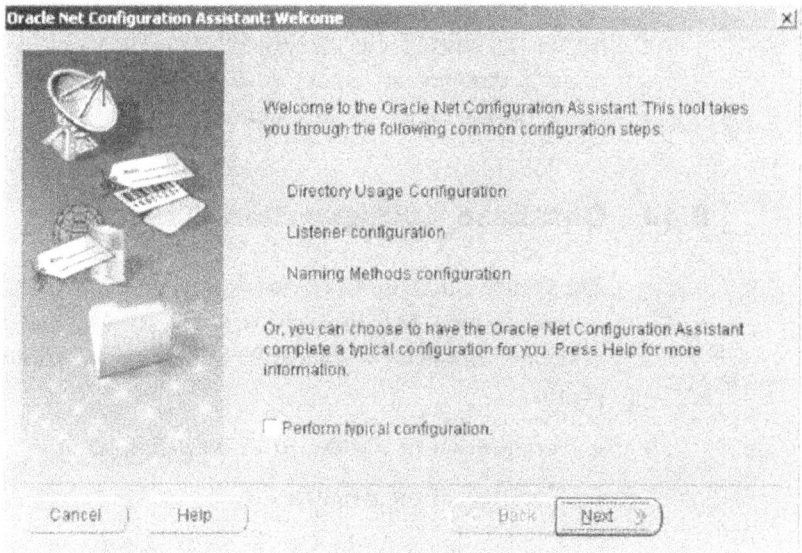

Similarly, using the Oracle Net Configuration Assistant, other
components like agents, including the database agent, could be
configured. Once all the required agents and components have been
configured, this marks the end of the database installation process.

The configuration assistant includes database configuration and creation assistants. These components help in configuring and setting up of the database either as a stand-alone configuration or as a RAC configuration.

8.4   Database creation

Database creation can be done in one of two ways, either by using the GUI-based interface provided with the product, as stated in the previous section, or using a script file, which contains all the steps required to create a database. In the case of a RAC database, creation of the database is different from the regular stand-alone configuration because in the case of RAC, we have one database and two or more instances.

An advantage of using the GUI interface over script file method is that there are fewer steps to be remembered. This is because using the configuration assistant the steps are already predefined, and based on the selected template the type of database is automatically created, sized, and configured. However, the script file approach has an advantage over the GUI interface approach in the sense that the creator is able to see what is happening during the creation process and can physically monitor the process. Another advantage of this option is that the script can be done based on the needs of the enterprise.

8.4.1   Database Configuration Assistant

The Oracle Database Configuration Assistant (DBCA) helps in the creation of the database. It follows the standard naming and placement convention as defined in the OFA standards. DBCA provides three primary processing phases:

- Verification of the shared disk configuration
- Creation of the database
- Configuration of the Oracle network services

To create the database, the following steps have to be completed via the DBCA:

1.   As mentioned earlier in Figure 8.8, the DBCA could be launched automatically as part of the installation process or manually

Figure 8.10
Database
Configuration
Assistant data-
base selection
screen.

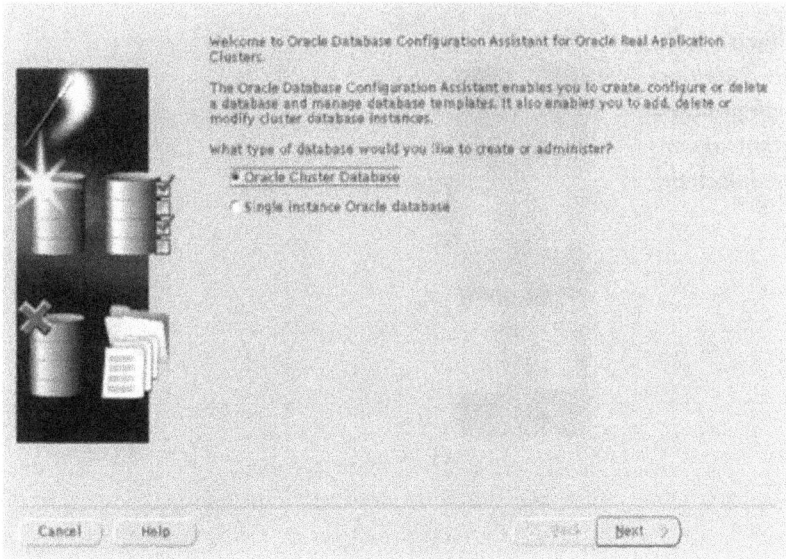

by directly executing the `dbca` command from the `$ORACLE_HOME/bin` directory in the case of a Unix platform. On a Windows platform, from the start menu select Programs, Oracle, and then configuration and migration tools. From this option, the DBCA option can be selected. Figure 8.10 is the DBCA selection screen; from this screen, the type of database to be installed is selected. The screen provides two choices, Oracle clustered database or single instance Oracle database. Select the Oracle cluster database option and click "next."

2.   The next screen is the operations window (Figure 8.11), which provides the options to either create a new database or to manage database creation templates provided by Oracle. From this screen, select "create a database option" and click "next."

9i

New Feature: With Version *9i*, Oracle has introduced templates that could be used to create databases. For example, there is a template for setting up a database that is more suited for an OLTP type of environment.

3.   The next screen is the node selection window. The appropriate node where RAC needs to be configured is selected. After making the appropriate selection, click "next."

4.   Following the node selection screen is the template selection screen. Figure 8.12 shows the Oracle templates that can be selected

Figure 8.11
Database Configuration Assistant operation selection.

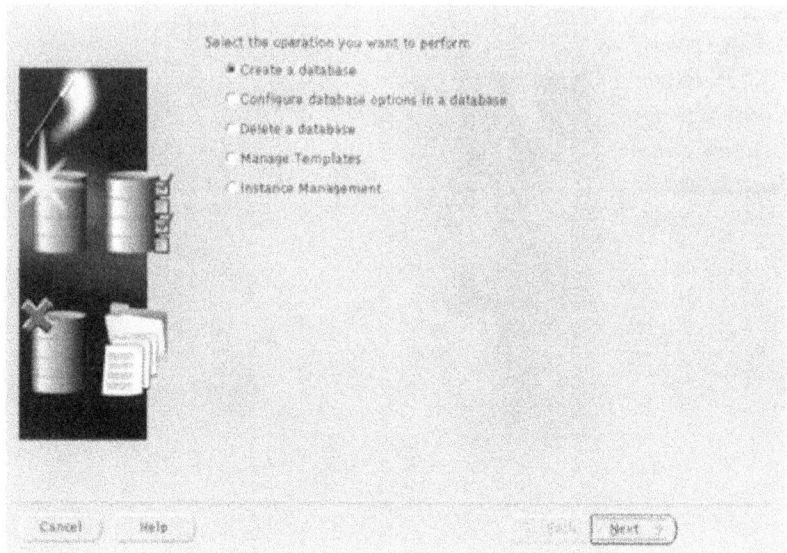

Figure 8.12
Selecting the template.

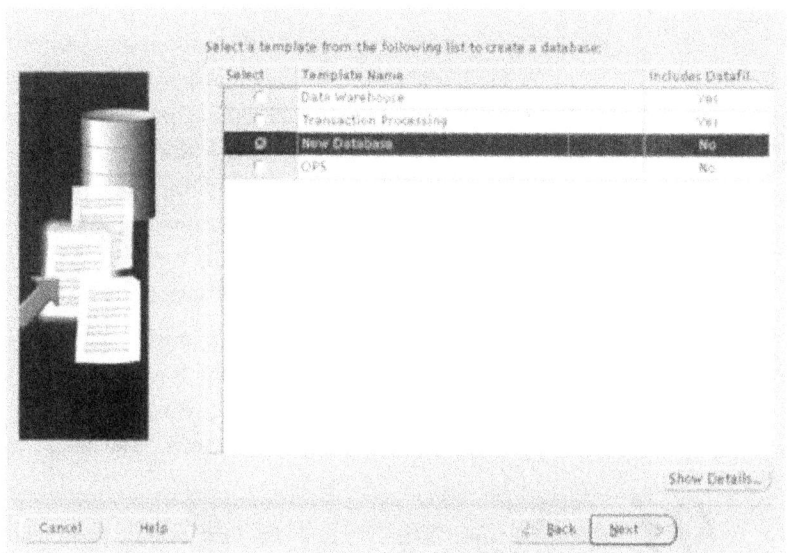

according to the functionality that the database will support. Oracle provides various predefined templates as part of the database configuration assistant that make it easy for the user to create predefined standard configurations depending on the type of application that the database will be used for.

5.   Based on the template selected, the template with the predefined configuration is displayed for validation. At this point the user could

either cancel certain selections that he or she feels are not required or select the "back" option to make a different choice.

6. The next screen is the database identification window. In the screen the global database name and Oracle system identifier prefix (SID) are entered in the appropriate fields. The global database name is typically of the form `name.domain`, for example, `proddb.summerskyus.com`, and the SID is used to uniquely identify the instance. In the case of RAC the specified SID is used as a prefix to the instance number. For example, `PRODDB` would become `PRODDB1` and `PRODDB2` for instance 1 and instance 2, respectively. These values could also be overridden, for example with `RAC1` and `RAC2`, respectively.

The next few screens take the user through the process of creating the database and configuring the additional features such as Java Virtual Machine (JVM) and intermedia.

7. The next window (Figure 8.13) is the client connection selection screen, which displays the option to select the type of connection that is intended. This allows the installation and configuration of either of the two connection options (shared server or dedicated server). If the database were to run from multiple clustered nodes, then the shared server mode would be ideal. However if only one

Figure 8.13
Client connection selection.

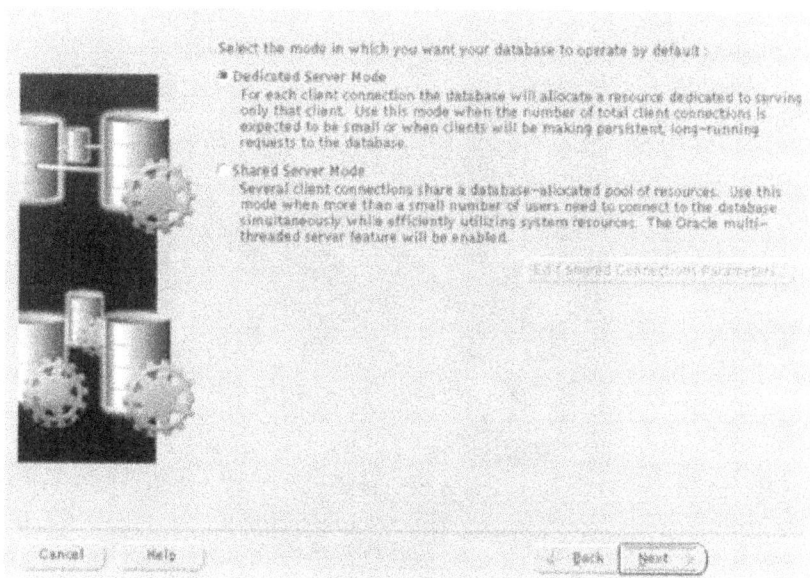

node is available, dedicated server would be the choice. After selecting the connection mode click "next."

8.   The next few screens displayed by the DBCA are for configuration of the initialization parameters such as the shared pool, buffer pool, file locations for the system parameter file, the user trace, system trace files, etc.

9.   After selecting the appropriate values for the initialization parameters, click "next" on the last parameter screen. A summary screen containing the initialization parameters will be displayed and after the initial review of the parameters, click "next."

10. DBCA now displays the database storage window. This window allows entering a filename for each type of file, for example the storage definition for the control file, for the various tablespaces, rollback segments, etc. Once all the storage for the various files has been defined, click "next."

11. The next screen shows the database creation options. Ensure that the "create database" check box is selected and click "finish."

12. Figure 8.14 is the final screen where the actual "create database" option is selected. On selection of the "finish" option, the DBCA begins creating the database according to the values specified. Once the process has finished, a new database is created which can be

Figure 8.14
Database creation screen.

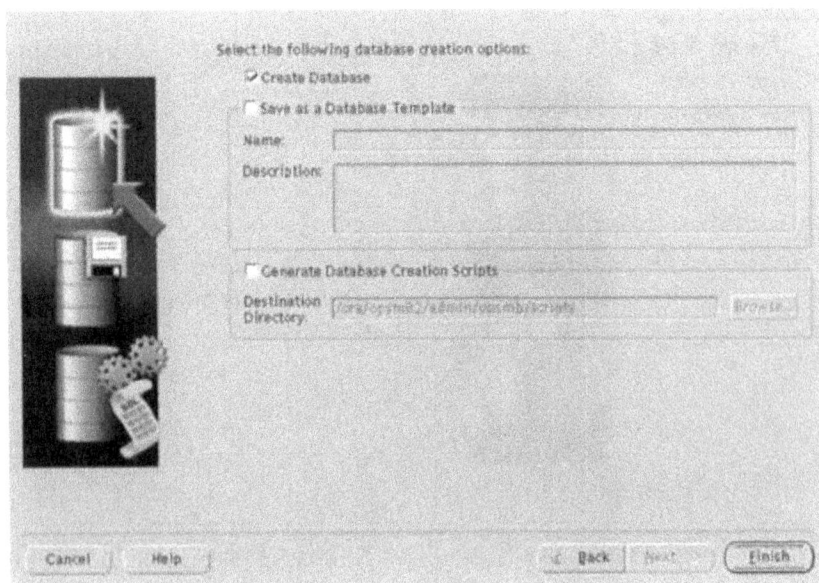

accessed using SQL*Plus or other applications designed to work with a RAC database.

8.4.2 Manual database configuration

In the previous section we looked at how, using the DBCA, the RAC database and the required instances could be created from a GUI interface. Another method, which is a more traditional way of creating databases and the corresponding instances is through the script file method with certain manual steps. Apart from executing a script file that contains the definitions required for creating the instance and the database, there are other steps that would require manual intervention and control. When installing and configuring the database manually the following would be the sequence of steps and tasks:

1.   Determine sizes of the initial tablespaces. Table 8.3 provides the recommended sizes for the various tablespaces.

2.   Create `crdbRAC1.sql` script and `initPRODDB.ora` files to install the new RAC instance.

Note: `CrdbRAC1.sql`, `CrdbRAC2.sql`, and `initPRODDB.ora` source files have been provided in Appendix 2.

3.   Create a RAC1 instance and PRODDB database.

    a.   Create all directories based on OFA standards for the new instance.

    b.   Create a `crdbRAC1.sql` script to create the subdirectory and `initPRODDB.ora` file to the `$ORACLE_BASE/admin/RAC1/pfile` directory.

    c.   Ensure that the following parameters in `initPRODDB.ora` have the following values:

```
RAC1.instance_number    = 1
RAC1.thread             = 1
RAC1.instance_name    = RAC1
RAC1.service_names    = RAC1.SUMMERSKYUS.COM
RAC1.undo_tablespace  = UNDO_RAC1
```

Table 8.3   *Recommended Sizes for the Initial Tablespaces*

Tablespace	Size (MB)
SYSTEM	1000
UNDO_RAC1	5000
UNDO_RAC2	5000
TEMP	2000
TOOLS	2000
USERS	1000
INDX	200
DRSYS	200
CONTROL FILE 1	300
CONTROL FILE 2	300
CONTROL FILE 3	300
Server parameter file	5
EXAMPLE	160
CWMLITE	100
XML	50
ODM	250
INDX	70
Srvcfg for the SRVM configuration repository	100

    d. Ensure that the following parameters for the RAC2 instance have the following values:

```
RAC2.instance_number    = 2
RAC2.thread             = 2
RAC2.instance_name      = RAC2
RAC2.service_names      = RAC2.SUMMERSKYUS.COM
RAC2.undo_tablespace    = UNDO_RAC2
```

    e. Set ORACLE_SID to the new SID, and ORACLE_HOME.

    f. Create the password file for remote admin:

```
orapwd file=$ORACLE_HOME/dbs/orapwRAC1
entries=32
```

```
password=oracle
orapwd file=$ORACLE_HOME/dbs/orapwRAC2
entries=32
password=oracle
```

g. Invoke SQL*Plus, and execute crdbRAC1.sql after logging in as oracle on ORA-DB1.

```
oracle$ sqlplus /nolog
SQL>@crdbRAC1.sql
```

h. Convert the pfile into an spfile (binary) and move it to a shared raw device partition:

```
oracle$ sqlplus /nolog
SQL> CREATE SPFILE='/dev/vx/rdsk/oraracdg/
partition200m_1' from pfile;
```

i. Create a symbolic link for this new shared spfile:

```
ln --s /dev/vx/rdsk/oraracdg/paritition200m_1 $ORACLE_HOME/dbs/
spfilePRODDB.ora
```

j. Invoke SQL*Plus and start the instance:

```
SQL> startup
ORACLE instance started.

Total System Global Area        450937896  bytes
Fixed Size                         730152  bytes
Variable Size                   285212672  bytes
Database Buffers                163840000  bytes
Redo Buffers                      1155072  bytes
Database mounted.
Database opened.
SQL>
```

k. Verify the parameter definitions:

```
SQL>select sid, name, value from v$spparameter;
```

l. Check spool file for errors and resolve.

4. Create RAC2 instance:

a. Invoke SQL*Plus; and execute crdbRAC2.sql after logging in as oracle on ORA-DB1:

```
oracle$ sqlplus /nolog
SQL>@crdbRAC2.sql
```

b. Issue the following command to enable the second thread on ORA-DB1:

```
SQL>ALTER DATABASE ENABLE THREAD 2;
```

c. Shut down the instance:

```
oracle$ sqlplus /nolog
```

```
SQL>shutdown immediate
```

    d. Create a symbolic link from $ORACLE_HOME/dbs to $ORACLE_ BASE/admin/PRODDB/pfile for the initPRODDB.ora file:

```
ln -s $ORACLE_BASE/admin/PRODDB/pfile/initPRODDB.ora $ORACLE_HOME/
dbs/initRAC1.ora
```

    e. Create a symbolic link from $ORACLE_HOME/dbs to $ORACLE _BASE/admin/PRODDB/pfile for the initPRODDB.ora file:

```
ln -s $ORACLE_BASE/admin/PRODDB/pfile/initPRODDB.ora $ORACLE_HOME/
dbs/initRA2.ora
```

    f. From ORA-DB2 connect to RAC1 via SQL*Plus and restart RAC1:

```
oracle$sqlplus /nolog
SQL>connect as sys@RAC1 /as sysdba
SQL>shutdown immediate

SQL> startup
ORACLE instance started.

Total System Global Area      450937896  bytes
Fixed Size                       730152  bytes
Variable Size                 285212672  bytes
Database Buffers              163840000  bytes
Redo Buffers                    1155072  bytes
Database mounted.
Database opened.
SQL>
```

    g. By default, the ORA-DB1/RAC1 instance threads are created with mode PUBLIC. To change the mode to PRIVATE (disabling and enabling the threads will change them to PRIVATE):

```
oracle$ sqlplus /nolog
SQL>
SQL>ALTER DATABASE DISABLE THREAD 1;
SQL>ALTER DATABASE ENABLE THREAD 1;
```

    h. From ORA-DB1 connect to RAC1 via SQL*Plus and restart the instance:

```
oracle$ sqlplus /nolog
SQL>connect as sys@RAC1 /as sysdba
SQL>shutdown immediate

SQL> startup
ORACLE instance started.

Total System Global Area      450937896  bytes
Fixed Size                       730152  bytes
Variable Size                 285212672  bytes
Database Buffers              163840000  bytes
```

```
Redo Buffers                        1155072  bytes
Database mounted.
Database opened.
SQL>
```

5. Full export of the database.

    a. Invoke SQL*Plus and connect as SYS/<password> as sysdba.

    b. Create user FULLEXPORT identified by <password> default tablespaces users temporary tablespace temp:

```
exp userid=fullexport/<password> file=fullexportRAC.dmp
log=fullexportRAC.log
```

6. Bounce both the instances, RAC1 and RAC2.

    a. Instance RAC1:

```
oracle$sqlplus /nolog
SQL>connect as sys@RAC1 /as sysdba
SQL>shutdown immediate

SQL> startup
ORACLE instance started.

Total System Global Area        450937896  bytes
Fixed Size                         730152  bytes
Variable Size                   285212672  bytes
Database Buffers                163840000  bytes
Redo Buffers                      1155072  bytes
Database mounted.
Database opened.
SQL>
```

    b. Instance RAC2:

```
oracle$ sqlplus
SQL*Plus: Release 9.2.0.1.0 - Production on Wed
 Oct 9 18:07:16 2002
Copyright (c) 1982, 2002, Oracle Corporation.  All
 rights reserved.

SQL>connect as sys@RAC2 /as sysdba
SQL>shutdown immediate

SQL> startup
ORACLE instance started.

Total System Global Area        450937896  bytes
Fixed Size                         730152  bytes
Variable Size                   285212672  bytes
Database Buffers                163840000  bytes
Redo Buffers                      1155072  bytes
```

```
Database mounted.
Database opened.
SQL>
```

7. Database verification.

a. RAC1 and RAC2 instances:

```
oracle$sqlplus /nolog
SQL>connect as sys@RAC1 /as sysdba
SQL>select * from v$active_instances;

oracle$sqlplus /nolog
SQL>connect as sys@RAC2 /as sysdba
SQL>select * from v$active_instances;
```

b. Verify if the database files have been created:

```
oracle$sqlplus /nolog
SQL>connect as sys@RAC1 /as sysdba
SQL>select file_id, status, file_name from
  dba_data_files;
```

c. Verify tablespaces:

```
oracle$sqlplus /nolog
SQL>connect as sys@RAC1 /as sysdba
SQL>select tablespace_name, status, contents
  from dba_tablespaces;
```

This completes the creation of the basic database. As part of the database configuration the next step is selecting the appropriate database options to ensure that it has been created based on requirements.

8.5   Database configuration

8.5.1   Cluster configuration

1.   The first and foremost step in the cluster configuration is to ensure that the node is aware of the database. To provide this communication, it is required that the oratab file in the /etc directory is updated with the following entry:

```
<DATABASE NAME>:<ORACLE_HOME>:<REBOOT STATUS>
```

DATABASE_NAME is the name of the database that is being configured. Please note that this is the database name and not the SID name normally entered in a single stand-alone configuration.

ORACLE_HOME is the Oracle home and the Oracle version that the database is created under. This is specfied by the directory path of ORACLE_HOME.

REBOOT_STATUS is a Y/N indicator to inform the operating system if the database is to be automatically started when the node is started.

For example:

```
PRODDB:/app/home/oracle/product/9.2.0:N
```

PRODDB is the name of the clustered database, /app/home/ oracle/product/9.2.0 is the ORACLE-HOME directory, and N indicates that the database should not be started when the node is bounced. What this means is that the database will be started either by a manual process or through some other automated processes using scripts.

The oratab file is located in the /var/opt/oracle directory on Sun Solaris and HP Tru64 platforms.

2. The second step is to ensure that all nodes participating in the clustered configuration are available. This is verified using the lsnodes command.

```
oracle$ lsnodes
ora-db2.summerskyus.com
ora-db1.summerskyus.com
```

The above command will list all the nodes defined to be part of the clustered configuration at the O/S level.

3. The third step is to make the database and instances cluster aware. This is done by completing the following steps:

a. Ensure that the global service daemon (GSD) has been started. GSD is started by using the GSD control (gsdctl) utility. For example:

```
oracle$ gsdctl start
Successfully started the daemon on the local node.

    Usage: gsdctl [options]
    Where options include:
      start  start the gsd
       stop  stop the gsd
       stat  query the status of the gsd
```

Note: GSD must be started on all the nodes in a RAC environment so that the manageability features and tools operate properly.

9iR2

New Feature: `gsdctl` is a new utility introduced in Oracle 9*i* Release 2. Prior to this release, issuing the gsd command started the process.

b. Check if the server configuration parameter file (`srvConfig.loc`) is present. This file is to configure parameters that would be shared across multiple instances. The server configuration file contains the raw device or file system that is visible from two or more instances and will contain cluster-specific parameters. On most platforms the file is located in the `/var/opt/oracle` directory. The file contains the raw device partition where the server configuration file will be visible from all the instances in the RAC cluster.

```
oracle$ ls -ltr
total 8
-rw-r--r--          1 root      other   55 Aug 12 15:45
                                             oraInst.loc
-rw-rw-r--          1 oracle    other   60 Aug 23 10:48
                                             srvConfig.loc
-rw-rw-r--          1 oracle    other  820 Sep 21 17:14
                                             oratab
oracle$ more srvConfig.loc

srvconfig_loc=/dev/vx/rdsk/oraracdg/srvm_
  shared_config_100m
```

c. If this is the first RAC database and instances are being installed on this cluster, the server configuration file needs to be initialized. The file can be initialized in one of many ways. For example, the file can be initialized by resetting its contents or by importing data from an already created text file. The server configuration file has the following commands:

```
oracle$ srvconfig
Usage: srvconfig [options]
```

where options include:

```
-help               display command-line help message
-?same as -help option
-init               initialize configuration repository
```

```
-init -f            force initialization of configurat-
                    ion repository
-exp <file>         export configuration repository
                    contents to given text file
-imp <file>         import given text file contents to
                    the configuration repository
-conv<file>         convert given config file contents into 9.0 style
                    configuration
-version            display repository version information
```

To reset the server configuration file, the following command can be used:

```
oracle$ srvconfig --init
```

d. After the configuration file has been reset, the next step is to update the configuration file with the database and instance information. This is done using the server control utility (srvctl). The GSD process receives requests from srvctl to execute administrative job tasks, such as startup or shutdown of instances. OEM and Oracle Intelligent Agent (discussed in step 6) use the configuration information that srvctl to discover and monitor nodes in the cluster.

The first step in this process is to add the database that supports this clustered environment that is being configured. This is done with the following command:

```
oracle$ srvctl add database -d <database name>
-o <oracle home directory>

oracle$ srvctl add database -d PRODDB -o /app/home/oracle/product/9.2.0
Successful addition of cluster database: PRODDB
```

The above command adds the database PRODDB to the configuration file with the ORACLE-HOME information.

The second step is to add the instances that will share the database defined above. To add the instances to the server configuration file, the following command will be used:

```
oracle$ srvctl add instance -d <database name> -i
  <instance name> -n <node name>

oracle$ srvctl add instance -d PRODDB -i RAC1
-n ora-db1
Instance successfully added to node: ora-db1
```

The above command adds the instance named RAC1 that is configured to be used with the common shared database PRODDB and will run on node ora-db1.

From the same node the other instances participating in the clustered configuration can be added to the configuration file. Once all the instances and databases have been added, the srvctl utility can be used to check the configuration or check the status of the clustered databases and their respective instances:

```
srvctl config <database name>
```

The above command will verify which databases have been configured in the configuration file. For example, to check if the configuration of the PRODDB made it into the configuration file, the following command can be issued:

```
oracle$ srvctl config -d PRODDB
```

Similarly, to check the configuration files for the instances running on a specific node, the following command will help:

```
oracle$ srvctl config -d PRODDB
ora-db1 RAC1
ora-db2 RAC2
```

By checking the status of the server control, the instance level detail and the corresponding node information will be displayed:

```
srvctl status database -d <database name>
```

The above command will check the status of a given database:

```
oracle$ srvctl status database -d PRODDB
instance RAC1 is running on node ora-db1
instance RAC2 is running on node ora-db2
```

> **Note:** A list of parameters and definitions for using the srvctl utility can be found in Appendix 1.

4.   Configure Net8 support.

   a.   Having a shared disk configuration, two separate listeners are required, one for each instance. There are no hard and fast rules in naming the listeners. Since they run on two different nodes they could be called the same, or for administration purposes if they need to be easily identified they could be specifically named to match the instance, etc. They are LISTENER_RAC1 and LISTENER_RAC2 for ORA-DB1 and ORA-DB2 respectively.

b.   The following information is added to the `listener.ora` file
located in the `TNS_ADMIN` directory:

```
LISTENER=
(DESCRIPTION_LIST=
  (DESCRIPTION=
   (ADDRESS_LIST=
     (ADDRESS=(PROTOCOL=IPC)(KEY=EXTPROC))
   )
   (ADDRESS_LIST =
  (ADDRESS=(PROTOCOL=TCP)(HOST=15.152.2.10)
  (PORT=1521))
   )
  )
)

SID_LIST_LISTENER=
  (SID_LIST=
   (SID_DESC=
     (SID_NAME=PLSExtProc)
     (ORACLE_HOME=/apps/oracle/product/9.2.0.)
     (PROGRAM=extproc)
  )
  (SID_DESC=
   (ORACLE_HOME=/apps/oracle/product/9.2.0)
   (SID_NAME=RAC1)
  )
)
```

c.   The `/etc/services` file needs to reflect that new ports used
for the new `LISTENER_SID`.

d.   Similar to the listener, the tnsnames file should also be maintained
specifically on each instance. If there is only one `ORACLE_HOME`
for multiple instances (e.g., in an HP Tru64 environment), in such
a situation there needs to be only one tnsnames file. The following
information is added to the `$TNS_ADMIN/tnsnames.ora` file
on the database server and on the client machines:

```
PRODDB.SUMMERSKYUS.COM=
  (DESCRIPTION=
   (ADDRESS_LIST=
   (LOAD_BALANCING=ON)
   (FAILOVER=ON)
   (ADDRESS=(PROTOCOL=TCP)(HOST=15.152.2.10)
  (port=1521))
   (ADDRESS=(PROTOCOL=TCP)(HOST=15.152.2.20)
  (port=1521))
   (CONNECT_DATA=
   (SERVICE_NAME=PRODDB.SUMMERSKYUS.COM)
   (FAILOVER_MODE=(TYPE=SELECT)(METHOD=BASIC)
  )
  )
)
```

```
RAC1.SUMMERSKYUS.COM=
(DESCRIPTION=
  (SDU=8192)
  (TDU=8192)
    (ADDRESS_LIST=
      (ADDRESS=(PROTOCOL=TCP)(HOST=15.152.2.10)
        (PORT=1521))
    )
    (CONNECT_DATA=
      (SERVICE_NAME=PRODDB.SUMMERSKYUS.COM)
      (INSTANCE_NAME=RAC1)
    )
  )
RAC2.SUMMERSKYUS.COM=
  (DESCRIPTION=
    (ADDRESS_LIST=
      (ADDRESS=(PROTOCOL=TCP)(HOST=15.152.2.20)
        (PORT=1521))
    )
    (CONNECT_DATA=
      (SERVICE_NAME=PRODDB.SUMMERSKYUS.COM)
      (INSTANCE_NAME=RAC2)
    )
  )
```

e. Test connection using SQL*Plus:

```
sqlplus username/password@RAC1
sqlplus username/password@RAC2
```

5. Configure STATSPACK, which is an Oracle-provided utility used to gather performance statistics for a specific period of time. The statistics gathered are stored in a specific tablespace and schema. Reports could be generated from these stored data for specific run periods. This new utility from Oracle replaces the traditional utility called utlebstat/ultestat. While both these utilities are available, STATSPACK provides a more formated and detailed information not present in utlestat.

Note: A detailed explanation of the installation and configuration process including samples of outputs is discussed in detail in Chapter 13 later in this book.

6. Configure the intelligent agent, which is a daemon process that runs on the database server to help Oracle Enterprise Manager (OEM) to communicate with the database. This is an snmp agent provided by

Oracle called dbsnmp. This agent, when started, allows remote monitoring of the database via OEM.

The intelligent agent process can be started and stopped using the `agentctl` utility:

```
oracle$ agentctl
```

Usage:

```
agentctl start|stop|status|restart [agent]
agentctl start|stop|status    blackout [<target>]
  [-d/uration <timefmt>] [-s/ubsystem <subsystems>]
```

The following are valid options for blackouts:

```
<target>  name of the target. Defaults to node target.
<timefmt>  is specified as [days] hh:mm
<subsystem> is specified as [jobs events collections]
      defaults to all subsystems

oracle $ agentctl status

DBSNMP for Solaris: Version 9.2.0.1.0 - Production on
  09-OCT-2002 08:56:41

Copyright (c) 2002 Oracle Corporation. All rights
  reserved.

Could not contact agent. It may not be running.

oracle $ agentctl start

DBSNMP for Solaris: Version 9.2.0.1.0 - Production on
  09-OCT-2002 08:56:54

Copyright (c) 2002 Oracle Corporation. All rights
  reserved.

Starting Oracle Intelligent Agent......
Agent started

oracle $ agentctl status

DBSNMP for Solaris: Version 9.2.0.1.0 - Production on
  09-OCT-2002 08:57:34

Copyright (c) 2002 Oracle Corporation. All rights
  reserved.

Version          : DBSNMP for Solaris: Version
                   9.2.0.1.0 - Production
Oracle Home      : /apps/oracle/product/9.2.0
Started by user  : oracle
Agent is running since 10/09/02 08:57:09
```

9i

New Feature: Prior to Oracle *9i*, the intelligent process was controlled through the listener control utility. In other words, all administrative tasks, like starting and stopping the agent, were done via the listener control utility (lsnrctl) using the dbsnmp_agent command. In Oracle *9i* a new utility called agent control (agentctl) replaces the dbsnmp_agent and the agent eliminates the dependency on the lsnrctl that existed in the previous version.

8.5.2   Parameter file configuration

If you have worked with an Oracle database, then the parameter file is not something that is new to you. Oracle requires the parameter file to find certain initial definitions during startup of the database. One common parameter is the location of the control file, because without the control file, it would be difficult to start the database.

In the case of a single instance configuration, all parameters are located in one file. Prior to Oracle *9i*, these parameters were stored in an ASCII text file and were read once before instance startup. If a subsequent change was required later on, a restart of the instance was needed for the change to take effect.

9i

New Feature: With the introduction of Oracle *9i*, Oracle has changed the ASCII-based parameter file into a binary file and most of the parameters can be changed dynamically while the instance is active.

In the case of a multi-instance Oracle configuration like OPS, Oracle required that each instance maintain its own parameter file and another parameter file that contained common parameters applicable to all instances participating in the clustered configuration. The parameter file that contained the common parameters got included at runtime with the individual parameter file.

Now with the introduction of the binary server parameter file concept in Oracle *9i*, Oracle has brought about a change in how these parameters are defined. This way, in the case of a RAC implementation, instead of having instance-specific parameter files, one parameter file that contains both the common parameters and instance-specific parameters can be used. However, the syntax for the parameter definition has changed. Parameters that are common to all instances are defined with a "*" in front of the parameter, and the instance-specific parameter is defined with the instance name in front of the parameter.

For example, when defining the location of the control file, the parameter CONTROL_FILES is defined as follows:

```
*.CONTROL_FILES=
  (/dev/vx/rdsk/oraracdg/partition300m_3,
    /dev/vx/rdsk/oraracdg/partition300m_10)
*.OPEN_CURSORS=400
*.DB_BLOCK_SIZE=8192
*.OPTIMIZER_MODE=CHOOSE
```

Notice the "*" in front of the parameter. This indicates that the parameter is applicable to both instances.

However, when defining the instance number, which is specific for every instance, the parameter is suffixed with the instance name:

```
RAC1.INSTANCE_NUMBER=1
RAC1.INSTANCE_NAME=RAC1
RAC1.INSTANCE_THREAD=1
```

Once these parameters have been added to the parameter file, there are two options: it could be retained in the location that contains the init.ora file in the traditional ASCII format, or at a suitable location from where it could be converted into a server parameter file stored in binary format.

The disadvantage of the server parameter file is that changes to the parameters, including additions and deletions, can only be done online while the instance is up.

A common file should be available to all instances from a common shared location. The server parameter file is no different. For this purpose it is important to identify a common shared area where the parameter file can be stored. This is true when RAC is implemented on systems that support clustered file systems or require raw device partitions.

The next step is to convert the existing ASCII parameter file (init.ora) to the binary file and store the file in the shared location:

```
oracle$ sqlplus '/as sysdba';
SQL*Plus: Release 9.2.0.1.0 - Production on Tue Oct 1 23:17:53 2002
Copyright (c) 1982, 2002, Oracle Corporation. All rights reserved.

Connected to:
Oracle9i Enterprise Edition Release 9.2.0.1.0 - 64bit Production
With the Partitioning, Real Application Clusters, OLAP and Oracle Data
  Mining options
JServer Release 9.2.0.1.0 - Production
```

```
SQL> show user
USER is "SYS"
SQL> create spfile='/new location' from pfile
File Create
```

Similar to a non-clustered database configuration where a soft link is created to the $ORACLE_HOME/dbs directory, under RAC also such a definition is required. However, unlike a stand-alone configuration in the case of a RAC implementation, each instance will have an instance-specific parameter file soft-linked from the shared disk to the $ORACLE_HOME/dbs directory:

```
ln -s <path/parameter file> <$ORACLE_HOME/dbs/
  <parameter file>
```

The above command from the operating system prompt will create the soft link from its current shared disk to this area.

For example, the symbolic link for the initPRODDB.ora could be created as illustrated below:

```
oracle$ ln -s $ORACLE_BASE/admin/PRODDB/pfile/initPRODDB.ora
  $ORACLE_HOME/dbs/initRAC1.ora
```

8.5.3 Password file configuration

Oracle requires a password file to create and maintain passwords for schema owners with sysdba and sysoper privileges, for example the sys user. This file is important and should be current for the database to start. If the database structure was to change, this indirectly affects the control file, causing it to refresh the password file information and a new password file is required. What this implies is that every time the database is opened, the password file is verified against the control file.

A password file for each instance can be created using the following command:

```
orapwd file=<path/file_name> entries=<no of entries> password=<pass-
  password>
```

For example, a password file for the RAC1 instance is created as below:

```
oracle$ orapwd file=$ORACLE_HOME/dbs/orapwRAC1 entries=32 pass-
  word=oracle
```

8.6   Database administration

Space management, instance management, schema management, reorganization, etc., are all common database administration functions that are also applicable in a RAC configuration. This section will look at some of the administration activities around the various tasks listed above and will also look at some day-to-day basic tasks like starting and stopping of instances and configuration of SQL*Net.

8.6.1   Space management

Space management depends on the type of storage used for implementing a RAC configuration. For example, when using locally managed tablespaces and automatic segment management on raw devices, it is important that the tablespaces should not be created with autoextend or unlimited clauses. Raw partitions are fixed in size, which means that once the maximum size at which the partition has been created is reached, it cannot grow further. However, in the case of a CFS configuration, unlimited tablespace quota and autoextend do not have such restrictions.

8.6.2   Automatic undo management (AUM)

Under this feature, Oracle manages the segment free and used space with bitmaps, as opposed to free lists and free list groups. Automatic segment-space management is simpler to administer than free lists and it provides improved space utilization. To use AUM the following parameters have to be defined in the parameter file:

- UNDO_MANAGEMENT=<AUTO>: This parameter enables the undo management feature and tells Oracle at instance startup that AUM has been requested.

- UNDO_TABLESPACE=<filename>: This parameter is used to assign the name of the UNDO tablespace for the instance. It is recommended that each instance will have its own UNDO tablespace. The drawback of not setting this parameter in the parameter file and making it available to Oracle during instance startup is that Oracle will use the first available UNDO tablespace.

Using the AUM option for tablespace management ignores most of the storage definition values. For example, the FREE LISTS, FREE LIST GROUPS, and PCTUSED are ignored for bitmap segments. These columns contain NULL values in the database dictionary views. However, PCTFREE can be specified for bitmap segments.

UNDO tablespace files can be switched by using the following command:

```
ALTER SYSTEM SET UNDO_TABLESPACE = <tablesapce name>
```

This command will switch the undo tablespace to this new tablespace.

8.6.3   SYSTEM rollback segment

The only external rollback segment used by Oracle with AUM is the SYSTEM rollback segment. Each database has only one SYSTEM rollback segment and RAC uses the same SYSTEM rollback segment for all instances.

8.6.4   Schema management

Management of user definitions or objects such as tables, views, indexes, etc., created by a user is called schema management. This includes reorganization of tables and indexes.

8.6.5   Setting environment variables

On Unix platforms, certain commands or group of commands can be redefined by using environment variables. For example, ORACLE_HOME is an environment variable that points to the Oracle home directory. Similarly, if the node has multiple instances, before accessing any specific instance via SQL*Plus, it is required that the SID environment variable point to the SID that is of interest or the SID be specified as part of the connect command.

The following command will set the environment variable for the SID:

```
oracle$ ORACLE_SID=RAC1
oracle$ export ORACLE_SID
```

8.6.6   Instance management

In this section the various instance management operations and verification process will be discussed. Many of the instance management operations like starting, stopping of instances, starting, stopping of listener, etc., are similar to the operations on a single stand-alone configuration of Oracle.

Shutting down an instance

This operation is similar to shutdown processes on a regular stand alone configuration:

```
oracle$ sqlplus '/as sysdba'
SQL> shutdown immediate;
```

This command shuts down the instance immediately after all the transactions that are active on the instance have committed their work:

```
SQL>shutdown abort;
```

This command shuts down the instance abnormally. Oracle forces all user processes running in that instance to log off the database. The user that was terminated by this abnormal operation receives the following error message "ORA-1092: Oracle instance terminated. Disconnection forced." However, if the user process is not currently accessing the database, the user receives the following error message: "ORA-1012 Not logged on."

When the instance is shut down abnormally, Oracle has to perform recovery on instance restart or, in the case of RAC, as the surviving instances will perform the recovery task:

```
SQL>shutdown transactional
```

This command with the LOCAL option will shut down the instance after all the active transactions on the instance have either committed or rolled back. If the LOCAL option is not specified, then the shutdown transaction has a global effect, in the sense that it waits until the active transactions on all other instances have issued either a commit or rollback operation.

Starting an instance

The following command will start the local instance or the instance where the environment variable is currently pointing:

```
oracle$ sqlplus '/as sysdba'
SQL*Plus: Release 9.2.0.1.0 - Production on Wed Oct 9 18:07:16 2002
Copyright (c) 1982, 2002, Oracle Corporation.  All rights reserved.

Connected to an idle instance.

SQL> startup
ORACLE instance started.
```

```
Total System Global Area      450937896 bytes
Fixed Size     730152     bytes
Variable Size              285212672      bytes
Database Buffers           163840000      bytes
Redo Buffers 1155072     bytes
Database mounted.
Database opened.
SQL>
```

Quiescing a RAC database

The quiescing of a RAC database is similar to quiescing a single stand-alone database, except for certain limitations. When quiescing a database from an instance, the other instances cannot open the database. For example, when an ALTER SYSTEM QUIESCE RESTRICTED statement is issued and Oracle has not completed processing this statement, the database cannot be opened from the current or any other instance participating in the clustered configuration.

Verifying the instances

From any of the instances participating in the clustered configuration, the following command will display a list of instances.

```
SQL> SELECT * FROM V$ACTIVE_INSTANCES;
```

- INST_NUMBER identifies the instance number.

- INST_NAME identifies the host name and instance name.

8.7 Adding nodes in RAC

One of the great advantages of the clustered configuration is to add or remove nodes from the cluster without affecting the other already existing instances in the cluster. This provides scalability to the applications using RAC. However, when adding nodes to the cluster and before allowing it to participate as an instance in the clustered configuration, certain pre-requisites or procedures have to be completed, as follows:

1. The node joining the cluster should have a cloned image of the operating system that matches the other nodes in the cluster. The cloned image should contain the same version including all patch sets applied. This step is a very important step; the operating system image should be an exact clone of the other nodes.

2. The server configuration file (on a Unix operating system) should be manually updated on the new node by copying it from an existing

node. The creation of the server configuration file is illustrated in Section 8.5.1 cluster configuration under step 3.

3. Depending on the original implementation, the disks have to be configured to use the clustered file system or for raw devices.

4. Once step 3 is complete and the node is part of the cluster ensure that all nodes are running and the new node is visible to all other nodes. This could be accomplished by using the `lsnodes-l` command on a Unix operating system.

5. (Perform this step only if using Oracle 10*g*). Using the OUI install the Oracle Cluster ready services (CRS) software on the new node. If the node has any other cluster software installed they should be disabled before CRS is installed.

6. (Perform this step only if using Oracle 10*g*). From an existing node, run the `clscfg -add` command, which configures the new node for the cluster.

7. Run the OUI to install RAC

8. On Unix platform, run the `root.sh` script on the new node to set up the configuration locations.

9. Create the instance either manually as described in Section 8.4.2 above or by running the DBCA utility.

10g   New Feature: CFS is a new service provided by Oracle in version 10*g*. That overrides the cluster ware product provided by most vendors. When using version 10*g* of RAC, the vendor provided cluster ware should be disabled.

8.8   Conclusion

In this chapter we looked at the various preconditions that need to be completed for the installation configuration and administration of a RAC database. During this process of installing the database we looked at the storage subsystem configuration, and raw devices, clustered file systems, and VERITAS clustered file systems, etc., were discussed and compared. In particular the steps required to configure a raw partition were discussed and tested.

Basic level administrative functionality around the installation and configuration of the listener, SQL*Net, and intelligent agent has been provided. A detailed discussion on the high availability and failover scenarios will be discussed in Chapter 10 (Availability and Scalability).

The chapter worked through the various steps of installing a RAC environment, and looked at certain cluster configurations like server control, global service daemon, etc., required for clustered database functioning. Finally, basic instance management commands like startup, shutdown, and quiesce operations were discussed.

In the next chapter we will look at the various data dictionaries, focusing specifically on RAC functionality. Their usefulness in everyday tasks and the information they provide will also be discussed.

9

Parameters and Views

9.1   Introduction

In the previous chapter we looked at the installation and configuration of a RAC environment. During this process we looked at the creation of a RAC database using DBCA versus the traditional manual method. Script creation continues to have several advantages over the GUI-based DBCA utility provided by Oracle, because the script provides an in-depth view of what happens at each stage of the database creation. This level of detailed information is hidden when the DBCA utility is used. Then we also looked at configuring the instances to be cluster aware.

During these discussions we also looked at database administration and configuration commands that are useful for day-to-day operational functions of a database administrator.

What good is a database and a clustered solution, when the characteristics of the database cannot be observed, analyzed, and tuned to satisfy the requirements of the business that it supports? The interfaces required for the observation, analysis, and tuning of RAC, are provided through the data dictionary views.

A photograph of a landscape provides an illustration of the area or imagination of the photographer from the actual characteristics of the area. Similarly, the data dictionary view provides a user-friendly presentation of the data from its underlying physical tables.

Data dictionary view contains a set of underlying system tables that Oracle maintains. The data dictionary views provide some of the cryptic data that is stored in these tables, in a more clean and optimized manner, to the administrators. These values are analyzed to manage the clustered database.

Data dictionary views are also available in a single stand-alone configuration of Oracle. However, in the case of clustered databases that have multiple instances talking to a common shared database, additional identification such as an instance number helps to identify how each instance is performing relative to the others and which specific instances could potentially be causing the problem, if any. This helps in drilling down the actual area of the problem.

In this chapter, the various data dictionary views that are more commonly required and used in a RAC implementation will be analyzed and discussed. While many of the views are used for basic day-to-day administrational activities, others are used to determine the health of the database. Only the functionalities of these views will be discussed in this chapter. The details of how some of the performance-related views will be used are covered later in Chapter 13 (Performance Tuning).

9.2   Types of views

There are basically two types of views provided by Oracle, called static views and dynamic views. The static views normally contain the administrative details, e.g., metadata information useful for day-to-day administration of the database. The dynamic views contain data that is dynamic in nature, i.e., the data in these views change either after the database is restarted, or in certain cases when a session leaves the database.

Static views can be of various kinds based on the functionality and permissions available for viewing these views. They are ALL_, DBA_, and USER_. The USER_ views only contain information pertaining to the user. To determine the various views pertaining to the specific category, the view called DICTIONARY provides a list under each category.

For example, the query below provides a list of all static dictionary views that are classified under ALL_ prefix:

```
SQL> SELECT TABLE_NAME FROM DICTIONARY WHERE TABLE_NAME LIKE 'ALL_%';

TABLE_NAME

-------------------------------

ALL_COL_PRIVS
ALL_COL_PRIVS_MADE
ALL_COL_PRIVS_RECD
ALL_CONSTRAINTS
ALL_CONS_COLUMNS
ALL_CONS_OBJ_COLUMNS
```

```
ALL_CONTEXT
ALL_DB_LINKS
ALL_DEF_AUDIT_OPTS
ALL_DEPENDENCIES
ALL_DIMENSIONS

...

...

ALL_HISTOGRAMS
ALL_JOBS
ALL_OUTLINES
ALL_OUTLINE_HINTS
ALL_SNAPSHOT_REFRESH_TIMES
```

The above is a listing of static views that begin with ALL_.

The dynamic views are dynamic in nature for two reasons. The first reason is that one or more views have derived columns from one or more underlying tables or views. The second reason is that many of the values in these views are volatile; they are only retained for the duration that the instance or session is active, and cleared once the instance is bounced or the session completes.

On a stand-alone configuration all dynamic views start with V$; for example, V$INSTANCE provides details about the instance. In this case, V$ views only provide visibility to information pertaining to a specific instance. In a RAC environment, two or more instances are configured to provide access to a common physical database. All dynamic views have a corresponding GV$ (global V$) dynamic view, and querying a GV$ view retrieves the V$ view information from all qualified instances. Instance level information in the GV$ views is identified by the additional column INST_ID, which displays the instance number from which the associated V$ view information was obtained.

GV$ views are visible only if the PARALLEL_MAX_SERVERS parameter is set to a value greater than zero on all instances mounting the database.

The following query will list all the dynamic views available in a specific release of Oracle:

```
SQL> SELECT TABLE_NAME FROM DICTIONARY WHERE TABLE_NAME LIKE 'GV$%';

TABLE_NAME

--------------------------------

GV$OPEN_CURSOR
GV$SUBCACHE
GV$DB_OBJECT_CACHE
```

```
GV$DB_PIPES
GV$VERSION
GV$CONTROLFILE
GV$DATABASE
GV$THREAD
GV$LOG
GV$STANDBY_LOG
GV$DATA FILE

...
...

GV$MAP_ELEMENT
GV$MAP_EXT_ELEMENT
GV$MAP_COMP_LIST
GV$MAP_SUBELEMENT
GV$MAP_FILE_IO_STACK
GV$MAP_LIBRARY
```

> **Note:** The static views are self-explanatory in the sense that the name describes its contents. For example, DBA_TABLES will list all the tables in the database with the corresponding ownership details that a user with DBA role assigned could view. ALL_TABLES will provide a list of all tables that are viewable by the user and that does not require DBA role privileges; similarly, the USER_TABLES will provide a list of tables that belong to the current user's schema.

While there is sufficient documentation available for static tables, the information pertaining to the dynamic views is comparatively scarce. Hence this chapter will only discuss the dynamic views that are required for the day-to-day administration and tuning of the RAC instances.

Dynamic views

These views are called dynamic views because they record real-time values that show and provide visibility to the current state of the database. While the static views provide the status and composition of the data dictionary, the dynamic V$ and GV$ views provide details on the health of the database. For example, what volume of data is contained in each table, does the table contain chained rows, how much data is being read and written to various tables, how much data is being pinned into the database buffer cache and how much is being reloaded? All such information provides a view of the current health of the database and helps the database administrator to take correct action to improve the performance by fixing the anomalies.

Depending on the type of information contained in these views, data in these view columns is obtained by one of the following methods:

1. Cardinality information pertaining to the various tables is gathered by using the ANALYZE or DBMS_STATS package. While ANALYZE has been the procedure used for a while, it is currently a deprecated method and is only available for backward compatibility. This procedure is being replaced with a new package DBMS_STATS. For example, the following command will gather schema level statistics for schema owner 'MVALLATH':

```
EXECUTE DBMS_STATS.GATHER_SCHEMA_STATS (OWNNAME=> 'MVALLATH',
  granularity=>'ALL, cascade=>TRUE);
```

2. Performance-related information, for example, number of selects, number of hits and misses on the data dictionary cache, or the segment level wait information, is only provided if the TIMED_STATISTICS parameter is set to TRUE. The TIMED_STATISTICS parameter can be set in one of two ways, dynamically using an ALTER command as below:

```
ALTER SYSTEM SET TIMED_STATISTICS=TRUE;
```

This will reset the value when the instance is restarted. Another way of setting this parameter is by permanently setting the value in the init<SID>.ora file. For example, the init<SID>.ora file will contain among other parameters the following:

```
*.JOB_QUEUE_PROCESSES = 2
*.OPEN_CURSORS = 1024
*.COMPATIBLE = 9.2.0.2
*.AUDIT_TRIAL = FALSE
*.TIMED_STATISTICS = TRUE
```

There is a general myth regarding this parameter, namely that TIMED_STATISTICS would consume CPU resources and hence should not be set to TRUE. The overhead by enabling this parameter is not significant. A considerable amount of write activity to the data dictionary occurs irrespective of this parameter being set. However, unless this parameter is set, no real-time data regarding the database characteristics is gathered for analysis and tuning. Also the benefits obtained by enabling this parameter outweighs the disadvantages of using this parameter.

338 9.2 Types of views

In the sections below we will discuss the various dynamic views that would be helpful in day-to-day administration and maintenance of RAC. This chapter will provide a great detail of information with respect to the views themselves and the underlying tables, with minor examples. A detailed discussion on its usability with respect to performance tuning of RAC configurations will be available in Chapters 13, 14, and 15 later in this book.

GV$ACTIVE_INSTANCES

This view helps map instance names to instance numbers for all instances that have the database currently mounted, i.e., the instance should be active and functioning. Instances that are offline or dismounted are not visible in this view.

Based on X$ Table: X$KSIMSI

Column	Datatype	Description
INST_ID	NUMBER	A unique number assigned to the instance via the parameter file when the instance was first created.
INST_NUMBER	NUMBER	The instance number.
INST_NAME	VARCHAR2(180)	The name assigned to the instance, for example, RAC1, RAC2, etc., and is represented in the following format: node_name.domain_ name:instance_name

```
SQL> COL INST_ID FORMAT 99
SQL> COL INST_NUMBER FORMAT 99
SQL> COL INST_NAME FORMAT A60
SQL> SELECT INST_ID, INST_NUMBER, INST_NAME FROM GV$ACTIVE_INSTANCES;
------------------------------------------------
21ora-db1.summerskyus.com:RAC1
22ora-db2.summerskyus.com:RAC2
11ora-db1.summerskyus.com:RAC1
12ora-db2.summerskyus.com:RAC2
```

GV$ARCHIVE

Archive logs are copies of redo log files, when a log file switch is completed; a copy of the redo log file is made to the archive log file destination specified in the parameter file. This view contains information on redo log files that are ready for archiving.

> **Note:** The information contained in this dynamic view is also present in the GV$LOG file and is a better view for archive-log-related information.

Based on X$ Tables: X$KCCLE and X$KCCDI

Column	Datatype	Description
INST_ID	NUMBER	A unique number assigned to the instance via the parameter file when the instance was first created.
GROUP#	NUMBER	Log file group number.
THREAD#	NUMBER	Log file thread number.
SEQUENCE#	NUMBER	Log file sequence number.
ISCURRENT	VARCHAR2(3)	Indicates if this is the current online redo log. *Note:* This is a new column introduced in Oracle 9*i*.
CURRENT	VARCHAR2(3)	Contains the same value as ISCURRENT. *Note:* This column is obsolete in Oracle 9*i* and is retained for backward compatibility.
FIRST_CHANGE#	NUMBER	First SCN stored in the current log.

GV$ARCHIVE_DEST

This view provides a list of all archive log destinations defined in the parameter file, the details such as the current value, the archive log mode, and current status.

Based on X$ Table: X$KCRRDEST

Column	Datatype	Description
INST_ID	NUMBER	A unique number assigned to the instance via the parameter file when the instance was first created.
DEST_ID	NUMBER	Identifies the log archive destination parameter. The number of destinations could be between 1 to 10.
DEST_NAME	VARCHAR2(256)	Specifies the parameter used to configure this archive log file. For example LOG_ARCHIVE_DEST_1

STATUS	VARCHAR2(9)	Identifies the current status of the destination. The potential values for this column include: VALID: Initialized and available INACTIVE: No destination information DEFERRED: Manually disabled by the user ERROR: Error during open or copy DISABLED: Disabled after error BAD PARAM: Parameter has errors ALTERNATE: Destination is an alternate state FULL: Exceeded quota size for the destination
BINDING	VARCHAR2(9)	Specifies how failure will affect the archival operation. The valid values for the column include: MANDATORY: Successful archival is required OPTIONAL: Successful archival is not required and is based on the parameter LOG_ARCHIVE_MIN_SUCCEED_DEST
NAME_SPACE	VARCHAR2(7)	Identifies the scope of the parameter setting. The valid values for this column include: SYSTEM: System definition SESSION: Session definition
TARGET	VARCHAR2(7)	Specifies whether the archive destination is local or remote to the primary database. The valid values for this column include: PRIMARY: This value indicates that the destination is local STANDBY: This value indicates that the destination is at a remote location, which could be system configured for STANDBY/DATA GUARD purposes
ARCHIVER	VARCHAR2(10)	Identifies the archiver process relative to the database where the query is issued. The valid values for this column include: ARCn FOREGROUND LGWR RFS

SCHEDULE	VARCHAR2(8)	Indicates whether the archival of this destination is INACTIVE, PENDING, ACTIVE or LATENT.
DESTINATION	VARCHAR2(256)	Specifies the physical location for the archived logs. This is the value for the parameter defined in the DEST_NAME column.
LOG_SEQUENCE	NUMBER	Identifies the sequence number of the last archived redo log to be archived.
REOPEN_SECS	NUMBER	Identifies the retry time (in seconds) after error.
DELAY_MINS	NUMBER	Identifies the delay interval (in minutes) before the archived redo log is automatically applied to a standby database.
NET_TIMEOUT	NUMBER	Number of seconds the log writer process will wait for status from the network server of a network operation issued by the log writer process.
PROCESS	VARCHAR2(10)	Identifies the archiver process relative to the primary database, even if the query is issued on the standby database: ARCn FOREGROUND LGWR
REGISTER	VARCHAR2(3)	Indicates whether the archived redo log is registered in the remote destination control file. If the archived redo log is registered, it is available to the managed recovery operation. The valid values are: YES: The archived redo log file has been registered in the remote destination control file NO: The archived redo log file has not been registered
FAIL_DATE	DATE	Date and time when the last error was encountered.
FAIL_SEQUENCE	NUMBER	Sequence number of the archived redo log being archived when the last error occurred.
FAIL_BLOCK	NUMBER	Block number of the archived redo log being archived when the last error occurred.

FAILURE_COUNT	NUMBER	Current number of contiguous archival operation failures that have occurred for the destination.
MAX_FAILURE	NUMBER	Contains the number of times log transport services should attempt to re-establish communication and resume archival operations with a failed destination.
ERROR	VARCHAR2(256)	Displays the error text message of the last error.
ALTERNATE	VARCHAR2(256)	Specifies an alternative destination if any defined in the parameter file.
DEPENDENCY	VARCHAR2(256)	Indicates the dependent archive destination.
REMOTE_TEMPLATE	VARCHAR2(256)	Indicates the details of the template that is to be used to derive the location to be recorded.
QUOTA_SIZE	NUMBER	Quotas allocated for the archive log file at the remote destination and is expressed in bytes.
QUOTA_USED	NUMBER	Indicates the size of all the archived redo logs currently residing on the specified destination.
MOUNTID	NUMBER	Instance mount identifier.
TRASMIT_MODE	VARCHAR2(12)	Indicates the current network transmission mode defined for the transfer of archive redo log file to a remote destination: ASYNC=PARALLEL SYNC=NOPARALLEL
ASYNC_BLOCKS	NUMBER	Number of blocks specified for the ASYNC attribute.
AFFIRM	VARCHAR2(3)	Specifies disk I/O mode.
TYPE	VARCHAR2(7)	Indicates whether the archived log destination definition is PUBLIC or PRIVATE. Only PUBLIC destinations can be modified at runtime using the ALTER SYSTEM SET or ALTER SESSION SET statements. PUBLIC is the default type.
SP_NAME (Introduced in Oracle 10g)	VAARCHAR2(30)	Service provider name

GV$ARCHIVED_LOG

This view displays archived log information from the control file, including archive log names. An archive log record is inserted after the online redo log is successfully archived or cleared. If the log is archived twice, there will be two archived log records with the same THREAD#, SEQUENCE# and FIRST_CHANGE#, however with a different name.

An archive log record is also inserted when an archive log is restored from a backup set or a copy and whenever a copy of a log is made with the RMAN copy command.

Column	Datatype	Description
INST_ID	NUMBER	A unique number assigned to the instance via the parameter file when the instance was first created.
RECID	NUMBER	Archived log record ID.
STAMP	NUMBER	Archived log record stamp.
NAME	VARCHAR2(513)	Archived log file name. If the column contains a NULL, then it indicates that the log file was cleared before it was archived.
DEST_ID	NUMBER	The original destination from which the archive log was generated.
THREAD#	NUMBER	Redo thread number.
SEQUENCE#	NUMBER	Redo log sequence number.
RESETLOGS_CHANGE#	NUMBER	Resetlogs change# of the database when this log was written.
RESETLOGS_TIME	DATE	Resetlogs time of the database when the log was written.
FIRST_CHANGE#	NUMBER	First change# in the archived logs.
FIRST_TIME	DATE	Timestamp of the first change.
NEXT_CHANGE#	NUMBER	First change in the next log.
NEXT_TIME	DATE	Timestamp of the next change.
BLOCKS	NUMBER	Size of the archived log in blocks.
BLOCK_SIZE	NUMBER	Redo log block size. This is the logical block size of the archived log, which is the same as the logical block size of the online log from which this archived log was copied. The online log logical block size is a platform-specific value that is not adjustable by the user.
CREATOR	VARCHAR2(7)	Identifies the creator of the archive log.
REGISTRAR	VARCHAR2(7)	Identifies the registrar of the archive log.
STANDBY_DEST	VARCHAR2(3)	Indicates if the entry is an archive log destination.

ARCHIVED	VARCHAR2(3)	Indicates that the online redo was archived or that RMAN only inspected the log and created a record for future application of redo logs during recovery.
APPLIED (Introduced in Oracle 9i)	VARCHAR2(3)	Indicates whether or not the archive log has been applied to its corresponding standby database. YES: Indicates that it has been applied NO: Indicates it has not been applied
DELETED	VARCHAR2(3)	Specifies whether an RMAN delete command has physically deleted the archived log file from disk, as well as logically removing it from the control of the target database and from the recovery catalog.
STATUS (Introduced in Oracle 9i)	VARCHAR2(1)	The status of this archived log. Possible values are: A: Available D: Deleted U: Unavailable X: Expired
COMPLETION_TIME	DATE	Time when the archiving was completed.
DICTIONARY_BEGIN (Introduced in Oracle 9i)	VARCHAR2(3)	Indicates whether or not this log contains the start of a LogMiner dictionary. The valid values are: YES: This log contains the start of a LogMiner dictionary NO: This log does not contain the start of a LogMiner dictionary
DICTIONARY_END (Introduced in Oracle 9i)	VARCHAR2(3)	Indicates whether or not this log contains the end of a LogMiner dictionary. The valid values are: YES: This log contains the end of a LogMiner dictionary NO: This log does not contain the end of a LogMiner dictionary
END_OF_REDO (Introduced in Oracle 9i)	VARCHAR2(3)	Indicates whether or not this archived redo log contains the end of all redo information from the primary database. The valid values are: YES: This log contains the end of all redo information NO: This log does not contain the end of all redo information

BACKUP_COUNT (Introduced in Oracle 9i)	NUMBER	Indicates the number of times that has been backed up. Values range from 0 to 15. If the file has been backed up more than 15 times the value remains.
ARCHIVAL_THREAD# (Introduced in Oracle 9i)	NUMBER	Indicates the redo thread number of the instance that performed the archival operation. This column differs from the THREAD# column only when a closed thread is archived by another instance.
ACTIVIATION# (Introduced in Oracle 9i)	NUMBER	This is used if Oracle Data Guard has been configured and indicates processes to manage any logfile transfer gaps using the FAL_ CLIENT and FAL_SERVER parameters on the primary and Data Guard database. It indicates the number assigned to the database instantiation.
IS_RECOVERY_DEST _FILE (Introduced in Oracle 10g)	VARCHAR2(3)	Indicates whether the file was created in the recovery area destination (YES) or not (NO)
COMPRESSED (Introduced in Oracle 10g)	VARCHAR2(3)	Indicates whether the archived log is compressed (YES) or not (NO)

GV$ARCHIVE_PROCESSES

This view provides information about the current state of the various archive processes on the cluster. This view would be helpful for debugging or analyzing delays in the archive process.

Based on X$ Table: X$KCRRARCH

Column	Datatype	Description
INST_ID	NUMBER	A unique number assigned to the instance via the parameter file when the instance was first created.
PROCESS	NUMBER	The identifier for the ARCH process for the instance, numbered 0–9.
STATUS	VARCHAR2(10)	The current status of the ARCH process. This column indicates if the archive process corresponding to the process number has been configured or defined in the parameter file. The possible values for this column are: STOPPED: Never scheduled or configured SCHEDULED: Currently in the scheduled state but not started

		STARTING: Currently in the process of starting; this is a state after scheduled
		ACTIVE: Indicates that the specific ARCH process has been configured
		STOPPING: The archive run is complete and is currently stopping before going back to a scheduled status
		TERMINATED: ARCH process was terminated abnormally either by process crash or by a system failure including instance crash
LOG_SEQUENCE	NUMBER	Indicates the current log sequence number being archived. There are two possible values:
		The actual log sequence number
		Zero (indicates that the ARCH process is idle)
STATE	VARCHAR2(4)	This is the current state of the ARCH process. Possible values are:
		IDLE: ARCH process is pausing before the next schedule
		BUSY: ARCH process is currently in the middle of archiving

GV$BGPROCESS

This view provides a description of all the background processes used by Oracle on each instance.

Based on X$ Table: X$KSBDP and X$KSBDD

Column	Datatype	Description
INST_ID	NUMBER	A unique number assigned to the instance via the parameter file when the instance was first created.
PADDR	RAW(4)	Address of the process state object. A raw value in this column indicates that the background process has been configured.
NAME	VARCHAR2(5)	Name of the background process.
DESCRIPTION	VARCHAR2(64)	Description of the background process.
ERROR	NUMBER	Error encountered.

GV$BH

This view specifically contains information pertaining to RAC and provides the status and number of local forced writes and forced reads for every buffer in the buffer cache. It is a very important view and provides critical information used for performance monitoring of the RAC instances.

Based on X$ Tables: X$BH and X$LE

Column	Datatype	Description
INST_ID	NUMBER	A unique number assigned to the instance via the parameter file when the instance was first created.
FILE#	NUMBER	Data file identifier. The value in this column could be used to join against the DBA_DATA_FILES or V$DBFILES.
BLOCK#	NUMBER	Block number.
CLASS#	NUMBER	Class number.
STATUS	VARCHAR2(1)	Status of the buffer: FREE: Not currently in use XCUR: Exclusive SCUR: Shared current CR: Consistent read READ: Being read from disk MREC: In media recovery mode IREC: In instance recovery mode PI: Past image
XNC	NUMBER	Obsolete in Oracle 9i. Retained for backward compatibility. In 9i this column has no value.
LOCK_ELEMENT_ADDR	RAW(4)	The address of the lock element that is locking this buffer. If two buffers have the same LOCK_ELEMENT_ADDR value lock_element_addr then they are being protected by the same lock.
LOCK_ELEMENT_NAME	NUMBER	The address of the lock element that is locking this buffer.
LOCK_ELEMENT_CLASS	NUMBER	The address of the lock element that is locking this buffer.
FORCED_READS	NUMBER	Number of times the block had to be reread from disk because another instance had forced it out of this instance's cache by requesting the lock on this block in lock mode.
FORCED_WRITES	NUMBER	Number of times DBWn had to write this block to disk because this instance had dirtied the block and another instance had requested the lock on the block in conflicting mode.

DIRTY	VARCHAR2(1)	Y indicates that the block was dirtied or modified.
TEMP	VARCHAR2(1)	Y indicates that the block is a temporary block.
PING	VARCHAR2(1)	Y indicates that the block was pinged.
STALE	VARCHAR2(1)	Y indicates that the block is now stale in the current instance.
DIRECT	VARCHAR2(1)	Y indicates that the direct block.
NEW	VARCHAR2(1)	This column has no value in Oracle 9*i*. Its obsolete.
OBJD	NUMBER	Database object number of the block that the buffer represents.
TS#	NUMBER	Tablespace number that the block belongs to. The value in this column could be joined with the V$TABLESPACE view to determine the actual tablespace the block belongs to.

Columns FORCED_READS and FORCED_WRITES together represent the number of disk I/Os an instance has to perform on each block in the cache due to conflicting lock requests by other instances. These I/Os are wasteful, since they occur only due to lock activity and thus they need to be ignored.

GV$CR_BLOCK_SERVER

This view displays statistics on the block server background process (BSPn) used in cache fusion with RAC.

Based on X$ Table: X$KCLCRST

Column	Datatype	Description
INST_ID	NUMBER	A unique number assigned to the instance via the parameter file when the instance was first created.
CR_REQUESTS	NUMBER	Number of requests received for a version of a block at a specific SCN.
CURRENT_REQUESTS	NUMBER	Number of requests for the most recent version of a block.
DATA_REQUESTS	NUMBER	Number of current or CR requests for data blocks.
UNDO_REQUESTS	NUMBER	Number of CR requests for undo blocks.
TX_REQUESTS	NUMBER	Number of CR requests for undo segment header blocks.

CURRENT_RESULTS	NUMBER	Number of requests for which no changes were rolled out of the block returned to the requesting instance.
PRIVATE_RESULTS	NUMBER	Number of requests for which changes were rolled out of the block returned to the requesting instance. Only zero-XID transactions can use the block.
ZERO_RESULTS	NUMBER	Number of requests for which changes were rolled out of the block returned to the requesting instance. Only zero-XID transactions can use the block.
DISK_READ_RESULTS	NUMBER	Number of requests for which the requesting instance had to read the requested block from disk.
FAIL_RESULTS	NUMBER	Number of requests that failed; the requesting transaction must reissue the request.
FAIRNESS_DOWN_CONVERTS	NUMBER	Number of times an instance receiving a request has down-converted an X lock on a block because it was not modifying the block.
FAIRNESS_CLEARS	NUMBER	Number of times the "fairness counter" was cleared. This counter tracks the number of times a block was modified after it was served.
FREE_GC_ELEMENTS	NUMBER	Number of times a request was received from another instance and the X lock had no buffers.
FLUSHES	NUMBER	Number of times the log has been flushed by a BSPn process.
LIGHT_WORKS	NUMBER	Number of times the light-work rule was evoked. This rule prevents the BSP background process from going to disk while responding to CR requests for data, undo, or undo segment header blocks. This rule can prevent the BSPn process from completing its response to the CR request.

GV$CACHE

This is another view that contains performance-related data for RAC. This view contains information from the block header of each block in the SGA of the current instance as related to particular database objects.

Column	Datatype	Description
INST_ID	NUMBER	A unique number assigned to the instance via the parameter file when the instance was first created.
FILE#	NUMBER	Data file identifier. The value in this column could be used to join against the DBA_DATA_FILES or V$DBFILES.
BLOCK#	NUMBER	Block number.
CLASS#	NUMBER	The class number.
STATUS	VARCHAR2(1)	Status of the buffer: FREE: Not currently in use XCUR: Exclusive SCUR: Shared current CR: Consistent read READ: Being read from disk MREC: In media recovery mode IREC: In instance recovery mode PI: Past image
XNC	NUMBER	Obsolete in Oracle 9*i*. Retained for backward compatibility. In 9*i* this column has no value.
FORCED_READS	NUMBER	Number of times the block had to be reread from disk because another instance had forced it out of this instance's cache by requesting the lock on this block in lock mode.
FORCED_WRITES	NUMBER	Number of times DBWR had to write this block to disk because this instance had dirtied the block and another instance had requested the lock on the block in conflicting mode.
NAME	VARCHAR2(30)	Name of the database object containing the block.
PARTITION_NAME	VARCHAR2(30)	The name of the partition; NULL for non-partitioned objects.

KIND	VARCHAR2(12)	Type of database object. The column contains the following potential values:

1: INDEX
2: TABLE
3: CLUSTER
4: VIEW
5: SYNONYM
6: SEQUENCE
7: PROCEDURE
8: FUNCTION
9: PACKAGE
10: NONEXISTENT
11: PACKAGE BODY
12: TRIGGER
13: TYPE
14: TYPE BODY
19: TABLE PARTITION
20: INDEX PARTITION
21: LOB
22: LIBRARY

OWNER#	NUMBER	Owner number.
LOCK_ELEMENT_ADDR	RAW(4)	The address of the lock element that is locking this buffer. If two buffers have the same LOCK_ELEMENT_ADDR value then the same lock is protecting them.
LOCK_ELEMENT_NAME	NUMBER	The address of the lock element that is locking this buffer.

GV$CACHE_LOCK

This is a RAC view and contains information similar to that found in the GV$CACHE view; however, it contains platform-specific lock manager identifiers. This information may be useful if the platform-specific lock manager provides tools for monitoring the PCM lock operations that are occurring. For example, first query to find the lock element address using INDX and CLASS, then query GV$BH to find the buffers that are covered by the lock.

Column	Datatype	Description
INST_ID	NUMBER	A unique number assigned to the instance via the parameter file when the instance was first created.

FILE#	NUMBER	Block number.
STATUS	VARCHAR2(4)	Status of block: FREE: Not currently in use XCUR: Exclusive SCUR: Shared current CR: Consistent read READ: Being read from disk MREC: In media recovery mode IREC: In instance recovery mode
XNC	NUMBER	Number of parallel cache management PCM lock conversions due to contention with another instance.
NAME	VARCHAR2(30)	Name of the database object containing the block.
KIND	VARCHAR2(12)	Type of database object:

1: INDEX
2: TABLE
3: CLUSTER
4: VIEW
5: SYNONYM
6: SEQUENCE
7: PROCEDURE
8: FUNCTION
9: PACKAGE
10: NONEXISTENT
11: PACKAGE BODY
12: TRIGGER
13: TYPE
14: TYPE BODY
19: TABLE PARTITION
20: INDEX PARTITION
21: LOB
22: LIBRARY
Null: UNKNOWN

OWNER#	NUMBER	Owner number.
LOCK_ELEMENT_ADDR	RAW(4)	The address of the lock element that contains the PCM lock that is covering the buffer. If two or more buffers have the same address, then these buffers are covered by the same PCM lock.
LOCK_ELEMENT_NAME	NUMBER	The address of the lock element that contains the PCM lock that is covering the buffer. If two or more buffers

		have the same address, then these buffers are covered by the same PCM lock.
FORCED_READS	NUMBER	Number of times the block had to be reread from disk because another instance had forced it out of this instance's cache by requesting the lock on this block in lock mode.
FORCED_WRITES	NUMBER	Number of times DBWR had to write this block to disk because this instance had dirtied the block and another instance had requested the lock on the block in conflicting mode.
INDX	NUMBER	Platform-specific lock manager identifier.
CLASS	NUMBER	Platform-specific lock manager identifier.

GV$CACHE_TRANSFER

This is a RAC-specific view. This view is also identical to the GV$CACHE view; however, it only displays blocks that have been pinged at least once. It contains information from the block header of each block in the SGA of the current instance as related to particular database objects.

Column	Datatype	Description
INST_ID	NUMBER	A unique number assigned to the instance via the parameter file when the instance was first created.
FILE#	NUMBER	Data file identifier. The value in this column could be used to join against the DBA_ DATA_ FILES or V$DBFILES.
BLOCK#	NUMBER	Block number.
CLASS#	NUMBER	Class number.
STATUS	VARCHAR2(1)	Status of the buffer: FREE: Not currently in use XCUR: Exclusive SCUR: Shared current CR: Consistent read READ: Being read from disk MREC: In media recovery mode

		IREC: In instance recovery mode
		PI: Past image
XNC	NUMBER	Obsolete in Oracle 9i. Retained for backward compatibility. In 9i this column has no value.
FORCED_READS	NUMBER	Number of times the block had to be reread from disk because another instance had forced it out of this instance's cache by requesting the lock on this block in lock mode.
FORCED_WRITES	NUMBER	Number of times DBWn had to write this block to disk because this instance had dirtied the block and another instance had requested the lock on the block in conflicting mode.
NAME	VARCHAR2(30)	Name of the database object containing the block.
PARTITION_NAME	VARCHAR2(30)	The name of the partition; NULL for non-partitioned objects.
KIND	VARCHAR2(12)	Type of database object. The column contains the following potential values:

1: INDEX
2: TABLE
3: CLUSTER
4: VIEW
5: SYNONYM
6: SEQUENCE
7: PROCEDURE
8: FUNCTION
9: PACKAGE
10: NONEXISTENT
11: PACKAGE BODY
12: TRIGGER
13: TYPE
14: TYPE BODY
19: TABLE PARTITION
20: INDEX PARTITION
21: LOB
22: LIBRARY

OWNER#	NUMBER	Owner number.
GC_ELEMENT_ADDR	RAW(4)	The address of the lock element that is locking this buffer.

| | | If two buffers have the same LOCK_ELEMENT_ADDR value then the same lock is protecting them. |
| GC_ELEMENT_NAME | NUMBER | The address of the lock element that is locking this buffer. |

GV$DB_CACHE_ADVICE

This view contains rows that predict the number of physical reads for the cache size corresponding to each row. The rows also compute a "physical read factor," which is the ratio of the number of estimated reads to the number of reads actually performed by the real buffer cache during the measurement interval.

Based on X$ Tables: X$KCBSC and X$KCBWBPD

Column	Datatype	Description
INST_ID	NUMBER	A unique number assigned to the instance via the parameter file when the instance was first created.
ID	NUMBER	Buffer pool identifier; values range from 1 to 8.
NAME	VARCHAR2(20)	Buffer pool name.
BLOCK_SIZE	NUMBER	Block size in bytes for buffers in this pool. Possible values: the standard block size, the power of 2 non-standard block size, 2048, 4096, 8192, 16,384, 32,768.
ADVICE_STATUS	VARCHAR2(3)	Status of the advisory: ON indicates it is currently running OFF indicates it is disabled
SIZE_FOR_ESTIMATE	NUMBER	Cache size for predication (in megabytes).
BUFFERS_FOR_ ESTIMATE	NUMBER	Cache size for prediction (in terms of buffers).
EST_PHYSICAL _READ_FACTOR	NUMBER	Physical read factor for this cache size, which is the ratio of the number of estimated physical reads to the number of reads in the real cache. If there are no

		physical reads in the real cache, the value of this column is null.
ESTD_PHYSICAL_READS NUMBER		Estimated number of physical reads for this cache size.

New Feature: This view is new with Oracle Version 9.1.0 and is populated only if the DB_CACHE parameter is used instead of the DB_BLOCK_BUFFERS parameter and the DB_CACHE_ADVICE parameter is enabled.

GV$DB_OBJECT_CACHE

This view displays database objects that are cached in the library cache. Objects include tables, indexes, clusters, synonym definitions, PL/SQL procedures and packages, and triggers.

Based on X$ Table: X$KGLOB

Column	Datatype	Description
INST_ID	NUMBER	A unique number assigned to the instance via the parameter file when the instance was first created.
OWNER	VARCHAR2(64)	Owner of the object.
NAME	VARCHAR2(1000)	Name of the object.
DB_LINE	VARCHAR2(64)	Database link name.
NAMESPACE	VARCHAR2(28)	Library cache namespace of the object: TABLE/PROCEDURE, BODY, TRIGGER, INDEX, CLUSTER, OBJECT
TYPE	VARCHAR2(28)	Type of the object: INDEX, TABLE CLUSTER VIEW, SET, SYNONYM, SEQUENCE, PROCEDURE, FUNCTION, PACKAGE, PACKAGE BODY, TRIGGER, CLASS, OBJECT, USER, DBLINK
SHARABLE_MEM	NUMBER	Amount of sharable memory in the shared pool consumed by the object.
LOADS	NUMBER	Number of times the object has been loaded. This count also increases when an object has been invalidated.
EXECUTIONS	NUMBER	Execution counts, column not used.

LOCKS	NUMBER	Number of users currently locking this object.
PINS	NUMBER	Number of users currently pinning this object.
KEPT	VARCHAR2(3)	Indicates if the object has been kept with the package DBMS_SHARED_POOL_KEEP. Valid values are: YES: Has been kept NO: Has not been kept
CHILD_LATCH	NUMBER	Child latch number that is protecting the object.

GV$ENQUEUE_LOCK

This view describes the locks pertaining to enqueue state objects. You will notice that the columns in this view are identical to the columns in GV$LOCK view; however, the contents vary. While GV$LOCK describes locks held by the Oracle server and outstanding requests for a lock or latch, the GV$ENQUEUE_LOCK describes locks pertaining to enqueue state objects.

Based on X$ Tables: X$KSQEQ, X$KSUSE, and X$KSQRS

Column	Datatype	Description
INST_ID	NUMBER	A unique number assigned to the instance via the parameter file when the instance was first created.
ADDR	RAW(4)	Address of lock state object.
KADDR	RAW(4)	Address of lock.
SID	NUMBER	Identifier for session holding or acquiring the lock.
TYPE	VARCHAR2(2)	Type of lock. Lists users and system types that can have locks.
ID1	NUMBER	Lock identifier #1 (depends on type).
ID2	NUMBER	Lock identifier #2 (depends on type).
LMODE	NUMBER	Lock mode in which the session holds the lock:
		0: None 1: Null (NULL) 2: Row S (SS) 3: Row X (SX) 4: Share (S) 5: S/Row: X (SSX) 6: Exclusive (X)

REQUEST	NUMBER	Lock mode in which the process requests the lock: 0: None 1: Null (NULL) 2: Row S (SS) 3: Row X (SX) 4: Share (S) 5: S/Row: X (SSX) 6: Exclusive (X)
CTIME	NUMBER	Time since current mode was granted.
BLOCK	NUMBER	The lock is blocking another lock.

GV$ENQUEUE_STAT

This view displays statistics on the number of enqueue (lock) requests for each type lock.

Based on X$ Table: X$KSQST

Column	Datatype	Description
INST_ID	NUMBER	A unique number assigned to the instance via the parameter file when the instance was first created.
EQ_TYPE	VARCHAR2(2)	Type of enqueue requested.
TOTAL_REQ#	NUMBER	Total number of enqueue requests or enqueue conversions for this type of enqueue.
TOTAL_WAIT#	NUMBER	Total number of times an enqueue request or conversion resulted in a wait.
SUCC_REQ#	NUMBER	Number of times an enqueue request or conversion was granted.
FAILED_REQ#	NUMBER	Number of times an enqueue request or conversion failed.
CUM_WAIT_TIME	NUMBER	Total number of times (in milliseconds) spent waiting for the enqueue or enqueue conversion.

GV$EVENT_NAME

This view provides a listing of all events and parameter definitions.

Based on X$ Table: X$KSLED

Column	Datatype	Description
INST_ID	NUMBER	A unique number assigned to the instance via the parameter file when the instance was first created.
EVENT#	NUMBER	The number of the wait event.
NAME	VARCHAR2(64)	The name of the event.

PARAMETER1	VARCHAR2(64)	The description of the first parameter for the wait event.
PARAMETER2	VARCHAR2(64)	The description of the second parameter for wait event.
PARAMETER3	VARCHAR2(64)	The description of the third parameter for the wait event.
CLASS# (Introduced in Oracle 10g)	NUMBER	Number of the class of the wait event
CLASS (Introduced in Oracle 10g)	VARCHAR2 (64)	Name of the class of the wait event

Note: Details about the various events names and the respective values for the various parameter columns can be found in the Oracle reference manual.

GV$FALSE_PING

This view is for RAC implementations and displays buffers that may be getting false pings. Buffers identified as getting false pings can be remapped in GC_FILES_TO_LOCKS to reduce lock collisions.

Column	Datatype	Description
INST_ID	NUMBER	A unique number assigned to the instance via the parameter file when the instance was first created.
FILE#	NUMBER	Data file identifier number. The value in this column could be used to join against the V$DATA_FILE to get the name of the file.
BLOCK#	NUMBER	Block number.
STATUS	VARCHAR2(1)	Status of block: FREE: Not currently in use XCUR: Exclusive SCUR: Shared current CR: Consistent read READ: Being read from disk MREC: In media recovery mode IREC: In instance recovery mode
XNC	NUMBER	Number of PCM lock conversion from Exclusive mode due to contention with another instance. This column is

		obsolete but is retained for historical compatibility.
FORCED_READS	NUMBER	Number of times the block had to reread from disk because another instance had forced it out of this instance's cache by requesting the PCM lock on the block in exclusive mode.
FORCED_WRITES	NUMBER	Number of times DBWR had to write this block to disk because this instance had dirtied the block and another instance had requested the lock on the block in conflicting mode.
NAME	VARCHAR2(30)	Name of the database object containing the block.
PARTITION_NAME	VARCHAR2(30)	The name of the partition; NULL for non-partitioned objects.
KIND	VARCHAR2(12)	Type of database object. The column contains the following potential values: 1: INDEX 2: TABLE 3: CLUSTER 4: VIEW 5: SYNONYM 6: SEQUENCE 7: PROCEDURE 8: FUNCTION 9: PACKAGE 10: NONEXISTENT 11: PACKAGE BODY 12: TRIGGER 13: TYPE 14: TYPE BODY 19: TABLE PARTITION 20: INDEX PARTITION 21: LOB 22: LIBRARY
OWNER#	NUMBER	Owner number.
LOCK_ELEMENT_ADDR	RAW(4)	The address of the lock element that is locking this buffer. If two buffers have the same LOCK_ELEMENT_ADDR value then the same lock is protecting them.
LOCK_ELEMENT_NAME	NUMBER	The address of the lock element that is locking this buffer.

> **Note:** In a RAC environment the parameter `GC_FILES_TO_LOCKS` should not be used. If this parameter is configured, the cache fusion technology available in RAC is disabled and the OPS behavior is invoked. This means transfer of blocks will happen using the pinging mechanism.

GV$FILE_CACHE_TRANSFER

A very useful view in a RAC environment that displays the number of blocks pinged per data file. This information in turn can be used to determine access patterns to existing data files and decide new mappings from data file blocks to PCM locks.

Based on X$ Tables: X$KCFIO and X$KCCFE

Column	Datatype	Description
INST_ID	NUMBER	A unique number assigned to the instance via the parameter file when the instance was first created.
FILE_NUMBER	NUMBER	Number of the data file.
X_2_NULL	NUMBER	Number of lock conversions from Exclusive to NULL for all blocks in the file.
X_2_NULL_FORCED_WRITE	NUMBER	Number of forced writes that occur for blocks of the specified file due to Exclusive-to-NULL conversions.
X_2_NULL_FORCED_STATE	NUMBER	Number of times a block in the file was made STALE due to Exclusive-to-NULL conversions.
X_2_S	NUMBER	Number of lock conversions from Exclusive to Shared for all blocks in the file
X_2_S_FORCED_WRITES	NUMBER	Number of forced writes that occur for blocks of the specified file due to Exclusive-to-Shared conversion.
S_2_NULL	NUMBER	Number of lock conversion from Shared to NULL for all blocks in the file.
S_2_NULL_FORCED_STALE	NUMBER	Number of times a block in the file was made STALE due to Shared-to-NULL conversions.

RBR	NUMBER	Number of times the instance received a reuse block range cross-instance call for this file.
RBR_FORCED_WRITE	NUMBER	Number of blocks written due to reuse of block range cross-instance calls for this file.
RBR_FORCED_STALE	NUMBER	Number of times a block in this file was made STALE due to reuse of block range cross-instance calls.
NULL_2_K	NUMBER	Number of lock conversions from NULL to Exclusive for all blocks of the specified file.
S_2_X	NUMBER	Number of lock conversions from Shared to Exclusive for all blocks of the specified file.
NULL_2_S	NUMBER	Number of lock conversions from NULL to Shared for all blocks of the specified file.

GV$GCSHVMASTER_INFO

Provides information regarding cache fusion in a RAC environment. It describes the current and previous master instances and the number of times GCS resources have been remastered, except those belonging to files mapped to a particular master.

Based on X$ Table: X$KJDRPCMHV

Column	Datatype	Description
INST_ID	NUMBER	A unique number assigned to the instance via the parameter file when the instance was first created.
HV_ID	NUMBER	PCM hash value ID.
CURRENT_MASTER	NUMBER	Master instance of this PCM hash value ID.
PREVIOUS_MASTER	NUMBER	Previous master instance of this PCM hash value ID.
REMASTER_CNT	NUMBER	Number of times this has been remastered.

GV$GCSPFMASTER_INFO

This view is for RAC and describes the current and previous master instances and the number of times GCS resources belonging to files mapped to instances have been remastered.

Based on X$ Table: X$KJDRPCMPF

Column	Datatype	Description
INST_ID	NUMBER	A unique number assigned to the instance via the parameter file when the instance was first created.
FILE_ID	NUMBER	File number.
CURRENT_MASTER	NUMBER	Master instance of this file.
PREVIOUS_MASTER	NUMBER	Previous master instance of this file.
REMASTER_CNT	NUMBER	Number of times this has been remastered.

GV$GC_ELEMENT

This view is used in RAC. It contains entries for each PCM lock that is used by the buffer cache. The name of the PCM lock that corresponds to a lock element is ("BL,"indx,class).

Based on X$ Table: X$LE

Column	Datatype	Description
INST_ID	NUMBER	A unique number assigned to the instance via the parameter file when the instance was first created.
GC_ELEMENT_ADDR	RAW(4)	Address of the lock element that contains the PCM lock that is covering the buffer. If two or more buffers have the same address, then these buffers are covered by the same PCM lock.
INDX	NUMBER	Platform-specific lock manager identifier.
CLASS	NUMBER	Platform-specific lock manager identifier.
GC_ELEMENT_NAME	NUMBER	Name of the lock that contains the PCM lock that is covering the buffer.
MODE_HELD	NUMBER	Platform-dependent value for lock mode held, often 3 = share and 5 = exclusive.
BLOCK_COUNT	NUMBER	Number of blocks covered by PCM lock.
RELEASING	NUMBER	Nonzero if PCM lock is being downgraded.

ACQUIRING	NUMBER	Nonzero if PCM lock is being upgraded.
INVALID	NUMBER	Nonzero if PCM lock is invalid.
FLAGS	NUMBER	Process level flags for the lock element.

GV$GC_ELEMENTS_WITH_COLLISIONS

This view is specific to a RAC implementation. This view helps identify the locks that protect multiple buffers, each of which has been either force-written or force-read at least 10 times.

Based on V$ View: V$BH

Column	Datatype	Description
INST_ID	NUMBER	A unique number assigned to the instance via the parameter file when the instance was first created.
GC_ELEMENT_ADDR	RAW(4)	Address of the lock element that contains the PCM lock covering the buffer. If two or more buffers have the same address, then these buffers are covered by the same PCM lock.

GV$GES_BLOCKING_ENQUEUE

This is a RAC-specific view and provides information on all locks currently known to the lock manager that are being blocked or blocking others. The output of this view is a subset of the output from GV$GES_ENQUEUE.

Based on V$ View: V$GES_ENQUEUE

Column	Datatype	Description
INST_ID	NUMBER	A unique number assigned to the instance via the parameter file when the instance was first created.
HANDLE	RAW(4)	Lock pointer.
GRANT_LEVEL	VARCHAR2(9)	Granted level of the lock.
REQUEST_LEVEL	VARCHAR2(9)	Requested level of the lock.
RESOURCE_NAME1	VARCHAR2(30)	Resource name for the lock.
RESOURCE_NAME2	VARCHAR2(30)	Resource name for the lock.
PID	NUMBER	Process identifier which holds the lock.
TRANSACTION_ID0	NUMBER	Lower 4 bytes of the transaction identifier to which the lock belongs.

TRANSACTION_ID1	NUMBER	Upper 4 bytes of the transaction identifier to which the lock belongs.
GROUP_ID	NUMBER	Group identifier for the lock.
OPEN_OPT_DEADLOCK	NUMBER	1 if deadlock open option is set, otherwise 0.
OPEN_OPT_PERSISTENT	NUMBER	1 if persistent open option is set, otherwise 0.
OPEN_OPT_PROCESS_OWNED	NUMBER	1 if process_owned open option is set, otherwise 0.
OPEN_OPT_NO_XID	NUMBER	1 if NO_XID open option is set, otherwise 0.
CONVERT_OPT_GETVALUE	NUMBER	1 if GETVALUE convert option is set, otherwise 0.
CONVERT_OPT_PUTVALUE	NUMBER	1 if PUTVALUE convert option is set, otherwise 0.
CONVERT_OPT_NOVALUE	NUMBER	1 if NOVALUE convert option is set, otherwise 0.
CONVERT_OPT_DUBVALUE	NUMBER	1 if DUBVALUE convert option is set, otherwise 0.
CONVERT_OPT_NOQUEUE	NUMBER	1 if NOQUEUE convert option is set, otherwise 0.
CONVERT_OPT_EXPRESS	NUMBER	1 if EXPRESS convert option is set, otherwise 0.
CONVERT_OPT _NODEADLOCKWAIT	NUMBER	1 if NODEADLOCKWAIT convert option is set, otherwise 0.
CONVERT_OPT _NODEADLOCKBLOCK	NUMBER	1 if NODEADLOCKBLOCK convert option is set, otherwise 0.
WHICH_QUEUE	NUMBER	In which queue the lock is currently located: 0 for NULL queue 1 for GRANTED queue 2 for CONVERT queue
STATE	VARCHAR2(64)	State of lock as owner sees it.
AST_EVENT0	NUMBER	Last AST event.
OWNER_NODE	NUMBER	Node identifier.
BLOCKED	NUMBER	1 if the lock request is blocked by others, otherwise 0.
BLOCKER	NUMBER	1 if this lock is blocking others, otherwise 0.

GV$GES_CONVERT_LOCAL

This view provides information regarding average convert time, count information, and timed statistics for local GES enqueue operations.

Column	Datatype	Description
INST_ID	NUMBER	A unique number assigned to the instance via the parameter file when the instance was first created.
CONVERT_TYPE	VARCHAR2(64)	Conversion type, for example: 1: CREATE TABLE 2: INSERT 3: SELECT . . . 12: DROP TABLE 13: CREATE SEQUENCE . . . 97: CREATE PACKAGE BODY 98: ALTER PACKAGE BODY 99: DROP PACKAGE BODY
AVERAGE_CONVERT _TIME	NUMBER	Average conversion time for each type of lock operation. The value is displayed in hundredths of a second.
CONVERT_COUNT	NUMBER	The number of operations.

GV$GES_CONVERT_REMOTE

This view displays the average convert time, count information, and timed statistics for remote GES enqueue operations.

Column	Datatype	Description
INST_ID	NUMBER	A unique number assigned to the instance via the parameter file when the instance was first created.
CONVERT_TYPE	VARCHAR2(64)	Conversion types (for a listing of the conversion types refer to Table 9.1).
AVERAGE_ CONVERT_TIME	NUMBER	Average conversion time for each type of lock operation. The value is displayed in hundredths of a second.
CONVERT_COUNT	NUMBER	The number of operations.

Table 9.1   *GES Conversion Types*

Type	Description
NULL->SS	NULL mode to subshared mode
NULL->SX	NULL mode to shared exclusive mode
NULL-> S	NULL mode to shared mode
NULL->SSX	NULL mode to subshared exclusive mode

(continued)

Table 9.1   *Continued*

Type	Description
NULL->X	NULL mode to exclusive mode
SS->SX	Subshared mode to shared exclusive mode
SS->X	NULL mode to exclusive mode
SS->SX	Subshared mode to shared exclusive mode
SS->S	Subshared mode to shared mode
SS->SSX	Subshared mode to subshared exclusive mode
SS->.X	Subshared mode to exclusive mode
SX->S	Shared exclusive mode to shared mode
SX->SSX	Shared exclusive mode to subshared exclusive mode
SX->X	Shared exclusive mode to exclusive mode
S->SX	Shared mode to shared exclusive mode
S->SSX	Shared mode to subshared exclusive mode
S->X	Shared mode to exclusive mode
SSX->X	Subshared exclusive mode to exclusive mode

GV$GES_ENQUEUE

This is a RAC view and describes all locks currently known to the lock manager.

Based on X$ Table: X$KJILKFT

Column	Datatype	Description
INST_ID	NUMBER	A unique number assigned to the instance via the parameter file when the instance was first created.
HANDLE	RAW(4)	Lock pointer.
GRANT_LEVEL	VARCHAR2(9)	Granted level of the lock.
REQUEST_LEVEL	VARCHAR2(9)	Requested level of the lock.
RESOURCE_NAME1	VARCHAR2(30)	Resource name for the lock.
RESOURCE_NAME2	VARCHAR2(30)	Resource name for the lock.
PID	NUMBER	Process identifier which holds the lock.

TRANSACTION_ID0	NUMBER	Lower 4 bytes of the transaction identifier to which the lock belongs.
TRANSACTION_ID1	NUMBER	Upper 4 bytes of the transaction identifier to which the lock belongs.
GROUP_ID	NUMBER	Group identifier for the lock.
OPEN_OPT_DEADLOCK	NUMBER	1 if DEADLOCK open option is set, otherwise 0.
OPEN_OPT_PERSISTENT	NUMBER	1 if PERSISTENT open option is set, otherwise 0.
OPEN_OPT_PROCESS_OWNED	NUMBER	1 if PROCESS_OWNED open option is set, otherwise 0.
OPEN_OPT_NO_XID	NUMBER	1 if NO_XID open option is set, otherwise 0.
CONVERT_OPT_GETVALUE	NUMBER	1 if GETVALUE convert option is set, otherwise 0.
CONVERT_OPT_PUTVALUE	NUMBER	1 if PUTVALUE convert option is set otherwise 0.
CONVERT_OPT_NOVALUE	NUMBER	1 if NOVALUE convert option is set otherwise 0.
CONVERT_OPT_DUBVALUE	NUMBER	1 if DUBVALUE convert option is set otherwise 0.
CONVERT_OPT_NOQUEUE	NUMBER	1 if NOQUEUE convert option is set otherwise 0.
CONVERT_OPT_EXPRESS	NUMBER	1 if EXPRESS convert option is set otherwise 0.
CONVERT_OPT _NODEADLOCKWAIT	NUMBER	1 if NODEADLOCKWAIT convert option is set, otherwise 0.
CONVERT_OPT _NODEADLOCKBLOCK	NUMBER	1 if NODEADLOCK-BLOCK convert option is set, otherwise 0.
WHICH_QUEUE	NUMBER	In which queue the lock is currently located: 0 for NULL queue 1 for GRANTED queue 2 for CONVERT queue
STATE	VARCHAR2 (64)	State of lock as owner sees it.
AST_EVENT0	NUMBER	Last AST event.
OWNER_NODE	NUMBER	Node identifier.
BLOCKED	NUMBER	1 if the lock request is blocked by others, otherwise 0.
BLOCKER	NUMBER	1 if this lock is blocking others, otherwise 0.

GV$GES_RESOURCE

This view is present in RAC and displays information of all resources currently known to the lock manager.

Column	Datatype	Description
INST_ID	NUMBER	A unique number assigned to the instance via the parameter file when the instance was first created.
RESP	RAW(4)	Resource pointer.
RESOURCE_NAME	VARCHAR2(30)	Resource name in hexadecimal for the lock.
ON_COVERT_Q	NUMBER	1 if no convert queue, 0 otherwise.
ON_GRANT_Q	NUMBER	1 if no granted queue, 0 otherwise.
PERSISTENT_RES	NUMBER	1 if it is a persistent resource, 0 otherwise.
RDOMAIN_NAME	VARCHAR2(25)	Recovery domain name.
RDOMAINP	RAW(4)	Recovery domain pointer.
MASTER_NODE	NUMBER	Master node ID.
NEXT_CVT_LEVEL	VARCHAR2(9)	Next lock level to convert on global convert queue.
VALUE_BLK_STATE	VARCHAR2(32)	State of the value block.
VALUE_BLK	VARCHAR2(64)	First 64 bytes of the value block.

GV$GES_STATISTICS

This is present in RAC and displays miscellaneous GES statistics.

Column	Datatype	Description
INST_ID	NUMBER	A unique number assigned to the instance via the parameter file when the instance was first created.
STATISTIC#	NUMBER	Statistic number.
NAME	VARCHAR2(64)	Name of the statistic.
VALUE	NUMBER	Value associated with the statistic.

GV$HVMASTER_INFO

TThis is a RAC only view and describes the current and previous master instances and the number of times that GES resources have been remastered. This view is used to monitor the remastering of instances during instance failures and when the resources held by the instance are distributed to the other available instances.

Based on X$ Table: X$KJDRHV

Column	Datatype	Description
INST_ID	NUMBER	A unique number assigned to the instance via the parameter file when the instance was first created.
HV_ID	NUMBER	Hash value ID.
CURRENT_MASTER	NUMBER	Master instance of this hash value ID.
PREVIOUS_MASTER	NUMBER	Previous master of this hash value ID.
REMASTER_CNT	NUMBER	Number of times this has been remastered.

GV$MTTR_TARGET_ADVICE

This view is introduced in Oracle 9i. It contains rows that predict the number of physical I/Os for the MTTR corresponding to each row. The rows also compute a physical I/O factor, which is the ratio of the number of estimated I/Os to the number of I/Os actually performed by the current MTTR setting during the measurement interval.

Based on X$ Table: X$KCBMMAV

Column	Datatype	Description
INST_ID	NUMBER	A unique number assigned to the instance via the parameter file when the instance was first created.
MTTR_TARGET_FOR _ESTIMATE	NUMBER	MTTR setting being simulated. Equal to the current MTTR setting if this is the first row of the view.
ADVICE_STATUS	VARCHAR2(5)	Current status of MTTR simulation: ON: Simulation is on READY: Ready for simulation OFF: Simulation is off
DIRTY_LIMIT	NUMBER	Dirty buffer limit derived from the MTTR being simulated.
ESTD_CACHE_WRITES	NUMBER	Estimated number of cache physical writes under this MTTR.
ESTD_CACHE _WRITE_FACTOR	NUMBER	Estimated cache physical write ratio under this MTTR. It is the ratio of the estimated number of cache writes to the number of cache writes under the current MTTR setting.

ESTD_TOTAL_WRITES	NUMBER	Estimated total number of physical writes under this MTTR.
ESTD_TOTAL_WRITE_FACTOR	NUMBER	Estimated total physical write ratio under this MTTR. It is the ratio of the estimated total number of physical writes to the total number of physical writes under the current MTTR setting.
ESTD_TOTAL_IOS	NUMBER	Estimated total number of I/Os under this MTTR.
ESTD_TOTAL_IO_FACTOR	NUMBER	Estimated total I/O ratio under this MTTR. It is the ratio of the estimated total number of I/Os to the total number of I/Os under the current MTTR setting.

GV$PGASTAT

This view provides PGA memory usage statistics as well as statistics about the automatic PGA memory manager when it is enabled. This view contains cumulative values since instance startup.

Based on X$ Table: X$QESMMSGA

Column	Datatype	Description
INST_ID	NUMBER	A unique number assigned to the instance via the parameter file when the instance was first created.
NAME	VARCHAR2(64)	Name of the statistic.
VALUE	NUMBER	Statistic value.
UNITS	VARCHAR2(12)	Unit for the value. Depending on the type of statistics the units could be either in microseconds, bytes, or percent.

GV$PGA_TARGET_ADVICE

This view is introduced in Oracle 9*i* to support the usage of a new parameter called PGA_AGGREGATE_TARGET. This view predicts how the cache hit percentage and overallocation count statistics displayed by the V$PGASTAT performance view would be impacted if the value of the PGA_AGGREGATE TARGET parameter is changed. The prediction is performed for various values of the PGA_AGGREGATE TARGET parameter selected around its current value. The advice statistics are generated by stimulating the past workload run by the instance.

Based on X$ Table: X$QESMMAHIST

Column	Datatype	Description
INST_ID	NUMBER	A unique number assigned to the instance via the parameter file when the instance was first created.
PGA_TARGET_ FOR_ESTIMATE	NUMBER	Value of PGA_AGGREGATE_ TARGET for this predication (in bytes).
PGA_TARGET_FACTOR	NUMBER	PGA_TARGET_FOR_ESTIMATE/ the current value of the PGA_ AGGREGATE_TARGET parameter.
ADVICE_STATUS	VARCHAR2(3)	Indicates whether the advice is enabled or disabled depending on the value of the STATISTICS_ LEVEL parameter.
BYTES_PROCESSED	NUMBER	Total bytes processed by all the work areas considered by this advice.
ESTD_EXTRA_BYTES_RW	NUMBER	Estimated number of extra bytes that would be read or written if PGA_ AGGREGATE_TARGET was not set to the value of the PGA_TARGET_ FOR_ESTIMATE column. This number is derived from the estimated number and size of work areas which would run in one-pass for the value of PGA_AGGREGATE_TARGET.
ESTD_PGA_CACHE_HIT _PERCENTAGE	NUMBER	Estimated value of the cache hit percentage statistic when PGA_ AGGREGATE_TARGET equals PGA_ TARGET_FOR_ESTIMATE. This column is derived from the above two columns and is equal to: BYTES PROCESSED/(BYTES_ PROCESSED + ESTD_EXTRA_ BYTES_RW)
ESTD_OVERALLOC_COUNT	NUMBER	Estimated number of PGA memory overallocations if the value of PGA_AGGREGATE_TARGET is set to PGA_TARGET_FOR_ESTIMATE column. A nonzero value means that the PGA_TARGET_FOR_ESTIMATE is not large enough to run the work area workload. Hence, the DBA should not set PGA_AGGREGATE_ TARGET to PGA_TARGET_FOR_ ESTIMATE column, since Oracle will not be able to honor that target.

GV$SEGMENT_STATISTICS

Displays information about segment level statistics. This view is new in Oracle *9i* Release 2 and contains good information that will allow easy tuning of the tablespaces based on issues.

Based on X$ Tables: OBJ$, USER$, X$KSOLSFTS, TS$

Column	Datatype	Description
INST_ID	NUMBER	A unique number assigned to the instance via the parameter file when the instance was first created.
OWNER	VARCHAR2(30)	Owner of the object.
OBJECT_NAME	VARCHAR2(30)	Name of the object.
SUBOBJECT_NAME	VARCHAR2(30)	Name of the subobject.
TABLESPACE_NAME	VARCHAR2(30)	Name of the tablespace to which the object belongs.
TS#	NUMBER	Tablespace number.
OBJ#	NUMBER	Dictionary object number of the object.
DATAOBJ#	NUMBER	Data object number of the object.
OBJECT_TYPE	VARCHAR2(18)	Type of the object.
STATISTIC_NAME	VARCHAR2(64)	Name of the statistic.
STATISTIC#	NUMBER	Statistic number.
VALUE	NUMBER	Statistic value.

GV$SESSION_WAIT

This view lists the resources or events for which active sessions are waiting.

Based on X$ Tables: X$KSUSECST and X$KSLED

Column	Datatype	Description
INST_ID	NUMBER	A unique number assigned to the instance via the parameter file when the instance was first created.
SID	NUMBER	Session identifier.
SEQ#	NUMBER	Sequence number that uniquely identifies the wait. Incremented for each wait.
EVENT	VARCHAR2(64)	Resource or event for which the session is waiting.
P1TEXT	VARCHAR2	Description of first additional parameter.
P1	NUMBER	First additional parameter.

P1RAW	RAW(4)	First additional parameter. Same as P1, displayed in hexadecimal.
P2TEXT	VARCHAR2	Description of second parameter.
P2	NUMBER	Second additional parameter.
P2RAW	RAW(4)	Second additional parameter. Same as P2, displayed in hexadecimal.
P3TEXT	VARCHAR2	Description of third parameter.
P3	NUMBER	Third additional parameter.
P3RAW	RAW(4)	Third additional parameter. Same as P3 displayed in hexidecimal.
WAIT_CLASS# (Introduced in Oracle 10g)	NUMBER	Wait class number
WAIT_CLASS (Introduced in Oracle 10g)	VARCHAR2(64)	Name of the wait class
WAIT_TIME (Introduced in Oracle 10g)	NUMBER	A nonzero value is the session's last wait time. A zero value indicates that session is currently active.
WAIT_TIME	NUMBER	A nonzero value is the session's last wait time. A zero value means the session is currently waiting.
SECONDS_IN_WAIT	NUMBER	The number of seconds in wait event.
STATE	VARCHAR2	Wait state: 0: waiting 1: waited for short time 2: waited for unknown time > 0: waited for a known time

GV$SESSTAT

This view shows cumulative user session-wide statistics since the beginning of each session. The data in this view only remains for the life of the session, that is, when the session completes, at which time the data pertaining to the session is cleared from this view.

Based on X$ Table: X$KSUSESTA

Column	Datatype	Description
INST_ID	NUMBER	A unique number assigned to the instance via the parameter file when the instance was first created.

```
SID               NUMBER        Session identifier.
STATISTIC#        NUMBER        Statistic number.
VALUE             NUMBER        Statistic value.
```

Note: Statistics numbers are not guaranteed to remain constant from one release to another. It is therefore advised that the statistics name is used in place of the statistics number.

GV$SHARED_POOL_ADVICE

This view displays information about estimated parse time savings in the shared pool for different sizes. The sizes range from 50% to 200% of the current shared pool size, in equal intervals. The value of the interval depends on the current size of the shared pool.

Based on X$ Tables: X$KSMSPR and X$KGHLU

Column	Datatype	Description
INST_ID	NUMBER	A unique number assigned to the instance via the parameter file when the instance was first created.
SHARED_POOL_SIZE_FOR _ESTIMATE	NUMBER	Shared pool size for the estimate. The value is displayed in megabytes.
SHARED_POOL_SIZE_FACTOR	NUMBER	Size factor with respect to the current shared pool size.
ESTD_LC_SIZE	NUMBER	Estimated memory in use by the library cache. This value is displayed in megabytes.
ESTD_LC_MEMORY_OBJECTS	NUMBER	Estimated number of library cache memory objects in the shared pool of the specified size.
ESTD_LC_TIME_SAVED	NUMBER	Estimated elapsed parse time saved owing to library cache memory objects being found in a shared pool of the specified size. This is the time that would have been spent in reloading the required objects in the shared pool had they been aged out due to insufficient amount of available free memory.
ESTD_LC_TIME _SAVED_FACTOR	NUMBER	Estimated parse time saved factor with respect to the current shared-pool size.

ESTD_LC_MEMORY _OBJECT_HITS	NUMBER	Estimated number of times a library cache memory object was found in a shared pool of the specified size.

GV$SYSSTAT

This view provides the system statistics information of all instances. The description of the statistic associated with each statistic number could be obtained from V$STATNAME view.

Based on X$ Table: X$KSUSGSTA

Column	Datatype	Description
INST_ID	NUMBER	A unique number assigned to the instance via the parameter file when the instance was first created.
STATISTIC#	NUMBER	Statistic number.
NAME	VARCHAR2(64)	Statistic name.
CLASS	NUMBER	Represents one or more statistics class. The following classes are additive: 1: User 2: Redo 3: Enqueue 4: Cache 16: O/S 32: Parallel server 64: SQL 128: Debug
VALUE	NUMBER	Statistic value.

GV$SYSTEM_EVENT

This view contains information on total waits for an event since the instance was started. The data is maintained at the system level for the duration that the instances are up.

Based on X$ Tables: X$KSLEI and X$KSLED

Column	Datatype	Description
INST_ID	NUMBER	A unique number assigned to the instance via the parameter file when the instance was first created.
EVENT	VARCHAR2(64)	The name of the wait event.
TOTAL_WAITS	NUMBER	The total number of waits for the event.
TOTAL_TIMEOUTS	NUMBER	The total number of timeouts for this event.

TIME_WAITED	NUMBER	The total amount of time waited for this event, in hundredths of a second.
AVERAGE_WAIT	NUMBER	The average amount of time waited for this event, in hundredths of a second.

9.3   Parameters

The list below includes some of the common parameters required for RAC and general performance tuning of the Oracle 9*i* database.

ACTIVE_INSTANCE_COUNT	This parameter is used to configure a RAC environment in an active passive configuration. This parameter when set to 1 determines that the first instance that starts up becomes the primary instance. This parameter has no meaning in a three or more node RAC configuration.
9i CLUSTER_DATABASE (Introduced in Oracle 9*i* Release 1)	Specifies if the clustered database option has been enabled.
9i CLUSTER_DATABASE_INSTANCES (Introduced in Oracle 9*i* Release 1)	This specifies the number of instances participating in the clustered configuration. This parameter should be set identical on all participating instances. Oracle computes the default LARGE_ POOL_SIZE based on the value of this parameter.
9i CLUSTER_INTERCONNECTS (Introduced in Oracle 9*i* Release 1)	Specifies information regarding any additional cluster interconnects available to use.
CURSOR_SHARING	This parameter can have three possible values: FORCE: Forces statements to share a cursor in spite of minor differences SIMILAR: Statements that differ in some literals, however are otherwise identical to share a cursor EXACT: Allows only statements with identical text to share the same cursor
CURSOR_SPACE_FOR_TIME	Allows additional space allocation for cursors. Allowed values are: TRUE: Shared SQL areas are kept pinned in the shared pool, which enhances execution of cursor FALSE: Shared SQL areas are deallocated from the library cache to make room for new SQL statements
9i DB_nK_CACHE_SIZE (Introduced in Oracle 9*i* Release 1)	Specifies the size of the cache for the *n*K buffers, where *n* = 2, 4, 8, 16, 32 and can be specified in kilobytes, megabytes,

and gigabytes. This parameter is set based on the DB_BLOCK_SIZE parameter, which in turn is dependent on the O/S block size.

DB_BLOCK_SIZE

Specifies the size of the Oracle database block.

Typically, the block size values are 2048 and 4096.

In a RAC implementation this parameter affects the maximum value of the FREELISTS storage parameter for tables and indexes. However, the FREELISTS and FREELIST GROUP parameter do not apply if the locally managed storage option is used.

9i

DB_CACHE_ADVICE
(Introduced in Oracle 9i Release 1)

Enables or disables statistics gathering used for predicting behavior with different cache sizes through GV$DB_ CACHE_ADVICE view.

Valid values are:

OFF: Advisory is turned off

READY: Advisory is turned off, but the memory remains allocated

ON: Advisory is turned on

Turning on Advisory incurs CPU and memory overheads.

9i

DB_CACHE_SIZE
(Introduced in Oracle 9i Release 1)

Specifies the size of the default buffer pool for buffers with the primary block size.

Note: The DB_CACHE_SIZE parameter replaces the DB_BLOCK_BUFFERS parameter used in previous versions of Oracle.

DB_MULTIBLOCK_READ_COUNT

Specifies the maximum number of blocks read in one I/O operation during a sequential scan.

In a RAC environment, setting this value to an optimal value is critical, else this affects the GCS resource traffic across the cluster interconnect. Idle values for an OLTP system are in the range of 4 to 16.

9i

DB_KEEP_CACHE_SIZE
(Introduced in Oracle 9i Release 1)

Specifies the size of the keep buffer pool. The size of the buffers in the keep buffer pool is of the primary block size.

DB_NAME

Specifies a database identifier of up to 8 characters in length. It should contain the same value that was specified during the database creation.

In a RAC environment this is the shared physical database name and not the instance name.

9i DB_RECYCLE_CACHE_SIZE
(Introduced in Oracle 9*i* Release 1)

Specifies the size of the recycle buffer pool.

DB_WRITER_PROCESSES

Specifies the initial number of database writer processes for an instance. This is useful for systems that modify data heavily. In Oracle 9*i* this value can be of range 1 to 20 and is displayed as DBWn processes (DBW0 to DBW9) and (DBWa to DBWj).

DBWR_IO_SLAVES

This parameter is helpful on systems that have only one DBW0 process and specifies the number of I/O server processes used by the DBW0 process.
The DBWn process should be preferred over the I/O slave processes.

ENQUEUE_RESOURCES

Sets the number of resources that can be concurrently locked by the lock manager. If no value is specified, Oracle allocates a value based on the SESSIONS parameter. Oracle will automatically allocate additional enqueues from the shared pool as needed if the number specified by ENQUEUE_RESOURCES is exceeded.
In a RAC environment the resource usage could be verified by querying the GV$RESOURCE_LIMIT view.

9i FAST_START_MTTR_TARGET
(Introduced in Oracle 9*i* Release 1)

Specifies the number of seconds the database takes to perform crash recovery of a single instance. This parameter replaces FAST_START_IO_TARGET and LOG_CHECKPOINT_INTERVAL. However, setting these parameters in Oracle 9*i* will override the FAST_START_MTTR_TARGET parameter.

GC_FILES_TO_LOCKS

This parameter has been provided for backward compatibility, when set it disables the cache fusion processing in a RAC environment.

HASH_JOIN_ENABLED

Specifies whether the optimizer should consider using a hash join as a join method. If set to TRUE, the optimizer compares the cost of a hash join with other types of joins and chooses hashing if it gives the lowest cost.
The parameter should be set to TRUE in a data-warehousing environment.

HASH_AREA_SIZE

Specifies the maximum amount of memory in bytes to be used for hash joins. This parameter is more relevant to

	parallel execution operations. The default value for this parameter is derived from twice the SORT_AREA_SIZE.
INSTANCE_GROUPS	This parameter is specific to a RAC implementation when the parallel mode of operation is used. It is used in conjunction with the PARALLEL_INSTANCE_GROUP parameter.
	It specifies one or more instance groups and assigns the current instance to those groups.
INSTANCE_NAME	When two or more instances can be configured in a RAC environment against common shared physical database, this parameter specifies the unique name of this instance.
	It should be noted that only in a RAC configuration is there a distinction of unique names between the database and the instance. In a single-instance configuration, the instance name is often the same as the database name.
INSTANCE_NUMBER	Specifies a unique number that maps the instance to one free list group for each database object created with storage parameter FREELIST GROUPS.
LOG_BUFFER	Specifies the amount of memory that Oracle uses when buffering redo entries to a redo log file.
	A larger value for LOG_BUFFER will reduce redo log file I/O, especially when there are long or a large number of transactions. On busy systems a value of 65,536 or higher is reasonable.
LOG_CHECKPOINT_INTERVAL	Specifies the frequency of checkpoints in terms of the number of redo log file blocks that can exist between an incremental checkpoint and the last block written to the redo log. The number refers to physical operating system blocks and not database blocks.
LOG_CHECKPOINT_TIMEOUT	Specifies the amount of time that has passed since the incremental checkpoint at the position where the last write to the redo log occurred.
LOCK_CHECKPOINTS_TO_ALERT	Setting the value of this parameter to TRUE helps monitor the checkpoint activity. Every time a checkpoint occurs it writes entries to the alert log file.

9iR2

LOG_PARALLELISM (Introduced in Oracle 9i Release 2)	Specifies the level of concurrency for redo allocation within Oracle. On systems that have 16 or more processors and there is a very high contention on the redo allocation latch, setting the value of this parameter between 2 and 8 would help increase the throughput of certain update-intensive workloads.
MAX_COMMIT_PROPAGATION_DELAY	This parameter is specific to RAC and is used to specify the maximum amount of time allowed before the SCN held in the SGA of an instance is refreshed by the LGWR process.
OPTIMIZER_DYNAMIC_SAMPLING	Controls the level of dynamic sampling performed by the optmizer.
OPTIMIZER_INDEX_CACHING	Setting this parameter to an appropriate value helps adjust the behavior of cost-based optimizer to favor nested loop joins and IN-list iterators.
OPTIMIZER_INDEX_COST_ADJ	Setting this parameter to an appropriate value helps tune the optimizer behavior for access path selection to be more or less index friendly, i.e., make the optimizer to use the index access path over a full table scan.
OPTIMIZER_MAX_PERMUTATIONS	Restricts the number of permutations of the tables the optimizer will consider in queries with joins. The default value for this parameter has been reduced in Oracle 9i from 80,000 to 2000.
OPTIMIZER_MODE	This parameter establishes the default behavior for choosing an optimization approach for the instance. RULE: Chooses the rule-based approach for all SQL statements regardless of the presence of statistics. *Note:* This is a desupported option in Oracle 10*g*. CHOOSE: The optimizer chooses between cost-based approach and a rule-based approach based on whether statistics are available. *Note:* This is a desupported option in Oracle 10*g*. FIRST_ROWS_n: The optimizer uses a cost-based approach regardless of the presence of statistics and optimizes with a goal of best response time to return the first *n* rows.

FIRST_ROWS: The optimizer uses a mix of cost and heuristics to find a best plan for fast delivery of the first few rows. ALL_ROWS: The optimizer uses a cost-based approach for all SQL statements in the session regardless of the presence of statistics and optimizes with a goal of best throughput.

Note: ALL-ROWS is the default OPTIMIZER-MODE option starting with Oracle 10*g*.

ORACLE_TRACE_ENABLE

Setting this parameter to a value of TRUE helps perform trace collection of server event data by using:

Oracle trace manager

Oracle command line interface, or

By specifying a collection name in the ORACLE_TRACE_COLLECTION_NAME parameter

9i

PGA_AGGREGATE_TARGET
(Introduced in Oracle 9*i* Release 1)

Specifies the target aggregate PGA memory available to all server processes attached to the instance. This parameter enables the automatic sizing of SQL working areas used by memory-intensive SQL operators such as sort, group by, hash-join, bitmap merge, and bitmap create.

Note: Oracle recommends using this parameter over the SORT_AREA_SIZE and SORT_AREA_RETAINED_SIZE by enabling automatic sizing of SQL working areas. SORT_AREA_RETAINED_SIZE is retained for backward compatibility.

SERVICE_NAMES

Specifies one or more names for the database service to which the instance is connected.

In a RAC implementation all instances should have this parameter set to at least one common value. This parameter plays an important role for implementation of the TAF option.

SESSION_CACHED_CURSORS

Specifies the number of session cursors to cache. Repeated parse calls of the same SQL statement cause the session cursors for that statement to be moved into the session cursor cache. Subsequent parse calls will find the cursor in the cache and would not be required to reopen the cursor.

9i   SGA_MAX_SIZE
       (Introduced in Oracle *9i* Release 1)
       STAR_TRANSFORMATION_
       ENABLED

Specifies the maximum size of the SGA for the lifetime of the instance.
Setting the value of this parameter to TRUE determines whether a cost-based query transformation will be applied to start queries.

9iR2   STATISTICS_LEVEL
         (Introduced in Oracle *9i* Release 2)

This parameter sets the statistics collection level of the database. The possible values for this parameter are:
ALL
TYPICAL
BASIC

THREAD

This parameter is specifically used in a RAC implementation and specifies the number of the redo threads to be used by an instance.

9i   TIMED_OS_STATISTICS
       (Introduced in Oracle *9i* Release 1)

Specifies the interval at which Oracle collects operating system statistics when a request is made from the client to the server or when a request completes.
Note: Collecting O/S level statistics is very expensive and should be done with caution under controlled testing.

TIMED_STATISTICS

Specifies whether or not statistics related to time are collected. When the value of this parameter is set to TRUE, the statistics are collected and stored in trace files or displayed in the GV$SESSTATS or GV$SYSSTATS views.

9i   TRACE_ENABLED
       (Introduced in Oracle *9i* Release 1)

This parameter controls tracing of the execution history or code path of Oracle. This parameter by default is enabled and helps retain diagnostics for the entire cluster.

TRANSACTION_AUDITING

This parameter by default is enabled and generates a special redo record that contains the user login name, username, the session ID, some O/S information, and client information. If set to FALSE, no redo record will be generated.

TRANSACTIONS

Specifies the maximum number of concurrent transactions. Greater values increase the size of the SGA and can increase the number of rollback segments allocated.

9i   UNDO_MANAGEMENT
       (Introduced in Oracle *9i* Release 1)

Specifies which undo space management mode the system should use. The values are:
AUTO: Instance starts automatic undo management
MANUAL: Undo management is managed by the DBAs and the space is allocated

9i UNDO_RETENTION
(Introduced in Oracle *9i* Release 1)

9i UNDO_TABLESPACE
(Introduced in Oracle *9i* Release 1)

9i WORKAREA_SIZE_POLICY
(Introduced in Oracle *9i* Release 1)

10g CREATE_STORED_OUTLINES
(Introduced in Oracle 10g Release 1)

10g DB_FLASHBACK_
RETENTION_TARGET
(Introduced in Oracle 10g Release 1)

10g DB_RECOVERY_FILE_DEST
(Introduced in Oracle 10g Release 1)

externally as rollback segments. MANUAL is the default value

Specifies the amount of committed undo information to retain in the database. Oracle allocates the required space to retain the data specified by this parameter. However, if additional undo space is required by an active transaction the space allocated for retention purposes will be used.

Specifies the undo tablespace to be used when an instance starts up. This parameter is valid only when automatic undo management has been enabled.

Specifies the policy for sizing work areas. This parameter controls the mode in which working areas are tuned.
Possible values are:
AUTO: Work areas used by memory-intensive operators are sized automatically, based on the PGA memory used by the system, the PGA memory is set using PGA_ AGGREGATE_TARGET parameter. This value can only be used when the PGA_ AGGREGATE_TARGET is defined
MANUAL: Work area sizing is done manually

Determines whether Oracle automatically creates and stores an outline for each query submitted during the session. Possible values are:
TRUE: Enables automatic outline creation for subsequent queries in the same session.
FALSE: Disables automatic outline creation during the session.
<category_name> Enables the behavior of TRUE except that any outline created during the session is stored in the category_name category.

Specifies the upper limit (in minutes) on how far back in time the database may be flashed back. How far back one can flashback a database depends on how much flashback data Oracle has kept in the recovery area.

Specifies the default location for the recovery area. The recovery area contains multiplexed copies of the current control files and online redo logs, as well as

10g DB_RECOVERY_FILE_DEST_SIZE
(Introduced in Oracle 10g Release 1)

10g DDL_WAIT_FOR_LOCKS
(Introduced in Oracle 10g Release 1)

archived redo logs, flashback logs and RMAN backups.
Specifies the hard limit on the total space to be used by target database recovery files.
Specifies whether DDL statements should wait and complete instead of timing out if the statement is not able to acquire all required locks. Possible values are:
TRUE: DDL statements wait until the statement acquires all required locks.
FALSE: DDL statements time out if the statement cannot obtain all required locks.

10g INSTANCE_TYPE
(Introduced in Oracle 10g Release 1)

Specifies whether the instance is a database instance or an automated storage management instance. Possible values are:
RDBMS: The instance is a database instance.
OSM: The instance is an Automated Storage Management instance.

10g STREAMS_POOL_SIZE
(Introduced in Oracle 10g Release 1)

Specifies the size of the streams pool, from which memory is allocated for Streams. If this parameter is not defined or is set to ZERO then 10% of the shared pool is allocated for streams.

9.4   Conclusion

This chapter has been a very generic chapter covering various definitions. These definitions are discussed to provide a foundation for a more detailed discussion in the performance-tuning chapter later in this book.

In this chapter we looked at the various dynamic performance views and discussed their usage in a RAC environment. We also looked at certain views and discussed the X$ tables that these views are based on. These discussions were to introduce the user to certain internals of performance management. As it was noticed, certain columns found in the tables are not directly reflected in the dynamic performance views.

This completes Part II of the book and in Part III we will cover operations. In Chapter 10, we will discuss the availabilty and scalability features of the RAC option, what it provides, when and how the RAC guard could be put to use, and its installation and configuration process.

Part III

Operations

10

Availability and Scalability

10.1   Introduction

In the previous chapter we browsed through definitions of the various data dictionary views and parameters pertaining to RAC. All dynamic views that are available in a single stand-alone configuration of Oracle are available from a global level. What this means is that these global views will provide visibility to all instances participating in the clustered configuration. DBAs could view the statistics of any instance from any other instance in the cluster. For example, to look at the users connected to instance RAC2 from instance RAC1, the global view GV$SESSION could be queried where the INST_ID has a value of 2, or by querying the entire view information from all views.

Oracle has introduced and maintains several initialization parameters that are specific to a RAC configuration. The previous chapter also discussed these parameter definitions. The usage of many of the parameters is covered later in the appropriate chapters of this book.

Availability of a football player of 94% indicates that the player has missed one game of a 16-game season. However, 99.97% availability of a computer system indicates a downtime of 2.5 hours in a year. Today's business requirements are to meet 99.99% or 99.999% availability, which indicates 0.5 hours or no downtime. To meet these high-availability requirements with no downtime in a year, the factor critical for success is for systems to provide automatic failover when one participating system fails, with minimal interruption to the user. If this does not occur, when a system or a participating node fails either in a clustered or non-clustered configuration, then a considerable amount of time will be used in migrating the user from the failed node to another (re-establishing the database connection, re-executing the query, user having to browse through the screen to his/her last view, etc.). When this failure happens more frequently there would be user frustrations and subsequently potential loss of business.

Availability of enterprise systems is not confined to the database tier, because it is not only the database tier that could fail. When an availability requirement of 99.999% is specified, it applies to the entire system. This includes the database tier, the application tier, the firewalls, interconnects, networks, LAN, storage subsystems, and the controllers to these storage subsystems, because every tier in the enterprise system is prone to failure. To meet the availability factor across the enterprise, it is required that every tier should consider meeting the same SLA requirements of 99.999%. As discussed in Chapter 2 (Hardware Concepts), the availability of the enterprise system could be achieved by providing a redundant architecture. This means that every subsystem or component should have redundant hardware, so that if one piece of hardware fails, the other redundant piece is available to provide the required functionality and continued business.

Figure 10.1 represents a two-node total redundancy system with failover options at every level of the equipment. This type of totally redundant configuration supports and provides a higher availability and

Figure 10.1
*Various levels of
redundancy for
high-availability
systems.*

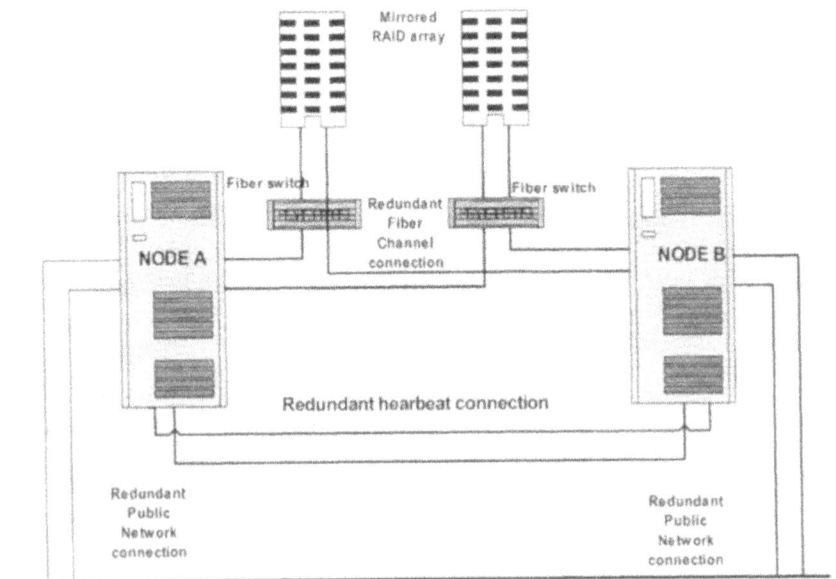

includes the following functions:

- When a node leaves the cluster, the remaining systems go through a cluster state transition and during this phase, automatically adjust to the new cluster membership.

- When one path to the storage device fails, the device can be accessed through an alternate path.

- If one communication path fails, systems that are part of the clustered configuration can still exchange information on the remaining communication paths.

- Using volume shadowing and a mirrored disk option provides availability at the disk subsystem/storage level. This means that when one disk fails, the information is still available on the other mirrored disk. For example, in a RAID 1 configuration, which is mirror only, a copy of the data is simultaneously saved on disks; that is, to the original disk and to the mirrored disk. When one of the disks is unusable, the system continues operation by accessing the other disk as if no loss was encountered. Because of this, users are not affected.

The high-availability scenario also applies to application systems accessing the clustered configuration. In the event of a server failure (due to hardware, application, or operator fault) another node, configured as the secondary node (in an active/passive configuration), automatically assumes the responsibilities of the primary node. At this point, users are switched to that node without operator intervention. This switch minimizes downtime.

A cluster is designed to avoid a single point of failure. Applications are distributed over more than one computer (in an active/active configuration), achieving a degree of parallelism and failure recovery and providing high availability. In this type of configuration, when one node in the cluster fails, other nodes automatically assume the responsibility of the primary node and the users are distributed across other available nodes.

While availability of the systems is very critical to the enterprise, equally critical is the potential that the application systems and the layered hardware architecture and technology selected are able to accommodate the increased usage. This implies that the hardware system should be able to scale without much difficulty. Very similar to availability requirements are the scalability requirements, which are seldom considered critical.

Businesses that start with a low capital investment, potentially start with hardware models that are small and at some point reach a saturation level where the specific hardware has reached its limitations and is unable to handle the increased users on the system. At this stage, either additional hardware needs to be purchased or the capacity of the current systems increased.

Increasing the capacity will take the enterprise a certain distance, allowing the business to continue and accept the increased growth of users. Now this increased growth of users obtained with the increased capacity of the existing hardware i.e. by adding additional resources such as CPU, storage, memory, etc., at some point reaches a stage when any further increase is not possible because every model or hardware platform is designed for a certain maximum resource capacity, after which the hardware must be replaced with higher specification models (vertical scaling). One of the biggest drawbacks of the vertical scalability model is that this model does not support availability. When this bigger hardware fails, the system is down and the application is not usable.

Figure 10.2 represents the vertical and horizontal scalability of the systems. When the computers are vertically scaled, the system configuration

Figure 10.2
Vertical and horizontal scalability representation.

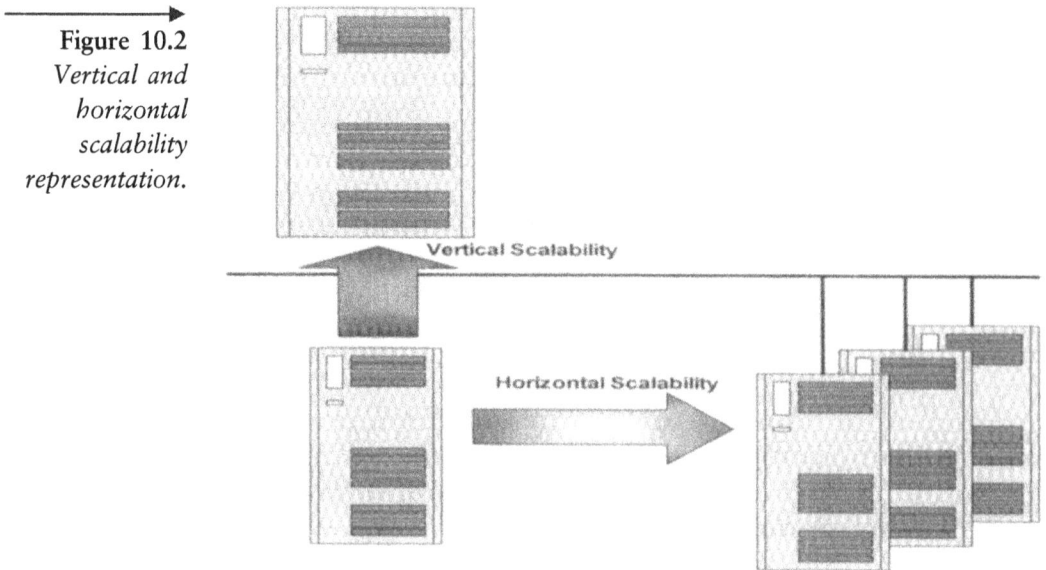

increases due to the computer now having additional resources compared to the standard configuration. Under the horizontal scalability, the size of the computer remains the same but another computer is added, almost doubling the resources and aiding in distribution of load between both computers. Horizontal scalability also provides higher availability because users can be migrated to the other available computer if one node fails.

Another option would be that additional hardware (nodes) could be added to the existing hardware. This provides for distribution of work (scalability) and when any node or hardware fails, the other systems in the configuration are available to carry on with the business (availability).

Availability and scalability of the enterprise systems is dependent on several factors including the hardware, the application, the database and other media. On the database tier, availability and scalability in an Oracle environment could be achieved from features such as Oracle Data Guard (ODG), Oracle Advanced Replication (OAR), or RAC.

ODG and OAR are high-availability options however, not within the true concept of immediate availability, but rather availability due to a disaster. Availability provided by RAC is more real-time availability, basically because of its clustered architecture and the fact that multiple nodes or instances share the common single copy of the physical database, providing data consistency and distribution to users accessing the database from multiple nodes or instances.

In this chapter we will discuss the various high-availability and scalability features provided by RAC. RAC provides a clustered database solution where two or more nodes share a common storage subsystem. The nodes are connected to each other via a high-speed cluster interconnect option, normally a Gigabit Ethernet. Each node contains an instance and is configured to be in an active state. The database that is configured on this common shared storage subsystem is accessible to the users from any instance.

Under RAC, when one of the participating systems fails, the users are migrated to another system, providing a failover mechanism. While this is a normal failover using the features of the clustered operating system, RAC provides additional failover opportunities by using features such as TAF, database connections and processes that had lost connection are reconnected and this failover is transparent to the user. In the next section we will look at availability.

10.2   Availability

10.2.1   Oracle Real Application Clusters

RAC allows multiple Oracle instances residing on different nodes to access the same physical database, as shown in Figure 10.3. GCS and GES maintain consistency across the caches of the different nodes. RAC protects against either node failure or communication failure to a subset of the nodes. With a RAC implementation, two different setups for availability are possible:

- *Failover only:* Workload runs only on one instance, with the second instance being used only for failover purposes. This requires no changes to the application.

- *Failover and scalability:* Workload runs on multiple instances simultaneously. While this allows the application to take advantage of the resource of the multiple nodes, it may require changes to the application in order to be able to scale. This is the case if the application has not been designed to work in such an environment where the process from the application attaches to the database through one or more instances to process information.

Note: To understand these cluster failover principles it is important that the reader has read through Chapter 2 (Hardware Concepts).

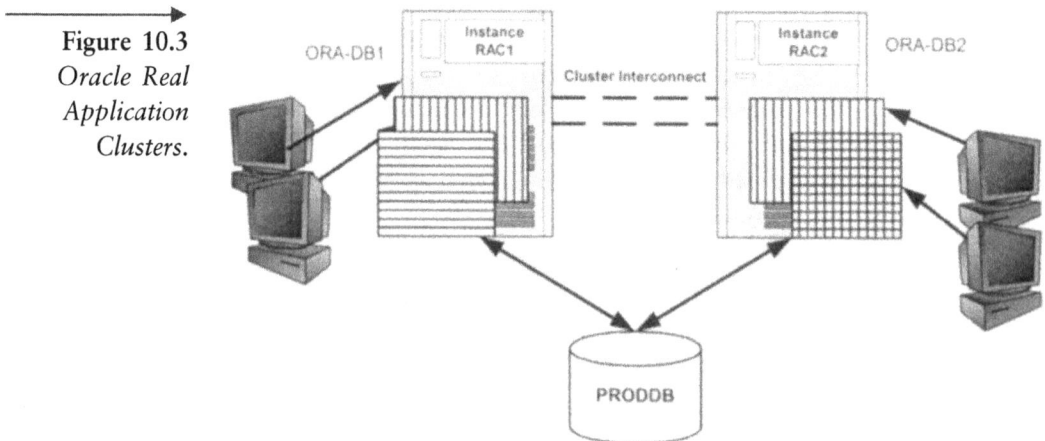

Figure 10.3
*Oracle Real
Application
Clusters.*

10.2.1 How does the failover mechanism work?

RAC relies on the CM of the clustered operating system for failure detection. The CM is a distributed kernel component that monitors whether cluster members can communicate with each other, and enforces the rules of cluster membership. The CM:

- Forms a cluster, adds members to a cluster and removes members from a cluster

- Tracks which members in a cluster are active

- Maintains a cluster membership list that is consistent on all cluster members

- Provides timely notification of membership changes

- Detects and handles possible cluster partitions

The CM ensures data integrity between communication failures by using a voting mechanism. That is, processing and I/O activity is allowed only when the cluster has a quorum. A quorum depends on a number of factors such as expected votes from the participating members in the cluster (node votes) and quorum disk votes.

- Node votes are the fixed number of votes that a given member contributes towards a quorum. Cluster members can have either 1 or 0 node votes. Each member with a vote (1) is considered a voting member of the cluster and with 0 is considered a non-voting member.

- Quorum disk votes are the fixed number of votes that a quorum disk contributes towards a quorum. Similar to the node vote, a quorum disk can also have either 1 or 0 votes.

> **Note:** While node votes are a common method of voting, certain cluster configurations use the quorum disk method to determine availability of cluster members.

The CM determines the availability of a member in a cluster using the heartbeat function. Using the heartbeat mechanism, the CM allows the nodes to communicate with the other nodes to determine availability on a continuous basis at preset intervals, e.g., 2 seconds on Sun and Linux clusters. This means that every 2 seconds every node validates the existence of another node in the cluster.

When the heartbeat from the node does not get through after a specified amount of time, a timeout occurs (configurable in most operating systems). At this point, the node that originally detected the failure declares that the other node is not responding and declares that the node is not available for communications and has failed. The node that detected the failure first attempts to reform the cluster. (*The heartbeat timeout parameter, like the heartbeat interval, varies from operating system to operating system; the default heartbeat timeout parameter on Sun clusters is 12 seconds and the default on Linux clusters is 10 seconds.*[1]) Reforming the cluster requires that the remaining nodes have enough members to form a quorum. If the remaining nodes form a quorum, the reorganization of the cluster membership happens. The reorganization process regroups the nodes that are accessible and removes the nodes that have failed. For example, in a four-node cluster, if one node fails, the CM will regroup among the remaining three nodes.

Similarly, when a node is added or joins the cluster after recovery, the CM performs this step to reform the cluster. The information regarding a node joining the cluster or leaving the cluster is exposed to the respective Oracle instances by the LMON process running on each cluster node.

As discussed previously in Chapter 4 (RAC Architecture), LMON is a background process that monitors the entire cluster to manage global resources. By constantly probing the other instances, it checks and manages instance deaths and the associated recovery for GCS. When a node joins or leaves the cluster, it handles reconfiguration of locks and resources. In particular, LMON handles the part of recovery associated with global resources. LMON-provided services are also known as Cluster Group Services (CGS).

The next step in the failover process is the database recovery operation. As part of this operation, Oracle will remaster the GCS of the failed instances amongst the available instances. Unlike the previous versions, where all services from both the failed and the available instances were reconfigured, in the case of Oracle 9*i* and above, only the services from the failed instance are reconfigured.

Once the reconfiguration of the services from the failed instances has completed, Oracle starts the cache recovery process by rolling forward

---

1   Oracle provides a daemon process called the "watchdog" for Linux environments for failover detection. The watchdog process provides the heartbeat functionality for Oracle Cluster Management Services (OCMS).

transactions. This is made possible by reading the redo log files of the failed instance. Because of the shared storage subsystem, redo log files of any specific instance are visible to other instances. This makes any one instance that detected the failure to read the redo log files and start the recovery process.

After completion of the cache recovery process, Oracle starts the transaction recovery, that is, rolling back all uncommitted transactions. Oracle records all the steps of the recovery process in the alert log file of the instance that is performing the recovery.

The following extract is from the alert log file of the recovering instance. It displays the steps that Oracle has to perform; for example, the log file tracks the reconfiguration and cleaning up of enqueue resources.

```
Sun Sep 29 13:55:14 2002
Reconfiguration started
List of nodes: 0,
  Global Resource Directory frozen
one node partition
  Communication channels re-established
  Master broadcasted resource hash value bitmaps
  Non-local Process blocks cleaned out
  Resources and enqueues cleaned out
  Resources remastered 7306
  20900 GCS shadows traversed, 4 cancelled, 4159 closed
  10401 GCS resources traversed, 0 cancelled
  13156 GCS resources on freelist, 22000 on array, 22000 allocated
  set master node info
  Submitted all remote-enqueue requests
  Update rdomain variables
  Dwn-cvts replayed, VALBLKs dubious
  All grantable enqueues granted
  20900 GCS shadows traversed, 0 replayed, 4162 unopened
  Submitted all GCS remote-cache requests
  0 write requests issued in 16738 GCS resources
  263 PIs marked suspect, 0 flush PI msgs
Sun Sep 29 13:55:16 2002
Reconfiguration complete
Post SMON to start 1st pass IR
Sun Sep 29 13:55:16 2002
instance recovery: looking for dead threads
Sun Sep 29 13:55:16 2002
Beginning instance recovery of 1 threads
Sun Sep 29 13:55:16 2002
Started first pass scan
Sun Sep 29 13:55:20 2002
Completed first pass scan
   200007 redo blocks read, 3240 data blocks need recovery
Sun Sep 29 13:55:25 2002
```

```
Started recovery at
  Thread 2: logseq 4, block 665405, scn 0.0
Recovery of Online Redo Log: Thread 2 Group 4 Seq 4 Reading mem 0
  Mem# 0 errs 0: /dev/vx/rdsk/oraracdg/partition1G_32
  Mem# 1 errs 0: /dev/vx/rdsk/oraracdg/partition1G_34
Sun Sep 29 13:55:31 2002
Ended recovery at
  Thread 2: logseq 4, block 865412, scn 0.6547319
  2474 data blocks read, 3715 data blocks written, 200007 redo blocks
  read
Ending instance recovery of 1 threads
```

After detection and during the remastering of GCS of the failed instance and cache recovery, most work in the surviving instance is paused and while transaction recovery takes place, work occurs at a slower pace. This point is considered full database availability, as now all data is accessible, including that which resided on the failed instance. The application is now responsible for reconnecting the users and repeating any uncommitted work they have done.

The output below is from the SMON trace file that indicates how SMON performs the recovery operations (basically by making available every segment that has completed recovery, for user access) when the recovering nodes try to recover the data that belongs to the failed instance:

```
SMON: about to recover undo segment 11
SMON: mark undo segment 11 as available
SMON: about to recover undo segment 12
SMON: mark undo segment 12 as available
SMON: about to recover undo segment 13
SMON: mark undo segment 13 as available
SMON: about to recover undo segment 14
SMON: mark undo segment 14 as available
SMON: about to recover undo segment 15
SMON: mark undo segment 15 as available
SMON: about to recover undo segment 16
SMON: mark undo segment 16 as available
SMON: about to recover undo segment 17
SMON: mark undo segment 17 as available
SMON: about to recover undo segment 18
SMON: mark undo segment 18 as available
SMON: about to recover undo segment 19
```

While RAC provides high availability of systems, the database servers, and the applications that use them, there are various features and options under RAC that provide even more support towards achieving the 99.999% availability of today's Internet-based business requirements. RAC allows for multiple nodes to participate in a clustered configuration providing continuous availability. When one of the participating nodes fails, the users are migrated to another node, thus providing a failover mechanism.

The best failover is the one that no one notices. Unfortunately, even though Oracle has been structured to recover very quickly, failures can severely disrupt users by dropping connections from the database. Work in progress at the time of the failure is most likely lost. If the user queried 1000 rows from the database and a failure on the node occurred while the user was scrolling through these rows on his/her terminal, the failure would cause the user to re-execute the query and browse through these rows again. This disruption could be eliminated for most situations by masking the failure with the TAF option.

10.2.3   The watchdog daemon on Linux

Oracle provides cluster management software (OCMS) with RAC Enterprise Edition to manage Linux clusters. The OCMS consists of two components: the watchdog daemon and the CM.

The watchdog daemon (watchdogd) uses a software-implemented watchdog timer to monitor selected system resources to prevent database corruption. The watchdog timer is a feature of the Linux kernel and comes as part of RAC.

The watchdog daemon monitors the CM and passes notifications to the watchdog timer at defined intervals. The behavior of the watchdog timer is partially controlled by the CONFIG_WATCHDOG_NOWAYOUT configuration parameter at the Linux kernel level.

The value of the CONFIG_WATCHDOG_NOWAYOUT configuration parameter should be set to Y. If the watchdog timer detects an Oracle instance or CM failure, it resets the instance to avoid possible database corruption.

The CM maintains the status of the nodes and the Oracle instances across the cluster. The CM process runs on each node of RAC. CM uses the following communication channels between nodes:

- Private network

- Quorum partition on the shared disk

During normal cluster operations, the CMs on each node of the cluster communicate with each other through heartbeat messages sent over the private network. The quorum partition is used as an emergency communication channel if a heartbeat message fails. A heartbeat message can fail for the following reasons:

- The CM terminates on a node

- The private network fails

- There is an abnormally heavy load on the node

The CM uses the quorum partition to determine the reason for the failure. From each node, the CM periodically updates the designated block on the quorum partition. Other nodes check the timestamp for each block. If the message from one of the nodes does not arrive, but the corresponding partition on the quorum has a current timestamp, the network path between this node and other nodes has failed.

Each Oracle instance registers with the local CM. The CM monitors the status of local Oracle instances and propagates this information to CMs on other nodes. If the Oracle instance fails on one of the nodes, the following events occur:

- The CM on the node with the failed Oracle instance informs the watchdog daemon about the failure.

- The watchdog daemon requests the watchdog timer to reset the failed node.

- The watchdog timer resets the node.

- The CMs on the surviving nodes inform their local Oracle instances that the failed node is removed from the cluster.

- Oracle instances in the surviving nodes starts the RAC reconfiguration procedure.

10.2.4   Transparent application failover

RAC provides near-continuous availability by hiding failures from end-user clients and application server clients. This provides continuous, uninterrupted data access. TAF in the database reroutes application clients to an available database node in the cluster when the connected node fails. Application clients do not see error messages describing loss of service.

TAF allows client application users to continue working after the application loses its connection to the database. While users may experience a brief pause during the time the database server fails over to a surviving cluster node, the session context is preserved. After failover completes, the application automatically reconnects to the database and, if desired, can continue retrieving data from SELECT statements initiated before the failure. After a failover, only the execution of interrupted SELECT statements can be resumed. All other calls are rolled back and OCI reports an error message that can be trapped and handled by the application.

Figure 10.4 illustrates the step-by-step scenario of the TAF configuration. When a node or instance fails, what steps are taken before the user continues to receive the data? In this configuration, if the user's connection to node ORA-DB1 dies, their transaction is rolled back; however, they can continue work without having to manually reconnect to the other instance, establish another transaction programmatically, and then execute the request again. This functionality of continuation of work is made possible using the TAF option.

To get a good understanding of how the TAF architecture works, it would be helpful to walk through a failover scenario using the earlier example, i.e. where a user is querying the database to retrieve 1000 rows from the database. Assume that the user is connected to node ORA-DB1 instance RAC1. By following the steps identified in Figure 10.4:

1.   The heartbeat mechanism between the various nodes in the cluster checks to see if another node in the cluster is available and is participating in the cluster configuration. As discussed earlier, this verification process happens on a continuous basis.

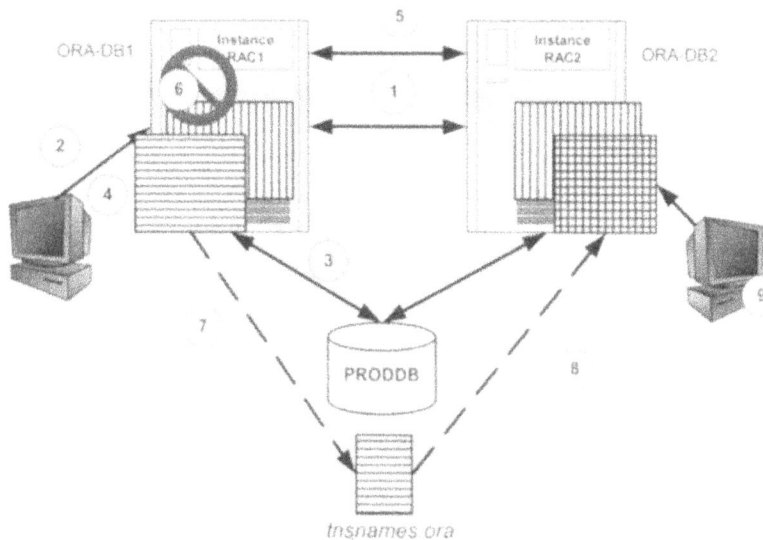

Figure 10.4
Oracle transparent application failover.

2. Let us assume that a user executes a query against the database to retrieve 1000 rows from the database via instance RAC1.

3. The initial 500 rows are retrieved from the PRODDB database via instance RAC1 and returned to the user for browsing through the graphical user interface (GUI). (The application only retrieves and displays no more than 500 rows every time.)

4. While the user is browsing through the first 500 rows, node ORA-DB1 fails.

5. Node ORA-DB2 checks for the heartbeat of the other participating node and deduces that node ORA-DB1 is not responding to the heartbeat request; it times out and declares that the node ORA-DB1 has failed.

6. The user is unaware of the failure and scrolls past the initial 500 rows. In order to retrieve and display the remaining 500 rows, the process tries to connect to instance RAC1 but detects that RAC1 is not available.

7. When the process tries to connect to the instance, using the entries in the tnsnames.ora file the user connection to the other available node ORA-DB2 is established.

8. The user is now connected to instance RAC2 on node ORA-DB2.

9. Oracle re-executes the query using the connection on instance RAC2 and displays the remaining rows to the user. If the data was available in the buffer cache, the rows are returned to the user instantaneously. However, if the rows are not available, Oracle has to perform an I/O operation. This would be delayed until the recovery process has completed.

In Figure 10.4, when node ORA-DB1 fails, any SELECT statements that had partially executed on instance RAC1 are migrated as part of the failover process and are displayed through instance RAC2, when the user process fails over to node ORA-DB2. All this happens transparently without any interruption to the user. It should be noted that along with the SELECT statement, the following are also failed over:

- Client/server connection

- User session state

- Prepared statements

- Active cursors that have begun to return results to the user

The benefits that TAF adds in meeting the high-availability requirements in today's machine-critical applications are overwhelming, and the first question that arises is, why did Oracle not introduce such a feature before or why is this feature not available among other databases? Though the mechanism is very useful in meeting today's high-availability requirements, implementing such a feature is complex, basically because *the database connections are not stateless.* This means that during failure, the database, the users, and the transactions are in a specific state of operation, such as:

- The process may be in a state of retrieving data from the database.

- The database has already established a connection via Oracle Net to an instance.

- A user connecting to the database has password and other user-authentication information.

- The session has language and character set information that is specific to the instance on which the user has established a connection.

- There are cursors open by various sessions that could be in an execution state.

- SELECT cursors are open and users have partially scrolled through the various rows using the client interface or the user application browser.

- INSERT, UPDATE, and DELETE (DML) statements and PL/SQL procedures are being executed.

It should be noted from the scenarios above that only SELECT statements are failed over from one node to another; transactional statements are not failed over by configuration of TAF. Transactional or DML statements can programmatically be transferred from node ORA-DB1 to node ORA-DB2 by proper validation of Oracle returned error messages and taking appropriate actions. (An example handling failover of DML statements is as shown in the Java example that appears later in this chapter.) This should be a preferred method to avoid any user interruptions, as well as keeping the database or system failures transparent to the user. Among the transactional statements, the following do not automatically failover when a node fails:

- PL/SQL server-side package variables

- Global temporary tables

- Effect of any ALTER SESSION statements

- Applications not using OCI8 and above

- Applications not using the JDBC thick driver

- Transactional statements, i.e., statements that include INSERT, UPDATE, and DELETE operations

While the failover is in process, it would be user friendly to inform the user via the application interface that the activity or command issued may take some time. This information could be communicated by validating the various error messages returned by Oracle as part of the node and connection failure. Some of the common Oracle error codes that should be handled by the application to track and transfer transactional statements include:

- ORA-01012: not logged on to Oracle

- ORA-01033: Oracle initialization or shutdown in progress

- ORA-01034: Oracle not available

- ORA-01089: immediate shutdown in progress—no operations are permitted

- ORA-03113: end-of-file on communication channel

- ORA-03114: not connected to ORACLE

- ORA-12203: TNS—unable to connect to destination

- ORA-12500: TNS—listener failed to start a dedicated server process

- ORA-12571: TNS—packet writer failure

TAF configuration

TAF can be configured using one of two methods.

- TNSNAMES-based configuration

- OCI API requests

TNSNAMES-based configuration

Under this method, configuring the TAF option involves adding Oracle Net parameters to the tnsnames.ora file and, when one of the participating nodes encounters failure, the use of parameter values to ascertain the next step in the failover process. The parameter that drives the TAF option is the FAILOVER_MODE under the CONNECT_DATA section of a connect descriptor. By using one or more of the subparameters listed in Table 10.1, full functionality of TAF is obtained.

Table 10.1   *TAF Subparameters*

Parameter	Description
BACKUP	Specifies a different net service name to be used to establish the backup connection. A backup should be specified when using PRECONNECT to pre-establish connections. Specifying a BACKUP is strongly recommended for BASIC methods; otherwise, reconnection may first attempt the instance that has just failed, adding additional delay until the client reconnects
TYPE	Specifies the type of failover. Three types of Net Oracle failover functionality are available by default to the Oracle call interface. SESSION: Fails over the session. With this option, only connection is established, no work in progress is transferred from the failed instance to the available instance. SELECT: Enables user with open cursors to continue fetching on them after failure. Oracle Net keeps track of any SELECT statements issued in the current transaction. It also keeps track of how many rows have been fetched back to the client for each cursor associated with a SELECT statement. If connection to the instance is lost, Oracle Net establishes a connection to a backup instance and continues with the execution of the SELECT statement from the point of failure
METHOD	Determines the speed of the failover from the primary to the secondary or backup node. BASIC: Establishes connections at failover time PRECONNECT: Pre-establishes connections. If this parameter is used, connection to the backup instance is made at the same time as the connection to the primary instance
RETRIES	Specifies the number of attempts to connect to the BACKUP node after a failure before giving up
DELAY	Specifies the amount of time in seconds to wait between attempts to connect to the BACKUP node after a failure before giving up

Another important parameter, or value, that should not be configured manually is the GLOBAL_DBNAME parameter in the SID_LIST_listener_name section of the listener.ora. Configuring this parameter in listener.ora disables TAF. If the GLOBAL_DBNAME parameter has been defined, the parameter should be deleted and the database should be allowed to dynamically register the global database names automatically.

TAF implementation

The TAF option using the `tnsnames.ora` file can be implemented in one of three ways:

- Connect-time failover and client load balancing
- Retrying a connection
- Pre-establishing a connection

Through examples, the various implementations options are explained.

Connect-time failover and client load balancing   Oracle Net connects randomly to one of the listener addresses on node ORA-DB1 or ORA-DB2. If the instance fails after the connection, Oracle Net fails over to the other node's instance, preserving any SELECT statements in progress.

The connect time failover example listed below is the basic method of tnsnames-based failover implementation. When the user session tries to connect to the instance on the first node (ORA-DB1) and determines that the instance is not responding or is not currently available, the session would immediately try the next host name defined in the list (namely ORA-DB2) to establish a connection. The failover from one instance to another is true for the connections that are made for the very first time or for connection retries that occur during an instance crash when a transaction is in progress.

```
PRODDB.SUMMERSKYUS.COM=
  (DESCRIPTION=
   (ADDRESS_LIST=
     (FAILOVER=ON)
     (LOAD_BALANCE=ON)
     (ADDRESS=(PROTOCOL=TCP)
       (HOST=ORA-DB2.SUMMERSKYUS.COM)
         (PORT=1521))
     (ADDRESS=(PROTOCOL=TCP)
        (HOST=ORA-DB1.SUMMERSKYUS.COM)
         (PORT=1521))
  )
  (CONNECT_DATA=
     (SERVICE_NAME=PRODDB.SUMMERSKYUS.COM)
     (ORACLE_HOME = /apps/oracle/product/9.2.0)
     (FAILOVER_MODE=(TYPE=SELECT)
        (METHOD=BASIC))
  )
  )
```

> **Note:** If the FAILOVER and LOAD_BALANCE commands are not placed together below the ADDRESS_LIST argument, during a failover, certain sessions could encounter an ORA-3113 end-of-file on communication channel error.

Retrying a connection With the RETRIES and DELAY parameters as part of the FAILOVER-MODE parameter. The purpose of this parameter is that the connections to the instances are automatically retried by the number of times specified by the parameter. In this scenario the connection is retried 20 times with a delay of 15 seconds between every retry. Unlike the other option where one node in the cluster fails and the connection is re-established on one of the other surviving nodes, under this option, the connection is retried on the same node and no backup node is defined as part of the configuration. Similarly there is no significance to the load-balancing parameter, which has been set to OFF.

These additional parameters are extremely useful when there are thousands of users connected to the instance of the failed node and all these users have to establish connections to the other available nodes. In the case of a dedicated connection, there is only a single thread to establish connections, and simultaneous connection requests from a large number of users could cause connection timeouts. The retry and delay parameters help to retry the connection, with a delay between retries to establish connections to the available node. This is less of an issue when the shared server is configured and used to establish connections to the database, because users are placed in a queue and when a connection becomes available the user establishes connection.

```
PRODDB.SUMMERSKYUS.COM=
  (DESCRIPTION=
   (ADDRESS_LIST=
    (FAILOVER=ON)
    (LOAD_BALANCE=OFF)
    (ADDRESS=(PROTOCOL=TCP)
     (HOST=ORA-DB2.SUMMERSKYUS.COM)
       (PORT=1521))
    (ADDRESS=(PROTOCOL=TCP)
      (HOST=ORA-DB1.SUMMERSKYUS.COM)
      (PORT=1521))
  )
  (CONNECT_DATA=
  (SERVICE_NAME=PRODDB.SUMMERSKYUS.COM)
  (ORACLE_HOME = /apps/oracle/product/9.2.0)
  (FAILOVER_MODE=(TYPE=SELECT)
```

```
(METHOD=BASIC)
(RETRIES=20)
(DELAY=15))
)
)
```

Pre-establishing a connection Another implementation option available under the TAF configuration is to set up a pre-established connection to the backup or secondary instance. One of the potential performance issues is the time required to re-establish a connection after the primary instance has failed, which depends on the time taken to establish a connection to the backup or secondary instance. This could be resolved by pre-establishing connections, which means that the initial and backup connections are explicitly specified. While there is a great advantage in pre-establishing the connection, this is not without drawbacks; pre-established connections consume resources. During some controlled failover testing, additional resource usage was noticed when using pre-established connections. This is because the process always validates the connection throughout its activity.

In the following example, the Oracle Net connects to the listener on ORA-DB1 and simultaneously also makes a connection to the other instance on ORA-DB2. While the process has to make two connections at the beginning of a transaction, the time required to establish a connection during the failover is reduced.

If ORA-DB1 fails after the connection, Oracle Net fails-over to ORA-DB2, preserving any SELECT statements in progress. Having the backup connection already in place, it can reduce the time needed for a failover.

Apart from the additional resource consumption, another drawback in using the preconnection method is that if the connection to the backup instance does not succeed during failover connect time, fail back to the original instance is not possible.

Pre-establishing a connection implies that the backup node is predefined or hard coded. This reduces the scope of availability, as the connection to the original nodes/instances is not dynamic like in the other methods.

```
PRODDB =
  (DESCRIPTION =
  (ADDRESS=
  (PROTOCOL=TCP)
  (HOST=ORA-DB1)
  (PORT=1521))
```

```
(CONNECT_DATA =
   (SERVICE_NAME = PRODDB.SUMMERSKYUS.COM)
   (INSTANCE_NAME=ORA-DB1RAC1)
   (FAILOVER_MODE=
(BACKUP=ORA-DB2RAC2.SUMMERSKYUS.COM)
(TYPE=SELECT)
(METHOD=PRECONNECT)))

ORA-DB2=
   (DESCRIPTION=
   (ADDRESS=
   (PROTOCOL=TCP)
   (HOST=ORA-DB2)
   (PORT=1521))
(CONNECT_DATA=
   (SERVICE_NAME=PRODDB.SUMMERSKYUS.COM)
   (INSTANCE_NAME=ORA-DB2RAC2)
   (FAILOVER_MODE=
(BACKUP=ORA-DB1RAC1.SUMMERSKYUS.COM)
(TYPE=SELECT)
(METHOD=PRECONNECT)))
```

OCI API requests

Under this method, implementing TAF involves using Oracle-provided APIs to accomplish what is normally performed through the tnsnames.ora file. However, under the OCI-based method, the application servers have a better control of what these APIs accomplish and provide appropriate actions based on the results from these calls.

When the OCI definitions are used, TAF is always active and there are no preset requirements of setting the mode to failover.

OCI-based TAF configuration is made possible by using the various failover type events provided through APIs. The failover events shown in Table 10.2 are part of the OracleOCIFailover interface.

TAF callbacks TAF callbacks are used to track and trace failures. They are called during the failover to notify the JDBC application regarding events that are generated. In this case, unlike the tnsnames-based TAF configuration, the application has some control over the failover operation.

To address the issue of failure while establishing a connection of the failover process, the callback function is invoked programmatically several times during the course of re-establishing the user's session.

The first call to the callback function occurs when Oracle first detects an instance connection loss. At this time the client may wish to replay ALTER SESSION commands and inform the user that failover has

Table 10.2   *Failover Events*

Failover Event	Description
FO_SESSION	The user session is reauthenticated on the server-side while open cursors in the OCI application need to be re-executed. This call is equivalent to FAILOVER_MODE=(TYPE=SESSION) defined in the tnsnames.ora file
FO_SELECT	The user session is reauthenticated on the server side; however, open cursors in the OCI can continue fetching. This implies that the client-side logic maintains the fetch state of each open cursor. This call is equivalent to FAILOVER_MODE=(TYPE=SELECT) defined in the tnsnames.ora file
FO_NONE	This is the default mode and implies no failover functionality is used. This call is equivalent to FAILOVER_MODE=(TYPE=NONE) defined in the tnsnames.ora file
FO_BEGIN	Indicates that failover has detected a lost connection and failover is starting
FO_END	Indicates successful completion of failover
FO_ABORT	Indicates that failover was unsuccessful and there is no option of retrying
FO_REAUTH	Indicates that a user handle has been reauthenticated
FO_ERROR	Indicates that failover was temporarily unsuccessful. This gives the application the opportunity to handle the error and retry failover In the case of an error while failing over to a new connection, the JDBC application is able to retry failover. Typically the application sleeps for a while and then it retries, either indefinitely or for a limited amount of time, by having the callback return FO_RETRY. The retry functionality is accomplished by using the FAILOVER_MODE=(RETRIES=<>, DELAY=<>) defined in the tnsnames.ora file
FO_EVENT_UNKOWN	Indicates a bad failover event

happened. If failover is unsuccessful, then the callback is called to inform the application that failover will not take place.

A detailed example will clearly demonstrate the advantages of utilizing the interface provided by Oracle, `OracleOCIFailover`:

```
public interface OracleOCIFailover{
// Possible Failover Types
public static final int FO_SESSION = 1;
public static final int FO_SELECT = 2;
public static final int FO_NONE  = 3;
public static final int;

// Possible Failover events registered with callback
public static final int FO_BEGIN = 1;
public static final int FO_END  = 2;
public static final int FO_ABORT = 3;
public static final int FO_REAUTH = 4;
public static final int FO_ERROR = 5;
public static final int FO_RETRY = 6;
public static final int FO_EVENT_UNKNOWN = 7;

public int callbackFn (Connection conn,
               Object ctxt, // Anything the user
                wants to save
               int type, // One of the above possible Failover
               Types
                int event ); // One of the above
                possible Failover Events
```

In the case of a failure of one of the instances, Oracle tries to restore the connections of the failed instance onto the active instance. This causes a possible delay, in which case the users are to be notified, as a business rule.

```
package rac.chapter10.taf;

//java imports
import java.sql.Connection;
import java.sql.Statement;
import java.sql.ResultSet;
import java.sql.SQLException;
import java.sql.DriverManager;

//Oracle imports
import oracle.jdbc.OracleConnection;
//log4j imports.
import org.apache.log4j.Category;

public class TAFDetailsExample {
  /* Connection object to handle the database connection*/
  private Connection con = null;
  /**
  * TAFCallbackFn class implements the interface provided
  * by Oracle in case of FailOver
  */
```

```java
private TAFCallbackFn clbFn = null;
/* Failover string */
private String strFailover = null;
/* Statement object to execute query */
private Statement stmt = null;
/* Result set object to hold the results of the query*/
private ResultSet rs = null;
/* used for getting an instance of log4j for this class.
*/
protected static Category cat =
Category.getInstance
(TAFDetailsExample.class.getName());

/**

* Constructor.
*/
public TAFDetailsExample() {
}

public static void main(String[] args) {
  TAFDetailsExample tafDE = new TAFDetailsExample();
  // This method handles database connections.
  tafDE.handleDBConnections();
  try {
    // This method is used to execute query
    tafDE.runQuery();
    cat.debug(tafDE.toString());
    // This method is used to free the resources
    allocated
    tafDE.closeConnections();
  } catch (SQLException e) {
    e.printStackTrace();
  }
}

/**
  * This method is used to clear all the resources
    allocated.
  * @throws SQLException
  */
void closeConnections() throws SQLException {
    rs.close();
    stmt.close();
    con.close();
    cat.debug("Allocated Resources are free now.");
}
/**
  *This method is used to handle the database connection
  *with specific connection strings.
  */

void handleDBConnections() {
    try {
```

```
        // Register the Oracle driver
        DriverManager.registerDriver(
            new oracle.jdbc.driver.OracleDriver());
    // Create a Connection to the database with specific connection
      string
    con = (OracleConnection)
        DriverManager.getConnection(
        "jdbc:oracle:oci:@PRODDBTRANS ",
        "user",
        "pwd");
      if (con != null)
        this.RegisterFailOver(); //register failover
    } catch (SQLException e) {
    cat.debug("Error Occurred while registering Failover.");
        e.printStackTrace();
    }
}
/**
 * This Function registers the class that implements the
 * Oracle OCIFailover Interface. This is done to notify Oracle that in
   case of a failure the callback function in the registered class is to
   be invoked.
 */

void RegisterFailOver() throws SQLException {
    clbFn = new TAFCallbackFn();
    strFailover = new String("Register Failover");
    // Registers the callback Function.
    ((OracleConnection) con).registerTAFCallback(clbFn, strFailover);
    cat.debug(" Failover Registered Successfully. ");
}
/**
 * This method is used to execute query.
 */

void runQuery() {
    try {
      stmt = con.createStatement();
    } catch (SQLException e) {
      e.printStackTrace();
    }
    long startTime = 0;
    long endTime = 0;
    /**
     * This loop is used for testing purposes only.
     */
    for (int i = 0; i < 20000; i++) {
      startTime = System.currentTimeMillis();
      try {
        /**
         * This query is just used for testing purposes.
```

```java
 * In a real time scenario the query is
   dynamically passed and can be any valid PL/SQL
   statement.
 */
String query = "SELECT USP.USPRL_ID," +
        "USP.USPRL_FIRST_NAME,      " +
        "USP.USPRL_LAST_NAME,       " +
        "USP.USPRL_CITY,            " +
        "USP.USPRL_STATE_ID,        " +
        "COMP.COMP_NAME,            " +
        "COMP.COMP_TYPE_CD,         " +
        "USP.USPRL_EMAIL,           " +
        "USP.USPRL_PHONE,           " +
        "US.USEC_TOTAL_LOGINS,      " +
        "USP.USPRL_ROLE_CD,         " +
        "COMP.COMP_SCAC_CODE,       " +
        "USP.USPRL_LOGIN_NAME,      " +
        "UL.USRLI_ID                " +
        "FROM USER_PROFILE USP,     " +
        "COMPANY COMP,              " +
        "USER_LOGIN UL,             " +
        "USER_SECURITY US           " +
        "WHERE UL.USRLI_ACTIVE_STATUS_CD=
         'ACTIVE'AND" +
        "UL.USRLI_LOGGED_IN_EUSR_ID=
         USP.USPRL_ID " +
        "AND USP.USPRL_COMP_ID =
         COMP.COMP_ID AND " +
        "USP.USPRL_ID = US.USEC_USPRL_ID
         ORDER BY " +
        "COMP.COMP_COMP_TYPE_CD, " +
        "COMP.COMP_NAME, USP.USPRL_LAST_NAME";

    rs = stmt.executeQuery(query);

} catch (SQLException e) {
    /**
     * The limitations for failover prevent INSERT, DELETE, UPDATE
     * and transactional statements from failing over.
     * The possible errors that Oracle could throw in such a
     * situation can be handled and we can get a new connection
     * and execute the statements keeping the failure transparent
       to the user.
     * The possible errors for handling are.
     */
if ((e.getErrorCode() == 1012) ||    // ORA-01012: not logged on to Oracle
    (e.getErrorCode() == 1033) ||    // ORA-01033: Oracle initialization
                                     // or shutdown in
                                        progress
    (e.getErrorCode() == 1034) ||    // ORA-01034: Oracle not available
    (e.getErrorCode() == 1089) ||    // ORA-01089: immediate shutdown in
                                     // progress, no
                                        operations are
                                     // permitted
```

```
(e.getErrorCode() == 3113) ||      // ORA-03113:
                                   //   end-of-file on
                                   // communication
                                   //   channel
(e.getErrorCode() == 3114) ||      // ORA-03114: not
                                   //   connected to Oracle
(e.getErrorCode() == 12203) ||     // ORA-12203:
                                   //   TNS---unable to
                                   //   connect
                                   // to destination
(e.getErrorCode() == 12500) ||     // ORA-12500:
                                   //   TNS---listener failed to
                                   // start a dedicated server process
(e.getErrorCode() == 12571))       // ORA-12571:
                                   //   TNS---packet writer
                                   // failure
        {
          cat.debug("Node failed while executing" +
                  "INSERT/DELETE/UPDATE/TRANSACTIONAL Statements");
            // Get another connection
            handleDBConnections();
            // re execute the query.
            runQuery();
        } else
        // The failure is not due to a node failure.
            e.printStackTrace();
      }
      endTime = System.currentTimeMillis();

      if (cat.isDebugEnabled())
         cat.debug("Execution Time for the query is  " +
                 (endTime - startTime) + " ms.");
   }
 }
 public String toString() {
    StringBuffer sb = new StringBuffer();
    try {
      sb.append("\nResultset values are " + "\n" + rs.getType());
    } catch (SQLException e) {
      e.printStackTrace();
    }
    return sb.toString();
 }
}
package rac.chapter10.taf;

//Java imports
import java.sql.Connection;
import java.sql.SQLException;

//log4j imports
import org.apache.log4j.Category;

//Oracle imports
import oracle.jdbc.OracleOCIFailover;
```

```java
public class TAFCallbackFn implements OracleOCIFailover {
 private static Category cat =
Category.getInstance(TAFCallbackFn.class.getName());
 public TAFCallbackFn() {
     }

/**
 * This callback function will be invoked on failure of a
 * node or lost connections
 * @param connection - The failed connection which will be restored
 * @param o - Used to hold the user Context object
 * @param i - failover type
 * @param i1 - failover event
 * @return - In case of an error return FO_RETRY else
 * return 0
 */
public int callbackFn(Connection connection, Object o,
 int type, int event) {
    String foType[] = {
        "SESSION",
        "SELECT",
        "NONE"
    };
    String foEvent[] = {
        "BEGIN",
        "END",
        "ABORT",
        "REAUTHORISE",
        "ERROR",
        "RETRY",
        "UNKNOWN"
    };
    try {
    cat.debug("The connection for which the failover occurred is :" +
              connection.getMetaData().toString());
    } catch (SQLException e) {
       e.printStackTrace();
    }
    cat.debug("FAILOVER TYPE is : " + foType[type-1]);
    cat.debug("FAILOVER EVENT is : " + foEvent[event-1]);

    switch (event) {
       case FO_BEGIN:
          cat.info("Failover event is begin ");
          break;

       case FO_END:
          cat.info("Failover event is end");
          return 0;

       case FO_ABORT:
          cat.info("Failover is aborted");
          break;

       case FO_REAUTH:
```

```
         cat.info("Failover needs reauthorization");
         break;
      case FO_ERROR:
      cat.info("Error  occurred  while  failing  over.  Retrying  " + "  to
      restore connection. ");
  try {
                          Thread.sleep(2000);//sleep for 2 seconds
           } catch (InterruptedException e) {  // Trap errors
         cat.error("Error while causing the currently
                 executing thread to sleep");
       }
         return FO_RETRY;
      default:
         cat.info("Default is returned");
   }
   cat.debug("Before returning from the Callback Function.");
   return 0;
 }
}
```

In the example above, the Oracle JDBC driver is registered and the connection is obtained from the `DriverManager`.

```
DriverManager.registerDriver(new
 oracle.jdbc.driver.OracleDriver());
con=OracleConnection)DriverManager.getConnection
("jdbc:oracle:oci:@PRODDB","user", "pwd");
```

Here PRODDB represents an entry in the `tnsnames.ora`, which has the connection strings. In this file, failover has been enabled (FAILOVER=ON) and type of failover indicates that all SELECT queries will be failed over (TYPE=SELECT):

```
PRODDB.SUMMERSKYUS.COM=
(DESCRIPTION=
 (ADDRESS_LIST=
  (FAILOVER=ON)
  (LOAD_BALANCE=ON)
  (ADDRESS=(PROTOCOL=TCP)
      (HOST=ORA-DB2.SUMMERSKYUS.COM)
        (PORT=1521))
  (ADDRESS=(PROTOCOL=TCP)
        (HOST=ORA-DB1.SUMMERSKYUS.COM)
        (PORT=1521))
 )
 (CONNECT_DATA=
  (SERVICE_NAME=PRODDB.SUMMERSKYUS.COM)
  (ORACLE_HOME = /apps/oracle/product/9.2.0)
  (FAILOVER_MODE=(TYPE=SELECT)
          (METHOD=BASIC)
          (RETRIES=20)
          (DELAY=15))
 )
)
```

After a connection is established, the class that is implementing the Oracle interface should be registered with Oracle:

```
clbFn = new TAFCallbackFn();
strFailover = new String("Register Failover");
((OracleConnection)con).registerTAFCallback
(clbFn, strFailover);
```

This notifies Oracle that in the case of a failure, the callback function, which is implemented in the class TAFCallbackFn, is to be called. Oracle also provides the failover type (SESSION, SELECT, or NONE) and the present failover event.

```
package rac.chapter10.taf;
//java imports
import java.sql.Connection;
import java.sql.Statement;
import java.sql.ResultSet;
import java.sql.SQLException;
import java.sql.DriverManager;

//Oracle imports
import oracle.jdbc.OracleConnection;
//log4j imports.
import org.apache.log4j.Category;
```

When the failover starts, Oracle sends the FO_BEGIN event, thus notifying the application that the failover has begun and behind the scenes tries to restore the connection. As explained earlier, if the failover type is SELECT, the query is re-executed and the cursor is positioned to the row where the failure occurred. Additionally, the session on the initial instance may have received session-specific commands (ALTER SESSION), which need to be re-executed before the failover process is activated and the user session is established to continue. As discussed in the earlier section, session-specific commands will not be automatically replayed on the failed over instance. Also, the callback is called each time a user handle besides the primary handle is reauthenticated on the new connection. Since each user handle represents a server-side session, the client program would need to replay the ALTER SESSION commands for that session.

All the above-mentioned limitations for failover need to be handled so that the failure is transparent to the user. The possible errors that can be thrown by Oracle in such a case are handled and the connection is re-established and the query is re-executed.

```
if ((e.getErrorCode() == 1012) ||// ORA-01012: not logged on to Oracle
(e.getErrorCode() == 1033) ||    // ORA-01033: Oracle initialization
```

```
                                   // or shutdown in progress
  (e.getErrorCode() == 1034) ||    // ORA-01034: Oracle not available
  (e.getErrorCode() == 1089) ||    // ORA-01089: immediate shutdown in
                                   // progress, no operations are per-
                                   // mitted
  (e.getErrorCode() == 03113) ||   // ORA-03113: end-of-file on communi-
                                   // cation channel
  (e.getErrorCode() == 03114) ||   // ORA-03114: not connected to Oracle
  (e.getErrorCode() == 12203) ||   // ORA-12203: TNS---unable to connect
                                   // to destination
  (e.getErrorCode() == 12500) ||   // ORA-12500: TNS---listener failed
                                   // to
                                   // start a dedicated server process
  (e.getErrorCode() == 12571))     // ORA-12571: TNS---
                                   // packet writer failure
      {
        cat.debug("Node failed while executing" +
              " TRANSACTIONAL Statements");
        // Get another connection
        handleDBConnections();
        // re execute the query.
        runQuery();
}
```

When the connection is established and the failover has ended, the FO_END event is sent back to the application saying that the failover has been completed.

Transitions may not always be smooth; if an error is encountered while restoring a connection to the failed over instance, the FO_ERROR event is sent to the application indicating the error and requesting the application to handle this error appropriately. Under these circumstances, the application could provide a retry functionality where the application will rest or sleep for a predefined interval of time and send back a FO_RETRY event. If during a subsequent attempt a similar error occurs, the application would retry again until the number of retry attempts specified by the property RETRIES in the tnsnames.ora file has been reached. The sleep or rest time is defined by the property DELAY also defined in the tnsnames.ora file.

```
case FO_ERROR:
    cat.info("Error Occurred while failing over. Retrying to restore
connection.");
try {
     Thread.sleep(2000);
   } catch (InterruptedException e) {  // Trap errors
     cat.error("Error while causing the currently executing thread to
     sleep");
   }
   return FO_RETRY;
```

An extract from a debug log below shows the scenario where a failure occurred and the query that executed on the primary instance in 47 ms failed over and re-executed the query in about 3026 ms (this includes the time for the session to failover, establish a new connection and re-execute the query). The entire failover operation is transparent to the user.

```
20:55:54,041 runQuery TAFDetailsExample.java 91 DEBUG: Execution Time
for the query is 47ms.
20:55:54,041 runQuery TAFDetailsExample.java 91 DEBUG: Execution Time
for the query is 47ms.
20:55:54,041 runQuery TAFDetailsExample.java 91 DEBUG: Execution Time
for the query is 32ms.
20:55:54,056 callbackFn TAFCallbackFn.java 45  DEBUG:
```

The connection for which the failover occurred is:

```
oracle.jdbc.driver.OracleDatabaseMetaData@6b13c7
20:55:54,056 callbackFn TAFCallbackFn.java 49 DEBUG: FAILOVER TYPE is :
SELECT
20:55:54,056 callbackFn TAFCallbackFn.java 50  DEBUG: FAILOVER EVENT is
: BEGIN
20:55:54,072 callbackFn TAFCallbackFn.java 57  INFO: Failover event is
begin
20:55:54,072 callbackFn TAFCallbackFn.java 89  DEBUG: Before returning
from the callBack Function.
20:55:56,121 callbackFn TAFCallbackFn.java 49 DEBUG: FAILOVER TYPE is :
SELECT
20:55:56,121 callbackFn TAFCallbackFn.java 50  DEBUG: FAILOVER EVENT is
: END
20:55:56,137 callbackFn TAFCallbackFn.java 61  INFO: Failover event is
end
20:55:56,138 callbackFn TAFCallbackFn.java 89  DEBUG: Before returning
from the callBack Function.
20:55:57,018 runQuery TAFDetailsExample.java 91 DEBUG: Execution Time
for the query is 3026ms.
```

TAF verification

Implementation of TAF could be verified by querying the Oracle-provided data dictionary views. V$SESSION has three columns, FAILOVER_MODE, FAILOVER_TYPE, and FAILED_OVER, that provide information pertaining to TAF implementation, and verification of results when the node in the cluster crashes and the session fails-over to one of the available nodes.

```
SELECT SID,
    USERNAME,
    FAILOVER_TYPE,
    FAILOVER_METHOD,
    FAILED_OVER
```

```
FROM V$SESSION
/
 SID  USERNAME     FAILOVER_TYPE FAILOVER_M  FAILED_OVER
 ----  ----------   -------------  ----------  -----------
 316  OLTP_USER     SELECT        BASIC        YES
 317  OLTP_USER     SELECT        BASIC        NO
 320  OLTP_USER     SELECT        BASIC        NO
 326  OLTP_USER     SELECT        BASIC        NO
1257  MVALLATH      NONE          NONE         NO
 328  OLTP_USER     SELECT        BASIC        YES
 330  OLTP_USER     SELECT        BASIC        YES
 332  OLTP_USER     SELECT        BASIC        YES
 337  OLTP_USER     SELECT        BASIC        NO
 338  OLTP_USER     SELECT        BASIC        NO
 341  OLTP_USER     SELECT        BASIC        YES
```

The above query provides the details and status of the failover operation. The output of the query indicates that five users' sessions have failed over (FAILED_OVER = YES) from the instance that had crashed. The user SCHEMA_OWNER has a connection to the database, but has not been set up to use the failover option and has the default FAILOVER_TYPE of NONE.

On systems where there are many sessions it would be better to look at the details by grouping the results. The following query gives a consolidated count on the operation:

```
SELECT MACHINE,
   FAILOVER_TYPE,
   FAILOVER_METHOD,
   FAILED_OVER,
   COUNT (*)
FROM V$SESSION
GROUP BY MACHINE,
    FAILOVER_TYPE,
    FAILOVER_METHOD,
    FAILED_OVER
```

When configuring TAF to have the TYPE=SELECT:

- The ordering of rows retrieved by a SELECT statement is not fixed; for this reason, queries that might be replayed should contain an ORDER BY clause. However, even without an ORDER BY clause, rows returned by the reissued query are nearly always returned in the initial order; known exceptions are queries that execute using the HASH JOIN or PARALLEL query features. If an ORDER BY clause is not used, OCI will check if the set of discarded rows matches those previously retrieved to ensure that the application does not generate incorrect results.

- Recovery time after a failover can be longer when using TYPE=SELECT. For example, if a query that retrieves 100,000 rows is interrupted by a failure after 99,989 rows have been fetched, then the client application will not be available for new work after a failover until 99,989 rows have first been refetched, discarded, and the last 11 rows of the query have been retrieved.

Other benefits of TAF

The main functionality of the TAF features is to failover users' sessions from the failed instance to another active instance. However by putting to use this same functionality there are other useful scenarios where TAF improves system availability. Some of these functions are:

- Transactional shutdown
- Quiescing the database

Shutdown Transactional

During maintenance windows, when an instance needs to be freed from user or client activity (for example, applying a database patch to an instance without interrupting service to the clients), TAF can come in handy. By using the shutdown transactional, shutting down selected nodes rather than an entire database, users can be migrated from one instance to another. This is done by using the TRANSACTIONAL clause of the SHUTDOWN statement, which removes a node from service so that the shutdown event is deferred until all existing transactions are completed. This routes newly submitted transactions to an alternate node.

For example, the output below indicates a SHUTDOWN TRANSACTIONAL operation:

```
SQL> SHUTDOWN TRANSACTIONAL
Database closed.
Database dismounted
ORACLE instance shut down
SQL>
```

Quiescing the database

Certain database administrative activities require isolation from concurrent user transactions or queries. To accomplish such a function, the quiesce database feature could be used. Quiescing the database prevents having to shut down the database and reopen it in restricted mode to perform these administrative tasks.

Quiescing of the database is accomplished by issuing the following command:

```
ALTER SYSTEM QUIESCE RESTRICTED.
```

The QUIESCE RESTRICTED clause allows administrative tasks to be performed in isolation from concurrent user transactions or queries. In a RAC implementation, this affects all instances, not just the one that issues the statement.

> **Note:** In a RAC implementation, quiescing of the database is allowed only if the database resource manager feature was activated at instance startup. The resource manager should be started on all instances. It is through the facilities of the database resource manager that non-DBA sessions are prevented from becoming active. It should be noted that while the quiesce statement is in effect, any changes to the current resource plan are queued until after the system is unquiesced.

After completion of DBA activities, the database could be unquiesced by issuing the following statement.

```
SQL>ALTER SYSTEM UNQUIESCE;
```

Once the database has been unquiesced the non-DBA activities are allowed to proceed.

10.2.5   Oracle Real Application Cluster Guard

This section will focus on the architecture and configuration of Oracle Real Application Cluster Guard (RACG). One of the great advantages or functionalities of RAC is to provide high availability. Availability can be provided either through an active/active configuration or an active/passive configuration. In the active/active configuration, both instances are active all the time and users can connect to either instance by connecting directly to the address of the instance or through a common load balance option using the load-balancing feature of Oracle Net. Active/passive configurations are where only one instance is active all the time and the other instance is provided for availability, in the sense that when one instance fails, users would automatically transfer to the other instance. RACG is one such tool that provides failover of the services from the failed node or instance to the other instance.

Oracle, in the previous versions of the product, provided a similar functionality through the failsafe feature. Oracle parallel failsafe was available on a limited set of clusters and required a separate installation. The primary difference between a failsafe option and the current RACG option is that, in the case of failsafe the failover instance is not active, it is made active after the primary instance has failed and when the actual failover happens. In the case of RACG, both instances are available all the time; however, users only connect to one active instance, and when the primary instance fails, the users are failed over to the secondary instance. Unlike the failsafe option, RACG combines the features of RAC and the vendor's cluster management services to provide an efficient failover.

Architecture

Figure 10.5 illustrates a two-node RACG configuration. Each node executes the vendor's CM, which in addition to its normal functions, is responsible for running and halting scripts automatically upon failover or when you issue the appropriate command.

Components of RACG

Packs

Each node contains a pack of software provided by Oracle. A pack is software that ensures the availability of the resources required to run an Oracle instance. A pack supports a single instance with access provided through listeners. A pack controls startups, shutdowns, and restarts of the processes under its control.

There is one pack for each instance. Packs contain the following components:

- RAC instance
- Listeners
- IP Addresses
- Pack functions
- Monitors
- Disk group manager

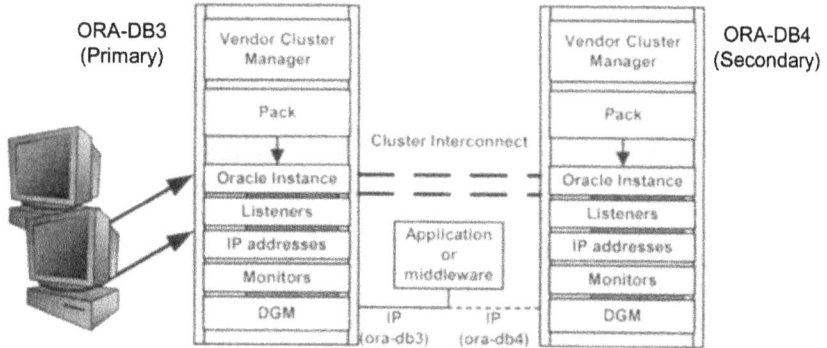

Figure 10.5
*Oracle Real
Application
Cluster Guard
architecture.*

RAC instance

In Figure 10.5, node ORA-DB3 is running in the primary instance role and node ORA-DB4 in the secondary instance role.

Listeners One or more listeners can be configured to accept Oracle Net connection requests. Public listeners support clients, and private listeners support tools such as OEM and RMAN and also provide access for database administration tasks. Private listeners can also be used by the DBA for administration tasks. In Figure 10.5, the public listener points to the IP address of node ORA-DB3, which is configured as the primary node.

IP addresses Clients can use the pack's relocatable IP address to access the resources managed by the pack. A relocatable IP address is a public IP address that is configured to be up or down by the RACG. A relocatable IP address is not associated with a specific physical server; it can float between physical servers. It is initially associated with only the primary node. If the primary node fails, then the address fails over to a different cluster node (a secondary node). The relocatable IP address is configured to be up as the first step when the pack is running and is configured to be down as the last step when the pack is halted.

A stationary, private IP address is configured for private tasks such as IPC, heartbeat, system management, and RMAN operations. A private listener supports access to the instance through the private IP address.

Public IP addresses are relocatable and can be moved between nodes to maintain availability to an active instance. However, private IP addresses are static and support connections to private listeners.

Pack functions   Packs do the following:

- Start and stop the relocatable IP address and public listener

- Start and stop the private listener

- Start and stop the Oracle instance

- Start and stop the monitors

A pack starts up the Oracle instance and monitors the instance. If it determines that the instance has expired, then it ensures that the resources associated with that instance are moved to the secondary node and subsequently enables service on the secondary node.

A pack can run on either the primary or the secondary node. When it is on its primary node, it starts up and shuts down everything. However, when the pack is on its foreign node, it only configures the relocatable IP address to be up or down.

Monitors

- *Instance monitor:* The instance monitor detects termination of the local instance and initiates failover to the secondary node or restarts the instance.

- *Listener monitor:* The function of the listener monitor is to check and restart the listeners. When the public listener fails to restart, the listener monitor exits and initiates a halt script, at which point RACG either begins failover or restarts the primary instance, depending on the state of the secondary node.

- *Heartbeat monitor:* The heartbeat monitor checks the availability of the Oracle instance. During normal operation, the heartbeat monitor on each instance updates its own local heartbeat and checks the heartbeat of the other instance. The heartbeat monitor on the primary instance also executes a customer-defined query to test whether the primary instance is capable of work. The local Oracle instance is considered unavailable if the heartbeat monitor fails to complete three consecutive attempts and there are no unusual circumstances, such as instance recovery or unusually large numbers of sessions logging on.

If the primary instance is unavailable and the primary instance role has not resumed normal function on its new node, then the heartbeat monitor initiates takeover. A takeover occurs when the secondary node executes failover of the primary instance role to itself.

Disk group manager A disk group manager (DGM) is required only on some platforms, to enable public access to the database disks by the current primary node.

Configuration

In Oracle 9*i*, RACG supports a large variety of clusters and is automatically installed with the RAC option. The typical configuration for RACG is a two-instance RAC database with ACTIVE_INSTANCE_COUNT = 1 defined in their parameter files. This enables one instance as the primary instance and one as the secondary instance. The primary instance masters the entire GRD and is the only instance to allow user connections through Oracle Net Services. The secondary instance takes over the primary role when the primary instance fails.

In addition, the pieces of software necessary to manage an instance are configured into packs. Each pack is a self-contained set of software that can enable and monitor all the components of a RACG instance on a node.

Types of configurations

Hub configuration A hub configuration consists of one node that serves as the secondary node for other nodes that serve as primary nodes for separate installations of RACG databases. The simplest possible hub configuration consists of three nodes.

Figure 10.6 illustrates that the primary instance for database A resides on node ORA-DB3, the primary instance for database B resides on node ORA-DB4, and the primary instance for database C resides on node ORA-DB5. The secondary instances for all three databases reside on node ORA-DB6.

In a stable state, all primary instances run on their preferred primary nodes. When a failure on a primary node occurs, the primary instance fails over to its secondary instance on node ORA-DB6. A single failover of a primary node to the secondary node has minimal impact; however, if this failure pattern repeats or if there are several failures there would a considerable impact on the performance of RAC. In the above configuration, if node ORA-DB6, which is configured as the secondary node for all the primary nodes fails, then all of the RACG installations lose resilience. In this configuration node ORA-DB6 is also the single point of failure.

Ring configuration Compared to the hub-based configuration, this configuration distributes the various primary and secondary instances amongst various nodes. No one node is a single point of failure.

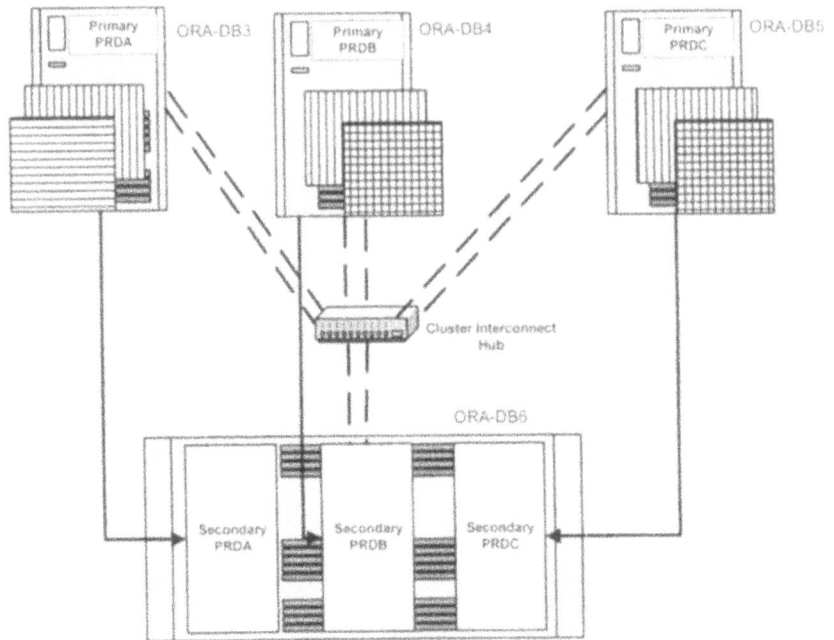

Figure 10.6
*Oracle Real
Application
Cluster Guard
hub configura-
tion.*

Figure 10.7 illustrates the RACG ring configuration. In this configuration three nodes are configured with each node containing a primary
and secondary instance that maps to a primary and secondary instance in
another node forming a ring/circle configuration.

The primary instance for database A resides on node ORA-DB3, while
the secondary instance for database A resides on node ORA-DB4. The
primary instance for database B resides on node ORA-DB4, while the
secondary instance for database B resides on node ORA-DB5.

The primary instance for database C resides on node ORA-DB5, while
the secondary instance for database C resides on node ORA-DB3.

Starting the RACG

The RACG software is controlled from the command line. To start RACG:

1.   Log in as the `root` user.

2.   Shut down all listeners associated with the RACG database on the
     cluster.

3.   Ensure that the `DB_NAME`, `ORACLE_SERVICE`, `ORACLE_HOME`, and if
     necessary, the `ORACLE_BASE` environment variables are set correctly.

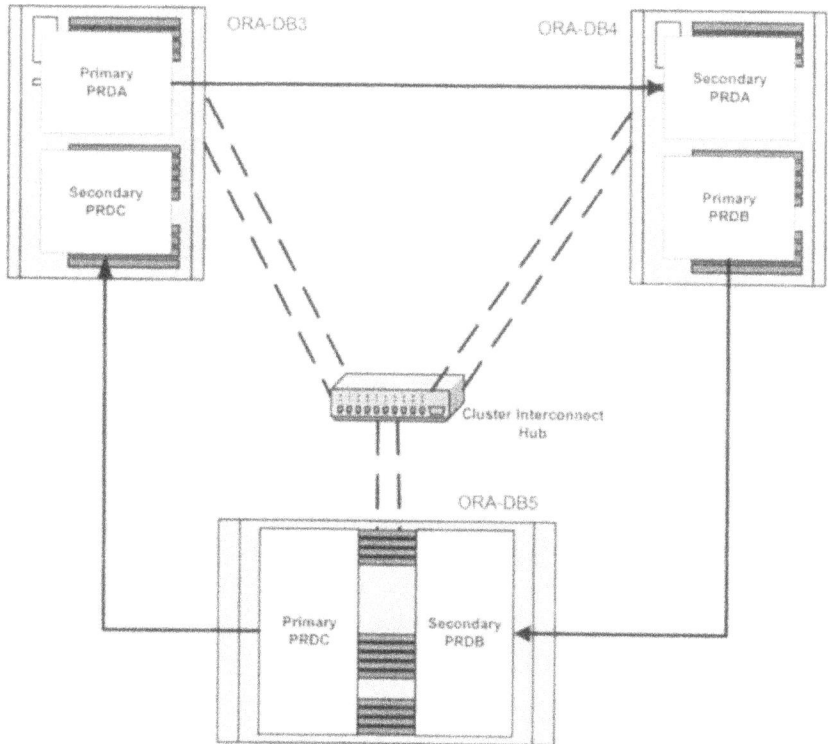

Figure 10.7
*Oracle Real
Application
Cluster Guard
ring configura-
tion.*

4.   Enter the following command:

```
# pfsctl
```

5.   Start RACG from the PFSCTL prompt:

```
PFSCTL> pfsboot
```

6.   Check the RACG packs log file for any errors:

```
$ORACLE_BASE/admin/db_name/pfs/pfsdump/
pfs_<ORACLE_SERVICE>_hostname.log
```

```
$ORACLE_HOME/pfs/db_name/log/pfs_<ORACLE_SERVICE>_hostname.log
```

7.   Check the Oracle heartbeat monitor logs for errors:

```
$ORACLE_BASE/admin/db_name/pfs/pfsdump/
pfs_<ORACLE_SERVICE>_hostname_ping.log
```

```
$ORACLE_HOME/pfs/db_name/log/
pfs_<ORACLE_SERVICE>_hostname_ping.log
```

Operation

Figure 10.8 illustrates the failure operation when the primary instance fails. During normal operation, both node ORA-DB3 and node ORA-DB4 are operational. Pack A is running on its primary node, node ORA-DB3, and has the primary instance role. It contains the primary instance and an IP address. Pack B is running on its primary node, node ORA-DB4, and has the secondary instance role. It contains the secondary instance and an IP address.

If the primary instance fails, then RACG automatically does the following:

- The secondary instance becomes the primary instance.

- Pack A starts on node ORA-DB4 in foreign mode. This means that only its relocatable IP address is configured to be up on node ORA-DB4.

Now both Pack A and Pack B are running on node ORA-DB4. Pack B contains the primary instance and its IP address. Pack A has only the relocatable IP address configured to be up. Nothing is running on node ORA-DB3.

A notification about the failure is sent to the PFS log. If the system is set up to notify an administrator of the failure, then the administrator can use the RESTORE command to restore the secondary instance role. At which point RACG starts Pack A on node ORA-DB3. Because the instance on node ORA-DB4 now has the primary instance role, the instance associated with Pack A assumes the secondary instance role when it restarts. When both instances are up and operating, the system has resilience.

Figure 10.8
Oracle Real Application Cluster Guard failover operation.

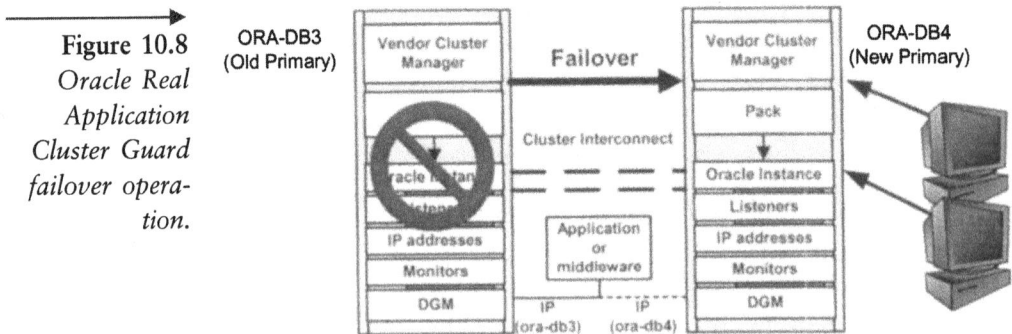

Restoration

After RACG fails over the primary instance role, the packs are on their home nodes, but the instance roles are reversed. If the primary instance needs to run on the preferred primary node, then this can be done by using the MOVE_PRIMARY and RESTORE commands.

Pack A is on node ORA-DB3 and has the secondary instance role. Pack B is on node ORA-DB4 and has the primary instance role. When the user enters the MOVE_PRIMARY command, RACG halts Pack B. The secondary instance, which is running on node ORA-DB3, becomes the primary instance. When the user enters the RESTORE command, RACG starts Pack B on node ORA-DB4. Pack B assumes the secondary instance role. The packs are now running on their home nodes with their original roles.

Advantages and disadvantages of RACG

The primary advantage of using the RACG configuration for high availability, is where one node is defined as the primary node and the other node is not being used. Under these circumstances, the second node is configured as the secondary node and is only used for a failover operation.

There are several disadvantages to this configuration:

1. The secondary node is not utilized until such time that the primary node fails. While the secondary node is up and operable, no user connections are permitted to this node.

2. There are several other alternative solutions to high availability such as ODG and OAR. The solutions not only provide high availability and failover, but also allow minimal use of the secondary node, for example, for read-only or reporting solutions.

3. For RACG to be operational, it requires RAC to be installed and configured, which is an expensive solution considering the fact that the secondary instance is not utilized.

4. While RACG configuration could be implemented on multiple nodes as illustrated in the hub and ring configuration scenarios, these configurations are very complex to set up, implement, and manage. The ideal configuration is a two-node configuration.

5. RACG operation requires several manual interferences to reinstate the original primary and secondary node configurations.

10.3   Scalability

The RAC scalability feature is its basic architecture and is made possible by the various features offered through the technology. RAC is a clustered database solution, where one copy of a physical database could be accessed from two or more nodes or instances. Which means that an instance or node could join or leave the cluster dynamically (provided the database has been created to provide for this feature). What this means is that when a node or instance crashes, Oracle will reconfigure the membership to the cluster and continue functioning as a cluster with fewer instances. Similarly, when a node or instance joins the cluster, it reconfigures the membership to the cluster and continues functioning as if some additional resource was dynamically added to the instance.

Some of the scalability features we have already discussed in the previous chapters include:

- *New cache fusion technology:* All data communication or sharing of global memory information happens via the high-speed cluster interconnect, providing sharing of data across instances and only writing to disk when it absolutely needs to.

- *Dynamic reconfiguration of resources:* When a node or instance joins or leaves the cluster, Oracle is able to dynamically register this fact and balance the additional resources to the instance that joined the cluster or the resources from the instance to the available instances when an instance leaves the cluster.

- *Fast recovery feature:* Due to the shared database architecture, any instance could recover the data that belonged to another instance by reading the redo logs of the instance.

- *Listener load balancing:* Where multiple users try to make connections to an Oracle instance and the local listener is busy, Oracle will automatically load balance to the other instance provided the load balancing parameter has been set to ON (LOAD_BALANCE = ON) in the tnsnames.ora file.

- *Addition of nodes or instances dynamically:* This provides for easy business growth. As the business grows and as more and more users access the available instance, making it highly resource intensive, additional instances could be added to the cluster dynamically, allowing distribution of workload to the new instances and thus providing scalability of the database servers. While more nodes or instances are added to the existing configuration, apart from the basic instance configuration no additional database-related activities or additional databases are required. These additional instances will share the already available common physical database.

- *Users from all nodes or instances access the common shared physical database to retrieve data simultaneously:* This means that multiple users from multiple instances could access the same piece of information simultaneously, and all lock-related activity, when users' processes from the various instances request for the same data, is handled by the GCS across the cluster interconnect.

10.3.1 Configuring RAC for scalability

RAC can be configured as an active/passive configuration, where one node is only active at any given point of time, while the other node is inactive or in a passive state and is used only when the active instance fails. The main goal for this kind of configuration is availability and failover; when one node in the cluster fails, users are migrated to the other instance on another node. This feature is implemented using the Oracle RACG. The drawback to such a configuration is that one instance is idle all the time (until the primary instance fails) and capital investment is not being utilized.

This type of configuration could be achieved without a RAC configuration where one Oracle instance is installed on shared storage mounted on one node, and when the node fails, the other node could remount the disks. The failed-over node then becomes the active node (this depends on the O/S failover capabilities).

> **Note:** When RAC is implemented using an active/passive state, the total node/instance count is always two and addition of further nodes is not possible.

The other type of configuration is where nodes have been configured to be in an active/active state. Which means all the instances are in a usable state and no instance is idle at a given point in time. This is where the true functionality of a RAC implementation is obtained. RAC, when configured to be in an active/active state, provides availability and scalability provided that certain parameters are configured during the database creation time.

```
CREATE DATBASE 'PRODDB'
MAXINSTANCES 8
MAXLOGFILES 48
MAXDATA FILES 1024
MAXLOGHISTORY 1024
CHARACTER SET UTF8
NATIONAL CHARACTER SET 'UTF8''
CONTROLFILE REUSE
```

All the parameters used in the database creation command help in the scalability of the database; considerable care should be taken in calculating the appropriate values for these parameters. These values should be arrived at based on the future capacity requirements of the enterprise. This is possible through various interviews, capacity planning and on factors like the number of new users that the system will have. This will help determine the additional number of instances would be required.

For example, the MAXINSTANCES parameter used during database creation defines the number of instances that the database server would ever have. This does not necessarily mean that during the initial setup there would be eight instances (in the example listed above) sharing a common shared physical database. It just means potentially many instances could simultaneously have this database mounted and open. This value takes precedence over the value of initialization parameter INSTANCES.

Setting this parameter to a higher value allows Oracle to create the control file with appropriate space allocated for these instances when they are actually added to the cluster. Another advantage of setting the MAXINSTANCES parameter to a higher value would be to help the plug-and-play capability of the instances. That is, instances could be easily added to the cluster without any significant change to the database.

The downside of not allocating a high value to the MAXINSTNACES parameter is that the control file will have to be re-created when additional instances above the MAXINSTANCES parameter are added to the cluster.

Note: The value of the MAXINSTANCES parameter should not be an arbitrary value; it should be arrived at by using capacity planning techniques and based on business requirements.

Similarly, based on the value of the MAXINSTANCES parameter, the MAXLOGFILES and MAXLOGHISTORY parameters are sized because these parameters are all related to the number of instances.

- MAXLOGFILES specifies the maximum number of redo log file groups that can ever be created for the database. During the control file creation, Oracle uses this value to allocate the names of these redo log files.

- MAXLOGHISTORY is useful only when using Oracle in ARCHIVELOG mode with RAC. It specifies the maximum number of archived redo log files for automatic media recovery of RAC. During the creation of the control file, Oracle uses this value to allocate the names of archived redo log files. The default value is a multiple of MAXINSTANCES value and depends on the O/S.

One of the main advantages of sizing these parameters appropriately is that instances could be added to the cluster dynamically, while all other basic configuration requirements have been taken care of.

10.4   Maximum availability architecture

In the previous sections we discussed the various system availability requirements and how some of these requirements are met with the standard out of the box implementation of RAC. This level of availability is normally sufficient for most organizations operating on a 24*7 schedule providing support for their day-to-day customers. However, there are organizations that have machine-critical, high-transaction processing, state-of-the-art technology databases that are required to be kept up all the time; to mention a few would be the stock exchange, the space station, etc, where every second of downtime is very expensive. These organizations require something called a maximum availability architecture (MAA).

MAA provides a redundant and robust architecture that prevents different outages or recovers from an outage within a small MTTR. The goal in this situation is to have no impact or minimal impact on availability while catastrophic outages can be repaired.

When Internet based business requirements stipulate an uptime of 99.999%, the hardware infrastructure is made redundant at all tiers, such as the network tier, application server tier, load balancing tier, etc. On the database tier, the clustered database technologies such as RAC provide continuous availability by having one instance up when one fails.

This level of redundancy is available or is concentrated at one location (primary data center) of the enterprise. What if a catastrophic outage (such as an act of god) caused the entire data center to collapse? The entire business operation is affected. The redundancy at the local data center does not provide much room for availability. From our example above, the stock exchange or the space station would be seriously affected if such a situation arose. This calls for a much higher level of redundancy.

MAA is obtained by providing redundancy to the already redundant architecture, that is the entire primary data center is made redundant by creating an identical operation infrastructure at a remote location. If the data center had two application servers, two database servers, two load balancers, two firewalls, the remote redundant site will also have the exact same set of hardware infrastructure. Fully functional and ready to be active when any catastrophic outage happens.

Changes to most of these tiers are less frequent compared to the database tier, where the data is consistently changing. In this case data needs to be moved to the remote location as close to real time as possible, that is data needs to be moved from the primary RAC database to a remote RAC database. This could be implemented using Oracle utilities such as ODG or OAR.

10.5   Conclusion

In this chapter, we discussed the various high-availability features in a clustered database solution such as RAC. Apart from the basic failover option provided by the clustered operating system, RAC provides some additional advanced features like TAF where the user sessions are migrated to another available instance and data is continuously provided. This failover without interruption to the user's original request happens behind the scene and is transparent to the user. We discussed how this feature could be implemented using the tnsnames-based configuration and how programmatically such a feature could be implemented using OCI APIs.

After the discussions on high availability we also discussed the scalability features of RAC. Multinode configuration of this clustered database provides availability because if one node fails, another node could support the user's requests. Similarly, in an active/active configuration, users could access the common shared database from any of the available nodes or instances. Another important feature provided by RAC is the plug-and-play option, where a node could be added to the cluster configuration dynamically; or when a node of the cluster is dropped, RAC continues to function by dynamically reconfiguring the resources amongst the available instances.

In this chapter we discussed the architecture, configuration, and operation of the RACG. RACG's ideal configuration is a two-node configuration, where one node is configured as the primary node and the second node is configured as the secondary node. While RACG is an enhancement to the failsafe feature available in the previous versions of Oracle, the requirement to have RAC makes this an expensive solution.

A detailed discussion regarding RACG can be found in the Oracle RAC documentation.[2]

In the next chapter, we will discuss the migration process; for example, the migration process for moving from a single instance configuration to a RAC configuration. Similarly, migrating from an OPS configuration to a RAC will also be discussed.

---

2   "Oracle Real Application Cluster Guard—Concepts and Administration."

Migrating to RAC

11.1   Introduction

In the previous chapter, we looked at the high-availability and scalability features of a clustered database solution such as RAC. RAC provides other normal features such as recoverability, manageability, and maintainability found in a stand-alone configuration of Oracle. However, availability and scalability are naturally derived from the architecture of the database configuration.

Hardware and operating system clustering provides failover opportunities when a member in the cluster fails, thus providing continuous availability of the application to the users. Apart from the clustered failover options available at the operating system level, Oracle provides additional failover options through the TAF implementation. TAF provides transparent failover of the users' sessions from the failed instance to one of the other available instances. Much of the working of TAF, its configuration, implementation, and some performance aspects, was also discussed in the previous chapter.

With the introduction of Oracle 9i and the enhancement to the clustered database solution from the earlier version of OPS, considerable improvements have been made regarding the cache fusion technology, allowing users to access data from any instance participating in the clustered configuration and Oracle to transfer the information across the cluster interconnect. This feature of cache fusion replaces the expensive pinging activity that occurred in the earlier versions of Oracle.

OPS implementations required that the applications were specifically designed to use the clustering technology. This is because when an instance requested records that were already being worked against on another specific instance, the blocks that contained these rows had to be written to disk before the requesting instance could read it. This activity of writing to disk to provide visibility to the other requesting instance is called pinging and is a very expensive operation. The tuning of these pinging activities is a highly complex process; architects had to specifically design applications or have the existing applications redesigned to reduce sharing of data across instances.

In Version 9*i*, Oracle completed its implementation of the cache fusion technology, where data is transferred via the interconnect to the requesting instance, compared to writing the data to disk to make it available to the other instance, which provided limitations to scalability. RAC makes this version of the cluster database solution usable by most applications.

In this chapter we will discuss the migration of a single instance Oracle database to Oracle 9*i* RAC. During this process we will look into details such as, if RAC is required, will migration be feasible and what kind of complexities if any could be encountered during this migration process.

We will also discuss upgrading from a previous version of the clustered database OPS to Oracle 9*i* RAC. While the migration path from OPS to RAC should be much easier compared to the migration from a single instance, there are certain areas during the migration process where precautionary measures should be taken depending on the type of environment/application that the current database has been supporting. The first step is the analysis or the requirements process.

11.2   Analysis process

During this process the organization needs to determine the business requirements, such as availability, scalability, and all other requirements defined in Chapter 1. If the organization determines that all these business requirements are critical to its everyday functioning as an enterprise for continued business and customer support, it would be ideal to investigate whether the current application could be migrated to a clustered solution.

A basic question is, has the application been designed for a clustered database solution? This was truer in the case of migrating from a single stand-alone configuration to the previous version of the clustered database platform OPS. With RAC, this requirement is of less importance. The main reason, as we have seen from the previous chapters, is because all the communications occur across the cluster interconnect.

Under OPS, all request sharing happened via processes pinging the information from disk, and in RAC this happens via the cluster interconnect. Due to the heavy disk activity, it is a requirement when implementing a clustered database solution with OPS that the application has specific design considerations that would lessen such high activity.

Scalability of the applications, as mentioned in Chapter 1 (Section 1.2.7), is an important database requirement. One of the database features that support this requirement is the data-partitioning feature. While partitioning is not a requirement for RAC, it would help in data distribution and therefore provides scalability. If the current database has already taken advantage of the data-partitioning feature or if the database implementation is changed to use the data-partitioning feature, it would be beneficial to the overall performance of the application.

Certain applications provide homegrown consistency locking mechanisms. RAC, with the clustered architecture, provides its own mechanism of lock management when users from more than one instance request the same information. It should be analyzed thoroughly to ensure that these home-grown locking solutions would function in a clustered database environment.

During this analysis process, one of the questions that should get answered is, why should you migrate to a clustered solution? If all the business requirements stipulated can be met by the existing configuration, or if a small change to the current configuration can help meet the requirement, would that be sufficient? This is a very important question, because when the cost-benefit analysis is determined before implementation, this will provide a most convincing answer. On the other hand, if this is not answered when the system is implemented and alive, when the real benefits expected are not released, it could be too late and a huge investment could be wasted.

Note: Most organizations do not pay much attention to this fact. They are carried away by the bells and whistles of the latest and greatest technology without taking a close look at the cost-benefit analysis or looking into the details of whether the technology is what is really needed, if it will provide the benefits they are looking for, etc.

There are several organizations today that have implemented the technology and have after a few years of struggle realized that it was not what they were looking for.

The next major step before the actual migration to this new platform is to determine the actual cost-benefit analysis.

11.3   Cost-benefit analysis

During this process the organization has to make a list of benefits that this technology will provide. This should be obtained not by mere theoretical means, but using prototyping and simulating methods. These prototypes and simulations should validate from all venues including:

- Current application architecture

- Current database structure

- Future database structure

- Future application architecture

- Expanded business

- Increased users

- Failover

- Scalability

- Manageability

- Recoverability

- Maintainability

All the possible reasons as to why this specific technology was selected should be examined to collect statistics that could be used in the costing model.

Before determining the benefits and the cost to obtain these benefits, it is important that a determination be made as to the time frame over which these are to be realized. Once these benefits, which are also called intangible benefits, have been validated and all the business requirements have been satisfied from the simulation or prototyping model, the next step is to arrive at the cost of implementing such a solution.

A costing model that determines the cost benefits over a certain number of years should be prepared, as shown in Table 11.1.

It should be noted that all the benefits that have been validated via prototyping and simulation should be spread over a span of five years. This cost is compared against the cost of the product and its implementation, basically the amount of money spent during year 0.

Once the cost-benefit analysis is completed and the results of analysis provide an indication that the entire migration process would be favorable

Table 11.1   *Costing Model*

Costs and Benefits	Year 0	Year 1	Year 2	Year 3	Year 4
Software cost					
Implementation cost					
Training cost					
Recurring maintenance cost					
Increased speed of activity					
Improved management					
Saved time in updating data					
Error reduction					
Increased flexibility					
Increased availability					
Increased scalability					
Increased manageability					
Hardware cost					
O/S training cost					
Recurring maintenance cost					
Improved management					
Increased flexibility					
Increased availability					
Increased scalability					
Increased manageability					

to the enterprise, the next step is to start preparing and planning on the actual migration itself.

11.4   Preparation phase

The first step during the preparation phase is to decide on the hardware and software requirements and the administrative issues related to each of these environments. Most of the discussions on the various hardware technologies, including storage and disk configuration, have been covered in detail in Chapter 2 (Hardware Concepts). From these discussions, an appropriate environment should be prepared, based on the requirements of the business and the cost-benefit analysis determined in the previous section. An appropriate clustered hardware solution and license for implementing RAC in a production environment should be purchased.

While deciding on the hardware, a fair question to ask is, what should the actual configuration be? While such a question does arise several times throughout the process, the actual configuration is determined and obtained through the capacity planning process.

11.5   Capacity planning

In this process, based on the planned growth rate of the enterprise, the growth rate in the number of users as a result of increased business is determined. Based on these growth rates, the appropriate hardware configurations are selected.

After analyzing the business requirements and their current application, database configuration, and the growth requirements, careful analysis should be performed to quantify the benefits of switching to a RAC environment. In the case of a new application and database configuration, a similar analysis should also be performed to quantify if RAC would be necessary to meet the requirements of the current and future business needs.

The first step in the quantification process is to analyze the current business requirements such as:

■   Are there requirements that justify or require the systems to be up and running 24 hours a day, every day of the year?

■   Are there sufficient business projections on the number of users that would be accessing the system, and what will the user growth rate be?

■   Will there be a steady growth rate that would indicate that the current system configurations might not be sufficient?

Once answers to these questions have been determined, a simulation model should be constructed to establish the scalability requirements for the planning or requirements team, and the architecture should be considered. These issues need to be resolved before moving to the next step.

Chapter 2 (Hardware Concepts) discusses in detail various technology options, like SMP, MPP, NUMA, and clustered SMP. The simulation should determine if any of these hardware architectures would be required or would be ideal for the implementation of the system. During this initial hardware architecture evaluation, the question should arise as to whether a single instance configuration would be sufficient or a clustered solution would be required. If a single instance configuration is deemed sufficient, then whether the system would need to be protected from disasters would need to be determined. If disaster protection is a requirement, then, protection could be provided by using the Oracle Data Guard feature (called Oracle Standby prior to Version 9.0).

Other considerations are:

■ Are there any reporting requirements? If so, what is the plan to accomplish them?

■ If the data guard solution is not sufficient, a more reliable, high-availability solution may be required.

■ Is clustered configuration a requirement? If so, what conditions necessitate this?

The application could be either the user-defined application used to perform a basic business function, such as a customer management system, or it could be a third-party product like the RDBMS. In both cases, consideration should be given to validating that "clusterizing" is the only option.

Applications to run in a clustered configuration (e.g., clustered SMP, NUMA clusters) should be clusterizable such that the benefits could be measured in terms of global performance or availability. (Availability basically refers to availability to service clients.) From the performance aspect, the initial measurements would be to determine the required throughput of the application. Under normal scenarios, performance is measured by the number of transactions that the system could process per second or the number of records that could be inserted into the system per hour. Performance can also be measured by the throughput of the system, utilizing a simple formula like the following:

$$\text{THROUGHPUT} = \frac{\text{No. of Operations Performed by the Application}}{\text{Unit of Time Used for Measurement}}$$

There are two levels of throughput measurement: the minimum throughput expectation and the maximum throughput required.

To complicate things a bit further, there could also be the ideal throughput required from the application, which is normally the average throughput. Lastly, the requirement could be twisted further by stating the percentage increase in throughput required to meet the expectations.

Another measurement of throughput can be determined by establishing the number of concurrent users or the maximum number of jobs that the application can handle. This measurement could be based on the following:

- The typical interaction between the user and the application, or job, that has been mentioned in the business requirements.

- Length of this typical interaction to complete the request or job by the user measured as the acceptable response time, which is measured in units of time.

So the throughput measurement based on the number of users could be:

$$\text{THROUGHPUT} = \frac{\text{No. of Concurrent Users (per Requirements)}}{\text{User Acceptable Response Time (UART)}}$$

If this formula is applied to the current application or to the simulation model, then throughput of the system could be measured for the application (which is the inverse of the above formula):

$$\text{UART} = \text{Throughput} \times \text{No. of Concurrent Users Supported}$$

The throughput derived above could be increased on the system in many different ways, such as:

1. Through changes made to the application; normally an expensive process because it may result in a rewriting of the entire application.

2. Increase of power of the hardware running the application; a situation of vertical scalability, and could also be an expensive process because hardware limitations could repeat after the current estimated users have been reached.

3. Clusterizing the application; probably the best opportunity in this situation due to the provision of horizontal scalability. Clusterizing enables the administrator to meet the increased demand of users as the business grows and requirements change (with higher numbers of concurrent users) by adding additional nodes to the cluster to help scale the application. This is done while providing the same amount of throughput and UART.

Once the clustering options have been decided upon, the next step will be to determine how this will be done. It is imperative to consider or create a goal that this activity will accomplish before establishing the best method to incorporate. It is often argued that maintenance should be simple; however, from the overall management perspective, the ultimate focus of the operation should be performance.

While maintenance is an important feature, performance plays a more important role in this process. Some options to consider during the clustering process are as follows. Is the application designed to be:

1. *Multiplexed:* Do multiple copies of the application run on each of the nodes in the cluster?

2. *Partitioned:* Is the application designed in such a manner that it could be broken up into several pieces based on functionality and mode of operation? For example, partitioning could be based on functionality like accounts payable, accounts receivable, and payroll, all based on the departments that will be accessing these functionalities. The other alternative is to partition the application by the mode of operation like OLTP and batch or application behavior.

3. *Hybrid scenario:* Is a combination of the above two options a way to get the best results of both worlds? A possible combination would be to partition the application based on one of the criteria best suited for the application and business, then to multiplex the partitioned pieces.

Items 1 and 2 above are true and feasible most of the time in the case of a business application or the client/server application. Because there are no specific protocols between clients, there is reliance on a central database server to serialize the transactions when maximizing the overall throughput and offering a consistent view of the database to all clients. This means that after the initial configuration, additional clients could be added without much difficulty; therefore, increasing linearly the client-side/application-side throughput.

The application server, the business application, or the client/server application is just one piece to the puzzle. The other main piece to the puzzle is the application or product that stores all the information and which contains the business rules: the database server. Very commonly, database, or RDBMS servers, are run on a single node and execute the application queries, packages, etc., and are not easily clusterizable. This is because the RDBMS constitutes instance structures (memory, processes) when accessing the database and has to guarantee the synchronization, serialization, consistency, and data reliability. Analyzing the implementation of Oracle in one of the three options above, multiplexing would require having multiple copies of the database on different storage systems so that the application would access one of the copies of the database. Normally, when such a configuration is implemented, the transferring of data between the many copies of the database is required to keep the database in sync. For such situations a replication tool comes as a choice. However, the synchronization overhead introduced to data contention and resolution can be so relevant that the application may scale down instead of scaling up.

Applying the second option listed above, partitioning of the database server would mean to physically find a common ground and make the databases into two separate databases. Each database would have a different data set or would support a specific business function. Implementation of such a configuration would entail that the clients are also partitioned, forcing certain clients to specific Oracle server nodes. This is feasible to a certain degree if there is a clear line between the various departments or organizations accessing these partitions. For example, accounts receivable, accounts payable, payroll, human resources, etc., could be partitioned to some extent. However, when consolidating these functions to provide a cohesive window of information to the management, there could be difficulty because of cross-functional data requirements (e.g., accounts payable needs to look at the data of accounts receivable, etc.).

The third option listed above would be to enlist a combination of the first two options. Unfortunately, because both options have their own limitations, a combined scenario would not be feasible either.

Implementing a database application on a clustered environment would completely depend on the clustered RDBMS technology that is used. The database is the backbone of every enterprise system and to get the best performance from the application, the database should be compatible or designed to run on a clustered hardware configuration (e.g., clustered SMP or NUMA servers). OPS and now the RAC version of Oracle RDBMS allow Oracle-based applications to scale up in a clustered configuration smoothly. This allows multiple Oracle instances to share one common database, which provides the option for the application to run on multiple nodes accessing any of the Oracle instances that communicate with one common physical database.

11.5.1 How to measure scaling

When the application is configured to run on a clustered system, the throughput, or global throughput, of an N-node clustered configuration could be measured. This would basically be:

$$T(n) = \text{SUM}t(i)$$

where $i = 1, \ldots, n$ and $t(i)$ is the throughput measured on one node in the clustered configuration.

Following the above, with different values of n, the value of T will change. This will aid in defining the throughput curve of the application, which basically indicates the scalability factor in a clustered configuration.

Other factors that could hinder, improve, or contribute to the performance of the system must be considered. This includes the various resources and the power of the computational hardware. Resources and computational power apply to each node in the cluster. Each node could be of a different configuration (though not done this way for many reasons); hence, the values could be different and may affect the overall scalability matrix. Adding these factors to the formula above would result in the following:

$$T(n) \approx nts(n)$$

where $T(n)$ is the global throughput of the application running on all N nodes and is measured by unit of time; t, as we indicated above, is the throughput for one node in the cluster; n is the number of nodes participating in the clustered configuration; and $s(n)$ is a coefficient that determines our overall cluster throughput.

This could be even further complicated, or more variables could be added to the puzzle, by studying factors such as the type of clustered hardware, the topology of the cluster, the type of application running on the clustered configuration, etc. Because certain hardware platforms perform better than others, these factors will also affect the scalability. For example, MPP architecture works well for a data warehouse implementation; however, for an OLTP implementation, a clustered SMP architecture would be better suited. With these factors added, the new formula would be:

$$T(n) \approx nts(c, n, a, k)$$

Figure 11.1
*Capacity
planning.*

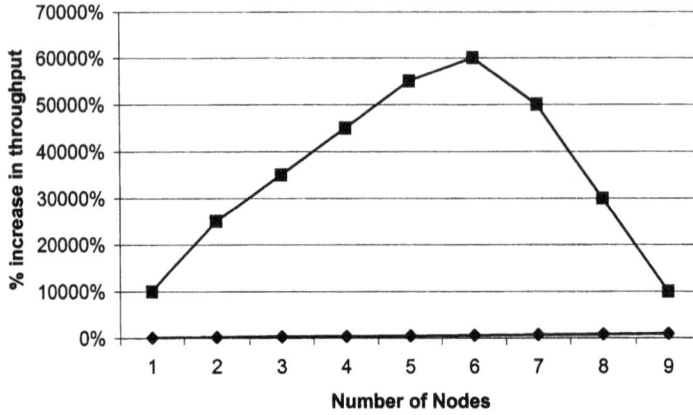

where c is the type of clustered hardware, n is the node number, a is the type of application running on the clustered configuration, and k is the topology of the cluster.

Because all of these additional factors cannot be measured, only the previous formulas are used.

The best-case scenario of scalability of an application would be when the application scales up with a constant factor of one, providing a consistent linear growth. However, this kind of scalability is not realistic. Rather, it is typical for applications to have sublinear growth with the increase in nodes. The growth continues until a certain limit has been reached, after which adding additional nodes to the clustered configuration would not show any further advantage. This is demonstrated by the graph in Figure 11.1, which indicates that there is a linear scale-up with the addition of new nodes; however, after a certain percentage of scalability has been reached, a point of no return is reached on investment, and the scalability reduces with the addition of more nodes.

Capacity planning for an enterprise system takes many iterative steps. Every time there is a change in usage pattern, capacity planning has to be visited in some form or the other.

11.6 Oracle single instance vs. clustered configuration

Every Oracle configuration starts with a single instance, in the sense that even in the clustered Oracle configuration like RAC, it starts with a single instance. From the basic level of database creation, database management, database performance tuning, etc., all operations start with a basic single instance configuration and move to a clustered configuration. It is very important in every aspect of database administration and maintenance that each instance is considered as an individual unit before considering it as a combined cluster.

Stand-alone, or single instance, configuration in an enterprise system does not provide all the functionalities discussed in Chapter 2, such as availability and scalability. One way of providing for availability is by using some of the high-availability options accessible from Oracle, for example, the ODG (previously called Hot Standby) where the data from the primary database is copied to the remote database. This is done by copying the redo logs when the redo log switch occurs. The difficulty with such a configuration is that there could be loss of data when the node that contains the primary database fails and the last set of redo logs are not copied over to the destination database. This creates an inconsistent environment.

Another high-availability option would be to use the OAR feature. This option is very similar to the ODG option; however, instead of copying the redo logs from the primary instance to the secondary, or target replicated environment, data could be transferred more frequently like a record, or a group of records. This feature, when compared to the ODG option, provides a much closer level of data consistency. This is due to the fact that in the case of failure of the node that contains the primary database, only the last few rows, or sets, of data are not transferred.

From a disaster recovery or reporting solution, the ODG and OAR feature are high-availability options. Where data consistency is not an immediate concern, such as in the case of disasters due to an "act of God," where the primary database is not available, a remote database created by either of these options could help provide a backup opportunity to the enterprise system.

Oracle's clustered, or multi-instance configurations comprise multiple nodes working as a cohesive unit with each node in the cluster consisting of two or more instances talking to a common shared database. As has been discussed, this feature is the RAC configuration.

11.7   Migrating from a single instance to RAC

Beginning with Oracle Version 9*i* Release 2, most of the hardware platforms, except a few, support the clustered file system for a RAC implementation. Others such as Sun Solaris and HP-UX do not support a clustered file system solution for RAC. If the hardware platform of choice is one of these platforms, it is required that RAC is implemented on raw devices (unless third party solutions, such as VERITAS CFS is used).

To migrate a single instance database to RAC, the following procedures are to be completed:

1. *Configuration of the hardware platform:* Based on the hardware platform selected, the appropriate cluster configuration directions should be followed from the vendor-specific documentation. Validate all tests to ensure that the hardware installed and configured is performing as per the specifications defined by the appropriate vendors.

2. *Creation of raw devices or configuration of the clustered file systems:* This depends on the clustered hardware platform selected and is based on Oracle's support for a clustered file system or a raw device. More details of raw device or clustered file system configuration are provided in Chapter 8 (Installation and Configuration). As discussed in Chapter 8, it is important that sufficient planning of the sizes of the various partitions be done prior to raw partitioning of these devices.

3. *Evaluation of partitioning strategy if not already present:* If the current database system does not have a data-partitioning strategy, consider the possibilities of partitioning the data based on a certain business attribute or function. For example, in a cable or satellite broadcasting system it could be the smart card or the set-top box number; in a customer management system it could be customer ID; in a logistics system, it could be the paying company ID. All these attributes could help group transactions records together, forming data partitions. If the current database has a partitioned schema, this schema could be implemented in a RAC environment.

4. *Evaluation of the optimizer mode in the current application:* If the current (legacy) application is configured to work with the rule-based optimizer, while migrating to Oracle 9i, it would be advantageous to move towards the cost-based optimizer. However, this migration is a crucial step, as all queries will have to be individually validated on a system with a cost-based optimizer and tuned for performance.

5. *Evaluation of tablespaces and log files of single instance:* Based on the raw device partition size analysis performed in step 1, determine

the appropriate tablespaces that could be mapped to these partitions.

6.   *Export of data from old database:* Export the current production data. The method of exporting data could depend on the platform, including the operating system and architecture on which the new database will be implemented. For example, if the new hardware platform is on a similar operating system, then a dd command on Unix or an ocopy command on Windows would help perform the trick, as raw devices are used.

However, if during this migration process, the database configuration is changed from a 32-bit version to a 64-bit version, it would be more appropriate to export the data from the 32-bit database and import it into the new database.

Similarly, if there were a character set conversion, for example from ASCII to UTF-8, in this case also the export method would be preferable over the dd or ocopy commands.

7.   *Install operating-system-dependent cluster software:* Somewhere along these steps it is important to install and configure the clustered software. The Unix technical operations group based on the hardware vendor configuration manuals performs this step. For the RAC implementation this is a very important step. Normally, for a stand-alone implementation of Oracle, this step is not performed and hence special system administrator skills is required when installing and configuring the cluster software. After successful installation of this software the following checks should be performed to ensure that the clusterware is properly functioning:

   a.   Throughput testing of the cluster interconnect.

   b.   Throughput testing between the database cluster and the application servers.

   c.   Heartbeat configuration testing including tracing of heartbeat activities.

   d.   Heartbeat timeout configuration testing, including tracing and validating occurrence of timeout at the specified intervals.

   f.   Crash recovery testing to ensure that the recovery of one node does not affect the other nodes in the cluster.

   g.   Crash recovery performance testing to ensure that the timings are as specified by the manufacturer.

All the above and other basic tests as stipulated by the manufacturer would ensure that all hardware validations have been completed as per vendor specifications. It is important to perform these steps at this stage to avoid any unknowns that may occur when additional hardware or software is added.

> **Note:** For Unix, the information for the installation and configuration of the cluster software should be found in the vendor-provided documentation. For installation and configuration of the cluster software for the Windows or Linux operating systems, Oracle provides all the required preinstall tools.

8. *Install Oracle 9i Enterprise Edition with the RAC and partitioning (optional) option:* Installation of the Oracle Enterprise Edition is dependent on the clustered operating system being installed. The complete steps for installation and configuration of the Oracle RDBMS software have been detailed in Chapter 8 (Installation and Configuration).

> **Note:** Certain features like the RAC option will not be visible from the Oracle installer unless the clustered operating system has been installed and configured correctly. The clustered operating system and its components should be visible to the OUI to provide visibility to the RAC option.

9. *Create a new database:* The next step after installation and configuration of the Oracle software is to install the database. For creation of the database, there are two options, either use the Oracle-provided DBCA utility or use the manual option for creating and configuring the Oracle database. Both these options have also been documented in Chapter 8 (Installation and Configuration).

10. *Import data from old database to the new database:* If the database structure including the physical layout, physical configuration, or the operating system has changed, it would be ideal to export the data from the current environment and import the data into this new environment.

11. *Adjust the parameter values:* When the database is initially created, the parameters all have default values, especially if the DBCA utility was used. Once the database has been created and all the required steps to bring the system online have been completed, then the next

step is to configure all the parameters to match the parameter values in the current active instance.

12. *Start the database:* The next step after the initial configuration of the parameters is to start the instances on their respective nodes. The following commands could be used to start the database instance. Since this is a clustered database, there are multiple instances accessing the common physical database and each instance is required to mount and open the database for shared access.

13. *Tune the instances:* Tuning the instances starts very similarly to tuning a single instance configuration. Tune one instance first and apply the same changes to the other instances. When an instance has been tuned, the next step is to tune both instances in a clustered environment.

> **Note:** There are no straightforward rules for tuning the instances or the clustered database. Tuning Oracle instances has come a long way from when it was considered to be an art and most of the tuning was achieved through trial and error. Today, Oracle provides a considerable amount of statistics that has changed the methodology to a scientific approach.

Tuning is also an iterative process, which means identifying problems, fixing them, then identifying new problems; once these are fixed, another set of problems are identified, and so forth.

A detailed analysis of the tuning of the instances, of the various areas of the clustered database, and of the clustered operating system will be discussed in Chapters 13, 14, and 15 on performance tuning.

11.8 Conclusion

In this chapter, we looked at the analysis, planning, and the actual migration from a stand-alone configuration to a clustered database solution. In these sections, we discussed how and why the upgrade should be done. The reasons should be supported by a cost-benefit analysis where the actual benefits of the migration should be thoroughly analyzed through prototyping and simulation models. After the basic analysis, the actual capacity of the hardware and software model should be determined through capacity modeling, where the configuration of the hardware is determined.

After the capacity planning, we discussed the steps involved in migrating a stand-alone configuration to RAC; most of the details in this discussion can be found in Chapter 8 where the installation and configuration details of RAC have been extensively covered; in this chapter we also discussed other aspects of the migration process such as partitioning, selection of the optimizer, etc.

The next chapter contains discussions on a very important area that is critical to any business organization, namely backup and recovery. In this chapter we will look into the details of installation and configuration using the various backup and recovery utilities like cold backups, hot backups, and RMAN.

Backup and Recovery

12.1   Introduction

In the previous chapter we discussed the various aspects considered during the migration process. There are three possible migration scenarios:

1.   Migrating from single instance to RAC.

2.   Migrating from OPS to RAC.

3.   Migrating from single instance to OPS.

Migrating a database from a single instance configuration to a RAC configuration is more complex compared to the migration from an OPS environment to RAC. However, the earlier migration (scenario 3 above, which was not discussed in the previous chapter) of a system from a stand-alone configuration to OPS was comparatively much more complex and involved a great amount of planning and architectural reconfiguration. This is primarily because of the complexity that was present with users sharing information from multiple instances, and the high pinging activity that is not present under Oracle 9*i*.

In this chapter we will discuss backup and recovery in a RAC environment. Backups are taken to protect against the future, that is, to protect against failure situations that could potentially happen. One may argue that the chances of these failures happening are 50–50; however, when it happens without these backups it would be impossible to get back the lost data. Once it is certain that backup is required, the next question is, how often are they to be backed up? This depends on the backup strategy defined for the organization.

When we mention recovery, it also covers failures of an instance or system, because Oracle has to recover from these failures. Availability of an Oracle database when an instance or node fails, has been discussed in detail in Chapter 10 (Availability and Scalability). This chapter, apart from the backup functionality, will discuss in detail the various failure scenarios and the recovery process during those failures.

12.2   Backup

Every single system is prone to failures: natural, mechanical, or electronic. This could be the human system, automobiles, computer hardware, elevators, application servers, applications, database servers, databases, networks, or network connectivity. Based on the critical nature of the item and its everyday use, these types of failures need an alternative way to provide the required service and/or a method to keep the systems up and functioning. For example, the human system can fail due to sickness; to avoid falling sick the human body needs exercise, good food, and general care, so the body's metabolism works efficiently and keeps the body healthy. An automobile can fail due to a simple problem like a flat tire. A backup option in this case would be a spare tire and some essential tools to replace the tire. In some unavoidable conditions an alternative to the automobile has to be used (bus or taxi). Electronic devices such as computer hardware are prone to failures; hardware comes in many forms throughout the entire enterprise configuration. Normally protection against hardware failures is obtained by providing redundancy at all tiers of the configuration. This helps because, when one component fails, the others will help continue operation.

On the database side, the storage system that physically stores the data needs to be protected. Mirroring the disk, where the data is copied to another disk to provide safety, and failover when a disk in the array fails, will provide the required redundancy against disk failures. The disk redundant configuration is achieved by following an appropriate RAID configuration, as discussed in Chapter 2 (Hardware Concepts).

What happens when a privileged user deletes rows from a table in a production database? What happens when this damage is only noticed after a few days? What happens when lightning hits the production center and the electric grid, causing a short circuit that damages the entire storage subsystem? In all these situations an alternative method over and beyond the redundant hardware architecture is required to get to the bottom of the problem for its resolution, namely, a process to retrieve and recover the lost data.

The answer to this is that a copy of the data needs to be saved regularly to another medium and stored in a remote location. Such a method of data storage will protect the enterprise from losing its valuable data. The method of copying data from a live system for storage in a remote location is called a *backup process*.

Backup and recovery methods for a database under RAC are similar to the procedures used in a single stand-alone configuration. RAC supports all the backup features of an Oracle database running in single-instance mode.

While defining database configuration specifications (RAC or non-RAC) the following should be considered:

- If loss of data is unacceptable, the ARCHIVELOG mode should be enabled.

- All instances in a RAC configuration should be set to automatic archiving.

- The archive destination for each instance needs to be available to each specific instance only during normal operation, but they have to be made available to the other instances performing recovery following a media failure.

- Multiple archive logs are written to the same destination. Hence, partitions should not be used for archive log files because in a raw device configuration, each archive will overwrite the previous one.

12.2.1 Backup strategies

If a backup and recovery strategy is not available, it is important that a good backup and recovery strategy is designed and tested. Various options available under Oracle are:

- Full offline backup.

- Hot backup.

- Backup using Recovery Manager (RMAN).

Full offline backup

A full offline backup procedure for a RAC environment is almost identical to a single-instance configuration. The major difference in a RAC environment is that all instances that are part of the clustered configuration should be shut down before the actual backup operation.

The procedure to perform a full offline backup is:

1. Query the V$DATAFILE view to obtain the names and locations
    of the data files. Spool the output to a file that could be read to
    perform the backup operation:

```
COL NAME FORMAT A50
SELECT FILE#,
  NAME,
  STATUS
FROM V$DATAFILE
/
```

2. Query the V$LOGFILE view to obtain the names and locations of
    the online redo log files. Spool the output to a file that can be read
    to perform the backup operation:

```
COL MEMBER FORMAT A50
SELECT * FROM V$LOGFILE
/
```

3. Query the V$CONTROLFILE view to obtain the names and locations
    of the control files. Spool the output to a file that can be read to
    perform the backup operation:

```
COL NAME FORMAT A50
SELECT * FROM V$CONTROLFILE
/
```

4. Shut down all instances (including the one used to query the data
    dictionary) that are currently accessing the database:

```
oracle$sqlplus /nolog
SQL>connect as sys@RAC1 /as sysdba
SQL>shutdown immediate
```

5. Save copies of the data files to an alternate location. This is done by
    using an operating system utility like ocopy when using raw devices
    or the standard copy utility available on most operating systems,
    when using clustered file systems to save all the data files, online
    redo log files and at least one copy of the control file to a backup
    location on disk.

6. Move the saved copies of the various files to backup media
    such as a tape. Depending on the backup and recovery strategy
    and the SLA requirements, retaining a copy of the latest backup
    set on disk would enable an easy restoration, if such a need
    arises.

        7.   Restart the instances:

```
oracle$sqlplus /nolog
SQL> startup
ORACLE instance started.
Total System Global Area   450937896 bytes
Fixed Size                    730152 bytes
Variable Size              285212672 bytes
Database Buffers           163840000 bytes
Redo Buffers                 1155072 bytes
Database mounted.
Database opened.
SQL>
```

For repeated use of this strategy the entire process is implemented using a script, provided such a script could shut down all instances before starting the backup operation.

Using the SRVCTL utility, startup and shutdown of remote instances could be controlled from a single instance, making this process easier.

Hot backup

Hot or online backup allows backup of all or part of the database while it is in operation. The procedure for a hot backup in a RAC configuration is similar to that followed in a single instance configuration. Unlike the full offline backups, hot backups can be performed only when the database has been configured to run in ARCHIVELOG mode.

The procedure to perform a hot backup is:

1.   Query the V$DATAFILES and the V$TABLESPACE view to obtain the names and locations of the data files. These views could be joined using the TS# column.

```
SELECT TS.NAME,
       DF.NAME
FROM V$DATAFILE DF,
     V$TABLESPACE TS
WHERE DF.TS# = TS.TS#
/
```

2.   Query the V$LOGFILE view to obtain the names and locations of the online redo log files.

```
COL MEMBER FORMAT A50
SELECT * FROM V$LOGFILE
/
```

3. Query the `V$CONTROLFILE` view to obtain the names and locations of the control files:

```
COL NAME FORMAT A50
SELECT * FROM V$CONTROLFILE
/
```

4. As a privileged user like `system`, issue the `ALTER TABLESPACE <tablespace_name> BEGIN BACKUP` command. This command prevents the file header from being updated when a log switch or checkpoint occurs.

5. Issue the appropriate operating system command for backing up the data files for this tablespace. Use the `ocopy` in backing up from a raw device partition or a regular operating system copy like `cp`[1] when backing up from a clustered file system.

6. Issue the `ALTER TABLESPACE <tablespace_name> END BACKUP` command.

7. Repeat steps 4 through 6 for all tablespaces to be backed up.

8. Back up the control files with the `ALTER DATABASE BACKUP CONTROLFILE TO...` command. For an added measure of safety, back up the control file to trace:

```
ALTER DATABASE BACKUP CONTROLFILE TO TRACE.
/
```

9. After all the tablespaces have been backed up, issue another `ALTER SYSTEM ARCHIVE LOG CURRENT` command to generate archive log files for all redo threads, including any unarchived logs from closed threads. Include the archived files generated by this step in your backup along with any other archived log files that were generated since the start of the backup.

> **Note:** OCOPY is an Oracle-provided copy utility that allows writing to continue while the backup is running. Please note that (when using raw devices) on a Windows operating system also, Windows-based copy commands such as `copy`, `xcopy` *cannot* be used for backup, as this does not allow files in use to be copied.

Usage of `ocopy`:

```
ocopy from_file [to_file [a | size_1 [size_n]]]
ocopy -b from_file to_drive
ocopy -r from_drive to_dir
```

---

1.   `cp` is a copy command used on Unix operating systems.

b: Splits the input file into multiple output files. This option is useful for backing up to devices that are smaller than the input file.

r: Combines multiple input files and writes to a single output file. This option is useful for restoring backups created with the -b option.

Backup verification

It is a good practice to verify the files backed up using user-managed backups, such as cold and hot backups discussed above. This verification process should be added to the backup and recovery strategy and should be periodically verified.

■ The best method to verify the usability of backups is to restore them to a separate host and attempt to open the database.

■ Another method is to check the physical data structure integrity of the offline data file. This could be done using Oracle-provided utilities such as DBVERIFY.

Recovery Manager

Recovery Manager (RMAN) is a component of the Oracle database that provides a tightly integrated method for creating, managing, restoring, and recovering Oracle database backups. This utility supports hot, cold, and incremental backups. RMAN provides an option to maintain a repository called the recovery catalog that contains information about backup files and archived log files. RMAN uses the recovery catalog to automate restore operation and media recovery.

RMAN determines the most efficient method of executing the requested backup, restore, or recovery operation and then executes these operations in conjunction with the Oracle database server. The RMAN process and the server automatically identify modifications to the structure of the database and dynamically adjust the required operation to adapt to the changes.

RMAN offers a wide variety of advantages over the traditional full and hot backup options that have been available in Oracle for a very long time. Some of the key features are:

■ Recovery at the block level.

■ Backup retention policy.

■ Persistent configuration.

■ Automatic channel allocation.

■ Resumable backup and restore.

- Multiplex archived log backups.

- Managing space when restoring archive logs.

- Archive log failover.

- Backup of server parameter file.

- Control file auto backup.

- Enterprise manager support.

RMAN components

Figure 12.1 illustrates the various components that constitute the RMAN process. The figure also illustrates how the various components interact with each other, with the RMAN process, and finally with a certain certified external media process (MML) that is used to back up the data to external media such as a tape device. Let us briefly look at some of RMAN components and how they interact with each other.

RMAN process   In order to use RMAN, the RMAN executable has to be invoked. It is through this executable that all functions of the backup and recovery process are handled. This implies that the RMAN process is the central component of the entire backup and recovery operation.

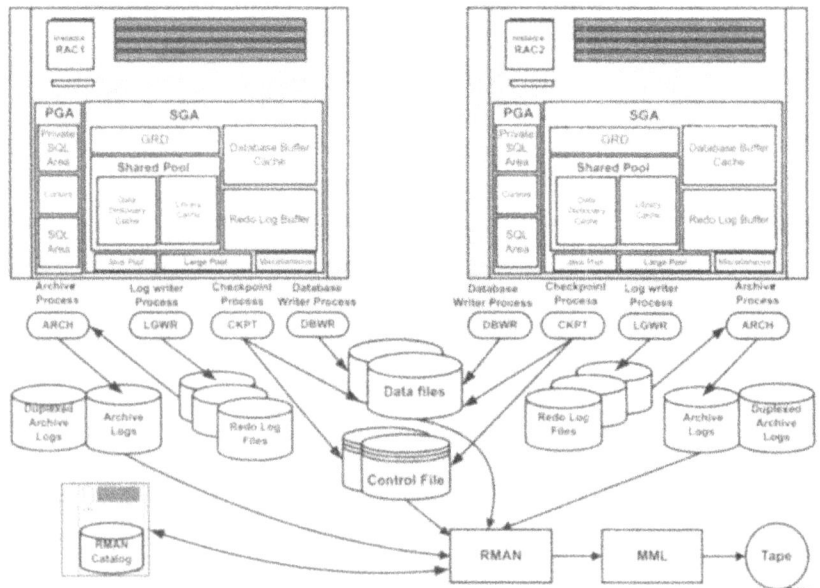

Figure 12.1
RMAN
components.

Channels In order to communicate with the I/O device such as a tape or a disk system, RMAN processes need to open a communication link between these devices, called channels. Based on the number of I/O devices that would be involved in the backup operation, several channels could be opened at the same time. These channels could be invoked for parallel or asynchronous access to these devices or could be configured to backup in a sequential order.

Target database The database that is being backed up by the RMAN process is called the target database. In Figure 12.1, RMAN interacts with one target database called PRODDB. Since this is a RAC implementation, this database could have two or more instances, for example RAC1 and RAC2. The main difference in the implementation of RMAN in a RAC environment compared to a stand-alone environment, is that each instance has a copy of redo log files and these redo log files are archived to an instance-specific archive log destination. These archive log destination disks should be visible from all instances in the clustered configuration. This has two purposes:

1. To provide visibility to RMAN to back up these archive log files.

2. To provide visibility for recovery purposes during media recovery when the instance that the archive log files belong to has crashed.

Recovery catalog database The recovery catalog, as illustrated in Figure 12.1, is optional and is a repository used by RMAN to store backup and recovery activities performed on the target database. The catalog database does not contain the actual physical backup files from the target database. Normally, to provide visibility of the information contained in the catalog databases when the target database is not available, the catalog is created as a separate database that is external to the target database.

Media management layer The media management layer (MML) is a third-party piece of software that manages the reading and writing of files to and from tape. For example, the VERITAS NetBackup and the Legato backup utilities are MML products. Due to the variety of tape media devices available in the market, RMAN depends on the various certified MML products to backup the files to tape.

Configuring RMAN

Oracle provides options for configuring RMAN, similar to those for installing and configuring a database. RMAN can be configured using the

command line or using the GUI-based interface that comes bundled with
the Oracle Enterprise Manager (OEM).

1.   Create a tablespace in the catalog database to hold the catalog data:

```
SQL> CREATE TABLESPACE rcvcat_data_p001
 2* DATA FILE '/u02/oradata/PRODDB/rcvcat_ts.dbf' SIZE 200m
SQL> /

Tablespace created.
```

2.   Create an RMAN user in the catalog database:

```
SQL> CREATE USER rmanadmin IDENTIFIED BY rmanadmin
2 TEMPORARY TABLESPACE temp
3 DEFAULT TABLESPACE rcvcat_data_p001 QUOTA UNLIMITED ON
  rcvcat_data_p001
SQL>/

User created.
```

3.   Grant the RMAN user a special role in the catalog database:

```
SQL> GRANT RECOVERY_CATALOG_OWNER TO rmanadmin;
SQL> GRANT CONNECT, RESOURCE TO rmanadmin;
Grant succeeded.
```

4.   Create user for RMAN in the target database:

```
SQL> CREATE USER rmantarget IDENTIFIED BY rmantarget TEMPORARY
  TABLESPACE temp DEFAULT TABLESPACE users;
```

5.   Grant the user the following privileges:

```
SQL>GRANT CONNECT, RESOURCE, UNLIMITED TABLESPACE TO rmantarget;
```

6.   Shut down the instance and subsequently start it in mount mode:

```
SQL>SHUTDOWN IMMEDIATE
SQL>STARTUP MOUNT
```

7.   Verify if the instance is in archive log mode – if not, set the database
     to archive log mode:

```
SELECT NAME,
   LOG_MODE
FROM V$DATABASE
/

NAME       LOG_MODE
---------  ------------
PRODDB     NOARCHIVELOG

SQL>ALTER  DATABASE ARCHIVELOG;
```

8. Verify if the log mode has changed by querying V$DATABASE:

```
SELECT NAME,
   LOG_MODE
FROM V$DATABASE
/

NAME       LOG_MODE
---------- ------------
PRODDB     ARCHIVELOG
```

9. Shut down instance:

```
SQL>SHUTDOWN IMMEDIATE
```

10. Assign the following parameters in the initPRODDB.ora file:

```
RAC1.log_archive_dest      = /archivelogs/arch/
RAC2.log_archive_dest      = /archivelogs/arch/

RAC1.log_archive_format    = 'RAC1_%T_%S.arc'
RAC2.log_archive_format    = 'RAC2_%T_%S.arc'
*.log_archive_start        = true
```

10g **New Feature:** The archive log-naming format specified by the ARCHIVE_LOG_FORMAT parameter can include the resetlogs ID as part of the format string. The resetlogs ID represents the current incarnation of the database. This allows RMAN for easier recovery of a database from a previous backup. The resetlogs ID is represented by the format string %r in the archive log name. For example LOG_ARCHIVE_FORMAT= RAC1_%T_%S_%r.arc' where %r represents the resetlogs ID. This is new with Oracle 10*g*.

11. Start the instance:

```
SQL>STARTUP
```

12. Test archive operation by performing a log switch on the target database:

```
SQL>ARCHIVE LOG LIST
Database log mode              Archive Mode
Automatic archival             Enabled
Archive destination            /archivelogs/arch/
Oldest online log sequence     31
Next log sequence to archive   33
Current log sequence           33
SQL>ALTER SYSTEM SWITCH LOGFILE
```

This should create log files in $ORACLE_BASE/admin/PRODDB/RAC1/ arch directory.

13.   Connect to the catalog database using RMAN and issue the create catalog command:

```
oracle$rman catalog rmanadmin/rmanadmin@rcatalog
Recovery Manager: Release 9.2.0.1.0 - Production

RMAN-06008: connected to recovery catalog database
RMAN-06428: recovery catalog is not installed
RMAN> CREATE CATALOG
RMAN-06431: recovery catalog created
```

14.   Connect to the target database and the catalog database using the RMAN and issue the register database command:

```
oracle$rman target sys/change_on_install@PRODDB catalog rman_user/
    rman_pass@RCATALOG

Recovery Manager: Release 9.2.0.2.0 - 64bit Production

Copyright (c) 1995, 2002, Oracle Corporation. All rights reserved.

RMAN-06005: connected to target database:PRODDB (DBID=1016892352)
RMAN-06008: connected to recovery catalog database

RMAN> REGISTER DATABASE;

RMAN-03022: compiling command: register
RMAN-03023: executing command: register
RMAN-08006: database registered in recovery catalog
RMAN-03023: executing command: full resync
RMAN-08002: starting full resync of recovery catalog
RMAN-08004: full resync complete
```

15.   Store scripts into the RMAN catalog:

```
RMAN>@rman_script_level0
RMAN>@rman_script_level1
RMAN>@rman_script_level2
```

16.   Based on the backup and recovery startegy defined for the organization, regular backups could be scheduled in one of two ways: by setting up command-level processes to run at scheduled intervals, or by using the GUI-based interface provided by OEM and its job scheduling interface.

Note: Sample RMAN scripts for setting up RMAN jobs are provided in Appendix 2 of this book. For detailed descriptions on installation and configuration procedures for RMAN please refer to Oracle-provided documentation sets for the appropriate version.

Configuring RMAN for RAC

Figure 12.1 specifies that RMAN depends on the archive log files, control files, and data files; this is true whether RMAN is configured for a stand-alone configuration or a RAC configuration. The data files and control files in a RAC implementation are required to be located on a shared storage subsystem. The files that are specific to the instance such as the archive log files can be stored on storage media that are visible to the instance. However, while these devices could be available for write activity to the node that owns the device, these devices should be available for read purposes to all instances participating in the cluster. The reason for this is because, in case a media recovery is required, the archive log files from the failed instance may need to be applied from one of the other available nodes or instances. This would be possible only if these devices are visible to the instance or node that is performing the recovery operation.

Another important point that is very critical to archiving log files in RAC implementations that use raw partitions is that the archive logs should be located on file systems and not on raw partitions. This is because raw partitions do not have the capability to store multiple files in these partitions and if archive logs are stored on a raw device partition, each new archive will overwrite the previous one.

Backup files from RMAN process could be written to disk or tape directly. Many organizations based on their backup strategy may decide to keep a few days of backup on disk for easy access. In this case the backup is stored on disk and then backed up from disk to tape. When disks are used for backup, these devices should also be visible from all instances participating in the cluster. In other words, these devices should also be mounted as shareable. In certain storage management solutions, such as NFS, there are considerable performance implications when the file systems are mounted to be shareable and such methods should be avoided.

10g **New Feature:** Starting with Oracle 10g a specific area in which Oracle can store and manage files related to backup and recovery could be created using the parameters DB_RECOVERY_FILE_DEST and DB_RECOVERY_FILE_DEST_SIZE.

Reporting in RMAN

RMAN provides a good reporting option. Using the RMAN utility, various details of the backup activity and other options can be obtained.

A 'report schema' command provides a list of the various tablespaces and data files configured for the target database.

```
RMAN> report schema
2> ;

using target database controlfile instead of recovery catalog
Report of database schema

File    K-bytes   Tablespace          RB segs   Datafile Name
----    -------   ---------------     -------   -------------
1        921600   SYSTEM                  ***   /dev/vx/rdsk/
                                                oraracdg/partition1G_3
2       2867200   UNDO_RAC1               ***   /dev/vx/rdsk/oraracdg/
                                                partition3G_2
3        921600   TOOLS                   ***   /dev/vx/rdsk/oraracdg/
                                                partition1G_16
4        921600   USERS                   ***   /dev/vx/rdsk/oraracdg/
                                                partition1G_13
5       2867200   UNDO_RAC2               ***   /dev/vx/rdsk/oraracdg/
                                                vertpartition3G_9
6        921600   ASAD_DATA_P001          ***   /dev/vx/rdsk/oraracdg/
                                                partition1G_44
7        921600   ASAD_DATA_P002          ***   /dev/vx/rdsk/oraracdg/
                                                partition1G_45
8        921600   ASAD_DATA_P003          ***   /dev/vx/rdsk/oraracdg/
                                                partition1G_47
9        921600   ORDHD_DATA_P001         ***   /dev/vx/rdsk/oraracdg/
                                                partition1G_12
10       921600   ORDHD_DATA_P002         ***   /dev/vx/rdsk/oraracdg/
                                                partition1G_14
11       921600   ORDHD_DATA_P003         ***   /dev/vx/rdsk/oraracdg/
                                                partition1G_17
12       921600   ORDLI_DATA_P001         ***   /dev/vx/rdsk/oraracdg/
                                                partition1G_10
```

This report provides a list of backup summary data; when the last backup was taken and what level of backup was taken (full, incremental, etc.):

```
RMAN> list backup summary;
List of Backups
===============
Key  TY  LV  S Device  Completion   #       #       Tag
                Type    Time         Pieces  Copies

1     B   0   A DISK    20-OCT-02    3       1       TAG20021020T135125
2     B   0   A DISK    20-OCT-02    2       1       TAG20021020T135125
3     B   0   A DISK    20-OCT-02    2       1       TAG20021020T135125
4     B   0   A DISK    20-OCT-02    5       1       TAG20021020T135125
5     B   1   A DISK    20-OCT-02    1       1       TAG20021020T144731
6     B   1   A DISK    20-OCT-02    1       1       TAG20021020T144731
7     B   1   A DISK    20-OCT-02    1       1       TAG20021020T144731
```

The following report lists all the data files that have changed since the last RMAN backup and are ready to be backed up:

```
RMAN> report need backup
2> ;

RMAN retention policy will be applied to the command
RMAN retention policy is set to redundancy 1
Report of files with less than 1 redundant backups
File    #bkps   Name
----    -----   ----------------------------------------
32      0       /dev/vx/rdsk/oraracdg/partition100m_54a
230     0       /dev/vx/rdsk/oraracdg/partition3G_5
231     0       /dev/vx/rdsk/oraracdg/partition500m_6b
232     0       /dev/vx/rdsk/oraracdg/partition500m_7b
233     0       /dev/vx/rdsk/oraracdg/partition3G_13
234     0       /dev/vx/rdsk/oraracdg/partition3G_14
235     0       /dev/vx/rdsk/oraracdg/partition1G_11
236     0       /dev/vx/rdsk/oraracdg/partition3G_6
237     0       /dev/vx/rdsk/oraracdg/partition300m_51
238     0       /dev/vx/rdsk/oraracdg/partition500m_12a
239     0       /dev/vx/rdsk/oraracdg/partition500m_13b
240     0       /dev/vx/rdsk/oraracdg/partition500m_14a
241     0       /dev/vx/rdsk/oraracdg/partition500m_15a
242     0       /dev/vx/rdsk/oraracdg/partition500m_17a
243     0       /dev/vx/rdsk/oraracdg/partition500m_17b
```

12.3   Backup and recovery strategy

Every organization will need to prepare a backup and recovery strategy and, more importantly, schedule the testing of this strategy at intervals. This is to ensure that as the business changes its operations and functioning, the strategic elements that were defined in the early stages are still valid. The actual strategy depends on the organizational needs, based on the criticallity of data and its availability. Since every organization will more or less tailor the backup and recovery strategies to what most fits their business requirements, no sample stratagies have been provided. If the reader would like to review some sample strategies, such information is available in the Oracle-provided documentation.

12.4   Redo internals

The ACID property of a transaction that relates to failures and recovery is the durability property. This property requires that once a user's transaction completes successfully (by the issue of a commit statement), the changes that are made must survive RDBMS failures. The e-mail system provides a good example; if the e-mail system fails, all sent e-mail would be retained in the inbox when the mailbox is opened at a later time. Similarly, Oracle is able to protect data loss from the database failures by logging the information in the redo log files. In this section, we will look into the various areas that affect the backup and recovery feature, by examining certain internal details.

12.4.1   Logging

Oracle uses the physiological logging mechanism for tracking changes to the database. Physiological logging blends the best of both worlds, namely physical logging and logical logging.

Physical logging

Under the physical logging method both the "before" and "after" image of the block is logged. This is achieved by keeping the changes made to a block or an entire copy of the block with the "before" image.

Logical logging

Under this method of logging, the actual operation that is performed, such as a DELETE or an UPDATE operation, is recorded. This is required because if the user requests an undo operation, all the required conditions for the statement have to be made available.

Physiological logging

This is a combination of both the physical logging and logical logging. Under this method, both the before and after image of the block along with the type of operation is stored. Oracle maintains redo records for all changes, which consist of one or more change vectors. A change vector is the physical change to a database block. A group of change vectors, which constitute a single atomic change to the database, is called a redo record.

12.4.2   Redo architecture

Oracle redo architecture consists of several components:

> **Note:** The complete architecture of the redo log files is visible if the dump of the redo log file is examined through its trace files.

SCN   This records the consistent version and defines the committed version of the database. An SCN is allocated and saved in the header of a redo record that commits the transaction. SCNs are also recorded in other data structures, such as data file headers, control file structures and block header structures. It is saved in the redo record header that commits the transaction. It may also be saved in a record when it is necessary to mark the redo as being allocated after a specific SCN.

> **Note:** The SCN is 48 bits long and thus can be allocated at a rate of 16,384 SCNs per second for over 534 years without running out of them.

RBA   The redo byte address (RBA) identifies the start of a redo record within an online redo log file. It acts as a pointer to where a particular change vector appears in the redo stream. It consists of three fields, the log sequence number, the block number within the log, and byte offset within the block. The RBA structure is 10 bytes long.

Change vector   As discussed earlier, a change vector is the physical change to a database block. The change vector has a header that gives the data block address (DBA) of the block, the segment, the SCN, the change type, the block class, and the operation.

Redo record   A group of change vectors, which constitute a single atomic change to the database, is called a redo record. This grouping allows multiple database blocks to be changed so that either all changes occur or no changes occur. A redo record is a change to the database state. Redo records are ordered by SCNs; this helps during recovery, when changes are applied in the order of the SCN.

Redo log files   The redo records that contain the changes to the database blocks are stored in redo log files. These files are a series of circular files where all changes are recorded. Its thread number, the sequence number within a thread, and the range of SCNs spanned by its redo records, identifies each log. The information in the redo log files is logically ordered by SCN to preserve the order in which changes were made.

In the redo log header this information is stored in the thread number, sequence number, low SCN, and next SCN fields. The low SCN is the SCN associated with the first redo record. The next SCN is the low SCN of the log with the next higher sequence number of the same thread. The current log for an enabled thread has an infinite next SCN, since there is no log with a higher sequence number.

The following dump output illustrates the above redo log header information.

```
LOG FILE #1:
(name #3) C:\ORACLE\ORADATA\...\REDO01.LOG
Thread 1 redo log links: forward: 2 backward: 0
siz: 0x32000 seq: 0x00000002 hws: 0x8 bsz: 512 nab: 0x723 flg: 0x0 dup: 1
Archive links: fwrd: 0 back: 0 Prev scn: 0x0000.0002e872
Low scn: 0x0000.00034541 10/25/2002 00:19:40
Next scn: 0x0000.00039c37 11/03/2002 19:32:42
FILE HEADER:
  Software vsn=153092096=0x9200000, Compatibility
  Vsn=153092096=0x9200000
  Db ID=2747698417=0xa3c68cf1, Db Name='ORA9IDB'
  Activation ID=2747712753=0xa3c6c4f1
  Control Seq=252=0xfc, File size=204800=0x32000
  File Number=1, Blksiz=512, File Type=2 LOG
descrip:"Thread 0001, Seq# 0000000002, SCN
  0x000000034541-0x000000039c37"
thread: 1 nab: 0x723 seq: 0x00000002 hws: 0x8 eot: 0 dis: 0
reset logs count: 0x1c601474 scn: 0x0000.0002e872
Low scn: 0x0000.00034541 10/25/2002 00:19:40
Next scn: 0x0000.00039c37 11/03/2002 19:32:42
Enabled scn: 0x0000.0002e872 10/23/2002 22:32:20
Thread closed scn: 0x0000.00039c36 10/25/2002 00:32:45
Log format vsn: 0x8000000 Disk cksum: 0x2370 Calc cksum: 0x2370
Terminal Recovery Stamp scn: 0x0000.00000000 01/01/1988 00:00:00
Most recent redo scn: 0x0000.00000000
Largest LWN: 0 blocks
Miscellaneous flags: 0x0
LOG FILE #2:
```

In a RAC environment, where multiple instances have their own redo log files and record database block changes pertaining to that instance, the order of SCN increase across threads/instances.

Redo threads The redo record information generated by an instance is called a thread of redo and is assigned a number. The thread number becomes significant in a multi-instance database configuration such as RAC. Each thread is written to its own private set of redo log files.

For each log file there is a control file record that describes the log file characteristics. The index of a log's control file record is referred to as its log number. Log numbers are unique across instances. The log file record in the control file has fields identifying the number of group members, as well as the head and tail of filenames in the group.

Checkpoint structure This is a data structure that defines a point in the redo stream, before which all changes to blocks have been written to disk. The checkpoint structure contains a checkpoint SCN, an enabled thread `bitvec` (a bit mask identifying what threads were enabled at the time of the checkpoint), a timestamp, the number of the thread that initiated the checkpoint, and an RBA.

The output below is an extract from a dump file of the online redo log file. This output provides visibility to the various redo architecture components, such as the RBA, SCN, DBA, and change vector.

```
REDO RECORD - Thread:1 RBA: 0x00001f.00000021.006c LEN: 0x0054 VLD: 0x01
SCN: 0x0000.070a75f4 SUBSCN: 1 11/21/2002 10:07:59
CHANGE #1 TYP:0 CLS:33 AFN:2 DBA:0x00800089 SCN:0x0000. 070a75f3 SEQ:
  1 OP:5.4
ktucm redo: slt: 0x0007 sqn: 0x00001bf6 srt: 0 sta: 9 flg: 0x2
ktucf redo: uba: 0x00800291.0718.18 ext: 2 spc: 3270 fbi: 0
```

12.4.3   Recovery architecture

Like the redo architecture, Oracle's recovery architecture is composed of various components and different algorithms for different functions. While these algorithms are provided to help in the recovery functions of the database, they are related to the redo architecture because recovery of the database depends on the redo log files and the presence of data in these files. The following section discusses the various algorithms and how these algorithms interact during a recovery operation.

Oracle's FIX rule algorithm

We discussed earlier that Oracles buffer contains data that was retrieved by various processes and which are in a consistent state of being modified; while these modifications happen, Oracle needs to ensure that other processes do not access the buffer or pages of data in memory. Oracle's FIX rule provides this functionality, that is, it prevents the access of the buffer or page until all the changes needed to take the buffer to the next consistent state have been applied.

Oracle relies on the O/S for implementing the FIX rule. In a Unix environment, this rule is implemented with semaphores. (Semaphores should be a familiar subject to database administrators who have installed, configured, and tuned an Oracle database system). If sufficient semaphores are not defined the following errors are normally noticed during instance startup, of which the ORA-3113 and ORA-27416 are common:

```
ORA-7250 "spcre: semget error, unable to get first semaphore set."
ORA-7279 "spcre: semget error, unable to get first semaphore set."
  ORA-7251 "spcre: semget error, could not allocate any semaphores."
ORA-7252 "spcre: semget error, could not allocate any semaphores."
  ORA-7339 "spcre: maximum number of semaphore sets exceeded."
ORA-3113 "end-of-file on communication channel" at instance startup.
ORA-27146 "post/wait initialization failed"
```

However, for others, *semaphores are a system resource that Oracle utilizes for interprocess communication.* How many semaphores does the Oracle RDBMS need? This depends on many factors, such as the number of process parameters defined in the `init<SID>.ora` file. The number of semaphores is normally set to two times the number of processes defined in the parameter file and the number depends on certain Unix kernel parameter settings.

On Unix the locking portion of the FIX rule is implemented by:

1.   Obtaining a page semaphore in exclusive mode prior to altering the page, or obtaining a page semaphore in shared or exclusive mode prior to reading the page.

2.   Holding the semaphore until the changes to be applied are recorded in a log buffer and the changes have been made to the page.

In order to ensure that the original state can be restored in the case of a failure, Oracle creates a redo record prior to changing the buffer. Oracle guarantees that when a page is unpinned after the page action completes, the redo records are consistent with the buffer state.

Several times during normal activity there could be potential failures of the page action, for example when a process dies while modifying a buffer. Under such circumstances there is an inconsistent page, and to bring the page back to a consistent state, Oracle needs to perform a block recovery. In order to perform this block level recovery, Oracle needs to apply the redo records to a copy of the block obtained from the data file.

Note: While in a Unix environment, Oracle depends on the semaphores to implement this rule; on an O/S such as Windows there is no concept of semaphores. On such environments it should be ensured that sufficient memory is allocated for Oracle to perform efficiently.

Write-ahead logging algorithm

It was stated earlier that, in order to ensure that the original state can be restored in the case of a failure, Oracle creates a redo record in the undo segment prior to changing the buffer. Apart from this, Oracle also needs to create the redo for the purpose of the undo change and the change itself. The redo change created during the process of modifying the record needs to be written to the redo log files in order for the change to complete.

This writing of the entry into the redo log files completes the change process to the record.

To ensure that writing all changes to the redo log file is complete, Oracle needs to ensure that the LGWR completes the process of writing the changes to the online redo log files prior to DBWR writing the dirty blocks to disk.

Log force at commit algorithm

When the user process completes its transaction with a commit statement, Oracle generates an SCN. This committed record is formed in the log buffer as a result of the completion of the change process. However, in order to make this change permanent, all redo entries up to and including the committed record need to be written to the online redo log files. The writing of the redo entries is optimized by Oracle by using the piggyback approach, such that any transaction that completes during the signaling of a write will be written at the same time. Grouping several transactions together performs this operation.

Online log switching algorithm

We have discussed in Chapter 3 (Oracle Database Concepts) how Oracle manages the redo log files, how the log switch happens, and the various criteria under which Oracle performs a log switch. One of the situations discussed where a log switch happens, is when Oracle encounters insufficient space in the current online redo log file. However, just having insufficient space cannot ensure that the log file can be switched; Oracle has to ensure the following:

1.   If the ARCHIVE LOG mode is enabled, the archiving process has to complete on the redo log file where Oracle will point to write the next redo operation when the current log file is full.

2.   The next log file should not contain changes required in the event of instance recovery being needed. This is determined by Oracle by ensuring that the thread checkpoint SCN is beyond the highest SCN allocated in the log to be switched into. When a delay happens due to this behavior, Oracle writes a "checkpoint not complete" message in the alert_<SID>.log file (e.g., alert_RAC2.log). If this happens frequently, the alternative is to add more redo log files, increase the size of the log files or the frequency of checkpoint activity.

Checkpoint algorithm

In Chapter 3 (Oracle Database Concepts) the various events and situations that trigger the checkpoint activity (log switch, shutdown, hot backup, etc.) were discussed in detail. There are various types of checkpoints such as:

- *Thread checkpoint:* It is only in RAC that the concept of threads is really utilized and hence this type of checkpoint pertains to a RAC implementation. All blocks dirtied prior to the checkpoint SCN in that thread for all online data files will be written to disk. This occurs each time a local checkpoint is initiated by the instance, for example, during log switch.

- *Database checkpoint:* The thread checkpoint that has the lowest checkpoint SCN for all enabled threads becomes the database checkpoint. All blocks in memory, which contain changes made prior to this SCN across all instances, must be written out to disk.

- *Data file checkpoint:* All blocks changed prior to the data file checkpoint SCN have been written to disk. Database checkpoints, hot backups, or when taking a tablespace offline, can signal data file checkpoint.

- *Incremental checkpoint:* Checks that happen more frequently are called incremental checkpoints. The DBWR process periodically writes out buffers from the checkpoint queues to advance the incremental checkpoint in memory. The CKPT process determines the lowest low RBA of all the buffers at the heads of the checkpoints queues and writes out this RBA to a thread-private location in the control file. Incremental checkpoints are used to reduce recovery time in the case of failure. During recovery, the recovery process chooses the highest incremental checkpoint RBA and the thread checkpoint RBA as the starting position for recovery.

  In Oracle 8*i* this feature was implemented using the `FAST_START_IO_TARGET` parameter. In Version 9*i*, Oracle has introduced another parameter called `FAST_START_MTTR_TARGET`, which writes records based on the recovery time required.

- *Mini-checkpoint:* This checkpoint occurs due to DDL operation such as `DROP TABLE`, `ALTER TABLE`, etc. Unlike the other types of checkpoints, the mini-checkpoint only affects blocks belonging to the object covered by the statement.

12.4.4   Redo architecture in RAC

The redo architecture in a RAC environment is no different compared to a stand-alone configuration. This is because all redo and recovery is instance-specific. Every instance will have a set of redo logs and archive logs that contain changes made by users on that instance. For example, as illustrated in Figure 12.1 above, RAC1 and RAC2 have their background process that write to their copy of the redo logs.

While each instance that participates in the clustered configuration has its own set of redo log files, each set of these redo log files is assigned a thread. The thread-to-instance relationship is assigned through the parameter file. It is during a recovery operation that these threading properties of the redo logs (in a RAC configuration) play an important part.

During a recovery operation, when one or more instances fail, the recovery operation is performed by one of the other instances that is available. A more detailed discussion about recovery operation is covered in the next section.

12.5   **Failure and recovery**

All application systems, including database systems, are prone to failures. While there are several reasons for these failures, and these failures should be minimized for continuous business operation, they still continue to occur. The database technology should be able to handle many of these failures, providing immediate recovery and placing the systems back in operation.

There are several failure scenarios in a RAC environment. Some of these scenarios could be found in the traditional stand-alone configuration, others are specific to the RAC environment.

Figure 12.2 illustrates the various areas of the system (operating system, hardware and database) that could fail. The various failure scenarios in a two-node configuration, as illustrated in Figure 12.2, are:

1.   Interconnect failure

2.   Node failure

3.   Instance failure

4.   Media failure

5.   GSD/GCS failure

6.   Instance hang or false failure

Let us briefly explain each of these failure scenarios and discuss the various recovery scenarios for these categories.

Figure 12.2
RAC configuration with points of failure.

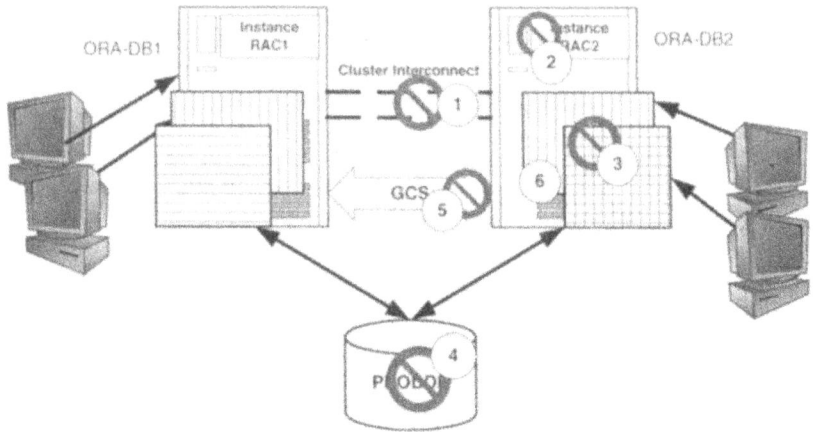

I. Interconnect failure

If the interconnect between the nodes fails, either because of a physical failure or a software failure in the communication or IPC layer, it appears to the cluster manager (CM) at each end of the interconnect that the node at the other end has failed. The CM software should use an alternative method, such as checking for a quorum disk or pinging the node, to evaluate the status of the system. It may shut down both nodes or just one of the nodes at the end of the failed connection. It will also fence the disks from any node it shuts down to prevent any further writes from being completed.

Recovery operations are not performed because of a cluster interconnect failure. The interconnect failure should cause the instance or node to fail, and only then is Oracle recovery performed. A typical situation under these circumstances would be when one instance (or both) loses communication with the other, and waits until it receives a failure signal. The failure of the cluster interconnect could cause a communication failure between the two nodes. And when the heartbeat mechanism between the two nodes is not successful, the CM, triggered by the heartbeat timeout parameter, signals a node failure. However, since there was no physical failure of the instance and/or node, the LMON process is unable to write to the disk regarding the status of the other instance.

While there is no physical failure of the instance and/or node, every instance would wait to receive a communication from the other instance that it is either up and alive and communication can continue or that the other instance is down and is not reachable. If, after a certain time, there is no response, one of the instances that is currently up will try to force shutdown of the other instance. These repeated tries will be logged in the alert log as illustrated below.

The output below is the instance activity as indicated in the alert log files, where another instance in the cluster is not reachable and the current instance is in a wait state before attempting recovery. It should be noted that after several attempts when the other instance does leave the cluster, the recovery operation begins.

The following output from the alert log indicates the various steps during a recovery operations.

```
Wed Nov 13 08:51:25 2002
Instance recovery: looking for dead threads
Instance recovery: lock domain invalid but no dead threads
Wed Nov 13 13:19:43 2002
Communications reconfiguration: instance 0
Wed Nov 13 13:19:51 2002
Evicting instance 1 from cluster
Wed Nov 13 13:20:11 2002
Waiting for instances to leave:
1
Wed Nov 13 13:20:31 2002
Waiting for instances to leave:
1
Wed Nov 13 13:20:51 2002
Waiting for instances to leave:
1
Wed Nov 13 14:49:30 2002
Reconfiguration started
List of nodes: 1,
Wed Nov 13 14:49:30 2002
Reconfiguration started
List of nodes: 1,
  Global Resource Directory frozen
one node partition
  Communication channels reestablished
  Master broadcasted resource hash value bitmaps
  Non-local Process blocks cleaned out
  Resources and enqueues cleaned out
  Resources remastered 7071
  26264 GCS shadows traversed, 0 cancelled, 51 closed
  22664 GCS resources traversed, 0 cancelled
  24964 GCS resources on freelist, 37877 on array, 37877 allocated
  set master node info
  Submitted all remote-enqueue requests
  Update rdomain variables
  Dwn-cvts replayed, VALBLKs dubious
```

```
  All grantable enqueues granted
  26264 GCS shadows traversed, 0 replayed, 51 unopened
  Submitted all GCS remote-cache requests
  0 write requests issued in 26213 GCS resources
  63 PIs marked suspect, 0 flush PI msgs
Wed Nov 13 14:49:32 2002
Reconfiguration complete
  Post SMON to start 1st pass IR
Wed Nov 13 14:49:32 2002
Instance recovery: looking for dead threads
Wed Nov 13 14:49:32 2002
Beginning instance recovery of 1 threads
Wed Nov 13 14:49:32 2002
Started first pass scan
Wed Nov 13 14:49:33 2002
Completed first pass scan
  27185 redo blocks read, 1197 data blocks need recovery
Wed Nov 13 14:49:34 2002
Started recovery at
  Thread 1: logseq 25, block 745265, scn 0.0
Recovery of Online Redo Log: Thread 1 Group 3 Seq 25 Reading mem 0
  Mem# 0 errs 0: /dev/vx/rdsk/oraracdg/partition1G_27
  Mem# 1 errs 0: /dev/vx/rdsk/oraracdg/partition1G_29
Wed Nov 13 14:49:35 2002
Completed redo application
Wed Nov 13 14:49:36 2002
Ended recovery at
  Thread 1: logseq 25, block 772450, scn 0.115066397
  813 data blocks read, 1212 data blocks written, 27185 redo blocks read
Ending instance recovery of 1 threads
SMON: about to recover undo segment 1
SMON: mark undo segment 1 as available
SMON: about to recover undo segment 2
.......
Wed Nov 13 15:03:21 2002
Reconfiguration started
List of nodes: 0,1,
  Global Resource Directory frozen
  Communication channels reestablished
  Master broadcasted resource hash value bitmaps
  Non-local Process blocks cleaned out
  Resources and enqueues cleaned out
  Resources remastered 6966
  26984 GCS shadows traversed, 0 cancelled, 601 closed
  26383 GCS resources traversed, 0 cancelled
  24887 GCS resources on freelist, 37877 on array, 37877 allocated
  set master node info
Wed Nov 13 15:03:24 2002
Reconfiguration complete
Wed Nov 13 15:03:24 2002
Instance recovery: looking for dead threads
Instance recovery: lock domain invalid but no dead threads
```

Under such circumstances where the communication between instances fails and one instance is not responding to other's requests, there are considerable performance delays. This is due to the fact that the Oracle kernel is repeatedly trying to shut down the unreachable instance in order to perform recovery.

These circumstances call for a manual intervention, where the database administrator would be required to shut down one of the instances to allow business to continue. To avoid this manual intervention, there are two possible actions:

1. Write a cluster validation code to check for the availability of GCS and GES communication between nodes. This allows for detecting and shutting down an instance when the CM is unable to perform such a task. The validation routine would be an update command that continually loops through a block that performs an update of a record in a table when a single data block is covered by a single PCM lock. This block would run on all the nodes at each end of the interconnect. By running this routine on every possible pair of nodes where each pair is updating a different block, an abnormal delay in obtaining the lock would indicate a problem with the remote GCS or the interconnect between the nodes. The process could be updating the record based on who detected the problem and could force a shutdown of the instance.

2. Another method that would be much more clear and straight-forward is to provide redundant interconnects between each pair of nodes. The additional interconnect will act as a standby to the primary interconnect and will be used when the primary inter-connect fails. However, the possibility of having additional interconnects depends on the hardware vendor. The additional interconnects should be an important part of the deployment architecture, to provide true high availability of the database cluster. If this is not provided, the cluster interconnect becomes a single point of failure.

Once the instance has been shut down, the instance recovery operation begins.

2. Node failure

RAC comprises two or more instances sharing a common single copy of a physical database. Each instance is normally attached or configured to run on a specific node. In RAC, if the entire node fails, the instance that includes GCS elements stored in its shared pool as well as the GCS processes running on that node will fail. Under such circumstances, the GCS must reconfigure itself in order to remaster the locks that were being managed by the failed node before instance recovery can occur.

Many cluster hardware vendors use a disk-based quorum system that allows each node to determine which other nodes are currently active members of the cluster. These systems also allow a node to remove itself from the cluster or to remove other nodes from the cluster. The latter is accomplished through a type of voting system, managed through the shared quorum disk, that allows nodes to determine which node will remain active if one or more of the nodes become disconnected from the cluster interconnect.

RAC relies on the CM of the operating system for failure detection. Using the heartbeat mechanism, the CM allows the nodes to communicate with the other nodes that are available on a continuous basis at preset intervals, e.g., 2 seconds on Sun and Tru64 clusters.[2] At each heartbeat, every member instance gives its status of the other members' availability. It they all agree, nothing further is done until the next heartbeat. If two or more instances report a different instance configuration among each other (e.g., because the cluster interconnect is broken between a pair of nodes), then one member arbitrates among the different membership configurations. Once this configuration is tested, the arbitrating instance uses the shared disk to publish the proposed configuration to the other instances. All active instances then examine the published configuration, and, if necessary, terminate themselves.

Another important failure detection criterion is the heartbeat timeout condition. After a predefined timeout period (configurable on most operating systems), remaining nodes detect the failure and attempt to reform the cluster. (*The heartbeat timeout parameter, like the heartbeat interval, varies from operating system to operating system; the default heartbeat timeout parameter on Sun clusters is 12 seconds and the default on Linux clusters is 10 seconds.*) Based on the timeout interval and the heartbeat interval, the CM will validate the existence of the other node several times (*in the case of Sun clusters about four times and in the case of Linux clusters about three times*). If the remaining nodes form a quorum, the other nodes will reorganize the cluster membership.

---

2.   In the case of Linux and Windows clusters, an Oracle-provided CM is used and the heartbeat mechanism is wrapped with another process called the watchdog process provided by Oracle to give this functionality.

The reorganization process regroups the nodes that are accessible and removes the nodes that have failed. For example, in a four-node cluster, if one node fails, the CM will regroup among the remaining three nodes. The CM performs this step when a node is added to a cluster or a node is removed from a cluster. This information is exposed to the respective Oracle instances by the LMON process running on each cluster node.

Up to this point the CM at the operating system level did the failure detection; since a node failure also involves an instance failure, there are further steps involved before the surviving instances can perform the recovery operation. Instance failure involves database recovery followed by instance recovery.

3. Instance failures

RAC has many instances talking to a common shared physical database. Since several instances are involved in this configuration, one or more instances (or all) are prone to failure. If all instances participating in the configuration fail, the database is in an unusable state; this is called a crash or database crash and the recovery process associated with this failure is called a crash recovery. However, if only one or more, but not all, of these instances fail, this is known as an instance failure and the recovery process associated with this failure is called an instance recovery.

We will now discuss both failure scenarios.

Database crash

All instances in a configuration could fail due to several reasons like a kernel-level exception. When all instances in the clustered configuration fail, the database is in an unusable state; however, this would not necessarily indicate that there is a problem with the database.

Recovery of an instance from a crash is similar to a recovery operation in a single instance configuration, where each instance would perform its instance recovery.

Instance failure

Instance failure could happen in several ways. The common reason for an instance failure is when the node itself fails. The node failure, as discussed above, could be due to several reasons, including power surge, operator error, etc. Other reasons for an instance failure could be because a certain background process fails or dies, or when there is a kernel-level exception encountered by the instance causing an ORA-0600 or ORA-07445 error. A failure by issuing a SHUTDOWN ABORT command by a database administrator could also cause an instance failure.

Instance failures occur where:

- The instance is totally down and users do not have any access to the instance.

- The instance is up, but when connecting to it there is a hang situation or user gets no response.

In the case where the instance is not available, users could continue access to the database in an active/active configuration, provided the failover option has been enabled in the application. The failover option, as discussed in Chapter 10 (Availability and Scalability), could be enabled either by using the OCI inside the application or by using the SQL client, where the failover options are configured in the tnsnames.ora file.

Recovery from an instance failure happens from another instance that is up and running, that is part of the cluster configuration, and whose heartbeat mechanism deduces the failure first and informs the LMON process on the node. The LMON process on each cluster node communicates with the CM on the respective node and exposes that information to the respective instances.

LMON provides the monitoring function by continually sending messages from the node on which it runs, often by writing to the shared disk. When the node fails to perform the functions and when LMON stops sending messages to other active instances, the other nodes consider that the node is no longer a member of the cluster. Such a failure causes a change in a node's membership status within the cluster.

The LMON process controls the recovery of the failed instance by taking over its redo log files and performing instance recovery.

Instance recovery is complete when Oracle has performed the following steps:

- Rolling back all uncommitted transactions of the failed instance, called *transaction recovery*.

- Replaying the online redo log files of the failed instance, called *cache recovery*.

How does Oracle know that recovery is required for a given data file?
The SCN is a logical clock that increments with time. The SCN describes
a "version" or a committed version of the database. When a database
checkpoints, an SCN (called the checkpoint SCN) is written to the data file
headers. This is called the start SCN. There is also an SCN value in the
control file for every data file, which is called the stop SCN. The stop SCN
is set to infinity while the database is open and running. There is another
data structure called the checkpoint counter in each data file header and
also in the control file for each data file entry. The checkpoint counter
increments every time a checkpoint happens on a data file and the start
SCN value is updated. When a data file is in hot backup mode, the
checkpoint information in the file header is frozen but the checkpoint
counter still gets updated.

When the database is shut down gracefully, with the SHUTDOWN
NORMAL or SHUTDOWN IMMEDIATE command, Oracle performs a
checkpoint and copies the start SCN value of each data file to its
corresponding stop SCN value in the control file before the actual
shutdown of the database.

When the database is started, Oracle performs two checks (among
other consistency checks):

1.   To see if the start SCN value in every data file header matches with
      its corresponding stop SCN value in the control file.

2.   To see if the checkpoint counter values match.

If both these checks are successful, then Oracle determines that no
recovery is required for that data file. These two checks are done for all
data files that are online.

If the start SCN of a specific data file does not match the stop SCN
value in the control file, then at least a crash recovery is required. This can
happen when the database is shut down with the SHUTDOWN ABORT
statement or if the instance crashes. After the first check, Oracle performs
the second check on the data files by checking the checkpoint counters. If
the checkpoint counter check fails, then Oracle knows that the data file
has been replaced with a backup copy (while the instance was down) and
therefore, media recovery is required.

Note: Crash recovery is performed by applying the redo records in the
online log files to the data files. However, media recovery may require
applying the archived redo log files as well.

Figure 12.3
Instance
recovery.

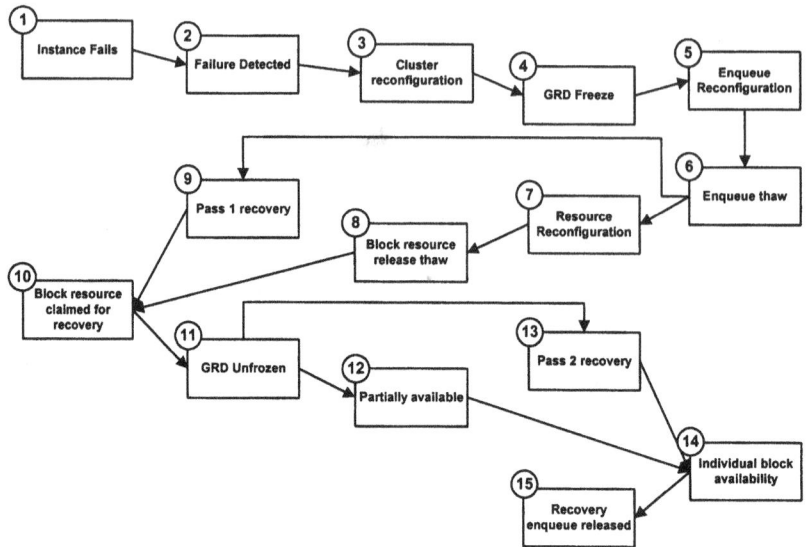

Figure 12.3 illustrates the flow during the various stages of the recovery process during an instance failure. Instance failure, as we have discussed above, is a scenario where one or more, but not all, instances have failed. We will now discuss these various steps of the recovery process in detail.

1.   *Instance fails:* This is the first stage in the process, when an instance fails and recovery becomes a necessity. As illustrated above, an instance could fail for various reasons including operator error, when the database administrator executes the SHUTDOWN ABORT statement, or when the node that the instance is running on crashes.

2.   *Failure detected:* The CM of the clustered operating system does the detection of a node failure or an instance failure. The CM is able to accomplish this with the help of certain parameters such as the heartbeat interval and the heartbeat timeout parameter. The heartbeat interval parameter invokes a watchdog[3] process that wakes up at a stipulated time interval and checks the existence of the other members in the cluster. On most O/Ss this interval is configurable, and can be changed with the help of the systems administrators. This value is normally specified in seconds. Setting a very small value could cause some performance problems. Though

---

3.   The watchdog process is only present in environments where Oracle has provided the CM layer of the product, for example Linux.

the overhead of this process running is really insignificant, on very busy systems, frequent running of this process could turn out to be expensive. Setting this parameter to an ideal value is important and is achieved by constant monitoring of the activities on the system and the amount of overhead this particular process is causing.

When the instance fails, the watchdog process or the heartbeat validation interval does not get a response from the other instance within the time stipulated in the heartbeat timeout parameter; the CM clears and declares that the instance is down. From the first time that the CM does not get a response from the heartbeat check, to the time that the CM declares that the node has failed, repeated checks are done to ensure that the initial message was not a false message.

The timeout interval, like the heartbeat interval parameter, should not be set low. Unlike the heartbeat interval parameter, in the case of the timeout interval it is not a performance concern; rather, a potential to cause false failure detections because the cluster might inversely determine that a node is failing due to transient failures if the timeout interval is set too low. The false failure detections can occur on busy systems, where the node is processing tasks that are highly CPU intensive. While the system should reserve a percentage of its resources for these kinds of activities, occasionally when systems are high on resources with high CPU utilization, the response to the heartbeat function could be delayed and hence, if the heartbeat timeout is set very low, could cause the CM to assume that the node is not available when actually it is up and running.

3. *Cluster reconfiguration:* When a failure is detected, the cluster reorganization occurs. During this process, Oracle alters the node's cluster membership status. This involves Oracle taking care of the fact that a node has left the cluster. The GCS and GES provide the CM interfaces to the software and expose the cluster membership map to the Oracle instances when nodes are added or deleted from the cluster. The LMON process performs this exposure of the information to the remaining Oracle instances.

LMON performs this task by continually sending messages from the node it runs on and often writing to the shared disk. When such write activity does not happen for a prolonged period of time, it provides evidence to the surviving nodes that the node is no longer a member of the cluster. Such a failure causes a change in a node's membership status within the cluster and LMON initiates the recovery actions, which include remastering of GCS and GES resources and instance recovery.

The cluster reconfiguration process, along with other activities performed by Oracle processes, are recorded in the respective background process trace files and in the instance-specific alert log files.

```
*** 2002-11-16 23:48:02.753
kjxgmpoll reconfig bitmap: 1
*** 2002-11-16 23:48:02.753
kjxgmrcfg: Reconfiguration started, reason 1
kjxgmcs: Setting state to 6 0.
*** 2002-11-16 23:48:02.880
  Name Service frozen
kjxgmcs: Setting state to 6 1.
kjxgfipccb: msg 0x1038c6a88, mbo 0x1038c6a80, type 22, ack 0, ref 0, stat 6
kjxgfipccb: Send cancelled, stat 6 inst 0, type 22, tkt (3744,204)
kjxgfipccb: msg 0x1038c6938, mbo 0x1038c6930, type 22, ack 0, ref 0, stat 6
kjxgfipccb: Send cancelled, stat 6 inst 0, type 22, tkt (3416,204)
kjxgfipccb: msg 0x1038c67e8, mbo 0x1038c67e0, type 22, ack 0, ref 0, stat 6
kjxgfipccb: Send cancelled, stat 6 inst 0, type 22, tkt (3088,204)
kjxgfipccb: msg 0x1038c6bd8, mbo 0x1038c6bd0, type 22, ack 0, ref 0, stat 6
kjxgfipccb: Send cancelled, stat 6 inst 0, type 22, tkt (2760,204)
kjxgfipccb: msg 0x1038c7118, mbo 0x1038c7110, type 22, ack 0, ref 0, stat 6
kjxgfipccb: Send cancelled, stat 6 inst 0, type 22, tkt (2432,204)
kjxgfipccb: msg 0x1038c6fc8, mbo 0x1038c6fc0, type 22, ack 0, ref 0, stat 6
kjxgfipccb: Send cancelled, stat 6 inst 0, type 22, tkt (2104,204)
kjxgfipccb: msg 0x1038c7268, mbo 0x1038c7260, type 22, ack 0, ref 0, stat 6
kjxgfipccb: Send cancelled, stat 6 inst 0, type 22, tkt (1776,204)
kjxgfipccb: msg 0x1038c6e78, mbo 0x1038c6e70, type 22, ack 0, ref 0, stat 6
kjxgfipccb: Send cancelled, stat 6 inst 0, type 22, tkt (1448,204)
kjxgfipccb: msg 0x1038c6d28, mbo 0x1038c6d20, type 22, ack 0, ref 0, stat 6
kjxgfipccb: Send cancelled, stat 6 inst 0, type 22, tkt (1120,204)
kjxgfipccb: msg 0x1038c7a48, mbo 0x1038c7a40, type 22, ack 0, ref 0, stat 6
kjxgfipccb: Send cancelled, stat 6 inst 0, type 22, tkt (792,204)
kjxgfipccb: msg 0x1038c7508, mbo 0x1038c7500, type 22, ack 0, ref 0, stat 6
kjxgfipccb: Send cancelled, stat 6 inst 0, type 22, tkt (464,204)
kjxgfipccb: msg 0x1038c73b8, mbo 0x1038c73b0, type 22, ack 0, ref 0, stat 6
kjxgfipccb: Send cancelled, stat 6 inst 0, type 22, tkt (136,204)
*** 2002-11-16 23:48:03.104
Obtained RR update lock for sequence 6, RR seq 6
*** 2002-11-16 23:48:04.611
Voting results, upd 1, seq 7, bitmap: 1
kjxgmps: proposing substate 2
kjxgmcs: Setting state to 7 2.
  Performed the unique instance identification check
kjxgmps: proposing substate 3
kjxgmcs: Setting state to 7 3.
  Name Service recovery started
  Deleted all dead-instance name entries
```

```
kjxgmps: proposing substate 4
kjxgmcs: Setting state to 7 4.
  Multicasted all local name entries for publish
  Replayed all pending requests
kjxgmps: proposing substate 5
kjxgmcs: Setting state to 7 5.
  Name Service normal
  Name Service recovery done
*** 2002-11-16 23:48:04.612
kjxgmps: proposing substate 6
kjxgmcs: Setting state to 7 6.
kjfmact: call ksimdic on instance (0)
*** 2002-11-16 23:48:04.613
*** 2002-11-16 23:48:04.614
Reconfiguration started
Synchronization timeout interval: 660 sec
List of nodes: 1,
  Global Resource Directory frozen
node 1
* kjshashcfg: I'm the only node in the cluster (node 1)
Active Sendback Threshold = 50%
Communication channels reestablished
Master broadcasted resource hash value bitmaps
Non-local Process blocks cleaned out
Resources and enqueues cleaned out
Resources remastered 2413
35334 GCS shadows traversed, 0 cancelled, 1151 closed
17968 GCS resources traversed, 0 cancelled
20107 GCS resources on freelist, 37877 on array, 37877 allocated
set master node info
Submitted all remote-enqueue requests
Update rdomain variables
Dwn-cvts replayed, VALBLKs dubious
All grantable enqueues granted
*** 2002-11-16 23:48:05.412
35334 GCS shadows traversed, 0 replayed, 1151 unopened
Submitted all GCS cache requests
0 write requests issued in 34183 GCS resources
29 PIs marked suspect, 0 flush PI msgs
*** 2002-11-16 23:48:06.007
Reconfiguration complete
Post SMON to start 1st pass IR
*** 2002-11-16 23:52:28.376
kjxgmpoll reconfig bitmap: 0 1
*** 2002-11-16 23:52:28.376
kjxgmrcfg: Reconfiguration started, reason 1
kjxgmcs: Setting state to 7 0.
*** 2002-11-16 23:52:28.474
  Name Service frozen
kjxgmcs: Setting state to 7 1.
*** 2002-11-16 23:52:28.881
Obtained RR update lock for sequence 7, RR seq 7
*** 2002-11-16 23:52:28.887
```

```
Voting results, upd 1, seq 8, bitmap: 0 1
kjxgmps: proposing substate 2
kjxgmcs: Setting state to 8 2.
  Performed the unique instance identification check
kjxgmps: proposing substate 3
kjxgmcs: Setting state to 8 3.
  Name Service recovery started
  Deleted all dead-instance name entries
kjxgmps: proposing substate 4
kjxgmcs: Setting state to 8 4.
  Multicasted all local name entries for publish
  Replayed all pending requests
kjxgmps: proposing substate 5
kjxgmcs: Setting state to 8 5.
  Name Service normal
  Name Service recovery done
*** 2002-11-16 23:52:28.896
kjxgmps: proposing substate 6
kjxgmcs: Setting state to 8 6.
*** 2002-11-16 23:52:29.116
*** 2002-11-16 23:52:29.116
Reconfiguration started
Synchronization timeout interval: 660 sec
List of nodes: 0,1,
```

During this stage of recovery when the reconfiguration of cluster membership takes place, the RAC environment is in a state of system pause and most client transactions are suspended until Oracle completes recovery processing.

Analyzing the LMON trace. In general, the LMON trace file listed above contains the recovery and reconfiguration information on locks, resources, and states of its instance group.

The six *substates* in the Cluster Group Service (CGS) that are listed in the trace file are:

- State 0: Waiting for the instance reconfiguration.

- State 1: Received the instance reconfiguration event.

- State 2: Agreed on the instance membership.

- States 3, 4, 5: CGS name service recovery.

- State 6: GES/GCS (lock/resource) recovery.

Each state is identified as a pair of incarnation number and its current substate. "Setting state to 7 6" means that the instance is currently at incarnation 7 and substate 6.

"kjxgfipccb" is the callback on the completion of a CGS message send. If the delivery of message fails, a log would be generated. Associated with the log are message buffer pointer, recovery state object, message type and others.

"Synchronization timeout interval" is the timeout value for GES to signal an abort on its recovery process. Since the recovery process is distributed, at each step, each instance waits for others to complete the corresponding step before moving to the next one. This value has a minimum of 10 minutes and is computed according the number of resources.

4.   *GRD freeze:* The first step in the cluster reconfiguration process, before beginning the actual recovery process, is for the CM to ensure that the GRD is not distributed and hence freezes activity on the GRD so that no future writes or updates happen to the GRD on the node that is currently performing the recovery. This step is also recorded in the alert logs. Since the GRD is maintained by the GCS and GES processes, all GCS and GES resources and also the write requests are frozen. During this step of the temporary freeze, Oracle takes control of the situation and balances the resources among the available instances.

```
Sat Nov 16 23:48:04 2002
Reconfiguration started
List of nodes: 1,
Global Resource Directory frozen
one node partition
Communication channels reestablished
```

5.   *Enqueue reconfiguration:* Enqueue resources are reconfigured among the available instances.

6.   *Enqueue thaw:* After the reconfiguration of resources among the available instances, Oracle makes the enqueue resources available. At this point the process forks to perform two tasks in parallel, resource reconfiguration and pass 1 recovery.

7.   *Resource reconfiguration:* This phase of the recovery is important in a RAC environment where the GCS commences recovery and remastering of the block resources, which involves rebuilding lost resource masters on surviving instances.

Remastering of resources is exhaustive by itself because of the various scenarios under which remastering of resources takes place. The following output from the alert log illustrates the reconfiguration steps:

```
Sat Nov 16 23:48:04 2002
Reconfiguration started
```

```
List of nodes: 1,
  Global Resource Directory frozen
one node partition
  Communication channels reestablished
  Master broadcasted resource hash value bitmaps
  Non-local Process blocks cleaned out
  Resources and enqueues cleaned out
  Resources remastered 2413
  35334 GCS shadows traversed, 0 cancelled, 1151 closed
  17968 GCS resources traversed, 0 cancelled
  20107 GCS resources on freelist, 37877 on array, 37877 allocated
  set master node info
  Submitted all remote-enqueue requests
  Update rdomain variables
  Dwn-cvts replayed, VALBLKs dubious
  All grantable enqueues granted
  35334 GCS shadows traversed, 0 replayed, 1151 unopened
  Submitted all GCS remote-cache requests
  0 write requests issued in 34183 GCS resources
  29 PIs marked suspect, 0 flush PI msgs
Sat Nov 16 23:48:06 2002
Reconfiguration complete
```

8.   *Resource release:* Once the remastering of resources is completed, the next step is to complete processing of pending activities. Once this is completed, all resources that were locked during the recovery process are released or the locks are downgraded (converted to a lower level).

9.   *Pass 1 recovery:* This step of the recovery process is performed in parallel with steps 7 and 8. SMON will merge the redo thread ordered by SCN to ensure that changes are written in an orderly fashion. SMON will also find BWR in the redo stream and remove entries that are no longer needed for recovery, because they are PI of blocks already written to disk. A recovery set is produced that only contains blocks modified by the failed instance with no subsequent BWR to indicate that the blocks were later written. Each entry in the recovery list is ordered by first-dirty SCN to specify the order to acquire instance recovery locks. Reading the log files and identifying the blocks that need to be recovered completes the first pass of the recovery process.

```
Post SMON to start 1st pass IR
Sat Nov 16 23:48:06 2002
Instance recovery: looking for dead threads
Sat Nov 16 23:48:06 2002
Beginning instance recovery of 1 threads
Sat Nov 16 23:48:06 2002
Started first pass scan
```

```
Sat Nov 16 23:48:06 2002
Completed first pass scan
 5101 redo blocks read, 490 data blocks need recovery
Sat Nov 16 23:48:07 2002
Started recovery at
 Thread 1: logseq 29, block 2, scn 0.115795034
Recovery of Online Redo Log: Thread 1 Group 1 Seq 29 Reading mem 0
 Mem# 0 errs 0: /dev/vx/rdsk/oraracdg/partition1G_31
 Mem# 1 errs 0: /dev/vx/rdsk/oraracdg/partition1G_21
Sat Nov 16 23:48:08 2002
Completed redo application
Sat Nov 16 23:48:08 2002
Ended recovery at
 Thread 1: logseq 29, block 5103, scn 0.115820072
 420 data blocks read, 500 data blocks written, 5101 redo blocks read
Ending instance recovery of 1 threads
```

10. *Block resource claimed for recovery*: Once pass 1 of the recovery process completes and the GCS reconfiguration has completed, the recovery process continues by:

a. Obtaining buffer space for the recovery set, possibly by performing write operation to make room.

b. Claiming resources on the blocks identified during pass 1.

c. Obtaining a source buffer, either from an instance's buffer cache or by a disk read.

During this phase, the recovering SMON process will inform each lock element's master node for each block in the recovery list that it will be taking ownership of the block and lock for recovery. Blocks become available as they have been recovered. The lock recovery is based on the ownership of the lock element. This depends on one of the various scenarios of lock conditions:

Scenario 1: Let us assume that all instances in the cluster are holding a lock status of NL0; SMON acquires the lock element in XL0 mode, reads the block from disk and applies redo changes, and subsequently writes out the recovery buffer when complete.

Scenario 2: In this situation, the SMON process of the recovering instance has a lock mode of NL0 and the second instance has a lock status of XL0; however, the failed instance has a status similar to the recovery node, i.e., NL0. In this case, no recovery is required because the current copy of the buffer already exists on another instance.

Scenario 3: In this situation, let us assume that the recovering instance has a lock status of NL0; the second instance has a lock status of XG0.

However, the failed instance has a status similar to the recovery node. In this case also, no recovery is required because a current copy of the buffer already exists on another instance. SMON will remove the block entry from the recovery set and the recovery buffer is released. The recovery instance has a lock status of NG1; however, the second instance that originally had a XG0 status now holds NL0 status after writing the block to disk.

Scenario 4: Now, what if the recovering instance has lock status of NL0; the second instance has a lock status of NG1. However, the failed instance has a status similar to the recovery node. In this case the consistent read image of the latest PI is obtained, based on SCN. The redo changes are applied and the recovery buffer is written when complete. The recovery instance has a lock element of XG0 and the second instance continues to retain the NG1 status on the block.

Scenario 5: The recovering instance has a lock status of SL0 or XL0 and the other instance has no lock being held. In this case, no recovery is needed because a current copy of the buffer already exists on another instance. SMON will remove the block from the recovery set. The lock status will not change.

Scenario 6: The recovery instance holds a lock status of XG0 and the second instance has a lock status of NG1. SMON initiates the write of the current block. No recovery is performed by the recovery instance. The recovery buffer is released and the PI count is decremented when the block write has completed.

Scenario 7: The recovery instance holds a lock status of NG1 and the second instance holds a lock with status of XG0. In this case, SMON initiates a write of the current block on the second instance. No recovery is performed by the recovery instance. The recovery buffer is released and the PI count is decremented when the block write has completed.

Scenario 8: The recovering instance holds a lock status of NG1, and the second instance holds a lock status of NG0. In this case a consistent read copy of the block is obtained from the highest PI based on SCN. Redo changes are applied and the recovery buffer is written when complete.

11. *GRD unfrozen:* After the necessary resources are obtained, and the recovering instance has all the resources it needs to complete pass 2 with no further intervention, the block cache space in the GRD is unfrozen.

The following extract from the alert log illustrates the activities around the GRD:

```
Sat Nov 16 23:52:29 2002
Reconfiguration started
List of nodes: 0,1,
  Global Resource Directory frozen
  Communication channels reestablished
  Master broadcasted resource hash value bitmaps
  Non-local Process blocks cleaned out
  Resources and enqueues cleaned out
  Resources remastered 2415
  35334 GCS shadows traversed, 0 cancelled, 1118 closed
  34216 GCS resources traversed, 0 cancelled
  20096 GCS resources on freelist, 37877 on array, 37877 allocated
  set master node info
  Submitted all remote-enqueue requests
  Update rdomain variables
  Dwn-cvts replayed, VALBLKs dubious
  All grantable enqueues granted
  35334 GCS shadows traversed, 16435 replayed, 1118 unopened
  Submitted all GCS remote-cache requests
  0 write requests issued in 17781 GCS resources
  0 PIs marked suspect, 0 flush PI msgs

Sat Nov 16 23:52:30 2002
Reconfiguration complete
```

At this stage, the recovery process splits into two parallel phases while certain areas of the system are being made partially available; the second phase of the recovery begins.

12.   *Partial availability:* At this stage of the recovery process the system is partially available for use. The blocks not in recovery can be operated on as before. Blocks being recovered are blocked by the resource held in the recovering instance.

13.   *Pass 2 recovery:* The second phase of recovery continues, taking care of all the blocks identified during pass 1, recovering and writing each block, then releasing recovery resources. During the second phase the redo threads of the failed instances are once again merged by SCN and instead of performing a block level recovery in memory, during this phase the redo is applied to the data files.

14.   *Block availability:* Since the second pass of recovery recovers individual blocks, these blocks are made available for user access as they are recovered a block at a time.

15.   *Recovery enqueue release:* When all the blocks have been recovered and written and the recovery resources released, the system is completely available and the recovery enqueue is released.

During normal instance recovery operation, there is a potential that one or more (including the recovering instance) of the other instances could also encounter failure. If this happens, Oracle has to handle the situation appropriately, based on the type of failure:

- If recovery fails without the death of the recovering instance, instance recovery is restarted.

- If during the process of recovery the recovering process dies, one of the surviving instances will acquire the instance recovery enqueue and start the recovery process.

- If during the recovery process, another non-recovering instance fails, SMON will abort the recovery, release the instance recovery (IR) enqueue and reattempt instance recovery.

- During the recovery process, if I/O errors are encountered, the related fies are taken offline and the recovery is restarted.

- If one of the blocks that SMON is trying to recover is corrupted during redo application, Oracle performs online block recovery to clean up the block in order for instance recovery to continue.

4. Media failures

Media failures comprise the failure of the various components of the database, such as data files, tablespaces, and the entire database itself. They occur when the Oracle file storage medium is damaged and prevents Oracle from reading or writing data, resulting in the loss of one or more database files. These failures could affect one or all types of files necessary for the operation of an Oracle database, including data files, online redo log files, archived redo log files, and control files.

The reasons for media failures could be bad disk, controller failures, mirrored disk failures, block corruptions, and power surge. Depending on the type of failure, a data file, tablespace, or the database controls the access to the database. The extent of damage to the specific area will determine the amount of time that the media would be offline and the access will be interrupted.

Database operation after a media failure of online redo log files or control files depends on whether the online redo log or control file is setup with multiplexing. Storing the multiplexed files on separate disks protects the copies from failures. For example, if a media failure damages a single disk of a multiplexed online redo log file, then database operation will continue from the other disk without significant interruption. On the other hand, if the files were not multiplexed, damage to the single copy of the redo log file could cause the database operation to halt and may cause permanent loss of data.

In the case of data files, failures could be categorized as read failures or write failures. Read failures are because Oracle is unable to read a data file; this causes an O/S level error message to be returned back to the application. On the other hand, if there are write failures, i.e., when Oracle cannot write to a data file, for example if the database is in ARCHIVELOG mode, then Oracle will return an error in the DBWR trace file and will take the data file offline automatically, and users will be allowed access to the remaining data files. If the write failure was against the system tablespace, the data file that maps to the tablespace is taken offline and the instance that encountered the error is shut down.

Write failures on a data file, when the database is not in ARCHIVELOG mode, cause the DBWR process to fail and this causes a crash on the instance. In this case, if the problem is temporary, then a crash or instance recovery will fix the instance and the instance is restarted. However, if the damage is permanent, the entire database would have to be restored from a most recent copy of the backup.

In a RAC environment, media failure could mean access to the database interrupted from one or more or all instances.

Recovery of media failures also depends on the type of media failure and accordingly either a data file recovery, tablespace recovery, or database recovery is performed.

Data file recovery

When the failure is at the data file level, normally caused by damage or corruption in the data file, a data file recovery is performed. Data file recovery is used to restore a file that is taken offline with immediate option because of an I/O error or to restore a file after disk failure.

The command used to recover a data file is:

```
SQL>recover datafile '<filename>'[filename2, filename3>;
```

Tablespace recovery

Tablespace recovery is the one form of media recovery that is specified at a logical level. This is because a tablespace is only related to the media via the data file. Tablespace by itself is an indirect reference or logical name given to one or more data files. Since tablespaces could be mapped to a data file during a tablespace recovery operation, Oracle queries the data dictionary to determine the tablespace to data file mapping. Up to 16 data files assigned to a tablespace can be recovered simultaneously.

The command used for tablespace recovery is:

```
SQL>recover tablespace <tablespace_name. (tablespace_name)...;
```

Database recovery

Recovery at this level recovers certain or all of the data files in a database. This operation could also be used to recover a damaged control file. A complete database recovery operation returns all data files and the control file to the same point in time through the redo application.

Database recovery is invoked by the following command:

```
SQL>recover database (until time 'xxxx'/change xxxx/cancel);
```

Database recovery could be a complete recovery, where the entire database is brought to the current point in time; or incomplete recovery, where the whole database is brought to a point behind the current time, after which, rolling forward to the same point restores all data files.

If the current or latest version of the control file is not available, database recovery can still be performed using the RESETLOGS option. Using this option will also bring the database to the current state. This is possible because when the database is opened with RESETLOGS, a comparison is done between the data files in the control file and those in the data dictionary table. If a data file is found to be in sys.file$ table but not in the control file, then an entry will be created for it in the control file with the name MISSINGnnnn, where nnnn is the file_id. The file will be marked offline as needing recovery. This file, if it exists, can then be renamed to its correct using the following syntax:

```
SQL>alter database rename file 'MISSINGnnnn' to '<file_name>';
```

Following this statement the data file is recovered and brought online.

Conversely, if the data file listed in the control file is not found by querying the sys.file$ table then it is removed from the control file.

Thread recovery

A thread is a stream of redo, for example, all redo log files for a given instance. In a single stand-alone configuration there is usually only one thread, although it is possible to specify more, under certain circumstances.

An instance has one thread associated with it, and recovery under this situation would be like any stand-alone configuration. What is the difference in a RAC environment? In a RAC environment, multiple threads are usually seen; there is generally one thread per instance, and the thread applicable to a specific instance is defined in the server parameter or int<SID>.ora file.

In a crash recovery, redo is applied one thread at a time because only one instance at a time can dirty a block in cache; in between block modifications the block is written to disk. Therefore a block in a current online file can read redo for at most one thread. This assumption cannot be made in media recovery as more than one instance may have made changes to a block, so changes must be applied to blocks in ascending SCN order, switching between threads where necessary.

In a RAC environment, where instances could be added or taken off the cluster dynamically, when an instance is added to the cluster, a thread enable record is written, a new thread of redo is created. Similarly, a thread is disabled when an instance is taken offline through a shutdown operation. The shutdown operation places an end of thread (EOT) flag on the log header.

Figure 12.4 illustrates the thread recovery scenario. In this scenario there are three instances, RAC1, RAC2, and RAC3, that form the RAC configuration. Each instance has set of redo log files and is assigned thread 1, thread 2, and thread 3 respectively.

Figure 12.4
Thread recovery.

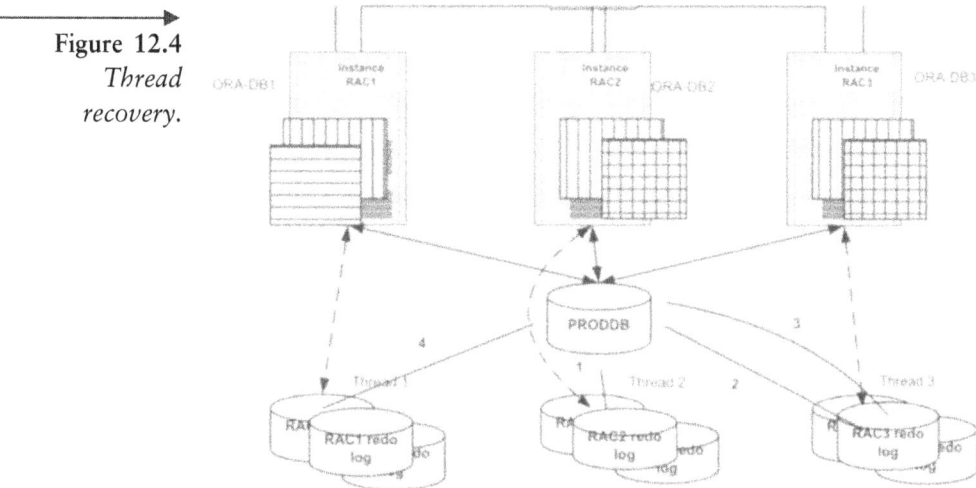

As discussed above, if multiple instances fail, or during a crash recovery, all instances have to synchronize the redo log files by the SCN number during the recovery operation. For example, in Figure 12.4, SCN #1 was applied to the database from thread 2, which belongs to instance RAC2, followed by SCN #2 from thread 3, which belongs to instance RAC 3, and SCN #3 also from thread 3, before applying SCN #4 from thread 1, which is assigned to instance RAC1.

Steps of media recovery

Oracle has to perform several steps during a media recovery from validating the first data file up to the recovery of the last data file. Determining if the archive logs have to be applied etc. is also carried out during this process. All database operations are sequenced using the database SCN number. Similarly, during a recovery operation, the SCN plays an even more important role because data has to be recovered in the order in which it was created.

1.   The first step during the media recovery process is to determine the lowest data file header checkpoint SCN of all data files being recovered. This information is stored in every data file header record.

     The output below is from a data file header dump and indicates the various markers validated during a media recovery process.

```
DATA FILE #1:
(name #233) /dev/vx/rdsk/oraracdg/partition1G_3
creation size=0 block size=8192 status=0xe head=233 tail=233 dup=1
 tablespace 0, index=1 krfil=1 prev_file=0
 unrecoverable scn: 0x0000.00000000 01/01/1988 00:00:00
 Checkpoint cnt:139 scn: 0x0000.06ffc050 11/20/2002 20:38:14
 Stop scn: 0xffff.ffffffff 11/16/2002 19:01:17
 Creation Checkpointed at scn:  0x0000.00000006 08/21/2002 17:04:05
 thread:0 rba:(0x0.0.0)
 enabled threads: 00000000 00000000 00000000 00000000
  00000000 00000000 00000000 00000000
 Offline scn: 0x0000.065acf1d prev_range: 0
 Online Checkpointed at scn:  0x0000.065acf1e 10/19/2002 09:43:15
 thread:1 rba:(0x1.2.0)
 enabled threads: 01000000 00000000 00000000 00000000 00000000
  00000000 00000000 00000000
 Hot Backup end marker scn: 0x0000.00000000
 aux_file is NOT DEFINED
 FILE HEADER:
 Software vsn=153092096=0x9200000, Compatibility
  Vsn=134217728=0x8000000
 Db ID=3598885999=0xd682a46f, Db Name='PRODDB'
 Activation ID=0=0x0
```

```
Control Seq=2182=0x886, File size=115200=0x1c200
File Number=1, Blksiz=8192, File Type=3 DATA
Tablespace #0 - SYSTEM  rel_fn:1
Creation   at   scn: 0x0000.00000006 08/21/2002 17:04:05
Backup taken at scn: 0x0000.00000000 01/01/1988 00:00:00 thread:0
  reset logs count:0x1c5a1a33 scn: 0x0000.065acf1e recovered at 11/16/
   2002 19:02:50
status:0x4 root dba:0x004000b3 chkpt cnt: 139 ctl cnt:138
begin-hot-backup file size: 0
Checkpointed at scn:  0x0000.06ffc050 11/20/2002 20:38:14
  thread:2 rba:(0x15.31aa6.10)
  enabled threads:  01100000 00000000 00000000 00000000 00000000
  00000000 00000000 00000000
Backup Checkpointed at scn:  0x0000.00000000
thread:0 rba:(0x0.0.0)
enabled threads:  00000000 00000000 00000000 00000000 00000000 00000000
  00000000 00000000
External cache id: 0x0 0x0 0x0 0x0
Absolute fuzzy scn: 0x0000.00000000
Recovery fuzzy scn: 0x0000.00000000 01/01/1988 00:00:00
Terminal Recovery Stamp scn: 0x0000.00000000 01/01/1988 00:00:00
```

If a data file's checkpoint is in its offline range, then the offline-end checkpoint is used instead of the data file header checkpoint as its media-recovery-start SCN.

Like the start SCN, Oracle uses the stop SCN on all data files to determine the highest SCN to allow recovery to terminate. This prevents a needless search beyond the SCN that actually needs to be applied.

During the media recovery process, Oracle automatically opens any enabled thread of redo and if the required redo records are not found in the current set of redo log files, the database administrator is prompted for the archived redo log files.

2. Oracle places an exclusive MR (media recovery) lock on the files undergoing recovery. This prevents two or more processes from starting media recovery operation simultaneously. The lock is acquired by the session that started the operation and is placed in a shared mode so that no other session can acquire the lock in exclusive mode.

3. The MR fuzzy bit is set to prevent the files from being opened in an inconsistent state.

4. The redo records from the various redo threads are merged to ensure that the redo records are applied in the right order using the ascending SCN.

5.   During the media recovery operation, checkpointing occurs as normal, updating the checkpoint SCN in the data file headers. This helps if there is a failure during the recovery process because it can be restarted from this SCN.

6.   This process continues until a stop SCN is encountered for a file, which means that the file was taken offline, or made read-only at this SCN and has no redo beyond this point. With the database open, taking a data file offline produces a finite stop SCN for that data file; if this is not done, there is no way for Oracle to determine when to stop the recovery process for a data file.

7.   Similarly, the recovery process continues until the current logs in all threads have been applied. The end of thread (EOT) flag that is part of the redo log header file of the last log guarantees that this has been accomplished.

The following output from a redo log header provides indication of the EOT marker found in the redo log file:

```
LOG FILE #6:
  (name #242) /dev/vx/rdsk/oracledg/partition1G_100
  (name #243) /dev/vx/rdsk/oracledg/partition1G_400
Thread 2 redo log links: forward: 0 backward: 5
siz: 0x190000 seq: 0x00000015 hws: 0x4 bsz: 512 nab:
  0xffffffff flg: 0x8 dup: 2
Archive links: fwrd: 3 back: 0 Prev scn: 0x0000.06e63c4e
Low scn: 0x0000.06e6e496 11/16/2002 20:32:19
Next scn: 0xffff.ffffffff 01/01/1988 00:00:00
FILE HEADER:
  Software vsn=153092096=0x9200000, Compatibility
  Vsn=153092096=0x9200000
  Db ID=3598885999=0xd682a46f, Db Name='PRODDB'
  Activation ID=3604082283=0xd6d1ee6b
  Control Seq=2181=0x885, File size=1638400=0x190000
  File Number=6, Blksiz=512, File Type=2 LOG
descrip:"Thread 0002, Seq# 0000000021, SCN
  0x000006e6e496-0xffffffffffff"
thread: 2 nab: 0xffffffff seq: 0x00000015 hws: 0x4 eot: 2 dis: 0
reset logs count: 0x1c5a1a33 scn: 0x0000.065acf1e
Low scn: 0x0000.06e6e496 11/16/2002 20:32:19
Next scn: 0xffff.ffffffff 01/01/1988 00:00:00
Enabled scn: 0x0000.065acfa2 10/19/2002 09:46:06
Thread closed scn: 0x0000.06ffc03e 11/20/2002 20:37:25
Log format vsn: 0x8000000 Disk cksum: 0xb28f Calc cksum: 0xb28f
Terminal Recovery Stamp scn: 0x0000.00000000 01/01/1988 00:00:00
Most recent redo scn: 0x0000.00000000
Largest LWN: 0 blocks
Miscellaneous flags: 0x0
```

5. GCS and GES failure

The GCS and GES services that comprise the LMS, LMD, and GRD processes provide the communication of requests over the cluster interconnect. These processes are also prone to failures. This could potentially happen when one or more of the processes participating in this configuration fails, or fails to respond within a predefined amount of time. Failures such as these could be as a result of failure of any of the related processes, a memory fault, or some other cause. The LMON on one of the surviving nodes should detect the problem and start the reconfiguration process. While this is occurring, no lock activity can take place, and some users will be forced to wait to obtain required PCM locks or other resources.

The recovery that occurs as a result of the GCS or GES process dying is termed online block recovery. This is another kind of recovery that is unique to the RAC implementation. Online block recovery occurs when a data buffer becomes corrupt in an instance's cache. Block recovery could also occur if either a foreground process dies while applying changes or if an error is generated during redo application. If the block recovery is to be performed as a result of the foreground process dying, then PMON initiates online block recovery. However, if this is not the case, then the foreground process attempts to make an online recovery of the block.

Under normal circumstances, this involves finding the block's predecessor and applying redo records to this predecessor from the online logs of the local instance. However, under the cache fusion architecture, copies of blocks are available in the cache of other instances and therefore the predecessor is the most recent PI for the buffer that exists in the cache of another instance. If, under certain circumstances, there is no PI for the corrupted buffer, the block image from the disk data is used as the predecessor image before changes from the online redo logs are used.

6. Instance hang or false failure

Under very unusual circumstances, probably due to an exception at the Oracle kernel level, an instance could encounter a hang condition, in which case the instance is up and running but no activity against this instance is possible. Users or processes that access this instance could encounter a hung connection and no response is received. In such a situation, the instance is neither down nor available for access. The other surviving instance may not receive a response from the hung instance; however, it cannot declare that the instance is not available because the required activity of the LMON process, such as writing to the shared disk, did not complete. Since the surviving instance did not receive any failure signal, it attempts to shut down the non-responding instance and is unable to because of the reasons stated above. In these situations the only opportunity is to perform a hard failure of either the entire node holding the hung instance or the instance itself. In either situation human interruption is required.

In the case of forcing a hard failure of the node holding the hung instance, the systems administrator will have to perform a bounce of the node; when the node is back up and alive the instance can be started.

In the case where the instance shutdown is preferred, no graceful shutdown is possible; instead, an operating-system-level intervention by shutting down one of the critical background processes such as SMON will cause an instance crash.

Recovery in both these scenarios is an instance recovery. All steps discussed in the section on instance failures apply to this type of failure.

12.6   Flashback queries

In Oracle 9*i*, with the introduction of the undo tablespace management feature, that replaces the rollback segment approach, Oracle has also added the feature of retention. With the retention feature, the previous images of data could be retained for a user-specified period of time. The feature that supports the visibility to the previous queries and data from the undo tablespace is called "flashback."

Using the flashback query feature provides visibility to data at a point-in-time in the past, and this data could be used to compare the data in the present. In the case of an UPDATE operation, the flashback query option provides visibility to the data exactly as it appeared before the UPDATE statement was executed.

How much of the past data is visible depends on the UNDO_ RETENTION parameter defined in the init<SID>.ora file. To retrieve these rows, Oracle has provided certain built-in packages such as DBMS_FLASH BACK and a set of standard procedures.

Benefits of using flashback query

■   Saving SCNs and flashing back to those SCNs, instead of saving data sets and retrieving them later, could gain application performance.

- Flashback queries are online operations, in the sense that while normal activity against the database is in progress, users could perform flashback query transactions against the UNDO tablespace without affecting the normal activity. This is possible because flashback query normally goes back in time and different sessions can flash back to different flashback times or SCNs on the same object concurrently.

- Apart from defining an appropriate value for the UNDO_RETENTION parameter, no additional management activity is required to perform flashback queries.

While flashback queries are good to retrieve and audit certain operations in the past, this feature cannot be used to undo any activity. It only helps identify changes during a period of time or changes performed by a specific SCN.

10g

New Feature: There are significant enhancements to the flashback functionality in Oracle 10g,

1. FLASHBACK DATABASE: will help bring the database to a prior point in time by undoing all the changes that have taken place since that time.
2. FLASHBACK TRANSACTION HISTORY: using the DBA_ TRANSACTION_QUERY view provided, changes to the database can be examined at the transaction level.
3. FLASHBACK TABLE: this statement helps quickly recover a table to a point in time in the past, eliminating the need to restore from a backup.
4   FLASHBACK DROP: Provides a way to restore accidentally dropped tables. When tables are dropped Oracle places them in a recycle bin from which they can later be recovered.

Flashback queries in RAC

Each instance in a two or more instance configuration such as RAC maintains its undo activity in their respective UNDO tablespaces. Similarly, each instance configures in its respective init<SID>.ora file the UNDO_RETENTION parameter that provides the threshold value on how many days' worth of undo data is retained, and makes the flashback query features specific to every instance.

12.7   Oracle LogMiner

Oracle's LogMiner is a tool to basically mine the redo log files. Through this mining operation, several purposes could be accomplished. For example, if a user accidentally deletes rows from the database, instead of retrieving the rows from a backup system (if the archive log files or the redo log files are easily available) through this mining operation, the rows could be easily retrieved. LogMiner provides both the redo and undo functionality, that is, when the DML statements are retrieved by mining the redo logs files, the statements retrieved could be utilized to perform a redo operation or an undo operation. It can be used to provide a historical view of the database without the need for point-in-time recovery.

Like most of the Oracle interfaces, LogMiner can be implemented and used either through the command line interface or using the GUI interface provided as part of the OEM product.

Figure 12.5 illustrates the various LogMiner components and how they interact with the other background processes of Oracle. The LogMiner uses the various external sources such as the online catalog, dynamic

Figure 12.5
LogMiner components.

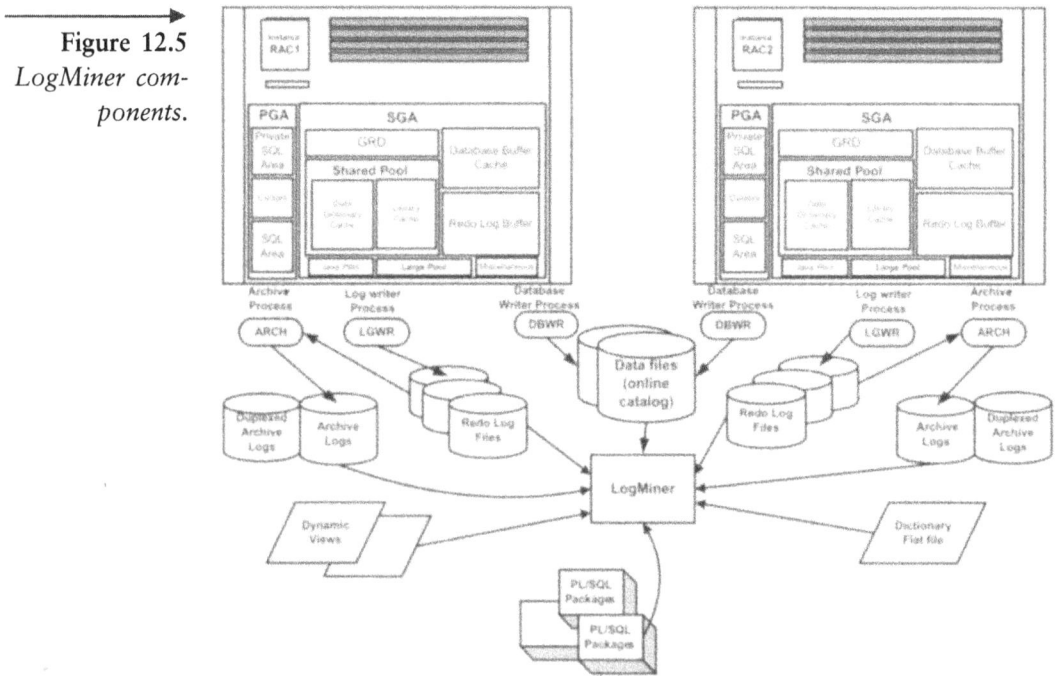

views, PL/SQL packages, and dictionary flat file to complete the required mining operation against the online redo log files or the archive redo log files.

LogMiner components

The LogMiner process is composed of the following components:

- PL/SQL packages
- Online redo log files
- Archive redo log files
- Dynamic views
- Online catalog
- Data dictionary

PL/SQL packages   Since LogMiner comes bundled with the RDBMS, the required LogMiner PL/SQL packages are installed when the database is created. To enable LogMiner, the following two PL/SQL scripts need to execute as user `sys`:

- `$ORACLE_HOME/rdbms/admin/dbmslmd.sql`
- `$ORACLE_HOME/rdbms/admin/dbmslm.sql`

These scripts contain all the packages required for the various steps of the LogMiner process.

Online redo log files   Most of the information required with respect to the past activity on the database is contained in the redo log files. If the activity had happened before, and a couple of redo log files switches have occurred, the information would be contained in the archive redo log files.

Archive redo log files   If the information expected is not contained in the online redo log files, the next alternative is to look for the information in the archive redo log files. It could be that the activity had happened a while ago and the archive redo log files that contain this information have been transferred to a permanent backup medium and the files deleted from disk. In this case, to retrieve the specific data, the archive log files for the period of time should be restored before performing this activity.

Dynamic views   With the default database installation, the following dynamic views are also created. These views are used to access the information that LogMiner retrieves from the redo log files. The following dynamic views are populated when a LogMiner session is started:

```
V$LOGMNR_CONTENTS
V$LOGMNR_DICTIONARY
V$LOGMNR_LOGS
V$LOGMNR_PARAMETERS
```

Online catalog   With this option, LogMiner uses the database's internal data dictionary as the LogMiner dictionary. To use the internal online dictionary, the database should be mounted and open. It is also required that the redo log files belong to the same database that the online dictionary belongs to.

Dictionary in a flat file   LogMiner could use a dictionary extracted to a text file. Since there is no direct access to the online dictionary, the database could be mounted or unmounted.

Using LogMiner

LogMiner can be used to:

- Audit past database activity, such as to determine the types and number of DML operations against a specific table and by a specific user.

- Track down corruption activity in the redo log files, find when this corruption occurred, and who caused this corruption.

- Pinpoint where to perform object-level recovery by SCN, either by using the SCN or by using date and time of transaction.

- Gather information about resource utilization and historical performance.

- Diagnose and debug problems within an application.

Mining the log files

LogMiner functions can be performed either by using the command line option or by using the GUI interface provided with the OEM product.

Command line interface   The following are the steps to mine a redo log file.

1.   LogMiner is started using the DBMS_LOGMNR.START_LOGMNR procedure. While executing this procedure, information such as the type of dictionary is specified. For example:

     a.   When using the online catalog,

```
EXECUTE DBMS_LOGMNR_START_LOGMNR
(options=>DBMS_LOGMNR_D.DICT_FROM_ONLINE_CATALOG);
```

> b. When using the dictionary flat file,

```
EXECUTE DBMS_LOGMNR_START_LOGMNR (DICTFILENAME=> 'opt/Oracle/logmnr/
   dictionary.ora');
```

> 2. Analyze the output using the Oracle-provided dynamic views. The V$LOGMNR_CONTENTS query is queried. This view provides the insight into the redo log files. The query executed against this view reads the redo log files and constructs one or more at a time in the V$LOGMNR_CONTENTS view. Every time the query is issued, LogMiner reads the entire redo log files again and returns the results to the view. This continues until all the data filtering criteria have been met.

> For example, to mine the redo log files and retrieve data from the salary table where salary for a specific value or higher was inserted the following is performed.

```
SELECT SQL_REDO, SQL_UNDO
FROM V$LOGMNR_CONTENTS
WHERE USERNAME = 'OLTP_USER_P'
AND TABLENAME = 'USER_PROFILE';


INSERT INTO USER_PROFILE
(USPRL_ID, USER_NAME, EMAIL,
ADDRESS) VALUES (498458,
'MVALLATH', 'murali.vallath@
summersky.biz','53494,
RAC drive, Big City,';
2 rows selected
```

```
SQL_REDO              SQL_UNDO
DELETE FROM USER_PROFILE WHERE
USPRL_ID= 498458 AND ROWID =
'AAABgPAAFAAACtEAAE';


INSERT INTO USER_PROFILE
(USPRL_ID, USER_NAME, EMAIL,
ADDRESS) VALUES (498458,
'MVALLATH', 'murali.vallath@
summersky.biz', '53494,
RAC drive, Big City,';
DELETE FROM USER_PROFILE
WHERE USPRL_ID=498458 AND
ROWID= 'AAABgPAAFAAACtEAAE';
```

> **Graphical user interface**   Oracle provides the LogMiner options to view the OEM product. The tool provides all functionalities that are available through the command line interface. However, OEM predefines most of the underlying scripts and provides immediate mining opportunities.

> Accessing the redo log files from the OEM product requires that the user performing the mining activity has SYSDBA privileges.

> After the tool has connected to the database (in a RAC environment, the tool is connected directly to the database and not to the instance), mining opportunities are provided to all redo log files that belong to all instances participating in the clustered configuration.

> Figure 12.6 is a snapshot view of the create query interface screen provided for LogMiner from the OEM product. The figure illustrates how selecting from the drop-down list of criteria (for example, user, owner, table name, etc.) helps in construction of the query.

Figure 12.6
LogMiner OEM
create query
interface.

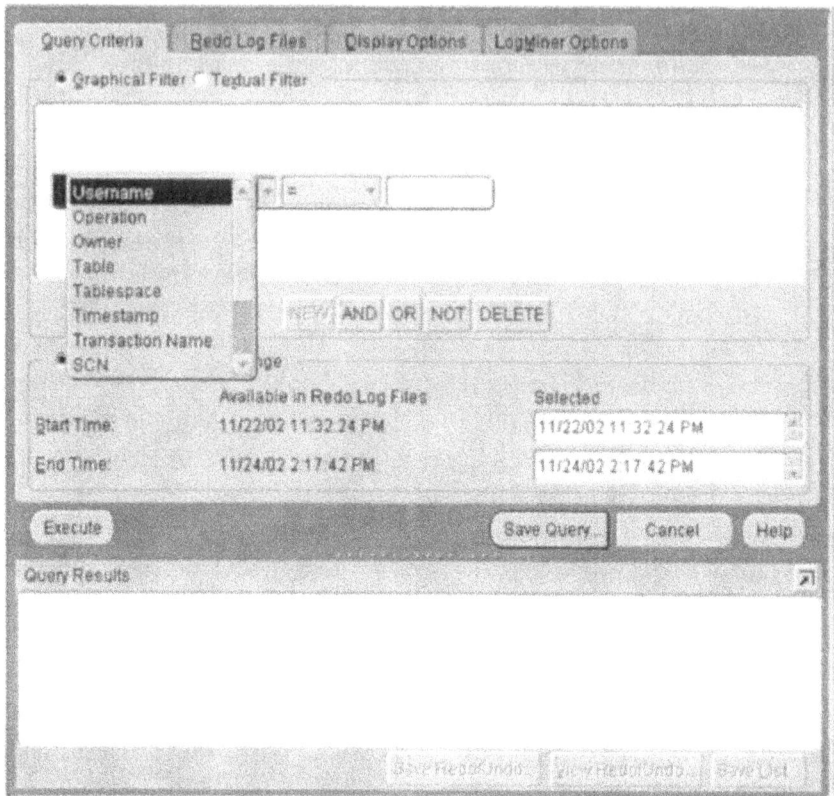

Figure 12.6
LogMiner OEM create query interface.

Once the user has created the required query condition and clicks on the "execute" button (if only the default selection criteria are required), the data from the current redo log files is filtered and displayed in a neat presentable format.

If additional conditions are to be specified, the tabs in the create query interface can be utilized to select the redo log files, and to specify the display criteria and LogMiner options such as formatting of output. For example, under this last tab option, OEM provides some additional options such as skipping redo log file corruptions, querying only committed transactions, etc. These options help filter good and clean data.

Figure 12.7 is a snapshot of the OEM LogMiner options interface. Through this interface, the selection is further trimmed down to provide a closer filtered data set from the online redo log files.

Once the conditions and options have been selected and the "execute" button is clicked, OEM will retrieve all queries from the redo log files that meet the selection criteria and display them on the interface.

Figure 12.7
*LogMiner OEM
options
interface.*

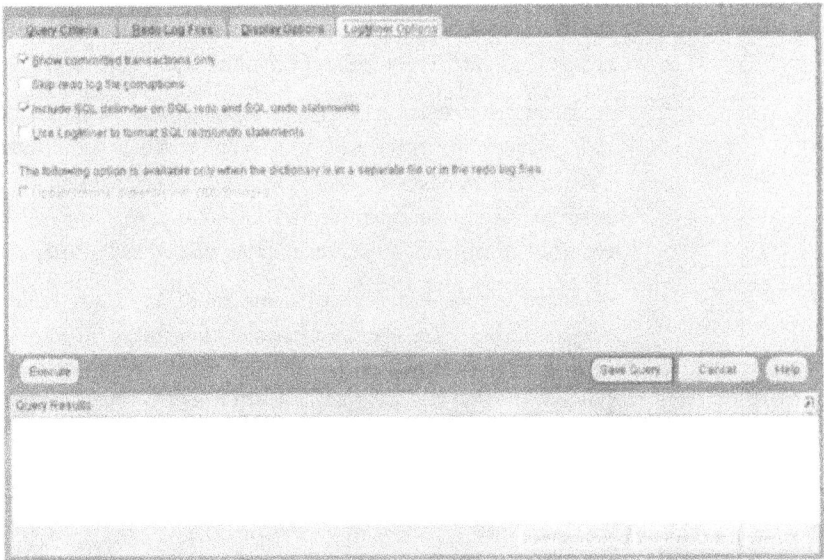

LogMining a RAC environment

Each instance in a two or more instance configuration such as RAC has its own set of online redo log files and a set of archive redo log files. Since LogMiner is used to mine the redo log files and the archive redo log files, separate requests against each of the instances need to be performed to retrieve all the rows.

12.5   Conclusion

In this chapter we looked at some of the critical administrative functions that database administrators perform in their day-to-day work schedule. Backing up a database protects against potential loss or corruption of the data due to various reasons that may or may not be within human control. To provide this solution, we looked at the various types of backup options in Oracle and focused on RMAN. RMAN provides a comprehensive solution leading towards a 24 hours a day, 7 days a week operation, where no downtime is required for backing up the data. RMAN provides this functionality through the various backup strategies such as full, cumulative, and incremental backups. Incremental backups allow the opportunity for frequent backups, because Oracle only backs up data blocks that have changed since the previous backup.

We discussed the fact that while developing a compressive backup and recovery strategy is important, it is equally important to schedule testing of the backup and recovery strategy to ensure that the changes in business conditions and economic conditions have not invalidated this strategy.

Backups are taken to help recover the database from failures. Under this subject we discussed the various kinds of failures in a stand-alone Oracle configuration and the additional kinds of failures in a RAC configuration, for example the GCS failures. During these failure scenarios we also discussed how the data is recovered under these circumstances.

Recovery is not always done from backups and not always done by Oracle. There are certain features available in Oracle where a database administrator could perform operations by going back into the past and retrieving database activities. Tools such as flashback queries and LogMiner provide this opportunity.

In Chapter 15, we will start discussions on performance tuning of a RAC configuration. However, before we dive into this subject, let us discuss the various tools that would help make the performance tuning activity easy. The next chapter will discuss the tools and utilities used in performance tuning.

13

Performance Tuning: Tools and Utilities

13.1   Introduction

In the previous chapter we discussed backup and recovery. We discussed why backup was one of the critical parts of any Information Technology implementation. Hardware redundancy provides availability to the computer system by making hardware components available as backup when the main components fail. In the case of data that is stored on the various hardware devices, such as operating system and database files, copies of these devices are required to be maintained at remote locations. When the main device fails, the data could be restored from these remote copies. We discussed various backup methods, hot, cold, and backups using RMAN. RMAN provides a more real-time backup method where backups could be performed while the database is operational without requiring any part of the database to be down or unusable.

We also looked at the various scenarios when a database, instance, node, and memory structures could fail, how during these various failure situations the various recovery methods are applied, and how Oracle performs the recovery.

Backup is important; equally important is the performance of the database system because there would no requirement for a backup system if the current database system is not usable because of its poor performance. User satisfaction is critical to the success of the enterprise system. On slowly performing systems, user satisfaction is seldom achievable.

Performance tuning is a very wide subject. There are several approaches to tuning a system. Tuning could be approached artistically like a violinist who tightens the strings to get the required sound, or where the performance engineer could make changes to the system by trying to improve the performance by trial and error. On the other hand, the performance engineer or DBA could take a more scientific approach to tuning, where he or she would collect statistics:

■ From areas of the application that are performing slowly.

■ During various times of the day when more users are using the system.

■ From heavily used functional areas of the application, etc.

Based on the data collected, the database performance engineer could take a more methodical approach to tuning the system. A methodical approach based on data and evidence is a better method of problem solving, more like a criminal investigation officer. Analysis should be backed by evidence. In this case, the collected data would help to understand the reasons for the slowness or poor performance.

Every reason should be backed by data and a scientific approach should be taken to tune the system, because there is a reason why a system is slow. Slow performance could be due to bad configuration, bad code, bad hardware, bad eyes, or bad anything. Unless there is foolproof evidence of why it is slow, no scientific approach to finding the root cause of the problem is possible. The old ancestral methodology that "tuning a computer system is an art" is not completely true, because tuning is not a hit-or-miss situation; it is to be approached in a scientific manner with supporting data.

Performance tuning will be covered in this and the next two chapters. In this chapter, we will look at the various tools for Oracle database tuning, its implementation and configuration and in the subsequent two chapters we will go into the specifics of tuning the database and overall tuning of a RAC system.

13.2   UTLBSTAT/UTLESTAT

The UTLBSTAT/UTLESTAT scripts are designed to provide a summary of Oracle activity over a reasonable period of time (>10 minutes). UTLBSTAT creates a snapshot of some of the internal Oracle dynamic performance views (V$ views). UTLESTAT creates a second snapshot of these views and reports on the differences between the two snapshots to a file called report.txt.

The UTLBSTAT/UTLESTAT scripts are shipped as standard with all Oracle releases. In Version 8.1.6 there is a new tool called STATSPACK which has improved functionality over what UTLBSTAT/UTLESTAT offer. Using STATSPACK you can collect more statistical information and store the performance statistics data permanently in Oracle tables enabling snapshot reporting.

13.3   STATSPACK

Oracle officially introduced a new utility for capturing performance data in Oracle Version 8.1.6 called STATSPACK. STATSPACK is a successor to the UTLBSTAT/UTLESTAT processes and works on a similar concept of capturing snapshots of the various performance views and comparing them against previous snapshots. UTLBSTAT/UTLESTAT capture statistics into temporary tables at the beginning, and after the UTLESTAT process reports on the differences between the two snapshots in the report.txt file, it deletes the snapshot data. STATSPACK does not delete the snapshot collection, thus providing access to historical information.

STATSPACK fundamentally differs from UTLBSTAT/UTLESTAT tuning scripts by collecting more information, and also by storing the performance statistics data permanently in Oracle tables, which can later be used for reporting and analysis. The data collected can be analyzed using the report provided, which includes an "instance health and load" summary page, high-resource SQL statements, as well as the traditional wait events and initialization parameters.

Permanent tables owned by PERFSTAT (a user created by the STATSPACK utility) store performance statistics. Instead of creating/dropping tables each time, data is inserted into the pre-existing tables. This makes historical data comparisons easier. STATSPACK also separates the data collection from the report generation. Data is collected when a "snapshot" is taken; viewing the data collected is in the hands of the performance engineer when he/she runs the script to generate the performance report.

There is a fundamental difference between the ways the two utilities compute certain information. For example, the STATSPACK utility increments a transaction counter on a commit or a rollback operation to calculate the number of transactions:

```
'user commits' + 'user rollbacks'
```

UTLBSTAT/UTLESTAT considers a transaction to complete with a commit only, and so assumes that transactions = "user commits." For this reason, comparing per transaction statistics between STATSPACK and

`UTLBSTAT`/`UTLESTAT` may result in significantly different transaction ratios.

With STATSPACK, Oracle separated the data collection phase from the reporting phase to allow for greater flexibility to establish performance baselines as well as to conduct trend reporting. Apart from this basic enhancement, STATSPACK provides visibility into various areas of database performance that is not provided by the `UTLBSTAT`/`UTLESTAT` utility. The reporting capability provides comparative views between two snapshot periods, and provides a high-level summary page indicating the overall health of the database for the given snapshot period followed by details on the performance characteristics.

Over the various releases of Oracle, the STATSPACK report has been considerably enhanced, providing even greater detail of information and insight to the actual performance problem.

13.3.1 Installing STATSPACK

With Oracle providing all the required scripts, STATSPACK installation has been made an easy task. All scripts are located in the `ORACLE_HOME/rdbms/admin` directory and the scripts are created when Oracle is installed on the server. STATSPACK scripts can be identified easily as they are prefixed with `sp*.sql`.

Prerequisites

Before the actual installation process, it is necessary to ensure that the basic requirements of installation have been identified and verified.

It should be ensured that the STATSPACK scripts are available in the appropriate directories:

- On a Unix platform, use the following command:

`ls -ltr $ORACLE_HOME/rdbms/admin/sp*.sql`

- On a Windows platform they should be available in a similar location at

`%ORACLE_HOME/rdbms/admin/sp*.sql`

As we have discussed earlier, the STATSPACK captures snapshots of performance statistics and stores them in permanent tables. Hence considerable effort should be provided in sizing the appropriate tablespaces based on the period of time that the data should be retained for historical purposes. For easy maintenance, it would be advisable to create tablespaces, to allow dropping and re-creation without affecting regular business data.

```
SQL>SPACK_DATA_P001
create tablespace SPACK_DATA_P001 datafile
'/dev/vx/rdsk/oraracdg/partition_500m1a' size 450M
    extent management local uniform size 1M
       segment space management auto;
```

During the process of gathering these snapshots and during subsequent reporting, Oracle performs a considerable number of sort operations. Based on the intervals at which the various snapshots are captured and how busy the system has been during this period, the amount of sort activity could be very high. In order to isolate the sort activity performed by STATSPACK from the sort activity performed by the regular application, it is advisable to create a separate TEMP tablespace exclusively for STATSPACK:

```
SQL>SPACK_TEMP_P001
```

Understanding the STATSPACK scripts

STATSPACK scripts are modularized. The main driver script called `spcreate.sql` controls the installation of the STATSPACK utility and this script calls the `spcusr.sql`, `spctab.sql`, and `spcpkg.sql` scripts. In order to report any errors during the installation, these scripts generate `.lis` files, which are verified to ensure that the installation has completed successfully.

Figure 13.1 illustrates the script interface and their dependency matrix. While the straight lines indicate how each of the scripts are called, the

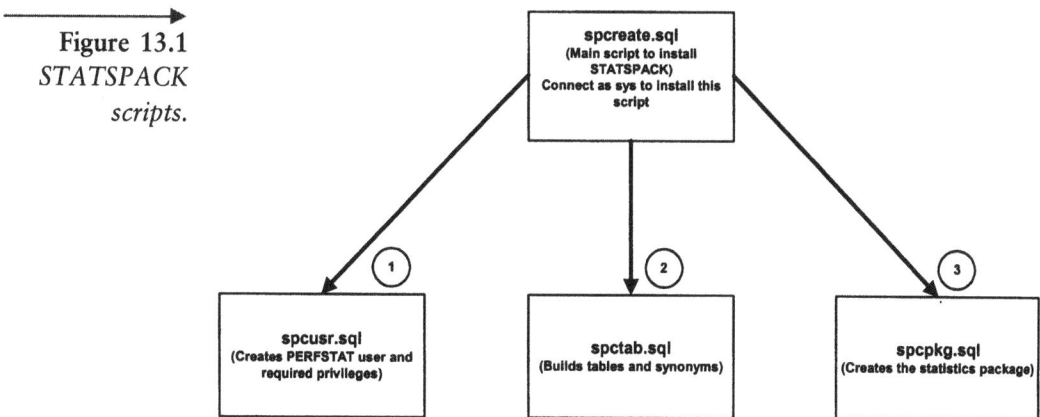

Figure 13.1
STATSPACK
scripts.

Table 13.1   *STATSPACK Scripts*

Script	Purpose
`spurge.sql`	Deletes data pertaining to specific snapshots or a range of snapshots
`spreport.sql`	Generates a report on the overall database performance between two snapshot periods
`spauto.sql`	Creates a DBMS_JOB scheduled at regular intervals and collects snapshots of the database performance
`sptrunc.sql`	Truncates all the tables, moving the high water mark to the beginning
`spdrop.sql`	Used to uninstall STATSPACK
`sprepins.sql`	Generates a report on information from a different instance. This is helpful in a RAC environment where reports from multiple instances are required
`sprepsql.sql`	Generates a report providing SQL run time statistics for a specific SQL statement

numbers indicate the order in which they are executed from the `spcreate.sql` script. The order also indicates the dependency of each script on the next.

There are few other scripts that do not have any direct dependency on the above scripts but require the previous set of scripts to be completed successfully before they can be run.

Table 13.1 provides a list of certain important STATSPACK scripts and their purposes. The script that is commonly used is `spreport.sql`, which provides a report on the overall database performance between two snapshot periods.

Installation

STATSPACK installation requires that the user running the scripts has the `SYSDBA` privileges. It is idle to run the scripts as user `sys`.

1.   Connect using SQL*Plus as user `sys`:

```
sqlplus
SQL> connect as sys/<password> as sysdba
SQL>
```

2. Execute the following script:

SQL> @$ORACLE_HOME/rdbms/admin/spcreate.sql

This script will in turn run the three other scripts, `spcusr.sql`, `spctab.sql`, and `spcpack.sql` to create the user, tables, and the packages that constitute the STATSPACK utility.

During the execution process, the only user inputs that are required is the name of the default tablespace where the STATSPACK-specific tables are to be created and the temporary tablespace required for the temp sort area.

> **Note:** `spcusr.sql` will create the `PERFSTAT` user with a default password of `PERFSTAT`. After the user is created, the script automatically connects as the `PERFSTAT` user before executing the remaining scripts.

In a RAC implementation, since the underlying database is the same for all instances, the `spcreate.sql` script should only be executed once. However, for gathering statistics, the required `spauto.sql` script could be executed individually on all instances participating in the clustered configuration. This is because the data relevant to the instance performance needs to be gathered individually by each instance.

13.3.2 Configuration

After the successful execution of the scripts provided, the STATSPACK utility is installed and after verification of all the `.lis` files to ensure that the installation did not generate any errors, the next step is configuring STATSPACK to collect statistics.

The configuration process is to ensure that the STATSPACK scripts are executed to collect snapshots of the database performance. Having the correct settings will prove extremely valuable to establish effective performance baselines or troubleshooting a performance issue.

To determine the amount of data that a STATSPACK snapshot will collect, Oracle has divided this data gathering process based on two different conditions:

- Snapshot level, which will determine the granularity and volume of snapshot information to be collected.

- SQL threshold, which will determine the amount of SQL to be captured when snapshot level 5 or greater is used.

Snapshot level

Oracle provides up to five levels of information gathering, depending on the granularity of the data that is to be collected. The higher the level, the more information is gathered. The data gathered is later analyzed using a report generated by the `spreport.sql` script.

Level 0: General performance

This level can be used to gather general performance information about the database. General performance information pertaining to the following areas is collected:

- Wait statistics
- System events
- System statistics
- Rollback segment data
- Row cache
- SGA
- Latch statistics
- Background events
- Session events
- Lock statistics
- Buffer pool statistics
- Resource limit
- Enqueue statistics

   If enabled, statistics will also be gathered for the following:

- Automatic undo management
- Buffer cache advisory data
- Auto PGA memory management
- Cluster DB statistics

Level 5: Level 0 + SQL statements

Level 5 will gather all the information from the previous level, plus it will collect performance data on high-resource SQL statements. This is also the default snapshot level.

When this snapshot level is chosen, there are additional SQL-related configuration parameter settings that can be adjusted. These parameters are called SQL thresholds. These parameters and their allowable settings are discussed later.

The STATSPACK information gatherer at this level and beyond collects high-performance SQL statements, which are retrieved by probing the shared pool of the instance. The larger the size of the pool, the greater the number of statements likely to be cached, and the STATSPACK information gatherer has to browse through more areas to capture all the complex queries.

The duration of a snapshot generation at this level is directly affected by the size assigned to the SHARED_POOL_SIZE initialization parameter setting for the database. A low value assigned to the SHARED_POOL_SIZE will result in a shorter duration of this snapshot, whereas a high value will result in a longer duration.

Level 6: Level 5 + SQL plans and plan usage

Level 6 will gather all the information from the previous level, plus it will collect execution plans and the plan usage as they relate to the high-performing SQL queries captured in the previous level.

The higher the level (in order to capture the performance statistics and store them in the STATSPACK tables) the more resources are required by the information gatherer. Also the more data that is to be stored, the more the space and insert time to store the data is needed; hence unless information with this much detail is required most of the time, basic level 5 information should be sufficient. Higher levels could be utilized to drill down after a specific problem has been identified.

Level 7: Level 6 + segment level statistics

Level 7 will gather all the information from the previous level, plus it will collect performance data on highly used segments. *At this level any RAC-specific segment-level statistics are also collected.*

Segment-level information collected at this level helps make decisions about modification of physical layout on certain segments or tablespaces.

```
Top 5 CR Blocks Served (RAC) per Segment for DB: PRODDB Instance: RAC1
  Snaps:
-> End Global Cache CR Blocks Served Threshold: 1000
                                            CU
                      Subobject    Obj.      Blocks
Owner       Tablespace Object Name  Name      Type    Served  %Total
--------    ---------- ----------   ----------  ------  ------  ------
MVALLATH    USPRL_PK_  PK_USPRL     _INDX_P003  INDEX   1,065    12.9
MVALLATH    INDX_TBS20 COMP_INDX7               INDEX     963   11.72
MVALLATH    USERS      PK_USEC                  INDEX     704    8.57
MVALLATH    COMP_DATA_ COMPANY      _DATA_P003  TABLE     525    6.39
MVALLATH    USRLI_DATA USER_LOGIN   _DATA_P001  TABLE     437    5.32
-------------------------------------------------------------------

Top 5 CU Blocks Served (RAC) per Segment for DB: PRODDB Instance: RAC
  Snaps:
-> End Global Cache CU Blocks Served Threshold: 1000
                                            CU
                      Subobject    Obj.      Blocks
Owner       Tablespace Object Name  Name      Type    Served  %Total
--------    ---------- ------------ ---------  ------  ------  ------
MVALLATH    COMP_DATA_ COMPANY      _DATA_P002 TABLE  21,536   58.40
MVALLATH    COMP_DATA_ COMPANY      _DATA_P003 TABLE   5,755   15.61
MVALLATH    USPRL_DATA USER_PROFILE _DATA_P002 TABLE   2,537    6.88
MVALLATH    USERS      PK_USRLI     INDEX        662    1.80
MVALLATH    INDX_TBS30 USRLI_INDX1  _INDX_P001 INDEX    631    1.71
-------------------------------------------------------------------
```

Level 10: Level 7 + parent–child latches

Level 10 will gather all the information from the previous level, plus it will collect parent–child latch information.

Due to the extensive detail of statistics collected at this level, gathering snapshot information at this level should be done with great caution.

SQL threshold

While capturing high-resource SQL queries, certain additional criteria or threshold values can be defined, for example, capture SQL queries with number of executions greater than 500.

Defining threshold values for various criteria provides additional levels of filtering when capturing SQL queries that have performance issues.

Table 13.2 *Threshold parameter descriptions and values*

Threshold Parameter Description	Default Value
Number of executions of the SQL statement	100
Number of disk reads performed by the SQL statement	1000
Number of parse calls performed by the SQL statement	1000
Number of buffer gets performed by the SQL statement	10,000
Size of shareable memory used by the SQL statement	1 MB
Version count for the SQL statement	20
Number of global cache consistent read blocks served (RAC)	1000
Number of global cache current blocks served (RAC)	1000

Table 13.3 *STATSPACK Parameters and Values*

Parameter	Description	Range of Values	Default Values
I_snap_level	Snapshot level	0, 5, 6, 7, 10	5
I_uncomment	Comment to accompany snapshot	Text	Blank
I_executions_th	Number of times SQL statement executed	Integer ≥ 0	100
I_disk_reads_th	Number of disk reads that a statement makes	Integer ≥ 0	1000
I_parse_calls_th	Number of parse calls the statement makes	Integer ≥ 0	1000
I_buffer_gets_th	Number of buffer gets the statement makes	Integer ≥ 0	10,000
I_sharable_mem_th	Amount of shareable memory	Integer ≥ 0	1 MB
I_session_id	Session ID to capture session granular statistics	Valid SID from V$SESSION	0
I_modify_parameter	Save the parameters specified for future	True, False	False

Table 13.2 provides a list of threshold descriptions and their default values. Thresholds can be set during snapshot collection. If no value is specified for the threshold parameters, the default values shown are applied.

Table 13.3 provides a list of parameters that can be used with the STATSPACK utility during snapshot collection. If the parameters and a corresponding value are not used, the default values shown are applied during snapshot gathering.

13.3.3   Execution

Snapshots to collect statistics can be gathered in one of two ways:

- Interactively, by executing the following command:

```
SQL> EXECUTE STATSPACK.SNAP();
```

or by passing in a value to one of the parameters listed in Table 13.3. For example using the I_snap_level parameter to collect snapshot at a specific level (0, 5, 6, 7, 10)

```
SQL> EXECUTE STATSPACK.SNAP(I_snap_level=>n)
```

where 'n' could have a value of 0, 5, 6, 7, or 10.

- Through an automated script that is executed at fixed intervals either through the Oracle provided DBMS_JOB package or through an operating-system-based utility such as cron shell or perl script. Oracle provides, along with the other STATSPACK scripts, a script spauto.sql to automate the snapshot collection using the DBMS_JOB package. If the spauto.sql script is executed for automated snapshot collection, the data is gathered every hour by the hour:

```
SQL>$ORACLE_HOME/rdbms/admin/spauto.sql
```

13.3.4   Reporting

The STATSPACK utility has been installed and configured, and snapshots have been taken at various intervals. Now the data gathered needs to be analyzed after extracting the data through a report generator. Oracle provides a report generator with STATSPACK. This script will provide the overall health of the database between two snapshot periods.

To generate this report, the `spreport.sql` script is executed, and the script requests for snapshot information: basically the starting and ending snapshot information that needs to be compared and the interval during which the performance summary of the instance is required.

```
SQL> @$ORACLE_HOME/rdbms/admin/spreport.sql

Current Instance
~~~~~~~~~~~~~~~~

3598885999 PRODDB          2 RAC1

Instances in this STATSPACK schema
~~~~~~~~~~~~~~~~~~~~~~~~~~~~~~~~~~~~

3598885999      1 PRODDB      RAC1      ora-db1.summerskyus.com
3598885999      2 PRODDB      RAC2      ora-db2.summerskyus.com


Using 3598885999 for database Id

Using         2 for instance number

Completed Snapshots

                                        Snap        Snap
Instance    DB Name      Id       Snap Started      Level    Comment
--------    -------     -----   ----------------   ------    -------
RAC2        PRODDB      3509    22 Nov 2002 12:02     10
                        3515    22 Nov 2002 14:03     10
                        3520    22 Nov 2002 15:04     10
                        3526    22 Nov 2002 16:04     10
                        3527    22 Nov 2002 17:01     10


Specify the Begin and End Snapshot Ids
~~~~~~~~~~~~~~~~~~~~~~~~~~~~~~~~~~~~~~~~

Enter value for begin_snap: 3509
Begin Snapshot Id specified: 3509

Enter value for end_snap: 3526
End   Snapshot Id specified: 3526

Specify the Report Name
~~~~~~~~~~~~~~~~~~~~~~~~~
The default report file name is sp_3509_3526.  To use this name, press
   <return> to continue, otherwise enter an alternative.
Enter value for report_name:
```

Analysing the report

If no value is specified for the report a default name is used.

The output shown below is the first page of the STATSPACK report and provides the overall health of the instance, which includes:

- *Instance characteristics:* This includes the database name, instance name, Oracle version, and the snapshot information.

- *Cache sizes:* This section shows the various cache sizes based on the initRAC1.ora parameters.

- *Load profile:* This section provides the database load characteristics during the snapshot period. It provides insight into potential problems with the instance. For example, a high hard parse could indicate that the SQL queries may be using literals and requires a parse operation because of using different values during every execution. There are a large number of physical reads per second, which could also mean that the queries have not been tuned well or the queries are performing full table scans instead of index-based retrieval.

- *Instance efficiency percentages (ratios):* The various performance ratios and their respective values during this snapshot period are listed.

- *Shared pool statistics:* Indicates the amount of shared pool consumed during the snapshot period.

- *Top 5 Timed (wait) events:* This is a very important section of the STATSPACK report and provides the top 5 reasons why an instance is behaving the way it is. The top 5 waits indicate the overall health of the database. This section also provides the CPU information for this snapshot period; inclusion of CPU statistics in the STATSPACK report is new in Oracle *9i*.

```
        STATSPACK report for

DB Name      DB Id Instance Inst Num   Release Cluster           Host
------      ----- -------- -------    ------- -------           ----
PRODDB  3598885999    RAC1          1 9.2.0.2.0    YES       ora-db1.
                                                          summerskyus.com


Snap Id       Snap Time               Sessions  Curs/Sess  Comment
-------      ---------       ------------------ ---------  ------
Begin Snap:     3509  22-Nov-02 12:00:02     #######         .0
End Snap:       3526  22-Nov-02 16:00:04     #######         .0
Elapsed:                    240.03 (mins)


Cache Sizes (end)
~~~~~~~~~~~~~~~~~
     Buffer Cache:    1,024M    Std Block Size:       8K
```

```
        Shared Pool Size:        256M        Log Buffer:    976K
Load Profile
~~~~~~~~~~~~~
                              Per Second          Per Transaction
                            --------------        ----------------
Redo size:                     3,103.00             1,360.33
Logical reads:                16,323.94             2,772.35
Block changes:                   119.86                18.70
Physical reads:                3,495.09               121.35
Physical writes:                  28.42                11.50
User calls:                      114.31                50.11
Parses:                          168.06                73.68
Hard parses:                    3958.01               199.00
Sorts:                          1287.61               126.09
Logons:                       10,348.00                98.76
Executes:                        174.20                76.37
Transactions:                      2.28


  % Blocks changed per Read:  0.31  Recursive Call %: 87.42
Rollback per transaction% : 13.50  Rows per Sort    :   3.79

Instance Efficiency Percentages (Target 100%)
~~~~~~~~~~~~~~~~~~~~~~~~~~~~~~~~~~~~~~~~~~~~~~~~~~~~~

   Buffer Nowait  %:  100.00       Redo NoWait  %:  100.00
      Buffer Hit  %:  100.00    In-memory Sort % :  100.00
     Library Hit  %:  100.00        Soft Parse  %:  100.00
  Execute to Parse %:    3.52        Latch Hit % :   99.98
Parse CPU to Parse Elapsd %:92.06  % Non-Parse CPU:   97.95

Shared Pool Statistics       Begin   End
                             ------  ------
             Memory Usage %:   40.38   41.62
   % SQL with executions>1:   66.67   66.39
  % Memory for SQL w/exec>1:   63.38   64.26

Top 5 Timed Events
~~~~~~~~~~~~~~~~~~~~~
                %Total
Event                      Waits      Time (s)    Ela Time
----------------------     ------     --------    --------
CPU time                                5,085       49.68
enqueue                    17,618       3,442       33.63
global cache null to x     30,079         399        3.90
global cache cr request   105,492         353        3.45
log file sync              36,619         272        2.66
         ------------------------------------------------------------
```

- *Workload characteristics:* The output section below provides RAC-specific information; this information is not found in a STATSPACK report generated for a stand-alone configuration.

```
Cluster Statistics for DB: PRODDB  Instance: RAC1  Snaps: 3509 -3526
Global Cache Service - Workload Characteristics
--------------------------------------------------
Ave global cache get time (ms):                              2.7
Ave global cache convert time (ms):                         10.2

Ave build time for CR block (ms):                            0.1
Ave flush time for CR block (ms):                            2.5
Ave send time for CR block (ms):                             0.2
Ave time to process CR block request (ms):                   2.8
Ave receive time for CR block (ms):                          3.7

Ave pin time for current block (ms):                         9.1
Ave flush time for current block (ms):                       0.9
Ave send time for current block (ms):                        0.2
Ave time to process current block request (ms):             10.2
Ave receive time for current block (ms):                    10.6

Global cache hit ratio:                                      0.2
Ratio of current block defers:                               0.1
% of messages sent for buffer gets:                          0.2
% of remote buffer gets:                                     0.2
Ratio of I/O for coherence:                                  0.2
Ratio of local vs remote work:                               0.4
Ratio of fusion vs physical writes:                          0.0

Global Enqueue Service Statistics
---------------------------------
Ave global lock get time (ms):                               1.9
Ave global lock convert time (ms):                          48.8
Ratio of global lock gets vs global lock releases:           1.1

GCS and GES Messaging statistics
--------------------------------
Ave message sent queue time (ms):                            0.1
Ave message sent queue time on ksxp (ms):                    0.6
Ave message received queue time (ms):                        0.0
Ave GCS message process time (ms):                           0.2
Ave GES message process time (ms):                           0.0
% of direct sent messages:                                  94.2
% of indirect sent messages:                                 5.1
% of flow controlled messages:                               0.7
--------------------------------------------------------------

GES Statistics for DB: PRODDB  Instance: RAC1  Snaps: 3509-3526
Statistic                               Total      per        per
                                                  Second     Trans
-----------------------------------     -----    ------     ------
dynamically allocated gcs resourc           0      0.0        0.0
dynamically allocated gcs shadows            0      0.0        0.0
flow control messages received               0      0.0        0.0
flow control messages sent                   0      0.0        0.0
gcs ast xid                                 11      0.0        0.0
gcs blocked converts                    34,077      2.4        1.0
gcs blocked cr converts                 64,259      4.5        2.0
gcs compatible basts                        12      0.0        0.0
```

```
gcs compatible cr basts (global)        3,595      0.2      0.1
gcs compatible cr basts (local)            21      0.0      0.0
gcs cr basts to PIs                         0      0.0      0.0
gcs cr serve without current lock           0      0.0      0.0
gcs error msgs                              0      0.0      0.0
gcs flush pi msgs                       1,358      0.1      0.0
gcs forward cr to pinged instance           0      0.0      0.0
gcs immediate (compatible) conver       2,272      0.2      0.1
gcs immediate (null) converts           3,857      0.3      0.1
gcs immediate cr (compatible) con          24      0.0      0.0
gcs immediate cr (null) converts       32,803      2.3      1.0
gcs msgs process time(ms)              35,540      2.5      1.1
gcs msgs received                     157,776     11.0      4.8
gcs out-of-order msgs                       0      0.0      0.0
gcs pings refused                          18      0.0      0.0
gcs queued converts                         4      0.0      0.0
gcs recovery claim msgs                     0      0.0      0.0
gcs refuse xid                              3      0.0      0.0
gcs retry convert request                   0      0.0      0.0
gcs side channel msgs actual            1,636      0.1      0.0
gcs side channel msgs logical         144,217     10.0      4.4
gcs write notification msgs                 2      0.0      0.0
gcs write request msgs                  1,954      0.1      0.1
gcs writes refused                         32      0.0      0.0
ges msgs process time(ms)               8,398      0.6      0.3
ges msgs received                     211,190     14.7      6.4
implicit batch messages received          905      0.1      0.0
implicit batch messages sent              431      0.0      0.0
lmd msg send time(ms)                   3,394      0.2      0.1
lms(s) msg send time(ms)                  112      0.0      0.0
messages flow controlled                2,052      0.1      0.1
messages received actual              365,272     25.4     11.1
messages received logical             368,964     25.6     11.2
messages sent directly                277,620     19.3      8.5
messages sent indirectly               14,960      1.0      0.5
msgs causing lmd to send msgs          62,250      4.3      1.9
msgs causing lms(s) to send msgs       14,573      1.0      0.4
msgs received queue time (ms)           8,999      0.6      0.3
msgs received queued                  368,963     25.6     11.2
msgs sent queue time (ms)               1,363      0.1      0.0
msgs sent queue time on ksxp (ms)     174,191     12.1      5.3
msgs sent queued                       15,004      1.0      0.5
msgs sent queued on ksxp              292,726     20.3      8.9
process batch messages received           474      0.0      0.0
process batch messages sent               211      0.0      0.0
          --------------------------------------------------------
```

```
Wait Events for DB: PRODDB  Instance: RAC1  Snaps:
   3509 -3526
-> s  - second
-> cs - centisecond -     100th of a second
-> ms - millisecond -    1000th of a second
```

```
-> us - microsecond - 1000000th of a second
-> ordered by wait time desc, waits desc (idle events last)
```

Event	Waits	Timeouts	Total Wait Time (s)	Avg wait (ms)	Waits /txn
enqueue	17,618	1,775	3,442	195	0.5
global cache null to x	30,079	23	399	13	0.9
global cache cr request	105,492	101	353	3	3.2
log file sync	36,619	49	272	7	1.1
DFS lock handle	92,013	29	235	3	2.8
control file parallel write	4,659	0	53	11	0.1
buffer busy global cache	1,152	0	44	38	0.0
log file parallel write	36,209	36,201	42	1	1.1
control file sequential read	18,309	0	35	2	0.6
PX Deq: Execute Reply	10,797	0	31	3	0.3
PX Deq: Parse Reply	13,099	0	30	2	0.4
PX qref latch	29	29	28	981	0.0
direct path read	2,625	0	26	10	0.1
PX Deq: Join ACK	13,793	6,592	26	2	0.4
buffer busy global CR	1,617	0	19	12	0.0
global cache open x	2,592	0	13	5	0.1
global cache s to x	8,153	3	13	2	0.2
SQL*Net more data to client	164,396	0	10	0	5.0
PX Deq: Signal ACK	3,990	1,357	10	3	0.1
PX Deq: reap credit	210,299	195,058	8	0	6.4
IPC send completion sync	6,707	0	8	1	0.2
global cache busy	193	0	7	35	0.0
wait for master scn	9,528	0	6	1	0.3
buffer busy waits	289	0	5	18	0.0
db file parallel write	1,803	0	5	3	0.1
db file sequential read	424	0	4	9	0.0
direct path write	6,032	0	4	1	0.2
global cache open s	1,944	0	4	2	0.1
row cache lock	126	0	3	27	0.0
process startup	12	1	3	261	0.0
global cache null to s	875	0	3	3	0.0
library cache lock	4,903	0	2	0	0.1
latch free	519	228	1	3	0.0
CGS wait for IPC msg	50,310	46,897	1	0	1.5
name-service call wait	4	1	1	304	0.0
ksxr poll remote instances	37,777	23,639	1	0	1.1
SQL*Net break/reset to clien	240	0	0	2	0.0
KJC: Wait for msg sends to c	939	0	0	0	0.0
PX Deq Credit: send blkd	27	0	0	2	0.0
library cache pin	39	0	0	1	0.0
LGWR wait for redo copy	43	0	0	0	0.0
buffer deadlock	84	83	0	0	0.0
cr request retry	47	47	0	0	0.0
lock escalate retry	18	18	0	0	0.0

```
SQL*Net message from
  client                    1,611,345        0    201,600    125   49.0
PX Idle Wait                   33,509   26,541     72,502   2164    1.0
gcs remote message            443,378  288,380     27,927     63   13.5
ges remote message            487,520  268,165     14,028     29   14.8
PX Deq: Execution Msg          28,974    1,101      7,113    246    0.9
```

Wait Events for DB: PRODDB Instance: RAC1 Snaps: 3509 -3526

-> s - second
-> cs - centisecond -   100th of a second
-> ms - millisecond -   1000th of a second
-> us - microsecond - 1000000th of a second
-> ordered by wait time desc, waits desc (idle events last)

Event	Waits	Timeouts	Total Wait Time (s)	Avg wait (ms)	Waits /txn
jobq slave wait	172	166	512	2975	0.0
SQL*Net more data from clien	3,786	0	224	59	0.1
SQL*Net message to client	1,611,349	0	3	0	49.0

Background Wait Events for DB: PRODDB Instance: RAC1 Snaps: 3509 -3526
-> ordered by wait time desc, waits desc (idle events last)

Event	Waits	Timeouts	Total Wait Time (s)	Avg wait (ms)	Waits /txn
log file sync	2,952	27	71	24	0.1
control file parallel write	4,659	0	53	11	0.1
log file parallel write	36,209	36,201	42	1	1.1
control file sequential read	17,281	0	35	2	0.5
DFS lock handle	830	0	4	5	0.0
row cache lock	25	0	3	118	0.0
db file parallel write	925	0	2	3	0.0
enqueue	1,388	0	1	1	0.0
process startup	8	0	1	164	0.0
CGS wait for IPC msg	50,310	46,897	1	0	1.5
global cache null to x	11	0	0	1	0.0
latch free	15	1	0	1	0.0
global cache cr request	8	0	0	1	0.0
rdbms ipc reply	13	0	0	0	0.0
buffer busy waits	6	0	0	1	0.0
LGWR wait for redo copy	43	0	0	0	0.0
global cache null to s	2	0	0	1	0.0
library cache lock	2	0	0	1	0.0
global cache s to x	1	0	0	1	0.0

```
global cache open x                1        0        0        1    0.0
KJC: Wait for msg                  2        0        0        0    0.0
   sends to c
rdbms ipc message            206,156  126,240   95,578      464    6.3
ges remote message           487,521  268,166   14,028       29   14.8
gcs remote message           208,763  146,147   13,966       67    6.4
smon timer                        52       43   13,265   ######    0.0
```

> **Note:** For more discussions about many of the above statistics and wait events, please refer to the subsequent chapters on performance tuning.

13.4   Oracle Enterprise Manager

Oracle Enterprise Manager (OEM) comes bundled with the Oracle Enterprise Edition and can be installed on the same node as the database server or can be installed separately on another machine, which is the preferred approach. For example, if the database server is on a Unix operating system, OEM could very well be installed on this machine. However, due to the more textual nature of the operating system, invoking the GUI interface of OEM would require some emulation tools such as X-Windows. Due to this dependency and the unfriendly nature, OEM is normally installed as two separate tiers, the OEM repository and the OEM console/client. While the client is normally installed on a Windows-based workstation, the repository could be installed on any operating system, including Unix.

OEM can be installed from the Oracle Universal Installer (OUI) by selecting the Oracle 9*i* Management and Integration option.

OEM comprises a three-tier configuration: the target database that needs to be controlled or monitored from OEM, the middle tier or the management server (also called the repository) where all the target database information is collected and stored, and the client or console tier used to display the information.

The repository is used to capture and store information pertaining to the target tier.

The front tier is the console and is used to monitor the database (target tiers) via the management server, or directly using the local tnsnames.ora file. If the direct approach is used, it bypasses the management server and the tool only supports the basic functionality such as database administration. Storing the information in the management server provides additional functionality, such as sending a page to a DBA when any alert is encountered and collecting target tier statistics when the DBA is not monitoring the console for historical information.

The target tier comprises the instance, the database, and the intelligent agent that runs in the background and helps communicate database-related information back to the server. The intelligent agent also contains a data gatherer that is used to gather data on a continuous basis even when no-one is monitoring the console.

Figure 13.2 illustrates the OEM component architecture. It represents the three-tier configuration consisting of the console or the user interface tier, middle tier or the management server tier, and the end tier or the target database tier. The end tier can consist of multiple databases and instances across one or more environments and locations that the OEM will monitor and manage. OEM also supports each target tier being on different operating systems.

OEM provides a good deal of troubleshooting opportunities, provided the product has been configured correctly. Compared to the single stand-alone configuration, installation and configuration of OEM for

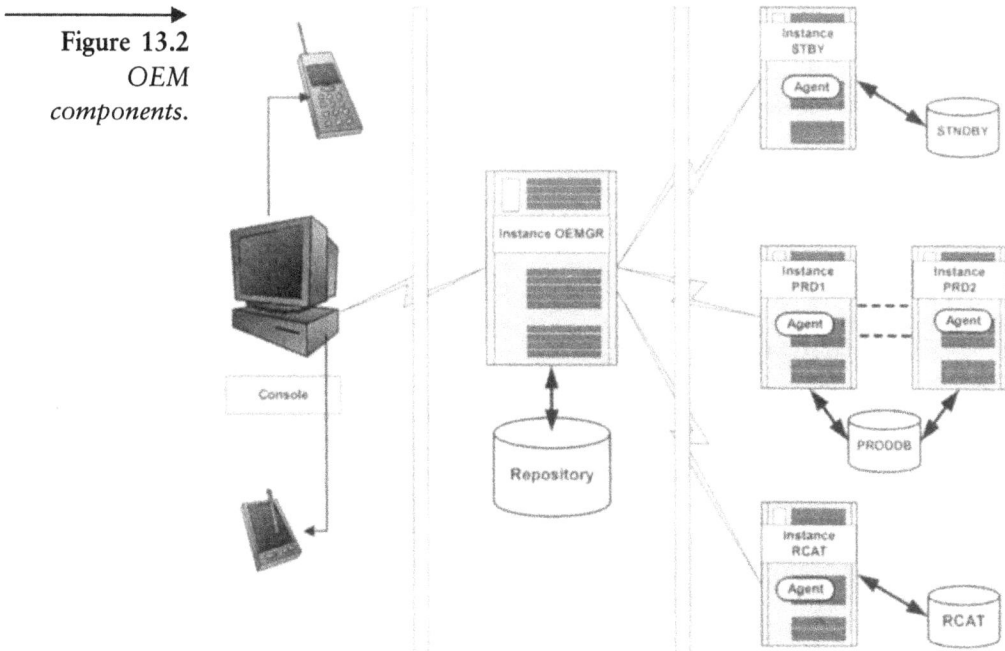

Figure 13.2
OEM
components.

troubleshooting and monitoring a clustered database environment requires certain additional processes.

13.4.1   Installation

To install the OEM console tier and the middle tier, using the OUI, the Oracle 9*i* Management and Integration option is selected, as shown in Figure 13.3. This screen lists the available products that come bundled with the Enterprise Edition of the database server.

Once this option is selected, the next screen appears (Figure 13.4), which contains more specific installation options such as the Oracle Management Server and Oracle Internet Directory. The Oracle Management Server is selected to install the OEM repository and the console. Depending on the product that is to be installed, the appropriate option is selected or, by selecting the custom option, Oracle provides the option to install one or all the products.

Note: Installation of the Oracle Internet Directory is not directly related to configuration and performance tuning of RAC and hence is not discussed.

Figure 13.3
Installation product selection.

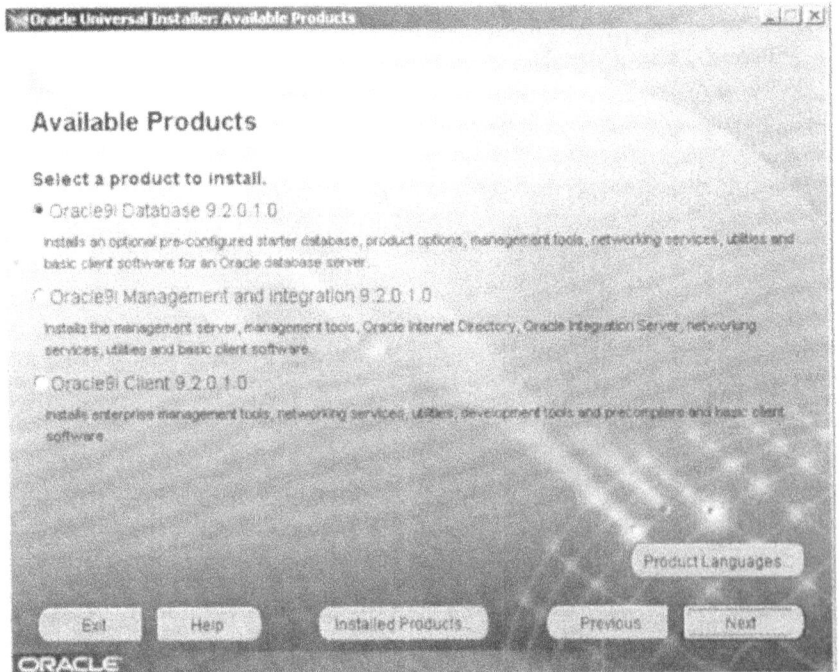

Figure 13.4
OEM installa-
tion type
selection.

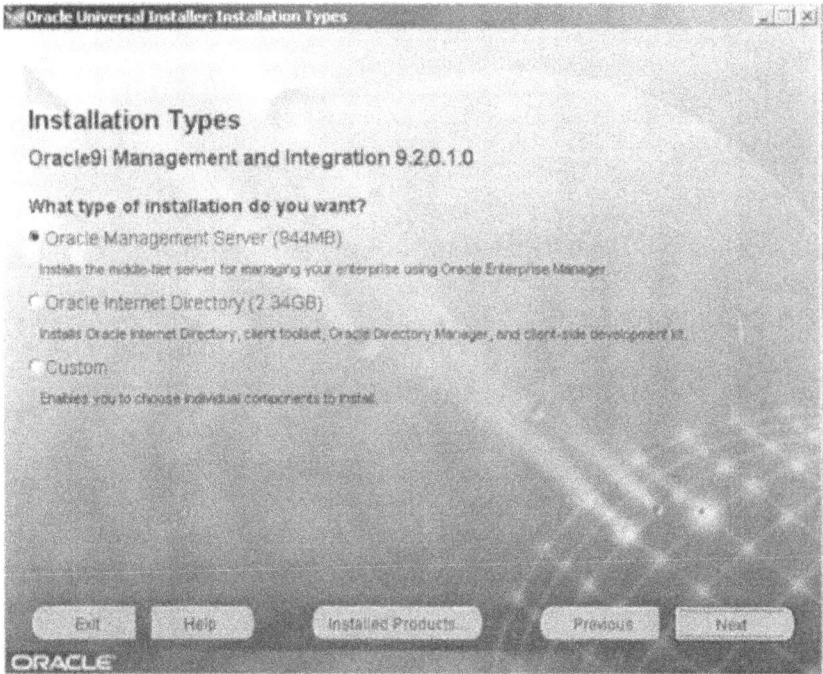

After the selection of this option, OEM is installed along with the client portion of the product. After the basic installation of the product, the next set of screens help in the configuration of the management server.

Figure 13.5 shows the management server configuration assistant. In this screen the information pertaining to the credentials of the management server, including the host name/address and repository owner's information, is entered.

Through a series of similar configuration screens the management server is installed.

13.4.2   Configuring OEM for RAC

The management server should be able to discover the existence of the various databases that are to be managed via OEM. While discovering and managing individual instances could be as easy as telling the Enterprise Manager of the node information, such as the IP address of the node or the node name, on which the databases reside, selecting and configuring a clustered database requires additional steps.

Figure 13.5
*Management
server
configuration.*

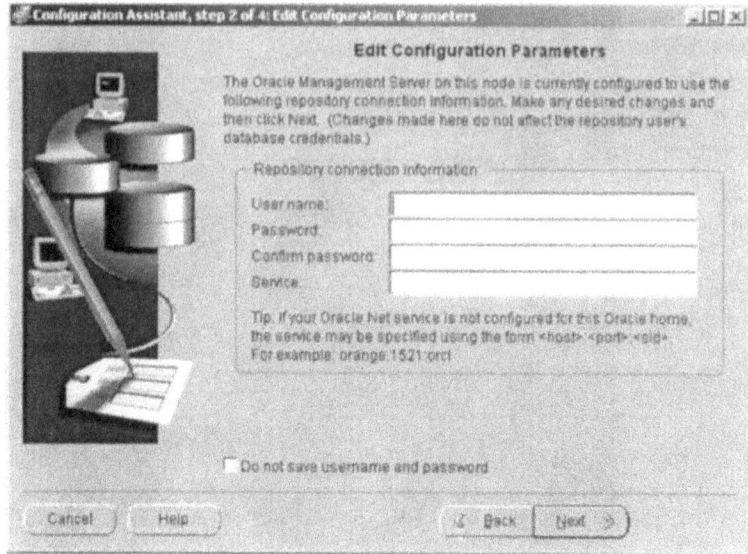

Note: If these additional steps are not followed, the database and the multiple instances will not be visible to OEM as a clustered database, but rather as one instance with the database attached to it and the others as separate instances.

Prerequisite

Prior to configuration of the various products required for the discovery of the clustered database, it is required that the RAC database and the other subcomponents listed in Chapter 8 (Installation and Configuration) have been installed and configured.

Configuring the agent

The intelligent agent is a primary component for the discovery of both a stand-alone configuration and a clustered configuration of the database. The agent is installed by invoking the agent control (agentctl) utility available in the ORACLE_HOME/bin directory on the database server machine. The following are the steps for installing and configuring the agent:

1. The agent needs visibility of all nodes containing the instances participating in the clustered database configuration. This can be verified on most Unix platforms with the following command:

```
ora-db1:RAC1:oracle # lsnodes
ora-db1.summerskyus.com
```

```
ora-db2.summerskyus.com
ora-db1:RAC1:oracle #
```

2.   The next step is to verify if the database has been configured to be in a clustered state, that is, the database and all instances have been mapped to each other in the server control utility provided by Oracle as part of RAC. This can be verified on most Unix platforms with the following command:

```
ora-db2:RAC2:oracle # srvctl status database -d PRODDB
Instance RAC1 is running on node ora-db1.summerskyus.com
Instance RAC2 is running on node ora-db2.summerskyus.com
```

3.   The listener should be aware of all the instances participating in the clustered configuration. This is verified with the following command:

```
ora-db1:RAC1:oracle # lsnrctl status
LSNRCTL for Solaris: Version 9.2.0.2.0 - Production on 06-DEC-2002
   11:57:30

Copyright (c) 1991, 2002, Oracle Corporation.  All rights reserved.

Connecting to (DESCRIPTION=(ADDRESS=(PROTOCOL=IPC)(KEY=EXTPROC)))

STATUS of the LISTENER
------------------------
Alias            LISTENER
Version          TNSLSNR for Solaris: Version 9.2.0.2.0 - Production
Start Date       22-NOV-2002 00:36:11
Uptime           3 days 16 hr. 54 min. 21 sec
Trace Level      Off
Security         OFF
SNMP             OFF
Listener Parameter File  /apps/oracle/product/9.2.0/network/admin/
                         listener.ora
Listener Log File        /apps/oracle/product/9.2.0/network/log/lis-
                         tener.log
Listening Endpoints Summary...
  (DESCRIPTION=(ADDRESS=(PROTOCOL=ipc)(KEY=EXTPROC)))
  (DESCRIPTION=(ADDRESS=(PROTOCOL=tcp)(HOST= (ora-db1)(PORT=1521))))
Services Summary...
Service "PLSExtProc" has 1 instance(s).
  Instance "PLSExtProc", status UNKNOWN, has 1 handler(s) for this
  service...
Service "RAC1" has 1 instance(s).
  Instance "RAC1", status UNKNOWN, has 1 handler(s) for this service...
Service "RAC1.summerskyus.com" has 1 instance(s).
  Instance "RAC1", status READY, has 1 handler(s) for this service...
Service "PRODDB" has 1 instance(s).
```

```
 Instance "PRODDB", status UNKNOWN, has 1 handler(s) for this service...
Service "PRODDB.SUMMERSKYUS.COM" has 1 instance(s).
 Instance "RAC1", status READY, has 1 handler(s) for this service...
The command completed successfully
ora-db1:RAC1:oracle #
```

In the above output, of the two instances participating in the clustered configuration the listener has registered only one instance. This is because the following two parameters have not been configured.

The LOCAL_LISTENER and REMOTE_LISTENER parameters point to their respective host names as illustrated below:

```
RAC1.local_listener="(ADDRESS=(PROTOCOL=TCP)
  (HOST=ora-db1.summerskyus.com)(PORT=1521))"

RAC1.remote_listener="(ADDRESS=(PROTOCOL=TCP)
  (HOST=ora-db2.summerskyus.com)(PORT=1521))"
```

LOCAL_LISTENER is the listener for the local instance and REMOTE_LISTENER is the listener on the remote instance(s) participating in the clustered configuration. On implementations with two or more instances, there would be multiple remote listener parameter definitions.

It is good to set these parameters in the parameter file so that they register automatically during startup and shutdown of instances. However, these parameters can be set dynamically using the following commands:

```
ALTER SYSTEM SET LOCAL_LISTENER="(ADDRESS=(PROTOCOL=TCP)
  (HOST=ora-db1.summerskyus.com)(PORT=1521))"

ALTER SYSTEM SET REMOTE_LISTENER="(ADDRESS=(PROTOCOL=TCP)
  (HOST=ora-db2.summerskyus.com)(PORT=1521))"
```

Once these parameters have been set with the appropriate values, the listener will register the remote instances.

Note: Registration does not occur until the next time the PMON discovery routine executes. By default, this happens at 60-second intervals. This normally occurs when a listener is started after the Oracle instance and every time that listener fails and is restarted. The 60-second delay can be overridden using the system-level SQL statement ALTER SYSTEM REGISTER. This statement forces PMON to register the service immediately.

Checking the status of the listener again will reveal all instances participating in the clustered configuration having registered with the local listener on the local instance:

```
ora-db1:RAC1:oracle # lsnrctl status
LSNRCTL for Solaris: Version 9.2.0.2.0 - Production on 06-DEC-2002
   11:59:30

Copyright (c) 1991, 2002, Oracle Corporation.  All rights reserved.

Connecting to (DESCRIPTION=(ADDRESS=(PROTOCOL=IPC)(KEY=EXTPROC)))

STATUS of the LISTENER
------------------------
Alias          LISTENER
Version        TNSLSNR for Solaris: Version 9.2.0.2.0 - Production
Start Date     06-DEC-2002 11:54:20
Uptime         0 days 0 hr. 5 min. 10 sec
Trace Level    OFF
Security       OFF
SNMP           OFF

Listener Parameter File/apps/oracle/product/9.2.0/network/admin/lis-
                tener.ora
Listener Log File/apps/oracle/product/9.2.0/network/log/listener.log
Listening Endpoints Summary...
  (DESCRIPTION=(ADDRESS=(PROTOCOL=ipc)(KEY=EXTPROC)))
  (DESCRIPTION=(ADDRESS=(PROTOCOL=tcp)(HOST=ora-db1)
  (PORT=1521)))
Services Summary...
Service "PLSExtProc" has 1 instance(s).
  Instance "PLSExtProc", status UNKNOWN, has 1 handler(s) for this
   service...
Service "RAC1" has 1 instance(s).
  Instance "RAC1", status UNKNOWN, has 1 handler(s) for this service...
Service "RAC1.summerskyus.com" has 1 instance(s).
  Instance "RAC1", status READY, has 1 handler(s) for this service...
Service "RAC2.summerskyus.com" has 1 instance(s).
  Instance "RAC2", status READY, has 1 handler(s) for this service...
Service "PRODDB" has 1 instance(s).
  Instance "PRODDB", status UNKNOWN, has 1 handler(s) for this service...
Service "PRODDB.SUMMERSKYUS.COM" has 2 instance(s).
  Instance "RAC1", status READY, has 1 handler(s) for this service...
  Instance "RAC2", status READY, has 1 handler(s) for this service...
The command completed successfully
ora-db1:RAC1:oracle #
```

9i

New Feature: LOCAL_LISTENER and REMOTE_LISTENER parameters are new in Oracle 9*i* Release 1. In this release, these parameters can only be defined by setting them in the init<SID>.ora file and these parameters take effect during instance startup. Oracle Release 2 has provided dynamic configuration of these parameters using the ALTER SYSTEM SET REMOTE_LISTENER command.

4.   The GSD should also be available for the intelligent agent to have visibility to the clustered database configuration. This is verified using the following command:

```
ora-db2:RAC2:oracle # gsdctl stat
GSD is running on the local node
```

5.   The tnsnames.ora file on the database server should be set up and configured to provide visibility to all instances.

6.   Once all the above agents and daemons have been verified, the intelligent agent can be started. This can be done with the following command:

```
ora-db1:RAC1:oracle # agentctl start
DBSNMP for Solaris: Version 9.2.0.1.0 - Production on 06-DEC-2002
  11:55:24

Copyright (c) 2002 Oracle Corporation. All rights reserved.
Starting Oracle Intelligent Agent......
Agent started
```

Another component that is required by the management server for collecting database statistics is the data gatherer.

9i   **New Feature:** In prior versions of Oracle, the data gatherer was configured as a separate daemon process on the database server. In Oracle *9i*, the data gatherer is part of the intelligent agent and is installed and started when the agent is started.

Note: Verification and configuration of all the above components is to be performed on all nodes participating in the clustered configuration. Once this is completed, the clustered database and the corresponding instances can be discovered via OEM. Steps required for configuration, starting, and stopping of the intelligent agent have been discussed in Chapter 8 (Installation and Configuration).

Figure 13.6 illustrates the selection and discovery of the instances of an Oracle database.

Figure 13.6
OEM Node
Discovery
Wizard.

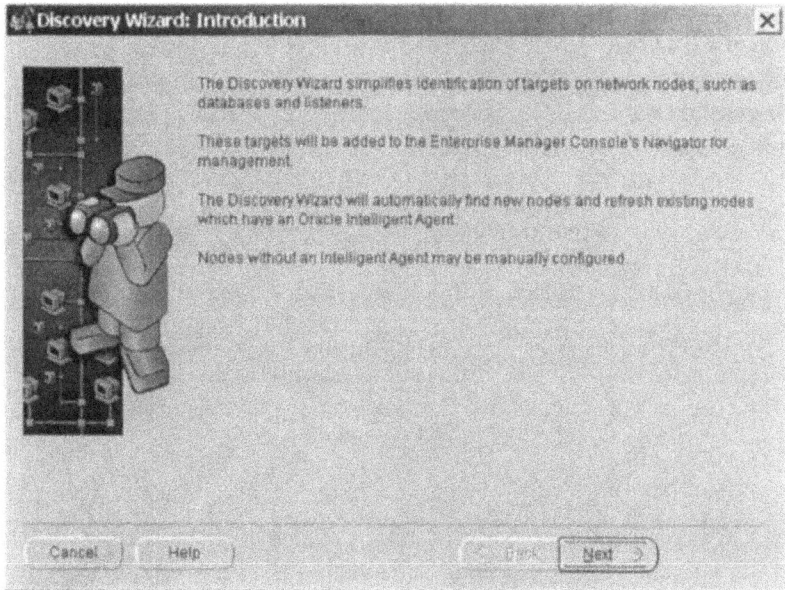

Figure 13.6
OEM Node
Discovery
Wizard.

Performance manager

Apart from the database administration and maintenance functionality, OEM also contains the performance manager (this feature requires the Performance and tuning pack to be installed). In version 9*i*, Oracle has enhanced OEM to provide visibility to a clustered database.

Database health screen

This health screen provides a complete view on the overall health of the database. The summary screen contains views to the CPU, memory and disk usage charts. The bottom of the screen displays information containing the various wait statistics, including waits across the cluster interconnects.

Figure 13.7 is a screen capture of the OEM database performance overview chart for a single instance. This chart provides overall performance characteristics of the instance being monitored. These characteristics are displayed based on threshold parameters defined for each view. This requires that the DBA be familiar with their values under normal and peak load conditions so that an appropriate value can be determined for what constitutes an abnormal condition. Once the appropriate thresholds have been set in the performance overview chart, any time poor throughput or response time is reported, the appropriate area will be flagged red. For example in Figure 13.7, the database memory

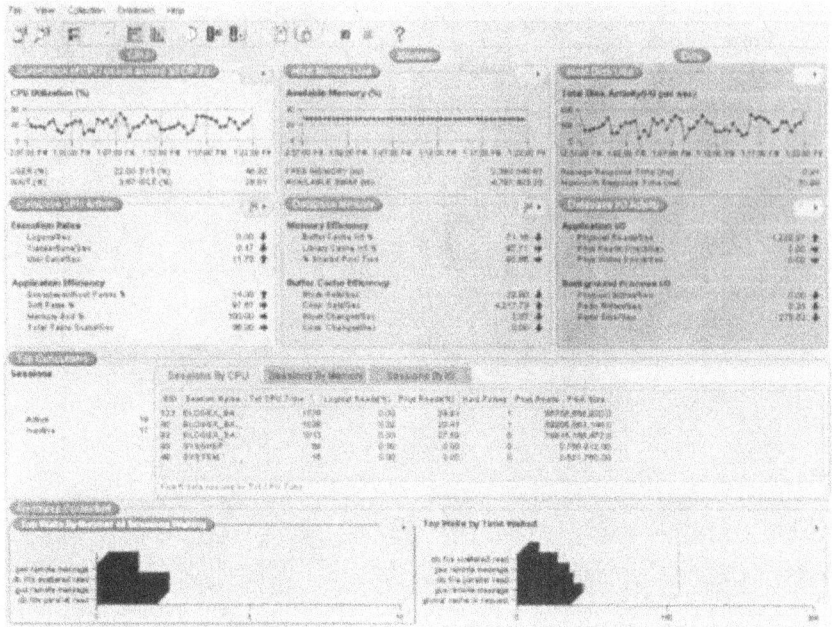

Figure 13.7
*OEM Database
performance
overview chart.*

chart has been flagged red, which indicates that the efficiency of the buffer has gone below the threshold value defined for this area. This will point the DBA in the right direction for diagnosing the problem.

While this screen provides an overall health of the database, individual performance views could be drilled down to get more finite information on certain performance issues.

CPU utilization chart   Figure 13.8 provides the CPU utilization chart of all CPUs on the system. The view provides breakdown charts on CPU utilization by user processes, system calls, idle time, and wait time

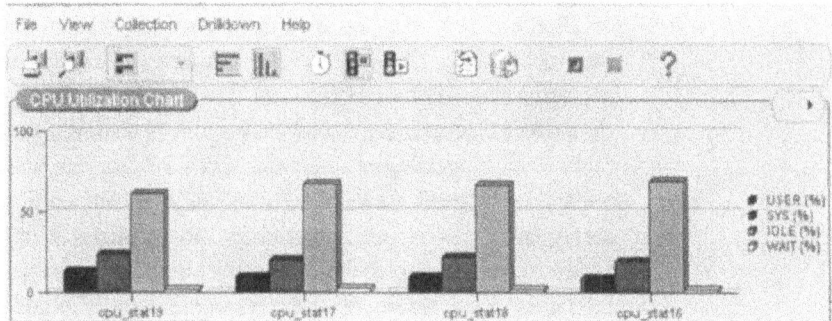

Figure 13.8
*OEM CPU
utilization chart.*

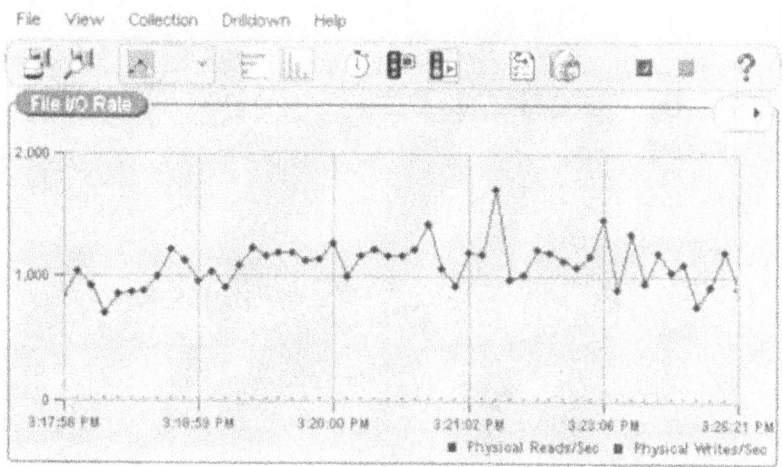

Figure 13.9
OEM file I/O rate chart.

encountered by the instance. The chart indicates that the node has four CPUs and each CPU is 60% idle. The user activity on this system only measures about 20% of the total workload. The CPU chart could be further drilled down by individual processes and or sessions that are currently utilizing CPU on the node.

File I/O rate chart   Figure 13.9 illustrates the file I/O rate on the current instance. Since this is an instance-specific view, it does not reflect the I/O activity of the entire system. Data from the I/O activity could be saved for historical purposes and could be used to determine user patterns on the system, such as what part of the day or which day of the week or month the I/O activity is the highest. This is obtained by preparing a trend analysis.

Global cache CR request   This chart is a drilldown from the database health overview chart and displays the global cache CR request wait event activity. This event is only visible in a RAC environment where more than one instance is configured to be active. This event reflects interconnect traffic activity and validates the functioning of cache fusion technology in RAC.

Figure 13.10 illustrates the global cache activities across the cluster interconnect. High activity on this chart could indicate potential latency issues, badly performing queries, or mixed access user patterns where users are requesting the same information from various instances, causing high global cache activity while sharing information.

Figure 13.10
*OEM global
cache* CR
*request activity
chart.*

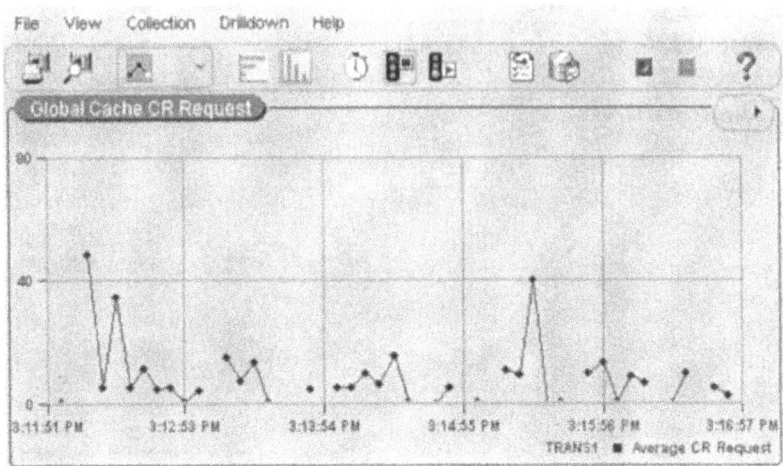

13.5 EXPLAIN PLAN

Transactional activity in a system comprises SELECT, INSERT, UPDATE, and DELETE operations. In order to perform these operations, Oracle generates an execution plan for the statement. The execution plan is generated either based on a set of predefined rules (RBO) or based on the statistics available during the time of creating an execution plan (CBO). Since these execution plans are generated based on the information available in the SQL statement (attributes in the WHERE clause) these plans need to be examined in detail to ensure that they are correct. If this is not the case, appropriate information can be provided either by modifying the statement in such a manner to provide the appropriate selection criteria, or by providing hints to inform the optimizer of an alternative approach to executing the query (such as providing hints).

Hints are like clues to a detective investigating a case. They provide information to help the detective to complete the task more efficiently and quickly.

One such method of looking at the execution plan generated by Oracle is by creating an EXPLAIN PLAN. An EXPLAIN PLAN for an SQL statement is generated using certain environmental settings such as enabling the AUTOTRACE feature and then executing the statement. The syntax to enable AUTOTRACE is

```
SET AUTOT[RACE] {OFF | ON TRACE[ONLY]} [EXP[LAIN]] [STAT[ISTICS]]
```

To set the AUTOTRACE feature the user is required to have the PLUSTRACE role. In order to create the PLUSTRACE role the plustrce.sql script needs to be executed as user sys. This script is located in ORACLE_HOME/sqlplus/admin directory.

The command used to generate the EXPLAIN PLAN is

```
SQL> SET AUTOTRACE TRACEONLY;
SQL> SET TIMING ON;
```

This command sets the environment conditions and required variables. Subsequently, if the SQL statement is executed, the execution plan or EXPLAIN PLAN for the statement is generated.

```
SELECT UP.USPRL_ID,
       UP.USPRL_FIRST_NAME,
       UP.USPRL_LAST_NAME,
       UP.USPRL_CITY,
       UP.USPRL_STATE_ID,
       UP.USPRL_LOGIN_NAME,
       UP.USPRL_EMAIL,
       UP.USPRL_PHONE,
       UP.USPRL_ROLE_CD,
       CMP.COMP_NAME,
       CMP.COMP_SCAC_CODE,
       US.USEC_TOTAL_LOGINS,
       UL.USRLI_ID
FROM   USER_PROFILE  UP,
       COMPANY       CMP,
       USER_LOGIN    UL,
       USER_SECURITY US
WHERE UL.USRLI_ACTIVE_STATUS_CD  = 'Active'
       AND UL.USRLI_LOGGED_IN_USPRL_ID = UP.USPRL_ID
       AND UP.USPRL_COMP_ID     = CMP.COMP_ID
       AND UP.USPRL_ID          = US.USEC_USPRL_ID
ORDER BY CMP.COMP_TYPE_CD,
       CMP.COMP_NAME,
       UP.USPRL_LAST_NAME

Elapsed: 00:00:09.80

Execution Plan
----------------------------------------------------------
0      SELECT STATEMENT Optimizer=CHOOSE (Cost=11 Card=19 Bytes=3078)
1    0   SORT (ORDER BY) (Cost=11 Card=19 Bytes=3078)
2    1    TABLE ACCESS (BY GLOBAL INDEX ROWID) OF 'USER_SECURITY' (Cost=2
          Card=1 Bytes=8)
3    2      NESTED LOOPS (Cost=8 Card=19 Bytes=3078)
4    3       NESTED LOOPS (Cost=7 Card=19 Bytes=2926)
5    4        NESTED LOOPS (Cost=6 Card=19 Bytes=2204)
6    5         VIEW OF 'index$_join$_003' (Cost=4 Card=19 Bytes=342)
7    6          HASH JOIN
8    7           INDEX (FAST FULL SCAN) OF 'PK_USRLI' (UNIQUE) (Cost=3
                 Card=19 Bytes=342)
```

```
9    7              INDEX (FAST FULL SCAN) OF 'USRLI_INDX1' (NON-UNIQUE)
                    (Cost=3 Card=19 Bytes=342)
10   5             TABLE ACCESS (BY LOCAL INDEX ROWID) OF 'USER_PROFILE'
                    (Cost=2 Card=1 Bytes=98)
11   10             INDEX (UNIQUE SCAN) OF 'PK_USPRL' (UNIQUE)
12   4            TABLE ACCESS (BY LOCAL INDEX ROWID) OF 'COMPANY' (Cost=2
                    Card=1425 Bytes=54150)
13   12             INDEX (UNIQUE SCAN) OF 'PK_COMP' (UNIQUE)
14   3           INDEX (RANGE SCAN) OF 'USEC_INDX1' (NON-UNIQUE)
Statistics
-------------------------------------------------------
        0 recursive calls
      394 db block gets
   433218 consistent gets
     8366 physical reads
        0 redo size
    27787 bytes sent via SQL*Net to client
     1007 bytes received via SQL*Net from client
       34 SQL*Net roundtrips to/from client
        1 sorts (memory)
        0 sorts (disk)
      487 rows processed
```

Note: For a detailed explanation on how to interpret the EXPLAIN PLAN for an SQL query please refer to Metalink note number **46234.1.**

13.6   SQL Trace

SQL Trace is a utility that comes bundled with the Oracle database server. This utility is used to generate SQL Trace information while the database is being used for a specific session. The output generated in the form of trace files from the process contains the execution plans used by the SQL queries. This information generated in the trace files is used to help improve the query performance.

SQL Trace is generated at the system level by enabling an init<SID>.ora parameter SQL_TRACE = TRUE or at the session level with the following statement:

SQL>ALTER SESSION SET SQL_TRACE = TRUE;

Either method of SQL tracing generates output files for every session containing trace information in the directory specified by the USER_DUMP_DEST parameter.

Setting this parameter before executing SQL queries at the session level will generate trace files for only queries executed by this session. The files are generated in the same user dump destination.

The trace files generated are basic raw files and not easily readable. However, Oracle provides a utility called TKPROF, which can be utilized to format the trace files into a more readable form using the following command:

```
Usage: tkprof tracefile outputfile [explain= ] [table= ]
       [print= ] [insert= ] [sys= ] [sort= ]

table=schema.tablename Use 'schema.tablename' with 'explain=' option.
explain=user/password  Connect to ORACLE and issue EXPLAIN PLAN.
print=integer  List only the first 'integer' SQL statements.
aggregate=yes|no
insert=filename List SQL statements and data inside INSERT statements.
sys=no  TKPROF does not list SQL statements run as user SYS.
record=filename  Record non-recursive statements found in the trace file.
waits=yes|no  Record summary for any wait events found in the trace file.
sort=option  Set of zero or more of the following sort options:
 prscnt   number of times parse was called
 prscpu   cpu time parsing
 prsela   elapsed time parsing
 prsdsk   number of disk reads during parse
 prsqry   number of buffers for consistent read during parse
 prscu    number of buffers for current read during parse
 prsmis   number of misses in library cache during parse
 execnt   number of execute was called
 execpu   cpu time spent executing
 exeela   elapsed time executing
 exedsk   number of disk reads during execute
 exeqry   number of buffers for consistent read during execute
 execu    number of buffers for current read during execute
 exerow   number of rows processed during execute
 exemis   number of library cache misses during execute
 fchcnt   number of times fetch was called
 fchcpu   cpu time spent fetching
 fchela   elapsed time fetching
 fchdsk   number of disk reads during fetch
 fchqry   number of buffers for consistent read during fetch
 fchcu    number of buffers for current read during fetch
 fchrow   number of rows fetched
 userid   userid of user that parsed the cursor

tkprof <trace filename> <output file name>, explain=<schema name>/
  <password>@SID table=<schema name>.<temp table name> <additional
  parameters>
```

> **Note:** A sample out can be found in the next section.

13.7   Oracle event interface

SQL Trace is a simple straightforward approach to getting to the execution plan generated by Oracle for the various SQL queries. The information provided by these trace files is only minimal. While SQL_TRACE is a good start to getting to the basic execution behavior, it seldom provides any details on the actual reasons for the performance characteristics or the reasons why the optimizer showed a specific behavior during query execution.

Oracle provides certain events that can be enabled at the system or session level to capture information for all sessions or at the session level.

Event 10046

Enabling event 10046 at various levels provides varying details about the execution plans, performance characteristics, and other related information.

Level I

This is enabled at the system level using the following statement:

```
ALTER SYSTEM SET EVENTS '10046 TRACE NAME CONTEXT FOREVER, LEVEL 1';
```

or at the session level

```
ALTER SESSION SET EVENTS '10046 TRACE NAME CONTEXT FOREVER, LEVEL 1'
```

Setting event 10046 at level 1 is equivalent to setting the SQL_TRACE parameter to TRUE in the init<SID>.ora file or enabling trace at a session level. The output produced by this event is generated in the user dump destination directory. The trace file could be interpreted in a more readable format using the TKPROF similar to the SQL_TRACE feature listed above.

The following is the output generated by tracing event 10046 at level 1 on the SQL query:

call	count	cpu	elapsed	disk	query	current	rows
Parse	2205	0.14	0.15	0	1608	0	0
Execute	6880	3.19	4.14	0	0	0	0
Fetch	6880	3.19	6.24	67	38590	0	6880
total	15965	6.52	10.54	67	40198	0	6880

Misses in library cache during parse: 0

```
Optimizer goal: CHOOSE
Parsing user id: 33  (MVALLATH)
  Rows    Row Source Operation
 -----   --------------------------------------------------
   487   SORT ORDER BY (cr=3218 r=67 w=66 time=374942 us)
   487    TABLE ACCESS BY GLOBAL INDEX ROWID USER_SECURITY PARTITION: 1 1
          (cr=3218 r=67 w=66 time=366031 us)
   978     NESTED LOOPS  (cr=3130 r=67 w=66 time=362323 us)
   490      NESTED LOOPS  (cr=2638 r=67 w=66 time=350329 us)
   490       NESTED LOOPS  (cr=1656 r=67 w=66 time=337860 us)
   490        VIEW  (cr=674 r=67 w=66 time=322853 us)
   490         HASH JOIN  (cr=674 r=67 w=66 time=321329 us)
 56373         INDEX FAST FULL SCAN PK_USRLI PARTITION: 1 1
 (cr=190 r=1 w=0 time=44521 us)(object id 24891)
   490         INDEX FAST FULL SCAN USRLI_INDX1 (cr=484 r=0 w=0 time=73787 us)
 (object id 24706)
   490        TABLE ACCESS BY LOCAL INDEX ROWID USER_PROFILE
 PARTITION: 1 1 (cr=982 r=0 w=0 time=11879 us)
   490         INDEX UNIQUE SCAN PK_USPRL PARTITION: 1 1
 (cr=492 r=0 w=0 time=5923 us)(object id 24741)
   490       TABLE ACCESS BY LOCAL INDEX ROWID COMPANY
 PARTITION: 1 1 (cr=982 r=0 w=0 time=9774 us)
   490        INDEX UNIQUE SCAN PK_COMP PARTITION: 1 1
 (cr=492 r=0 w=0 time=4757 us)(object id 24813)
   487      INDEX RANGE SCAN USEC_INDX1 (cr=492 r=0 w=0
 time=8898 us)(object id 24694)

  Rows  Execution Plan
  ----  --------------------------------------------------
     0  SELECT STATEMENT   GOAL: CHOOSE
   487   SORT (ORDER BY)
   487    TABLE ACCESS   GOAL: ANALYZED (BY GLOBAL INDEX ROWID) OF
           'USER_SECURITY' PARTITION: START=1 STOP=1
   978     NESTED LOOPS
   490      NESTED LOOPS
   490       NESTED LOOPS
   490        VIEW OF 'index$_join$_003'
   490         HASH JOIN
156373          INDEX   GOAL: ANALYZED (FAST FULL SCAN) OF
           'PK_USRLI' (UNIQUE) PARTITION: START=1 STOP=1
   490          INDEX   GOAL: ANALYZED (FAST FULL SCAN) OF
           'USRLI_INDX1' (NON-UNIQUE)
   490        TABLE ACCESS   GOAL: ANALYZED (BY LOCAL INDEX ROWID) OF
           'USER_PROFILE' PARTITION: START=1 STOP=1
   490         INDEX   GOAL: ANALYZED (UNIQUE SCAN) OF 'PK_USPRL'
           (UNIQUE) PARTITION: START=1 STOP=1
   490       TABLE ACCESS   GOAL: ANALYZED (BY LOCAL INDEX ROWID) OF
           'COMPANY' PARTITION: START=1 STOP=1
   490        INDEX   GOAL: ANALYZED (UNIQUE SCAN) OF 'PK_COMP'
           (UNIQUE) PARTITION: START=1 STOP=1
   487     INDEX   GOAL: ANALYZED (RANGE SCAN) OF 'USEC_INDX1'
           (NON-UNIQUE)
```

Interpreting the trace output generated using TKPROF:

- *Call:* Statistics for each cursor's activity are divided into three areas:

  Parse: Statistics from parsing the cursor. This includes information for plan generation, etc.

  Execute: Statistics for the execution phase of a cursor.

  Fetch: Statistics for actually fetching the rows.

- *Count:* Number of times a particular activity is performed on this particular cursor.

- *CPU:* CPU time used by this cursor.

- *Elapsed:* Elapsed time for this cursor.

- *Disk:* This indicates the number of blocks read ´ ⌐m disk. Generally, it is preferable to see blocks being read from the buffer cache rather than disk.

- *Query:* This column is incremented if a buffer is read in consistent mode. A consistent mode buffer is one that has been generated to give a consistent read snapshot for a long-running transaction. The buffer actually contains this status in its header.

- *Current:* This column is incremented if a buffer is found in the buffer cache that is new enough for the current transaction and is in current mode (and it is not a CR buffer). This applies to buffers that have been read into the cache as well as buffers that already exist in the cache in current mode.

- *Rows:* Rows retrieved by this step.

Further in the output generated from tracing event 10046, please note the rows column in the execution plan. This indicates the number of rows that the buffer is carrying around during each of these steps. The highest number of rows is in

```
156373    INDEX GOAL: ANALYZED (FAST FULL SCAN) OF 'PK_USRLI' (UNIQUE)
          PARTITION: START=1 STOP=1
```

This could be where the actual performance problem lies. The main question that arises when examining the trace file would be, why are 156,373 rows being retrieved and filtered through at this step when the actual number of rows returned is only 487?

Such detailed information is not found in a regular EXPLAIN PLAN created from the AUTOTRACE feature.

Level 4

Level 1 tracing of event 10046 provides the basic SQL queries; sometimes to re-create the issue or to re-execute the query, these basic raw queries and their EXPLAIN PLAN(s) are not sufficient, especially if the query is using bind variables. Using bind variables is an excellent practice and should be in the best practices guide of the organization. For debugging and query tuning purposes it would be helpful to determine the values used during the query execution. To determine the bind variables and the corresponding bind values, event 10046 at level 4 would capture the information.

Similar to level 1, level 4 can be enabled at the system or session level using the following statements:

```
ALTER SYSTEM SET EVENTS '10046 TRACE NAME CONTEXT FOREVER, LEVEL 4';
ALTER SESSION SET EVENTS '10046 TRACE NAME CONTEXT FOREVER, LEVEL 4';
```

Level 8

Many times the query performs poorly due to several reasons other than the way in which the query is written. For example, slow performance could be due to the way the table has been stored on disk, poor distribution of data on the disk, too many tables sharing the same data files, data heavily scattered, or because the query is performing full table scans. There are no other reasons for the slow performance; however, the EXPLAIN PLAN(s) generated by the previous methods do not provide the actual reasons for the slowness. Under such circumstances, it would be good to enable event 10046 at level 8 to capture the additional information.

Similar to level 1 and level 4, level 8 can be enabled at the system or session levels through the following statements:

```
ALTER SYSTEM SET EVENTS '10046 TRACE NAME CONTEXT FOREVER, LEVEL 8';
ALTER SESSION SET EVENTS '10046 TRACE NAME CONTEXT FOREVER, LEVEL 8';
```

The following is the additional information generated by event 10046 at level 8:

```
Elapsed times include waiting on following events:
Event waited on                    Times    Max.     Total
                                   Waited   Wait     Waited
------------------------------------------------------------
db file sequential read            38479   230.02   3846.51
SQL*Net message to client          13760     0.00      0.04
SQL*Net message from client        13760     3.45   3238.44
```

```
global cache cr request          1355    0.20       3.02
library cache lock                 31    0.00       0.00
SQL*Net more data from client      31    0.00       0.00
KJC: Wait for msg sends            12    0.00       0.00
    to complete
global cache s to x                11    0.03       0.04
buffer busy global CR               4    0.00       0.00
latch free                          3    0.02       0.05
buffer busy global cache            1    0.01       0.01
**********************************************************
```

The above output lists the various wait events encountered during the query execution time. Now from the above it is certain that there are several wait situations that could have caused a performance slowdown for the query, and the query itself may not be the problem.

For example, the highest value in the "times waited" column is for db file sequential read. This wait indicates that the query requests a sequential access on the table to retrieve rows and is waiting for the read to complete. It indicates that the database is performing single block reads. This could happen when reading from an index, rollback segment, or sort area, rebuilding a control file, and while dumping data file headers. This wait could raise several questions like, should there be an index lookup, is the table small enough that full table scans would be more efficient? If the wait is consistently increasing for several sessions on this specific query, further drilldown by looking into the segment-level information may be helpful.

An SQL*Net message from the client indicates that the Oracle process is waiting for a message from the client (the application tier). This could be due to several factors; in particular the time waited may be misleading because this also includes idle waits. However, this may not be the case on a busy systems where it could indicate network latency. To improve the SQL*Net from and to the client would require tuning the SQL*Net traffic. Enabling trace at this level and examining the session data unit (SDU) and transport data unit (TDU) values will tune the settings for this parameter. The network value could be set in the tnsnames.ora file on the client side of the application.

Level 12

Level 12 provides a combined output of all the above levels. At this level, the execution plans, bind variables, bind values (generated with level 4), and the wait events (generated with level 8) are provided in the trace files. Most often, enabling event 10046 at level 12 will provide a comprehensive method of looking at the problem in hand. However, the output generated at this level could be large and may require considerable amount of disk space. Enabling a trace at this level should be done only after ensuring sufficient space is available.

Similar to the other levels, level 12 can be enabled at the system or session levels through the following statements:

```
ALTER SYSTEM SET EVENTS '10046 TRACE NAME CONTEXT FOREVER, LEVEL 12';
ALTER SESSION SET EVENTS '10046 TRACE NAME CONTEXT FOREVER, LEVEL 12';
```

Event 10053

Many times, when the query is being tuned for performance and after generating the EXPLAIN PLAN, trace files, turning on event 10046, looking at wait statistics, etc., the following questions arise during the query tuning or application execution process. Why is the execution plan being generated in this fashion? Why is the runtime performance different from interactive performance?

Under these circumstances, if the database has been configured to use the CBO, event 10053 will capture the actual steps that the CBO has taken to generate the execution plan.

Enabling event 10053 is similar to enabling any other event, that is, by using an ALTER SYSTEM or ALTER SESSION statement. However, unlike event 10046 that was discussed in the previous section, event 10053 can generate trace information only at two levels, level 1 and level 2:

```
ALTER SYSTEM SET EVENTS '10053 TRACE NAME CONTEXT FOREVER, LEVEL 1';
ALTER SESSION SET EVENTS '10053 TRACE NAME CONTEXT FOREVER, LEVEL 2';
```

The following is a partial output of the optimizer behavior generated from event 10053 at level 1:

```
****************************************
OPTIMIZER STATISTICS AND COMPUTATIONS
****************************************
GENERAL PLANS
***********************
Join order[1]: USER_LOGIN [UL] COMPANY [CMP] USER_PROFILE [UP]
  USER_SECURITY [US]
Now joining: COMPANY [CMP] *******
NL Join
 Outer table: cost: 4 cdn: 19 rcz: 18 resp: 4
 Inner table: COMPANY
   Access path: tsc Resc: 11
   Join: Resc: 213 Resp: 213
Join cardinality: 27075 = outer (19) * inner (1425) * sel (1.0000e+00)
  [flag=0]
 Best NL cost: 214 resp: 213
Join result: cost: 214 cdn: 27075 rcz: 56
```

```
Now joining: USER_PROFILE [UP] *******
NL Join
  Outer table: cost: 214  cdn: 27075  rcz: 56  resp:  213
  Inner table: USER_PROFILE
    Access path: tsc  Resc: 11
    Join: Resc: 298038 Resp:  298038
OPTIMIZER PERCENT INDEX CACHING = 90
  Access path: index (unique)
    Index: PK_USPRL
  TABLE: USER_PROFILE
    RSC_CPU: 0   RSC_IO: 1
  IX_SEL:  6.4350e-04  TB_SEL:  6.4350e-04
    Join:  resc: 1567  resp: 1567
OPTIMIZER PERCENT INDEX CACHING = 90
  Access path: index (join index)
    Index: USPRL_INDX1
  TABLE: USER_PROFILE
    RSC_CPU: 0   RSC_IO: 2
  IX_SEL:  0.0000e+00  TB_SEL:  3.0581e-03
    Join:  resc: 2921  resp: 2921
OPTIMIZER PERCENT INDEX CACHING = 90
  Access path: index (eq-unique)
    Index: PK_USPRL
  TABLE: USER_PROFILE
    RSC_CPU: 0   RSC_IO: 1
  IX_SEL:  0.0000e+00  TB_SEL:  0.0000e+00
    Join:  resc: 1567  resp: 1567
Join cardinality: 19 = outer (27075) * inner (1554) * sel (4.5158e-07)
  [flag=0]
  Best NL cost: 1567  resp: 1567
SM Join
  Outer table:
    resc: 213  cdn: 27075  rcz: 56  deg: 1  resp: 213
  Inner table: USER_PROFILE
    resc: 11  cdn: 1554  rcz: 98  deg: 1  resp: 11
    using join:1 distribution:2 #groups:1
    SORT resource     Sort statistics
      Sort width:        29 Area size:     712704 Max Area size:     712704
    Degree: 1
      Blocks to Sort:      239 Row size:        72 Rows:      27075
      Initial runs:        3 Merge passes:     1 IO Cost / pass:      284
      Total IO sort cost: 262
      Total CPU sort cost: 0
      Total Temp space used: 3711000
    SORT resource     Sort statistics
      Sort width:   29 Area size:   712704 Max Area size:   712704  Degree: 1
      Blocks to Sort:      23 Row size:        118 Rows:      1554
      Initial runs:   1 Merge passes:    1 IO Cost / pass: 28
      Total IO sort cost: 26
      Total CPU sort cost: 0
      Total Temp space used: 0
  Merge join  Cost: 511 Resp: 511
HA Join
```

```
Outer table:
  resc: 213 cdn: 27075 rcz: 56 deg: 1 resp: 213
Inner table: USER_PROFILE
  resc: 11 cdn: 1554 rcz: 98 deg: 1 resp: 11
  using join:8 distribution:2 #groups:1
 Hash join one ptn Resc: 68   Deg: 1   (sides swapped)
  hash_area: 256 (max=256) buildfrag: 257  probefrag: 21 ppasses:  2
 Hash join  Resc: 292  Resp: 292
 Outer table:
  resc: 11 cdn: 1554 rcz: 98 deg: 1 resp: 11
 Inner table: COMPANY
  resc: 213 cdn: 27075 rcz: 56 deg: 1 resp: 213
  using join:8 distribution:2 #groups:1
 Hash join one ptn Resc: 8  Deg: 1
   hash_area: 256 (max=256) buildfrag: 257 probefrag: 225 ppasses: 2
 Hash join  Resc: 232  Resp: 232
Join result: cost: 233  cdn: 19  rcz: 154
Now joining: USER_SECURITY [US] *******
NL Join
 Outer table: cost: 233 cdn: 19 rcz: 154  resp: 232
 Inner table: USER_SECURITY
  Access path: tsc Resc: 11
  Join: Resc: 441 Resp: 441
OPTIMIZER PERCENT INDEX CACHING = 90
 Access path: index (join index)
  Index: USEC_INDX1
 TABLE: USER_SECURITY
  RSC_CPU: 0  RSC_IO: 1
IX_SEL: 0.0000e+00 TB_SEL: 6.4893e-04
  Join: resc: 233 resp: 233
Join cardinality: 19 = outer (19) * inner (1559) * sel (6.4893e-04)
 [flag=0]
 Best NL cost: 234 resp: 233
SM Join
 Outer table:
  resc: 232 cdn: 19 rcz: 154 deg: 1 resp: 232
Inner table: USER_SECURITY
  resc: 11 cdn: 1559 rcz: 8 deg: 1 resp: 11
  using join:1 distribution:2 #groups:1
  SORT resource      Sort statistics
   Sort width:    29 Area size: 712704 Max Area size: 712704  Degree: 1
   Blocks to Sort:      1 Row size:       180 Rows:      19
   Initial runs:    1 Merge passes: 1 IO Cost / pass:    6
   Total IO sort cost: 4
   Total CPU sort cost: 0
   Total Temp space used: 0
  SORT resource      Sort statistics
   Sort width:   29 Area size:  712704 Max Area size:  712704  Degree: 1
   Blocks to Sort:      4 Row size:       19 Rows:      1559
   Initial runs: 1 Merge passes:    1 IO Cost / pass:    9
   Total IO sort cost: 6
   Total CPU sort cost: 0
   Total Temp space used: 0
```

```
 Merge join  Cost: 253 Resp:  253
HA Join
 Outer table:
  resc: 232  cdn: 19  rcz: 154  deg: 1  resp: 232
 Inner table: USER_SECURITY
  resc: 11 cdn: 1559 rcz: 8 deg: 1 resp: 11
  using join:8 distribution:2 #groups:1
 Hash join one ptn Resc: 1  Deg: 1
  hash_area: 256 (max=256) buildfrag: 257  probefrag:  4 ppasses:   2
 Hash join  Resc: 244  Resp: 244
ORDER BY sort
 SORT resource     Sort statistics
  Sort width:     29 Area size:  712704 Max Area size:   712704  Degree: 1
  Blocks to Sort:     1 Row size:      189 Rows:        19
  Initial runs:     1 Merge passes:     1 IO Cost / pass:   6
  Total IO sort cost: 4
  Total CPU sort cost: 0
  Total Temp space used: 0

Join result: cost: 237  cdn: 19  rcz: 162
Best so far: TABLE#: 0 CST:    4  CDN:      19 BYTES:     342
Best so far: TABLE#: 1 CST:  214  CDN:  27075 BYTES:  1516200
Best so far: TABLE#: 2 CST:  233  CDN:      19 BYTES:    2926
Best so far: TABLE#: 3 CST:  237  CDN:      19 BYTES:    3078



***********************

Join order[2]: USER_LOGIN [UL] COMPANY [CMP] USER_SECURITY [US]
  USER_PROFILE [UP]
Now joining: USER_SECURITY [US] *******
```

The trace output from event 10053 illustrates how the CBO actually performs the cost computation process during the generation of an execution plan for a query.

Please note that unlike the RBO where the execution plan is generated based on the predefined rules, in a CBO the execution plan is generated based on the best access path after generating all the possible ordering of objects.

For example, in the above illustration the first join order is similar to what was specified in the SQL query:

```
Join order[1]: USER_LOGIN [UL] COMPANY [CMP] USER_PROFILE [UP]
  USER_SECURITY [US]
```

Subsequently, Oracle creates a different join order and calculates the cost of its execution path:

```
Join order[2]: USER_LOGIN [UL] COMPANY [CMP] USER_SECURITY [US]
  USER_PROFILE [UP]
```

For every join operation, Oracle computes the cost of accessing the rows for a nested loop join (NL join), sort merge join (SM join), and hash join (HA join) operation.

For example, from the illustration above:

```
NL Join
  Outer table: cost: 4 cdn: 19 rcz: 18 resp: 4
  Inner table: COMPANY
    Access path: tsc Resc: 11
    Join: Resc: 213 Resp: 213
Join cardinality: 27075 = outer (19) * inner (1425) * sel (1.0000e+00)
  [flag=0]
```

From these three access methods, Oracle selects the operation that takes the least cost for execution. This is illustrated below by the "best so far" entry after each join order cost computation.

```
Best so far: TABLE#: 0 CST:   4 CDN:     19 BYTES:      342
Best so far: TABLE#: 1 CST: 214 CDN: 27075 BYTES: 1516200
Best so far: TABLE#: 2 CST: 233 CDN:     19 BYTES:     2926
Best so far: TABLE#: 3 CST: 237 CDN:     19 BYTES:     3078
```

For the query used in this illustration, Oracle created 14 different join order checks. However, if the best cost computed for a specific join order is not better than the previous, Oracle does not calculate the best cost for that specific join order.

Note: In complex queries where there are several tables being joined, Oracle has to compute join orders for all possible table combinations, which could be time consuming. If queries are not being reused, for example when literals are used instead of bind variables, Oracle has to compute these join orders every single time and could create several performance problems.

Similarly, to avoid several join orders in a complex query with several table joins, the /*ORDERED*/ hint becomes very helpful. This hint will enforce the join order and based on the hint Oracle will use the user specified join order for query execution.

13.8   Oracle's Wait interface

In the STATSPACK report discussions above, we mentioned the top 5 waits encountered by the database/application during a specific snapshot period. These wait events are retrieved by the STATSPACK process from certain data dictionary views and stored in the STATSPACK-specific tables in the PERFSTAT schema.

Oracle's wait interface (OWI) helps to identify all wait events. This helps track the number of waits and the amount of time waited for each event throughout the life of a session.

The data dictionary views that constitute the wait interface include:

- GV$SYSTEM_EVENT

- GV$SESSION_EVENT

- GV$SESSION_WAIT

- GV$EVENT_NAME

- GV$SYSSTAT

- GV$SESSTAT

Unlike the STATSPACK report that only reports information at the overall system level like that provided by querying the GV$SYSTEM_EVENT view, data dictionary views such as the GV$SESSION_EVENT and GV$SESSION_WAIT provide information at the session level.

Note: The definitions of these data dictionary views can be found in Chapter 9 (Parameters and Views).

Unlike the information in the GV$SYSTEM_EVENT, which is retained until the instance is bounced, the data available in session views is lost after the session has disconnected from the database. Due to the dynamic nature of these views and due to short span of a session's existence, collecting data from these views by querying them directly may be difficult. The workaround for this situation would be to capture the data in these views and store them in user-defined tables.

Caution: The implementation of these queries to capture data could cause serious performance risks in a live production system. They should be used intelligently. These scripts should be used with great caution and should be turned on only under extreme conditions and should be turned off immediately.

In order to retain the session statistics it is required that these statistics be written to a separate table before the session disconnects from the database. This could be implemented using the BEFORE LOGOFF ON

DATABASE trigger. The BEFORE LOGOFF ON DATABASE trigger is created at the database level and is configured to capture all events from the session-related views and insert them into their respective tables.

Note: The scripts required for creating the MVPERFAUDIT user, the tables, and respective triggers to capture data are included in Appendix 2 of this book.

The procedure mv_perfaudit_create.sql creates three tables, MV_AUDIT_SESSION_EVENT, MV_AUDIT_SESSION_WAIT, and MV_AUDIT_SESSION_STAT. The script also contains three trigger creation scripts used to populate the above three tables. Apart from the session information contained in the GV$SESSION_WAIT and GV$SESSION_EVENT tables, the procedure also captures additional information from the GV$SESSION view, including the SQL_ADDRESS of the statement that is related to the wait event. Using this address, the actual SQL text of the query can be obtained by joining the MV_AUDIT_SESSION_EVENT table against the V$SQL view.

```
COL EVENT format a30
COL USERNAME format a15
COL TIMEOUTS format 99999
COL WAIT format 99999
COL WAITED format 99999
COL SID format 9999

SELECT  mvase_sid SID,
        mvase_username USERNAME,
        mvase_sql_address SQL_ADDRESS,
        mvase_event EVENT,
         mvase_total_timeouts TIMEOUTS,
         mvase_total_waits WAIT,
         mvase_time_waited WAITED,
        mvase_failed_over FO
FROM    mv_audit_session_event
WHERE   mvase_username IS NOT NULL
ORDER BY mvase_sid;
/
```

SID	SQL_ADDRESS	EVENT	TIMEOUTS	WAIT	WAITED	FO
32	0000000442A622A0	jobq slave wait	1	2	573	NO
32	0000000442A622A0	log file sync	0	1	0	NO
32	0000000442A622A0	db file sequential read	939	1145	1252	NO
32	0000000442A622A0	SQL*Net message to client	0	15	0	NO
32	0000000442A622A0	SQL*Net message from client	0	14	7126	NO
32	0000000442A622A0	db file sequential read	0	1	7	NO

```
32   0000000442A622A0  SQL*Net message to client        0   31      0 NO
32   0000000442A622A0  SQL*Net more data to client      0    1      0 NO
32   0000000442A622A0  SQL*Net message from client      0   30   5793 NO
32   0000000442A622A0  db file sequential read        239  145    122 NO
32   0000000442A622A0  SQL*Net message to client        0   35      0 NO
```

Note: The USERNAME column has been suppressed from the output, for formatting purposes.

The above query output indicates that the session with SID 32 had encountered the above mentioned wait events while performing certain SQL operations. For example, the query below joins the MV_AUDIT_SESSION_ EVENT table to GV$SQL view to obtain the SQL text that the session was executing which had encountered the above-mentioned waits.

```
SELECT SQL_TEXT
FROM  GV$SQL, MV_AUDIT_SESSION_EVENT
WHERE ADDRESS=MVASE_SQL_ADDRESS
AND  MVASE_SID=32
```

Similarly, the wait table MV_AUDIT_SESSION_WAIT could be queried to retrieve the various details of the waits, including the reasons for the waits. For example, the wait could be on a table when retrieving rows, could be on the SQL*Net where the Oracle process is waiting for more information from the client, or is waiting to send a message to the client.

```
COL SID FORMAT 9999
COL USERNAME FORMAT A15
COL EVENT FORMAT A30
COL P1 FORMAT 9999
COL P2 FORMAT 9999
COL P3 FORMAT 9999
Select MVASW_SID SID,
       MVASW_USERNAME USERNAME,
       MVASW_SQL_ADDRESS SQL_ADDRESS,
       MVASW_EVENT EVENT,
       MVASW_P1 P1,
       MVASW_P2 P2,
       MVASW_P3 P3,
       MVASW_WAIT_TIME WAIT,
       MVASW_FAILED_OVER FO
FROM   MV_AUDIT_SESSION_WAIT
WHERE  MVASW_USERNAME IS NOT NULL
AND    (MVASW_EVENT LIKE 'global%'
OR     MVASW_EVENT LIKE 'db%'
OR     MVASW_EVENT LIKE 'gcs%'
OR     MVASW_EVENT LIKE 'ges%'
```

```
OR      MVASW_EVENT LIKE '%buffer%')
ORDER BY SID
/
```

SID	SQL_ADDRESS	EVENT	P1	P2	P3	WT	FO
30	0000000443D7CF48	db file sequential read	18	56903	1	0	NO
32	0000000442A622A0	db file sequential read	194	20683	1	0	NO
32	000000442174720	db file sequential read	18	25804	1	0	NO
32	00000004421739C0	db file sequential read	18	11786	1	0	NO
32	0000000443AB2528	global cache null to x	18	25804	17917873152	0	NO
36	0000000442178608	db file sequential read	18	24480	1	0	NO
36	0000000442178608	global cache s to x	18	1164	17934759808	0	NO
39	00000004421781C8	global cache open x	18	28712	17968379616	0	NO
90	00000004448FE370	db file sequential read	18	15422	1	0	NO
99	0000000443D7DDD8	global cache null to x	18	11888	17045147456	0	NO
120	00000004448F9728	db file sequential read	18	11891	1	0	NO
125	00000004448F8FA0	db file sequential read	18	11864	1	0	NO
125	00000004448FE370	global cache cr request	18	23689	17028513088	0	NO

The output above indicates the various wait events and the objects that the process waited against. For example, the query above has filtered out only the events that contain %db% and others related specifically to RAC. The db file sequential read on session 32 was encountered in the previous query from the MV_AUDIT_SESSION_EVENT table. This query illustrates the reasons for the wait.

The contents of P1, P2, and P3 vary from event to event. The actual meaning for these events could be obtained by querying MVASW_P1TEXT, MVASW_P2TEXT, and MVASW_P3TEXT from the MV_AUDIT_SESSION_ WAIT for column contents of P1, P2, and P3, respectively. The same information could also be obtained by querying the GV$EVENT_NAME view:

```
COL EVENT# FORMAT 9999
COL NAME FORMAT A30
COL PARAMETER1 FORMAT A12
COL PARAMETER2 FORMAT A12
COL PARAMETER3 FORMAT A12
SELECT
      EVENT#,
      NAME,
      PARAMETER1,
      PARAMETER2,
      PARAMETER3
FROM   GV$EVENT_NAME
WHERE (NAME LIKE 'db%'
OR     NAME LIKE '%parse%'
OR     NAME LIKE '%cpu%'
OR     NAME LIKE '%global%')
/
```

EVENT#	NAME	PARAMETER1	PARAMETER2	PARAMETER3
150	buffer busy global cache	file#	block#	id
151	buffer busy global CR	file#	block#	id
191	db file sequential read	file#	block#	blocks
192	db file scattered read	file#	block#	blocks
193	db file single write	file#	block#	blocks
194	db file parallel write	requests	interrupt	timeout
195	db file parallel read	files	blocks	requests
196	global cache open s	file#	block#	le
197	global cache open x	file#	block#	le
198	global cache null to s	file#	block#	le
199	global cache null to x	file#	block#	le
200	global cache s to x	file#	block#	le
201	global cache cr request	file#	block#	le
202	global cache cr disk request	file#	block#	le
203	global cache busy	file#	block#	id
205	global cache bg acks	count	loops	
206	global cache pending ast	le		
207	global cache retry prepare	file#	block#	
150	buffer busy global cache	file#	block#	id
151	buffer busy global CR	file#	block#	id
191	db file sequential read	file#	block#	blocks
192	db file scattered read	file#	block#	blocks
193	db file single write	file#	block#	blocks
194	db file parallel write	requests	interrupt	timeout
195	db file parallel read	files	blocks	requests
196	global cache open s	file#	block#	le
197	global cache open x	file#	block#	le
198	global cache null to s	file#	block#	le
199	global cache null to x	file#	block#	le
200	global cache s to x	file#	block#	le
201	global cache cr request	file#	block#	le
202	global cache cr disk	block#	le	

From the output above it is found that the parameters for db file sequential read are file#, block#, and blocks. Applying these values to the output from the MV_AUDIT_SESSION_WAIT table above, session 32 had encountered waits on two files, file# 194 and file# 18. Further analysis indicates that session 32 had encountered waits on file# 18 twice; however, in both the situations the blocks that it waited on were different (block# 25804 and block# 11786).

Session 32 also encountered waits on global cache locks reported through the global cache null to x wait. This wait is a lock conversion for a local read-only mode to exclusive mode. Further analysis of the statistics collected in the MV_AUDIT_SESSION_WAIT table determined that this wait was also encountered on file# 18 on block# 25804.

The next step would be to identify the actual files and the tablespaces that map to these objects. Once the tablespaces are identified, the next step would be to identify which tables or indexes are contained in these tablespaces.

In this case, as illustrated below, by querying the V$DATAFILE, V$TABLESPACE, and DBA_TABLES view, we can see that the files are shared by more than one table and the blocks contention are on these tables:

```
COL FILE# FORMAT 9999
COL FNAME FORMAT A44
COL TNAME FORMAT A25
COL TABLE_NAME FORMAT A30
SELECT
      F.FILE#,
       F.NAME FNAME,
        T.NAME TNAME,
      TABLE_NAME
FROM  V$DATAFILE F,
      V$TABLESPACE T,
      DBA_TABLES
WHERE F.TS#=T.TS#
AND   (F.FILE#=194
OR    F.FILE#=18)
AND   T.NAME = TABLESPACE_NAME
```

FILE#	FNAME	TNAME	TABLE_NAME
18	/dev/vx/rdsk/oraracdg/partition500m_1a	TBS190_DATA_P001	USER_PROFILE
18	/dev/vx/rdsk/oraracdg/partition500m_1a	TBS190_DATA_P001	COMPANY
194	/dev/vx/rdsk/oraracdg/partition500m_4a	TBS200_DATA_P001	USER_LOGIN
194	/dev/vx/rdsk/oraracdg/partition500m_4a	TBS200_DATA_P001	USER_SECURITY

Occasional contentions need not be of concern. However, if this contention is repeatable, the reasons need to be identified. From the above analysis there are two potential areas where the problem could be mapped. Either the contention is because the raw device partition is mapped to the same set of disks or it could be because the tables are hot tables and need to be moved into their respective tablespaces to use different files to store the data.

So far we have discussed the OWI with respect to the database, in the sense that it concerns the information reported by GV$SESSION_EVENT, GV$SYSTEM_EVENT, and GV$SESSION_WAIT. These wait activities more or less relate to the database configuration or the behavior of SQL queries or the distribution of data in the database.

It is not just the database and the data that can report issues concerning bad performance; performance data from the operating system can also help in troubleshooting and problem solving. The OWI reports on system-level activities or waits at the system level such as CPU, memory etc. Similar to the database statistics reported by the other three views, the wait activities for the CPU and memory could be obtained by querying the GV$SYSSTAT and GV$SESSTAT.

Similar to GV$SYSTEM_EVENT, which reports on the wait events at the instance level, GV$SYSSTAT also reports operating system statistics at the instance level. This means that the statistics generated from this view only provide an overall health of the database. Also the data provided by this view covers the time since the instance was last bounced as indicated by the GV$INSTANCE view.

```
COL NAME FORMAT A40
SELECT
INST_ID,
      NAME,
      VALUE
FROM    GV$SYSSTAT
WHERE  (NAME LIKE 'db%'
OR      NAME LIKE '%prase%'
OR      NAME LIKE '%cpu%'
OR      NAME LIKE '%global%')
```

INST_ID	NAME	VALUE
1	recursive cpu usage	1134363
1	global lock sync gets	4144288
1	global lock async gets	231936
1	global lock get time	206027
1	global lock sync converts	207121
1	global lock async converts	318799
1	global lock convert time	112312
1	global lock releases	4310681
1	db block gets	93786250
1	db block changes	57229650
1	global cache gets	67304228

```
INST_ID  NAME                                        VALUE
-------  -----------------------------------------   -------
1        global cache get time                       56519113
1        global cache converts                        1014750
1        global cache convert time                    1136498
1        global cache cr blocks received              1816738
1        global cache cr block receive time            759748
1        global cache current blocks received        10089455
1        global cache current block                   56747428
           receive time
1        global cache cr blocks served                1692951
1        global cache cr block build time               13719
1        global cache cr block flush time              215520
1        global cache cr block send time                38087

INST_ID  NAME                                        VALUE
-------  -----------------------------------------   -------
1        global cache current blocks served          28210721
1        global cache current block pin time           910030
1        global cache current block flush time         103497
1        global cache current block send time          828097
1        global cache freelist waits                        3
1        global cache defers                           119262
1        global cache convert timeouts                      0
1        global cache blocks lost                         178
1        global cache claim blocks lost                     0
1        parse time cpu                                 76791
1        parse time elapsed                            579757
1        parse count (total)                         13209035
1        parse count (hard)                             23307
1        parse count (failures)                           133
1        OS Wait-cpu (latency) time                         0
2        recursive cpu usage                          1113997
2        global lock sync gets                        3291355
```

As we have discussed earlier, in this case also, the session-based information is lost when the user disconnects his or her session from the database. Hence, the data from the GV$SESSTAT needs to be stored in a permanent table, for example, in MV_AUDIT_SESSION_STAT for future analysis.

```
COL SID FORMAT 999
COL USERNAME FORMAT A15
COL STAT# FORMAT 9999
COL NAME FORMAT A35
COL VALUE FORMAT
SELECT
MVASS_SID SID,
      MVASS_SQL_ADDRESS SQL_ADDRESS,
      MVASS_STATISTIC# STAT#,
      NAME,
      MVASS_VALUE VALUE
```

```
FROM   MV_AUDIT_SESSION_STAT,
       GV$STATNAME
WHERE MVASS_STATISTIC# = STATISTIC#
AND    MVASS_USERNAME IS NOT NULL
AND    MVASS_VALUE > 0
ORDER BY MVASS_SID
/
```

SID	SQL_ADDRESS	STAT#	NAME	VALUE
100	000000044668AD30	232	parse count (total)	1
100	000000044668AD30	219	PX local messages recv'd	2
100	000000044668AD30	218	PX local messages sent	2
100	000000044668AD30	1	logons current	1
100	000000044668AD30	0	logons cumulative	1
100	000000044668AD30	34	global lock releases	1
100	000000044668AD30	28	global lock sync gets	2
100	000000044668AD30	27	enqueue releases	1
100	000000044668AD30	25	enqueue requests	2
100	000000044668AD30	21	session pga memory max	4502576
100	000000044668AD30	20	session pga memory	4502576

SID	SQL_ADDRESS	STAT#	NAME	VALUE
100	000000044668AD30	16	session uga memory max	60968
100	000000044668AD30	235	execute count	1
100	000000044668AD30	34	global lock releases	1
100	000000044668AD30	28	global lock sync gets	2
100	000000044668AD30	27	enqueue releases	1
100	000000044668AD30	25	enqueue requests	2
100	000000044668AD30	21	session pga memory max	4502576
100	000000044668AD30	20	session pga memory	4502576
100	000000044668AD30	16	session uga memory max	60968
100	000000044668AD30	15	session uga memory	60968
100	000000044668AD30	14	process last non-idle time	1040613274

SID	SQL_ADDRESS	STAT#	NAME	VALUE
100	000000044668AD30	13	session connect time	1040613274
100	000000044668AD30	15	session uga memory	60968
100	000000044668AD30	14	process last non-idle time	1040613274
100	000000044668AD30	13	session connect time	1040613274

The above output indicates the session statistics of the system. It indicates the amount of memory and CPU (not shown in the output) consumed by the session. Data from this output could be utilized for sizing the Oracle memory and if there is high CPU usage, consider tuning the query.

13.9   Conclusion

In this chapter we looked at the various tools and options for gathering data that could be utilized for performance tuning the database. UTLBSTAT/UTLESTAT have played a significant role in performance tuning of Oracle databases and applications from earlier versions of Oracle. With Oracle Version 8.1.6 and above, many users have switched to the STATSPACK utility to generate these performance statistics.

In Oracle Version 9*i*, OEM has been enhanced considerably to provide a clustered database view, which helps in performance monitoring of RAC instances. The installation and configuration of OEM was discussed in detail.

One of the main aspects of an application performing well is to ensure that the persistence layer, which comprises SQL statements accessing the database, performs well. While there are several products available from various vendors today, Oracle provides several options for tuning SQL queries. Under this category the EXPLAIN PLAN, SQL_TRACE, event 10046, and event 10053 were discussed with trace outputs.

The OWI was also discussed at length. The wait interface that comprises GV$SESSION_EVENT, GV$SYSTEM_EVENT, GV$SESSION_WAIT, GV$SYSSTAT, and GV$SESSTAT was discussed in length. The discussion also included examples regarding analyzing this data for improving the performance of the system.

RAC comprises many instances of Oracle with one common database. While the ultimate goal of the enterprise system is to have the clustered solution perform well, this cannot happen unless the individual instances perform well. In the next chapter we will discuss a methodical approach to tuning a single instance configuration.

14

Tuning a Single Instance

14.1   Introduction

In the previous chapter we discussed some of the basic tools and utilities available from Oracle for performance monitoring. Tools such as OEM provide a good GUI with drilldown features to determine the specific areas of performance concern. Utilities such as the STATSPACK provide visibility to the health of the database over a specific period of time. The data gathered from STATSPACK can be retained for a user-defined period of time and utilized to a generate trend analysis.

Other opportunities for drilling down into the reasons relating to performance issues with SQL statements were discussed. In this discussion, the EXPLAIN PLAN, SQL Trace, and Oracle event interface provided visibility into some of the ways that Oracle computed the execution plan and how the queries could be tuned to ensure that it is more efficient.

Subsequently, we discussed OWI. The OWI is the method that provides visibility in getting to the bottom of a problem. While the ratios provide the cosmetics by almost always showing good performance when actually the system may be performing slowly, the OWI will help identify where the problem is and the cause of the problem.

All these tools and utilities provide visibility into the methods of accessing data that could be analyzed to determine why the system, application or database is performing poorly.

Performance tuning of any application, including the database, is an iterative process in the sense that it never completes. There is a constant requirement to continuously monitor and tune to maintain the overall health of the database. While at certain periods an aggressive performance tuning of the application and database may be required, during other times it is just routine continuous monitoring and tuning.

As we have discussed in the previous chapter, performance tuning is not an art; the systems are tuned based on data that is collected during the periods of poor performance as evidence, and the data collected provides an indication where the actual problem could potentially reside. However, many times it is not that simple. For the continuous monitoring and tuning of systems, a process or method should be adopted that helps streamline the activity. As in most repeatable situations, a methodology should be adopted, and once it has been validated and approved it needs to be practiced. This methodology should be iterated all day, every day, to continuously tune the systems.

In this chapter we will look into the scientific approach of troubleshooting, performance tuning, and maintaining a healthy database system. Tuning a RAC implementation has many tiers. However, since a RAC configuration comprises one or more instances connected to a shared database, tuning of a RAC configuration starts with tuning a single instance. This single instance should be tuned similar to tuning a stand-alone configuration of the database and once this is tuned the other tiers, network, interconnect, cluster manager, etc., are to be incorporated into the tuning process.

14.2   **Methodology**

Problem-solving tasks of any nature need to be approached in a systematic and controlled manner. There needs to be a defined procedure or an action plan and this procedure needs to be followed step-by-step from start to finish. During every step of the process, data is collected and analyzed, and the results are fed into the next step, which in turn is performed in a similar step-by-step approach. Hence methodology is the procedure or process followed from start to finish, from identification of the problem to problem solving and documentation. A methodology is a procedure or process that is repeatable as a whole or in increments through iterations.

During all of these analysis steps, the determination of the cause or reasons for a behavior or problem should be based on quantitative analysis and not on guesswork.

The performance tuning methodology can be broadly categorized into seven steps:

1.   Problem statement

2.   Information gathering

3.   Area identification

4.   Area drilldown

5.   Problem resolution

6.   Testing against baseline

7.   Repeating the process

While each of the above steps is very broad, a methodical approach will help identify and solve the problem in question, namely performance.

Which area of the system is having a performance problem? Where do we start? Should the tuning process start with the operating system, network, database, instance, or the application? Obviously it is the users of the application tier that are complaining that the system is slow. Users access the application, and the application through some kind of persistence layer communicates to the database to store and retrieve information. However, when the user who made the request does not get the response to the request in a sufficiently fair amount of time, they complain that the system is slow.

Well, this method will help provide a well-performing application system. However, certain iterations may have to be performed from bottom up. That is, starting with the hardware platform, tuning the storage subsystem, tuning the database configuration, tuning the instance, etc. Addressing the tuning issue using this approach could bring some amount of change or performance improvement to the system with less or no impact to the actual application code. However, if the application is poorly written, it does not matter how much tuning is done at the bottom tier, the underlying issue will remain the same.

14.2.1   Getting to the obvious

The application tier could be a very broad area and could have many components, all components communicating through the same persistence layer to the Oracle database. In order to get to the bottom of the problem, namely performance, each area of the application needs to be examined and tuned methodically. To differentiate the various components, the application needs to be divided into smaller areas.

14.2.2 Divide into quadrants

One approach towards a very broad problem is to divide the application into quadrants, starting with the most complex area in the first quadrant (most of the time the most complex quadrant or the most commonly used quadrant is also the worst-performing quadrant), followed by the area that is equally or less complex in the second quadrant, and so on. However, depending on how large the application is and how many areas of functionality the application covers, these four broad areas may not be sufficient. If this were the case, the next step would be to break each of the complex quadrants into four smaller quadrants (subquadrants) or functional areas. This second level of breakdown does not need to be done for all the quadrants from the first level and can be limited to only the most complex ones. After this second level of breakdown, the most complex or the worst-performing functionality of the application that fits into the first quadrant is selected for performance testing.

Following the methodology listed above, and through an iterative process, each of the subquadrants and the functionality described in the main quadrant will have to be tested. Starting with the first quadrant, the various areas of the application will be tuned, and when the main or more complex or most frequently used component has been tuned, the next component in line is selected and tuned. After all the four quadrants have been visited, the process starts all over again. This is because after the first pass, even though the findings of the first quadrant were validated against the components in the other quadrants, when performance of all quadrants improves, the first quadrant continues to show performance degradation and probably has room to grow.

Figure 14.1 illustrates the quadrant approach to dividing the application for a systematic approach to performance tuning. The quadrants are approached in a clockwise pattern with the most critical or worst-performing piece of the application occupying quadrant 1.

While intensive tuning may not be the goal through every iteration, each quadrant, based on the functionality supported and the amount of processing combined with the interaction with other tiers, may have room for further tuning or may have areas that are not present in the component of the first quadrant and hence may be a candidate for further tuning.

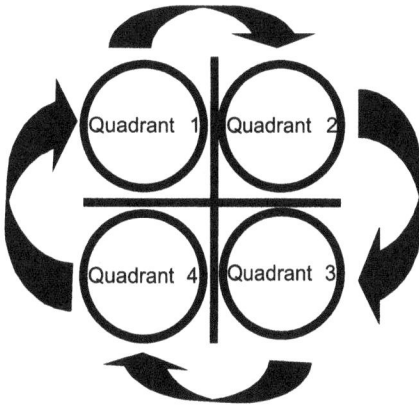

Figure 14.1
Dividing into quadrants.

Now that we have identified which component of the application needs immediate attention, the next step would be, where do we start? Obviously the most important piece is where the rubber meets the road. Hence in the case of an application that interacts with the database, the first step would be to look into the persistence layer.

In the previous section, we discussed taking a bottom-up approach. This may be an alternative if the database administrator or the performance engineer suspects that the underlying storage subsystem is where the problem resides.

From a database tuning perspective, the persistence layer would be the first layer to which considerable attention should be given. However, areas that do not have any direct impact on the database such as application partitioning, looking at the configuration of the application server (e.g., WebLogic, Oracle 9*i* AS, WebSphere, etc.[1]), tuning the various parameters of the application tier such as the number of connections, number of threads or queue sizes of the application server, are all areas that could also be addressed. However, in the context of this chapter the discussion will be focused around the database and the layers that interact with the database.

The persistence layer is the tier that interacts with the database and comprises SQL statements, which communicate with the database to store and retrieve information based on users' requests. These SQL statements depend on the database, its tables, and other objects that it contains, and store data to respond to the requests.

I.   WebLogic is a product owned by BEA Systems; WebSphere is a product owned by International Business Machines and Oracle 9*i* AS is a product owned by Oracle corporation.

In the previous chapter, the various utilities and tools of tuning SQL statements such as EXPLAIN PLAN, SQL Trace and the event interface were discussed. With the help of the SQL Trace or the event interface, all SQL statements executed through the various quadrants could be captured and profiled. These statements could be individually examined and tuned on an ongoing basis and a matrix could be developed, providing a trend of improved or degraded performance.

During a controlled load testing, the database statistics captured using various tools such as the STATSPACK provide insight into the worst-performing SQL queries. The STATSPACK utility discussed in Chapter 13 also provides other statistics as indications of why the database is performing or responding poorly.

14.3   Application tuning

Per our methodology discussed earlier, the tuning of an application starts here. If the performance engineer has no clue regarding what the application does (either because he is new to the organization or because he is a consultant) or has no insight into the various tiers of the application, the first and foremost requirement is to get a basic understanding of the application. Get an overview or basic understanding of the user behavior before taking the step of tuning any quadrant or any piece of the system.

Once a basic understanding of the application is obtained, the next step is to select a tool that could be used for load testing the application. There are several off-the-shelf products available, for example LoadRunner, e-Load, etc.[2] Before starting the tuning process, it is important to capture a performance baseline using the load-testing tool that would be used throughout the testing process for comparison. As the testing progresses and when several areas of the application are changed in some form or the other, it would always be helpful to compare any future testing against this baseline to ensure that progress in the right direction is being achieved.

Every time improved performance is achieved due to changes in the application, changes in the system configuration, etc., the new test result becomes the new baseline. This also helps maintain a progress report as

---

2.   LoadRunner is a product owned by Mercury Interactive; e-Load is a product owned by Emperix.

tuning progresses through the various iterations and through the other quadrants.

The application interacts with the database through its persistence layer. Let us start the analysis from this layer. The buck starts here!

One of the common problems identified during application tuning is that the application connects and disconnects for each database interaction. This is a common problem with stateless middleware in application servers. This mistake has over twice the magnitude of impact on performance, and it is totally unscalable. A possible solution here is to have a three-tier architecture where users or clients connect to the middle tier, which has permanent connections to the database. In this way, different users can use a single permanent connection to the database.

In order to tune the database, there should be sufficient evidence that the database is performing slowly, and which areas of the database are performing slower than expected. In order to gather the data for analysis, certain parameters have to be enabled in the init<SID>.ora file.

TIMED_STATISTICS

This is a very important parameter and turning this off will disable most of the statistics-gathering useful for a scientific analysis on the performance of the system. Check if the parameter has been enabled in the parameter file and if it is not enabled, this needs to be turned on. Enabling certain parameters may also automatically enable certain other parameters. For example, enabling the parameter STATISTICS_LEVEL to a value of TYPICAL automatically enables TIMED_STATISTICS to TRUE.

The myth that enabling the TIMED_STATISTICS parameter causes significant performance degradation is false. The overhead from enabling this parameter is so insignificant that, compared to the benefits that this parameter would provide, there should be no hesitation in enabling it. As we have discussed, tuning is not an art, it is scientific, and for scientific analysis there should be evidence in the form of data or statistics. To gather statistics, this parameter should be enabled.

TIMED_OS_STATISTICS

The TIMED_STATISTICS parameter will only enable gathering of statistics at the database and instance level. Starting with Version 9*i*, Oracle has introduced a new parameter called TIMED_OS_STATISTICS. This parameter will enable collection of operating system level statistics.

STATISTICS_LEVEL

This parameter sets the amount of statistics that will be collected. This is a new parameter in Oracle 9*i* and could be set to one of these three values, BASIC, TYPICAL, or ALL. TYPICAL is the default; when the value is set to TYPICAL or ALL it automatically enables the STATISTICS_LEVEL parameter.

Setting the STATISTICS_LEVEL to ALL will enable the collection of O/S-level statistics. This should be done only under controlled conditions because it could degrade performance to a great extent.

V$STATISTICS_LEVEL

The V$STATISTICS_LEVEL view provides the status of the statistics or advisories controlled by the STATISTICS_LEVEL initialization parameter. Most of the advice views will provide statistical advice when the STATSTICS_LEVEL is set to TYPICAL or ALL.

```
COL NAME FORMAT A30
COL VIEW_NAME FORMAT A25
SELECT
  STATISTICS_NAME NAME,
  SESSION_STATUS SES_STATUS,
  SYSTEM_STATUS SYS_STATUS,
  ACTIVATION_LEVEL ALEVEL,
  STATISTICS_VIEW_NAME VIEW_NAME,
  SESSION_SETTABLE SESTABLE
FROM V$STATISTICS_LEVEL
/
```

NAME	SES_STAT	SYS_STAT	ALEVEL	VIEW_NAME	SES
Buffer Cache Advice	ENABLED	ENABLED	TYPICAL	V$DB_CACHE_ADVICE	NO
MTTR Advice	ENABLED	ENABLED	TYPICAL	V$MTTR_TARGET _ADVICE	NO
Timed Statistics	ENABLED	ENABLED	TYPICAL		YES
Timed OS Statistics	DISABLED	DISABLED	ALL		YES
Segment Level Statistics	ENABLED	ENABLED	TYPICAL	V$SEGSTAT	NO
PGA Advice	ENABLED	ENABLED	TYPICAL	V$PGA_TARGET _ADVICE	NO
Plan Execution Statistic	DISABLED	DISABLED	ALL	V$SQL_PLAN _STATISTICS	YES
Shared Pool Advice	ENABLED	ENABLED	TYPICAL	V$SHARED _POOL_ADVICE	NO

```
8 rows selected.
```

The query that was used as an example in Chapter 13 to discuss how the tools behave, is probably a good starting point here:

```
SELECT UP.USPRL_ID,
       UP.USPRL_FIRST_NAME,
       UP.USPRL_LAST_NAME,
       UP.USPRL_CITY,
       UP.USPRL_STATE_ID,
       UP.USPRL_LOGIN_NAME,
       UP.USPRL_EMAIL,
       UP.USPRL_PHONE,
       UP.USPRL_ROLE_CD,
       CMP.COMP_NAME,
       CMP.COMP_SCAC_CODE,
       US.USEC_TOTAL_LOGINS,
       UL.USRLI_ID
FROM   USER_PROFILE   UP,
       COMPANY        CMP,
       USER_LOGIN     UL,
       USER_SECURITY US
WHERE UL.USRLI_ACTIVE_STATUS_CD = 'Active'
  AND UL.USRLI_LOGGED_IN_USPRL_ID = UP.USPRL_ID
  AND UP.USPRL_COMP_ID          = CMP.COMP_ID
  AND UP.USPRL_ID               = US.USEC_USPRL_ID
ORDER BY CMP.COMP_TYPE_CD,
       CMP.COMP_NAME,
       UP.USPRL_LAST_NAME


Execution Plan
--------------------------------------------------------------
0       SELECT STATEMENT Optimizer=CHOOSE (Cost=11 Card=19
        Bytes=3078)
1    0    SORT (ORDER BY) (Cost=11 Card=19 Bytes=3078)
2    1     TABLE ACCESS (BY GLOBAL INDEX ROWID) OF
            'USER_SECURITY'
          (Cost=2 Card=1 Bytes=8)
3    2       NESTED LOOPS (Cost=8 Card=19 Bytes=3078)
4    3        NESTED LOOPS (Cost=7 Card=19 Bytes=2926)
5    4         NESTED LOOPS (Cost=6 Card=19 Bytes=2204)
6    5           VIEW OF 'index$_join$_003'
          (Cost=4 Card=19 Bytes=342)
7    6             HASH JOIN
8    7               INDEX (FAST FULL SCAN) OF 'PK_USRLI' (UNIQUE)
          (Cost=3 Card=19 Bytes=342)
9    7               INDEX (FAST FULL SCAN) OF 'USRLI_INDX1'
          (NON-UNIQUE) (Cost=3 Card=19 Bytes=342)
10   5             TABLE ACCESS (BY LOCAL INDEX ROWID) OF
          'USER_PROFILE' (Cost=2 Card=1 Bytes=98)
11   10              INDEX (UNIQUE SCAN) OF 'PK_USPRL' (UNIQUE)
12   4          TABLE ACCESS (BY LOCAL INDEX ROWID) OF 'COMPANY'
          (Cost=2 Card=1425 Bytes=54150)
```

```
13  12              INDEX (UNIQUE SCAN) OF 'PK_COMP' (UNIQUE)
14  3               INDEX (RANGE SCAN) OF 'USEC_INDX1' (NON-UNIQUE)
```

Statistics

```
        0   recursive calls
      394   db block gets
   433218   consistent gets
     8366   physical reads
        0   redo size
    27787   bytes sent via SQL*Net to client
     1007   bytes received via SQL*Net from client
       34   SQL*Net roundtrips to/from client
        1   sorts (memory)
        0   sorts (disk)
      487   rows processed
```

The above output is generated from an EXPLAIN PLAN that was created for the query listed above. Looking at the statistics generated, the first question that probably arises would be, why are there 433,218 consistent gets and 8366 physical reads to get 487 rows back to the user? This tells us that Oracle had to filter through 433,218 rows of data to finally retrieve 487 rows that actually met the result set. During this process, Oracle also had to perform 8366 disk reads.

14.3.1   What are consistent gets?

Consistent gets indicate the rows found in memory; Oracle had scanned through the large volume of rows in memory, filtering out what was not needed. Basically rows were retrieved from memory or buffer instead of from the physical media such as a disk. Since there is no physical operation to retrieve the row, it could be considered a logical operation, hence it is also called a logical I/O (LIO). However, when data is retrieved from disk (physical) these rows are also loaded into the buffer cache, thus it should also be measured as an LIO influencer.

The following descriptions or statistics indicate an LIO operation:

- Buffer gets

- Consistent gets

- Db-block gets

- Buffer pinned count

Retrieving from memory has always been less expensive compared to retrieving from disk. In the case of retrieving from disk there are physical disk seeks and read time involved. When it comes to LIO operations in

Oracle, they are cheaper compared to physical I/O (PIO); however, LIOs are not cheap enough to be ignored.

Oracle depends on the operating system to manage the buffer, which means that every time an Oracle process needs to search for a row in the buffer there is a latch involved. A latch means to place a lock in memory. This means whenever a row is to be retrieved and validated, there is a latch and a lock every single time, which consumes a high amount of CPU cycles. Now getting a latch and lock is not a straightforward task either. When an Oracle process needs a latch, the O/S may not have any to give, which means it has to wait.

The other value from the query statistics above that catches one's attention, is the physical reads or PIOs. As we have discussed earlier, PIOs are even more expensive. PIOs can be tuned by examining the query and the underlying tables to ensure that there are indexes and the optimizer is using the correct path when generating the execution plan. Event 10053 discussed in Chapter 13 could be a helpful method to get this accomplished.

The EXPLAIN PLAN generated using the AUTOTRACE function could also be generated using the SQL_TRACE = TRUE parameter or by using the 10046 events.

In this situation the query needs to be tuned or rewritten to reduce the LIO. Query tuning may involve rewriting the query, adding a missing index to the table, or adding a hint to the query to use a different execution path.

14.3.2   Hard parses

Hard parses is another area to look into. If Oracle is encountering a large number of hard parses, this could also significantly affect the overall performance of the system. Hard parses are mainly caused because the queries are not being shared or, more precisely, reused. This means that if the query has been executed for the first time, and the query has been parsed, the query is loaded into the shared pool or the library cache. Subsequently, when the query is executed again, Oracle should find the query in the shared pool and should be able to reuse it. However, if it is not found, the query has to be parsed again. This could happen because the query was not identical to the previous query, they were inefficiently written, or the query was not frequently used and hence was aged out of the shared pool, providing space for more frequently used queries.

The number of hard parses in the system can be obtained using the following query:

```
SELECT
  PA.SID,
  PA.VALUE "Hard Parses",
EX.VALUE "Execute Count"
  FROM V$SESSTAT PA,
V$SESSTAT EX
  WHERE PA.SID=EX.SID
  AND PA.STATISTIC# =(SELECT STATISTIC#
                      FROM V$STATNAME
                      WHERE NAME ='parse count (hard)')
AND EX.STATISTIC# =(SELECT STATISTIC#
                    FROM V$STATNAME
                    WHERE NAME ='execute count')
AND PA.VALUE > 0
/
```

```
 SID   Hard Parses   Execute Count
----   -----------   -------------
  13            28             853
  14             1              14
  15             4            4939
  16            15             360
  17            22           14389
  20             1           13806
  21            33          207273
  22            22           95052
  23            26          172151
  24            58          186645
  25            25           98134

 SID   Hard Parses   Execute Count
----   -----------   -------------
  26            93          178495
  28             1           74224
  30             1           89114
  32             9            2185
  36             2          114054
  41            14           10116
  53             6           65957
  61             6              20
  72             1          143838

20 rows selected.
```

Bad or inefficient SQL is the cause of hard parses. Inefficient queries include those that do not use bind variables. Not using bind variables causes SQL queries to be parsed every single time, because literals in queries make each one different from a query that was executed previously, and that is already saved in the library cache of the instance.

Inefficient queries with hard-coded values/literals are something that are within the control of the developer and should be rewritten to use bind variables. In the case of Java applications, the method would be to use prepared statements.

In the SQL query example above, the literal `Active` has been hard coded, and subsequently the code when requiring data with `USRLI_ACTIVE_STATUS_CD` of inactive will execute another statement with the literal `Inactive` hard coded. That means there would be two variations of the same query in the shared pool. Now what if this is transactional data, for example an order number in an order management system? The variations could be many.

```
WHERE UL.USRLI_ACTIVE_STATUS_CD = 'Active'
  AND UL.USRLI_LOGGED_IN_USPRL_ID = UP.USPRL_ID
  AND UP.USPRL_COMP_ID            = CMP.COMP_ID
  AND UP.USPRL_ID                 = US.USEC_USPRL_ID
```

If this query was to use bind variables it would probably be rewritten as

```
WHERE UL.USRLI_ACTIVE_STATUS_CD = :STATUS_CD
  AND UL.USRLI_LOGGED_IN_USPRL_ID = UP.USPRL_ID
  AND UP.USPRL_COMP_ID = CMP.COMP_ID
  AND UP.USPRL_ID = US.USEC_USPRL_ID
```

In the rewritten query, `:STATUS_CD` is a bind variable. During execution time, this variable could have different values depending on what the application business logic requires.

In a Java application, bind variables are denoted by the use of prepared statements. If the query were to use prepared statements, it would probably be rewritten as

```
package rac.chapter14;
//Java Imports
import java.sql.Connection;
import java.sql.ResultSet;
import java.sql.PreparedStatement;

//Oracle Imports
import oracle.jdbc.OracleConnection;
public class BetterPerformance {
...
...


    void runQuery() throws SQLException {
    void runQuery() throws SQLException {
    String query = "SELECT UP.USPRL_ID, " +
                   "UP.USPRL_FIRST_NAME, " +
                   "UP.USPRL_LAST_NAME, " +
```

```
                        "UP.USPRL_CITY, " +
                        "UP.USPRL_STATE_ID, " +
                        "UP.USPRL_LOGIN_NAME, " +
                        "UP.USPRL_EMAIL, " +
                        "UP.USPRL_PHONE, " +
                        "UP.USPRL_ROLE_CD, " +
                        "CMP.COMP_NAME, " +
                        "CMP.COMP_SCAC_CODE, " +
                        "US.USEC_TOTAL_LOGINS, " +
                        "UL.USRLI_ID " +
        "FROM           USER_PROFILE UP, " +
                        "COMPANY CMP, " +
                        "USER_LOGIN UL, " +
                        "USER_SECURITY US " +
                        "WHERE    UL.USRLI_ACTIVE_STA-
                        TUS_CD = ? " +
        "AND            UL.USRLI_LOGGED_IN_USPRL_
        ID=UP.USPRL_ID"+
        "AND            UP.USPRL_COMP_ID=CMP.COMP_ID
                        " +
        "AND            UP.USPRL_ID = US.USEC_USPRL_ID
                        " +
        "ORDER BY CMP.COMP_TYPE_CD,
                        CMP.COMP_NAME,
                        UP.USPRL_LAST_NAME";
    pStmt = conn.prepareStatement(query);
    pStmt.setString(1,"Active");
    rs = pStmt.executeQuery();
  }
  ...
  ...
```

In both these situations, using bind variables and prepared statements, the query itself is the same and would be reused most of the time that a user executes this query from the shared pool.

While using bind variables or prepared statements would be an efficient practice, Oracle provides parameters that can help improve efficiency of SQL queries.

CURSOR_SHARING

To help with the bad SQL and to improve Oracle execution and reusability of the queries that use literals, Oracle has introduced a parameter in Version 8.0 called CURSOR_SHARING. By enabling this parameter, Oracle will generate bind variables for all literals that it encounters, which means queries are now shareable.

SESSION_CACHED_CURSORS

This parameter specifies the number of session cursors to cache. When the cursors are cached, subsequent calls of the same SQL statement will move the cursor to the session cursor cache. Subsequently, when the same SQL statement is executed, the parse calls will find the cursor in the cache and use the already open cursor.

Like the shared pool algorithm, Oracle uses the LRU algorithm to remove entries in the session cursor cache.

V$SQL_PLAN_STATISTICS

This is a new dynamic view introduced in Oracle 9*i* and captures the execution statistics for each operation in the execution plan. The statistics are collected for all cached cursors. Data in this view is collected only if the STATISTICS_LEVEL has been set to ALL.

14.3.3 Tuning parallel operators

```
SELECT SID, DECODE(EVENT,'PARALLEL QUERY DEQUEUE WAIT',
  'PQ DEQ WAIT',
  'PARALLEL QUERY QREF LATCH',
  'PQ REF LATCH', EVENT) EV,
  SEQ#, P1,P2,P3,WAIT_TIME
FROM V$SESSION_WAIT
ORDER BY 1;
```

Below is the output from this query. For the purpose of displaying all information, only column P1 has been displayed. Event "PX Deq Credit: send blkd" is a parallel query event and indicates that parallel query execution.

SID	EV	SEQ#	P1
1	pmon timer	39681	300
2	rdbms ipc message	44068	300
3	rdbms ipc message	46729	300
4	rdbms ipc message	13379	300
5	smon timer	2285	300
6	rdbms ipc message	78	180000
7	rdbms ipc message	1	6000
8	rdbms ipc message	1	6000
9	rdbms ipc message	1	6000
10	**PX Deq Credit: send blkd**	1090	268566527
11	SQL*Net message from client	8105	1111838976
12	**PX Deq Credit: send blkd**	195	268566527
13	SQL*Net more data to client	11382	1650815232
14	SQL*Net message from client	11600	675562835

```
15   PX Deq Credit: send blkd              187    268566527
16   rdbms ipc message                       1         6000
17   PX Deq Credit: send blkd              193    268566527
```

1.   When all of the above methods do not provide sufficient information to help diagnose the problem, the next method is to try and obtain more detailed information about the session activity by doing a trace of the session. This could be done by tracing the current session's activity by enabling event 10046 at level 12.

```
ALTER SESSION SET EVENTS '10046 TRACE NAME CONTEXT
FOREVER, LEVEL 12';
```

The trace file is normally generated in the location defined by the user dump destination in the parameter file. The output of the trace file looks like this (please note that PX Deq: Join ACK and other waits that start with PX all indicate that general parallel execution activity):

```
WAIT #1: nam='process startup' ela= 2 p1=80 p2=1 p3=0
WAIT #1: nam='process startup' ela= 1 p1=80 p2=2 p3=0
WAIT #1: nam='process startup' ela= 1 p1=80 p2=3 p3=0
WAIT #1: nam='PX Deq: Join ACK' ela= 1 p1=268500992 p2=1 p3=0
WAIT #1: nam='PX Deq: Join ACK' ela= 0 p1=268500993 p2=1 p3=0
WAIT #1: nam='PX Deq: Join ACK' ela= 0 p1=268500995 p2=1 p3=0
WAIT #1: nam='PX Deq Credit: send blkd' ela= 0 p1=268500995
 p2=1 p3=0
WAIT #1: nam='PX Deq Credit: send blkd' ela= 0 p1=268500995
 p2=2 p3=0
WAIT #1: nam='PX Deq: Parse Reply' ela= 0 p1=200 p2=1 p3=0
WAIT #1: nam='PX Deq: Parse Reply' ela= 0 p1=200 p2=2 p3=0
WAIT #1: nam='PX Deq: Parse Reply' ela= 0 p1=200 p2=1 p3=0
WAIT #1: nam='PX Deq: Parse Reply' ela= 0 p1=200 p2=1 p3=0
EXEC #1:c=2,e=10,p=0,cr=0,cu=3,mis=0,r=0,dep=0,og=3,
 tim=3704363918
WAIT #1: nam='SQL*Net message to client' ela= 0
 p1=1650815232 p2=1 p3=0
```

14.4   Instance tuning

Though the approach to these discussions is divided into several areas, performance tuning is an overall strategy. Many times a change to a specific area can affect other areas of the database. For example, tuning the SQL queries and ensuring the query is using bind variables may require that you reduce the size of the shared pool, because there would be more shared queries, which would mean fewer queries to be cached and hence a smaller shared pool. On the other hand, adding an index could improve the query performance, but could reduce the performance of a DML operation, because Oracle has to perform an extra I/O to update this new index.

Under this section, let us look at tuning some of the instance-specific areas in a RAC instance. Once the instance-specific parameters have been tuned, these changes can be applied to the other instances.

14.4.1   Memory management

Each instance uses the memory of the node and operating system in which it resides. The normal practice is to allocate about 80% of the system's memory for use by Oracle. The memory at the O/S level is allocated by setting certain kernel parameters that configure the shared memory and semaphores. Oracle uses certain parameters defined in the initialization file to utilize the memory allocated by the O/S kernel. The following parameters and dynamic views directly or indirectly influence the memory management of an instance.

SHARED_POOL

The shared pool contains the library cache and dictionary cache areas. The library cache is where Oracle will store the shared SQL queries and the dictionary cache contains the data-dictionary-related information. Sizing the SHARED_POOL depends on the SQL queries of the application, how many SQL queries are present and how large each query would be. Normally, a large shared pool may be required when the SQL queries do not use bind variables and instead use hard-coded values or literals while accessing information from the database.

Oracle provides advice on the shared pool size through the V$SHARED_POOL_ADVICE dynamic view. The statistics or advice is only provided if the STATISTICS_LEVEL parameter has been enabled and has been set to TYPICAL.

```
SQL> show parameter shared
/

NAME                            TYPE         VALUE
------------------------------- -----------  ----------
hi_shared_memory_address        integer      0
max_shared_servers              integer      20
shared_memory_address           integer      0
shared_pool_reserved_size       big integer  107374182
shared_pool_size                big integer  2147483648
shared_server_sessions          integer      0
shared_servers                  integer      0
```

V$SHARED_POOL_ADVICE

As mentioned above, the shared pool contains SQL statements; sizing of the shared pool is directly related to the quality of these SQL statements. The higher the size of the shared pool, the lower will be number of parses, because if sufficient memory is available then these SQL statements will not be aged out of the cache. The V$SHARED_POOL_ADVICE view provides information about library cache memory and provides additional help by predicting the effect of increasing or decreasing the amount of shared pool.

```
SELECT
      SHARED_POOL_SIZE_FOR_ESTIMATE SPSE,
      SHARED_POOL_SIZE_FACTOR SPSF,
      ESTD_LC_SIZE ELS,
      ESTD_LC_MEMORY_OBJECTS ELMO,
      ESTD_LC_TIME_SAVED ELTS,
      ESTD_LC_TIME_SAVED_FACTOR ELTSF,
      ESTD_LC_MEMORY_OBJECT_HITS ELMOH
FROM V$SHARED_POOL_ADVICE
/
```

SPSE	SPSF	ELS	ELMO	ELTS	ELTSF	ELMOH
1216	.5938	422	66163	109519	1	9175821
1424	.6953	422	66163	109519	1	9175821
1632	.7969	422	66163	109519	1	9175821
1840	.8984	422	66163	109519	1	9175821
2048	1	422	66163	109519	1	9175821
2256	1.1016	422	66163	109519	1	9175821
2464	1.2031	422	66163	109519	1	9175821
2672	1.3047	422	66163	109519	1	9175821
2880	1.4063	422	66163	109519	1	9175821
3088	1.5078	422	66163	109519	1	9175821
3296	1.6094	422	66163	109519	1	9175821
SPSE	SPSF	ELS	ELMO	ELTS	ELTSF	ELMOH
3504	1.7109	422	66163	109519	1	9175821
3712	1.8125	422	66163	109519	1	9175821
3920	1.9141	422	66163	109519	1	9175821
4128	2.0156	422	66163	109519	1	9175821

```
15 rows selected.
```

The value of 1 in the SHARED_POOL_SIZE_FACTOR column indicates the current shared pool size. The rows above this value indicate that the number of parse counts would be significantly high if the value was less than the current SHARED_POOL size and the rows below this number indicate that the parse counts would reduce when this value is increased.

The data dictionary view also reports on the library cache information. Through the ESTD_LC_TIME_SAVED (ELTS) column it provides the amount of parse time that is saved because the library cache had already cached the information. Conversely, this is the amount of time (in seconds) that Oracle would have spent reloading the query into the library cache if the shared pool was not set to the current value.

The query below against the V$DB_OBJECT_CACHE view provides an indication on the number of database objects that have been cached. The output from the query provides the number of various objects by type that is currently in a KEEP state and how many are not. For example, there are four INDEX objects retained and 111 objects not retained. Similarly, none of the cursors has been kept. This view also provides information such as the number of times the object had to be loaded back because of space restrictions.

```
SELECT
     TYPE,
     KEPT,
     COUNT (*),
     SUM (SHARABLE_MEM)
FROM V$DB_OBJECT_CACHE
GROUP BY TYPE,
         KEPT
/
```

TYPE	KEP	COUNT(*)	SUM(SHARABLE_MEM)
TYPE	NO	288	4768575
VIEW	NO	434	1103864
INDEX	NO	111	657241
INDEX	YES	4	5066
TABLE	NO	387	1467592
TABLE	YES	21	53696
CURSOR	NO	9120	123875555
CLUSTER	NO	4	8131
CLUSTER	YES	6	12741
LIBRARY	NO	8	10378
PACKAGE	NO	40	1213688

TYPE	KEP	COUNT(*)	SUM(SHARABLE_MEM)
PACKAGE	YES	2	483702
PUB_SUB	NO	11	16950
SYNONYM	NO	350	1631810
TRIGGER	NO	49	271407
FUNCTION	NO	62	1101355
OPERATOR	NO	2	6762
SEQUENCE	NO	21	54017
PROCEDURE	NO	1	20480

```
NOT LOADED        NO          4861                       0
NON-EXISTENT      NO            47                   61729
PACKAGE BODY      NO            36                 1182198

TYPE              KEP    COUNT(*)      SUM(SHARABLE_MEM)
----------        ----   --------      ------------------
PACKAGE BODY      YES           2                   95670
```

23 rows selected.

V$LIBRARY_CACHE_MEMORY

Continuing with the options of tuning the shared pool, the V$LIBRARY_CACHE_MEMORY dynamic view provides the amount of memory allocated to the library cache memory objects in different namespaces.

```
SELECT
     LC_NAMESPACE NAMESPACE,
     LC_INUSE_MEMORY_OBJECTS USED_BY_OBJ,
     LC_INUSE_MEMORY_SIZE USED_SIZE,
     LC_FREEABLE_MEMORY_OBJECTS AVL_FOR_OBJ,
     LC_FREEABLE_MEMORY_SIZE FREE_SIZE
FROM V$LIBRARY_CACHE_MEMORY
/
```

NAMESPACE	USED_BY_OBJ	USED_SIZE	AVL_FOR_OBJ	FREE_SIZE
BODY	6	0	76	1
CLUSTER	13	0	8	0
INDEX	14	0	220	0
JAVA DATA	0	0	0	0
JAVA RESOURCE	0	0	0	0
JAVA SOURCE	0	0	0	0
OBJECT	0	0	0	0
OTHER/SYSTEM	0	0	22	0
PIPE	0	0	0	0
SQL AREA	31	0	12803	105
TABLE/PROCEDURE	139	0	4197	16
NAMESPACE	USED_BY_OBJ	USED_SIZE	AVL_FOR_OBJ	FREE_SIZE
TRIGGER	46	0	152	0

12 rows selected.

V$LIBRARYCACHE

The query below will provide statistics that will help determine the performance of the library cache. Two of the key columns that should be monitored are RELOADS and INVALIDATIONS. RELOADS indicates the number of times the objects had to be reloaded into the library cache because they were not kept in memory. The reasons for this would be because of objects aging out of the library cache, objects not being used for a long time, or being flushed out because there was insufficient memory. Since RELOADS also contains the count for the load that occurred the very first time before the object was pinned, it should be observed if this value is growing. If the reloads were due to objects being flushed out, increasing the shared pool would be a potential option.

INVALIDATIONS occur when the objects become invalid because the underlying dependent objects may have been modified or may have changed the status to invalid. Invalidations of objects cause the objects to be reparsed after the underlying dependent objects have become valid again.

```
COL PINS FORMAT 99999999
COL RELOADS FORMAT 9999999
COL GETHITS FORMAT 9999999
COL PINHITS FORMAT 999999999
COL INVAL FORMAT 9999999
SELECT NAMESPACE,
       GETS,
       GETHITS,
       PINS,
       PINHITS,
       RELOADS,
       INVALIDATIONS INVAL
FROM V$LIBRARYCACHE
/
```

NAMESPACE	GETS	GETHITS	PINS	PINHITS	RELOADS	INVAL
SQL AREA	399001	382726	20997285	20972663	1084	8154
TABLE/PROCEDURE	7381256	7373683	10108219	10087081	4937	0
BODY	26869	26823	26869	26815	8	0
TRIGGER	1021324	1021012	1021591	1020945	27	0
INDEX	104208	103909	54768	54408	8	0
CLUSTER	6235	6221	5365	5343	0	0
OBJECT	0	0	0	0	0	0
PIPE	0	0	0	0	0	0
JAVA SOURCE	0	0	0	0	0	0
JAVA RESOURCE	0	0	0	0	0	0
JAVA DATA	0	0	0	0	0	0

```
11 rows selected.
```

DB_CACHE_SIZE

DB_CACHE_SIZE is a new parameter introduced in Version 9*i* that replaces the DB_BLOCK_BUFFERS parameter and defines the default buffer pool size. In situations where multiple block sizes are defined, normally the default cache size corresponds to the default database block size.

For every block size defined, a corresponding DB_CACHE_SIZE is to be created. This is to ensure that the data retrieved using a specific block size has a corresponding memory area and all rows are of the same block size.

Similar to the advice available for the shared pool, Oracle also provides advice for the DB_CACHE_SIZE. In order to enable the advice feature, the following two parameters should be enabled, the DB_CACHE_ADVICE parameter should be set to ON and the STATISTICS_LEVEL should be set to TYPICAL.

DB_CACHE_ADVICE

Turning this parameter ON enables statistics collection for the different cache sizes and Oracle populates the V$DB_CACHE_ADVICE view. This parameter is automatically enabled when the STATISTICS_LEVEL is set to TYPICAL or ALL.

V$DB_CACHE_ADVICE

Below is a query[3] that provides information from this view. Similar to V$SHARED_POOL_ADVICE, this query also provides advice on the optimal sizing of the DB_CACHE_SIZE parameter. In the output below, where the column EST_PHYSICAL_READ_FACTOR has a value of 1, the DB_CACHE_SIZE has been set to 512 MB. At this value the number of the estimated number of physical reads is 2,266,628. Setting this value lower than the current value would increase the number of physical reads. Increasing the value of DB_CACHE_SIZE to say 720 MB would reduce the physical reads, though not significantly, as indicated below.

```
column size_for_estimate        format 999,999,999 heading
                                  'Cache Size (m)'
column buffers_for_estimate      format 999,999,999 heading 'Buffers'
column estd_physical_            format 999.90 heading
  read_factor                     'Estd Phys|Read Factor'
column estd_physical_reads       format 999,999,999,999 heading 'Estd
Phys|Reads'
SELECT
     SIZE_FOR_ESTIMATE,
     BUFFERS_FOR_ESTIMATE,
     ESTD_PHYSICAL_READ_FACTOR,
     ESTD_PHYSICAL_READS
```

---

3.   This query has been taken from the Oracle Performance Tuning documentation Version 9*i* Release 2.

```
FROM V$DB_CACHE_ADVICE
WHERE NAME='DEFAULT' AND
      BLOCK_SIZE =
        ( SELECT VALUE
          FROM V$PARAMETER
          WHERE NAME = 'DB_BLOCK_SIZE' )
AND ADVICE_STATUS = 'ON'
/
```

Cache Size (m)	Buffers	Estd Phys Read Factor	Estd Phys Reads
48	5,739	89.43	202,695,043
96	11,478	84.00	190,395,258
144	17,217	80.78	183,093,708
192	22,956	77.80	176,354,748
240	28,695	75.91	172,069,835
288	34,434	51.73	117,244,628
336	40,173	10.25	23,238,498
384	45,912	4.77	10,812,383
432	51,651	1.81	4,100,150
480	57,390	1.21	2,732,271

Cache Size (m)	Buffers	Estd Phys Read Factor	Estd Phys Reads
512	61,216	1.00	2,266,628
528	63,129	.90	2,040,032
576	68,868	.70	1,586,507
624	74,607	.62	1,409,380
672	80,346	.56	1,268,110
720	86,085	.53	1,195,732
768	91,824	.51	1,145,432
816	97,563	.50	1,135,638
864	103,302	.50	1,133,148
912	109,041	.50	1,132,152

Cache Size (m)	Buffers	Estd Phys Read Factor	Estd Phys Reads
960	114,780	.50	1,132,152

```
21 rows selected.
```

DB_KEEP_CACHE_SIZE

This parameter is used to specify the size of the keep buffer pool. Oracle does not support multiple cache sizes for the keep cache. DB_KEEP_CACHE_SIZE is based on the default block size. If a value of this parameter is not specified in the parameter, Oracle assigns a value of ZERO. This parameter replaces the BUFFER_POOL_KEEP parameter.

DB_RECYCLE_CACHE_SIZE

Similar to the DB_KEEP_CACHE_SIZE parameter, this parameter is used to specify the size of the recycle buffer pool. DB_RECYCLE_CACHE_SIZE is also based on the default block size. Multiple block sizes do not change the size of this parameter. This parameter replaces the BUFFER_POOL_RECYCLE parameter.

V$BUFFER_POOL

This view and the query below provide information about all buffer pools available for the instance. The output indicates that the instance is currently only configured with a single DB_CACHE_SIZE or buffer pool.

```
SELECT
     NAME,
     BLOCK_SIZE,
     BUFFERS,
     SET_COUNT,
     LO_SETID,
     HI_SETID
FROM V$BUFFER_POOL;


NAME     BLOCK_SIZE   BUFFERS SET_COUNT  LO_SETID HI_SETID
----     ----------  --------- -------- --------- --------
DEFAULT      8192     122432         2         5        6
```

V$SGA_DYNAMIC_COMPONENTS

This view and the query below display information about the last 100 completed SGA resize operations. However, this does not include any work-in-progress operations.

```
SELECT
     COMPONENT,
     CURRENT_SIZE,
     OPER_COUNT,
     GRANULE_SIZE
FROM V$SGA_DYNAMIC_COMPONENTS;


COMPONENT       CURRENT_SIZE   OPER_COUNT    GRANULE_SIZE
-----------     ------------   ----------    ------------
shared pool       2147483648            0        16777216
large pool         117440512            0        16777216
buffer cache      1073741824            0        16777216
```

PGA_AGGREGATE_TARGET

This parameter replaces the SORT_AREA and SORT_AREA_RETAINED_SIZE parameter available in the previous versions of Oracle. This parameter specifies the target aggregate PGA memory available to all server processes attached to the instance. This parameter enables the automatic setting of the SQL work area used for sort/merge operations during SQL query execution.

Similar to the DB_CACHE_SIZE and the SHARED_POOL parameters, Oracle also provides advice on the PGA_AGGREGATE_TARGET provided the WORKAREA_SIZE_POLICY parameter has been defined.

V$PGASTAT

This view provides the PGA memory usage statistics and is a cumulative value since instance startup. The value from this view provides a great detail of information in sizing the PGA_AGGREGATE_TARGET.

```
COL NAME FORMAT A45
SELECT * FROM V$PGASTAT;

NAME                                            VALUE  UNIT
----------------------------------------    ---------  -------
aggregate PGA target parameter              524288000  bytes
aggregate PGA auto target                   442920960  bytes
global memory bound                          26214400  bytes
total PGA inuse                              32146432  bytes
total PGA allocated                         48112640  bytes
maximum PGA allocated                       49292288  bytes
total freeable PGA memory                    3997696  bytes
PGA memory freed back to OS                  1179648  bytes
total PGA used for auto workareas                  0  bytes

NAME                                            VALUE  UNIT
----------------------------------------    ---------  -------
maximum PGA used for auto workareas           376832  bytes
total PGA used for manual workareas                0  bytes
maximum PGA used for manual workareas              0  bytes
over allocation count                              0  bytes
processed                                    5899264  bytes
extra bytes read/written                           0  bytes
cache hit percentage                             100  percent

16 rows selected.
```

V$PGA_TARGET_ADVICE

This dynamic view provides statistics on the impact on the PGA when the PGA_AGGREGATE_TARGET parameter is changed.

```
SELECT
      PGA_TARGET_FOR_ESTIMATE PTFE,
      PGA_TARGET_FACTOR PTF,
      ADVICE_STATUS ADS,
      BYTES_PROCESSED BP,
      ESTD_EXTRA_BYTES_RW EEBR,
      ESTD_PGA_CACHE_HIT_PERCENTAGE EPCHP,
      ESTD_OVERALLOC_COUNT EOC
FROM V$PGA_TARGET_ADVICE
/
```

PTFE	PTF	ADS	BP	EEBR	EPCHP	EOC
26214400	.125	ON	35991552	30892032	54	10
52428800	.25	ON	35991552	7723008	82	0
104857600	.5	ON	35991552	0	100	0
157286400	.75	ON	35991552	0	100	0
209715200	1	ON	35991552	0	100	0
251658240	1.2	ON	35991552	0	100	0
293601280	1.4	ON	35991552	0	100	0
335544320	1.6	ON	35991552	0	100	0
377487360	1.8	ON	35991552	0	100	0
419430400	2	ON	35991552	0	100	0
629145600	3	ON	35991552	0	100	0
838860800	4	ON	35991552	0	100	0
1258291200	6	ON	35991552	0	100	0
1677721600	8	ON	35991552	0	100	0

```
14 rows selected.
```

SGA_MAX_SIZE

Setting this parameter allows dynamic allocation of memory configuration parameters such as the SHARED_POOL, DB_CACHE_SIZE, etc. If this parameter is not set, Oracle calculates this value based on the combined values of the other memory configuration parameters and this becomes the upper bound value of the SGA_MAX_SIZE. In this case, changing the values of the other parameters is not possible.

OPTIMIZER_INDX_COST_ADJ

This parameter affects the cost calculation of an index. If the default value of this parameter is set to 100%, then it causes the optimizer to evaluate index-based access at regular cost. Setting the value of this parameter to 50% computes the cost of index-based access to half the normal access method. If this value is set very low, say around 5%, the optimizer will prefer index scans over full table scans thus improving overall performance of queries.

OPTIMIZER_INDEX_CACHING

Setting this parameter higher than its default value of 0 helps adjust the behavior of cost-based optimizer to favor nested loop joins over in-list iterators.

Setting this parameter to a higher value, say between 90 and 95, makes nested loop joins and in-list iterators look less expensive to the optimizer. As a result, it will be more likely to pick nested loop joins over hash or sort-merge joins and to pick indexes using in-list iterators over other indexes or full table scans.

The following query lists all long-running operations on the database. The output from this query indicates a high number of hash joins and sort-merge operations on the database.

```
COL IID FORMAT 99
COL OPNAME FORMAT A11
COL SOFAR FORMAT 9999999
COL TOTAL FORMAT 9999999
COL UNITS FORMAT A8
COL TR FORMAT 999999
COL ES FORMAT 999999

SELECT
      INST_ID IID,
      OPNAME,
      SOFAR,
      TOTALWORK TOTAL,
      UNITS,
      START_TIME,
      TIME_REMAINING TR,
      ELAPSED_SECONDS ES
FROM GV$SESSION_LONGOPS
WHERE TIME_REMAINING> 0;
/
```

INST_ID	OPNAME	SOFAR	TW	UNITS	START_TIME	TR	ES
2	Hash Join	915	945	Blocks	04-DEC-2002 14:58:07	43	1299
2	Hash Join	885	945	Blocks	04-DEC-2002 14:59:58	82	1203
2	Hash Join	930	945	Blocks	04-DEC-2002 15:00:17	19	1190
2	Hash Join	810	945	Blocks	04-DEC-2002 15:00:20	193	1159
2	Hash Join	915	945	Blocks	04-DEC-2002 15:00:57	38	1144
2	Hash Join	810	945	Blocks	04-DEC-2002 15:02:38	170	1018
1	Sort Output	157	2047	Blocks	04-DEC-2002 15:13:24	5008	41
1	Sort Output	436	2047	Blocks	04-DEC-2002 15:12:28	1696	459
1	Sort Output	162	2047	Blocks	04-DEC-2002 15:12:56	4945	425
1	Sort Output	157	2047	Blocks	04-DEC-2002 15:13:24	5044	419
1	Sort Output	148	2047	Blocks	04-DEC-2002 15:13:39	4978	388
1	Sort Output	148	2047	Blocks	04-DEC-2002 15:13:48	4991	389

```
2 Sort Output    317 2047  Blocks  04-DEC-2002 15:22:23  8879 1627
2 Sort Output    317 2047  Blocks  04-DEC-2002 15:22:23  8896 1630
2 Sort Output    317 2047  Blocks  04-DEC-2002 15:22:38  8983 1646
2 Sort Output    317 2047  Blocks  04-DEC-2002 15:22:41  8999 1649
2 Sort Output    317 2047  Blocks  04-DEC-2002 15:22:50  8983 1646
```

Setting OPTIMIZER_INDX_COST_ADJ to 5 and OPTIMIZER_INDEX_ CACHING to 95 changes the optimizer behavior, and the new execution plans generated by Oracle for the same query eliminates these high latencies during query operations.

```
SELECT
     OPNAME,
     SOFAR,
     START_TIME,
     TIME_REMAINING,
     ELAPSED_SECONDS
FROM V$SESSION_LONGOPS;
/
```

```
OPNAME            SOFAR  START_TIME           TIME_REMAINING  ELAPSED_SECONDS
---------------  -------  --------------------  --------------  ---------------
Instance Recove  1638400  06-DEC-2002 17:03:43              0               31
Instance Recove        1  06-DEC-2002 17:03:43              0               39
Sort Output         2444  06-DEC-2002 17:08:34              0               12
Sort Output         2444  06-DEC-2002 17:08:34              0               12
```

The GV$SESSION_LONGOPS view provides visibility to the time taken to execute long-running operations under Oracle, providing the estimated total time and the time taken so far. The output from this query helps determine what kind of operations in the system take a long time to complete.

14.4.2   Log management

All the files and tablespaces, with the exception of redo log files, undo tablespaces, and archive log files, are shared across all instances. Redo log files, undo tablespaces, and archive log files store instance-specific information and hence there are multiple copies of these files, actually a set per instance. Having stated this, tuning of these files and their corresponding parameter falls under the category of tuning an instance.

In a RAC implementation that uses raw partitions to store data files, redo log files are also placed on these shared raw partitions. All tuning parameters and conditions also apply to tuning redo log files on a RAC instance.

Tuning this area of the instance has a corresponding effect on tuning the recovery management of the instance. This is because the redo log files, undo tablespaces, and archive log files play an important part in recovery management of both the instance and the database during instance failure or database failure.

Some of the parameters and dynamic views that help in tuning the log and recovery management of an instance will be discussed below.

FAST_START_MTTR_TARGET

This parameter is new in Oracle 9*i* and replaces the FAST_START_ IO_TARGET and LOG_CHECKPOINT_INTERVAL parameters available in the previous versions of Oracle. This parameter enables specification of the number of seconds that the database should take to perform crash recovery of a single instance.

It allows the administrator to establish a distance between LGWR and the checkpoint position based on the estimated time to apply redo information (in seconds). After instance startup, Oracle 9*i* will use estimates of redo read and data block read/write to determine how best to reach the FAST_START_MTTR_TARGET and translate that into dynamic settings for FAST_START_IO_TARGET and LOG_CHECKPOINT_ INTERVAL. As the instance remains active/up, and actual read/write time statistics accumulate and the initial "best guess" estimates are replaced by real data. The dynamic settings for LOG_CHECKPOINT_ INTERVAL and FAST_START_IO_TARGET adapt to reflect changes in the average I/O times. This effectively makes instance recovery time self-tuning and responsive to changes in the operating environment.

The maximum value for FAST_START_MTTR_TARGET is 3600 (1 hour). When values are set that exceed this value, they are rounded down. There is no predefined minimum value; however, when values are set too low it may not be possible to achieve the required MTTR target, as this is limited by the low limit of the target number of dirty buffers, which is 1000. Added to this value is the time taken to mount the database.

If the value is set too low, then the effective MTTR target will be the best MTTR target the system can achieve. If the value is set high, the effective MTTR is estimated based on the whole buffer cache being dirty. The ESTIMATED_MTTR column in the V$INSTANCE_RECOVERY view can be used to view the effective MTTR. If the parameter setting, shown by the TARGET_MTTR column, is consistently different to the effective MTTR it should be adjusted, since this means it is set at an unrealistic value.

If `FAST_START_MTTR_TARGET` is set to a low value, then the database will be writing to disk very frequently and this could easily result in system slowdown. The parameter should therefore be adjusted such that the system is not doing excessive checkpoints but, at the same time, the recovery time is still within acceptable limits.

The output below is an extract from the alert log file and indicates that the `FAST_START_MTTR_TARGET` has been set to 100 and has enabled `LOG_CHECKPOINT_INTERVAL`:

```
Wed Dec 25 11:17:57 2002
ALTER SYSTEM SET fast_start_mttr_target=100
SCOPE=MEMORY;
Wed Dec 25 11:18:26 2002
LOG_CHECKPOINT_INTERVAL was set when MTTR advisory was
switched on.
Wed Dec 25 11:20:37 2002
```

V$INSTANCE_RECOVERY

This view provides estimates of the amount of time it would take for a recovery to complete. The two columns `ESTIMATED_MTTR` and `TARGET_MTTR` provide an insight as to the actual amount of time it would take for crash recovery to complete. While the `TARGET_MTTR` is the value defined by the parameter `FAST_START_MTTR_TARGET`, the `ESTIMATED_MTTR` is the actual value based on the number of redo blocks being generated.

For example, an update operation to update one column of a 605,000 row table increased the `ESTIMATED_MTTR` value from 77 to 112, showing that it requires more MTTR to recover compared to the actual value specified by the `FAST_START_MTTR_TARGET` parameter. In order to maintain this recovery time, Oracle performs more frequent checkpoints that force writing of changes to the redo log files.

```
SELECT
      RECOVERY_ESTIMATED_IOS RECEIOS,
      ACTUAL_REDO_BLKS,
      TARGET_REDO_BLKS,
      TARGET_MTTR TMTTR,
      ESTIMATED_MTTR EMTTR,
      CKPT_BLOCK_WRITES CKPTBLKWRITS
FROM
V$INSTANCE_RECOVERY
/
```

RECEIOS	ACTUAL_REDO_BLKS	TARGET_REDO_BLKS	TMTTR	EMTTR	CKPTBLKWRITS
4836	77860	200000	100	77	0

```
SQL> /
```

RECEIOS	ACTUAL_REDO_BLKS	TARGET_REDO_BLKS	TMTTR	EMTTR	CKPTBLKWRITS
11220	221258	200000	100	96	35193

```
SQL> /
```

RECEIOS	ACTUAL_REDO_BLKS	TARGET_REDO_BLKS	TMTTR	EMTTR	CKPTBLKWRITS
12081	200023	200000	100	101	40762

```
SQL> /
```

RECEIOS	ACTUAL_REDO_BLKS	TARGET_REDO_BLKS	TMTTR	EMTTR	CKPTBLKWRITS
12118	185539	200000	100	112	43465

While MTTR is important to maintain service level agreements, setting the FAST_START_MTTR_TARGET to a small value could hinder performance due to frequent checkpoints.

V$MTTR_TARGET_ADVICE

Oracle also provides another dynamic view for tuning the MTTR value. This view is populated only if the FAST_START_MTTR_TARGET parameter is enabled. This advisor contains estimates on the number of physical I/Os for the MTTR corresponding to each row.

Like all other advisors, this advisor also provides estimates for various values of the MTTR_TARGET. For example, setting the FAST_START_MTTR_TARGET value to 150 would support a dirty buffer limit of 28,298 blocks, compared to 9875 blocks if the parameter were set to 100.

```
SELECT
     MTTR_TARGET_FOR_ESTIMATE MTE,
     DIRTY_LIMIT DL,
     ESTD_CACHE_WRITES ECW,
     ESTD_TOTAL_WRITES ETW,
     ESTD_TOTAL_IOS ETI

FROM
V$MTTR_TARGET_ADVICE
/
```

```
SQL>/
     MTE          DL         ECW         ETW         ETI
   ------      ------      ------      ------      -------
       76        1000      103686      103686       126144
      100        9875       91355       91355       113813
      150       28298       91355       91355       113813
      200       46721       91355       91355       113813
```

14.4.3 Undo management

Under Oracle 9*i*, with the new undo management architecture, every transaction that starts is allocated an undo segment of its own. If there are no undo segments available, a new undo segment is created automatically. However, if there is no space available for a new undo segment to be created, then Oracle assigns the transaction to a segment that is currently in use by another transaction.

When an instance is started, 10 undo segments are created; subsequently, for every five sessions, Oracle creates one undo segment. As mentioned earlier, when a new transaction is unable to identify an undo segment, it creates one. This way, on busy systems that started with 10 undo segments, this number of segments would grow very large, depending on the number of concurrent transactions and the duration of these transactions. A transaction retains an undo segment through the life of the transaction.

After undo segments are created, and as the database warms up and more and more users and transactions get started, a shutdown of the instance will reduce the number of undo segments back to the original 10. Subsequently, when the instance is started, only 10 segments are available and Oracle once again starts building the undo segments.

This is an expensive operation and shutting down instances frequently is discouraged. Since undo segments are automatically created, there is no significant maintenance involved. Undo segments could be monitored using the following dynamic performance views.

V$UNDOSTAT

This dynamic view helps in the determination of the amount of undo space required for the current workload. The values in the underlying fixed table (X$KTUSMST) are used by Oracle for automatic undo management. The view and the underlying X$ table retain the data spanning a 7-day cycle storing a maximum of 1008 rows. The view provides information such as the query length, transaction concurrency, and the amount of space consumed.

```
COL QUERYLEN FORMAT 9999999
COL STEALCNT FORMAT 9999999
SELECT
      END_TIME,
      UNDOBLKS,
      TXNCOUNT,
      MAXQUERYLEN QUERYLEN,
      MAXCONCURRENCY TXNCONCURRENCY,
      EXPSTEALCNT STEALCNT
FROM V$UNDOSTAT;
```

END_TIME	UNDOBLKS	TXNCOUNT	QUERYLEN	TXNCONCURRENCY	STEALCNT
19-DEC-2002 05:40:35	0	0	0	0	0
19-DEC-2002 04:00:35	5	558434	236	10	0
19-DEC-2002 03:50:35	15	558380	227	5	0
19-DEC-2002 03:40:35	16	558309	226	11	0
19-DEC-2002 02:10:35	164	555686	231	2	0
19-DEC-2002 02:00:35	26	554496	227	2	0
19-DEC-2002 01:50:35	152	554381	225	1	0
19-DEC-2002 01:40:35	1	554196	224	1	0
19-DEC-2002 01:30:35	1	554185	225	1	0
19-DEC-2002 01:20:35	11	554172	228	1	0
19-DEC-2002 01:10:35	3	554085	224	1	0
19-DEC-2002 01:00:35	13	554048	228	1	0
19-DEC-2002 00:50:35	13	553953	228	1	0
19-DEC-2002 00:40:35	8	553870	225	1	0
END_TIME	UNDOBLKS	TXNCOUNT	QUERYLEN	TXNCONCURRENCY	STEALCNT
19-DEC-2002 00:30:35	24	553817	225	1	0
19-DEC-2002 00:20:35	2	553697	228	1	0

DBA_UNDO_EXTENTS

The data in this view provides details on the number of extents for the undo segments across all the undo tablespaces. Please note that in the clustered database each instance is assigned an undo tablespace and this view reports on all undo tablespaces.

The view provides information on the currently active segments, blocks allocated to these active unexpired segments, and the tablespaces they belong to.

```
COL TABLESPACE_NAME FORMAT A20
COL SEGMENT_NAME FORMAT A20
SELECT
       SEGMENT_NAME,
       TABLESPACE_NAME,
       BLOCKS,
       STATUS
FROM DBA_UNDO_EXTENTS
/
```

SEGMENT_NAME	TABLESPACE_NAME	BLOCKS	STATUS
_SYSSMU10$	UNDO_RAC1	8	EXPIRED
_SYSSMU10$	UNDO_RAC1	128	UNEXPIRED
_SYSSMU11$	UNDO_RAC2	7	EXPIRED
_SYSSMU11$	UNDO_RAC2	8	EXPIRED
_SYSSMU11$	UNDO_RAC2	128	UNEXPIRED
_SYSSMU12$	UNDO_RAC2	7	EXPIRED
_SYSSMU12$	UNDO_RAC2	8	EXPIRED
_SYSSMU13$	UNDO_RAC2	7	EXPIRED
_SYSSMU13$	UNDO_RAC2	8	EXPIRED
_SYSSMU14$	UNDO_RAC2	7	EXPIRED
_SYSSMU14$	UNDO_RAC2	8	EXPIRED
SEGMENT_NAME	TABLESPACE_NAME	BLOCKS	STATUS
_SYSSMU20$	UNDO_RAC2	8	EXPIRED

V$ROLLNAME

This view acts as a cross-reference between the undo segment number and the actual undo segment.

```
SELECT USN,NAME FROM V$ROLLNAME;
```

USN	NAME
0	SYSTEM
11	_SYSSMU11$
12	_SYSSMU12$
13	_SYSSMU13$
14	_SYSSMU14$
15	_SYSSMU15$
16	_SYSSMU16$
17	_SYSSMU17$
18	_SYSSMU18$
19	_SYSSMU19$
20	_SYSSMU20$

UNDO$

In its internal tables, Oracle maintains various status values for the undo segments, as it passes through various stages of its operation. The status column has the following values:

1.   Invalid

2.   Defined but not in use

3.   Online

4.   Offline

5.   Needs recovery

6.   Partially available

```
COL INST# FORMAT 9999
COL NAME FORMAT A15

SELECT
     INST#,
     US#,
     NAME,
     STATUS$,
     XACTSQN,
     UNDOSQN,
     OPTIMAL
FROM UNDO$
/
```

~INST#	US#	NAME	STATUS$	XACTSQN	UNDOSQN	OPTIMAL
0	0	SYSTEM	3	0	0	
1	1	_SYSSMU1$	3	15046	3235	
1	2	_SYSSMU2$	3	17047	3399	
1	3	_SYSSMU3$	3	13821	2866	
1	4	_SYSSMU4$	3	13653	3803	
1	5	_SYSSMU5$	3	14259	2741	
1	6	_SYSSMU6$	3	14222	2781	
1	7	_SYSSMU7$	3	15171	3050	
1	8	_SYSSMU8$	3	13846	2446	

~INST#	US#	NAME	STATUS$	XACTSQN	UNDOSQN	OPTIMAL
1	33	_SYSSMU33$	1	2665	590	
1	34	SYSSMU34$	1	2725	600	
1	35	SYSSMU35$	1	1879	524	

~INST#	US#	NAME	STATUS$	XACTSQN	UNDOSQN	OPTIMAL
2	36	SYSSMU36$	1	1867	474	
2	77	SYSSMU77$	1	247	67	

```
2  78  SYSSMU78$           1      253       72
2  79  SYSSMU79$           1      265       75
2  80  SYSSMU80$           1      273       72
2  81  SYSSMU81$           1      264       74
2  82  SYSSMU82$           1      240       68
2  83  SYSSMU83$           1      237       64
2  84  SYSSMU84$           1      215       59
```

Undo and rollback activity is also reported by the STATSPACK reports:

```
Rollback Segment Stats for DB: PRODDB instance: RAC1 Snaps:
```

RBS No	Trans Table Gets	Pct Waits	Undo Bytes Written	Wraps	Shrinks	Extends
0	65.0	0.00	1,638	0	0	0
1	7,735.0	0.00	1,465,096	3	1	1
2	6,850.0	0.03	1,246,388	6	2	2
3	7,566.0	0.01	1,486,626	30	2	8
4	7,225.0	0.03	1,501,720	31	3	8
5	8,098.0	0.00	1,310,916	3	1	1
6	7,426.0	0.01	1,797,526	4	1	0
7	6,906.0	0.00	1,135,420	21	1	1
8	6,813.0	0.01	1,220,012	5	2	2
9	8,093.0	0.01	1,633,094	4	1	1
10	7,986.0	0.00	1,406,398	5	1	1

In the output above, a high value for "Pct Waits" suggests more rollback segments may be required. RBS stats may not be accurate between begin and end snaps when using auto undo management, as RBS may be dynamically created and dropped as needed.

14.5   Database tuning

In the previous section the discussion was around instance tuning, where basically tuning of the memory parameters and instance-specific areas was the goal. In this section we will look at tuning some of the physical characteristics, such as the database, the storage, and the segments. Memory management is to ensure that Oracle efficiently utilizes data that is in memory. The tuning of the physical layer is equally important, because the data is retrieved from disk before being loaded into memory. If the physical characteristics of the database did not help in providing an efficient data retrieval mechanism, there could be considerable performance issues across all instances participating in the clustered database configuration.

Statistics play a very important part in tuning this tier of the database. Statistical data is important for all areas of tuning; however, in the case of physical attributes, unless there is physical evidence that there are performance issues with a specific area, it is difficult to fix.

Similar to the instance tuning, there are parameters and views that would help tune the database layer. The STATSPACK utility that was discussed in Chapter 13 is a great source that would help in tuning the physical attributes of the database.

DB_BLOCK_SIZE

While tuning the database, the first and foremost important consideration is selecting the appropriate DB_BLOCK_SIZE. Fortunately, with Oracle 9*i*, database administrators have the opportunity to have multiple blocks. The primary block size, which is also called the default DB_BLOCK_SIZE cannot be changed once it is determined. Oracle allows for creation of four additional block sizes per database implementation: 4, 8, 16, and 32 KB.

The DB_BLOCK_SIZE determines the amount of data that could be retrieved per block retrieval. A large block size would be helpful for a decision support systems (DSS)/data warehouse implementation, where data is retrieved in large volumes, mostly through full table scans. A smaller block size of, say, 8 KB would be good enough for an online transaction processing (OLTP) application, where data is retrieved mostly in the form of singleton selections based on more specific selection criteria.

Block sizes also affect the segment-level performance. Segment-level performance issues can be obtained by collecting a STATSPACK snapshot at level 7 or through Oracle-provided views such as V$SEGMENT_ STATISTICS and V$SEGSTAT.

The common indication that there could be potential problems at the segment level is the "buffer busy waits" event noticed in the STATSPACK report. The other areas reported in the STATSPACK report that related to the segment-level statistics is the logical Reads and physical reads:

```
Top 5 Logical Reads per Segment for DB: PRODDB  Instance:
RAC1 Snaps:
-> End Segment Logical Reads Threshold: 10000
```

Owner	Tablespace	Object Name	Subobject Name	Obj. Type	Logical Reads	%Total
SOWNER	COMP_DATA_	COMPANY	_DATA_P002	TABLE	937,312	24.31
SOWNER	COMP_DATA_	COMPANY	_DATA_P001	TABLE	427,264	11.08
SOWNER	INDX_TBS30	USPRL_INDX3		INDEX	260,272	6.75
SOWNER	DATA_TBS30	REGION_DETAIL	_DATA_P001	TABLE	226,784	5.88
SOWNER	COMP_DATA_	COMPANY	_DATA_P003	TABLE	176,016	4.56

```
Top 5 Physical Reads per Segment for DB: PRODDB  Instance:
RAC1 Snaps:
-> End Segment Physical Reads Threshold: 1000
```

Owner	Tablespace	Object Name	Subobject Name	Obj. Type	Physical Reads	%Total
SOWNER	COMP_DATA_	COMPANY	_DATA_P002	TABLE	253,560	46.31
SOWNER	COMP_DATA_	COMPANY	_DATA_P001	TABLE	99,660	18.20
SOWNER	COMP_DATA_	COMPANY	_DATA_P003	TABLE	84,533	15.44
SOWNER	USPRL_DATA	USER_PROFILE	_DATA_P002	TABLE	70,094	12.80
SOWNER	USPRL_DATA	USER_PROFILE	_DATA_P001	TABLE	21,919	4.00

```
Top 5 Buf. Busy Waits per Segment for DB: PRODDB
Instance:RAC1 Snaps:
-> End Segment Buffer Busy Waits Threshold: 100
```

Owner	Tablespace	Object Name	Subobject Name	Object Type	Buffer Busy Waits	%Total
SOWNER	COMP_DATA_	COMPANY	_DATA_P001	TABLE	358	34.82
SOWNER	USERS	PK_USPRL		INDEX	243	23.64
SOWNER	COMP_DATA_	COMPANY	_DATA_P003	TABLE	207	20.14
SOWNER	INDX_TBS20	USPRL_INDX1	_INDX_P001	INDEX	64	6.23
SOWNER	INDX_TBS30	USRLI_INDX1	_INDX_P001	INDEX	39	3.79

Prior to Oracle 9*i*, to get to the bottom of the issue that cased these wait events, one had to hop through various tables and layers of information.

Another method to obtain this information is to directly query certain new dynamic views:

V$SEGMENT_STATISTICS

Starting with Oracle 9*i* Release 2, Oracle provides real-time segment-level statistical information. This view helps the database administrator to drill down into certain wait events noticed at the system level and associate them with a specific table or index.

Like other statistics gathering options, segment-level information is only provided if the STATISTICS_LEVEL parameter and the TIMED_ STATISTICS parameter has been enabled.

Oracle collects the following statistical information at the segment level:

```
SELECT STATISTIC_NAME FROM V$SEGSTAT_NAME;

STATISTIC_NAME
---------------------------------
ITL waits
buffer busy waits
db block changes
global cache cr blocks served
global cache current blocks served
logical reads
physical reads
physical reads direct
physical writes
physical writes direct
row lock waits

11 rows selected.
```

From the above list the "buffer busy waits" are normally of concern to most database administrators. To track down all the objects that have had "buffer busy waits" since the instance startup, the following query will be helpful:

```
COL OBJECT_NAME FORMAT A15
COL TABLESPACE_NAME FORMAT A20
COL OBJECT_TYPE FORMAT A25
COL STATISTIC_NAME FORMAT A20
COL VALUE FORMAT 9999999
SELECT
     OBJECT_NAME,
     TABLESPACE_NAME,
     OBJECT_TYPE,
     VALUE
FROM V$SEGMENT_STATISTICS
WHERE STATISTIC_NAME ='buffer busy waits'
AND VALUE >0
ORDER BY VALUE
/

OBJECT_NAME TABLESPACE_NAME     OBJECT_TYPE          VALUE
----------- ----------------    -----------------    ------
USPRL_INDX3 INDX_TBS3001_P001   INDEX                 1691
COMPANY     COMP_DATA_P002      TABLE SUBPARTITION    2531
USER_LOGIN  USLI_DATA_P002      TABLE PARTITION       4704
EVNTP_INDX1 INDX_TBS2034_P001   INDEX PARTITION      10538
```

> **Note:** The definition and cause of this event, and its remedy, are discussed later in this chapter.

V$SEGSTAT

This is another view that provides segment-level statistics on a real-time basis. This view is also new in Oracle 9*i* Release 2.

The information contained in this view is similar to what is contained in the V$SEGMENT_STATISTICS view. However, when using the V$SEGSTAT view, the values in the various columns will have to be joined with other object views to get the actual names of objects.

For example, to get the tablespace name associated with the data in the V$SEGSTAT view, the TS# column needs to be joined with the V$TABLESPACE view.

```
COL NAME FORMAT A25
COL STATISTIC_NAME FORMAT A25
COL VALUE FORMAT 999999999999
SELECT
        NAME,
        STATISTIC_NAME,
        VALUE
FROM V$SEGSTAT VSS,
V$TABLESPACE VTS
WHERE VSS.TS# = VTS.TS#
AND VALUE > 0
ORDER BY VALUE
```

The outcome of segment-level analysis is to eliminate the problem encountered by frequent waits at the segment level. The two parameters, among others, that would be worth investigating are the INITTRANS and the MAXTRANS parameters at the table and index definitions.

To confirm this finding, another wait event that could be examined is the "enqueue" wait. To determine the specific type of enqueue that is being waited on, the following query and a snapshot of the data on some of the enqueue types should help us drill down further.

```
SELECT
        EQ_TYPE,
        TOTAL_REQ#,
        TOTAL_WAIT#,
        FAILED_REQ#,
        CUM_WAIT_TIME
FROM V$ENQUEUE_STAT
ORDER BY TOTAL_WAIT#
/
```

EQ	TOTAL_REQ	TOTAL_WAIT	FAILED_REQ	CUM_WAIT_TIME
SQ	2017	27	0	409205
MR	34979	34	0	150
TS	88	53	1	205
HW	35475	230	0	2807
IR	1515	389	0	59010
JQ	984	969	10	3574
PS	6443	2808	1068	245641
TT	103161	3180	0	24616
US	4227	3677	0	19460
TA	4877	4754	0	51993
FB	9926	5118	0	8412

EQ	TOTAL_REQ	TOTAL_WAIT	FAILED_REQ	CUM_WAIT_TIME
CF	682320	5649	0	43608
TM	2048657	10556	1	567503
TX	1914970	28237	0	145181

From the above query and the data, it is obvious that the TX (transaction) and TM (DML enqueue) have encountered the highest numbers of requests (TOTAL_REQ) and waits (TOTAL_WAIT). The TX enqueue confirms our earlier finding that the INITRANS and the MAXTRANS parameters may require some adjustment. Another enqueue that has a high cumulative wait time (CUM_WAIT_TIME) is the SQ (sequence number) enqueue.

This is usually an application-related issue pertaining to row locking. However, under RAC, processing can magnify the effect of TX enqueue waits. Performance bottlenecks on leaf blocks of right-growing indexes may also appear as TX enqueue waits while index block splits are in progress.

TX enqueue performance issues along with "buffer busy waits" can be reduced by setting the value of the INITRANS parameter to be equal to the number of CPUs per node multiplied by the number of nodes in the cluster multiplied by 0.75, or to a higher value based on the number of transactions interfering with the objects in question. However, setting the INITRANS or MAXTRANS parameters to a value greater than 99 could cause performance problems. Setting a higher value causes overallocation of space for the transaction block header, which in turn causes less space to be available for the data layer variable header and causes more I/O operation.

DML_LOCKS

Under OPS, it was recommended that this parameter be set to a value of 0 to help improve performance. While this was true, when DML_LOCKS was set to 0, Oracle did not permit any DDL operations on the objects and hence caused severe maintenance concerns. When this parameter was set to 0, the database administrators had to shut down the instance, modify this parameter, make the changes, and set the DML_LOCKS back to its original value and bounce the instance again.

One of the reasons for TM enqueues that were noticed in the earlier example was too few locks. If the DML_LOCKS parameter is not set to 0 (which is not recommended because of maintenance-related difficulties) the number of locks is calculated based on the number of sessions, number of transactions, and the average number of objects that it would access directly or indirectly.

For example, if the instance is configured for 400 sessions, and if each session can execute a query that joins four tables, then each table on average will have at least one index that is accessed by the query. The data related to the table could be residing in at least one data partition and the index in at least one index partition, which means

400 Sessions × 8 Object (4 Tables + 4 Indexes)   = 3200
3200 × 2 Partitions (1 Table partition + 1 Index partition) 6400

The DML_LOCKS parameter in this situation should be set to 6400 or higher.

ENQUEUE_RESOURCES

Another related parameter that helps enqueue activity is the ENQUEUE_RESOURCES. This parameter sets the number of resources that are concurrently locked. While DML_LOCKS allows a certain number of locks per session, the ENQUEUE_RESOURCE parameter allows the setting of these locks. Both these parameters go hand in hand.

At database startup time, Oracle allocates the number of enqueues specified by the ENQUEUE_RESOURCE parameter. The default value for this parameter is derived from the SESSIONS parameter and should be greater than DML_LOCKS + 20. For 4 to 10 sessions, the default value is the number of database files + ((SESSIONS−3) × 5) + 20. For more than 10 sessions it is the number of database files + ((SESSIONS−10) × 2) + 55.

The usage of ENQUEUE_RESOURCES can be obtained by monitoring the V$RESOURCE_LIMIT view.

V$RESOURCE_LIMIT

This view provides visibility to some of the threshold settings and the current consumption values for some of the critical resources.

Some resources, those used by the distributed lock manager (DLM) for example, have a soft limit, which is the initial allocation, and a hard limit, which is theoretically infinite (although in practice it is limited by SGA size). During SGA reservation/initialization, a place is reserved in SGA for the INITIAL_ALLOCATION of resources, but if this allocation is exceeded, additional resources are allocated up to the value indicated in the LIMIT_VALUE against a specific resource. Certain resources such as the ges_ress, ges_locks, dml_locks, etc., have a maximum LIMIT_VALUE defined as UNLIMITED (UNLIMITED = 4,294,967,295).

The following query generates the output containing the current utilization of resources.

```
COL CU FORMAT 9999999
COL MU FORMAT 9999999
COL IA FORMAT A10
COL LV FORMAT A10
SELECT
     RESOURCE_NAME,
     CURRENT_UTILIZATION CU,
     MAX_UTILIZATION MU,
     INITIAL_ALLOCATION IA,
     LIMIT_VALUE LV
FROM V$RESOURCE_LIMIT
/
```

RESOURCE_NAME	CU	MU	IA	LV
processes	28	175	300	300
sessions	21	186	335	335
enqueue_locks	268	307	4564	4564
enqueue_resources	268	315	3532	UNLIMITED
ges_procs	27	173	301	301
ges_ress	18194	24068	13085	UNLIMITED
ges_locks	18534	26493	16625	UNLIMITED
ges_cache_ress	55	1146	0	UNLIMITED
ges_reg_msgs	75	1825	830	UNLIMITED
ges_big_msgs	27	576	830	UNLIMITED
ges_rsv_msgs	0	0	600	600
RESOURCE_NAME	CU	MU	IA	LV
gcs_resources	58457	102224	134675	134675
gcs_shadows	10824	62624	134675	134675
dml_locks	0	200	3000	UNLIMITED
temporary_table_locks	0	1	UNLIMITED	UNLIMITED
transactions	11	45	368	UNLIMITED
branches	0	1	368	UNLIMITED
cmtcallbk	0	1	368	UNLIMITED

```
sort_segment_locks          0    53 UNLIMITED  UNLIMITED
max_rollback_segments      11    27         74         74
max_shared_servers          0     0         20         20
parallel_max_servers        9    11         41         41
```

22 rows selected

The CURRENT_UTILIZATION (CU) column indicates whether the value indicated in the INITIAL_ALLOCATION (IA) column has been exceeded. When the initial allocation value is exceeded, the additional required resources are allocated from the shared pool, where they compete for space with other resources.

V$ROWCACHE

This dynamic view is used to measure the caching behavior of the dictionary cache. The dictionary cache is part of the shared pool and does not have any tunable parameters other than the SHARED_POOL initialization parameter itself. This means that if the shared pool has not been sized correctly there is a direct impact on the dictionary cache.

```
COLUMN PARAMETER FORMAT A21
COLUMN PCT_SUCC_GETS FORMAT 999.9
COLUMN UPDATES FORMAT 999,999,999

SELECT PARAMETER
     , SUM(GETS)
     , SUM(GETMISSES)
     , 100*SUM(GETS - GETMISSES) / SUM(GETS)  PCT_
     SUCC_GETS
     , SUM(MODIFICATIONS) UPDATES
 FROM V$ROWCACHE
WHERE GETS > 0
GROUP BY PARAMETER;
```

PARAMETER	SUM(GETS)	SUM(GETMISSES)	PCT_SUCC_GETS	UPDATES
dc_constraints	462	214	53.7	456
dc_files	5008999	1193	100.0	51
dc_free_extents	9	4	55.6	9
dc_global_oids	78108	303	99.6	0
dc_histogram_defs	3111931	182217	94.1	2,487
dc_object_ids	945364	5088	99.5	396
dc_objects	134090	8963	93.3	8,498
dc_profiles	24694	5	100.0	0
dc_rollback_segments	1759820	236	100.0	107
dc_segments	116673	1725	98.5	1,049
dc_sequences	2742	829	69.8	2,742

PARAMETER	SUM(GETS)	SUM(GETMISSES)	PCT_SUCC_GETS	UPDATES
dc_table_scns	10	10	0	0

```
dc_tablespace_quotas        6990            530          92.4       4,272
dc_tablespaces           4002024            534         100.0          34
dc_used_extents                3              3             0           3
dc_user_grants            233901             83         100.0           0
dc_usernames               99176             66          99.9           0
dc_users                15175456            107         100.0           2
18 rows selected.
```

In the output above, the various values provided are indications of inefficient use of the dictionary cache. For example, the high gets on the dc_users parameter indicate that there is frequent log-in and log-out activity, which could be reduced by having the application perform on a single sign-on option. This means that the application could have several user accounts, but the application itself has only one user sign-on password.

Applications not using locally managed tablespaces could experience high dc_used_extents, dc_segments, and dc_free_extents counts. This is due to frequent access to the dictionary to update the latest extent information. Using LMT reduces this activity because all tablespace management is performed locally at the tablespace level.

A common parameter that should be of concern in a RAC environment is the dc_sequences. This indicates that there are not enough cache sizes defined for the various sequences used by the application. Tuning the cache sizes on the sequences should help reduce the gets on this parameter.

14.6   Operating system tuning

14.6.1   CPU utilization

CPU utilization is the amount of time that the active CPUs on the system are working on running processes. CPU utilization statistics presented by the sar -u command (on a Unix system) is displayed as a composite of the %System, %User, and %Idle times, where the addition of all three parameters will equate to 100%. A lower %Idle time indicates a higher workload.

System and user statistics represent the proportion of time the CPUs are working on system-related activities or user-based programs, respectively. In a normal workload, %System should not consume more than 20% of CPU utilization. CPU utilization information is made more meaningful when combined with the run queue length and run queue occupancy statistics. For example, if the server is running close to the 95% utilization level, does this indicate an immediate CPU deficiency on the server? The answer is, we don't know yet. If this is a single CPU system and the run queue is consistently at a value of 1 then the answer is, it's difficult to arrive at any definite conclusion. If the run queue length consistently exceeds the number of CPUs on the system and the run queue occupancy is consistently high together with a high CPU utilization rate, then this would indicate a CPU deficiency.

An ideal situation for the server would be to consistently run under the 90% utilization level with a stable workload. In this situation, the investment in CPU power is justified, since the utilization rate is high, yet it is not at its maximum. The reality of most servers is that workload fluctuates throughout an entire day and rarely shows as stable. The measurement of CPU utilization can help in identifying shortfalls in CPU processing power. This is especially true during peak periods where the demand of CPU resources can exceed those available and cause system wide performance degradation. The sar -u command will generate the CPU utilization statistics.

The graphical output shown in Figure 14.2 is generated from the data gathered using the sar -u command over a 2-hour time frame. The output was fed into MS Excel[4] to generate this graph. It shows that the system has had several spikes with 100% CPU utilization at several periods, and is worth drilling down into. It can also be noticed that the user activity has been low, however, the system usage has been high.

Figure 14.2
Unix sar *report parsed through MS Excel tool.*

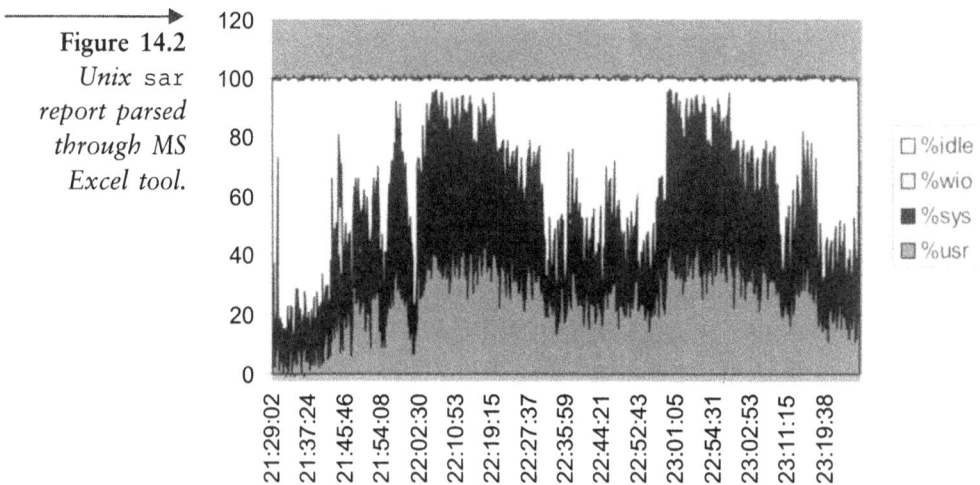

There are several ways to identify CPU top sessions on a system; for example, by using the basic Unix `ps` command. The options used with the `ps` command will also be specific to the type of Unix being run on the server. In general, looking at the accumulated CPU time and the percentage of CPU time the processes are consuming, this is expressed as a percentage of total CPU resources.

```
ora-db2:RAC2:oracle # ps -ef -o pgid,time,pcpu,comm |
sort -r -k 3| more


  PGID       TIME     %CPU    COMMAND
     0   16:48:20      0.8    fsflush
  2139   09:16:42      0.3    /opt/SysShep4/perl/bin/perl
 16163   03:43:34      0.2    oracleRAC2
  7409       0:00      0.1    ps
 15916       2:55      0.1    ora_smon_RAC2
  2013   02:25:32      0.1    dlmd
     0       0:00      0.0    vxnotify
    15       1:26      0.0    vxconfigd
  2094       0:11      0.0    sshd
  7409       0:00      0.0    sort
 26850       0:00      0.0    sh
     0       0:04      0.0    sched
  1558       0:00      0.0    rpc.ucmmstate
     0       0:00      0.0    pageout
 26343       0:00      0.0    oracleRAC2
 11741      31:43      0.0    oracleRAC2
 15918       0:00      0.0    ora_reco_RAC2
```

14.6.2   CPU from Oracle perspective

On a database server, running the `ps` command can yield program names which are fairly non-descriptive. Usually, the output as shown in the previous section would only be helpful to determine the Oracle instance that the process is running against. To relate Unix processes with the Oracle sessions, querying the V$SESSION table where the V$SESSION.PROCESS column equals the Unix process ID will provide a lead into the details. The SID and SERIAL# values can be selected from the V$SESSION table and used for further investigation inside the database to see which SQL statements are being executed by which user.

Starting with Oracle 9i, Oracle captures operating-system-level performance statistics and stores them with other Oracle-related data. This

data could be viewed using the Oracle-provided dynamic views. The query
below provides a list of CPU-related information captured by Oracle:

```
SELECT
      STATISTIC#,
      NAME
FROM   V$STATNAME
WHERE  NAME LIKE '%CPU%'
/

STATISTIC#  NAME
----------  -----------------------------------
        11  CPU used when call started
        12  CPU used by this session
       248  OS User level CPU time
       249  OS System call CPU time
       250  OS Other system trap CPU time
```

Using the above, one could query the Oracle instance and sort for the
top Oracle CPU-consuming sessions independent of the activity at the Unix
level. The users who are using the most CPU resources can be obtained
using the following query:

```
COL NAME FORMAT A30
COL USERNAME FORMAT A20
SELECT
      VSN.NAME,
      VS.USERNAME,
      VSS.VALUE/600 "CPU(MIN)"
FROM V$SESSTAT VSS,
      V$STATNAME VSN,
      V$SESSION VS
WHERE VSS.STATISTIC#=VSN.STATISTIC#
AND VS.SID=VSS.SID
AND VSN.NAME LIKE '%CPU%'
AND VSS.VALUE > 60000
GROUP BY VSN.NAME,
      VS.USERNAME,
      VSS.VALUE/600
/

NAME                             USERNAME           CPU(MIN)
------------------------         ----------         ----------
CPU used by this session         MVALLATH           2191.69333
CPU used by this session         SYSSHEP              164.24
CPU used when call started       MVALLATH           2191.69333
CPU used when call started       SYSSHEP              164.24
```

> **Note:** The CPU activity is also reported in the STATSPACK report under
> the instance activity area.

From the above query, user MVALLATH is consuming most of the CPU. With the session, process, and user name information, the details of the activities could be obtained by determining the activities or queries that user MVALLATH had performed from the data gathered either from the STATSPACK snapshot taken during this period or if the database administrator has been collecting the V$SESSION_EVENT and V$SESSION_WAIT information as described in Chapter 13.

From the query executed by MVALLATH discussed in Chapter 13, a large number of consistent gets and physical reads were performed. Consistent gets are logical operations or reading data from memory (also called buffer gets). In Chapter 5, we discussed how Oracle stores the data in the buffer cache. Searching through the buffer table causes latch serialization. Latch serialization consumes CPU cycles. A latch is nothing but a lock in memory, to protect memory structures from concurrent access by multiple processes. Every time Oracle needs a latch, it is going to spin CPU cycles requesting and releasing locks. This is expensive, and when many queries have a similar behavior, it could take the system to its knees, showing 100% CPU utilization.

In this case and any time where queries show high LIO operations, every effort should be provided to tune these queries, either by rewriting the queries to be more efficient or by providing hints to help the optimizer to generate a better execution plan.

Note: This query was probably not the only query being executed by the user during this period of high CPU utilization; however, it is just used as an example to explain one of the many causes.

Another reason for high CPU utilization could be an insufficient number of latches available. This can be set by tuning the DB_BLOCK_LRU_LATCHES parameter. This parameter can be set to its maximum value of between 2 and 12 times the number of CPUs.

14.6.3 Analyzing disk I/O

Analyzing disk I/O from operating system

Disk I/O can be another area that needs some attention, especially during the initial configuration and testing. Monitoring disk I/O in a clustered environment provides information regarding the mount points and if the disks have been sliced across or have been partitioned vertically against one controller.

Oracle data files, based on the content of usage and how busy they get (based on user access patterns), need to be placed on controller or mount points that do not get affected by other data files and I/O activity from other such busy files.

The output below is an example of looking at I/O activity. The iostat utility provides disk, tape I/O activity and CPU utilization information.

```
ora-db2:RAC2:oracle # iostat --xpm
                    extended device statistics
device      r/s      w/s kr/s kw/s wait actv   svc_t %w %b
sd0,a     239.0      0.0  0.0  0.0  0.0  0.0     3.7  0  0
sd0,e    1392.0      1.4  0.0  1.7  0.0  0.0     6.3  0  1
sd0,g       0.0      0.0  0.0  0.0  0.0  0.0     0.0  0  0
sd1,c     202.5      0.0  0.0  0.0  0.0  0.0   292.0  2  0
sd1,g       0.0      1.4  0.0  1.7  0.0  0.0     6.7  0  1
ssd435,c    0.0      0.0  0.0  0.0  0.0  0.0     0.0  0  0
ssd435,d    0.0   4949.3  0.0  0.0  0.0  0.0    19.0  0  0
ssd435,e    0.0      0.0  0.0  0.0  0.0  0.0     0.0  0  0
ssd436,c  239.8     48.1  0.0  0.0  0.0  0.0  3494.0  4  0
```

- device column provides the name of the disk for which statistic is listed.

- r/s column indicates the reads per second from the device.

- w/s column indicates the writes per second to the device.

- kr/s column indicates the kilobytes read per second from the device.

- kw/s column indicates the kilobytes written per second.

- wait is the average number of transactions waiting for service. This indicates the queue length.

- actv is the average number of transactions actively being serviced. The number indicates that the transactions are no longer in the queue and have not completed.

- svc_t is the average service time, in milliseconds.

- %w is the percentage of time there are transactions waiting for service.

- %b is the percentage of time the disk is busy. Busy disks indicate that transactions are in progress on the disk.

From the output generated using `iostat` above, the service time is a good indicator of disk activity and disk response times. For example the following output

```
sd0,e     1392.0    1.4    0.0    1.7  0.0  0.0    6.3   0   1
```

indicates that there were 1392.0 disk reads per second and the service time was only 6.3 milliseconds. However, the following output

```
sd1,c      202.5    0.0    0.0    0.0  0.0  0.0  292.0   2   0
ssd436,c   239.8   48.1    0.0    0.0  0.0  0.0 3494.0   4   0
```

indicates that there were 202.5 disk reads per second with a service time of 292.0 milliseconds on disk `sd1,c`, which is a poor response time. Disk `ssd436,c` on the other hand shows 3494.0 milliseconds of service time with 4% wait for 239 disk reads and 48 disk writes, which is significantly on the high side, and should be classified as a hot disk. High service times could indicate that some of the most significantly used tables, indexes, etc., reside on this disk and need to be distributed to other disks to reduce I/O contention.

Analyzing disk I/O from Oracle

I/O activity in Oracle can be obtained either by using the STATSPACK report, where the I/O activity at the tablespace level and the I/O activity at the data file level are reported separately from each other, or by querying against the Oracle database directly.

```
Tablespace IO Stats for DB: PRODDB  Instance: RAC1  Snaps: 3509 -3526
->ordered by IOs (Reads + Writes) desc

Tablespace
------------------------------
```

	Reads	Av Reads/s	Av Rd(ms)	Av Blks/Rd	Writes	Av Writes/s	Buffer Waits	Av Buf Wt(ms)
TEMP_OLTP	3,263	0	18.5	13.5	7,585	1	0	0.0
UNDO_RAC1	0	0	0.0		2,303	0	23	0.4
INDX_TBS3010_P001	0	0	0.0		562	0	263	41.1
USERS	55	0	8.9	1.0	166	0	1,706	28.7
SPACK_DATA_P001	15	0	9.3	1.0	135	0	0	0.0

```
File IO Stats for DB: PRODDB  Instance: RAC1  Snaps:
->ordered by Tablespace, File
```

Tablespace	Filename							
	Reads	Av Reads/s	Av Rd(ms)	Av Blks/Rd	Writes	Av Writes/s	Buffer Waits	Av Buf Wt(ms)
DATA_TBS3004_P001	/dev/vx/rdsk/oraracdg/partition300m_59							
	17	0	1.8	1.0	56	0	0	
DATA_TBS3008_P001	/dev/vx/rdsk/oraracdg/partition300m_61							
	0	0			64	0	0	
INDX_TBS2007_P001	/dev/vx/rdsk/oraracdg/partition200m_7							
	4	0	7.5	1.0	1	0	3	16.7
INDX_TBS2008_P001	/dev/vx/rdsk/oraracdg/partition200m_8							
	0	0			9	0	0	
INDX_TBS2009_P001	/dev/vx/rdsk/oraracdg/partition200m_9							
	0	0			5	0	0	
INDX_TBS2010_P001	/dev/vx/rdsk/oraracdg/partition200m_60							
	6	0	6.7	1.0	9	0	0	
INDX_TBS2011_P001	/dev/vx/rdsk/oraracdg/partition200m_10							
	6	0	10.0	1.0	8	0	0	

Wait event statistics of the STATSPACK report are also a good source of information on I/O-related performance issues. For example, in the following extract of the STATSPACK report the I/O-related waits have been highlighted:

```
-> ordered by wait time desc, waits desc (idle events last)
```

Event	Waits	Timeouts	Total Wait Time(s)	Avg wait (ms)	Waits /txn
enqueue	**17,618**	**1,775**	**3,442**	**195**	**0.5**
log file sync	**36,619**	**49**	**272**	**7**	**1.1**
DFS lock handle	92,013	29	235	3	2.8
control file parallel write	**4,659**	**0**	**53**	**11**	**0.1**
log file parallel write	36,209	36,201	42	1	1.1
control file sequential read	**18,309**	**0**	**35**	**2**	**0.6**
PX Deq: Execute Reply	10,797	0	31	3	0.3
PX Deq: Parse Reply	13,099	0	30	2	0.4
PX qref latch	29	29	28	981	0.0
direct path read	**2,625**	**0**	**26**	**10**	**0.1**
PX Deq:Join ACK	13,793	6,592	26	2	0.4
SQL*Net more data to client	164,396	0	10	0	5.0
PX Deq: Signal ACK	3,990	1,357	10	3	0.1
PX Deq: reap credit	210,299	195,058	8	0	6.4
IPC send completion sync	6,707	0	8	1	0.2
buffer busy waits	**289**	**0**	**5**	**18**	**0.0**
db file parallel write	**1,803**	**0**	**5**	**3**	**0.1**

db file sequential read	**424**	**0**	**4**	**9**	**0.0**
direct path write	6,032	0	4	1	0.2
row cache lock	126	0	3	27	0.0
process startup	12	1	3	261	0.0
library cache lock	4,903	0	2	0	0.1
latch free	**519**	**228**	**1**	**3**	**0.0**
name-service call wait	4	1	1	304	0.0
SQL*Net break/ reset to client	240	0	0	2	0.0
KJC: Wait for msg sends to client	939	0	0	0	0.0
PXDeq Credit: send blkd	27	0	0	2	0.0
library cache pin	39	0	0	1	0.0
LGWR wait for redo copy	43	0	0	0	0.0
buffer deadlock	84	83	0	0	0.0
cr request retry	47	47	0	0	0.0
lock escalate retry	18	18	0	0	0.0
SQL*Net message from client	1,611,345	0	201,600	125	49.0
PX Idle Wait	33,509	26,541	72,502	2164	1.0
PX Deq: Execution Msg	28,974	1,101	7,113	246	0.9

Log file sync

This wait is encountered when a user session commits (or rolls back), and the session's redo information must be flushed to the redo log file by the LGWR. The server process performing the commit or rollback waits under this event for the write to the redo log to be completed.

This wait event occurs because of frequent commits, or because the I/O bandwidth is insufficient. If the case is one of frequent commits (average wait time is low but the number of waits is high), then consideration should be given to using batch commits, e.g., commits after every 50 inserts. If, however, I/O is the bottleneck, then with the help of a system administrator the I/O bandwidth of the system should be enhanced to deal with the load. One possible way is to ensure that the log files on spindles are isolated from other data files. In Chapter 2 (Hardware Concepts) there is some discussion around placing redo log files on RAID 1 to help improve write times.

Direct path write

Direct path write refers to the writing of buffers from PGA directly to disk as opposed to the background process, DBWR, writing them from the buffer cache to disk. Direct path writes happen in the following situations:

- The PGA is too small and the sort has to be performed on disk, as opposed to in memory.

- Parallel operations such as parallel DML, parallel create table as select, where the parallel slaves write data from PGA to disk.

Direct path inserts/Certain LOB operations

When a process makes a direct path write request, it waits on this event while the request is serviced. The reason for this wait event is an inadequately sized PGA and/or insufficient I/O bandwidth. Use the PGA advisor for tuning the PGA, and if this does not remedy the problem consider I/O bandwidth enhancement.

Direct path read

Direct path read implies that blocks are being read from disk directly into the PGA and not the SGA. This kind of read generally takes place in the following two situations:

- Parallel queries are being performed where the query slaves are reading data directly into the PGA.

- A large sort is being processed that cannot fit into the area allocated in the PGA for sorting. As a result, the sort has to be done on disk in the TEMP tablespace. After the sort is complete, the data is read back into PGA directly from disk.

Direct I/O has been enabled

A process that is attempting to read blocks into the PGA makes an I/O request call and then waits for the call to be serviced. This wait event indicates that data buffers are being processed faster than the I/O subsystem can read them into the PGA.

This event points to two possible problems, the PGA is too small, or the I/O subsystem is not sized adequately. This could be confirmed either through OEM or by querying V$PGA_TARGET_ADVICE. If the PGA is too small, then increasing the initialization parameter PGA_AGGREGATE_ TARGET to the value recommended by the advisor would be helpful.

If the PGA advisor reveals that the PGA is appropriately sized, then the cause must be full table scans performing more parallel queries than the I/O subsystem can handle. Once again, the two possible remedies are reducing I/O workload or enhancing I/O bandwidth.

Buffer busy wait

This event occurs when two or more processes are trying to access the same buffer in the buffer cache. There are four types of buffer that may be in contention:

- *Segment data block buffer:* Data block of a table or index.

- *Segment header buffer:* Header block of a table or index.

- *Undo block buffer:* Data block of a rollback (undo) segment.

- *Undo header buffer:* Header of a rollback (undo) segment.

Not using AUM and/or automatic segment space management features of Oracle may be the reason for this wait event. Use of these features will help reduce contention for undo segments or their headers. Another possible reason for this wait event is the contention of the segment data block buffer, which is caused by indexes that are right-growing (this can happen when sequences are used to generate numbers being inserted), or by SQL statements performing large-range scans on indexes. The waits caused by sequence-generated indexes could be reduced by using reverse key indexes in a RAC environment.

If locally managed tablespaces are not used, then the symptom could be due to lack of free lists on tables that support many concurrent INSERT operations.

Latch free

A latch is a lock used by Oracle to protect memory structures. The latch free event occurs when a server process attempts to get a latch, but the latch is unavailable. There are different types of latches used for various purposes in Oracle. To resolve the problem of excessive latch free wait events, the type of latch being contended for has to be first identified, as the causes and remedy for the various types of latches are distinct. For example, tuning some of the parameters such as redo log buffer and redo copy latches help tune latch-related redo log files.

Shared pool or library cache latch

This latch can result in excessive waits due to unnecessary parsing of SQL statements. This can happen for several reasons, such as:

- Statements not using bind variables.

- Insufficient size of cursor cache.

- Cursors being closed explicitly after each execution.

- Frequent log-on/log-offs.
- The shared pool being too small.

To alleviate the problem, consider the following in the order shown:

1. Tune the shared pool using the shared pool advisor from the OEM performance management screens or using the V$SHARED_POOL_ADVICE dynamic performance view.

2. Set the initialization parameter CURSOR_SHARING=FORCE to force sharing of cursors among similar SQL statements not using bind variables.

Cache buffer LRU chain

This latch protects the lists of buffers in the buffer cache. It is acquired when modified (dirty) blocks are written to disk or when a server process is searching for blocks to write. Contention for this latch indicates excessive buffer cache throughput, such as cache-based sorts, inefficient SQL that accesses incorrect indexes (large index range scans), or many full table scans. When adding, moving, or removing a buffer from a list, a latch must be obtained.

Cache buffer chains

This latch is acquired when a user process tries to locate a block in the buffer cache. Contention for this latch indicates that multiple users are contending for the same blocks. Any resolution to this problem must include a reduction in contention for the same blocks. This can be achieved by tuning the SQL so that it performs fewer block accesses, and if this does not help, then by using a higher PCTFREE for the segment in question. This will mean that there are fewer rows per block in the segment, and therefore this makes it less likely that the blocks will have contention.

14.7   Conclusion

In this chapter we looked at the instance and database tuning of a single instance. In spite of the database being configured for RAC, only one instance is up during this tuning process. This part of the tuning phase is very critical, because if all instances are tuned at the same time it would be difficult to analyze whether the problems arising are from the instance level or because of the added cluster tier of the database. This phase of the tuning process will determine if the clustered tuning will help in any respect, because if scalability is difficult on a single instance database configuration, or if the single instance database is I/O bound, the scalability factor that is expected from the RAC implementation may be even more difficult to achieve.

Single stand-alone configuration has many areas that need to be visited for configuration and tuning, like the application tier, the instance tier, and the database tier. In a more busy application, the network tier is also something that needs to be considered during this tuning phase.

In the next chapter, we will discuss tuning the clustered database configuration. The discussions will be with respect to the same areas like the application, instance, and the database; however, we will be looking at it from a different perspective, namely a clustered configuration.

15

Performance Tuning: Cluster

15.1   Introduction

In the previous chapter, the discussion was centered around tuning a single instance configuration of the Oracle database. We stated that a methodology should be created/defined and followed during performance testing of the application and the database. We discussed how the application could be divided into quadrants and performance testing each quadrant through an iterative cycle. There are two ways of approaching the performance tuning of the application. One way is a top-down approach where the application tier is performance tuned first, then the instance, and subsequently the database. Another way is a bottom-up approach where the storage system is tuned first, followed by the database, instance, and application. While the second approach has less impact on the application, using the top-down approach is more robust.

We discussed the tuning aspects of the application tier, followed by the Oracle instance, and then looked at the areas to tune in a database tier by discussing the various I/O-related wait events. There were also discussions regarding areas of the system that are influenced by certain waits and what remedies could be applied to reduce their impact.

Clustered instance and database tuning should commence only after the single instance tuning has completed. There is an old quote, "A stitch in time saves nine." If you do not complete the single instance tuning before tuning the cluster, it will be a terrible mistake, and if this approach is taken, you will need to include additional days/weeks in the implementation project plan in case it needs to start all over again.

A clustered database configuration comprises a single instance database configuration first, and then further instances are added to help provide scalability of the application. The important components in the clustered database configuration are the interconnect that communicates between instances and the storage that is shared from multiple instances.

Normally, in a complete application development life cycle, it would be best practice to start tuning the application first. However, when migrating from a single instance configuration to a clustered configuration, or when the single instance configuration has been tuned to a great extent, to reduce the impact on the overall applications it would be a better practice to start tuning bottom up. As mentioned, the two important components in a RAC configuration are the cluster interconnect and the shared storage subsystem. Our goal here is to start with the storage subsystem and then move into the cluster interconnect, and then into the instance and database tuning.

15.2   Storage subsystem

The storage subsystem and the distribution of disks play an important part in the overall performance of any system. In the case of Oracle databases, the appropriate sizing, stripe widths, and the appropriate placements of files, etc., are also very important.

In Chapter 2 (Hardware Concepts) we discussed that redo log files should be isolated from the rest of the data files. Since redo log files are write-intensive and have no read activity, they would be configured on RAID 1 type storage systems.

In a RAC configuration, this takes another important twist, because each instance maintains its own copy of the redo log files. When configuring the redo logs files in a RAC configuration, not only should the redo log files be isolated from the data files, they should also be isolated from the redo log files of the other instances.

During allocation of disks and storage areas, and while creating data files, it is important to isolate data files that belong to hot tables, or tables that are highly transaction oriented, from other similar files.

From the operating system, the `iostat` is a good measure to determine disk activity. The STATSPACK report also indicates and helps to determine hot table spaces so that they can be moved to appropriate storage areas.

OEM provides certain GUI-based views of the disk utilization. The disk utilization chart in Figure 15.1 is a good example of the information available from OEM. The chart indicates that the activity on the various disks is not distributed; certain disks are busy, while there is absolutely no

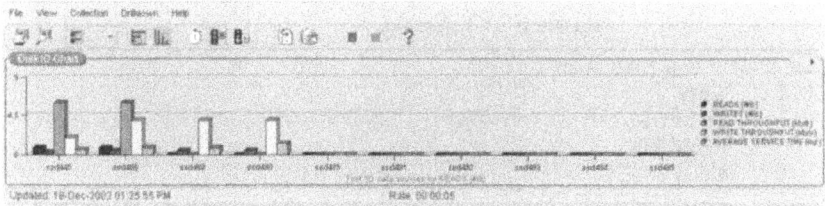

Figure 15.1
OEM disk utilization chart.

activity on the other disks. Good rule-of-thumb guidelines for distributing I/O are:

- Separate redo log groups on different disks.

- Separate members of a group on different disks.

- Separate data files and redo log files on different disks.

- Separate (or stripe) table data on different disks.

- Separate tables and indexes on different disks.

- Store temporary segments on different disks.

- Store undo segments on different disks.

Similarly, the output generated from the I/O activity screen provides the overall I/O on any specific instance. Figure 15.2 indicates that the peak I/O activity is mostly reads on the systems and averages between 800 and 1800 reads per second.

Oracle provides dynamic views that can be queried to determine the hot data files. For example, the following query provides a list of data files

Figure 15.2
OEM file I/O rate chart.

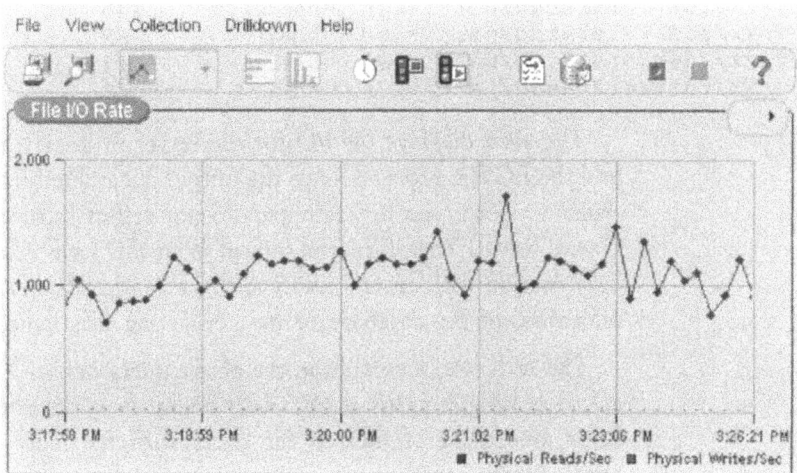

and their I/O activity:

```
COL NAME FORMAT A45
SELECT NAME,
       PHYRDS,
       PHYWRTS,
       AVGIOTIM
FROM   V$DATAFILE DF,
       V$FILESTAT FS
WHERE DF.FILE#=FS.FILE#
/
```

NAME	PHYRDS	PHYWRTS	AVGIOTIM
/dev/vx/rdsk/oraracdg/partition_1G3	976	16	0
/dev/vx/rdsk/oraracdg/partition_3G2	23	1283	0
/dev/vx/rdsk/oraracdg/partition_1G16	3	0	1
/dev/vx/rdsk/oraracdg/partition_1G13	4799	267	0
/dev/vx/rdsk/oraracdg/partition_3G9	3	0	1
/dev/vx/rdsk/oraracdg/partition_1G44	35	0	0
/dev/vx/rdsk/oraracdg/partition_1G45	4	0	0
/dev/vx/rdsk/oraracdg/partition_1G47	4	0	1
/dev/vx/rdsk/oraracdg/partition_1G12	308	0	0
/dev/vx/rdsk/oraracdg/partition_1G14	4	0	1
/dev/vx/rdsk/oraracdg/partition_1G17	4	0	0

NAME	PHYRDS	PHYWRTS	AVGIOTIM
/dev/vx/rdsk/oraracdg/partition_1G10	276	0	0
/dev/vx/rdsk/oraracdg/partition_1G15	156	0	0
/dev/vx/rdsk/oraracdg/partition_1G18	4	0	0
/dev/vx/rdsk/oraracdg/partition_1G4	148	0	0
/dev/vx/rdsk/oraracdg/partition_1G5	148	0	0
/dev/vx/rdsk/oraracdg/partition_1G6	1444	0	0
/dev/vx/rdsk/oraracdg/partition_500m1a	691	0	0
/dev/vx/rdsk/oraracdg/partition_200m3	140	0	0
/dev/vx/rdsk/oraracdg/partition_200m4	92	0	0
/dev/vx/rdsk/oraracdg/partition_200m5	14	0	0
/dev/vx/rdsk/oraracdg/partition_200m6	12	0	0

The view displays the I/O for the server processes, the DBWR process, and the LGWR process. Since the output is gathered from Oracle-provided dynamic views, the I/O activities do not reflect those not initiated by the Oracle server. Therefore, the output from this script should be analyzed in combination with an O/S utility such as iostat to investigate whether the relocation of the database or the competing files is necessary.

The AVGIOTIM column in the above query helps identify any disks that are processing requests at obviously higher or lower rates than others. This helps movement of files to the disks with the most appropriate speeds based on the contents.

If data files have been isolated and distributed and the redo log files have been distributed, but there continues to be a significant number of I/O related issues, then thought should be given to the indexing, partitioning, and data distribution factors of the application. Similarly, looking at the speeds of the actual physical disks could also be helpful.

15.3   Cluster interconnect

This is a very important piece of the clustered configuration in Oracle 9*i* RAC. Oracle depends a lot on the cluster interconnect for movement of data between the instances. Chapter 5 (Transaction Management) provides detailed explanation on how global data movement occurs.

The important test on the cluster interconnect should start with a test of the hardware configuration. Tests to determine the transfer rate specification versus the actual implemented packet size should be made to ensure the installation has been carried out as per specification.

In a two-node RAC configuration, the cluster interconnect is a direct link between two nodes (e.g., between ORA-DB1 and ORA-DB2). However, in a configuration of more than two nodes, this direct connection between the nodes is not possible, hence a switch would be required to act as a bridge between the nodes participating in the clustered configuration. Now while determining the performance of a system with more than two nodes, the speed of the switch has to be obtained independently of the speed of the interconnect to determine the true latency of the switch and the interconnect.

In Chapter 2 (Hardware Concepts) the various types of cluster interconnects have been discussed. The speed of the cluster interconnect solely depends on the hardware vendor and the layered operating system. Oracle depends on the operating system and the hardware for sending packets of information across the cluster interconnect. For example, one type of cluster interconnect supported between Sun 4800s is the UDP protocol. However, Solaris in this specific version of the interconnect protocol has an O/S limitation of a 64 KB packet size for data transfer. To transfer 256 KB worth of data across this interconnect protocol would take this configuration over four round trips. On a high-transaction system where there is a large amount of interconnect traffic, because of user activity on the various instances participating in the clustered configuration, this could cause a serious performance issue.

After the initial hardware and operating-system-level tests to confirm the packet size across the interconnect, subsequent tests could be done from the Oracle database to ensure that there is not any significant added latency from using cache-to-cache data transfer or the cache fusion technology. The query below provides the average latency of a consistent block request on the system. The data in these views show a cumulative figure since the last time the Oracle instance was bounced. Hence, this does not reflect the true performance of the interconnect or give a true picture of the latency in transferring data. To get a more realistic picture of the performance, it would be good to bounce all the Oracle instances and test again.

To obtain good performance it is important that the latency across the cluster interconnect be as low as possible. In Chapter 2 (Hardware Concepts) there is information about interconnects that support latency as low as 0.005 nanoseconds.

Latencies on the cluster interconnect could be caused by:

- A large number of processes in the run queues waiting for CPU or scheduling delays.

- Platform-specific O/S parameter settings that affect IPC buffering or process scheduling.

- Slow, busy, or faulty interconnects.

Oracle recommends that the average latency of a consistent block request should typically be about 15 ms depending on the system configuration and volume. *The average latency of a consistent block request is the average latency of a consistent-read request round trip from the requesting instance to the holding instance and back to the requesting instance.*

```
set numwidth 20
column "AVG CR BLOCK RECEIVE TIME (ms)" format 9999999.9
select
      b1.inst_id,
      b2.value "GCS CR BLOCKS RECEIVED",
      b1.value "GCS CR BLOCK RECEIVE TIME",
      ((b1.value / b2.value) * 10) "AVG CR BLOCK RECEIVE
      TIME (ms)"
from   gv$sysstat b1,
gv$sysstat b2
where b1.name = 'global cache cr block receive time'
and    b2.name = 'global cache cr blocks received'
and    b1.inst_id = b2.inst_id;
```

INST_ID	GCS CR BLOCKS RECEIVED	GCS CR BLOCK RECEIVE TIME	AVG CR BLOCK RECEIVE TIME (ms)
1	2758	112394	443.78
2	1346	1457	10.8

2 rows selected.

In the output above, it can be noticed that the AVG CR BLOCK RECEIVE TIME is 443.78 ms; this is significantly high when the expected average latency as recommended by Oracle should be 15 ms. A high value is possible if the CPU has limited idle time and the system typically processes long-running queries. However, it is possible to have an average latency of less than 1 ms with user-mode IPC. Latency can also be influenced by a high value of the DB_MULTI_BLOCK_READ_COUNT parameter. This is because a requesting process can issue more than one request for a block depending on the setting of this parameter. Correspondingly, the requesting process may have to wait longer. This kind of high latency requires further investigation of the cluster interconnect configuration and tests should be performed at the operating system level.

Apart from the basic packet transfer tests that can be performed at the O/S level, there are other checks and tests that can be done to ensure that the cluster interconnect has been configured correctly.

- There are redundant private high-speed interconnects between the nodes participating in the cluster. One interconnect is the primary and the other acts as the secondary when the primary fails, providing continuous availability.

- The user network connection does not interfere with the cluster interconnect traffic. That is, they are isolated from each other.

- The heartbeat verification occurs on a separate interconnect and is configured with a redundant path should one fail, without interruption. The heartbeat communication should be via the network that is outside the user networking or the private interconnects discussed above.

The following operating system commands can provide information on the cluster interconnect configuration:

- The netstat command displays network-related data structures. The output below, netstat-i, indicates that there are three network adapters configured.

```
ha-db1:RAC1:oracle # netstat -i

Name  Mtu  Net/Dest      Address       Ipkts     Ierrs Opkts     Oerrs Collis Queue
lo0   8232 loopback      localhost     1348906   0     1348906   0     0      0
ge2   1500 ora-db1       ora-db1       71804657  0     86959594  0     0      0
ge1   1500 172.16.1.0    172.16.1.1    74815149  0     83336461  0     0      0
ge0   1500 172.16.0.128  172.16.0.129  8501769   0     6064307   0     0      0
```

ge2: Primary adapter

ge1: Primary interconnect adapter

ge0: Secondary interconnect adapter

lo0: The output also indicates that there is a loopback option configured. Verification of whether Oracle is using the loopback option should also be verified using the ORADEBUG command and is discussed later in this section. The use of the loopback IP depends on the integrity of the routing table defined on each of the nodes. Modification of the routing table can result in the inoperability of the interconnect. Without the cluster interconnect between the nodes, RAC traffic cannot continue and could dramatically reduce database performance or halt database operations.

■   On certain Unix versions the usage of the transport layer can be verified by using the scstat command.

```
# scstat -W
-- Cluster Transport Paths --
                Endpoint                    Endpoint              Status
---------  ----------------------    ----------------------    --------
Transport  ora-db1.summerskyus.com:  ora-db2.summerskyus.com:  Path
  path:      ge1                       ge1                        online
Transport  ora-db1.summerskyus.com:  ora-db2.summerskyus.com:  Path
  path:      ge0                       ge0                        online
```

■   Another useful command for verification of the network is the ifconfig command:

```
ora-db1:RAC1:oracle # ifconfig -a
```

Checks can also be done from the Oracle instance to ensure proper configuration of the interconnect protocol. If the following commands are executed as user sys, a trace file is generated in the user dump destination directory that contains certain diagnostic information pertaining to the UDP/IPC configurations:

```
SQL> ORADEBUG SETMYPID
     ORADEBUG IPC
     EXIT
```

The following is an extract from the trace file pertaining to the interconnect protocol. The output confirms that the cluster interconnect is being used for instance-to-instance message transfer.

```
SSKGXPT 0x3671e28 flags SSKGXPT_READPENDING    info for network 0
        socket no 9    IP 172.16.193.1         UDP 59084
        sflags SSKGXPT_WRITESSKGXPT_UP
        info for network 1
        socket no 0    IP 0.0.0.0      UDP 0
        sflags SSKGXPT_DOWN
context timestamp 0x4402d
        no ports
```

Note: The above output is from a Sun 4800 and indicates the IP address and that the protocol used is UDP. On certain operating systems such as Tru64 the trace output does not reveal the Cluster interconnect information.

Oracle's alert log (output listed below) is another great source of information:

```
Mon Dec 2 11:21:58 2002
cluster interconnect IPC version:Oracle UDP/IP with Sun RSM disabled
IPC Vendor 1 proto 2 Version 1.0
```

The following NDD command at the operating system level will confirm the actual UDP size definition. The following output is from a Sun environment:

```
ora-db1:RAC1:oracle # ndd -get /dev/udp
name to get/set ? udp_xmit_hiwat
value ?
length ?
8192
name to get/set ? udp_recv_hiwat
value ?
length ?
8192
```

The output above reveals that the UDP has been configured for an 8 KB packet size. Applying this finding to the data gathered from the Oracle's views indicates that it would take 14,050 trips for all the blocks to be transferred across the cluster interconnect ($112,394/8 = 14,050$). If this were set to be 64 KB then the number of round trips would be signi-ficantly reduced (112,394/64 = 1756 trips).

The STATSPACK report is also a good source of information to determine the interconnect latency. For example the following extract indicates high timeouts during "gcs remote message" transfer.

Event	Waits	Timeouts	Total Wait Time (s)	Avg wait (ms)	Waits /txn
gcs remote message	391,629	377,590	7,017	18	2,163.7
ges remote message	77,311	74,159	3,488	45	427.1
gcs remote message	209,188	186,286	3,505	17	817.1
ges remote message	77,257	73,797	3,489	45	301.8
gcs remote message	599,108	323,177	6,943	12	303.5
ges remote message	81,552	72,571	3,485	43	41.3

The output above indicates high timeouts between remote message transfers; it can also be noticed that the number of waits and waits per transaction is significantly high.

Another parameter that affects the interconnect traffic is the DB_FILE_MULTIBLOCK_READ_COUNT. This parameter helps read a certain number of blocks at a time from disk. When data needs to be transferred across the cluster interconnect, this parameter determines the size of the block that each instance would request from the other during read transfers.

Sizing this parameter should be based on the interconnect latency and the packet sizes as defined by the hardware vendor, and after considering the operating system limitations (e.g., the Sun UDP max setting is only 64 KB).

Kernel parameters that define the UDP parameter settings in the respective hardware environments are shown in Table 15.1.

> **Note:** In Oracle 9i (9.2.0.1), there is a 32 KB size limitation set by Oracle on the amount of information that can be transferred across the cluster interconnect. In Oracle 9i (9.2.0.2) this limitation has been removed and now the amount of information that can be transferred across the cluster interconnect depends on limitations defined by the hardware vendor.

CLUSTER_INTERCONNECTS

This parameter provides Oracle with information on the availability of additional cluster interconnects that could be used for cache fusion activity

Table 15.1   *Kernel Parameters*

Hardware	Parameter
SUN (ndd)	`udp_recv_hiwat`
	`udp_recv_hiwat`
Linux	`/proc/sys/net/core/rmem_default`
	`/proc/sys/net/core/rmem_max`
	`/proc/sys/net/core/wmem_default`
	`/proc/sys/net/core/wmem_max`
Tru64 (sysconfig)	`udp_recvspace`
	`udp_sendspace`
HP (ndd)	`tcp_xmit_hiwater_def`
	`tcp_recv_hiwater_def`

across the cluster interconnect. The parameter overrides the default interconnect settings at the operating system level with a preferred cluster traffic network.

While this parameter does provide certain advantages on systems where high interconnect latency is noticed by helping reduce such latency, configuring this parameter could affect the interconnect high-availability feature. In other words, an interconnect failure that is normally unnoticeable would instead cause an Oracle cluster failure as Oracle still attempts to access the network interface.

15.4   Cluster instance tuning

Tuning of the instance in a RAC configuration is different from a single instance configuration. In Chapter 5 (Transaction Management) we discussed how the data is maintained by recording the block requests and changes in the GRD and how the GCS is responsible for maintaining the data consistency across the instances participating in the clustered configuration. This feature of Oracle adds additional opportunities for tuning the instance.

All views that are available at the single stand-alone configuration level are also available as a global view. These views are qualified with a prefix "G." For example, the V$SYSTEM_EVENT dynamic performance global view would be GV$SYSTEM_EVENT and would contain statistics from all instances participating in the clustered database configuration.

In the examples discussed in the previous chapters, we looked at using session-level statistics to get to the bottom of an issue. It is important to capture cluster-level wait statistics at the session level. However, since session-level information is only retained by Oracle for the duration of the session, it is important to store such information for future analysis. As indicated in Chapter 13, session-level statistics can be captured by using a log-off trigger, when the session-level data is saved from V$SESSION_EVENT, V$SESSION_WAIT and V$SESSTAT views into permanent tables for future analysis.

The query and its output below should be familiar from Chapter 13, where we discussed the instance-level wait events. In this section, we continue our discussions on the same query output, this time looking into the cluster-related wait events:

```
COL SID FORMAT 9999
COL USERNAME FORMAT A15
COL EVENT FORMAT A30
COL P1 FORMAT 9999
COL P2 FORMAT 9999
COL P3 FORMAT 9999

SELECT MVASW_SID SID,
       MVASW_USERNAME USERNAME,
       MVASW_SQL_ADDRESS SQL_ADDRESS,
       MVASW_EVENT EVENT,
       MVASW_P1 P1,
       MVASW_P2 P2,
       MVASW_P3 P3,
       MVASW_WAIT_TIME WAIT,
       MVASW_FAILED_OVER FO
FROM  MV_AUDIT_SESSION_WAIT
WHERE MVASW_USERNAME IS NOT NULL
AND  (MVASW_EVENT LIKE 'global%'
OR    MVASW_EVENT LIKE 'db%'
OR    MVASW_EVENT LIKE 'gcs%'
OR    MVASW_EVENT LIKE 'ges%'
OR    MVASW_EVENT LIKE '%buffer%')
ORDER BY SID
/
```

```
SID SQL_ADDRESS        EVENT                    P1   P2          P3 WT FO
--- ---------------- ------------------------ --- ----- ----------- -- --
 30 0000000443D7CF48 db file sequential read  18 56903           1  0 NO
 32 0000000442A622A0 db file sequential read 194 20683           1  0 NO
 32 0000000442174720 db file sequential read  18 25804           1  0 NO
 32 00000004421739C0 db file sequential read  18 11786           1  0 NO
 32 0000000443AB2528 global cache null to x    18 25804 17917873152  0 NO
 36 0000000442178608 db file sequential read  18 24480           1  0 NO
 36 0000000442178608 global cache s to x       18  1164 17934759808  0 NO
 39 00000004421781C8 global cache open x       18 28712 17968379616  0 NO
 45 00000004421760F8 db file sequential read  18 16482           1  0 NO
 50 00000004448FA0C8 db file sequential read  18 11787           1  0 NO
 77 0000000443D27A68 global cache null to x    18 19651 16978156672  0 NO
 90 00000004448FE370 db file sequential read  18 15422           1  0 NO
 99 0000000443D7DDD8 global cache null to x    18 11888 17045147456  0 NO
106 0000000444901728 global cache s to x       18  7053 17397452288  0 NO
109 00000004448FE370 db file sequential read  18 17213           1  0 NO
117 0000000444901728 global cache null to s    18  7053 17397452288  0 NO
120 00000004448F9728 db file sequential read  18 11891           1  0 NO
125 00000004448F8FA0 db file sequential read  18 11864           1  0 NO
125 00000004448FE370 global cache cr request   18 23689 17028513088  0 NO
```

                                                    19 rows selected.

Global cache CR request

This event indicates the time waited when a session is looking for a consistent-read (CR) version of a block (indicated by block# in column P2 that belongs to the file indicated in column P1 in the output above) and cannot find it in its local cache and hence has made a request against a remote instance for the block. However, the transferred block has not yet arrived at the requesting instance. It also implies that the current block is not cached locally. This event ends when the session gets the block or permission to read the block from disk.

This event may not always indicate a problem in the GCS requests. Some of the issues where these wait events can be found are when:

1.   Data blocks are being modified frequently on all instances.

2.   Requests for block resulted in a cache miss.

3.   LMS cannot keep up with the high number of CR requests.

4.   There are latency issues with the interconnect.

5.   There are full table scans.

High waits on this event could be reduced by looking at the system and scheduling delays; for example, ensuring that the LMSx processes get enough CPU. Another rather critical factor when it comes to the RAC architecture is the interconnect latency/bandwidth. Wait times could be reduced by ensuring that a high-speed interconnect with low latency is used.

Global cache `NULL` to x and global cache `NULL` to s

These events are waited for when a block (indicated by block# in column P2 that belongs to the file indicated in column P1 in the output above) was used by an instance, transferred to another instance, and then requested again by the original instance. Processes waiting for these events are usually waiting for a block to be transferred from the instance that last modified it. If one-instance requests cached data blocks from other instances, then it is normal that these events consume a greater proportion of the total wait time. The event ends when the session gets the block from a remote instance or has proper access mode to modify the block.

The wait time for this event depends on:

- The "busyness" of the block that is being requested by the session.

- The processing power available at the send side (e.g., CPU).

- Interconnect speed at requester/sender side, which is determined by the interconnect latency factor.

If this event is listed in the top 5 wait events, and the average wait time is less than 30 ms, the waits are to be considered as part of the normal activity. However, if the average is above the 30 ms threshold, attention should be given to reducing the wait times by:

- Looking for system load and scheduling delays; this could be obtained for example by ensuring the LMSX processes has enough CPU resources available.

- Ensuring that a high-speed interconnect with low latency is being used and validated.

- Identifying the busy blocks and the related objects by querying the V$SEGMENT_STATISTICS dynamic performance view.

Global cache open x

This event is associated with the initial access of a particular data block (indicated by block# in column P2 that belongs to the file indicated in column P1 in the output above) by an instance. If the duration of the wait is short, then the completion of the wait is most likely followed by a read from disk. If these events reflect a high wait time, this indicates that the block is currently not cached in the local instance or in a remote instance and requires a disk read to complete the request.

Global cache open s

Similar to the event described above, in this case the session waits to receive the resource identified by file# in the P1 column and block# identified by P2 in a shared mode.

Buffer busy due to global cache

This is the counterpart wait event to the "buffer busy wait" encountered and discussed in the previous chapter. However, the buffer busy wait encountered due to global cache is due to waits encountered at the global cache level. This wait is encountered on file# indicated by the value in the P1 column and block# indicated by the value in the P2 column.

Enqueues

These are shared memory structures (locks) that serialize access to database resources. They can be associated with a session or transaction. Enqueue names are displayed in the LOCK_TYPE column of the DBA_LOCK and DBA_LOCK_INTERNAL data dictionary views.

A resource uniquely identifies an object that can be locked by different sessions within an instance (local resource) or between instances (global resource). Each session that tries to lock the resource will have an enqueue on the resource.

The enqueue wait tracked by the V$SESSION_WAIT view indicates that the session is waiting for a local enqueue. The parameters P1 and P2 indicate the name of the enqueue and mode respectively. The possible modes are shown in Table 15.2.

Table 15.2   *Enqueue Mode Descriptions*

Mode Value	Description
1	Null mode
2	Subshare
3	Subexclusive
4	Share
5	Share/subexclusive
6	Exclusive

Querying the P1RAW column in the V$SESSION_WAIT view or MVASW_P1RAW column in the MV_AUDIT_SESSION_WAIT table for event enqueue can provide an indication as to which data object the enqueue is mapped against:

```
SELECT MVASW_EVENT,
       MVASW_P1RAW
FROM   MV_AUDIT_SESSION_WAIT
WHERE  MVASW_EVENT = 'enqueue';

EVENT      P1RAW
-------    ----------------
enqueue    0000000050530006
enqueue    0000000050530006
enqueue    0000000050530006
enqueue    0000000050530006
enqueue    0000000050530006
enqueue    0000000050530006
enqueue    0000000050530006
enqueue    0000000050530006
```

The P1RAW column stores the information in hexadecimal format and can be interpreted in the following manner:

- First 6 bytes indicate the type of object enqueue is waiting for.

- Second 2 bytes indicate the type of locks being held. Type 4 indicates a shared lock and type 6 indicates an exclusive lock.

15.5   Workload characteristics

The following output from the STATSPACK utility provides workload characteristics of the instance captured over the snapshot period. The average time against all events is the overall system-level performance characteristics.

```
Global Cache Service - Workload Characteristics
-----------------------------------------------
Ave global cache get time (ms):                 1.3
Ave global cache convert time (ms):             8.2

Ave build time for CR block (ms):               0.1
Ave flush time for CR block (ms):               1.1
Ave send time for CR block (ms):                0.2
Ave time to process CR block request (ms):      1.5
Ave receive time for CR block (ms):             4.9

Ave pin time for current block (ms):            0.3
Ave flush time for current block (ms):          0.0
Ave send time for current block (ms):           0.2
```

```
Ave time to process current block request (ms):        0.6
Ave receive time for current block (ms):             634.6

Global cache hit ratio:                                0.2
Ratio of current block defers:                         0.1
% of messages sent for buffer gets:                    0.2
% of remote buffer gets:                               0.2
Ratio of I/O for coherence:                            0.2
Ratio of local vs remote work:                         0.4
Ratio of fusion vs physical writes:                    0.0

Global Enqueue Service Statistics
---------------------------------
Ave global lock get time (ms):                         1.9
Ave global lock convert time (ms):                    48.8
Ratio of global lock gets vs global lock releases:     1.1
```

From the above output, the one wait event that stands out from the others is the "Ave receive time for current block (ms)." This is a measure of the average time a block has taken to arrive at the requesting instance from the time that the block was originally requested. A high value in the column indicates that there could be potential cluster interconnect issues including high latency. This needs to be resolved by looking at the cluster interconnect configuration as described under Section 15.3 above.

Table 15.3 is an Oracle-provided table indicating the acceptable latency on certain critical average waits listed in the STATSPACK report above. A large deviation from these figures almost always indicates performance issues directly or indirectly related to the cluster interconnect. In a RAC configuration, an abnormally high value could also mean frequent block transfers across the cluster interconnect; under such circumstances, consider resizing the DB_FILE_MULTIBLOCK_READ_COUNT.

Table 15.3 *Acceptable STATSPACK Latency Values[a]*

Latency	Lower Bound (ms)	Typical (ms)	Upper Bound (ms)
Ave global cache get time	0.3	3	10
Ave global cache convert time	0.3	6	15
Ave receive time for CR block	0.3	4	12
Ave time to process current block request	0.1	3	23
Ave receive time for current block	0.3	8	30

[a]*Source:* Oracle Corporation

This parameter dictates the number of blocks that each instance would try to read from the requesting instance during a given request. However, a very small value could affect the single instance performance.

Latencies displayed in the STATSPACK report are the average values and are arrived at based on the values of other latencies also found in the STATSPACK report.

Table 15.4 provides the methods used to arrive at the average latency measurements reported in the STATSPACK report. The table also provides the acceptable values for the various latencies.

Global cache hit ratio

This is an overall indicator of how much work is being done at the buffer cache level to maintain the global cache. It represents the hit as a result of global cache operation. This hit ratio is a derivate of the buffer cache hit ratio and the local cache hit ratio and is determined using the following formula:

Global cache hit = (Buffer cache hit ratio − Local cache hit ratio)

Table 15.4   *STATSPACK Latency Values[a]*

Latency	How to Calculate (in ms)	Typical Values (ms)	Upper Limit (ms)
Ave global lock get time	(Global lock get time) × 10/(Global lock sync gets + Global lock async gets)	20–30	60
Ave global lock convert time	(Global lock convert time) × 10/(Global lock sync converts + Global lock async converts)	10–20	100
Ave global cache get time	(Global cache get time) × 10/(Global cache gets)	2–3	10
Ave global cache convert time	(Global cache convert time) × 10/(Global cache converts)	6–8	15
Ave global cache CR request time	(Global cache CR block receive time) × 10/(Global cache CR blocks received)	5–30	50

[a]Source: Oracle Corporation

The hit ratio could be improved by:

- Ensuring efficient access to local data, for example by using automatic segment space management (ASSM) in tablespace definitions, or if the application uses the Oracle sequences extensively, increasing the sequence cache size.

- Avoiding long full table scan operations, especially in an OLTP environment. This could be accomplished by ensuring that the SQL queries are well tuned.

- Minimizing contention for a small set of buffers. The hot buffers could be identified by querying the V$SEGMENT_STATISTICS view and identifying the hot objects.

KJC: Wait for msg send to complete

This wait event is triggered when a foreground or background process wants to send a message to the other instance. The event ends when the message has reached the destination. A high wait average on this event indicates:

- High system load.
- High CPU usage.
- Scheduling latencies which could be related to long run queues.
- High interconnect latency.

Other events shown in the output above are:

Ratio of current block defers

Indicator of how often Oracle defers the shipping of a block because of active transactions on the local instance.

Ratio of I/O for coherence

Indicator of how much global cache gets are resolved by physical reads.

15.6   Statistics affecting RAC

GV$SESSTAT provides information on statistics that affect the performance of the clustered instances. Of the various statistics collected at the session and system level in the GV$SESSTAT and GV$SYSSTAT respectively, the statistics that belong to classes 4, 8, 32, and 40 should be of primary concern in a RAC implementation.

The listing below is a comprehensive view of the various statistics that are directly related to the performance of the RAC instances.

```
COL NAME FORMAT A50
SELECT
      STATISTIC#,
      NAME,
      CLASS
FROM V$STATNAME
WHERE CLASS IN (4,8,32,40)


STATISTIC# NAME                                             CLASS
---------- -----------------------------------------        -----
        22 enqueue timeouts                                   4
        23 enqueue waits                                      4
        24 enqueue deadlocks                                  4
        25 enqueue requests                                   4
        26 enqueue conversions                                4
        27 enqueue releases                                   4
        28 global lock sync gets                             32
        29 global lock async gets                            32
        30 global lock get time                              32
        31 global lock sync converts                         32
        32 global lock async converts                        32
        33 global lock convert time                          32
        34 global lock releases                              32
        35 total file opens                                   8
        36 opens requiring cache replacement                  8
        37 opens of replaced files                            8
        38 gcs messages sent                                 32
        39 ges messages sent                                 32
        40 db block gets                                      8
        41 consistent gets                                    8
        42 physical reads                                     8
        43 db block changes                                   8
        44 consistent changes                                 8
        45 recovery blocks read                               8
        46 physical writes                                    8
        47 physical writes non checkpoint                     8
        48 summed dirty queue length                          8
        49 DBWR checkpoint buffers written                    8
        50 DBWR transaction table writes                      8
        51 DBWR undo block writes                             8
        52 DBWR revisited being-written buffer                8
        53 DBWR make free requests                            8
        54 DBWR free buffers found                            8
        55 DBWR lru scans                                     8
```

```
STATISTIC# NAME                                          CLASS
---------- ------------------------------------          -----
        56 DBWR summed scan depth                           8
        57 DBWR buffers scanned                             8
        58 DBWR checkpoints                                 8
        59 DBWR cross instance writes                      40
        60 DBWR fusion writes                              40
        61 remote instance undo block writes               40
        62 remote instance undo header writes              40
        63 prefetch clients - keep                          8
        64 prefetch clients - recycle                       8
        65 prefetch clients - default                       8
        66 prefetch clients - 2k                            8
        67 prefetch clients - 4k                            8
        68 prefetch clients - 8k                            8
        69 prefetch clients - 16k                           8
        70 prefetch clients - 32k                           8
        71 change write time                                8
        72 redo synch writes                                8
        73 redo synch time                                  8
        74 exchange deadlocks                               8
        75 free buffer requested                            8
        76 dirty buffers inspected                          8
        77 pinned buffers inspected                         8
        78 hot buffers moved to head of LRU                 8
        79 free buffer inspected                            8
        80 commit cleanout failures:                        8
              write disabled
        81 commit cleanout failures:                        8
              block lost
        82 commit cleanout failures:                        8
              cannot pin
        83 commit cleanout failures:                        8
              hot backup in progress
        84 commit cleanout failures:                        8
              buffer being written
        85 commit cleanout failures:                        8
              callback failure
        86 commit cleanouts                                 8
        87 commit cleanouts                                 8
              successfully completed
        88 recovery array reads                             8
        89 recovery array read time                         8
        90 CR blocks created                                8
        91 current blocks converted for CR                  8
        92 switch current to new buffer                     8
        93 write clones created in foreground               8
        94 write clones created in background               8
        95 prefetched blocks                                8
        96 prefetched blocks aged out before use            8
        97 physical reads direct                            8
        98 physical writes direct                           8
        99 physical reads direct (lob)                      8
       100 physical writes direct (lob)                     8
```

STATISTIC#	NAME	CLASS
101	cold recycle reads	8
102	consistent gets - examination	8
103	shared hash latch upgrades - no wait	8
104	shared hash latch upgrades - wait	8
108	next scns gotten without going to GES	32
109	Unnecessary process cleanup for SCN batching	32
110	calls to get snapshot scn: kcmgss	32
111	kcmgss waited for batching	32
112	kcmgss read scn without going to GES	32
113	kcmccs called get current scn	32
126	global cache gets	40
127	global cache get time	40
128	global cache converts	40
129	global cache convert time	40
130	global cache cr blocks received	40
131	global cache cr block receive time	40
132	global cache current blocks received	40
133	global cache current block receive time	40
134	global cache cr blocks served	40
135	global cache cr block build time	40
136	global cache cr block flush time	40
137	global cache cr block send time	40
138	global cache current blocks served	40
139	global cache current block pin time	40
140	global cache current block flush time	40
141	global cache current block send time	40
142	global cache freelist waits	40
143	global cache defers	40
144	global cache convert timeouts	40
145	global cache blocks lost	40
146	global cache claim blocks lost	40
147	global cache blocks corrupt	40
148	global cache prepare failures	40
149	global cache skip prepare failures	40
150	total number of slots	8
151	instance recovery database freeze count	32
152	background checkpoints started	8
153	background checkpoints completed	8
154	number of map operations	8
155	number of map misses	8
208	queries parallelized	32
209	DML statements parallelized	32
210	DDL statements parallelized	32
211	DFO trees parallelized	32
212	Parallel operations not downgraded	32
213	Parallel operations downgraded to serial	32
214	Parallel operations downgraded 75 to 99 pct	32
215	Parallel operations downgraded 50 to 75 pct	32

```
STATISTIC# NAME                                           CLASS
---------- ------------------------------------------     -----
       216 Parallel operations                               32
               downgraded 25 to 50 pct
       217 Parallel operations                               32
               downgraded 1 to 25 pct
       218 PX local messages sent                            32
       219 PX local messages recv'd                          32
       220 PX remote messages sent                           32
       221 PX remote messages recv'd                         32
       225 table lookup prefetch client count                 8

134 rows selected.
```

The statistics collected by V$SESSTAT and V$SYSSTAT by themselves do not reflect any direct relation to a problem; they are just clues. To drill down further, the class that the statistics belong to provides an indication including the type of block that could potentially be causing the problem.

Table 15.5 provides a list of classes and the types of blocks that the class is related to. This is helpful during performance analysis when the statistics collected from the V$SESSTAT and V$SYSSTAT views need to be mapped to the actual area of the database or table. The following are descriptions for some of the statistics listed in the output above.

Table 15.5   *Class Description*

Class	Type of Block
1	Data or index block
2	Sort block
3	Save undo block
4	Segment header
5	Save undo segment header
6	Free lists block
7	System undo segment header
8	System undo segment block
$7 + 2n$	Header of undo segment number n
$8 + 2n$	Block in undo segment number n
32	Parallel operation
40	Global cache segment

Global cache gets

This gets incremented every time a block is not found in any of the remote caches and results in a disk read. The number indicates the approximate number of disk I/Os performed.

Global cache get time

This indicates the total time spent by the process waiting to get the required permission to read the block from disk.

Global cache converts

This indicates the number of times the access permission on a block has changed due to lock conversion.

Global cache convert time

This relates to the global cache converts statistic and indicates the total elapsed time to get the conversion complete.

GV$BH

This view displays pinging statistics against the various SGA buffers. Because this view only provides statistics for the local instance, viewing information at a global level would not provide significant benefits.

A single block can appear in multiple rows of these tables. Each row represents a different copy of the block. Multiple versions created for read-consistent queries appear with the status CR. For tuning purposes, the current copy with a status of XCUR or SCUR that contains the greatest value of XNC should be considered.

GV$CACHE_LOCK

This view displays information from the block header of each block in the SGA of the current instance as related to the particular database objects.

GV$CACHE_TRANSFER

This view displays types and classes of blocks that Oracle has transferred over the cluster interconnect at least once. It contains information from the block header of each block in the SGA of the current instance as related to particular database objects, i.e., it represents a block in the buffer cache of the current instance. This can be used to help identify which blocks are being pinged between instances, using the XNC column, which shows the number of lock conversions from exclusive to NULL status. These conversions represent potential pings. This view only shows buffers with a nonzero XNC count.

If the NAME column is blank, it indicates that the buffer is associated with a temporary segment. The FORCED_WRITES and FORCED_READS columns determine which type of objects RAC instances share. Values in the FORCED_WRITES column provide counts of how often a certain block type experiences a transfer out of a local buffer cache because the current version was requested by another instance.

The data in the XNC column is probably the most important in this view as it maintains the count of the block-level locks. Each block starts with an XNC value of zero when it first enters the buffer cache. This value is incremented each time the instance releases the lock covering that block. If a PCM lock covers multiple blocks, they can have different values of XNC because they may enter the buffer cache at different times.

When an instance writes a block to disk and reuses that buffer for other data, XNC is reset to zero. If the block returns to the buffer cache while other versions of the block are still in the cache, it starts with the greatest value of XNC for any version of the same block rather than starting with zero.

15.7 Monitoring Cache Transfers

Cache transfer activity across the instances can be observed using the following set of queries. The queries below will help identify the objects that have high cache transfer activities between instances. It displays contention statistics of buffers that are currently in the buffer cache of the corresponding instance. This could be identified with objects that have a high number of exclusive to NULL conversions.

```
SELECT
      INST_ID,
      NAME,
      FILE#,
      CLASS#,
      MAX(XNC)
FROM GV$CACHE_TRANSFER
GROUP BY INST_ID,
      NAME,
      FILE#,
      CLASS#
/
```

From the output below, it is clear that the object COMPANY is the possible source of high cache transfer activity:

INST_ID	NAME	FILE#	CLASS#	MAX(XNC)
1	IDL_UB2$	1	4	231
1	PK_USPRL	4	1	47
1	PK_COMP	4	1	39
1	COMPANY	171	1	2849

Using the query below on the GV$CACHE_TRANSFER will help identify the frequency of lock conversions and the block-related information in the COMPANY table:

```
SELECT FILE#,
       BLOCK#,
       CLASS#,
       STATUS,
       XNC
FROM   GV$CACHE_TRANSFER
WHERE NAME = 'COMPANY'
AND    FILE# = 171
/
```

The output below displays the frequency of lock conversions for the object found in the previous query, namely the COMPANY table:

FILE#	BLOCK#	CLASS#	STAT	XNC
171	898	1	XCUR	1321
171	1945	1	XCUR	27
171	1976	1	XCUR	19
171	2039	1	XCUR	849

To drill down further, the query below is used to display the rows in the block found in the previous query. The DBMS_ROWID package is used to extract the block number from the ROWID pseudocolumn. This helps identify values that may be partitionable to avoid future contention. If the data cannot be partitioned and the data in these identified tables is updated frequently, then another alternative to reduce contention would be to reduce the number of rows per block to spread out the I/O activity over different blocks.

```
SELECT COMP_ID,
       COMP_NAME
FROM   COMPANY
WHERE DBMS_ROWID.ROWID_BLOCK_NUMBER(ROWID) = 898
/
```

The output below displays the rows contained in block 898:

```
COMP_ID   NAME
-------   ------------------------
   3949   SUMMERSKY DB CONSULTANTS
   3952   CATAMARAN INC.
   3957   PRIYAR BROTHERS INC.
   3961   DIGITAL BROADCASTING INC.
```

The GV$CACHE_TRANSFER view could also be used to determine the objects involved in forced reads across instances:

```
SELECT
      INST_ID,
      NAME,
      CLASS#,
      SUM(FORCED_READS)
FROM GV$CACHE_TRANSFER
WHERE CLASS# IN (4,8,32,40)
GROUP BY INST_ID,
    NAME,
        CLASS#
ORDER BY SUM(FORCED_READS)
```

The output below is a list of objects that are involved in forced reads across the instances:

```
NAME                      SUM(FORCED_READS)
------------------------  -----------------
USER_PROFILE                           1948
_SYSSMU16$                                1
PK_USPRL                                584
COMPANY                                 958
STATS$BG_EVENT_SUMMARY                  184
GV$CLASS_CACHE_TRANSFER
```

This view provides inter-instance cache transfer information on the number of blocks pinged based on a block class:

```
COL IID FORMAT       999
COL X2N FORMAT       99999999999
COL X2NFW FORMAT     99999999999
COL X2NFS FORMAT     99999999999
COL X2S FORMAT       99999999999
COL X2SF FORMAT      99999999999
COL S2N FORMAT       99999999999
COL S2NFS FORMAT     99999999999
COL N2S FORMAT       99999999999
COL S2X FORMAT       99999999999
COL N2X FORMAT       99999999999
```

```
SELECT
     VCCT.CLASS,
     VCCT.INST_ID IID,
     VCCT.X_2_NULL X2N,
     VCCT.X_2_NULL_FORCED_WRITE X2NFW,
     VCCT.X_2_NULL_FORCED_STALE X2NFS,
     VCCT.X_2_S X2S,
     VCCT.X_2_S_FORCED_WRITE X2SF,
     VCCT.S_2_NULL S2N,
     VCCT.S_2_NULL_FORCED_STALE S2NFS,
     VCCT.NULL_2_S N2S,
     VCCT.S_2_X S2X,
     VCCT.NULL_2_X N2X
FROM GV$CLASS_CACHE_TRANSFER VCCT
WHERE VCCT.CLASS IS NOT NULL
/
```

The query against the class cache transfer provides class-level statistics of the cache transfer information. The output below indicates that the cache transfer is more of the data block level rather than at the segment header level. There are some N to S lock conversions at the segment level.

CLASS	IID	X2N	X2NFW	X2NFS	X2S	X2SF	S2N	S2NFS	N2S	S2X	N2X
data block	1	758251	0	758250	173391	0	100550	100550	66682981	132974	1244082
sort block	1	0	0	0	0	0	0	0	0	0	0
save undo block	1	0	0	0	0	0	0	0	0	0	0
segment header	1	0	0	0	1	0	2	2	2765	5	8

GV$FILE_CACHE_TRANSFER

This view identifies and displays the number of cache transfers per object file. The information collected through this view would be helpful to determine the file access patterns.

```
COL NAME FORMAT A45
COL IID FORMAT 999
COL RBR FORMAT 9999
COL X2N FORMAT 99999999
COL X2NFW FORMAT 99999999
COL X2NFS FORMAT 99999999
COL X2S FORMAT 99999999
```

```
COL S2N FORMAT 99999999
COL N2S FORMAT 99999999
COL RFW FORMAT 99999999
COL RFS FORMAT 99999999
COL S2X FORMAT 99999999
COL N2X FORMAT 99999999
COL CRT FORMAT 99999999
COL CURT FORMAT 99999999
SELECT
      VDF.NAME,
      VTS.NAME TABLESPACE_NAME,
      VFCT.INST_ID IID,
      VFCT.X_2_NULL X2N,
      VFCT.X_2_NULL_FORCED_WRITE X2NFW,
      VFCT.X_2_NULL_FORCED_STALE X2NFS,
      VFCT.X_2_S X2S,
      VFCT.S_2_NULL S2N,
      VFCT.RBR,
      VFCT.RBR_FORCED_WRITE RFW,
      VFCT.RBR_FORCED_STALE RFS,
      VFCT.NULL_2_S N2S,
      VFCT.S_2_X S2X,
      VFCT.NULL_2_X N2X,
      VFCT.CR_TRANSFERS CRT,
      VFCT.CUR_TRANSFERS CURT
FROM  GV$FILE_CACHE_TRANSFER VFCT, V$DATAFILE VDF,
  V$TABLESPACE VTS
WHERE  VFCT.FILE_NUMBER = VDF.FILE#
AND    VDF.TS# = VTS.TS#
AND    VFCT.CUR_TRANSFERS > 0
/
```

The output from the query above provides a view of the cache transfer activity at the file level. It provides the details on the kind of locks that are being placed at the data file level, and are related to the cache transfer requests from other instances. The instance ID column helps correlate and map the lock conversion requests on the specific file from the different instances.

NAME					TABLESPACE_NAME			
IID	X2N	X2NFW	X2NFS	X2S	S2N	RBR	RFW	RFS
	N2S	S2X	N2X	CRT	CURT			
/dev/vx/rdsk/oraracdg/partition1G_3					SYSTEM			
1	33	2	33	96	36	2	0	0
	1938	137	35	196	721			
/dev/vx/rdsk/oraracdg/partition1G_3					SYSTEM			
2	13	0	13	51	86	2	4	4
	1709	43	38	428	867			

Table 15.6   *Lock Conversions*

Lock Conversion	Description
NULL to S (lock buffers for read)	A NULL to S conversion occurs when a block is selected by a query. The block may or may not be present in the SGA. If a current copy of the block is in the cache, then only a lock conversion takes place, and the lock is not read from disk again. After the conversion, the status of the block is shared current (SCUR)
NULL to X (lock buffers for write)	A NULL to X conversion occurs when reading the block into the SGA for a DML operation (INSERT, UPDATE, DELETE). If the lock is not already held in exclusive mode, the status of the block after the conversion is exclusive current (XCUR)
S to NULL (release the shared lock from a buffer)	An S to NULL conversion occurs when an instance has acquired a block for read-only mode (SCUR mode) and another instance wants to modify the same block. The status of the first instance changes from SCUR to consistent read (CR)
S to X (upgrade read lock to write lock)	An S to X conversion occurs when a block is read into SGA by a SELECT statement and then a DML statement is issued against the same block. The status of the block changes from SCUR to XCUR
X to NULL (make buffers consistent read)	An X to NULL conversion occurs when an instance is modifying a block and another instance wants to modify the same block. The lock on the first instance is converted from X to NULL, a write to disk takes place, and the status of the block in the first instance's SGA changes from XCUR to CR. A high and consistently increasing number of these conversions indicates data contention that is causing pings. If the contention is for the same row, applications on the two instances should be run on the same instance. If two instances are accessing different rows in the same block, partition the data to reduce these conversions
X to S (downgrade write lock to read)	An X to S conversion takes place when an instance has modified a block and another instance wants to read the current version of the same block. This causes an X to S conversion on the first instance. This type of lock conversion occurs only if the block has been written out to disk prior to the request for the downgrade. If the block is still in memory, the block server process builds a read-consistent image of the required block and transmits it to the requesting instance without requiring a lock conversion

GV$LOCK_ACTIVITY

This view displays the DLM lock operation activity of the current instance. Each row corresponds to a type of lock operation (described in Table 15.6).

```
                    SELECT *
                    FROM GV$LOCK_ACTIVITY
                    /
INST_ID   FROM   TO_V   ACTION_VAL                                    COUNTER
-------   ----   ----   ------------------------------------   --------
      1   NULL   S      Lock buffers for read                  70198319
      1   NULL   X      Lock buffers for write                    10533
      1   S      NULL   Make buffers CR (no write)             70033838
      1   S      X      Upgrade read lock to write                 1744
      1   X      NULL   Make buffers CR (write dirty buffers)      4175
      1   X      S      Downgrade write lock to read                311
                          (write dirty buffers)
      2   NULL   S      Lock buffers for read                      1616
      2   NULL   X      Lock buffers for write                       42
      2   S      NULL   Make buffers CR (no write)                  310
      2   S      X      Upgrade read lock to write                   27
      2   X      NULL   Make buffers CR (write dirty buffers)        11
      2   X      S      Downgrade write lock to read                 28
                          (write dirty buffers)
12 rows selected.
```

From the data provided by the GV$LOCK_ACTIVITY view, the NULL to X and S to X conversions should be monitored. The instances with the highest number of conversions indicate requests for data locked by other instances.

The GV$FILE_CACHE_TRANSFER view would be helpful to determine which files are participating in this processes.

15.7   Conclusion

In this chapter we looked at tuning the RAC cluster, starting with the cluster interconnect, which is one of two most important components that could affect performance. We looked at the wait events that affect the cluster in the section on clustered instance tuning. Later in the chapter we discussed the various dynamic performance views that can help determine and troubleshoot performance issues with the RAC implementation.

The next chapter will focus on diagnosis-related tools and utilities that can help in day-to-day operations. The outputs from these tools provide information to Oracle Support when a critical problem such as an ORA-600 error is encountered.

16

Problem Diagnosis

16.1   Introduction

In the previous chapter we discussed the tuning of the cluster. During these discussions we analyzed the performance of the cluster interconnect, the storage subsystem, and cache transfer that happens via the cluster interconnect. Oracle scalability is measured by the number of users that can be added with increased business and when more instances are added to the cluster. However, if the amount of traffic is not something that is controllable because of the poor performance of the interconnect, the system will never be able to perform as desired, and every additional instance will probably provide a negative rather than positive impact.

How many times have database administrators had to call Oracle Support for critical problems faced in their day-to-day functioning? Some of the common errors encountered are ORA-600 and ORA-7445. When these errors are encountered, it is always expected that Oracle Support be notified of these errors. These errors are normally machine critical.

In this chapter we will look at some of the diagnosis that will help in problem solving. Most of the information in this chapter is either from Oracle's technology network[1] or from Metalink.[2]

Apart from these machine-critical Oracle errors, there are others that are also worth investigating, especially in a RAC environment.

---

1.   Oracle Technology Network (OTN) can be accessed from http://otn.oracle.com. Subscription to OTN is free, and can be obtained by registering at the same site.

2.   Metalink can be accessed from http://metalink.oracle.com. Metalink access requires the user to have a customer support identification (CSI) number. This number can be obtained by subscribing to Oracle support services.

16.2   RAC diagnostics

RAC is a multi-instance clustered configuration. As we have discussed in the previous chapter, apart from the single-instance-related issues that could be encountered, RAC could have issues across multiple instances. Critical issues such as an instance hang or very bad performance may lead to no or little information, even after the regular investigation performed by the database administrator. Oracle provides a good utility that helps gather statistics across all instances. The data gathered through this utility will help diagnose where the potential problem could be.

RACDIAG.SQL

RACDIAG.SQL is a script provided and downloadable from Metalink note# 135714.1. This script contains queries that will help diagnose various areas of the RAC instance and the cluster. The script is originally intended to diagnose hung sessions; however, its potential is much greater.

Among these scripts and outputs generated by the RACDIAG.SQL utility, the section that contains information regarding WAITING SESSIONS is very important in providing details of any serious issues.

Oracle also provides another diagnostic utility specifically for OPS environments called OPSDIAG.SQL. The script can be obtained from Metalink note# 205809.1.

Apart from the RAC diagnostic scripts which help capture performance-related data, Oracle also provides another set of diagnostic steps for troubleshooting interinstance performance. Though Metalink note# 18489.1 is titled "Tuning inter-instance performance in RAC and OPS" it has a good amount of detail that helps troubleshoot interconnect issues.

Daemon processes

The various daemon processes such as the GSD and SRVCTL processes are critical to the cluster, providing visibility to the RAC database and the existence of the other instances. If there is trouble with any of these processes, tracing the activities of these processes could be enabled to diagnose details of the problem.

Tracing the daemon processes   Metalink note# 178683.1 contains steps for tracing GSD, SRVCTL, GSDCTL, and SRVCONFIG. Configuring the environment to trace these areas requires modifications to some of the Oracle-provided scripts. The following illustrates the tracing of the GSDCTL procedure where the status of the GSD is obtained. The first illustration is the actual extract from the file gsdctl located in the $ORACLE_HOME/bin directory:

```
# External Directory Variables set by the Installer
JREDIR=/apps/oracle/product/9.2.0/JRE
JLIBDIR=/apps/oracle/product/9.2.0/jlib
MY_ORACLE_HOME=/apps/oracle/product/9.2.0

# jar files
SRVMJAR=$JLIBDIR/srvm.jar

#NetCa config jar
NETCFGJAR=$JLIBDIR/netcfg.jar

# JRE Executable and Class File Variables
JRE=$JREDIR/bin/jre
JRECLASSES=$JREDIR/lib/classes.zip
JREJAR=$JREDIR/lib/rt.jar

CLASSPATH=$NETCFGJAR:$JREJAR:$SRVMJAR

# Set the shared library path for JNI shared libraries
# A few platforms use an environment variable other than
  LD_LIBRARY_PATH
SET_DEFAULT=YES
PLATFORM='uname'
case $PLATFORM in "HP-UX"|"HI-UX")
  SET_DEFAULT=NO
  SHLIB_PATH=$MY_ORACLE_HOME/lib32:$MY_ORACLE_HOME/
  srvm/lib:$SHLIB_PATH
  export SHLIB_PATH
esac
case $SET_DEFAULT in "YES")

LD_LIBRARY_PATH=$MY_ORACLE_HOME/lib32:$MY_ORACLE_HOME/
  srvm/lib:$LD_LIBRARY_PATH
export LD_LIBRARY_PATH
esac

# Run gsd control utility
-DTRACING.ENABLED=true -DTRACING.LEVEL=2
$JRE -DTRACING.ENABLED=true -DTRACING.LEVEL=2
  -classpath $CLASSPATH oracle.ops.mgmt.daemon.GSDCTLDriver
  "$@" $MY_ORACLE_HOME
exit $?
```

The highlighted area contains the actual changes to the gsdctl file that enables tracing. The following is the trace generated to the terminal when the status of the GSD is checked:

```
ora-db2:RAC2:oracle # gsdctl stat
/apps/oracle/product/9.2.0/bin/gsdctl:
 -DTRACING.ENABLED=true: not found
[main] [16:11:10:285] [GetActiveNodes.create:Compile]
 Going into GetActiveNodes constructor...
[main] [16:11:10:310] [sQueryCluster.<init>:Compile]
 Detected Cluster
[main] [16:11:10:311] [sQueryCluster.isCluster:Compile]
 Cluster existence = true
[main] [16:11:10:312] [NativeSystem.<init>:Compile]
 Going to load SRVM library
[main] [16:11:10:368] [NativeSystem.<init>:Compile]
 loaded libraries
[main] [16:11:10:374]
 [GetActiveNodes.initializeCluster:Compile]  Inside
 GetActiveNodes.initializeCluster
[main] [16:11:13:512] [NativeResult.<init>:Compile]
 NativeResult: The String obtained is1|Everything ok So Far
[main] [16:11:13:513] [NativeResult.<init>:Compile]
 The status string is: 1
[main] [16:11:13:515] [NativeResult.<init>:Compile]
 The result string is: Everything ok So Far 1
[main] [16:11:13:615] [NativeResult.<init>:Compile]
 NativeResult: The String obtained is1|^ora-db1.
 summerskyus.com^ora-db2.summerskyus.com|ora-
 db2.summerskyus.com|Everything ok So Far
[main] [16:11:13:616] [NativeResult.<init>:Compile]
 The status string is: 1
[main] [16:11:13:617] [NativeResult.<init>:Compile]
 The result string is: ^ora-db1.summerskyus.com^ora-db2.
 summerskyus.com 3
[main] [16:11:13:619] [GetActiveNodes.<init>:Compile]
 Started clusterware daemon thread
[main] [16:11:13:620] [GetActiveNodes.create:Compile]
 Out of GetActiveNodes constructor.
[GetActiveNodes thread] [16:11:13:621]
 [GetActiveNodes.initializeClusterWare:Compile]
 Inside GetActiveNodes.initializeClusterWare
[GetActiveNodes thread] [16:11:13:624]
 [sQueryCluster.<init>:Compile]  full:Acquire called by thread
 GetActiveNodes thread count=0
[main] [16:11:13:625] [sQueryCluster.<init>:Compile]
 Detected Cluster
[main] [16:11:13:626] [sQueryCluster.isCluster:Compile]
 Cluster existence = true
[main] [16:11:13:627] [NativeSystem.<init>:Compile]
 loaded libraries
[main] [16:11:13:629] [Semaphore.acquire:Compile]
 empty:Acquire called by thread main count=1
```

```
[main] [16:11:13:630] [Semaphore.release:Compile]
  full:Release called by thread main count=1
[GetActiveNodes thread] [16:11:13:632]
  [Semaphore.release:Compile]  empty:Release called by thread
  GetActiveNodes thread count=1
[GetActiveNodes thread] [16:11:13:633]
  [GetLiveDaemonCommand.execute:Compile]
  In Execute function of GetLiveDaemonCommand
[GetActiveNodes thread] [16:11:13:914]
  [GetLiveDaemonCommand.execute:Compile]
  GetLiveDaemonCommand: String returned from native
  1|2|!ora-db1.summerskyus.com!ora-db2.summerskyus.com
[GetActiveNodes thread] [16:11:13:916]
  [NativeResult.<init>:Compile]  NativeResult:
  The String obtained is1|2|!ora-db1.summerskyus.com!
  ora-db2.summerskyus.com
[GetActiveNodes thread] [16:11:13:917]
  [NativeResult.<init>:Compile]  The status string is: 1
[GetActiveNodes thread] [16:11:13:918]
  [NativeResult.<init>:Compile]  The result string is: 2 2
[GetActiveNodes thread] [16:11:13:919] [line# N/A]
  full:Acquire called by thread GetActiveNodes thread
  count=0
[main] [16:11:13:919] [NativeResult.<init>:Compile]
  NativeResult: The String obtained is1|2|!ora-db1.
  summerskyus.com!ora-db2.summerskyus.com
[main] [16:11:13:921] [NativeResult.<init>:Compile]
  The status string is: 1
[main] [16:11:13:922] [NativeResult.<init>:Compile]
  The result string is: 2 2
[main] [16:11:13:923] [ClusterResult.getDaemon:Compile]
  Number of dead daemons 2
GSD is running on the local node
ora-db2:RAC2:oracle #
```

It is to be noted that the trace file indicates the validation of the cluster (highlighted) and checks and confirms the accessibility of the clusterware.

Tracing Oracle Net The performance reports indicate that there are server performance issues with the network traffic. The SQL*Net message from the client and SQL*Net message to the client show a large number of waits. While these waits also include the idle time, there is a potential that there could be an Oracle Net issue. A quick and easy method to identify the problem is to enable tracing of the Oracle Net traffic.

The listener and tnsnames files could be traced to look at the network traffic. For example the following is an output of the listener trace file.

In this situation the tracing was enabled at level 6 by adding
TRACE_LEVEL_LISTENER = 6 to the listener.ora file:

```
ora-db2:RAC2:oracle # more listener.trc


TNSLSNR for Solaris: Version 9.2.0.1.0 - Production on
   08-NOV-2002 15:57:17
Copyright (c) 1991, 2002, Oracle Corporation.  All rights
   reserved.


[08-NOV-2002 15:57:17:171]
--- TRACE CONFIGURATION INFORMATION FOLLOWS ---
[08-NOV-2002 15:57:17:171] New trace stream is /apps/
   oracle/product/9.2.0/network/trace/listener.trc
[08-NOV-2002 15:57:17:171] New trace level is 6
[08-NOV-2002 15:57:17:171] --- TRACE CONFIGURATION
   INFORMATION ENDS ---
[08-NOV-2002 15:57:17:172]
--- PARAMETER SOURCE INFORMATION FOLLOWS ---
[08-NOV-2002 15:57:17:172] Attempted load of system
   pfile source/apps/oracle/product/9.2.0/network/
   admin/listener.ora
[08-NOV-2002 15:57:17:172] Parameter source loaded
   successfully
[08-NOV-2002 15:57:17:172]
[08-NOV-2002 15:57:17:172] Attempted load of command line source
[08-NOV-2002 15:57:17:172] Parameter source was not loaded
[08-NOV-2002 15:57:17:172]
[08-NOV-2002 15:57:17:172]  -> PARAMETER TABLE LOAD RESULTS
   FOLLOW <-
[08-NOV-2002 15:57:17:173] Successful parameter table load
[08-NOV-2002 15:57:17:173]  -> PARAMETER TABLE HAS THE FOLLOWING
   CONTENTS <-
[08-NOV-2002 15:57:17:173] TRACE_LEVEL_LISTENER = 6
[08-NOV-2002 15:57:17:173] LISTENER = (DESCRIPTION_LIST =
   (DESCRIPTION = (ADDRESS_LIST = (ADDRESS = (PROTOCOL =
   IPC)(KEY = E
XTPROC))) (ADDRESS_LIST = (ADDRESS = (PROTOCOL = TCP)
   (HOST = ora-db2.summerskyus.com)(PORT = 1521)))))
[08-NOV-2002 15:57:17:173] SID_LIST_LISTENER =
   (SID_LIST = (SID_DESC = (SID_NAME = PLSExtProc)
   (ORACLE_HOME = /apps/oracle/product/9.2.0)
   (PROGRAM = extproc)) (SID_DESC = (ORACLE_HOME =
   /apps/oracle/product/9.2.0) (SID_NAME = RAC2))
   (SID_DESC = (ORACLE_HOME=/apps/oracle/product/9.2.0)
   (SID_NAME = PRODDB))
[08-NOV-2002 15:57:17:173] --- PARAMETER SOURCE
   INFORMATION ENDS ---
[08-NOV-2002 15:57:17:173]
--- LOG CONFIGURATION INFORMATION FOLLOWS ---
```

```
[08-NOV-2002 15:57:17:174] Log stream will be "/apps/
  oracle/product/9.2.0/network/log/listener.log"
[08-NOV-2002 15:57:17:174] Log stream validation
  requested
[08-NOV-2002 15:57:17:174] Log stream is valid
[08-NOV-2002 15:57:17:174] --- LOG CONFIGURATION
  INFORMATION ENDS ---


[08-NOV-2002 15:57:17:191] nsinherit: doing connect
  handshake...
[08-NOV-2002 15:57:17:192] nlpcaini: entry
[08-NOV-2002 15:57:17:192] nlpcaini: No process
  parameters set
[08-NOV-2002 15:57:17:192] nlpcaini: exit
[08-NOV-2002 15:57:17:192] nsinherit: inheriting the
  connection...
[08-NOV-2002 15:57:17:193] nsmal: 776 bytes at 0x1003cb0d0
[08-NOV-2002 15:57:17:193] nsmal: 2592 bytes at 0x1003cb3f0
[08-NOV-2002 15:57:17:193] nsopen: opening transport...
[08-NOV-2002 15:57:17:193] ntpcon: entry
[08-NOV-2002 15:57:17:193] ntpcon: toc = 4
...
[08-NOV-2002 15:57:17:275] nspsend: 32 bytes
  to transport
[08-NOV-2002 15:57:17:275] nscon: sending 439 bytes
  connect data
[08-NOV-2002 15:57:17:275] nsdo: cid=0, opcode=67,
  *bl=439, *what=1, uflgs=0x4002, cflgs=0x0
[08-NOV-2002 15:57:17:275] nsdo: nsctx: state=2,
  flg=0x4204, mvd=0
[08-NOV-2002 15:57:17:275] nsdo: gtn=185, gtc=185,
  ptn=10, ptc=2011
[08-NOV-2002 15:57:17:276] nsdo: 439 bytes to NS buffer
[08-NOV-2002 15:57:17:276] nsdofls: DATA flags: 0x0
[08-NOV-2002 15:57:17:276] nsdofls: sending NSPTDA packet
[08-NOV-2002 15:57:17:276] nspsend: plen=449, type=6
[08-NOV-2002 15:57:17:276] ntpwr: entry
[08-NOV-2002 15:57:17:276] ntpwr: exit
[08-NOV-2002 15:57:17:276] nspsend: 449 bytes to
  transport
[08-NOV-2002 15:57:17:277] nsdoacts: flushing
  transport
[08-NOV-2002 15:57:17:277] ntpctl: entry
[08-NOV-2002 15:57:17:277] ntpctl: exit
[08-NOV-2002 15:57:17:277] nscon: doing connect
  handshake...
```

Looking through the above listener trace file indicates the various connections to the database and the steps taken by the connection request. During this process, bytes are transferred.

16.3   ORADEBUG utility

ORADEBUG is a powerful utility and provides a wealth of information. However, this utility has very little documentation available. This utility comes in handy to step deep into the internal structures of Oracle and understand the actual problem. The wonderful benefit of using this utility is that the information gathered using this is useful when calling Oracle Support. The information puts the problem closer to resolution. For example, in Chapter 15 (Performance Tuning: Cluster) there was a discussion about getting details regarding the IPC configuration, and this utility was used.

The ORADEBUG utility is invoked from an SQL*Plus session by simply connecting to it and executing the specific ORADEBUG command. For example to get help on the various commands available through ORADEBUG:

```
                SQL> oradebug help
HELP            [command]                 Describe one or all commands
SETMYPID                                  Debug current process
SETOSPID        <ospid>                   Set OS pid of process to debug
SETORAPID       <orapid>                  Set Oracle pid of process to
                ['force']                    debug
DUMP            <dump_name> <lvl>         Invoke named dump
                [addr]
DUMPSGA         [bytes]                   Dump fixed SGA
DUMPLIST                                  Print a list of available
                                             dumps
EVENT           <text>                    Set trace event in process
SESSION_EVENT   <text>                    Set trace event in session
DUMPVAR         <p|s|uga>                 Print/dump a fixed PGA/SGA/
                <name> [level]               UGA variable
SETVAR          <p|s|uga> <name> <value>  Modify a fixed PGA/SGA/UGA
                                             variable
PEEK            <addr> <len> [level]      Print/Dump memory
POKE            <addr> <len> <value>      Modify memory
WAKEUP          <orapid>                  Wake up Oracle process
SUSPEND                                   Suspend execution
RESUME                                    Resume execution
FLUSH                                     Flush pending writes to trace
                                             file
CLOSE_TRACE                               Close trace file
TRACEFILE_NAME                            Get name of trace file
LKDEBUG                                   Invoke global enqueue service
                                             debugger
NSDBX                                     Invoke CGS name-service
                                             debugger
```

```
-G             <Inst-List | def | all> Parallel oradebug command prefix
-R             <Inst-List | def | all> Parallel oradebug prefix (return
                                             output
SETINST        <instance# .. | all>     Set instance list in double quotes
SGATOFILE      <SGA dump dir>           Dump SGA to file; dirname in
                                             double quotes
DMPCOWSGA      <SGA dump dir>           Dump & map SGA as COW; dirname in
                                             double quotes
MAPCOWSGA      <SGA dump dir>           Map SGA as COW; dirname in double
                                             quotes
HANGANALYZE    [level]                  Analyze system hang
FFBEGIN                                 Flash Freeze the Instance
FFDEREGISTER                            FF deregister instance from
                                             cluster
FFTERMINST                              Call exit and terminate instance
FFRESUMEINST                            Resume the flash frozen instance
FFSTATUS                                Flash freeze status of instance
SKDSTTPCS      <ifname>                 Helps translate PCs to names
               <ofname>
WATCH          <address> <len>          Watch a region of memory
               <self|exist|all|
               target>
DELETE         <local|global|target>  Delete a watchpoint
               watchpoint <id>
SHOW           <local|global|target>  Show watchpoints
               watchpoints
CORE                                    Dump core without crashing
                                             process
IPC                                     Dump ipc information
UNLIMIT                                 Unlimit the size of the trace file
PROCSTAT                                Dump process statistics
CALL           <func> [arg1] ...        Invoke function with arguments
               [argn]
```

A more detailed list of all the debuggable commands is listed in Appendix 1.

In Version 9*i*, Oracle has introduced a new feature where the database or instance can be placed in a freeze state. This feature is enabled from the ORADEBUG utility and is discussed in the next section.

16.3.1   Flash Freeze

A common dilemma faced by database administrators is whether to identify the cause of a failure or to ensure that normal service is restored as quickly as possible. By invoking Flash Freeze for example, the database administrator can place a freeze on the instance, take a diagnostic snapshot (as illustrated in the output below) of the entire system at the time of failure, quickly restart the database, and then make a diagnostic analysis offline.

The output below enables the flash freeze option using ffbegin, at which point the instance is placed in a freeze state. Once the instance is placed in a freeze state, the ALTER SESSION... command below will generate a dump file in the user dump destination directory. Subsequent to the generation of the dump file the instance is resumed using the ffresumeinst command.

```
SQL> oradebug ffbegin
Statement processed.
SQL> alter session set events 'immediate trace name
  systemstate level 10';

Session altered.

SQL> oradebug ffresumeinst
Statement processed.
```

All activities performed through the ORADEBUG utility are recorded in the alert log file. In the case of the flash freeze command, the alert log records a considerable amount of activities where the various background and foreground processes are frozen. Subsequently the activation information is also listed when they are activated.

Other flash freeze related commands supported by the ORADEBUG utility are:

```
FFBEGIN             Flash Freeze the Instance
FFDEREGISTER        FF deregister instance from cluster
FFTERMINST          Call exit and terminate instance
FFRESUMEINST        Resume the flash frozen instance
FFSTATUS            Flash freeze status of instance
```

The output below is an extract from the alert.log file, illustrating the flash freeze activity:

```
...
Wed Sep 25 01:57:45 2002
Issuing ORADEBUG FFBEGIN to: Unix process pid: 3429,
  image: oracle@ora-db1.summerskyus.com (PMON)
Issuing ORADEBUG FFBEGIN to: Unix process pid: 3431,
  image: oracle@ora-db1.summerskyus.com (DIAG)
Wed Sep 25 01:57:45 2002
Issuing ORADEBUG FFBEGIN to: Unix process pid: 3433,
  image: oracle@ora-db1.summerskyus.com (LMON)
Wed Sep 25 01:57:45 2002
```

```
Unix process pid: 3429, image: oracle@ora-db1.
  summerskyus.com (PMON) flash frozen
ORADEBUG FFSTATUS: Flash Freeze is in effect
All processes in instance are frozen
Issuing ORADEBUG FFDEREGISTER to: Unix process pid: 3429,
  image: oracle@ora-db1.summerskyus.com (PMON)
Issuing ORADEBUG FFDEREGISTER to: Unix process pid: 3431,
  image: oracle@ora-db1.summerskyus.com (DIAG)
Wed Sep 25 01:58:06 2002
Unix process pid: 3472, image: oracle@ora-db1.
  summerskyus.com (P004) deregistered
Wed Sep 25 01:58:06 2002
Unix process pid: 3470, image: oracle@ora-db1.
  summerskyus.com (P003) deregistered
Wed Sep 25 01:58:06 2002
ORADEBUG FFSTATUS: Flash Freeze is in effect
ORADEBUG FFSTATUS: Instance has been deregistered
All processes in instance are frozen
Wed Sep 25 01:58:28 2002
Issuing ORADEBUG FFRESUMEINST to: Unix process pid: 3429,
  image: oracle@ora-db1.summerskyus.com (PMON)
Issuing ORADEBUG FFRESUMEINST to: Unix process pid: 3431,
  image: oracle@ora-db1.summerskyus.com (DIAG)
```

16.4   Critical ORA errors

ORA-600: internal error code, arguments: [...], [...]

An ORA-600 error indicates a kernel exception. When such an error is encountered, Oracle records certain details related to this error in the alert log file and also in a user trace file.

This error message could mean errors in different areas of the Oracle kernel. The actual area is identified by the arguments listed in the error message. For example:

```
ORA-600: internal error code, arguments: [784], [0x3BE577248],
  [0x3BE578B88],
```

For example, in the above ORA-600 error message the first argument 784 indicates that the error is related to the service layer. Similarly, depending on the range that the first argument falls into, the error is grouped under a specific category, as shown in Table 16.1.

If an ORA-600 error is encountered, Oracle Support needs to be notified. During the notification process, all related information, including copies of the alert log and trace files referenced in the alert log, needs to be uploaded for Oracle to analyze and provide the appropriate fix.

Table 16.1   ORA-600 *Argument and Layer Information*

Argument	Layer
0000	Service layer
2000	Cache layer component base
4000	Transaction layer
6000	Data layer
8000	Access layer
9000	Parallel server
10000	Control layer
12000	User/Oracle interface layer
14000	System-dependent layer (port specific)
15000	Security layer
17000	Generic layer
18000	K2 (2-phase commit)
19000	Object layer
21000	Replication layer
23000	OLTP layer

Before notifying Oracle of the error message, as database administrator, the first step is to determine if others have encountered this error. Such information could be obtained from Metalink. Oracle has provided an ORA-600 error lookup utility that will help in obtaining this.

Figure 16.1 is an input screen for the ORA-600 argument lookup. On selecting the Oracle version and providing the first argument, the lookup will search through Metalink and provide any information that is available on the specific error argument. Based on the message the fix may already be explained.

In certain cases, depending on the type of error and occurrence of the message, information pertaining to the argument may not be available. Under these circumstances a technical assistance request (TAR) is opened with Oracle Support.

The ORA-600 lookup is accessible via Metalink note #1537881.

ORA-7445:exception encountered core dump [...][...]

ORA-7445 is also a critical error; however, the criticality is not grouped at the same level as the ORA-600 errors. The ORA-7445 error indicates that the process may have performed an illegal operation and hence was terminated by the operating system.

Like the ORA-600 error, ORA-7445 also reports arguments to the error message. Unlike the ORA-600 error argument, the ORA-7445 argument is alphanumeric rather than numeric and normally reflects an Oracle-related internal function call.

This error can occur during the following situations:

■   When starting a program, for example SQL*Plus, import, export, etc.

■   Starting a database.

■   While making a connection to the database.

■   During normal database operations, such as a query or DML operation.

- Shutting down the database.

  Steps to take upon an ORA-7445 error:

- Check alert.log for other errors that are generated with the ORA-7445 message. For example, the following information was generated with an ORA-7445 message: please note the error ORA-00602, which indicates an internal programming exception.

```
Thu Oct 10 11:16:37 2002
Trace dumping is performing id=[cdmp_20021114111637]
Thu Oct 10 11:16:47 2002
Errors in file /apps/admin/PRODDB/RAC2/bdump/
  rac2_pmon_3908.trc:
ORA-00602: internal programming exception
ORA-07445: exception encountered: core dump[0000000101B3F298][SIGSEGV]
```

This kind of additional information helps Oracle Support to diagnose the problem quickly.

- Check for Oracle-generated trace files. Oracle generates the trace files in the same directory as the alert log file is generated. In the previous example, rac2_pmon_3908.trc file was generated in the bdump directory.

- If a trace file wasn't generated, one needs to be produced for Oracle to diagnose the cause of the error. Metalink note#1812.1 explains the process of getting a stack trace from a CORE file.

ORA-3113: end-of-file on communication channel

ORA-3113 is also a common error encountered when a connection to the server is lost. It basically means that the client program is not able to communicate with a shadow process. This error is normally accompanied by one of the following additional errors:

- ORA-1041: internal error. Hostdef extension doesn't exist.

- ORA-3114: not connected to Oracle.

- ORA-1012: not logged on.

- ORA-1034: Oracle not available.

An ORA-3113 error could be encountered in a RAC implementation when the TAF option is used for failover. This error happens if the tnsnames.ora file does not represent the FAILOVER and

LOAD_BALANCING arguments after the ADDRESS_LIST argument. For example:

```
PRODDB.summerskyus.com=
(DESCRIPTION=
  (ADDRESS_LIST=
    (FAILOVER=on)
    (LOAD_BALANCE=on)
    (ADDRESS=(PROTOCOL=TCP)
      (HOST=ora-db2.summerskyus.com)
        (PORT=1521))
    (ADDRESS=(PROTOCOL=TCP)
        (HOST=ora-db1.summerskyus.com)
        (PORT=1521))
  )
  (CONNECT_DATA=
    (SERVICE_NAME=PRODDB.summerskyus.com)
    (ORACLE_HOME = /apps/oracle/product/9.2.0)
    (FAILOVER_MODE=(TYPE=SELECT)
                  (METHOD=BASIC)
                  (RETRIES=20)
                  (DELAY=15))
  )
)
```

ORA-1041: internal error. Hostdef extension doesn't exist

The hostdef extension referred to is a structure that is added to the control structure for client/server communication.

It is accessed via a pointer in the original structure. When the communication between the client and the server goes awry, this can result in ORA-1041 and ORA-3113 errors.

ORA-29740: evicted by member string, group incarnation string

An ORA-29740 error occurs when a member is evicted from the group by another member of the cluster database for one of several reasons, which may include a communications error in the cluster, or failure to issue a heartbeat to the control file. This mechanism is in place to prevent problems from occurring that would affect the entire database. For example, instead of allowing a cluster-wide hang to occur, Oracle will evict the problematic instance(s) from the cluster. When an ORA-29740 error occurs, a surviving instance will remove the problem instance(s) from the cluster.

When the problem is detected, the instances "race" to get a lock on the control file (results record lock) for updating. The instance that obtains the lock tallies the votes of the instances to decide membership. A member is evicted if:

- A communications link is down.

- There is a split-brain (more than one subgroup) and the member is not in the largest subgroup.

- The member is perceived to be inactive.

The following is a sample message in the alert log of the evicted instance:

```
Fri Sep 27 17:11:51 2002
Errors in file /apps/oracle/export/PRODDB/lmon_26410_ tick2.trc:
ORA-29740: evicted by member %d, group incarnation %d
Fri Sep 27 17:11:53 2002
Trace dumping is performing id=[cdmp_20010928171153]
Fri Sep 27 17:11:57 2002
Instance terminated by LMON, pid = 26410
```

The key to resolving the ORA-29740 error is to review the LMON trace files from each of the instances. On the evicted instance we will see something like:

```
Fri Sep 27 17:11:57 2002
kjxgrdtrt: Evicted by 0, seq (3, 2)
```

This indicates which instance initiated the eviction.

On the evicting instance the following information is reported:

```
kjxgrrcfgchk: Initiating reconfig, reason 3
Fri Sep 27 17:11:57 2002
kjxgmrcfg: Reconfiguration started, reason 3
...
Fri Sep 27 17:11:57 2002
Obtained RR update lock for sequence 2, RR seq 2
Fri Sep 27 17:11:57 2002
Voting results, upd 0, seq 3, bitmap: 0
Evicting mem 1, stat 0x0047 err 0x0002
```

From the above information it is clear that the instance initiated a reconfiguration for reason 3. After reconfiguration has started and this instance obtains the RR lock (results record lock), this instance will tally the votes of the instances to decide membership.

In troubleshooting ORA-29740 errors, the "reason" will be very important. The possible reasons are as follows:

- Reason 0 = No reconfiguration.

- Reason 1 = The node monitor generated the reconfiguration.

- Reason 2 = An instance death was detected.

- Reason 3 = Communications failure.

- Reason 4 = Reconfiguration after suspend.

In the above output, the first section indicated the reason for the initiated reconfiguration. In this case the reason reported was #3, "communications failure." For ORA-29740 errors, the most likely reasons would be 1, 2, or 3.

Reason 1: The node monitor generated the reconfiguration

This can happen if:

- An instance joins the cluster.

- An instance leaves the cluster.

- A node is halted.

It should be easy to determine the cause of the error by reviewing the alert logs and LMON trace files from all instances. If an instance joins or leaves the cluster or a node is halted, then the ORA-29740 error is not a problem.

Reason 2: An instance death was detected

This can happen if an instance fails to issue a heartbeat to the control file. When the heartbeat is missing, LMON will issue a network ping to the instance not issuing the heartbeat. As long as the instance responds to the ping, LMON will consider the instance alive. If, however, the heartbeat is not issued for the length of time of the control file enqueue timeout, the instance is considered to be problematic and will be evicted. This latter scenario is generally not observed, since an ORA-600 [2103] failure will generally occur prior to the eviction.

Reason 3: Communications failure

This can occur where:

- The LMON processes lose communication between one another.

- One instance loses communication with the LMD process of another instance.

- An LMON process is blocked, spinning, or stuck and is not responding to the other instance(s) LMON process.

- An LMD process is blocked or spinning.

In this case the ORA-29740 error is recorded when there are communication issues between the instances. It is an indication that an instance has been evicted from the configuration when IPC sends a timeout. A communications failure between a foreground, or background processes other than LMON, and a remote LMD will also generate an ORA-29740 with reason 3. When this occurs, the trace file of the process experiencing the error will print a message:

```
Reporting communication error with instance:
```

If communication is lost at the cluster layer (e.g., network cables are pulled), the cluster software may also perform node evictions in the event of a cluster split-brain. Oracle will detect a possible split-brain and wait for cluster software to resolve the split-brain. If cluster software does not resolve the split-brain within a specified interval, Oracle proceeds with evictions.

16.5   Remote Diagnostic Agent (RDA)

RDA is a set of scripts to gather detailed information about an Oracle environment. The scripts are focused to collect information that will aid in problem diagnosis: however, the output is also very useful to see the overall system configuration.

When reporting critical errors to Oracle Support it is encouraged that the RDA is used because it gives a comprehensive picture of the environment. This can greatly reduce TAR resolution time by minimizing the number of requests from Oracle Support Services for more information. RDA does not modify your system in any way; it merely collects data useful for Oracle Support Services.

Since the operation of these scripts is system specific, Oracle provides different sets of scripts and downloadable scripts for the various operating systems.

- Metalink note# 139597.1 for Unix
- Metalink note# 153091.1 for Windows
- Metalink note# 171748.1 for Open VMS

When installing RDA for gathering information from a RAC implementation, depending on whether Oracle and the operating system files are installed individually for each node, it is good to download and configure RDA on all instances. If Oracle and the operating systems files are shared amongst all instances (e.g., in HP Tru64) only one installation of RDA is required.

16.6   Conclusion

In this chapter we looked at the various problem-solving diagnosis methods for different kinds of error situations. ORA-600 and ORA-7445 are errors that normally cause great concern to database administrators. Such concerns are genuine because these errors are critical and could mean downtime for the production instance in certain cases.

Oracle has provided various methods of troubleshooting the instance and the database to gather information. If any of the above-mentioned errors occur, it is advisable to collect the following information irrespective of what is already generated by Oracle:

1.   Gather information from all instances using the RDA utility.

2.   Try to freeze the instance and collect the system state dump, as illustrated in the flash freeze section above.

3.   Check the alert log file and ensure that the trace files have been generated.

4.   Locate the trace files and become familiar with the problem.

5.   Zip these files and upload them to Oracle Support when the TAR is initially created.

In the next chapter the discussions will focus on the variations of RAC architecture or implementation on the various operating systems. Oracle has variations between Windows, Linux, Unix, and VMS.

RAC Implementations

17.1   Introduction

In the previous chapter we discussed the various problem diagnosis scenarios. We discussed the various methods to diagnose some of the most common errors encountered during the day-to-day operations of the production environment. Subsequently, the discussion focused on some of the utilities provided by Oracle that will help diagnose the problem and help Oracle Support Services to get to the bottom of the issues much quicker.

In this chapter the discussions will be centered around RAC implementations on Linux and Windows operating systems, basically the differences and additional processes.

17.2   Linux

17.2.1   Oracle Clustered File System

The Oracle Clustered File System (OCFS) was developed by Oracle to simplify the management of RAC database data files on Linux and Windows operating systems.

Installation of the OCFS requires a private network configured and consists of these general steps:

1.   Like the Linux operating system, OCFS is developed by Oracle as open source software and is available with source code under the general public license (GPL). The latest version of the OCFS

packages could be obtained from either of the following websites

- `http://otn.oracle.com/tech/linux/content.html`

- `http://www.ocfs.org/ocfs/`

The package comprises three files:

- Support file that contains all the generic packages required for OCFS. The file is identified with a version of the release, for example `ocfs-support-1.0.9-4.i686.rpm`

- Tools file that contains all packages to install the various tools required for the configuration and management of OCFS. This file is also identified with a version number of the release, for example `ocfs-support-1.0.9-4.i686.rpm`

- A Linux kernel module, which is specific to the type version of the Linux kernel. For example if the type version of the Linux operating system is e12smp the file that needs to be downloaded would be `ocfs-2.4.9-e12smp-1.0.9-4.i686.rpm`

Note: The type version of the Linux operating system could be determined using the uname command, for example

```
# uname -a

Linux oradb1.summerskyus.com 2.4.9-e.12smp #1 SMP
```

2.   The OCFS packages (RPM files) are required to be installed in the appropriate `/lib/modules` tree in use by the operating system kernel as user `root` in a specific order. The packages are installed using the following syntax:

```
rpm -i <ocfs_rpm_package>
```

- Install the support RPM file

  - `rpm -iv ocfs-support-1.0.9-4.i686.rpm`

- Install the correct kernel module RPM file for the system

  - `rpm -iv ocfs-2.4.9-e-smp-1.0.9-4.i686.rpm`

- Install the tools RPM file

  - `rpm -iv ocfs-tools-1.0.9-4.i686.rpm`

> **Note:** It is important to install the kernel module RPM file before installing the tools file. If this order is not followed, the install processes will error with the following error message: `ocfs=1.09 is needed by ocfs-tools-1.0.9-4`

3. Next step is to configure the `ocfs.conf` located in the `/etc` directory. This can be performed using the Oracle provided `ocfstool` from an x-windows interface as user `root`. The tool is invoked using the following command `/usr/bin/ocfstool`

   Use the Generate Config option under the Tasks tab to configure the private network adapters used by the cluster. Once configured the `/etc/ocfs.conf` file would contain the following entries.

```
$ more /etc/ocfs.conf
#
# ocfs config
# Ensure this file exists in /etc#
     node_name = oradb1.summerskyus.com
     node_number =
     ip_address = 192.37.210.21
     ip_port = 7000
     comm_voting = 1
     guid = 21FA5FA6715E2AB31451000BCD41E12B
```

4. OCFS needs to be started every time the system is started. This is done by adding the following lines in the `/etc/rc.d/rc.local` file

```
/sbin/load_ocfs
/sbin/mount -a -t ocfs
```

5. Next step is to create the partitions for use by OCFS. This is done using the Linux `fdisk` utility.

```
fdisk /dev/d439
```

   Size of partitions should take into consideration the block size used during the format operation. Oracle supports a block size between 2K to 1MB range. The max partition size is derived using the formula.

```
block_size * 1M * 8 (Bitmap size is fixed to 1M)
```
   If the block size if 2K the partition size would be

```
(2 * 1024) * (1M * 1024 * 1024) *8 = 16GB
```

> **Note:** Like all files systems OCFS has an operational overhead, the overhead would be approximately 10MB which is used for the files metadata, the "system files" that is stored at the end of the disk and the

partition headers. This should be taken into consideration when creating smaller partitions.

6.   Once the partitions are created using the fdisk utility they have to be formatted under OCFS. This step could be performed using the ocfstool utility or manually from the command line. This step should also be performed as user root. This process also defines the block size for the partition. For optimal performance benefits it is recommended that the block size be set at 128K.

After invoking the ocfstool (`/usr/bin/ocfstool`), using the format option (Figure 17.1) under the tasks tab is used to format the partitions with OCFS.

7.   Next step is to mount the partitions. Prior to mounting these partitions the appropriate mount points (directories) need to be created.

```
mkdir --p /u01 /u02 /u03
```

Once the mount points are created, they could be mounted using the ocfstool utility or from the command line using the mount command

```
mount -t ocfs -L /dev1d439 /u01
```

Figure 17.1
OCFS Tool
Interface

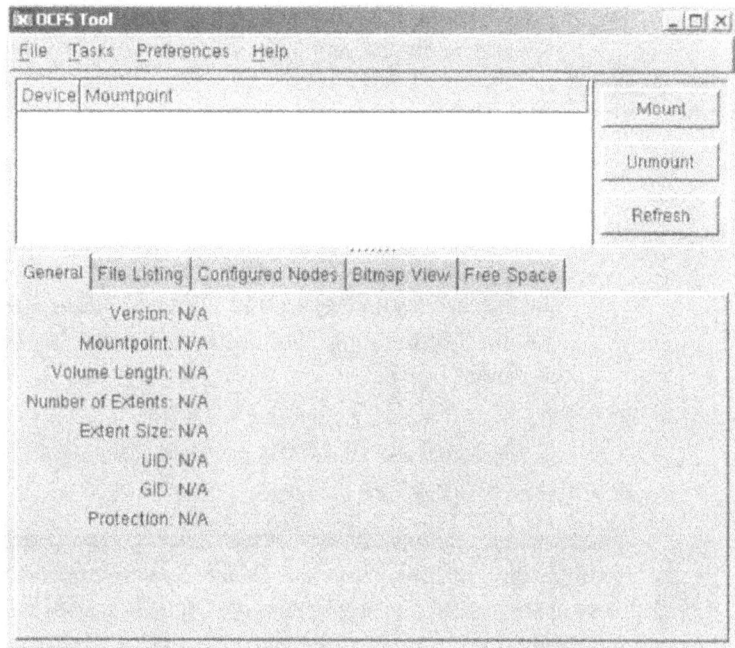

> **Note:** The mount points must be the same for all the nodes in the cluster.

8. The last step in the OCFS configuration is to add these definitions in the /etc/fstab file using the following syntax.

```
<partition device name> <mount point name> ocfs uid=1001,gid=100
```

> **Note:** The numbers following the uid and gid options correspond to the user id of the oracle user and the group id of the dba group verify that these values are correct for any RAC deployment where OCFS will be used.

17.2.2 Oracle Cluster Management Software

Oracle Cluster Management Software (OCMS) is included with the Oracle 9*i* Enterprise Edition for Linux. It provides cluster membership services, a global view of clusters, node monitoring, and cluster reconfiguration. It is a component of RAC on Linux and is installed automatically when RAC is selected. OCMS consists of the following components:

- Watchdog daemon
- Cluster manager

17.2.3 Watchdog daemon

The watchdog daemon (watchdogd) uses a software-implemented watchdog timer to monitor selected system resources to prevent database corruption. The watchdog timer is a feature of the Linux kernel. The watchdog daemon is part of RAC.

The watchdog daemon monitors the CM and passes notifications to the watchdog timer at defined intervals. The behavior of the Watchdog timer is partially controlled by the CONFIG_WATCHDOG_NOWAYOUT configuration parameter of the Linux kernel.

The value of the CONFIG_WATCHDOG_NOWAYOUT configuration parameter should be set to Y. If the watchdog timer detects an Oracle instance or CM failure, it resets the instance to avoid possible database corruption.

17.2.4   Cluster manager

The CM maintains the status of the nodes and the Oracle instances across the cluster. The CM process runs on each node of the cluster. Each node has one CM. The number of Oracle instances for each node is not limited by RAC. The CM uses the following communication channels between nodes:

- Private network.

- Quorum partition on the shared disk, also called a Quorum disk.

During normal cluster operations, the CMs on each node of the cluster communicate with each other through heartbeat messages sent over the private network. The quorum partition is used as an emergency communication channel if a heartbeat message fails. A heartbeat message can fail for the following reasons:

- The CM terminates on a node.

- The private network fails.

- There is an abnormally heavy load on the node.

The CM uses the quorum disk to determine the reason for the failure. From each node, the CM periodically updates the designated block on the quorum disk. Other nodes check the timestamp for each block. If the message from one of the nodes does not arrive, but the corresponding partition on the quorum has a current timestamp, the network path between this node and other nodes fails.

Figure 17.2 illustrates the Linux watchdog to Oracle instance communication hierarchy. Each Oracle instance registers with the local CM. The CM monitors the status of local Oracle instances and propagates this information to CMs on other nodes. If the Oracle instance fails on one of the nodes, the following events occur:

1.   The CM on the node with the failed Oracle instance informs the watchdog daemon about the failure.

2.   The watchdog daemon requests the watchdog timer/hangcheck timer to reset the failed node.

3.   The watchdog timer/hangcheck timer resets the node.

4.   The CMs on the surviving nodes inform their local Oracle instances that the failed node is removed from the cluster.

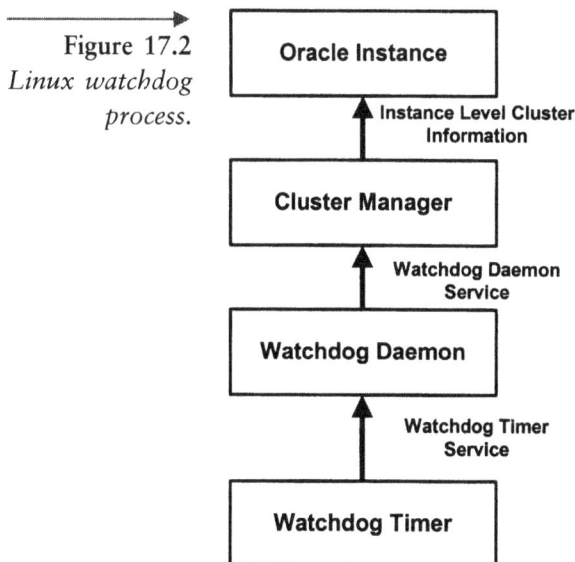

Figure 17.2
Linux watchdog process.

5. Oracle instances on the surviving nodes start the RAC reconfiguration procedure.

The nodes must reset if an Oracle instance fails. This ensures that:

- No physical I/O requests to the shared disks from the failed node occur after the Oracle instance fails.

- Surviving nodes can start the cluster reconfiguration procedure without corrupting the data on the shared disk.

9iR2

New Feature: The watchdog daemon process that existed in Oracle Release 9.1 impacted on system availability as it initiated system reboots under heavy workloads. Since then, this module has been removed from Oracle. In place of the watchdog daemon (`watchdogd`), Version 9.2.0.3 of the `oracm` for Linux now includes the use of a Linux kernel module called hangcheck-timer. The hangcheck-timer module monitors the Linux kernel for long operating system hangs, and reboots the node if this occurs, thereby preventing potential corruption of the database. This is the new I/O fencing mechanism for RAC on Linux.

OCMS Installation

Prior to installing the CM it is important the environment variable for ORACLE_HOME and the following directories are created on all the nodes in the cluster.

```
mkdir - p $ORACLE_HOME/oracm/log
mkdir - p $ORACLE_HOME/network/log
mkdir - p $ORACLE_HOME/network/trace
mkdir -p $ORACLE_HOME/rdbms/log
mkdir -p $ORACLE_HOME/rdbms/audit
mkdir -p $ORACLE_HOME/network/agent/log
mkdir $ORACLE_HOME/network/agent/reco
```

The CM comes bundled with the Oracle database software and is installed using the OUI. After invoking the Oracle installer, the CM option is selected from the available products screen.

Figure 17.3
Oracle Cluster
Manager

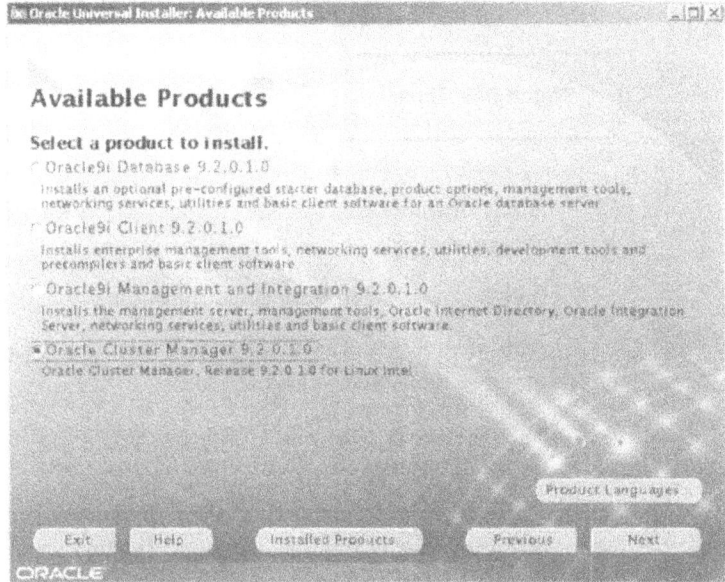

Once the Oracle CM has been selected, the next screen is used to define the public node information. This is done from the following screen.

Subsequent to the public node definition is the private node definition screen, followed by the watchdog definition screen and the quorum disk definition screen. Once this is defined, the CM manager is installed. These steps should be followed on all nodes in the cluster.

Note: The order of entering public and private should be paid attention to; they need to exactly correspond. For example the first public node that is entered must be the first private node entered and vice versa

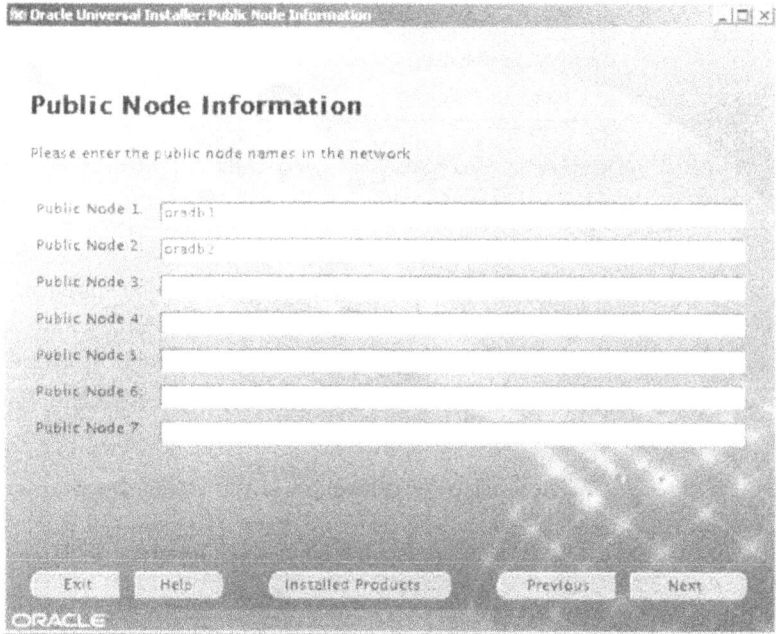

Figure 17.4
Public Node
Information

Once CM is installed, the cmcfg.ora file located in $ORACLE_HOME/ oracm/admin directory should have the following entries.

```
HeartBeat=15000
ClusterName=Oracle Cluster Manager, version 9i
PollInterval=1000
MissCount=20
PrivateNodeNames=oradb1_ic oradb2_ic
PublicNodeNames=oradb1 oradb2
ServicePort=9998
WatchdogSafetyMargin=5000
WatchdogTimerMargin=60000
CmDiskfile=
HostName=oradb1_ic
```

After CM for 9.2.0.1 is installed and configured, the next step is the installation of the RAC software. On completion of the RAC installation, the product could be upgraded to 9.2.0.3

9iR2 **New Feature:** The watchdog daemon process that existed in Oracle Release 9.1 impacted system availability as it initiated system reboots under heavy workloads. This module has since been removed from Oracle. In place of the watchdog daemon (watchdogd), Version 9.2.0.3 of the oracm for Linux now includes the use of a Linux kernel module called hangcheck-timer. The hangcheck-timer module monitors the Linux kernel for long operating system hangs, and reboots the node if this occurs, thereby preventing potential corruption of the database. This is the new I/O fencing mechanism for RAC on Linux.

Verify the miscount parameter for the CM in the cmcfg.ora file is set to a value greater than hangcheck-tick + hangcheck-margin (default should be OK at 210 seconds)

Quorum disk is required when using hangcheck timer. Create a partition on a raw device or if using OCFS create a partition using the steps defined above (section 17.2.1, Oracle Clustered File System). The required file could be created using the touch command for example:

```
touch/u12/quorum.dbf
```

When using hangchecktimer the cmcfg.ora file should look like this:

```
HeartBeat=15000
ClusterName=Oracle Cluster Manager, version 9i
PollInterval=1000
MissCount=20
PrivateNodeNames=oradb1_ic oradb2_ic
PublicNodeNames=oradb1 oradb2
ServicePort=9998
KernelModuleName=hangcheck-timer
CmDiskFile=/u12/quorum.dbf
HostName=oradb1_ic
```

17.2.5 Starting OCMS

The following sections describe how to start OCMS. Oracle Corporation supplies the $ORACLE_HOME/oracm/bin/ocmstart.sh sample startup script. Run this script as the root user.

Note: Once familiarity with the process is gained, the script can be used to automate the startup process.

Starting the watchdog daemon

To start the watchdog daemon, enter the following:

```
$ su root
# cd $ORACLE_HOME/oracm/bin
# watchdogd
```

The default watchdog daemon log file is $ORACLE_HOME/oracm/log/wdd.log.

Table 17.1 *Watchdog Daemon Arguments*

Argument	Valid Values	Default Value	Description
-l number	0 or 1	1	If the value is 0, no resources are registered for monitoring. This argument is used for debugging system configuration problems. If the value is 1, the CMs are registered for monitoring
-m number	5000 to 180,000 ms	5000	The watchdog daemon expects to receive heartbeat messages from all clients (oracm threads) within the time specified by this value. If a client fails to send a heartbeat message within this time, the watchdog daemon stops sending heartbeat messages to the kernel watchdog timer, causing the system to reset
-d string		/dev/watchdog	Path of the device file for the watchdog timer
-e string		`$ORACLE_HOME/ oracm/log/ wdd.log`	Filename of the watchdog daemon log file

Table 17.1 lists the various watchdog daemon arguments that are used during starting of the watchdog daemon process.

Configuring the cluster manager

The `$ORACLE_HOME/oracm/admin/cmcfg.ora` CM configuration file must be created on each node of the cluster before starting OCMS. The `cmcfg.ora` file should contain the following parameters:

- PublicNodeNames

- PrivateNodeNames

- CmDiskFile

- WatchdogTimerMargin/KernelModuleNames hangcheck-timer

- HostName

Before the creation of the CM configuration file the following should be verified:

- The `/etc/hosts` file on each node of the cluster has an entry for the public network (public name) and an entry for the private network (private name for each node).

- A private network is used for the RAC internode communication.

- The `CmDiskFile` parameter defines the location of the CM quorum disk.

- The `CmDiskFile` parameter on each node in a cluster must specify the same quorum disk.

The following example shows a `cmcfg.ora` file on the first node of a four node cluster:

```
PublicNodeNames=pubnode1 pubnode2 pubnode3 pubnode4
PrivateNodeNames=prinode1 prinode2 prinode3 prinode4
CmDiskFile=/dev/raw1
WatchdogTimerMargin=1000
HostName=prinode1
```

Table 17.2 lists all the CM parameters used for the creation of the CM configuration file.

Starting the cluster manager

To start the CM:

- Confirm that the watchdog daemon is running.

- Confirm that the host names specified by the `PublicNodeNames` and `PrivateNodeNames` parameters in the `cmcfg.ora` file are listed in the `/etc/hosts` file.

- As the `root` user, start the `oracm` process as a background process. To track activity, redirect any output to a log file. For example, the following script directs all the output messages and error messages to `$ORACLE_HOME/oracm/log/cm.out` file:

```
$ su root
# cd $ORACLE_HOME/oracm/bin
# oracm </dev/null >$ORACLE_HOME/oracm/log/cm.out 2>&1 &
```

The `oracm` process spawns multiple threads. The following command lists all the threads:

```
ps -elf
```

Table 17.3 describes the arguments used for the `oracm` executable.

Table **17.2**   *CM Parameters for the* `cmcfg.ora` *File*

Parameter	Valid Values	Default Value	Description
`CmDiskFile`	Directory path, up to 256 characters in length	No default value. Explicit value should be set	Specifies the pathname of the quorum partition
`MissCount`	2 to 1000	5	Specifies the time that the CM waits for a heartbeat from the remote node before declaring that node inactive. The time in seconds is determined by multiplying the value of the `MissCount` parameter by 3
`PublicNodeNames`	List of host names, up to 4096 characters in length	No default value	Specifies the list of all host names for the public network, separated by spaces. List host names in the same order on each node
`PrivateNodeNames`	List of host names, up to 4096 characters in length	No default value	Specifies the list of all host names for the private network, separated by spaces. List host names in the same order on each node
`HostName`	A host name, up to 256 characters in length	No default value	Specifies the local host name for the private network. Define this name in the `/etc/hosts` file
`ServiceName`	A service, up to 256 characters in length	CMSrvr	Specifies the service name to be used for communication between CM. If a CM cannot find the service name in the `/etc/services` file, it uses the port specified by the `ServicePort` parameter. ServiceName is a fixed-value parameter in this release. Use the `ServicePort` parameter if an alternative port for the CM is required
`ServicePort`	Any valid port number	9998	Specifies the number of the port to be used for communication between cluster managers when the ServiceName parameter does not specify a service

continued

Table 17.2   *Continued*

Parameter	Valid Values	Default Value	Description
WatchdogTimerMargin	1000 to 180,000 ms	No default value	The same as the value of the soft_margin parameter specified at Linux softdog startup. The value of the soft_margin parameter is specified in seconds and the value of the Watchdog TimerMargin parameter is specified in milliseconds. This parameter is part of the formula that specifies the time between when the CM on the local node detects an Oracle instance failure or join on any node and when it reports the cluster reconfiguration to the Oracle instance on the local node
WatchdogSafetyMargin	1000 to 180,000 ms	5000 ms	Specifies the time between when the CM detects a remote node failure and when the cluster reconfiguration is started. This parameter is part of the formula that specifies the time between when the CM on the local node detects an Oracle instance failure or join on any node and when it reports the cluster reconfiguration to the Oracle instance on the local node

Configuring timing for cluster reconfiguration

When a node fails, there is a delay before the RAC reconfiguration commences. Without this delay, simultaneous access of the same data block by the failed node and the node performing the recovery can cause database corruption. The length of the delay is defined by the sum of the following:

- Value of the WatchdogTimerMargin parameter.
- Value of the WatchdogSafetyMargin parameter.
- Value of the watchdog daemon -m command-line argument.

Table 17.3 *Arguments for the* oracm *Executable*

Argument	Values	Default Value	Description
/a:action	0,1	0	Specifies the action taken when the LMON process or another Oracle process that can write to the shared disk terminates abnormally. If action is set to 0 (the default), no action is taken. If action is set to 1, the CM requests the watchdog daemon to stop the node completely
/l:filename	Any	/$ORACLE_HOME/ oracm/log/ cm.log	Specifies the pathname of the log file for the CM. The maximum pathname length is 192 characters
/?	None	None	Shows help for the arguments of the oracm executable. If this argument is provided, CM will not start
/m	Any	25,000,000	The size of the oracm log file in bytes

If the default values for the Linux kernel soft_margin and CM parameters are used, the time between when the failure is detected and the start of the cluster reconfiguration is 70 seconds. For most workloads, this time can be significantly reduced. The following example shows how to decrease the time of the reconfiguration delay from 70 seconds to 20 seconds:

■ Set the value of the WatchdogTimerMargin (soft_margin) parameter to 10 seconds.

■ Leave the value of the WatchdogSafetyMargin parameter at the default value, 5000 ms.

■ Leave the value of the watchdog daemon -m command-line argument at the default value, 5000 ms.

To change the values of the WatchdogTimerMargin (soft_ margin) and the WatchdogSafetyMargin:

■ Stop the Oracle instance.

▪ Reload the `softdog` module with the new value of `soft_margin`. For example,

```
#/sbin/insmod softdog soft_margin=10
```

Change the value of the `WatchdogTimerMargin` in the CM configuration file `$ORACLE_HOME/oracm/admin/cmcfg.ora`. The value is modified by editing the parameter `WatchdogTimerMargin=50000`.

▪ Restart `watchdogd` with the -m command-line argument set to 5000.

▪ Restart the `oracm` executable.

▪ Restart the Oracle instance.

Note: The removal of the watchdogd and the introduction of the hangcheck-timer module require several parameter changes in the CM configuration file,

`$ORACLE_HOME/oracm/admin/cmcfg.ora`.

1. The following watchdogd related parameters are no longer valid and should be removed from all nodes in the cluster.
   ```
   WatchdogTimerMargin
   WatchdogSafetyMargin
   ```

2. A new parameter that identifies the hangcheck module to the oracm is required to be added to the `cmcfg.ora` file.
   ```
   kernelModuleNam=hangcheck-timer
   ```

3. The following parameter is now a required parameter. This informs the oracm to use the quorum partition.
   ```
   CMDiskFile=<quorum disk directory path>
   ```

4. The following new parameters have been introduced; these parameters are used when the hangcheck-timer module is loaded and indicates how long a RAC node must hang before the hangcheck-timer will reset the system.

hangcheck_tick – the hangcheck_tick is an interval indicating how often the hangcheck-timer checks on the health of the system.

hangcheck_margin – certain kernel activities may randomly introduce delays in the operation of the hangcheck-timer. hangcheck_margin provides a margin of error to prevent unnecessary system resets due to these delays.

The node reset occurs when the system hang time > (hangcheck_tick + hangcheck_margin)

Cluster manager starting options

OCMS supports node fencing by completely resetting the node if an Oracle instance fails and the CM thread malfunctions. This approach guarantees that the database is not corrupted.

However, it is not always necessary to reset the node if an Oracle instance fails. If the Oracle instance uses synchronous I/O, a node reset is not required. In addition, in some cases where the Oracle instance uses asynchronous I/O, it is not necessary to reset the node, depending on how asynchronous I/O is implemented in the Linux kernel.

The /a:action flag in the following command defines OCMS behavior when an Oracle process fails:

```
$ oracm /a:[action]
```

In this example:

- If the action argument is set to 0, the node does not reset. By default, the watchdog daemon starts with the -l 1 option and the oracm process starts with the /a:0 option. With these default values, the node resets only if the oracm or watchdogd process terminates. It does not reset if an Oracle process that can write to the disk terminates. This is safe if a certified Linux kernel is used that does not require node-reset.

- If the action argument is set to 1, the node resets if oracm, watchdogd, or an Oracle process that can write to the disk terminates. In these situations, a SHUTDOWN ABORT command on an Oracle instance resets the node and terminates all Oracle instances that are running on that node.

Note: Only the additional processes required for configuration of RAC on Linux have been discussed. All other steps discussed in Chapter 8 (Installation and Configuration) have to be followed for the complete installation of RAC on Linux.

17.3   Windows

In Oracle 9*i* Release 2 of RAC, Oracle introduced the cluster file system (CFS) for the Windows operating system. Installation of CFS on the Windows operating system eliminates the need for raw devices for RAC.

17.3.1   Cluster file system

CFS eliminates the requirement for Oracle database files to be linked to logical drives and enables all nodes to share a single Oracle home instead of requiring each node to have its own local copy. CFS volumes can span one shared disk or multiple shared disks for redundancy and performance enhancements.

The benefits of CFS are as follows:

- It is extensible without interrupting availability. Oracle homes and data files stored on CFS can be extended dynamically. Unlike raw partitions where each partition can only hold one partition (i.e., a partition is a file), with CFS multiple files can reside in one location.

- It eliminates the requirement for each node in a cluster to have its own local copy of the Oracle home.

- It takes full advantage of RAID volumes and storage area networks.

- It simplifies Oracle database administration. CFS provides a uniform view of files and directories across a cluster for both Oracle home files and Oracle database files.

- It provides uniform accessibility to archive logs in the event of physical node failures.

- When Oracle patches are applied, the updated Oracle home is visible to all nodes in the cluster.

- It guarantees consistency of metadata across all nodes in a cluster.

17.3.2   Before beginning

The procedures described in the following sections enable RAC to use CFS for database files and/or a shared Oracle home.

Before starting the installation process:

5.   Ensure that sufficient unallocated space is available on the shared disks.

6. Ensure that all the required administrative privileges are available for all nodes.

7. Make sure all the nodes to be part of the CFS are up and can communicate with each other in a TCP/IP environment.

8. Have the following hardware and network configuration information available:

   a. The public network names for each node (also known as host or TCP/IP names).

   b. If VIA hardware is used for cluster interconnects, the name of the VIA connection network interface card (NIC).

   c. The private network names of each node for the high-speed private interconnect. For optimal performance, a dedicated private interconnect for CFS should be used.

17.3.3 CFS-installed components and services

On successful installation of CFS, the following components and services are available:

Ocfs.sys

File system driver for Windows NT and Windows 2000. The correct O/S-specific version of the driver is installed depending on the Windows O/S.

OracleClusterVolumeService

CFS service that ensures consistent mount points across the cluster and provides configuration support for the file system driver. After installation, CFS service appears in the Windows Services panel.

OcfsFormat.exe

Utility that prepares volumes for use with the CFS. In order to enable a volume for use with CFS, it needs to be formatted by running this utility from one of the nodes in the cluster.

OcfsUtil.exe

Utility that is used for changing the cluster name for a given volume, managing the list of nodes configured on a volume, and creating node-specific files and directories.

OcfsOui.bat

Batch file that automatically runs from OUI during the installation of an Oracle home on CFS. It is called by OracleClusterVolumeService and it creates the needed node-specific directories and files on CFS for the Oracle home.

17.3.4   System requirements

- For accessibility requirements, Oracle Cluster Setup Wizard requires JAWS 4.0.2 or higher as the minimum configuration.

- CFS can be installed on a Windows workgroup or a Windows domain. For a domain, each node must be a member of the same domain or belong to a trusted domain.

- CFS does not support mixed clusters containing Windows NT and Windows 2000.

- Windows Terminal Services Client cannot be used to perform the installation.

- To guard against unnecessary troubleshooting, downtime, and performance problems, any node belonging to the CFS should not be:

  a)   A domain controller

  b)   Configured as a DHCP, WINS, or DNS server

- CFS supports nodes with multiple NICs and VIA hardware. A unique node name is assigned to each NIC. For performance and failover, multiple NICs with static IP addresses assigned to each are recommended.

- CFS supports up to 32 nodes in a cluster.

Table 17.4 provides the system requirements for installing CFS for RAC.

17.3.5   Cluster file system preinstallation steps

Under the Windows operating systems, raw partitions are referred to as logical drives.

> **Note:** For additional information on creating partitions, refer to the Windows online help from within the disk administration tools.

Table 17.4   *Hardware and O/S Requirements for CFS*

Component	Requirement
Processor	Pentium 266 or higher recommended
Operating system	Windows NT 4 Server with Service Pack 6 or higher Windows 2000 Server or Windows 2000 Advanced Server with Service Pack 2 or higher Not supported: Windows 2000 Datacenter Server
RAM	256 MB minimum
Virtual memory	Initial size 200 MB Maximum size 400 MB
Hard disk space	100 MB minimum for a volume to be usable for CFS 4 MB local disk space for CFS components
Networking protocol	TCP/IP
Video adapter	256 colors (required only for running installations and tools)

- Run Windows NT Disk Administrator or Windows 2000 Disk Management from one node to create an extended partition. For Windows 2000 only, use a basic disk. Dynamic disks are not supported.

- Create at least two partitions: one for the Oracle home and one for the Oracle database files.

  - In the prior version of RAC, a separate partition was required to be configured as a voting device. When CFS is used, this is not required. CFS stores the voting device in a file.

  - Caution should be taken when creating partitions. The number of partitions should be kept to the minimum. Increasing the number of partitions affects the overall performance of the system.

To create partitions

1. From one of the existing nodes of the cluster, run the Windows disk administration tool as follows:

   a. On Windows NT start Disk Administrator using the path: Start>Programs>Administrative Tools>Disk Administrator.

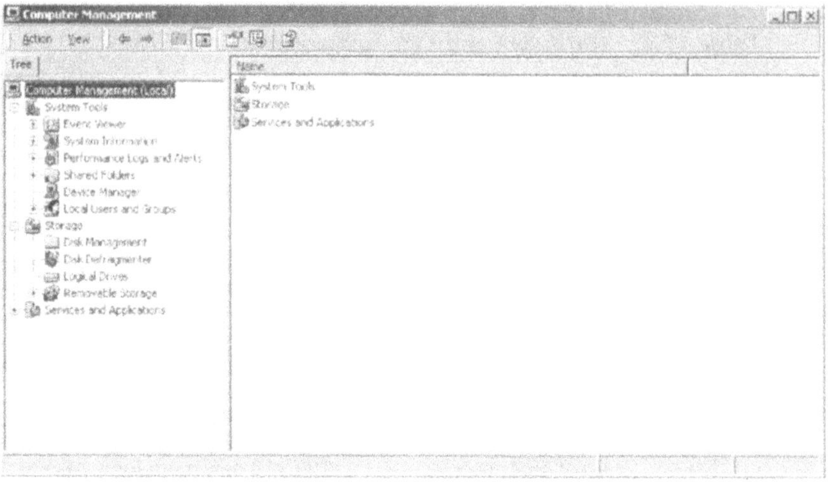

Figure 17.5
*Options under
Computer
Management
utility.*

b. On Windows 2000 start Disk Management using the path:
    Start>Settings>Control Panel>Administrative Tools>Computer
    Management. Figure 17.5 provides a view of the Computer
    Management list of functions. From this screen the Storage
    folder is expanded to select the Disk Management folder. For
    Windows 2000 only, use a basic disk as an extended partition
    for creating partitions.

2. From list of disk partitions the unallocated part of an extended
    partition is selected.

    a. For Windows NT choose Create Partition.

    b. For Windows 2000 choose Create Logical Drive. A wizard
        presents pages for configuring the logical drive.

3. Next is the Create Partition Wizard screen, shown in Figure 17.3.
    From this screen the actual size of the partition is defined. Oracle
    CFS requires that the partition created should be 100 MB or
    higher.

4. When creating the partition, caution should be taken not to assign
    any letter to the partition. Partition names are assigned through the
    Cluster Setup Wizard at a later stage in the process.

    a. Windows NT automatically assigns a drive letter. Remove the
        drive letter by right clicking on the new drive and selecting "Do
        not assign a drive letter" for the Assign Drive Letter option. Do
        this for any Oracle partitions.

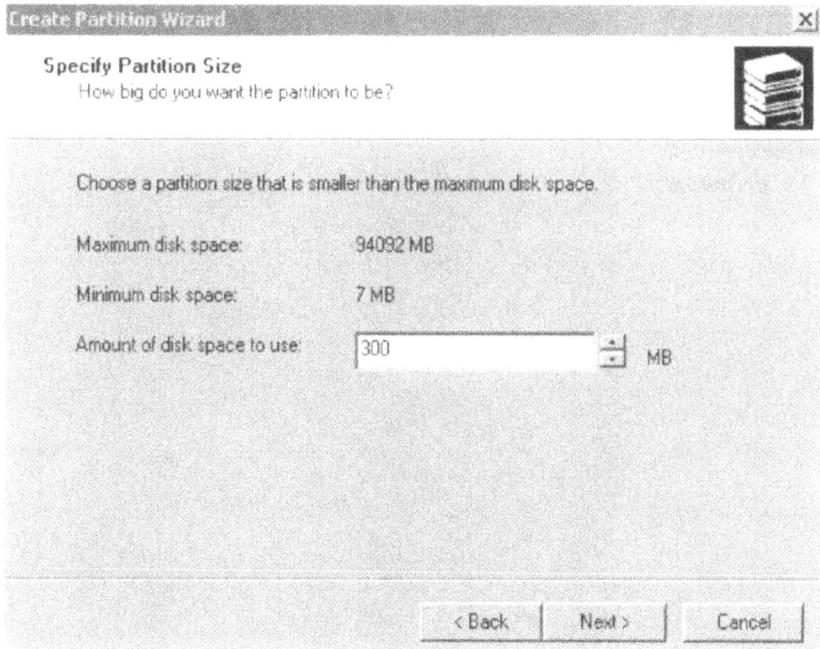

Figure 17.6
Defining the partition size.

b. For Windows 2000 choose the option "Do not assign a drive letter" and then click "Next" to continue. Figure 17.7 illustrates the screen where the drive letter is to be assigned for the partition. However, the path of the name definition for the partition is accomplished through the Cluster Setup Wizard option.

c. The next window prompts the user to determine if the partition needs to be formatted. In this screen "Do not format this partition" is selected.

d. Figure 17.8 provides a view of the last screen while defining a partition. From the screen the "Finish" option is selected, marking the completion of creating a partition (e.g., of size 300 MB as illustrated in the figure).

5. Choose "Commit Changes Now" from the Partition menu to save the new partition information.

6. Steps 2 through 4 are repeated for creation of any additional partitions. An optimal configuration would be with one partition created for Oracle home and another partition for the Oracle database files.

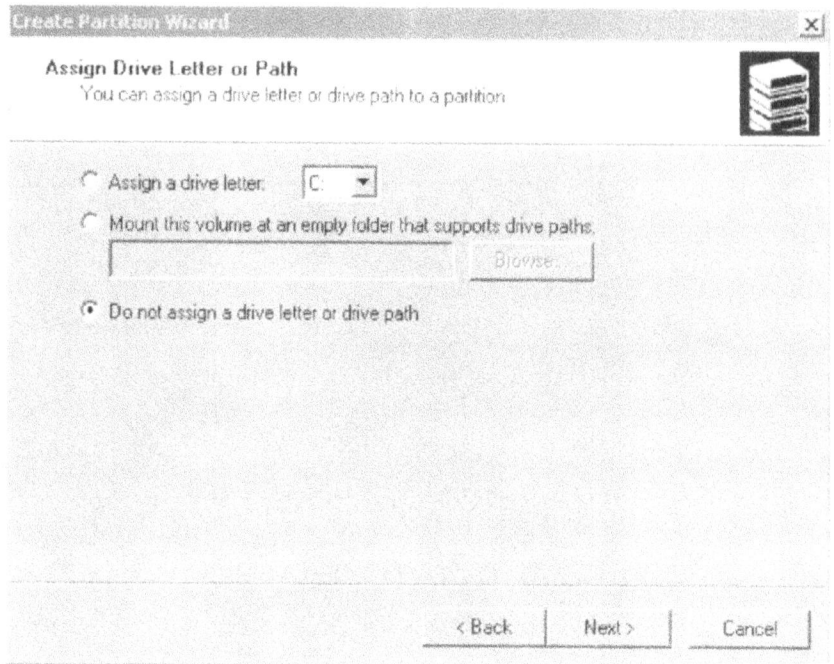

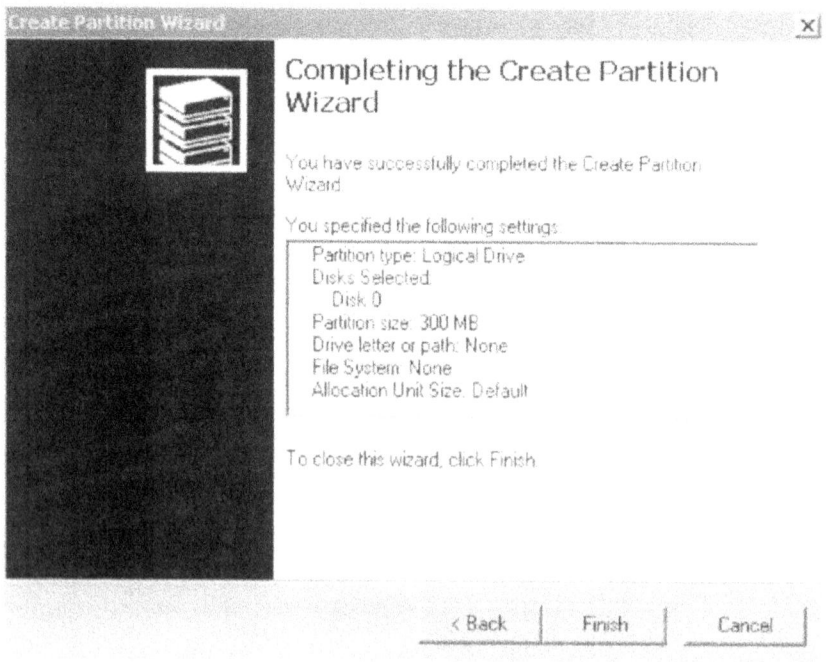

7. Once all the required partitions have been defined, it should be verified that these partitions are visible from all nodes participating in the cluster. As part of the verification process, it should be confirmed that no drive letter or path is assigned to a partition.

17.3.6   Installing cluster file system

This section describes the steps for the first installation of CFS.

Run `clustersetup.exe` from the `preinstall_rac\cluster-setup\` directory of the CFS product CD. Do not run `clustersetup.exe` from the Oracle *9i* Database product CD.

To install CFS:

1. From one of the nodes in the cluster, insert the CFS product CD, and navigate to the `\preinstall_rac\clustersetup\` directory and double-click `clustersetup.exe`. The welcome page for the Oracle Cluster Setup Wizard appears, as shown in Figure 17.6. Click "Next" to continue.

2. From the next screen choose "Create a cluster" and click "Next," at which point the Network Selection page appears.

Figure 17.9
CFS installation welcome screen.

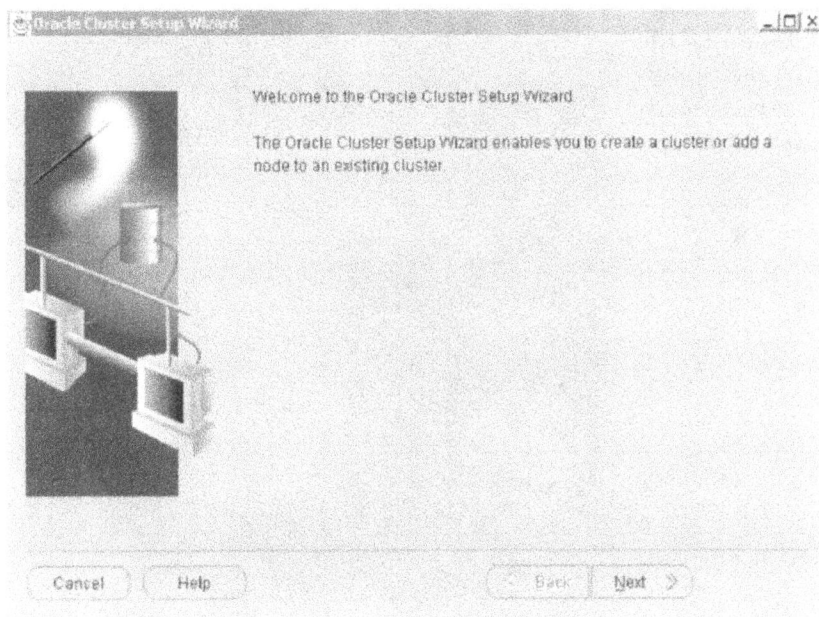

3. Choose "Use private network for interconnect" if the nodes have a high-speed private network connecting them. Otherwise, the public network can be selected. Click "Next." The Private Network Configuration page appears.

4. Enter the name for the cluster being created, and enter the names of the nodes. If a private network interconnect was selected in step 3, enter the public and private names for the nodes; otherwise, enter the public names. Figure 17.10 defines the public and private names for the nodes participating in the cluster. Once the names are assigned, click "Next," at which point the CFS options window appears.

5. Choose a CFS option for this cluster: "CFS for Oracle Home and Datafiles," "CFS for Oracle Home," or "CFS for Datafiles." Click "Next."

6. Depending on the CFS option selected, a page for selecting the disk partition and the drive letter appears:

   a. If "CFS for Oracle Home and Datafiles" is selected, then two pages appear sequentially: "CFS for Oracle Home" and "CFS for Datafiles."

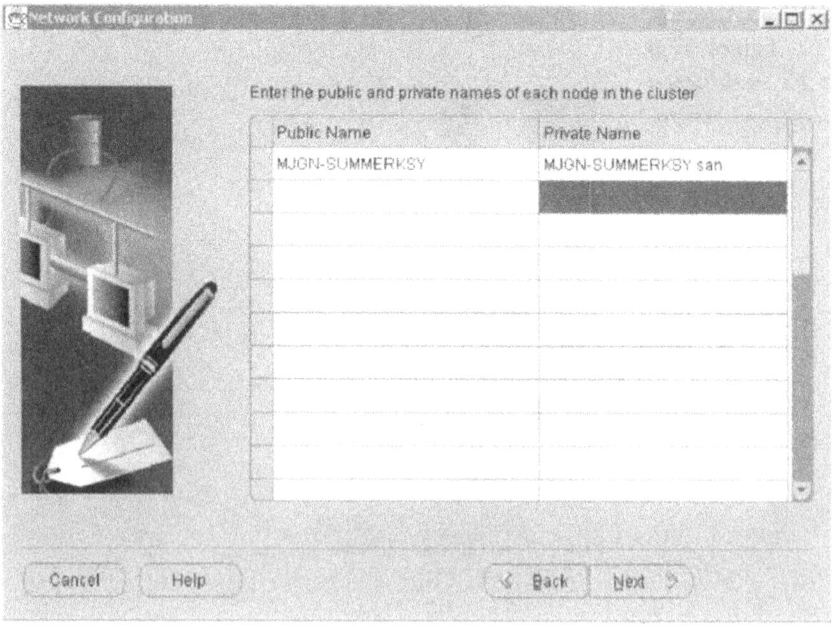

Figure 17.10
Public and private node name definition.

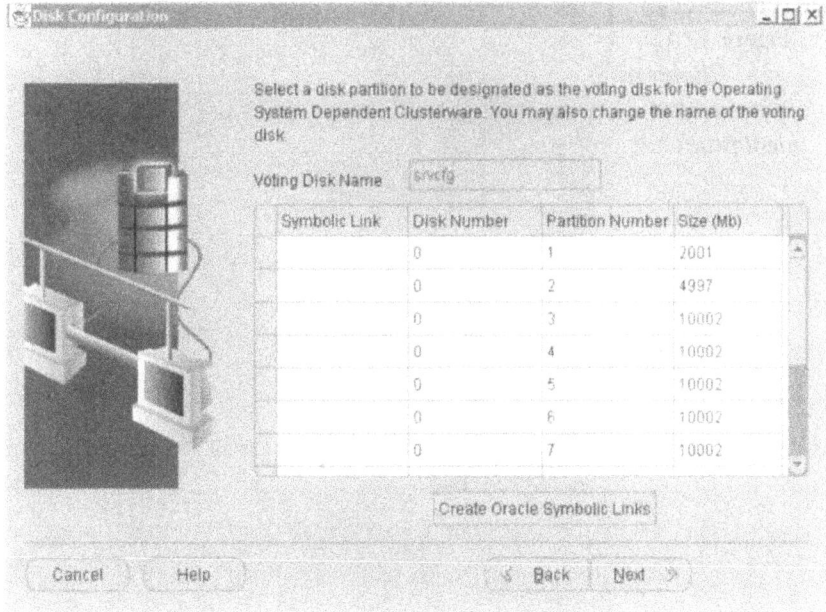

Figure 17.11
Voting disk selection.

b. If "CFS for Oracle Home" is selected, then the "CFS for Oracle Home" page appears followed by the Disk Configuration screen for configuring the voting disk (Figure 17.11). Select the appropriate disk for the voting disk, "srvcfg." CFS stores the voting device for operating-system-dependent (OSD) clusterware as a file on a CFS partition. Click "Next" when done.

c. If "CFS for Datafiles" is selected, then the "CFS for Datafiles" page appears.

7. Choose a partition of the required size from the list of available partitions and then choose a drive letter from the Drive Letter drop-down list. For the CFS option selected in step 5, the partition and drive letter combination will be assigned to the CFS drive letter for all of the volumes in the cluster.

8. For additional CFS volume definitions step 6 is repeated. Click "Next." If "CFS for Oracle Home and Datafiles" or "CFS for Datafiles" was selected in step 5, then skip to step 10.

9. If "CFS for Oracle Home" was selected in step 5 then the Disk Configuration page for configuring the voting disk appears because the Oracle database files will not use CFS.

Figure 17.12
*Cluster
interconnect
identification.*

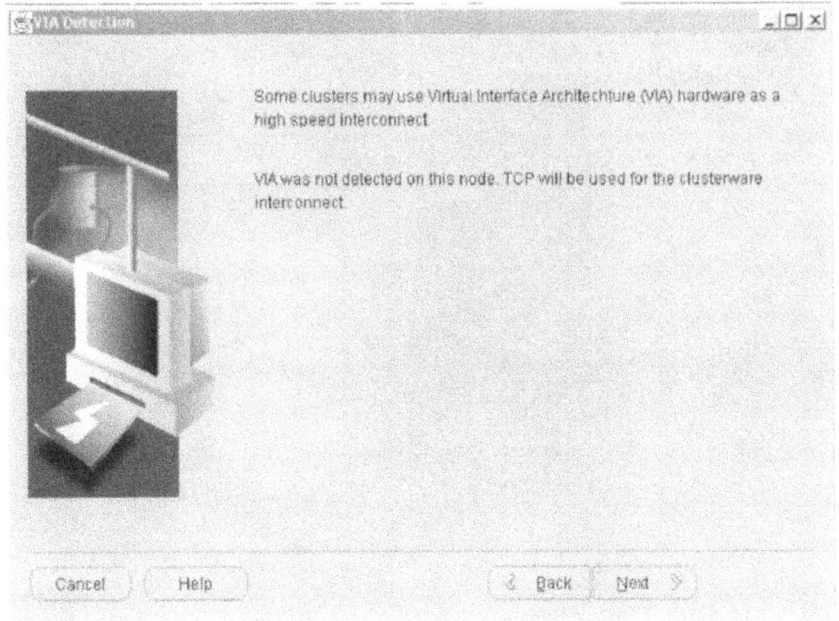

Figure 17.12
*Cluster
interconnect
identification.*

10. Click "Next." The installation wizard automatically checks that the cluster interconnect hardware such as VIA is configured. Figure 17.12 provides the status after the cluster interconnect identification has been performed by the CFS installation process. The installation process verifies the existence of VIA in the configuration.

    a. If VIA is not detected, TCP is used for the clusterware interconnect. Click "Next" and skip to step 13.

    b. If VIA is detected, then the VIA Selection page appears. Continue to step 11.

11. Choose "Yes" to use VIA for the interconnect and click "Next." The VIA Configuration page appears. Option "No" will inform the CFS installation process to use TCP/IP as the cluster interconnect.

12. Enter the name of the VIA connection and click "Next."

13. The Install Location page is the last page that appears. The default location is %systemroot%\osd9i. Click "Browse" to navigate to a different location if needed.

14. Click "Finish." A progress page displays the actions being performed. Figure 17.13 verifies the CFS configuration. Depending

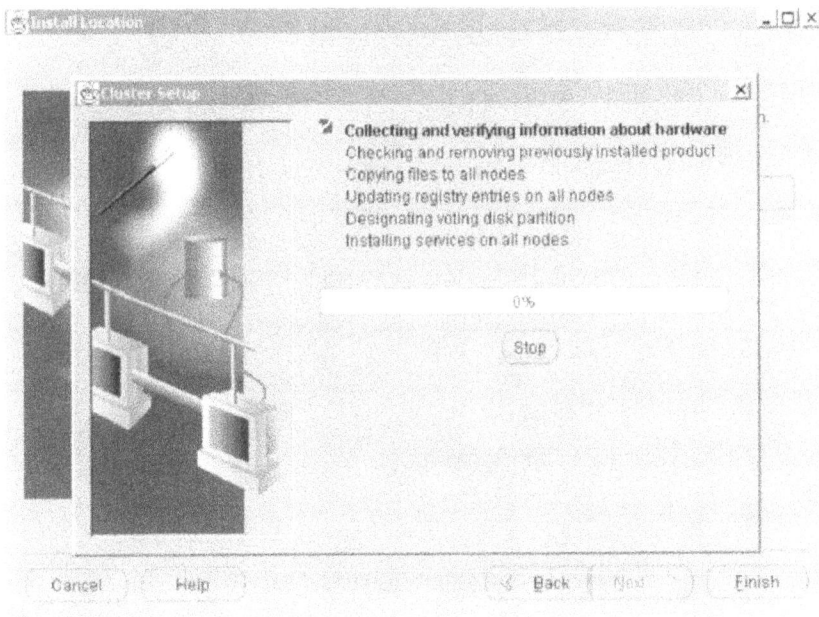

Figure 17.13
CFS verification.

on the number of partitions and the number of nodes defined in the configuration, this could take several minutes to complete.

17.3.7   Installing Oracle Real Application Clusters

The steps described in this section create a RAC database on the CFS. To perform these steps the following are required:

- To be logged in with administrative privileges.

- The CFS product CD.

- The Oracle 9*i* Enterprise Edition Release 2 (9.2.0.1.0) product CDs.

- The CFS drive letter that was specified earlier, for the Oracle home, and if "CFS for Datafiles" is created, then the CFS drive letter is specified for data files.

Task 1: Install Oracle RAC components

The steps required for installation of RAC are the same as defined in Chapter 8 (Installation and Configuration).

Task 2: Apply the patches

Before running DBCA to configure the database, the required patches for SRVM and DBCA should be applied. The patch documents are located in the \patch directory of the CFS product CD, or in the %ORACLE_HOME%\cfspatch directory of the Oracle home. Oracle provides the information required for installation of the server manager and the DBCA utility in their respective text files.

1. Perform the patch procedures described in srvm.txt to the SRVM patch.

2. Perform the patch procedure described in dbca.txt to apply the DBCA patch.

Task 3: Configure listener services

1. Stop the Oracle<oracle home name>TNSListener service from the Windows Services control panel.

    a. For example: OracleOraHome92TNSListener where the Oracle home name is OraHome92 and appears in the CFS under \oracle\ora92.

    b. On some systems the node name of the first node may be appended, for example OracleOraHome92TNSListener Listener_deptclust1.

2. Change Startup Type to Disabled for the listener service on each node, for all nodes in the cluster.

3. On each node, open an MS-DOS window and from the command prompt enter:

    lsnrctl start <listener_name>

    For example:

    O:\>lsnrctl start listener_deptclust1

    where listener_deptclust1 is the name of the listener configured for the node deptclust1 of the cluster named deptclust.

> **Note:** For the command-line argument, the listener name should match the listener configured for each node. For example: `listener_deptclust1`, `listener_deptclust2`, `listener_deptclust3`.

Perform this step on each node. The `lsnrctl` command creates the service for the listener provided as argument and starts the service. The listener service appears in the Services control panel for the node.

4. After the services for the listeners are created, the Startup Type for each service is changed to Automatic. Repeat this step for each node.

Task 4: Configure the Oracle RAC database

1. On the CFS drive that was created for data files, create an `oradata` directory at the root. This directory will be visible from all nodes in the CFS.
   For example: `P:\>md oradata`.

2. Open a new MS-DOS window and run DBCA from the command prompt as follows:

   `dbca -data fileDestination P:\oradata`

   The DBCA welcome page appears. Choose "Oracle cluster database" and click "Next."

3. Choose "Create database" and click "Next."

4. Select all nodes on the Node Selection page and click "Next."

> **Note:** The steps required for creation of a RAC database are discussed in Chapter 8 (Installation and Configuration).

17.3.8 Installing CFS on an existing cluster

If Release 2 (9.2.0.1.0) of RAC is installed, which does not contain the CFS feature, and it is determined that for easy maintenance the RAC installation needs to be upgraded to include CFS, the following section describes the steps involved.

Run the Oracle Cluster Setup Wizard from the CFS product CD to re-create the cluster to use CFS and choose "CFS for Datafiles" as the CFS option.

Preparation for installing CFS for Datafiles

Prior to installation of CFS the following should be performed:

- All databases running in the cluster should be stopped.
- Oracle services running on all nodes should be stopped.
- Oracle OSD clusterware services should also be stopped.

Task 1: Shut down databases

- Using the SRVCTL command the databases can be shut down from any of the participating nodes in the cluster. The following command shuts down the database:

  ```
  C:\> srvctl stop database -d <db_name>
  ```

  Control is not returned to the session that initiates a database shutdown until shutdown is complete.
  The database cannot be shut down if the database has any shared server processes that are maintaining session states.

- Alternatively, the SQL*Plus SHUTDOWN command could be used on each node on which the cluster database has an instance to shut down that instance.

Task 2: Stop Oracle services

Stop all Oracle database services. From the Services dialog box in the Windows Control Panel, stop these services (and others if applicable):

- OracleCMService9i
- OracleGSDService
- OracleService<SID>
- OracleTNSListener service on each node

Task 3: Back up database configuration information

Back up configuration information for existing databases by using the srvconfig utility:

```
C:\> srvconfig -exp %ORACLE_HOME%\conf_backup.txt
```

Task 4: Install CFS

- From the CFS product CD, run Cluster Setup Wizard as described in Section 17.3.6.

- Choose "CFS for Datafiles" as the CFS Option.

After the cluster is re-created, all nodes will have access to CFS for Datafiles.

Task 5: Restore database configuration information

- Initialize the SRVM configuration file by using the srvconfig utility as:

```
C:\> srvconfig -init
```

- Restore the backed up configuration information that was created in Task 3:

```
C:\> srvconfig -imp %ORACLE_HOME%\conf_backup.txt
```

Task 6: Start Oracle services

From the Services dialog box in Windows Control Panel on each node, start these services (and others if applicable):

- OracleCMService9i

- OracleGSDService

- OracleService<SID>

- OracleTNSListener service on each node.

17.3.9 Cluster file system features

Node-specific files and directories

CFS supports node-specific files and directories. This allows nodes in a cluster to see different views of the same files and directories although they have the same pathname on CFS. This feature supports products that are installed on the Oracle home (like Oracle Intelligent Agent) that need to have the same file name on different nodes but require a private copy on each node because node-specific information might be stored in these files.

Unique clustername integrity

CFS associates a unique clustername with a CFS volume. The clustername is automatically selected from the cluster manager registry, and if a valid non-default clustername is present in the value

HKEY_LOCAL_MACHINE\Software\Oracle\CM\ClusterName

then any volume formatted from this node will be available to nodes with the same clustername as this node. OcfsUtil provides a way to change the clustername for a volume to another clustername which makes the volume visible to all nodes in the cluster. Clustername allows a hardware cluster to be segregated into logical software clusters from a storage viewpoint. This is important for supporting a storage area network.

OcfsUtil command summary

OcfsUtil is a command-line utility that is used for:

- Changing the clustername for a given volume.
- Managing the list of nodes configured on a volume.
- Creating node-specific files and directories.

    Table 17.5 provides a list of OcfsUtil commands.

Table 17.5   OcfsUtil *Command Summary*

Command	Description and Syntax
ChangeClusterName	Enables the clustername for a volume to be changed, with the mount point <VolumeMount Point>, for example O:, to <NewClusterName> as specified. Specifying no <NewClusterName> resets the clustername to null clustername making the volume specified by VolumeMountPoint visible to all nodes that have hardware connectivity to it. Syntax: OcfsUtil /c ChangeClusterName /m <VolumeMountPoint> /n <NewClusterName>

continued

Table 17.5   *Continued*

Command	Description and Syntax
ChangeVolConfig	Prints the current volume's config map for the volume specified with mount point `<Volume MountPoint>`, for example, O:. If /d <NodeName> is specified, the NodeName will be removed from the config map. The config map is the list of nodes that have ever accessed this CFS. Syntax: OcfsUtil /c ChangeVolConfig /p /m <VolumeMountPoint> /d <NodeName>
NodeSpecificFile (Create) This command has three options: create, delete, or revert	Makes the file or directory (/d) specified by `<FullPath>` on the `<VolumeMountPoint>`, for example O:, into a node-specific file. The file or directory will have the same name on all nodes, but will have different contents and will be treated as a local file or directory. Syntax: OcfsUtil /c NodeSpecificFile /o <create/delete/revert>/m <MountPoint> /p <Path> /d and OcfsUtil /c NodeSpecificFile /o create /m <VolumeMountPoint> /p <FullPath> /d
NodeSpecificFile (Delete)	Deletes the node-specific file or directory specified by `<FullPath>` on the `<VolumeMount Point>` for example O:. Syntax: OcfsUtil /c NodeSpecificFile /o delete /m <VolumeMountPoint> /p <FullPath>
NodeSpecificFile (Revert)	Reverts the node-specific file or directory specified by `<FullPath>` on the `<VolumeMountPoint>`, for example O:, to a shared file and will point the file/directory to the contents of the node-specific file on `<NodeName>`. If no NodeName is specified, the reverted shared file directory will have the contents of the node on which the command is run. Syntax: OcfsUtil /c NodeSpecificFile /o revert /m <VolumeMountPoint> /p <FullPath> /n <NodeName>

17.3.10   Performance tuning

For CFS to perform optimally, do not store the Oracle home and the Oracle database files on the same partition or logical drive.

Allocation unit sizes

For volumes that have only Oracle database files, the allocation unit size should be set to greater than 1024 KB. For volumes on which the Oracle home is created, the allocation unit size should be set to 4 KB to 8 KB.

Use the Windows disk administration tool to set the file allocation unit size appropriate for the type of file access.

Table 17.6 provides the recommended allocation unit sizes. The default allocation for Windows is 4 KB.

Caching

For optimal performance, CFS does not cache data for Oracle database files. Instead it performs caching for both metadata and non-database files. Therefore, Oracle Corporation strongly recommends that third party products that require a file system to aggressively cache not be used with CFS. Doing so could cause conflicts with the caching mechanism used by CFS.

Networking recommendations

Public interconnects should not be used for the clustered database. Public interconnects experience busy network traffic. Do not use DHCP to dynamically assign IP addresses to the nodes running the clustered database. DHCP produces increased network traffic through leasing and revoking IP addresses.

Table 17.6   *Recommended Allocation Unit Sizes*

File Type	Recommended Allocation Unit Size
CFS for Oracle Home	4 KB to 8 KB
CFS for Datafiles	1024 KB minimum

Each node should have at least two NICs to provide a private interconnect for the internode cache fusion traffic. The private interconnect takes advantage of the performance gains provided by cache fusion.

The NICs should have dedicated IP addresses for optimal bandwidth. Alternatively, the NIC teaming where multiple physical NICs are configured as one logical NIC and multiple IP addresses are assigned to the single logical NIC. Using multiple NICs safeguards against the possibility of network card failure.

17.4   Conclusion

In this chapter we looked at the additional layered product requirements when installing RAC on operating systems such as Linux and Windows. During these discussions the installation process for both the Linux operating system and installation and configuration of the CFS for the Windows O/S was also discussed. CFS is a new file system feature introduced by Oracle in Version 9*i* Release 2 that removes the requirement of raw devices for RAC on Windows O/S.

This is the last chapter in the book. Part IV contains appendices.

Part IV

Appendices

Appendix I

Utilities

A1.1 GSDCTL: Global service daemon control

In Oracle 9*i* Release 2, Oracle has introduced another utility to manage the GSD process called the GSDCTL. Let us look at the GSD commands:

gsdctl start	Start the GSD
gsdctl stop	Stop the GSD
gsdctl stat	Check status of the GSD. Check to ensure that GSD is running

Usage

```
gsdctl stat
```

Example:

```
ora-db1:RAC1:oracle# gsdctl stat
GSD is running on the local node
ora-db1:RAC1:oracle#
```

A1.2 SRVCTL: Server control

In this section, let us look at the server control (SRVCTL) commands provided by Oracle to manage the clustered databases from the command line. The SRVCTL replaces and extends the capabilities of the OPS tool called OPSCTL, which supported only the START and STOP subcommands. In comparison to OPSCTL, the START and STOP subcommands have been extended with additional options and new subcommands have been added to support more functionality.

Unlike its predecessor, the SRVCTL utility also helps monitor the instances from the Oracle Enterprise Manager (OEM). It serves as a single point of control between the Oracle Intelligent Agent (OIA) and the nodes of the cluster. Only one node's OIA is used to communicate with the SRVCTL. That node communicates to the other nodes through Oracle Net.

Before invoking any commands to manage the RAC from the SRVCTL utility, it is required that the global services daemon (GSD) is configured and running on the node.

START subcommand

`srvctl start -d <db_name>`	Start specified RAC database
`-i <instance_name,>`	Start named instances if specified, otherwise entire RAC
`-n <node,...>`	Start instances on named nodes
`-s <stage,...>`	List of stages to start (stage = inst, lsnr)
`-x <stage,...>`	Except these stages
`-c <connect string>`	Connect string (default: /as sysdba)
`-o <options>`	Options to startup command (for example force or nomount)
`-S <status level>`	Intermediate status level for console
`-D <debug level>`	Debug level
`-h`	Print usage

Usage

This starts the instances that are configured for a database (e.g., PRODDB1) and listeners in a RAC:

```
srvctl start -d PRODDB1
```

To start the instance RAC1 and its listeners:

```
srvctl start -d PRODDB1 -i RAC1
```

To start only instance RAC1:

```
srvctl start -d PRODDB1 -i RAC1 -s inst
```

To start only listeners for instance RAC1:

```
srvctl start -d PRODDB1 -i RAC1 -s lsnr
```

Start all instances with debug output enabled:

```
srvctl start -d PRODDB1 -x lsnr -D 3
```

STOP subcommand

`srvctl stop -d <db_name>`	Stop specified RAC database
`-i <instance_name,>`	Stop named instances if specified, otherwise entire RAC
`-n <node,...>`	Stop instances on named nodes
`-s <stage,...>`	List of stages to stop (stage = inst, lsnr)
`-x <stage,...>`	Except these stages
`-c <connect string>`	Connect string (default: /as sysdba)
`-o <options>`	Options to shutdown command (e.g., force or nomount)
`-S <status level>`	Intermediate status level for console
`-D <debug level>`	Debug level
`-h`	Print usage

Usage

Stop instances and listeners in database PRODDB1:

```
srvctl stop -d PRODDB1
```

Stop only listeners:

```
srvctl stop -d PRODDB1 -s lsnr
```

Stop instance RAC1 with an option and with debug output:

```
srvctl stop -d PRODDB1 -i RAC1 -s inst -o immediate -D 3
```

Stop the instance on node ora-db1:

```
srvctl stop -p PRODDB1 -n ora-db1 -x lsnr
```

Stop database PRODDB1 with connection string system/manager:

```
srvctl stop -d PRODDB1 -c 'system/manager'
```

STATUS subcommand

```
srvctl status -d <db_name>
   -i <instance_name,>

   -n <node,...>
   -s <stage,...>

   -x <stage,...>
   -c <connect string>
   -S <status level>
   -D <debug level>
   -h
```

Check specified RAC database
Check named instances if specified, otherwise entire RAC
Check instances on named nodes
List of stages to check status (stage = inst, lsnr)
Except these stages
Connect string (default: /as sysdba)
Intermediate status level for console
Debug level
Print usage

Usage

Get status of database PRODDB1:

```
srvctl status -d PRODDB1
```

Get status of instance PRODDB1:

```
srvctl status -d PRODDB1 -i RAC1 -s inst
```

Get status of all listeners in database PRODDB1:

```
srvctl status -p PRODDB1 -s lsnr
```

CONFIG subcommand

```
srvctl status -d <db_name>

   -n <node,...>

   -D <debug level>
   -V
   -h
```

Show configuration for specified RAC database
Only show services on named nodes
Debug level
Show version
Print usage

Usage

List Real Application Clusters on the raw device:

```
srvctl config
```

Get configuration of database PRODDB1:

```
srvctl config -d PRODDB1
```

Get configuration of node ora-db1 (entries from all database configurations apply):

```
srvctl config -n ora-db1
```

Get configuration of node ora-db1 in database PRODDB1:

```
srvctl config -d PRODDB1 -n ora-db1
```

Display version:

```
srvctl config -V
```

ADD, DELETE, and RENAME subcommands

`srvctl add -d <db_name>`	Name of RAC to add to
`-i <instance_name,>`	Name of instance to add
`-n <node,...>`	Name of node on which to add instance
`-D <debug level>`	Debug level
`-h`	Print usage
`srvctl delete -d <db_name>`	Name of RAC to delete from
`-i <instance_name,>`	Name of instance to delete
`-D <debug level>`	Debug level
`-h`	Print usage
`srvctl rename -d <db_name>`	Name of RAC to rename
`-i <oldinstance_name,>`	Name of instance to rename
`-e <newinstance_name,>`	New name for instance
`-D <debug level>`	Debug level
`-h`	Print usage

Usage

Add database PRODDB1 to raw device:

```
srvctl add db -d PRODDB1 -o /disk1/ora9
```

Add an instance to PRODDB1:

```
srvctl add instance -d PRODDB1 -i RAC1 -n ora-db1
```

Delete instance OLDRACx from PRODDB1:

```
srvctl delete instance -d PRODDB1 -i RACx
```

Delete database PRODDB1:

```
srvctl delete db -d PRODDB1
```

Rename instance RACx as RAC1:

```
srvctl rename instance -d PRODDB1 -i RACx -e RAC1
```

MOVE, SET, and UNSET subcommands

`srvctl move -d <db_name>`	Name of RAC in which instance should be moved
`-i <instance_name,>`	Name of instance to move
`-n <newnode,...>`	New node for instance
`-D <debug level>`	Debug level
`-h`	Print usage
`srvctl set env -d` `<db_name>`	Name of RAC in which to set environment
`-t <name>=<value>`	Name and value of environment variable
`-i <instance_name,>`	Instance for which environment should be set
`-D <debug level>`	Debug level
`-h`	Print usage
`srvctl unset -d` `<db_name>`	Name of RAC to unset
`-t <name>`	Name of environment variable to unset
`-i <instance_name,>`	Instance for which environment variable should be unset

Usage

Move an instance RAC1 to new node ora-db2:

```
srvctl move instance -d PRODDB1 -i RAC1 -n ora-db2
```

Set Real Application Clusters environment:

```
srvctl set env -d PRODDB1 -t NLS_LANGUAGE=English
```

Set instance environment:

```
srvctl set env -d PRODDB1 -i RAC1 -t NLS_LANGUAGE=English
```

Unset Real Application Clusters environment:

```
srvctl unset env -d PRODDB1 -t NLS_LANGUAGE
```

GET subcommands

`srvctl get env -d <db_name>`	Name of RAC from which to get environment
`-i <instance_name,>`	Instance for which environment variables should be displayed
`-V`	Print version

Usage

Display all Real Application Clusters environment settings:

```
srvctl get env -d PRODDB1
```

Display all instance environment settings:

```
srvctl get env -d PRODDB1 -i RAC1
```

AI.3   ORADEBUG: Oracle debugger

```
Oracle9i Enterprise Edition Release 9.2.0.2.0 - 64bit
  Production
With the Partitioning, Real Application Clusters,
            OLAP and Oracle Data Mining options
JServer Release 9.2.0.2.0 - Production
SQL> oradebug help
```

HELP	[command]	Describe one or all commands
SETMYPID		Debug current process
SETOSPID	<ospid>	Set OS pid of process to debug
SETORAPID	<orapid> ['force']	Set Oracle pid of process to debug
DUMP	<dump_name> <lvl> [addr]	Invoke named dump
DUMPSGA	[bytes]	Dump fixed SGA
DUMPLIST		Print a list of available dumps
EVENT	<text>	Set trace event in process
SESSION_EVENT	<text>	Set trace event in session
DUMPVAR	<p|s|uga> <name> [level]	Print/dump a fixed PGA/SGA/UGA variable
SETVAR	<p|s|uga> <name> <value>	Modify a fixed PGA/SGA/UGA variable
PEEK	<addr> <len> [level]	Print/Dump memory
POKE	<addr> <len> <value>	Modify memory
WAKEUP	<orapid>	Wake up Oracle process
SUSPEND		Suspend execution
RESUME		Resume execution
FLUSH		Flush pending writes to trace file
CLOSE_TRACE		Close trace file
TRACEFILE_NAME		Get name of trace file
LKDEBUG		Invoke global enqueue service debugger
NSDBX		Invoke CGS name-service debugger
-G	<Inst-List | def | all>	Parallel oradebug command prefix
-R	<Inst-List | def | all>	Parallel oradebug prefix (return output
SETINST	<instance# .. | all>	Set instance list in double quotes
SGATOFILE	<SGA dump dir>	Dump SGA to file; dirname in double quotes
DMPCOWSGA	<SGA dump dir>	Dump & map SGA as COW; dirname in double quotes
MAPCOWSGA	<SGA dump dir>	Map SGA as COW; dirname in double quotes
HANGANALYZE	[level]	Analyze system hang
FFBEGIN		Flash Freeze the Instance
FFDEREGISTER		FF deregister instance from cluster
FFTERMINST		Call exit and terminate instance
FFRESUMEINST		Resume the flash frozen instance
FFSTATUS		Flash freeze status of instance
SKDSTTPCS	<ifname> <ofname>	Helps translate PCs to names
WATCH	<address> <len> <self| exist| all|target>	Watch a region of memory

```
DELETE      <local|global|              Delete a watchpoint
              target> watchpoint <id>
SHOW        <local|global| target>      Show watchpoints
              watchpoints
CORE                                    Dump core without crashing process
IPC                                     Dump ipc information
UNLIMIT                                 Unlimit the size of the trace file
PROCSTAT                                Dump process statistics
CALL        <func> [arg1] ... [argn]    Invoke function with arguments
SQL>
```

Appendix 2

Scripts

This appendix contains the scripts referred to throughout the book.

A2.1 Database creation scripts

A2.1.1 Creation of instance one and database

```
REM * crdbPRODDB_RAC1.SQL
REM *
REM * this script will create the PRODDB database and the
  data REM * dictionary for RAC implementation
REM * Author: Murali Vallath
REM * Date: 10-JULY-2002
REM *
set echo on
spool /apps/admin/PRODDB/create/crdbPRODDB_RAC1.lst
REM *
REM * Start the RAC1 instance
REM * (ORACLE_SID here must be set to RAC1).
REM *
startup nomount pfile=/apps/admin/PRODDB/pfile/
  initPRODDB.ora
REM *
REM * the command below creates the Oracle database PRODDB
REM * with specific parameters such as maxinstances,
  maxlogfiles
REM * etc.
REM * Subsequently it creates the SYSTEM tablespace
  followed by
REM * the redo log files for instance RAC1. Note there are
  3 log
REM * file groups and 2 members per group.
REM *
create database "PRODDB"
 maxinstances  8
 maxlogfiles  48
```

```
 maxdatafiles  1024
 maxloghistory 1024
 character set "UTF8"
 national character set "UTF8"
 controlfile reuse
 datafile
  '/dev/vx/rdsk/oraracdg/partition_1G3' size 900M
 logfile
group 1 ('/dev/vx/rdsk/oraracdg/partition_1G31',
        '/dev/vx/rdsk/oraracdg/partition_1G21')
  size 800M,
group 2 ('/dev/vx/rdsk/oraracdg/partition_1G23',
        '/dev/vx/rdsk/oraracdg/partition_1G25')
  size 800M,
group 3 ('/dev/vx/rdsk/oraracdg/partition_1G27',
        '/dev/vx/rdsk/oraracdg/partition_1G29')
  size 800M
default temporary tablespace TEMP tempfile
        '/dev/vx/rdsk/oraracdg/partition_1G9'
  size 900M
undo tablespace UNDO_RAC1 datafile
        '/dev/vx/rdsk/oraracdg/partition_3G2'
  size 2800M;


connect sys/change_on_install as sysdba
alter tablespace system default storage (pctincrease 0);
REM *
REM * install data dictionary views:
REM *
@$ORACLE_HOME/rdbms/admin/catalog.sql
@$ORACLE_HOME/rdbms/admin/catproc.sql
@$ORACLE_HOME/rdbms/admin/catblock.sql
@$ORACLE_HOME/rdbms/admin/catperf.sql
@$ORACLE_HOME/rdbms/admin/dbmspool.sql
REM *
REM * UTL data dictionary views:
REM *
@$ORACLE_HOME/rdbms/admin/utllockt.sql
@$ORACLE_HOME/rdbms/admin/utlxplan.sql
@$ORACLE_HOME/rdbms/admin/utltkprf.sql
@$ORACLE_HOME/rdbms/admin/utlchain.sql
@$ORACLE_HOME/rdbms/admin/utlvalid.sql
@$ORACLE_HOME/rdbms/admin/catio.sql
REM *
REM * XA compliant. Creates views needed to
REM * do XA recovery scan of prepared and heuristically
REM * completed transactions.
REM *
@$ORACLE_HOME/rdbms/admin/xaview.sql
REM *
REM * Execute the data dictionary scripts related to Real
REM * Application Clusters
REM *
```

```
@$ORACLE_HOME/rdbms/admin/catparr.sql
@$ORACLE_HOME/rdbms/admin/catclust.sql
REM * For Advanced Queuing (install if required)
REM *
#@$ORACLE_HOME/rdbms/admin/catqueue.sql

REM * For Replication (install if required)
REM *
#@$ORACLE_HOME/rdbms/admin/catrep.sql

REM * Exception table for constraint violation.
REM *
@$ORACLE_HOME/rdbms/admin/utlexcpt.sql

REM * Create a tablespace for database tools.
REM *
create tablespace tools datafile
      '/dev/vx/rdsk/oraracdg/partition_1G16' size 900M
      extent management local uniform size 1M
        segment space management auto;

REM *Create a tablespace for miscellaneous database user
REM *activity.
REM *
create tablespace users datafile
      '/dev/vx/rdsk/oraracdg/partition_1G13' size 900M
      extent management local uniform size 1M
        segment space management auto;

REM * Alter SYS and SYSTEM users.
REM *
alter user sys
identified by sys_orarac
temporary tablespace temp;

alter user system
identified by system_orarac
default tablespace system
temporary tablespace temp;

REM * Grant privileges and create synonyms on utility tables and
  REM * views.
REM *
grant all on sys.plan_table to public;
create public synonym plan_table for sys.plan_table;

grant all on sys.chained_rows to public;
create public synonym chained_rows for sys.chained_rows;

grant all on sys.invalid_rows to public;
create public synonym invalid_rows for sys.invalid_rows;

REM * Run the following to get rid of Profile warning message
  in REM * SQL Plus
```

```
REM *
connect system/system_orarac
@$ORACLE_HOME/sqlplus/admin/pupbld.sql
spool off
exit
```

A2.1.2   Creation of instance two

```
REM * crdbPRODDB_RAC2.sql
REM * Author: Murali Vallath
REM * Date: 10-JUL-2002
REM *

spool /apps/admin/PRODDB/create/crdbPRODDB_RAC2.lst
set termout on
set echo on

REM * Create redo log files for the second instance or thread 2
REM *
alter database add logfile thread 2
group 4 ('/dev/vx/rdsk/oraracdg/partition_1G32',
         '/dev/vx/rdsk/oraracdg/partition_1G34')
   size 800M,
group 5 ('/dev/vx/rdsk/oraracdg/partition_1G37',
         '/dev/vx/rdsk/oraracdg/partition_1G39')
   size 800M,
group 6 ('/dev/vx/rdsk/oraracdg/partition_1G41',
         '/dev/vx/rdsk/oraracdg/partition_1G42')
   size 800M;

create undo tablespace UNDO_RAC2 datafile
         '/dev/vx/rdsk/oraracdg/partition_3G4'
   size 2800M;

spool off

exit
```

A2.2   Initialization parameter file

```
# initPRODDB.ora
# Author: Murali Vallath
# Date: 10-JUL-2002
#
RAC1.instance_number  = 1
RAC1.thread    = 1
RAC1.instance_name = RAC1
```

```
RAC1.service_names = RAC1.SUMMERSKYUS.COM,PRODDB.SUMMERSKYUS.COM
RAC1.local_listener =''(ADDRESS=(PROTOCOL=TCP)(HOST
  =ora-db1.summerskyus.com)(PORT=1521))''
RAC1.remote_listener =''(ADDRESS=(PROTOCOL=TCP)(HOST=
  ora-db2.summerskyus.com)(PORT=1521))''


RAC2.instance_number = 2
RAC2.thread = 2
RAC2.instance_name = RAC2
RAC2.service_names = RAC2.SUMMERSKYUS.COM,
  PRODDB.SUMMERSKYUS.COM
RAC2.local_listener = ''(ADDRESS=(PROTOCOL=TCP)(HOST=
  ora-db2.summerskyus.com)(PORT=1521))''
RAC2.remote_listener =''(ADDRESS=(PROTOCOL=TCP)(HOST=
  ora-db1.summerskyus.com)(PORT=1521))''


*.DB_NAME      = PRODDB
*.DB_BLOCK_SIZE = 8192


*.CONTROL_FILES = (/dev/vx/rdsk/oraracdg/
  partition_300m71,
          /dev/vx/rdsk/oraracdg/partition_300m72,
          /dev/vx/rdsk/oraracdg/partition_300m73)


*.DB_FILES    = 512
*.DB_DOMAIN   = SUMMERSKYUS.COM


*.CLUSTER_DATABASE = TRUE
*.CLUSTER_DATABASE_INSTANCES = 2


*.dml_locks = 3600
*.optimizer_mode = CHOOSE
*.optimizer_index_caching = 90
*.optimizer_index_cost_adj = 5


*.undo_management = AUTO
RAC1.undo_tablespace = UNDO_RAC1
RAC2.undo_tablespace = UNDO_RAC2


*.db_file_multiblock_read_count = 8
*.db_cache_size = 1G
*.db_writer_processes = 2


*.shared_pool_size = 2G
*.sga_max_size = 3G


# shared_pool_reserved_size = 0
*.large_pool_size = 1048576
*.java_pool_size = 87643200
```

```
*.workarea_size_policy  = AUTO
*.pga_aggregate_target  = 80M

*.processes  = 300
*.log_buffer  = 999424

# RAC1.sql_trace  = true
# RAC2.sql_trace  = true
*.timed_statistics  = true

# This is set at 200000 to force a checkpoint every time a log
# switches.
# The logs are sized at 100M.

*.log_checkpoint_interval  = 200000
*.log_checkpoint_timeout  = 0
*.max_dump_file_size  = 102400

RAC1.log_archive_dest  = /archivelogs/arch/
RAC2.log_archive_dest  = /archivelogs/arch/

RAC1.log_archive_format  = 'RAC1_%T_%S.arc'
RAC2.log_archive_format  = 'RAC2_%T_%S.arc'
*.log_archive_start  = true

*.job_queue_processes  = 2
*.global_names  = TRUE
*.open_cursors  = 1024
*.compatible  = 9.2.0.2
*.remote_login_passwordfile = exclusive
*.max_enabled_roles  = 40
*.nls_date_format  = "DD-MON-YYYY HH24:MI:SS"

RAC1.background_dump_dest = /apps/admin/PRODDB/RAC1/bdump
RAC1.core_dump_dest  = /apps/admin/PRODDB/RAC1/cdump
RAC1.user_dump_dest  = /apps/admin/PRODDB/RAC1/udump

RAC2.background_dump_dest = /apps/admin/PRODDB/RAC2/bdump
RAC2.core_dump_dest  = /apps/admin/PRODDB/RAC2/cdump
RAC2.user_dump_dest  = /apps/admin/PRODDB/RAC2/udump

# Shared SQL is pinned in shared pool
*.cursor_space_for_time  = true

# Moved parsed SQL cursors to session cache
*.session_cached_cursors  = 150

*.parallel_min_servers  = 4
*.parallel_automatic_tuning = TRUE
```

```
*.audit_trail  = DB
*.audit_sys_operations  = TRUE
```

A 2.3   Oracle Net files

```
# tnsnames.ora
# Author: Murali Vallath
# Date: 10-JUL-2002
#
PRODDB.SUMMERSKYUS.COM =
  (DESCRIPTION=
    (SDU = 8192)
    (TDU = 8192)
    (ADDRESS_LIST=
      (failover=on)
      (load_balance=on)
      (ADDRESS=(PROTOCOL=TCP)(HOST=15.152.144.1)
  (PORT=1521))
      (ADDRESS=(PROTOCOL=TCP)(HOST=15.152.144.2)
  (PORT=1521))
  )
  (CONNECT_DATA=
    (SERVICE_NAME= PRODDB.SUMMERSKYUS.COM)
    (ORACLE_HOME = /apps/oracle/product/9.2.0)
    (FAILOVER_MODE=(TYPE=SELECT)(METHOD=BASIC)
      (RETRIES=5)(DELAY=1))
  )
)


# Generated by Oracle configuration tools.
# listener.ora
# Author: Murali Vallath
# Date: 10-JUL-2002
#


LISTENER=
  (DESCRIPTION_LIST=
   (DESCRIPTION=
     (ADDRESS_LIST=
       (ADDRESS=(PROTOCOL=IPC)(KEY=EXTPROC))
   )
   (ADDRESS_LIST =
  (ADDRESS=(PROTOCOL=TCP)
(HOST=ora-db1.SUMMERSKYUS.COM)
(PORT=1521)
(QUEUESIZE=20))
   )
  )
)
```

```
SID_LIST_LISTENER=
  (SID_LIST=
   (SID_DESC=
      (SID_NAME=PLSExtProc)
      (ORACLE_HOME=/apps/oracle/product/9.2.0)
      (PROGRAM=extproc)
   )
   (SID_DESC=
      (ORACLE_HOME=/apps/oracle/product/9.2.0)
      (SID_NAME=RAC1)
   )
   (SID_DESC=
     (ORACLE_HOME=/apps/oracle/product/9.2.0)
     (SID_NAME=PRODDB)
   )
)
```

A2.4   Capture session statistics

```
-- MV_CaptureSessionWaits.sql
-- This script contains all the objects required to
   capture
-- user session information on session logout from
-- gv$session_wait
--
-- This will only work with Oracle Real Application
   Clusters
-- NOTE: The script assumes that the user MVPERFAUDIT
   is present
-- Author: Murali Vallath
-- Date: 01-SEP-2002
-- Execute this procedure logged in as sys or system
--
SET ECHO ON
SET SPOOL MV_CaptureSessionWaits.lis
--
-- Drop the table if already present
--
DROP TABLE MVPERFAUDIT.MV_AUDIT_SESSION_WAIT;
--
-- Create the table to store the session wait information
--
CREATE TABLE MVPERFAUDIT.MV_AUDIT_SESSION_WAIT
( MVASW_SEQ                              NUMBER
,MVASW_INST_ID                          NUMBER
,MVASW_SID                              NUMBER
,MVASW_USERNAME                         VARCHAR2(30)
,MVASW_MACHINE                          VARCHAR2(64)
,MVASW_OSUSER                           VARCHAR2(30)
,MVASW_MODULE                           VARCHAR2(48)
,MVASW_SQL_ADDRESS                      RAW(8)
,MVASW_SEQ#                             NUMBER
```

```
,MVASW_EVENT                            VARCHAR2(64)
,MVASW_P1TEXT                           VARCHAR2(64)
,MVASW_P1                               NUMBER
,MVASW_P1RAW                            RAW(8)
,MVASW_P2TEXT                           VARCHAR2(64)
,MVASW_P2                               NUMBER
,MVASW_P2RAW                            RAW(8)
,MVASW_P3TEXT                           VARCHAR2(64)
,MVASW_P3                               NUMBER
,MVASW_P3RAW                            RAW(8)
,MVASW_WAIT_TIME                        NUMBER
,MVASW_SECONDS_IN_WAIT                  NUMBER
,MVASW_STATE                            VARCHAR2(19)
,MVASW_FAILOVER_TYPE                    VARCHAR2(13)
,MVASW_FAILOVER_METHOD                  VARCHAR2(10)
,MVASW_FAILED_OVER                      VARCHAR2(3)
,MVASW_SESSION_WAIT_DATE_TIME           DATE DEFAULT SYSDATE
) TABLESPACE TOOLS
/
--
-- Create the public synonym for the table and other
   privileges
--
CREATE PUBLIC SYNONYM MV_AUDIT_SESSION_WAIT for
   MVPERFAUDIT.MV_AUDIT_SESSION_WAIT;
GRANT INSERT,SELECT ON MVPERFAUDIT.MV_AUDIT_SESSION_WAIT TO PUBLIC;
--
Create sequence and grant rights to users
--
  CREATE SEQUENCE MVPERFAUDIT.MV_AUDIT_SESSION_WAIT_SEQ
  INCREMENT BY 1
  START WITH 1
  NOMAXVALUE
  NOMINVALUE
  NOCYCLE
  CACHE 200
  ORDER
/


CREATE PUBLIC SYNONYM MV_AUDIT_SESSION_WAIT_SEQ FOR
   MVPERFAUDIT.MV_AUDIT_SESSION_WAIT_SEQ;
GRANT SELECT ON MVPERFAUDIT.MV_AUDIT_SESSION_WAIT_SEQ
   TO PUBLIC;
--
-- Create the trigger to capture session wait statistics
--
CREATE OR REPLACE TRIGGER MV_AUDIT_SESSION_WAIT_TRG
BEFORE LOGOFF ON DATABASE
BEGIN

INSERT INTO MV_AUDIT_SESSION_WAIT
 SELECT
```

```
MV_AUDIT_SESSION_WAIT_SEQ.NEXTVAL
  ,GVSW.INST_ID
  ,GVSW.SID
  ,GVS.USERNAME
  ,GVS.MACHINE
  ,GVS.OSUSER
  ,GVS.MODULE
  ,GVS.SQL_ADDRESS
  ,GVSW.SEQ#
  ,GVSW.EVENT
  ,GVSW.P1TEXT
  ,GVSW.P1
  ,GVSW.P1RAW
  ,GVSW.P2TEXT
  ,GVSW.P2
  ,GVSW.P2RAW
  ,GVSW.P3TEXT
  ,GVSW.P3
  ,GVSW.P3RAW
  ,GVSW.WAIT_TIME
  ,GVSW.SECONDS_IN_WAIT
  ,GVSW.STATE
  ,GVS.FAILOVER_TYPE
  ,GVS.FAILOVER_METHOD
  ,GVS.FAILED_OVER
  ,SYSDATE
FROM GV$SESSION_WAIT GVSW, GV$SESSION GVS
  WHERE GVSW.SID = GVS.SID AND
    GVSW.INST_ID = GVS.INST_ID AND
    GVS.AUDSID = userenv('sessionid');
END;

========================================================

-- MV_CaptureSessionEvents.sql
-- This script contains all the objects required to
   capture
-- user session information on logout from
   gv$session_event
--
-- This will only work with Oracle Real Application
   Clusters
-- NOTE: The script assumes that the user MVPERFAUDIT
   is present
-- Author: Murali Vallath
-- Date: 01-SEP-2002
-- Execute this procedure logged in as sys or system
--
SET ECHO ON
SET SPOOL MV_CaptureSessionEvents.lis
--
-- Drop the table if already present
--
```

```
DROP TABLE MVPERFAUDIT.MV_AUDIT_SESSION_EVENT;
--
-- Create the table to store the session event information
--
CREATE TABLE MVPERFAUDIT.MV_AUDIT_SESSION_EVENT
  ( MVASE_ID                    NUMBER
  ,MVASE_INST_ID                NUMBER
  ,MVASE_SID                    NUMBER
  ,MVASE_USERNAME               VARCHAR2(30)
  ,MVASE_MACHINE                VARCHAR2(64)
  ,MVASE_OSUSER                 VARCHAR2(30)
  ,MVASE_MODULE                 VARCHAR2(48)
  ,MVASE_SQL_ADDRESS            RAW(8)
  ,MVASE_EVENT                  VARCHAR2(64)
  ,MVASE_TOTAL_WAITS            NUMBER
  ,MVASE_TOTAL_TIMEOUTS         NUMBER
  ,MVASE_TIME_WAITED            NUMBER
  ,MVASE_AVERAGE_WAIT           NUMBER
  ,MVASE_MAX_WAIT               NUMBER
  ,MVASE_TIME_WAITED_MICRO      NUMBER
  ,MVASE_FAILOVER_TYPE          VARCHAR2(13)
  ,MVASE_FAILOVER_METHOD        VARCHAR2(10)
  ,MVASE_FAILED_OVER            VARCHAR2(3)
  ,MVASE_SESSION_DATE_TIME      DATE DEFAULT SYSDATE
) TABLESPACE TOOLS
/


CREATE SEQUENCE MVPERFAUDIT.MV_AUDIT_SESSION_EVENT_SEQ
INCREMENT BY 1
START WITH 1
NOMAXVALUE
NOMINVALUE
NOCYCLE
CACHE 200
ORDER
/


CREATE PUBLIC SYNONYM MV_AUDIT_SESSION_EVENT for
  MVPERFAUDIT.MV_AUDIT_SESSION_EVENT;
CREATE PUBLIC SYNONYM MV_AUDIT_SESSION_EVENT_SEQ FOR
  MVPERFAUDIT.MV_AUDIT_SESSION_EVENT_SEQ;

GRANT INSERT,SELECT ON MVPERFAUDIT.MV_AUDIT_SESSION_EVENT
  TO PUBLIC;

GRANT SELECT ON MVPERFAUDIT.MV_AUDIT_SESSION_EVENT_SEQ
  TO PUBLIC;
--
-- Create the logout trigger to capture session event
  statistics
--
CREATE OR REPLACE TRIGGER MV_PERFAUDIT_SESSION_EVENT_TRG
```

```
BEFORE LOGOFF ON DATABASE
BEGIN
  INSERT INTO MV_AUDIT_SESSION_EVENT
    SELECT
      MV_AUDIT_SESSION_EVENT_SEQ.NEXTVAL,
      GVSE.INST_ID
      ,GVSE.SID
      ,GVS.USERNAME
    ,GVS.MACHINE
    ,GVS.OSUSER
    ,GVS.MODULE
    ,GVS.SQL_ADDRESS
      ,GVSE.EVENT
      ,GVSE.TOTAL_WAITS
      ,GVSE.TOTAL_TIMEOUTS
      ,GVSE.TIME_WAITED
      ,GVSE.AVERAGE_WAIT
      ,GVSE.MAX_WAIT
      ,GVSE.TIME_WAITED_MICRO
      ,GVS.FAILOVER_TYPE
      ,GVS.FAILOVER_METHOD
      ,GVS.FAILED_OVER
      ,SYSDATE
  FROM GV$SESSION_EVENT GVSE, GV$SESSION GVS
  WHERE GVSE.SID = GVS.SID AND
        GVSE.INST_ID = GVS.INST_ID AND
        GVS.AUDSID = userenv('sessionid');
END;
/
```

Appendix 3

References

The following articles, papers, presentations, and websites have been consulted during the author's study, research, and analysis. Much of this information has come in handy during the writing of this book. While every effort has been made to provide you with a list of reference material, any omission from this list is unintentional.

1. Got Waits? A Wait Approach to Performance Tuning and Optimization, Richmond Shee, IOUG Live 2001. http://www.ioug.org

2. High Availability Using Transparent Application Failover on Real Application Clusters, Murali Vallath, White Paper, Oracle Open World 2000. http://www.oracle.com

3. High Availability Using Transparent Application Failover on Real Application Clusters, Murali Vallath, Technical Feature, Oracle Scene, UKOUG Journal, Issue 12, Winter 2002. http://www.ukoug.org

4. Implementing RAID on Oracle Systems, Gaja Krishna Vaidyanatha, White Paper, Proceedings from Oracle Open World 2000.

5. IXORA, Steve Adams website. http://www.ixora.com.au

6. Monitoring Cache Transfers in Real Application Clusters, Murali Vallath, IOUG-SELECT, 2nd Issue, 2003. http://www.ioug.org

7. Multiple articles and papers from Metalink and Tech Net, Oracle Corporation. http://metalink.oracle.com

8. Oracle 9*i* Performance Management: The Oracle Method, Mughees A. Minhas, Oracle Corporation, Proceedings from Oracle World 2002. http://www.oracle.com

9. Oracle Documentation (Version 8.1.7, Version 9.1.0, Version 9.2.0), Oracle Technology Network, Oracle Corporation. http://technet.oracle.com

10. Oracle Performance Tuning 101, Gaja Krishna Vaidyanatha and Kirtikumar Deshpande, Osborne McGraw-Hill, 2001. http://www.osborne.com

11. Oracle SQL High Performance Tuning, Gary Harrison, Prentice Hall 2000. http://www.phptr.com

12. RAID: High-Performance, Reliable Secondary Storage, Peter M. Chen, Edward K. Lee, Garth A. Gibson, Randy H. Kartz, David A. Patterson, White Paper, ACM Computing Surveys

13. Scaling Oracle 8i, James Morle, Addison Wesley, 2000. http://www.aw.com/cseng/

14. Searching for Intelligence in the Cost Based Optimizer, Tim Gorman, White Paper, Evergreen Database Technologies Inc. http://www.egvdbt.com

15. The Expensive Parse Phase and the Cost of Using Synonyms, Murali Vallath, White Paper, IOUG Live 2001. http://www.ioug.org

16. Transaction Management in Oracle 9i, Stephen Haisley, Presentation, UKOUG 2002. http://www.ukoug2002.org

17. Tru64 UNIX — Oracle 9i Cluster Quick Reference, Tim Donar, Digital Press Books. http://www.digitalpressbooks.com

18. Why 99% Cache Hit Ratio Is Not OK, Cary Millsap, White Paper, 2001. http://www.hotsos.com

19. Why You Should Focus on LIOs Instead of PIOs, Cary Millsap, White Paper. http://www.hotsos.com

Appendix 4

Work Plan

A4.1   Introduction

A sample work plan that will help during a migration process from Oracle single instance to RAC is presented. This work plan is only provided as a guideline and is not indicative of any specific work plan. It should be used as a sample only, to act as a guideline in building a specific work plan for any specific migration process.

A4.2   Certification matrix

Table A4.1 is a matrix that should be completed to obtain and ensure that all the various software, hardware, and all layered products used for the migration project are certified and compatible with each other.

Table A4.1   *Certification Matrix*

OPS Certification Level
Oracle RDBMS:
Oracle RDBMS Version
Oracle RDBMS Patches:
Operating System
Version Number:
Cluster Manager Software

continued

Table A4.1 *Continued*

Version Number:
Hardware Configuration
Total Number of Host Nodes:
Db Cluster Alias
Database Host (Node 1)
Make:
Model:
Patch Level:
IP Address
Database Host (Node 2)
Make:
Model:
Patch Level:
IP Address
LAN Access Connectivity
Type:
Speed:

A4.3   Work plan RAC migration checklist

This is shown in Table A4.2.

Note: The work plan assumes usage of raw devices if file systems are used. Tasks 2, 3, 4 and 8 need to be replaced appropriately.

Table A4.2 *Work plan RAC migration checklist*

#	Tasks	Who	Status
1	Define business requirements, including capacity requirements based on anticipated growth.		

continued

Table A4.2 *Continued*

#	Tasks	Who	Status
2	Determine the size of raw partitions		
3	Create a raw partition matrix		
4	Create raw partitions		
5	Define logical volumes and volume groups		
6	Create shared file systems for Oracle		
7	Create shared file systems for archive logs		
8	Verify raw partitions		
9	Install Oracle		
10	Verify Oracle install		
11	Determine tablespace requirements, including sizes and the partitions they are to reside on, for the database		
12	Map data files to partitions. Usage of locally managed tablespaces should be preferred; this would avoid all the additional management that would normally be required in the case of dictionary-managed table spaces, including FREELISTS and FREELIST GROUPS		
13	Map tablespaces to data files		
14	Create `crdbRAC1.sql` script and `initRAC1.ora` (Samples of these scripts are shown in Appendix 2)		
15	Configure all external cluster-related processes including GSD, SRVCTL, and SRVCONFIG		
16	Create RAC1 instance and PRODDB database		
17	Create `crdbRAC2.sql` script and `initRAC2.ora` (Samples of these scripts are shown in Appendix 2)		
18	Full export of the database		
19	Configure Oracle Net Support		
20	Bounce both instances to ensure that all the setup completed to this point is OK		

continued

Table A4.2 *Continued*

#	Tasks	Who	Status
21	Database verification		
22	Create tablespaces		
23	Assign tables and indexes to mapped partitions		
24	Create database objects; this should be from the current production system (if one exists) or from the development system (if this is a new system). This will give a true picture of the performance characteristics		
25	Set up STATSPACK		
26	Set up OEM		
27	Load data from legacy configuration		
28	QA sanity check		
29	Load testing and tuning RAC1 and monitor using STATSPACK and OEM		
30	Tune parameters		
31	Verify testing results against the requirements		
32	Load testing and tuning RAC1 and RAC2 and monitor using STATSPACK and OEM		
33	Tune parameters		
34	Verify testing results against the requirements		
35	Setup DBMS_STATS package to collect stats		
36	Test load balancing of database cluster		
37	Test failover of database cluster using TAF		
38	Tune failover parameters		
39	Day in a life—test 1: to verify functioning of the cluster in a regular full day production-like simulation. Create backup and recovery strategy based on business requirements, including recovery criteria and procure management approval		

continued

Table A4.2 *Continued*

#	Tasks	Who	Status
40	Set up RMAN		
41	Start up backup processes		
42	Verify backup strategy		
43	Update startup/shutdown utilities		
44	Day in a life—Test 2: to verify functioning of the cluster in a regular full day production-like simulation with backup scripts running in the background at regular intervals and real user activity		
45	7-day burn down test—running a 24-hour, 7-day load test will simulate worst case user behavior for a week. This test will also test database and hardware anomalies, if any		
46	Verify testing results against the requirements		
47	Prepare and review report on testing and accomplishments		
48	Prepare and review configuration documentation		

About the Author

Murali Vallath has been using Oracle products for over 16 years. His work spans industries such as broadcasting, manufacturing and telephony and most recently transportation logistics. Vallath is no stranger to the software development life cycle; his solid understanding of IT covers requirement analysis, architecture, modeling, database design, application development, performance tuning and implementation.

Vallath is an Oracle Certified Database Administrator and has worked on a variety of database platforms for small to very large implementations, designing extensive databases for high volume, machine critical, real time OLTP systems. His expertise is with Oracle Parallel Server/Oracle Real Application Clusters and he has several implementations to his credit.

He is a frequent contributor to the Oracle-L list server and is known in the Oracle community for his dedication and leadership while he served as the President of the Charlotte Oracle Users Group.

Vallath is a regular speaker at national and international conferences, including the Oracle Open World, IOUG, UKOUG on Real Application Cluster and Oracle Performance Tuning related topics. He was the recipient of the Best Presenter of the Year Award in the DBA Track at the CLTOUG 2001 conference.

Vallath currently provides Oracle consulting services through Summersky Enterprises LLC (www.summersky.biz). The firm specializes in implementation and performance tuning of Oracle products, including OPS, RAC, data guard and replication. Prior to this he worked as Senior Database Architect at Elogex Inc. Apart from the regular performance tuning efforts at Elogex, he led the Performance Management SWAT team. His previous work and consulting experience includes Hinditron Computers in India, Digital Equipment Corporation, GTE Mobile, Navistar International and DST Interactive (formerly DBS Systems).

Vallath is a native of India and resides in Charlotte, N.C., with his wife (also an Oracle Certified Professional) and children Grishma, 8, and Nabhas, 7. When Vallath is not working on complex databases, his hobbies include photography and playing classical Indian music on the tabla, an Indian instrument.

Index

www.ingramcontent.com/pod-product-compliance
Lightning Source LLC
Chambersburg PA
CBHW080335220326
41598CB00030B/4517